Property of: Fil Sapienza

D1239676

THE
PROGRAMMER'S
PC
SOURCEBOOK

THE PROGRAMMER'S PC SOURCEBOOK

Reference Tables for IBM® PCs and Compatibles, PS/2™ Machines, and DOS

Thom Hogan

Microsoft
PRESS

PUBLISHED BY
Microsoft Press
A Division of Microsoft Corporation
16011 NE 36th Way, Box 97017, Redmond, Washington 98073-9717

Copyright 1988 by Thom Hogan
All rights reserved. No part of the contents of this book may be reproduced or transmitted
in any form or by any means without the written permission of the publisher.

Library of Congress Cataloging in Publication Data

Hogan, Thom, 1952-
        The programmer's PC sourcebook : charts and tables for the IBM PC,
compatibles, and the MS-DOS Operating System, including the new IBM
Personal System/2 computers / Thom Hogan.
        p.   cm.
Includes index.
ISBN 1-55615-118-7
        1. IBM microcomputers--Programming. 2. MS-DOS (Computer operating
system) 3. IBM Personal System/2 (Computer system) I. Title.
II. Title: Programmer's PC source book.
QA76.8.I1015H64 1988   87-36575
005.4'469--dc19   CIP

Printed and bound in the United States of America.

1 2 3 4 5 6 7 8 9 WAKWAK 3 2 1 0 9 8

Distributed to the book trade in the United States by Harper & Row.

Distributed to the book trade in Canada by General Publishing Company, Ltd.

Distributed to the book trade outside the United States and Canada by Penguin Books Ltd.

Penguin Books Ltd., Harmondsworth, Middlesex, England
Penguin Books Australia Ltd., Ringwood, Victoria, Australia
Penguin Books N.Z. Ltd., 182-190 Wairau Road, Auckland 10, New Zealand

British Cataloging in Publication Data available

To Roger Chapman and Alan Cooper,
two programmers I respect and admire

Contents

PART II: Software   37

SECTION 2: DOS Commands, Utilities, and Summaries   39

PART III: General PC Hardware

SECTION 7: Keyboards, Video Adapters, and Peripherals   393

Preface

Those of you who work in the microcomputer field know that the quantity of information available to you is far from manageable and is constantly increasing. If your reference library is like mine, it consists of shelf upon shelf of technical books and manuals. Some are indexed well, others are not. Some are clearly written, others are not. Often, finding the answer to a single question requires consulting three or four references on the subject to get the complete picture.

For several years I've known that I needed a distillation of all the important information about IBM personal computers—a summary of facts and detailed data. Knowing what I wanted, I proposed to Microsoft Press that I compile this book. They, too, had recognized the need for such a reference and quickly signed me to create it.

The PC Sourcebook includes information normally found in these key references:

- IBM personal computer Tech Refs (PC, XT, AT, PS/2)
- IBM BIOS Tech Ref
- IBM DOS Tech Ref
- MS-DOS Tech Ref
- Microsoft Windows Development Kit
- Microsoft Mouse Reference
- Lotus/Intel/Microsoft EMS Specifications
- Intel Microprocessor Handbooks

At the outset, both Microsoft Press and I would have described the effort required (and the size of the resulting book) as "moderate." Well, we were wrong. In the end, I took twice as much time as I had planned to compile and create the tables that make up this book. I ended up relying on more than 20 manuals and technical references, at least twice as many

books, and countless magazine articles. Often, it took two or more sources to create a "complete" table on a particular subject. In a few instances, I found that the source information wasn't published anywhere, even though it was "common knowledge" among my programming friends! The result of this work, as you can see, is a mammoth reference whose value, I hope, far outweighs the price you paid for it.

You will note that this is a first edition. Microsoft Press and I intend to update and expand the work as the world of IBM personal computers changes. Although I've tried to incorporate as much information as possible about new products, such as Microsoft Windows version 2.0 and IBM's PS/2 line of computers, some information was available only through the generosity of people working on prerelease products.

I'd like to ask you to let me know of changes and additions you'd like to see in future editions. Although I can't promise to incorporate all suggestions, I can promise to read and seriously consider each one. Send your ideas to:

Thom Hogan
Programmer's PC Sourcebook Suggestions
c/o Microsoft Press
16011 NE 36th Way, PO Box 97017
Redmond, WA 98073-9717

I hope that this work accomplishes the goal I intended to achieve. I hope you find this a useful compendium—a desktop reference that serves as your first stop for all information about IBM personal computers.

Acknowledgments

A number of people had a direct bearing on the publication of this book. Susan Lammers provided the initial enthusiasm, got the ball rolling, and rallied the troops when I started churning out tables. Ron Lamb provided timely feedback and suggestions. Marie Doyle and Evan Konecky shepherded the book through the final stages of production. Bob Combs did a commendable job of verifying and proofing the manuscript, and he provided helpful suggestions for keeping the book focused, yet complete. And a few hard-working, anonymous souls in Production spent a lot of time reformatting, renumbering, and entering corrected data into the final tables. In short, the whole crew at Microsoft Press was extremely helpful and—once the initial shock of such a mammoth undertaking wore off—tremendously enthusiastic. I salute them for contributing to the best author-publisher relationship I've encountered in my long technical-writing career.

Others deserve some acknowledgment as well. To the technical writers at Microsoft and IBM who provided the base information I distilled, I thank you for your excellent work in putting together the various technical references I used in compiling my data. That your employers publish such references is a sign of confidence and commitment, and I applaud that as well.

I can't begin to thank all the authors whose works I consulted at one point or another during this project, but Peter Norton, Ray Duncan, and Leo Scanlon deserve special mention for the consistent high quality (and quantity) of their works. And to all my friends who looked at portions of my outline and at partially completed tables: Thanks for your feedback—it made for a better reference.

Introduction

This book puts the basic hardware and software information about IBM PCs in one place.

What's the difference between the ASCII character definitions and the IBM PC's interpretation of them? Normally you'd have to consult two references to answer that question. Here, the answer is in one place. Suppose that you're tracing execution of a program on a single-step debugger, and your program hits a questionable call to a BIOS video function. To get the full information about what's happening, you want to know what's going into the 6845 (video controller) chip's registers, what the BIOS function does, and what data the function requires. Again, the answer to all your questions is in this book.

Whatever you need to know about an IBM PC—card sizes, cable connections, ROM BIOS routines, internal registers, DOS functions, and so on—you'll find at least the basic information here.

To provide you with a coherent summary of all the technical information scattered throughout the books on your shelves, this book:

- acts as a primary source for most information contained in the IBM and Microsoft technical references

- provides pointers to further information and to items too detailed for complete inclusion here

- organizes information about IBM personal computers in logical groups

Let's look at each of these functions individually.

Primary Source of IBM and Microsoft Information

Information in the IBM and Microsoft technical references often is spread over several volumes. The IBM personal-computer family has evolved in both software and hardware; thus, you find information about a particular BIOS function in as many as four or five places in the IBM references: the XT reference, the AT reference, the PS/2 reference, the options and adapters reference, and the BIOS reference.

This book distills the important information from the IBM and Microsoft technical and user references. Thus, in looking at a single BIOS-related table in this book, you see information that might have come from eight or nine different volumes. That is why I call this book a "primary" source of information—it's the first source you should turn to when you need to look something up. The full list of primary references is included in the bibliography at the end of the book.

Pointers to Further Information

The information in this book always points to the original source data. Furthermore, the book is fully cross-indexed so that every table also points to related tables elsewhere in the book.

The pointers to related information come in the form of *Source* and *See Also* notes at the bottom of each table.

- The *Source* note gives the name and page number(s) of the primary source used in compiling the table.

- The *See Also* note gives the numbers and names of other tables in this book that contain related information you might want to consult. (Read the section titled "Organization" for more on table numbering.)

Every effort has been made to ensure that the page numbers referenced in the *Source* notes are accurate. IBM does update its technical documentation from time to time, however, and thus a little "page creep" may find its way into this work. Sometimes, IBM retains page numbering in new editions (adding a page 1.1 and 1.2 between the original pages 1 and 2, for example); other times, IBM simply renumbers an entire section when it makes an update. Thus, the page numbers referenced here are exact if you use the same edition I consulted, or very close, if the primary source has been updated. Either way, you'll certainly find yourself in the correct section of the primary source.

Organization

To help you find information easily, as well as to help you see relationships among tables, this book is organized into three main parts:

- Part I includes miscellaneous general information.
- Part II includes software.
- Part III includes hardware.

Each part is further divided into one or more numbered sections. These numbers are used in identifying the tables, so the sections are numbered consecutively from the beginning of the book and without regard to part number, as you can see in the following abbreviated table of contents:

Part I: Miscellaneous Information
  Section 1:   General Information

Part II: Software
  Section 2:   DOS Commands, Utilities, and Summaries
  Section 3:   DOS Function Calls and Support Tables
  Section 4:   DOS BIOS Calls and Support Tables
  Section 5:   Other Interrupts, Mouse and EMS Support
  Section 6:   Microsoft Windows

Part III: General PC Hardware
  Section 7:   Keyboards, Video Adapters, and Peripherals
  Section 8:   Chips, Jumpers, Switches, and Registers
  Section 9:   Hardware Descriptions

All tables are numbered and, as stated earlier, I use those numbers in the *See Also* cross-referencing. The first number in each table is a section number. Thus you'll find information about DOS functions in tables that begin with a *3*. The second portion of a table number (separated from the section number by a period) is the number of the table within the section. DOS-reserved device names, for example, are found in Table 3.148, which means it is the 148th table in Section 3, the DOS functions section.

A word of note about the overall structure of this book: Programming for the BIOS and for hardware interrupts falls into the software part of the book because you're likely to encounter them while creating software. Physical items

such as pins, switches, and registers are found in the hardware part of the book. The distinction made here is arguably logical, but not necessarily the only one that could have been made.

How Tables Are Presented

In the figure at the top of the facing page you see a representative sample of a table.

At the top are the table number and table name in boldfaced type. They help you identify the table contents, with the number also serving as the cross-referencing used in this book.

If a table has been broken into subtables because of differences in implementation (as between the PC-XT and the PS/2), a subtable heading appears in italics immediately above each subtable.

Headings down the left side and across the top of a table are boxed and in italics to distinguish them from the information within the table. Where headings are grouped (bit numbers, for example, which are usually in groups of eight), a group header appears in italics immediately above the first item in the group, and the group is usually separated from the rest of the table by a slight space.

Entries are in boxed cells. In cases where groups of data are related, the group appears in a single box with each item on a separate line within the box. Within data entries, several abbreviations are consistently used:

MSB = most significant bit or byte
LSB = least significant bit or byte
LO = low order
HO = high order
000 = a binary value of zero, zero, zero
010 = a binary value of zero, one, zero
0X1 = a binary value of zero, don't care, one
1A (26) = the first value is hexadecimal; the parentheses contain the decimal equivalent
string = any group of text characters enclosed in quotes
command = any valid command (validity depends upon context)
label = a string that corresponds to the label formatting requirements
state = Boolean TRUE or FALSE value
char = character (a single byte of information)
int = integer number
filespec = a file's name and optional extension (type)
dbl word = double word (four bytes)
word = two bytes
R = reserved
O = obsolete

0.0. SOME REFERENCES USED IN COMPILING THIS BOOK

Reference	Edition	Part Number	Publisher	Used in Section
Advanced MS-DOS, by Ray Duncan	NA	ISBN 0-914845-77-2	Microsoft Press	2. DOS
DOS 3.3 Reference Manual	1st (Apr 87)	80X0667	IBM	2. DOS
DOS 3.3 Technical Reference	1st (Apr 87)	80X0945	IBM	2. DOS
IBM Technical Reference Options and Adapters Vol 1	1st (Apr 84)	6137804	IBM	7. Peripherals
IBM Technical Reference Options and Adapters Vol 2	1st (Apr 84)	6137806	IBM	7. Peripherals
Microprocessor and Peripheral Handbook Vol 1	1987	ISBN 1-55512-062-8	Intel	8. Chips
Microprocessor and Peripheral Handbook Vol 2	1987	ISBN 1-55512-062-8	Intel	8. Chips
Microsoft Windows 2.0 User's Guide	NA	NA	Microsoft	6. Windows
MS-DOS 3.3 Programmer's Reference	NA	410630014-330-R04-0787	Microsoft	2. DOS
PS/2 BIOS Technical Reference	1st (Apr 87)	84X1514	IBM	7.,8.,9. Hardware
PS/2 Model 30 Technical Reference	1st (Apr 87)	68X2201	IBM	7.,8.,9. Hardware
PS/2 Model 50 and 60 Technical Reference	1st (Apr 87)	68X2224	IBM	7.,8.,9. Hardware
Technical Reference PC AT	Rev (Mar 86)	6280099	IBM	7.,8.,9. Hardware
Technical Reference PC Network	1st (Sept 84)	6322916	IBM	7. Peripherals
Technical Reference PC/XT	1st (Jan 83)	6936763	IBM	7.,8.,9. Hardware
Technical Reference PC/XT and Portable PC	Mar 86	6280089	IBM	7.,8.,9. Hardware
Windows Programmer's Reference	NA	050-051053-200-10Z-1087	Microsoft	6. Windows

Notes: These references are updated periodically by their publishers. The page numbers referenced in this book are taken from the edition described above and are subject to change.

See Also: Bibliography

A special form of table is used for any function or interrupt call that uses registers to pass information. In such cases, you see a table formatted like the next example, with information showing exact register use. If a register is not used by a function or call, it is blank and you can assume that it is left unchanged by the function. Destroyed registers are explicitly identified in such tables. Presenting the register use as a consistently formatted table helps you visualize exactly how the function or call uses the registers.

3.045. FUNCTION 29H -- PARSE FILENAME

Prior to Calling Function

	High	Low
AX	29H	Parse control byte
BX		
CX		
DX		
SP		
BP		
SI	Offset of pointer to string to parse	
DI	Offset of pointer to buffer to contain unopened FCB	
IP		
flags		
CS		
DS	Segment of pointer to string to parse	
SS		
ES	Segment of pointer to buffer for unopened FCB	

Buffer | Empty

Upon Return From Function

	High	Low
AX		Status*
BX		
CX		
DX		
SP		
BP		
SI	Offset of pointer 1 byte past parsed string	
DI	Offset of pointer to unopened FCB	
IP		
flags		
CS		
DS	Segment of pointer 1 byte past parsed string	
SS		
ES	Segment of pointer to unopened FCB	

Notes: *00=FCB created, no wildcard characters; 01=FCB created, wildcard characters used in filename FFH=drive letter invalid

Source: IBM DOS 3.3 Technical Reference, pages 6-95 to 6-97

See Also:
2.51. Filename Separator Characters
3.001. INT 21H Functions by DOS Version Summary
3.123. Unopened FCB Format
3.142. Parse Control Byte

At the end of each table is a *Notes* section. Several categories of notes are possible, although not every table has each type:

- *Version Info:* tells you about differences in versions or between products.

- *Legend:* describes abbreviations used only in a single table.

- *Notes:* give general information or exceptions related to data in the table and contain the text of any footnotes in the table. Footnotes are usually identified by asterisks; one asterisk is the first footnote, two asterisks is the second, and so on. Entries with more than four asterisks use † for fifth entry, ¥ for sixth entry, § for seventh entry, and ∞ for eighth entry.

- *Source:* notes the primary source of the data in the table.

- *See Also:* refers you to related tables elsewhere in this book.

—PART—

I

MISCELLANEOUS
INFORMATION

SECTION

1

General Information

1.01. HEXADECIMAL TO DECIMAL NUMBER CONVERSION

Byte Values

Least Significant Digit

	0	1	2	3	4	5	6	7	8	9	A	B	C	D	E	F
00	0	1	2	3	4	5	6	7	8	9	10	11	12	13	14	15
10	16	17	18	19	20	21	22	23	24	25	26	27	28	29	30	31
20	32	33	34	35	36	37	38	39	40	41	42	43	44	45	46	47
30	48	49	50	51	52	53	54	55	56	57	58	59	60	61	62	63
40	64	65	66	67	68	69	70	71	72	73	74	75	76	77	78	79
50	80	81	82	83	84	85	86	87	88	89	90	91	92	93	94	95
60	96	97	98	99	100	101	102	103	104	105	106	107	108	109	110	111
70	112	113	114	115	116	117	118	119	120	121	122	123	124	125	126	127
80	128	129	130	131	132	133	134	135	136	137	138	139	140	141	142	143
90	144	145	146	147	148	149	150	151	152	153	154	155	156	157	158	159
A0	160	161	162	163	164	165	166	167	168	169	170	171	172	173	174	175
B0	176	177	178	179	180	181	182	183	184	185	186	187	188	189	190	191
C0	192	193	194	195	196	197	198	199	200	201	202	203	204	205	206	207
D0	208	209	210	211	212	213	214	215	216	217	218	219	220	221	222	223
E0	224	225	226	227	228	229	230	231	232	233	234	235	236	237	238	239
F0	240	241	242	243	244	245	246	247	248	249	250	251	252	253	254	255

Most Significant Digit labels the row headings (00–F0).

To Use This Table: To determine the decimal value of A4 hex, you look in the row labeled A0 (the most significant hex digit is A) and the column labeled 4 (the least significant hex digit is 4). The value at the intersection of these two headings (164) is the decimal value for A4.

Nibble		**Byte**		**Byte+Nibble**		**Word**	
Hex	Dec	Hex	Dec	Hex	Dec	Hex	Dec
0	0	00	0	000	0	0000	0
1	1	10	16	100	256	1000	4096
2	2	20	32	200	512	2000	8192
3	3	30	48	300	768	3000	12288
4	4	40	64	400	1024	4000	16384
5	5	50	80	500	1280	5000	20480
6	6	60	96	600	1536	6000	24576
7	7	70	112	700	1792	7000	28672
8	8	80	128	800	2048	8000	32768
9	9	90	144	900	2304	9000	36864
A	10	A0	160	A00	2560	A000	40960
B	11	B0	176	B00	2816	B000	45056
C	12	C0	192	C00	3072	C000	49152
D	13	D0	208	D00	3328	D000	53248
E	14	E0	224	E00	3584	E000	57344
F	15	F0	240	F00	3840	F000	61440

To Use This Table: To convert a two-byte (word) hexadecimal value to decimal, find the value associated with each hex digit place in the above table; add these numbers together. For example, the hex value A5D7 would be equal to 40960 (the A000 value) plus 1280 (the 500 value) plus 208 (the D0 value) plus 7, or 42455.

See Also:
1.06. Binary Number Conversions
1.09. Octal to Hexadecimal Number Conversion
1.12. Decimal to Hexadecimal Number Conversion

1.02. HEXADECIMAL TO BINARY NUMBER CONVERSION

Byte Values

Hex	Binary	Hex	Binary	Hex	Binary	Hex	Binary
0	0000 0000	40	0100 0000	80	1000 0000	C0	1100 0000
1	0000 0001	41	0100 0001	81	1000 0001	C1	1100 0001
2	0000 0010	42	0100 0010	82	1000 0010	C2	1100 0010
3	0000 0011	43	0100 0011	83	1000 0011	C3	1100 0011
4	0000 0100	44	0100 0100	84	1000 0100	C4	1100 0100
5	0000 0101	45	0100 0101	85	1000 0101	C5	1100 0101
6	0000 0110	46	0100 0110	86	1000 0110	C6	1100 0110
7	0000 0111	47	0100 0111	87	1000 0111	C7	1100 0111
8	0000 1000	48	0100 1000	88	1000 1000	C8	1100 1000
9	0000 1001	49	0100 1001	89	1000 1001	C9	1100 1001
A	0000 1010	4A	0100 1010	8A	1000 1010	CA	1100 1010
B	0000 1011	4B	0100 1011	8B	1000 1011	CB	1100 1011
C	0000 1100	4C	0100 1100	8C	1000 1100	CC	1100 1100
D	0000 1101	4D	0100 1101	8D	1000 1101	CD	1100 1101
E	0000 1110	4E	0100 1110	8E	1000 1110	CE	1100 1110
F	0000 1111	4F	0100 1111	8F	1000 1111	CF	1100 1111
10	0001 0000	50	0101 0000	90	1001 0000	D0	1101 0000
11	0001 0001	51	0101 0001	91	1001 0001	D1	1101 0001
12	0001 0010	52	0101 0010	92	1001 0010	D2	1101 0010
13	0001 0011	53	0101 0011	93	1001 0011	D3	1101 0011
14	0001 0100	54	0101 0100	94	1001 0100	D4	1101 0100
15	0001 0101	55	0101 0101	95	1001 0101	D5	1101 0101
16	0001 0110	56	0101 0110	96	1001 0110	D6	1101 0110
17	0001 0111	57	0101 0111	97	1001 0111	D7	1101 0111
18	0001 1000	58	0101 1000	98	1001 1000	D8	1101 1000
19	0001 1001	59	0101 1001	99	1001 1001	D9	1101 1001
1A	0001 1010	5A	0101 1010	9A	1001 1010	DA	1101 1010
1B	0001 1011	5B	0101 1011	9B	1001 1011	DB	1101 1011
1C	0001 1100	5C	0101 1100	9C	1001 1100	DC	1101 1100
1D	0001 1101	5D	0101 1101	9D	1001 1101	DD	1101 1101
1E	0001 1110	5E	0101 1110	9E	1001 1110	DE	1101 1110
1F	0001 1111	5F	0101 1111	9F	1001 1111	DF	1101 1111
20	0010 0000	60	0110 0000	A0	1010 0000	E0	1110 0000
21	0010 0001	61	0110 0001	A1	1010 0001	E1	1110 0001
22	0010 0010	62	0110 0010	A2	1010 0010	E2	1110 0010
23	0010 0011	63	0110 0011	A3	1010 0011	E3	1110 0011
24	0010 0100	64	0110 0100	A4	1010 0100	E4	1110 0100
25	0010 0101	65	0110 0101	A5	1010 0101	E5	1110 0101
26	0010 0110	66	0110 0110	A6	1010 0110	E6	1110 0110
27	0010 0111	67	0110 0111	A7	1010 0111	E7	1110 0111
28	0010 1000	68	0110 1000	A8	1010 1000	E8	1110 1000
29	0010 1001	69	0110 1001	A9	1010 1001	E9	1110 1001
2A	0010 1010	6A	0110 1010	AA	1010 1010	EA	1110 1010
2B	0010 1011	6B	0110 1011	AB	1010 1011	EB	1110 1011
2C	0010 1100	6C	0110 1100	AC	1010 1100	EC	1110 1100
2D	0010 1101	6D	0110 1101	AD	1010 1101	ED	1110 1101
2E	0010 1110	6E	0110 1110	AE	1010 1110	EE	1110 1110
2F	0010 1111	6F	0110 1111	AF	1010 1111	EF	1110 1111
30	0011 0000	70	0111 0000	B0	1011 0000	F0	1111 0000
31	0011 0001	71	0111 0001	B1	1011 0001	F1	1111 0001
32	0011 0010	72	0111 0010	B2	1011 0010	F2	1111 0010
33	0011 0011	73	0111 0011	B3	1011 0011	F3	1111 0011
34	0011 0100	74	0111 0100	B4	1011 0100	F4	1111 0100
35	0011 0101	75	0111 0101	B5	1011 0101	F5	1111 0101
36	0011 0110	76	0111 0110	B6	1011 0110	F6	1111 0110
37	0011 0111	77	0111 0111	B7	1011 0111	F7	1111 0111
38	0011 1000	78	0111 1000	B8	1011 1000	F8	1111 1000
39	0011 1001	79	0111 1001	B9	1011 1001	F9	1111 1001
3A	0011 1010	7A	0111 1010	BA	1011 1010	FA	1111 1010
3B	0011 1011	7B	0111 1011	BB	1011 1011	FB	1111 1011
3C	0011 1100	7C	0111 1100	BC	1011 1100	FC	1111 1100
3D	0011 1101	7D	0111 1101	BD	1011 1101	FD	1111 1101
3E	0011 1110	7E	0111 1110	BE	1011 1110	FE	1111 1110
3F	0011 1111	7F	0111 1111	BF	1011 1111	FF	1111 1111

Nibble Values

Hex	Binary	Hex	Binary
0	0000	8	1000
1	0001	9	1001
2	0010	A	1010
3	0011	B	1011
4	0100	C	1100
5	0101	D	1101
6	0110	E	1110
7	0111	F	1111

To Use This Table: Find the hexadecimal byte value you are looking up in one of left-most columns, and read its binary value in the same row in the column immediately to the right. For example, a hexadecimal value of 2B would result in a binary value of 0010 1011.

To Use This Table: To convert a long hexadecimal number into binary, simply use the table at the left to substitute for each hexadecimal digit. Thus a hexadecimal value of 9AF2 is 1001 1010 1111 0010 in binary.

See Also: 1.06. Binary Number Conversions
1.10. Octal to Binary Number Conversion
1.11. Decimal to Binary Number Conversion

1.03. HEXADECIMAL TO OCTAL NUMBER CONVERSION

Byte Values

Hex	Octal	Hex	Octal	Hex	Octal	Hex	Octal
0	000	40	100	80	200	C0	300
1	001	41	101	81	201	C1	301
2	002	42	102	82	202	C2	302
3	003	43	103	83	203	C3	303
4	004	44	104	84	204	C4	304
5	005	45	105	85	205	C5	305
6	006	46	106	86	206	C6	306
7	007	47	107	87	207	C7	307
8	010	48	110	88	210	C8	310
9	011	49	111	89	211	C9	311
A	012	4A	112	8A	212	CA	312
B	013	4B	113	8B	213	CB	313
C	014	4C	114	8C	214	CC	314
D	015	4D	115	8D	215	CD	315
E	016	4E	116	8E	216	CE	316
F	017	4F	117	8F	217	CF	317
10	20	50	120	90	220	D0	320
11	21	51	121	91	221	D1	321
12	22	52	122	92	222	D2	322
13	23	53	123	93	223	D3	323
14	24	54	124	94	224	D4	324
15	25	55	125	95	225	D5	325
16	26	56	126	96	226	D6	326
17	27	57	127	97	227	D7	327
18	30	58	130	98	230	D8	330
19	31	59	131	99	231	D9	331
1A	32	5A	132	9A	232	DA	332
1B	33	5B	133	9B	233	DB	333
1C	34	5C	134	9C	234	DC	334
1D	35	5D	135	9D	235	DD	335
1E	36	5E	136	9E	236	DE	336
1F	37	5F	137	9F	237	DF	337
20	40	60	140	A0	240	E0	340
21	41	61	141	A1	241	E1	341
22	42	62	142	A2	242	E2	342
23	43	63	143	A3	243	E3	343
24	44	64	144	A4	244	E4	344
25	45	65	145	A5	245	E5	345
26	46	66	146	A6	246	E6	346
27	47	67	147	A7	247	E7	347
28	50	68	150	A8	250	E8	350
29	51	69	151	A9	251	E9	351
2A	52	6A	152	AA	252	EA	352
2B	53	6B	153	AB	253	EB	353
2C	54	6C	154	AC	254	EC	354
2D	55	6D	155	AD	255	ED	355
2E	56	6E	156	AE	256	EE	356
2F	57	6F	157	AF	257	EF	357
30	60	70	160	B0	260	F0	360
31	61	71	161	B1	261	F1	361
32	62	72	162	B2	262	F2	362
33	63	73	163	B3	263	F3	363
34	64	74	164	B4	264	F4	364
35	65	75	165	B5	265	F5	365
36	66	76	166	B6	266	F6	366
37	67	77	167	B7	267	F7	367
38	70	78	170	B8	270	F8	370
39	71	79	171	B9	271	F9	371
3A	72	7A	172	BA	272	FA	372
3B	73	7B	173	BB	273	FB	373
3C	74	7C	174	BC	274	FC	374
3D	75	7D	175	BD	275	FD	375
3E	76	7E	176	BE	276	FE	376
3F	77	7F	177	BF	277	FF	377

Nibble Values

Hex	Octal
0	000
1	001
2	002
3	003
4	004
5	005
6	006
7	007
8	010
9	011
A	012
B	013
C	014
D	015
E	016
F	017

To Use This Table: Find the hexadecimal byte value you are looking up in one of the left-most columns and read its octal value in the same row in the column immediately to the right. For example, a hexadecimal value of 84 would result in an octal value of 204.

See Also:

1.08. Octal to Decimal Number Conversion
1.09. Octal to Hexadecimal Number Conversion
1.10. Octal to Binary Number Conversion
1.13. Decimal to Octal Number Conversion

1.04. HEXADECIMAL ADDITION TABLES

Results in Hexadecimal

	0	1	2	3	4	5	6	7	8	9	A	B	C	D	E	F
0	0	1	2	3	4	5	6	7	8	9	A	B	C	D	E	F
1		2	3	4	5	6	7	8	9	A	B	C	D	E	F	10
2			4	5	6	7	8	9	A	B	C	D	E	F	10	11
3				6	7	8	9	A	B	C	D	E	F	10	11	12
4					8	9	A	B	C	D	E	F	10	11	12	13
5						A	B	C	D	E	F	10	11	12	13	14
6							C	D	E	F	10	11	12	13	14	15
7								E	F	10	11	12	13	14	15	16
8									10	11	12	13	14	15	16	17
9										12	13	14	15	16	17	18
A											14	15	16	17	18	19
B												16	17	18	19	1A
C													18	19	1A	1B
D														1A	1B	1C
E															1C	1D
F																1E

Results in Decimal

	0	1	2	3	4	5	6	7	8	9	A	B	C	D	E	F
0	0	1	2	3	4	5	6	7	8	9	10	11	12	13	14	15
1		2	3	4	5	6	7	8	9	10	11	12	13	14	15	16
2			4	5	6	7	8	9	10	11	12	13	14	15	16	17
3				6	7	8	9	10	11	12	13	14	15	16	17	18
4					8	9	10	11	12	13	14	15	16	17	18	19
5						10	11	12	13	14	15	16	17	18	19	20
6							12	13	14	15	16	17	18	19	20	21
7								14	15	16	17	18	19	20	21	22
8									16	17	18	19	20	21	22	23
9										18	19	20	21	22	23	24
A											20	21	22	23	24	25
B												22	23	24	25	26
C													24	25	26	27
D														26	27	28
E															28	29
F																30

To Use This Table: Find the column/row intersection of the two hexadecimal nibble values you want to add -- the value in that cell is the result of adding the two hex nibbles together.

Table 1.04. Continued

Results in Hexadecimal

	10	20	30	40	50	60	70	80	90	A0	B0	C0	D0	E0	F0
10	20	30	40	50	60	70	80	90	A0	B0	C0	D0	E0	F0	100
20		40	50	60	70	80	90	A0	B0	C0	D0	E0	F0	100	110
30			60	70	80	90	A0	B0	C0	D0	E0	F0	100	110	120
40				80	90	A0	B0	C0	D0	E0	F0	100	110	120	130
50					A0	B0	C0	D0	E0	F0	100	110	120	130	140
60						C0	D0	E0	F0	100	110	120	130	140	150
70							E0	F0	100	110	120	130	140	150	160
80								100	110	120	130	140	150	160	170
90									120	130	140	150	160	170	180
A0										140	150	160	170	180	190
B0											160	170	180	190	1A0
C0												180	190	1A0	1B0
D0													1A0	1B0	1C0
E0														1C0	1D0
F0															1E0

Results in Decimal

	10	20	30	40	50	60	70	80	90	A0	B0	C0	D0	E0	F0
10	32	48	64	80	96	112	128	144	160	176	192	208	224	240	256
20		64	80	96	112	128	144	160	176	192	208	224	240	256	272
30			96	112	128	144	160	176	192	208	224	240	256	272	288
40				128	144	160	176	192	208	224	240	256	272	288	304
50					160	176	192	208	224	240	256	272	288	304	320
60						192	208	224	240	256	272	288	304	320	336
70							224	240	256	272	288	304	320	336	352
80								256	272	288	304	320	336	352	368
90									288	304	320	336	352	368	384
A0										320	336	352	368	384	400
B0											352	368	384	400	416
C0												384	400	416	432
D0													416	432	448
E0														448	464
F0															480

To Use This Table: Find the result at the intersection of the column and row that contain the hex numbers you are adding. If you are adding hexadecimal byte values that don't end in 0 (e.g., B4 + A6), first look up the results for the least significant digits (4 + 6 = A), then add this value to the results for the most significant digits (B0 + A0 = 150, so B4 + A6 = 15A). Remember to carry if necessary (B + B = 16, so BB + AB = 166).

See Also: 1.05. Hexadecimal Multiplication Tables

1.05. HEXADECIMAL MULTIPLICATION TABLES

Results in Hexadecimal

	0	1	2	3	4	5	6	7	8	9	A	B	C	D	E	F
0	0	0	0	0	0	0	0	0	0	0	0	0	0	0	0	0
1		1	2	3	4	5	6	7	8	9	A	B	C	D	E	F
2			4	6	8	A	C	E	10	12	14	16	18	1A	1C	1E
3				9	C	F	12	15	18	1B	1E	21	24	27	2A	2D
4					10	14	18	1C	20	24	28	2C	30	34	38	3C
5						19	1E	23	28	2D	32	37	3C	41	46	4B
6							24	2A	30	36	3C	42	48	4E	54	5A
7								31	38	3F	46	4D	54	5B	62	69
8									40	48	50	58	60	68	70	78
9										51	5A	63	6C	75	7E	87
A											64	6E	78	82	8C	96
B												79	84	8F	9A	A5
C													90	9C	A8	B4
D														A9	B6	C3
E															C4	D2
F																E1

Results in Decimal

	0	1	2	3	4	5	6	7	8	9	A	B	C	D	E	F
0	0	0	0	0	0	0	0	0	0	0	0	0	0	0	0	0
1		1	2	3	4	5	6	7	8	9	10	11	12	13	14	15
2			4	6	8	10	12	14	16	18	20	22	24	26	28	30
3				9	12	15	18	21	24	27	30	33	36	39	42	45
4					16	20	24	28	32	36	40	44	48	52	56	60
5						25	30	35	40	45	50	55	60	65	70	75
6							36	42	48	54	60	66	72	78	84	90
7								49	56	63	70	77	84	91	98	105
8									64	72	80	88	96	104	112	120
9										81	90	99	108	117	126	135
A											100	110	120	130	140	150
B												121	132	143	154	165
C													144	156	168	180
D														169	182	195
E															196	210
F																225

To Use This Table: Find the column/row intersection of the two hexadecimal nibble values you want to multiply -- the value in that cell is the result of multiplying the two hex nibbles together

See Also: 1.04. Hexadecimal Addition Tables

1.06. BINARY NUMBER CONVERSIONS

Binary	Decimal	Hex	Octal	Binary	Decimal	Hex	Octal
0000 0000	0	0	0	0100 0000	64	40	100
0000 0001	1	1	1	0100 0001	65	41	101
0000 0010	2	2	2	0100 0010	66	42	102
0000 0011	3	3	3	0100 0011	67	43	103
0000 0100	4	4	4	0100 0100	68	44	104
0000 0101	5	5	5	0100 0101	69	45	105
0000 0110	6	6	6	0100 0110	70	46	106
0000 0111	7	7	7	0100 0111	71	47	107
0000 1000	8	8	10	0100 1000	72	48	110
0000 1001	9	9	11	0100 1001	73	49	111
0000 1010	10	A	12	0100 1010	74	4A	112
0000 1011	11	B	13	0100 1011	75	4B	113
0000 1100	12	C	14	0100 1100	76	4C	114
0000 1101	13	D	15	0100 1101	77	4D	115
0000 1110	14	E	16	0100 1110	78	4E	116
0000 1111	15	F	17	0100 1111	79	4F	117
0001 0000	16	10	20	0101 0000	80	50	120
0001 0001	17	11	21	0101 0001	81	51	121
0001 0010	18	12	22	0101 0010	82	52	122
0001 0011	19	13	23	0101 0011	83	53	123
0001 0100	20	14	24	0101 0100	84	54	124
0001 0101	21	15	25	0101 0101	85	55	125
0001 0110	22	16	26	0101 0110	86	56	126
0001 0111	23	17	27	0101 0111	87	57	127
0001 1000	24	18	30	0101 1000	88	58	130
0001 1001	25	19	31	0101 1001	89	59	131
0001 1010	26	1A	32	0101 1010	90	5A	132
0001 1011	27	1B	33	0101 1011	91	5B	133
0001 1100	28	1C	34	0101 1100	92	5C	134
0001 1101	29	1D	35	0101 1101	93	5D	135
0001 1110	30	1E	36	0101 1110	94	5E	136
0001 1111	31	1F	37	0101 1111	95	5F	137
0010 0000	32	20	40	0110 0000	96	60	140
0010 0001	33	21	41	0110 0001	97	61	141
0010 0010	34	22	42	0110 0010	98	62	142
0010 0011	35	23	43	0110 0011	99	63	143
0010 0100	36	24	44	0110 0100	100	64	144
0010 0101	37	25	45	0110 0101	101	65	145
0010 0110	38	26	46	0110 0110	102	66	146
0010 0111	39	27	47	0110 0111	103	67	147
0010 1000	40	28	50	0110 1000	104	68	150
0010 1001	41	29	51	0110 1001	105	69	151
0010 1010	42	2A	52	0110 1010	106	6A	152
0010 1011	43	2B	53	0110 1011	107	6B	153
0010 1100	44	2C	54	0110 1100	108	6C	154
0010 1101	45	2D	55	0110 1101	109	6D	155
0010 1110	46	2E	56	0110 1110	110	6E	156
0010 1111	47	2F	57	0110 1111	111	6F	157
0011 0000	48	30	60	0111 0000	112	70	160
0011 0001	49	31	61	0111 0001	113	71	161
0011 0010	50	32	62	0111 0010	114	72	162
0011 0011	51	33	63	0111 0011	115	73	163
0011 0100	52	34	64	0111 0100	116	74	164
0011 0101	53	35	65	0111 0101	117	75	165
0011 0110	54	36	66	0111 0110	118	76	166
0011 0111	55	37	67	0111 0111	119	77	167
0011 1000	56	38	70	0111 1000	120	78	170
0011 1001	57	39	71	0111 1001	121	79	171
0011 1010	58	3A	72	0111 1010	122	7A	172
0011 1011	59	3B	73	0111 1011	123	7B	173
0011 1100	60	3C	74	0111 1100	124	7C	174
0011 1101	61	3D	75	0111 1101	125	7D	175
0011 1110	62	3E	76	0111 1110	126	7E	176
0011 1111	63	3F	77	0111 1111	127	7F	177

(Continued)

Table 1.06. Continued

Binary	Decimal	Hex	Octal	Binary	Decimal	Hex	Octal
1000 0000	128	80	200	1100 0000	192	C0	300
1000 0001	129	81	201	1100 0001	193	C1	301
1000 0010	130	82	202	1100 0010	194	C2	302
1000 0011	131	83	203	1100 0011	195	C3	303
1000 0100	132	84	204	1100 0100	196	C4	304
1000 0101	133	85	205	1100 0101	197	C5	305
1000 0110	134	86	206	1100 0110	198	C6	306
1000 0111	135	87	207	1100 0111	199	C7	307
1000 1000	136	88	210	1100 1000	200	C8	310
1000 1001	137	89	211	1100 1001	201	C9	311
1000 1010	138	8A	212	1100 1010	202	CA	312
1000 1011	139	8B	213	1100 1011	203	CB	313
1000 1100	140	8C	214	1100 1100	204	CC	314
1000 1101	141	8D	215	1100 1101	205	CD	315
1000 1110	142	8E	216	1100 1110	206	CE	316
1000 1111	143	8F	217	1100 1111	207	CF	317
1001 0000	144	90	220	1101 0000	208	D0	320
1001 0001	145	91	221	1101 0001	209	D1	321
1001 0010	146	92	222	1101 0010	210	D2	322
1001 0011	147	93	223	1101 0011	211	D3	323
1001 0100	148	94	224	1101 0100	212	D4	324
1001 0101	149	95	225	1101 0101	213	D5	325
1001 0110	150	96	226	1101 0110	214	D6	326
1001 0111	151	97	227	1101 0111	215	D7	327
1001 1000	152	98	230	1101 1000	216	D8	330
1001 1001	153	99	231	1101 1001	217	D9	331
1001 1010	154	9A	232	1101 1010	218	DA	332
1001 1011	155	9B	233	1101 1011	219	DB	333
1001 1100	156	9C	234	1101 1100	220	DC	334
1001 1101	157	9D	235	1101 1101	221	DD	335
1001 1110	158	9E	236	1101 1110	222	DE	336
1001 1111	159	9F	237	1101 1111	223	DF	337
1010 0000	160	A0	240	1110 0000	224	E0	340
1010 0001	161	A1	241	1110 0001	225	E1	341
1010 0010	162	A2	242	1110 0010	226	E2	342
1010 0011	163	A3	243	1110 0011	227	E3	343
1010 0100	164	A4	244	1110 0100	228	E4	344
1010 0101	165	A5	245	1110 0101	229	E5	345
1010 0110	166	A6	246	1110 0110	230	E6	346
1010 0111	167	A7	247	1110 0111	231	E7	347
1010 1000	168	A8	250	1110 1000	232	E8	350
1010 1001	169	A9	251	1110 1001	233	E9	351
1010 1010	170	AA	252	1110 1010	234	EA	352
1010 1011	171	AB	253	1110 1011	235	EB	353
1010 1100	172	AC	254	1110 1100	236	EC	354
1010 1101	173	AD	255	1110 1101	237	ED	355
1010 1110	174	AE	256	1110 1110	238	EE	356
1010 1111	175	AF	257	1110 1111	239	EF	357
1011 0000	176	B0	260	1111 0000	240	F0	360
1011 0001	177	B1	261	1111 0001	241	F1	361
1011 0010	178	B2	262	1111 0010	242	F2	362
1011 0011	179	B3	263	1111 0011	243	F3	363
1011 0100	180	B4	264	1111 0100	244	F4	364
1011 0101	181	B5	265	1111 0101	245	F5	365
1011 0110	182	B6	266	1111 0110	246	F6	366
1011 0111	183	B7	267	1111 0111	247	F7	367
1011 1000	184	B8	270	1111 1000	248	F8	370
1011 1001	185	B9	271	1111 1001	249	F9	371
1011 1010	186	BA	272	1111 1010	250	FA	372
1011 1011	187	BB	273	1111 1011	251	FB	373
1011 1100	188	BC	274	1111 1100	252	FC	374
1011 1101	189	BD	275	1111 1101	253	FD	375
1011 1110	190	BE	276	1111 1110	254	FE	376
1011 1111	191	BF	277	1111 1111	255	FF	377

To Use This Table: Find the value you want to look up by locating its binary equivalent in one of the left-most columns. Read the converted value in the appropriate column on the same row; e.g., the octal equivalent of binary 1110 is 16 (the third column).

See Also: 1.02. Hexadecimal to Binary Number Conversion
1.10. Octal to Binary Number Conversion
1.11. Decimal to Binary Number Conversion

1.07. BINARY TO SIGNED DECIMAL NUMBER CONVERSION

Binary	Decimal	Binary	Decimal	Binary	Decimal	Binary	Decimal
0000 0000	0	0100 0000	64	1000 0000	-128	1100 0000	-64
0000 0001	1	0100 0001	65	1000 0001	-127	1100 0001	-63
0000 0010	2	0100 0010	66	1000 0010	-126	1100 0010	-62
0000 0011	3	0100 0011	67	1000 0011	-125	1100 0011	-61
0000 0100	4	0100 0100	68	1000 0100	-124	1100 0100	-60
0000 0101	5	0100 0101	69	1000 0101	-123	1100 0101	-59
0000 0110	6	0100 0110	70	1000 0110	-122	1100 0110	-58
0000 0111	7	0100 0111	71	1000 0111	-121	1100 0111	-57
0000 1000	8	0100 1000	72	1000 1000	-120	1100 1000	-56
0000 1001	9	0100 1001	73	1000 1001	-119	1100 1001	-55
0000 1010	10	0100 1010	74	1000 1010	-118	1100 1010	-54
0000 1011	11	0100 1011	75	1000 1011	-117	1100 1011	-53
0000 1100	12	0100 1100	76	1000 1100	-116	1100 1100	-52
0000 1101	13	0100 1101	77	1000 1101	-115	1100 1101	-51
0000 1110	14	0100 1110	78	1000 1110	-114	1100 1110	-50
0000 1111	15	0100 1111	79	1000 1111	-113	1100 1111	-49
0001 0000	16	0101 0000	80	1001 0000	-112	1101 0000	-48
0001 0001	17	0101 0001	81	1001 0001	-111	1101 0001	-47
0001 0010	18	0101 0010	82	1001 0010	-110	1101 0010	-46
0001 0011	19	0101 0011	83	1001 0011	-109	1101 0011	-45
0001 0100	20	0101 0100	84	1001 0100	-108	1101 0100	-44
0001 0101	21	0101 0101	85	1001 0101	-107	1101 0101	-43
0001 0110	22	0101 0110	86	1001 0110	-106	1101 0110	-42
0001 0111	23	0101 0111	87	1001 0111	-105	1101 0111	-41
0001 1000	24	0101 1000	88	1001 1000	-104	1101 1000	-40
0001 1001	25	0101 1001	89	1001 1001	-103	1101 1001	-39
0001 1010	26	0101 1010	90	1001 1010	-102	1101 1010	-38
0001 1011	27	0101 1011	91	1001 1011	-101	1101 1011	-37
0001 1100	28	0101 1100	92	1001 1100	-100	1101 1100	-36
0001 1101	29	0101 1101	93	1001 1101	-99	1101 1101	-35
0001 1110	30	0101 1110	94	1001 1110	-98	1101 1110	-34
0001 1111	31	0101 1111	95	1001 1111	-97	1101 1111	-33
0010 0000	32	0110 0000	96	1010 0000	-96	1110 0000	-32
0010 0001	33	0110 0001	97	1010 0001	-95	1110 0001	-31
0010 0010	34	0110 0010	98	1010 0010	-94	1110 0010	-30
0010 0011	35	0110 0011	99	1010 0011	-93	1110 0011	-29
0010 0100	36	0110 0100	100	1010 0100	-92	1110 0100	-28
0010 0101	37	0110 0101	101	1010 0101	-91	1110 0101	-27
0010 0110	38	0110 0110	102	1010 0110	-90	1110 0110	-26
0010 0111	39	0110 0111	103	1010 0111	-89	1110 0111	-25
0010 1000	40	0110 1000	104	1010 1000	-88	1110 1000	-24
0010 1001	41	0110 1001	105	1010 1001	-87	1110 1001	-23
0010 1010	42	0110 1010	106	1010 1010	-86	1110 1010	-22
0010 1011	43	0110 1011	107	1010 1011	-85	1110 1011	-21
0010 1100	44	0110 1100	108	1010 1100	-84	1110 1100	-20
0010 1101	45	0110 1101	109	1010 1101	-83	1110 1101	-19
0010 1110	46	0110 1110	110	1010 1110	-82	1110 1110	-18
0010 1111	47	0110 1111	111	1010 1111	-81	1110 1111	-17
0011 0000	48	0111 0000	112	1011 0000	-80	1111 0000	-16
0011 0001	49	0111 0001	113	1011 0001	-79	1111 0001	-15
0011 0010	50	0111 0010	114	1011 0010	-78	1111 0010	-14
0011 0011	51	0111 0011	115	1011 0011	-77	1111 0011	-13
0011 0100	52	0111 0100	116	1011 0100	-76	1111 0100	-12
0011 0101	53	0111 0101	117	1011 0101	-75	1111 0101	-11
0011 0110	54	0111 0110	118	1011 0110	-74	1111 0110	-10
0011 0111	55	0111 0111	119	1011 0111	-73	1111 0111	-9
0011 1000	56	0111 1000	120	1011 1000	-72	1111 1000	-8
0011 1001	57	0111 1001	121	1011 1001	-71	1111 1001	-7
0011 1010	58	0111 1010	122	1011 1010	-70	1111 1010	-6
0011 1011	59	0111 1011	123	1011 1011	-69	1111 1011	-5
0011 1100	60	0111 1100	124	1011 1100	-68	1111 1100	-4
0011 1101	61	0111 1101	125	1011 1101	-67	1111 1101	-3
0011 1110	62	0111 1110	126	1011 1110	-66	1111 1110	-2
0011 1111	63	0111 1111	127	1011 1111	-65	1111 1111	-1

To Use This Table: Find the binary value you want to convert in one of the left columns. Read its corresponding signed decimal value in the same row in the column to the right.

See Also: 1.06. Binary Number Conversions

PC Sourcebook   13

1.08. OCTAL TO DECIMAL NUMBER CONVERSION

Octal	Dec	Octal	Dec	Octal	Dec	Octal	Dec
0	0	40	32	100	64	140	96
1	1	41	33	101	65	141	97
2	2	42	34	102	66	142	98
3	3	43	35	103	67	143	99
4	4	44	36	104	68	144	100
5	5	45	37	105	69	145	101
6	6	46	38	106	70	146	102
7	7	47	39	107	71	147	103
10	8	50	40	110	72	150	104
11	9	51	41	111	73	151	105
12	10	52	42	112	74	152	106
13	11	53	43	113	75	153	107
14	12	54	44	114	76	154	108
15	13	55	45	115	77	155	109
16	14	56	46	116	78	156	110
17	15	57	47	117	79	157	111
20	16	60	48	120	80	160	112
21	17	61	49	121	81	161	113
22	18	62	50	122	82	162	114
23	19	63	51	123	83	163	115
24	20	64	52	124	84	164	116
25	21	65	53	125	85	165	117
26	22	66	54	126	86	166	118
27	23	67	55	127	87	167	119
30	24	70	56	130	88	170	120
31	25	71	57	131	89	171	121
32	26	72	58	132	90	172	122
33	27	73	59	133	91	173	123
34	28	74	60	134	92	174	124
35	29	75	61	135	93	175	125
36	30	76	62	136	94	176	126
37	31	77	63	137	95	177	127

To Use This Table: Find the octal value in one of the left-most columns and read its corresponding decimal value in the column to its right in the same row

Notes: Octal is rarely used for values greater than 128 decimal

See Also: 1.03. Hexadecimal to Octal Number Conversion
1.06. Binary Number Conversions
1.13. Decimal to Octal Number Conversion

1.09. OCTAL TO HEXADECIMAL NUMBER CONVERSION

Octal	Hex	Octal	Hex	Octal	Hex	Octal	Hex
0	0	40	20	100	40	140	60
1	1	41	21	101	41	141	61
2	2	42	22	102	42	142	62
3	3	43	23	103	43	143	63
4	4	44	24	104	44	144	64
5	5	45	25	105	45	145	65
6	6	46	26	106	46	146	66
7	7	47	27	107	47	147	67
10	8	50	28	110	48	150	68
11	9	51	29	111	49	151	69
12	A	52	2A	112	4A	152	6A
13	B	53	2B	113	4B	153	6B
14	C	54	2C	114	4C	154	6C
15	D	55	2D	115	4D	155	6D
16	E	56	2E	116	4E	156	6E
17	F	57	2F	117	4F	157	6F
20	10	60	30	120	50	160	70
21	11	61	31	121	51	161	71
22	12	62	32	122	52	162	72
23	13	63	33	123	53	163	73
24	14	64	34	124	54	164	74
25	15	65	35	125	55	165	75
26	16	66	36	126	56	166	76
27	17	67	37	127	57	167	77
30	18	70	38	130	58	170	78
31	19	71	39	131	59	171	79
32	1A	72	3A	132	5A	172	7A
33	1B	73	3B	133	5B	173	7B
34	1C	74	3C	134	5C	174	7C
35	1D	75	3D	135	5D	175	7D
36	1E	76	3E	136	5E	176	7E
37	1F	77	3F	137	5F	177	7F

To Use This Table: Find the octal value in one of the left-most columns and read its corresponding hexadecimal value in the column to the right in the same row

Notes: Octal is rarely used for values greater than 128 decimal

See Also: 1.03. Hexadecimal to Octal Number Conversion

1.10. OCTAL TO BINARY NUMBER CONVERSION

Octal	Binary	Octal	Binary	Octal	Binary	Octal	Binary
0	0000 0000	40	0010 0000	100	0100 0000	140	0110 0000
1	0000 0001	41	0010 0001	101	0100 0001	141	0110 0001
2	0000 0010	42	0010 0010	102	0100 0010	142	0110 0010
3	0000 0011	43	0010 0011	103	0100 0011	143	0110 0011
4	0000 0100	44	0010 0100	104	0100 0100	144	0110 0100
5	0000 0101	45	0010 0101	105	0100 0101	145	0110 0101
6	0000 0110	46	0010 0110	106	0100 0110	146	0110 0110
7	0000 0111	47	0010 0111	107	0100 0111	147	0110 0111
10	0000 1000	50	0010 1000	110	0100 1000	150	0110 1000
11	0000 1001	51	0010 1001	111	0100 1001	151	0110 1001
12	0000 1010	52	0010 1010	112	0100 1010	152	0110 1010
13	0000 1011	53	0010 1011	113	0100 1011	153	0110 1011
14	0000 1100	54	0010 1100	114	0100 1100	154	0110 1100
15	0000 1101	55	0010 1101	115	0100 1101	155	0110 1101
16	0000 1110	56	0010 1110	116	0100 1110	156	0110 1110
17	0000 1111	57	0010 1111	117	0100 1111	157	0110 1111
20	0001 0000	60	0011 0000	120	0101 0000	160	0111 0000
21	0001 0001	61	0011 0001	121	0101 0001	161	0111 0001
22	0001 0010	62	0011 0010	122	0101 0010	162	0111 0010
23	0001 0011	63	0011 0011	123	0101 0011	163	0111 0011
24	0001 0100	64	0011 0100	124	0101 0100	164	0111 0100
25	0001 0101	65	0011 0101	125	0101 0101	165	0111 0101
26	0001 0110	66	0011 0110	126	0101 0110	166	0111 0110
27	0001 0111	67	0011 0111	127	0101 0111	167	0111 0111
30	0001 1000	70	0011 1000	130	0101 1000	170	0111 1000
31	0001 1001	71	0011 1001	131	0101 1001	171	0111 1001
32	0001 1010	72	0011 1010	132	0101 1010	172	0111 1010
33	0001 1011	73	0011 1011	133	0101 1011	173	0111 1011
34	0001 1100	74	0011 1100	134	0101 1100	174	0111 1100
35	0001 1101	75	0011 1101	135	0101 1101	175	0111 1101
36	0001 1110	76	0011 1110	136	0101 1110	176	0111 1110
37	0001 1111	77	0011 1111	137	0101 1111	177	0111 1111

To Use This Table: Find the octal value in one of the left-most columns and read its corresponding binary value in the column to the right in the same row

Notes: Octal is rarely used for values greater than 128 decimal

See Also: 1.06. Binary Number Conversions
1.08. Octal to Decimal Number Conversion
1.09. Octal to Hexadecimal Number Conversion

1.11 DECIMAL TO BINARY NUMBER CONVERSION

Dec	Binary	Dec	Binary	Dec	Binary	Dec	Binary
0	0000 0000	64	0100 0000	128	1000 0000	192	1100 0000
1	0000 0001	65	0100 0001	129	1000 0001	193	1100 0001
2	0000 0010	66	0100 0010	130	1000 0010	194	1100 0010
3	0000 0011	67	0100 0011	131	1000 0011	195	1100 0011
4	0000 0100	68	0100 0100	132	1000 0100	196	1100 0100
5	0000 0101	69	0100 0101	133	1000 0101	197	1100 0101
6	0000 0110	70	0100 0110	134	1000 0110	198	1100 0110
7	0000 0111	71	0100 0111	135	1000 0111	199	1100 0111
8	0000 1000	72	0100 1000	136	1000 1000	200	1100 1000
9	0000 1001	73	0100 1001	137	1000 1001	201	1100 1001
10	0000 1010	74	0100 1010	138	1000 1010	202	1100 1010
11	0000 1011	75	0100 1011	139	1000 1011	203	1100 1011
12	0000 1100	76	0100 1100	140	1000 1100	204	1100 1100
13	0000 1101	77	0100 1101	141	1000 1101	205	1100 1101
14	0000 1110	78	0100 1110	142	1000 1110	206	1100 1110
15	0000 1111	79	0100 1111	143	1000 1111	207	1100 1111
16	0001 0000	80	0101 0000	144	1001 0000	208	1101 0000
17	0001 0001	81	0101 0001	145	1001 0001	209	1101 0001
18	0001 0010	82	0101 0010	146	1001 0010	210	1101 0010
19	0001 0011	83	0101 0011	147	1001 0011	211	1101 0011
20	0001 0100	84	0101 0100	148	1001 0100	212	1101 0100
21	0001 0101	85	0101 0101	149	1001 0101	213	1101 0101
22	0001 0110	86	0101 0110	150	1001 0110	214	1101 0110
23	0001 0111	87	0101 0111	151	1001 0111	215	1101 0111
24	0001 1000	88	0101 1000	152	1001 1000	216	1101 1000
25	0001 1001	89	0101 1001	153	1001 1001	217	1101 1001
26	0001 1010	90	0101 1010	154	1001 1010	218	1101 1010
27	0001 1011	91	0101 1011	155	1001 1011	219	1101 1011
28	0001 1100	92	0101 1100	156	1001 1100	220	1101 1100
29	0001 1101	93	0101 1101	157	1001 1101	221	1101 1101
30	0001 1110	94	0101 1110	158	1001 1110	222	1101 1110
31	0001 1111	95	0101 1111	159	1001 1111	223	1101 1111
32	0010 0000	96	0110 0000	160	1010 0000	224	1110 0000
33	0010 0001	97	0110 0001	161	1010 0001	225	1110 0001
34	0010 0010	98	0110 0010	162	1010 0010	226	1110 0010
35	0010 0011	99	0110 0011	163	1010 0011	227	1110 0011
36	0010 0100	100	0110 0100	164	1010 0100	228	1110 0100
37	0010 0101	101	0110 0101	165	1010 0101	229	1110 0101
38	0010 0110	102	0110 0110	166	1010 0110	230	1110 0110
39	0010 0111	103	0110 0111	167	1010 0111	231	1110 0111
40	0010 1000	104	0110 1000	168	1010 1000	232	1110 1000
41	0010 1001	105	0110 1001	169	1010 1001	233	1110 1001
42	0010 1010	106	0110 1010	170	1010 1010	234	1110 1010
43	0010 1011	107	0110 1011	171	1010 1011	235	1110 1011
44	0010 1100	108	0110 1100	172	1010 1100	236	1110 1100
45	0010 1101	109	0110 1101	173	1010 1101	237	1110 1101
46	0010 1110	110	0110 1110	174	1010 1110	238	1110 1110
47	0010 1111	111	0110 1111	175	1010 1111	239	1110 1111
48	0011 0000	112	0111 0000	176	1011 0000	240	1111 0000
49	0011 0001	113	0111 0001	177	1011 0001	241	1111 0001
50	0011 0010	114	0111 0010	178	1011 0010	242	1111 0010
51	0011 0011	115	0111 0011	179	1011 0011	243	1111 0011
52	0011 0100	116	0111 0100	180	1011 0100	244	1111 0100
53	0011 0101	117	0111 0101	181	1011 0101	245	1111 0101
54	0011 0110	118	0111 0110	182	1011 0110	246	1111 0110
55	0011 0111	119	0111 0111	183	1011 0111	247	1111 0111
56	0011 1000	120	0111 1000	184	1011 1000	248	1111 1000
57	0011 1001	121	0111 1001	185	1011 1001	249	1111 1001
58	0011 1010	122	0111 1010	186	1011 1010	250	1111 1010
59	0011 1011	123	0111 1011	187	1011 1011	251	1111 1011
60	0011 1100	124	0111 1100	188	1011 1100	252	1111 1100
61	0011 1101	125	0111 1101	189	1011 1101	253	1111 1101
62	0011 1110	126	0111 1110	190	1011 1110	254	1111 1110
63	0011 1111	127	0111 1111	191	1011 1111	255	1111 1111

To Use This Table: Find the decimal byte value you are looking up in one of left columns and read its binary value in the same row in the column immediately to the right. For example, a decimal value of 43 would result in a binary value of 0010 1011.

See Also: 1.06. Binary Number Conversions
1.10. Octal to Binary Number Conversion

1.12. DECIMAL TO HEXADECIMAL NUMBER CONVERSION

Dec	Hex	Dec	Hex	Dec	Hex	Dec	Hex	Dec	Hex
1	1	27	1B	53	35	79	4F	600	258
2	2	28	1C	54	36	80	50	700	2BC
3	3	29	1D	55	37	81	51	800	320
4	4	30	1E	56	38	82	52	900	384
5	5	31	1F	57	39	83	53	1000	3E8
6	6	32	20	58	3A	84	54	2000	7D0
7	7	33	21	59	3B	85	55	3000	BB8
8	8	34	22	60	3C	86	56	4000	FA0
9	9	35	23	61	3D	87	57	5000	1388
10	A	36	24	62	3E	88	58	6000	1770
11	B	37	25	63	3F	89	59	7000	1B58
12	C	38	26	64	40	90	5A	8000	1F40
13	D	39	27	65	41	91	5B	9000	2328
14	E	40	28	66	42	92	5C	10000	2710
15	F	41	29	67	43	93	5D	20000	4E20
16	10	42	2A	68	44	94	5E	30000	7530
17	11	43	2B	69	45	95	5F	40000	9C40
18	12	44	2C	70	46	96	60	50000	C350
19	13	45	2D	71	47	97	61	60000	EA60
20	14	46	2E	72	48	98	62	70000	11170
21	15	47	2F	73	49	99	63	80000	13880
22	16	48	30	74	4A	100	64	90000	15F90
23	17	49	31	75	4B	200	C8	100000	186A0
24	18	50	32	76	4C	300	12C		
25	19	51	33	77	4D	400	190		
26	1A	52	34	78	4E	500	1F4		

To Use This Table:

Find the decimal value in the left column and read the corresponding hexadecimal value in the same row in the column to its right. If you are converting a decimal number larger than 100, you may have to perform the conversion in steps, adding the results together. For example, to convert 12345 into hex, first obtain the hex value of decimal 10000 (2710H), then add this to the value for 2000 decimal (7D0H), then add this to the value for 300 decimal (12CH), then add this to the value for 45 decimal (2DH). The proper result is 3039H; remember that the numbers you are adding are in hexadecimal. (See 1.04. Hexadecimal Addition Tables)

See Also:

1.01. Hexadecimal to Decimal Number Conversion
1.04. Hexadecimal Addition Tables

1.13. DECIMAL TO OCTAL NUMBER CONVERSION

Dec	Octal	Dec	Octal	Dec	Octal	Dec	Octal	Dec	Octal
1	1	27	33	53	65	79	117	600	1130
2	2	28	34	54	66	80	120	700	1274
3	3	29	35	55	67	81	121	800	1440
4	4	30	36	56	70	82	122	900	1604
5	5	31	37	57	71	83	123	1000	1750
6	6	32	40	58	72	84	124	2000	3720
7	7	33	41	59	73	85	125	3000	5670
8	10	34	42	60	74	86	126	4000	7640
9	11	35	43	61	75	87	127	5000	11610
10	12	36	44	62	76	88	130	6000	13560
11	13	37	45	63	77	89	131	7000	15530
12	14	38	46	64	100	90	132	8000	17500
13	15	39	47	65	101	91	133	9000	21450
14	16	40	50	66	102	92	134	10000	23420
15	17	41	51	67	103	93	135	20000	47040
16	20	42	52	68	104	94	136	30000	72460
17	21	43	53	69	105	95	137	40000	116100
18	22	44	54	70	106	96	140	50000	141520
19	23	45	55	71	107	97	141	60000	165140
20	24	46	56	72	110	98	142	70000	210560
21	25	47	57	73	111	99	143	80000	234200
22	26	48	60	74	112	100	144	90000	257620
23	27	49	61	75	113	200	310	100000	303240
24	30	50	62	76	114	300	454		
25	31	51	63	77	115	400	620		
26	32	52	64	78	116	500	764		

To Use This Table: Find the decimal value in the left column and read the corresponding octal value in the same row in the column to the right. If you are converting a decimal number larger than 100, you may have to perform the conversion in steps, adding the results together. For example, to convert 12345 into octal, first obtain the octal value of decimal 10000 (23420), then add this to the value for 2000 decimal (3720), then add this to the value for 300 decimal (454), then add this to the value for 45 decimal (55). The proper result is 30071; remember that the numbers you are adding are in octal.

See Also: 1.08. Octal to Decimal Number Conversion

1.14. TWO'S COMPLEMENTS

Binary	Complement	Binary	Complement	Binary	Complement	Binary	Complement
1111 1111	0000 0001	1011 1111	0100 0001	0111 1111	1000 0001	0011 1111	1100 0001
1111 1110	0000 0010	1011 1110	0100 0010	0111 1110	1000 0010	0011 1110	1100 0010
1111 1101	0000 0011	1011 1101	0100 0011	0111 1101	1000 0011	0011 1101	1100 0011
1111 1100	0000 0100	1011 1100	0100 0100	0111 1100	1000 0100	0011 1100	1100 0100
1111 1011	0000 0101	1011 1011	0100 0101	0111 1011	1000 0101	0011 1011	1100 0101
1111 1010	0000 0110	1011 1010	0100 0110	0111 1010	1000 0110	0011 1010	1100 0110
1111 1001	0000 0111	1011 1001	0100 0111	0111 1001	1000 0111	0011 1001	1100 0111
1111 1000	0000 1000	1011 1000	0100 1000	0111 1000	1000 1000	0011 1000	1100 1000
1111 0111	0000 1001	1011 0111	0100 1001	0111 0111	1000 1001	0011 0111	1100 1001
1111 0110	0000 1010	1011 0110	0100 1010	0111 0110	1000 1010	0011 0110	1100 1010
1111 0101	0000 1011	1011 0101	0100 1011	0111 0101	1000 1011	0011 0101	1100 1011
1111 0100	0000 1100	1011 0100	0100 1100	0111 0100	1000 1100	0011 0100	1100 1100
1111 0011	0000 1101	1011 0011	0100 1101	0111 0011	1000 1101	0011 0011	1100 1101
1111 0010	0000 1110	1011 0010	0100 1110	0111 0010	1000 1110	0011 0010	1100 1110
1111 0001	0000 1111	1011 0001	0100 1111	0111 0001	1000 1111	0011 0001	1100 1111
1111 0000	0001 0000	1011 0000	0101 0000	0111 0000	1001 0000	0011 0000	1101 0000
1110 1111	0001 0001	1010 1111	0101 0001	0110 1111	1001 0001	0010 1111	1101 0001
1110 1110	0001 0010	1010 1110	0101 0010	0110 1110	1001 0010	0010 1110	1101 0010
1110 1101	0001 0011	1010 1101	0101 0011	0110 1101	1001 0011	0010 1101	1101 0011
1110 1100	0001 0100	1010 1100	0101 0100	0110 1100	1001 0100	0010 1100	1101 0100
1110 1011	0001 0101	1010 1011	0101 0101	0110 1011	1001 0101	0010 1011	1101 0101
1110 1010	0001 0110	1010 1010	0101 0110	0110 1010	1001 0110	0010 1010	1101 0110
1110 1001	0001 0111	1010 1001	0101 0111	0110 1001	1001 0111	0010 1001	1101 0111
1110 1000	0001 1000	1010 1000	0101 1000	0110 1000	1001 1000	0010 1000	1101 1000
1110 0111	0001 1001	1010 0111	0101 1001	0110 0111	1001 1001	0010 0111	1101 1001
1110 0110	0001 1010	1010 0110	0101 1010	0110 0110	1001 1010	0010 0110	1101 1010
1110 0101	0001 1011	1010 0101	0101 1011	0110 0101	1001 1011	0010 0101	1101 1011
1110 0100	0001 1100	1010 0100	0101 1100	0110 0100	1001 1100	0010 0100	1101 1100
1110 0011	0001 1101	1010 0011	0101 1101	0110 0011	1001 1101	0010 0011	1101 1101
1110 0010	0001 1110	1010 0010	0101 1110	0110 0010	1001 1110	0010 0010	1101 1110
1110 0001	0001 1111	1010 0001	0101 1111	0110 0001	1001 1111	0010 0001	1101 1111
1110 0000	0010 0000	1010 0000	0110 0000	0110 0000	1010 0000	0010 0000	1110 0000
1101 1111	0010 0001	1001 1111	0110 0001	0101 1111	1010 0001	0001 1111	1110 0001
1101 1110	0010 0010	1001 1110	0110 0010	0101 1110	1010 0010	0001 1110	1110 0010
1101 1101	0010 0011	1001 1101	0110 0011	0101 1101	1010 0011	0001 1101	1110 0011
1101 1100	0010 0100	1001 1100	0110 0100	0101 1100	1010 0100	0001 1100	1110 0100
1101 1011	0010 0101	1001 1011	0110 0101	0101 1011	1010 0101	0001 1011	1110 0101
1101 1010	0010 0110	1001 1010	0110 0110	0101 1010	1010 0110	0001 1010	1110 0110
1101 1001	0010 0111	1001 1001	0110 0111	0101 1001	1010 0111	0001 1001	1110 0111
1101 1000	0010 1000	1001 1000	0110 1000	0101 1000	1010 1000	0001 1000	1110 1000
1101 0111	0010 1001	1001 0111	0110 1001	0101 0111	1010 1001	0001 0111	1110 1001
1101 0110	0010 1010	1001 0110	0110 1010	0101 0110	1010 1010	0001 0110	1110 1010
1101 0101	0010 1011	1001 0101	0110 1011	0101 0101	1010 1011	0001 0101	1110 1011
1101 0100	0010 1100	1001 0100	0110 1100	0101 0100	1010 1100	0001 0100	1110 1100
1101 0011	0010 1101	1001 0011	0110 1101	0101 0011	1010 1101	0001 0011	1110 1101
1101 0010	0010 1110	1001 0010	0110 1110	0101 0010	1010 1110	0001 0010	1110 1110
1101 0001	0010 1111	1001 0001	0110 1111	0101 0001	1010 1111	0001 0001	1110 1111
1101 0000	0011 0000	1001 0000	0111 0000	0101 0000	1011 0000	0001 0000	1111 0000
1100 1111	0011 0001	1000 1111	0111 0001	0100 1111	1011 0001	0000 1111	1111 0001
1100 1110	0011 0010	1000 1110	0111 0010	0100 1110	1011 0010	0000 1110	1111 0010
1100 1101	0011 0011	1000 1101	0111 0011	0100 1101	1011 0011	0000 1101	1111 0011
1100 1100	0011 0100	1000 1100	0111 0100	0100 1100	1011 0100	0000 1100	1111 0100
1100 1011	0011 0101	1000 1011	0111 0101	0100 1011	1011 0101	0000 1011	1111 0101
1100 1010	0011 0110	1000 1010	0111 0110	0100 1010	1011 0110	0000 1010	1111 0110
1100 1001	0011 0111	1000 1001	0111 0111	0100 1001	1011 0111	0000 1001	1111 0111
1100 1000	0011 1000	1000 1000	0111 1000	0100 1000	1011 1000	0000 1000	1111 1000
1100 0111	0011 1001	1000 0111	0111 1001	0100 0111	1011 1001	0000 0111	1111 1001
1100 0110	0011 1010	1000 0110	0111 1010	0100 0110	1011 1010	0000 0110	1111 1010
1100 0101	0011 1011	1000 0101	0111 1011	0100 0101	1011 1011	0000 0101	1111 1011
1100 0100	0011 1100	1000 0100	0111 1100	0100 0100	1011 1100	0000 0100	1111 1100
1100 0011	0011 1101	1000 0011	0111 1101	0100 0011	1011 1101	0000 0011	1111 1101
1100 0010	0011 1110	1000 0010	0111 1110	0100 0010	1011 1110	0000 0010	1111 1110
1100 0001	0011 1111	1000 0001	0111 1111	0100 0001	1011 1111	0000 0001	1111 1111
1100 0000	0100 0000	1000 0000	1000 0000	0100 0000	1100 0000	0000 0000	0000 0000

To Use This Table: Find the binary value you want to convert in one of the left columns. Read its corresponding two's complement value in the same row in the column to the right.

See Also: 1.06. Binary Number Conversions

1.15. COMMON 8086 FAMILY DATA FORMATS

	high word (address n+1)			low word (address n)		
	<--Most Significant					Least Significant-->
	<------ Byte 3 ------->	<------ Byte 2 ------->	<------ Byte 1 ------->	<------ Byte 0 ------->

Byte	7 6 5 4 3 2 1 0	
Word	15 14 13 12 11 10 9 8 7 6 5 4 3 2 1 0	
Double Word	31 30 29 28 27 26 25 24 23 22 21 20 19 18 17 16 15 14 13 12 11 10 9 8 7 6 5 4 3 2 1 0	

^
|
|
|
Sign Bit (if used)

Notes: Numbers in boxes are the bit numbers; note that the numbering of bits
starts with the least significant bit labeled as zero

Integer Storage Abilities

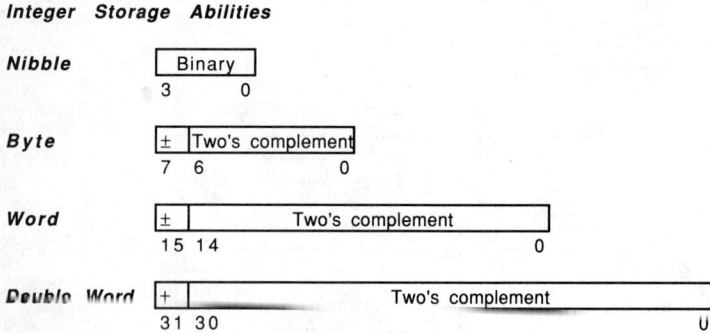

Nibble   Binary
               3   0

Byte   ± Two's complement
               7 6   0

Word   ± Two's complement
               15 14   0

Double Word + Two's complement
               31 30   0

Smallest Integer Value	Largest Integer Value
0	15
-128	127
-32,768	32,767
-2,147,483,648	2,147,483,647

Notes: Numbers beneath boxes indicate bit numbers (high=most significant)

See Also: 1.14. Two's Complements
                  1.16. Common Numeric Data Formats
                  1.17. Common String Formats

1.16. COMMON NUMERIC DATA FORMATS

8087 Word Integer

±	Two's complement

15 14   0

8087 Short Integer

±	Two's complement

31 30   0

8087 Long Integer

±	Two's complement

63 62   0

8087 Packed Decimal

±	Unused	18 consecutive 4-bit packed decimal values

79 78   72 71   0

1.0 assumed
/

8087 Short Real

±	Biased exponent (7FH)	Significand

31 30   23 22   0

1.0 assumed
/

8087 Long Real

±	Biased exponent (3FFH)	Significand

63 62   52 51   0

Explicit 1.0
|

8087 Temporary Real

±	Biased exponent (3FFFH)		Significand

79 78   64 63 62   0

1.0 assumed
/

IEEE Floating Point

±	Biased exponent (3FFH)	Significand

63 62   52 51   0

1.0 assumed
/

MASM Long Real (DQ)

Biased exponent (81H)	±	Significand

63   56 55 54   0

1.0 assumed
/

MASM Short Real (DD)

Biased exponent (81H)	±	Significand

31   24 23 22   0

Notes:

• Numbers beneath boxes indicate bit numbers (high=most significant)
• A bit value of 1 in the sign position (±) indicates the value is negative
• Exponent specifies the power of two by which the significand must be raised to obtain the value of a real number
• Significand specifies a binary value to be raised by the exponent
• Note that some data formats are "normalized" (i.e., have an assumed left-most bit of 1). Also, note that the decimal point in real numbers will be to the right of the left-most digit in the significand.
• The IEEE floating point format has an assumed high-order bit of 1 (i.e., is "normalized")
• Note that the exponent for IEEE floating point numbers is "biased" by an implementation-dependent amount. For the 8087, the real exponent = exponent - 1023.

Table 1.16. Continued

Layout of 8087 Data in Memory

	Byte Number	Legend
high	9	b=binary digit
	8	e=exponent bit
	7	s=significant bit
	6	t=two's complement bit
Position	5	±=sign bit
in	4	u=unused bit
Memory	3	
	2	
	1	
low	0	

Columns (bottom labels): Word Integer, Short Integer, Long Integer, Packed Decimal, Short Real, Long Real, Temporary Real, IEEE FP

To Use This Table: This table shows where each bit position is stored in memory, and what it is used for. Each letter or symbol in the boxes represents one bit (lower right is the least significant, upper left is most significant); each row represents one byte in memory.

Numeric Ranges Acceptable to Data Formats

	Smallest Value Accepted	Largest Value Accepted
8087 Word Integer	-32,768	32,767
8087 Short Integer	-2,147,483,648	2,147,483,647
8087 Long Integer	-9,223,372,036,854,775,808	9,223,372,036,854,775,807
8087 Packed Decimal	$-(10^{18})-1$	$(10^{18})-1$
8087 Short Real	8.43×10^{-37}	3.37×10^{38}
8087 Long Real	4.19×10^{-307}	1.67×10^{308}
8087 Temporary Real	3.4×10^{-4932}	1.2×10^{4932}
IEEE Floating Point	4.19×10^{-307}	1.67×10^{308}
MASM Long Real		
MASM Short Real		

Source: Intel 8087 Data Book, IEEE

See Also: 1.14. Two's Complements
1.15. Common 8086 Family Data Formats

1.17. COMMON STRING FORMATS

DOS Command Line — Length | String   (0, 1 ... 127)

DOS Display String (Int 21, Function 9) — String | $ (0 ... Length+1)

ASCIIZ — String | 0   (0 ... Length+1)

C * — String | 0   (0 ... Length+1)

Pascal* — StrLength | String   (0, 2 ... Length+2)

BASICA** (Microsoft BASIC) — Length | Pointer (0,1,2) --------> String (Pointer ... Pointer + Length)

Notes: •*Not all C and Pascal compilers follow these formats exactly, but this is the recognized standard for each
•**Note that for BASICA, the string and the information about it are not stored consecutively in memory

See Also: 1.15. Common 8086 Family Data Formats
1.16. Common Numeric Data Formats

1.18. COMMON MEMORY AREA TERMINOLOGY

Term	Bits	Possible Values	Description	Conventional Use
Bit	1	2	Binary digit - a single digital element	Boolean value
Nibble	4	16	One-half a byte is a "nibble"	Binary Coded Digit (0-9) or hex digit (0-F)
Byte	8	256	Standard "cell" of data, especially ASCII characters	ASCII character
Word	16	65536	8086 family of CPUs deal with this amount of data at a time	Short Integer; memory address (not including segment)
Double Word	32	4294967296	Smallest memory area that can handle an 8086 segment:offset address	Long integers or segment addresses
Paragraph	128	NA	16 consecutive bytes of data	Memory allocation blocks
Page	2048	NA	256 consecutive bytes of data	2 pages = 1 sector of data
Segment	NA	NA	65536 consecutive bytes of data	DS, CS, ES, or SS segment
Kilobyte	NA	NA	1024 bytes	NA
Megabyte	NA	NA	1048576 bytes	NA

See Also: 1.27. Powers of Two

1.19. BINARY CODED DECIMAL NUMBER FORMAT

Nibble (one BCD value)

Decimal	BCD
0	0000
1	0001
2	0010
3	0011
4	0100
5	0101
6	0110
7	0111
8	1000
9	1001

Byte (two BCD values)

Decimal	BCD	Decimal	BCD	Decimal	BCD	Decimal	BCD
00	0000 0000	25	0010 0101	50	0101 0000	75	0111 0101
01	0000 0001	26	0010 0110	51	0101 0001	76	0111 0110
02	0000 0010	27	0010 0111	52	0101 0010	77	0111 0111
03	0000 0011	28	0010 1000	53	0101 0011	78	0111 1000
04	0000 0100	29	0010 1001	54	0101 0100	79	0111 1001
05	0000 0101	30	0011 0000	55	0101 0101	80	1000 0000
06	0000 0110	31	0011 0001	56	0101 0110	81	1000 0001
07	0000 0111	32	0011 0010	57	0101 0111	82	1000 0010
08	0000 1000	33	0011 0011	58	0101 1000	83	1000 0011
09	0000 1001	34	0011 0100	59	0101 1001	84	1000 0100
10	0001 0000	35	0011 0101	60	0110 0000	85	1000 0101
11	0001 0001	36	0011 0110	61	0110 0001	86	1000 0110
12	0001 0010	37	0011 0111	62	0110 0010	87	1000 0111
13	0001 0011	38	0011 1000	63	0110 0011	88	1000 1000
14	0001 0100	39	0011 1001	64	0110 0100	89	1000 1001
15	0001 0101	40	0100 0000	65	0110 0101	90	1001 0000
16	0001 0110	41	0100 0001	66	0110 0110	91	1001 0001
17	0001 0111	42	0100 0010	67	0110 0111	92	1001 0010
18	0001 1000	43	0100 0011	68	0110 1000	93	1001 0011
19	0001 1001	44	0100 0100	69	0110 1001	94	1001 0100
20	0010 0000	45	0100 0101	70	0111 0000	95	1001 0101
21	0010 0001	46	0100 0110	71	0111 0001	96	1001 0110
22	0010 0010	47	0100 0111	72	0111 0010	97	1001 0111
23	0010 0011	48	0100 1000	73	0111 0011	98	1001 1000
24	0010 0100	49	0100 1001	74	0111 0100	99	1001 1001

Notes: Two binary coded digits may be stored in one byte, as shown in the lower table

See Also: 1.11. Decimal to Binary Number Conversion
                    1.15. Common 8086 Family Data Formats
                    1.16. Common Numeric Data Formats

1.20. ASCII CONTROL CODES

Dec	Hex	Binary	Mnemonic	Name	Definition
0	00	0000 0000	NUL	Null	Space filler character/used in output timing for some device drivers
1	01	0000 0001	SOH	Start of header	Marks beginning of message header
2	02	0000 0010	STX	Start of text	Marks beginning of data block (text)
3	03	0000 0011	ETX	End of text	Marks end of data block (text)
4	04	0000 0100	EOT	End of transmission	Marks end of transmission session
5	05	0000 0101	ENQ	Inquiry	Request for identification or information
6	06	0000 0110	ACK	Acknowledgement	"Yes" answer to queries or "ready for next transmission"/ used in asynchronous protocols for timing
7	07	0000 0111	BEL	Bell	Rings bell or audible alarm on terminal
8	08	0000 1000	BS	Backspace	Moves cursor position back one character
9	09	0000 1001	HT	Horizontal tab	Moves cursor position to next tab stop on line
10	0A	0000 1010	LF	Line feed	Moves cursor position down one line
11	0B	0000 1011	VT	Vertical tab	Moves cursor position down to next "tab line"
12	0C	0000 1100	FF	Form feed	Moves cursor position to top of next page
13	0D	0000 1101	CR	Carriage return	Moves cursor to left margin
14	0E	0000 1110	SO	Shift out	Next characters do not follow ASCII definitions
15	0F	0000 1111	SI	Shift in	Next characters revert to ASCII meaning
16	10	0001 0000	DLE	Data link escape	Used to control transmissions using "escape sequences"
17	11	0001 0001	DC1	Device control 1	Not defined; normally used for ON controls; usually user defined
18	12	0001 0010	DC2	Device control 2	Not defined; normally used for ON controls; usually user defined
19	13	0001 0011	DC3	Device control 3	Not defined; normally used for OFF controls; usually user defined
20	14	0001 0100	DC4	Device control 4	Not defined; normally used for OFF controls; usually user defined
21	15	0001 0101	NAK	Negative acknowledgment	"No" answer to questions or "errors found, retransmit"/used in asynchronous protocols
22	16	0001 0110	SYN	Synchronous idle	Sent by synchronous devices when idle to insure sync
23	17	0001 0111	ETB	End of transmission block	Marks block boundaries in transmission
24	18	0001 1000	CAN	Cancel	Indicates previous transmission should be disregarded
25	19	0001 1001	EM	End of medium	Marks end of physical media, as in paper tape
26	1A	0001 1010	SUB	Substitute	Used to replace a character known to be wrong
27	1B	0001 1011	ESC	Escape	Marks beginning of an Escape control sequence
28	1C	0001 1100	FS	File separator	Marker for major portion of transmission
29	1D	0001 1101	GS	Group separator	Marker for submajor portion of transmission
30	1E	0001 1110	RS	Record separator	Marker for minor portion of transmission
31	1F	0001 1111	US	Unit separator	Marker for most minor portion of transmission

Notes: •ASCII control codes are sometimes used to "formalize" a communications session between communications devices

•DC1, DC2, DC3, DC4, FS, GS, RS, and US all have user-defined meanings, and may vary in use between sessions or devices

•DC4 is often used as a general "stop transmission character"

•Codes used to control cursor position may be used to control print devices, and move the print head accordingly. Not all devices support the full set of positioning codes, however.

See Also: 1.21 ASCII Character Set

1.21. ASCII CHARACTER SET

Dec	Hex	Octal	Binary	Name	Character
0	00	0	0000 0000	NUL	None
1	01	1	0000 0001	SOH	^A*
2	02	2	0000 0010	STX	^B*
3	03	3	0000 0011	ETX	^C*
4	04	4	0000 0100	EOT	^D*
5	05	5	0000 0101	ENQ	^E*
6	06	6	0000 0110	ACK	^F*
7	07	7	0000 0111	BEL	^G*
8	08	10	0000 1000	BS	^H*
9	09	11	0000 1001	HT	^I*
10	0A	12	0000 1010	LF	^J*
11	0B	13	0000 1011	VT	^K*
12	0C	14	0000 1100	FF	^L*
13	0D	15	0000 1101	CR	^M*
14	0E	16	0000 1110	SO	^N*
15	0F	17	0000 1111	SI	^O*
16	10	20	0001 0000	DLE	^P*
17	11	21	0001 0001	DC1	^Q*
18	12	22	0001 0010	DC2	^R*
19	13	23	0001 0011	DC3	^S*
20	14	24	0001 0100	DC4	^T*
21	15	25	0001 0101	NAK	^U*
22	16	26	0001 0110	SYN	^V*
23	17	27	0001 0111	ETB	^W*
24	18	30	0001 1000	CAN	^X*
25	19	31	0001 1001	EM	^Y*
26	1A	32	0001 1010	SUB	^Z*
27	1B	33	0001 1011	ESC	^[*
28	1C	34	0001 1100	FS	^*
29	1D	35	0001 1101	GS	^]*
30	1E	36	0001 1110	RS	^^*
31	1F	37	0001 1111	US	^_*
32	20	40	0010 0000	space	Space
33	21	41	0010 0001	exclamation point	!
34	22	42	0010 0010	quotation mark	"
35	23	43	0010 0011	number sign	#
36	24	44	0010 0100	dollar sign	$
37	25	45	0010 0101	percent sign	%
38	26	46	0010 0110	ampersand	&
39	27	47	0010 0111	apostrophe	'
40	28	50	0010 1000	opening parenthesis	(
41	29	51	0010 1001	closing parenthesis	)
42	2A	52	0010 1010	asterisk	*
43	2B	53	0010 1011	plus sign	+
44	2C	54	0010 1100	comma	,
45	2D	55	0010 1101	hyphen or minus sign	-
46	2E	56	0010 1110	period	.
47	2F	57	0010 1111	slash	/
48	30	60	0011 0000	zero	0
49	31	61	0011 0001	one	1
50	32	62	0011 0010	two	2
51	33	63	0011 0011	three	3
52	34	64	0011 0100	four	4
53	35	65	0011 0101	five	5
54	36	66	0011 0110	six	6
55	37	67	0011 0111	seven	7
56	38	70	0011 1000	eight	8
57	39	71	0011 1001	nine	9
58	3A	72	0011 1010	colon	:
59	3B	73	0011 1011	semicolon	;
60	3C	74	0011 1100	less than sign	<
61	3D	75	0011 1101	equal sign	=
62	3E	76	0011 1110	greater than sign	>
63	3F	77	0011 1111	question mark	?

Dec	Hex	Octal	Binary	Name	Character
64	40	100	0100 0000	at sign	@
65	41	101	0100 0001	capital A	A
66	42	102	0100 0010	capital B	B
67	43	103	0100 0011	capital C	C
68	44	104	0100 0100	capital D	D
69	45	105	0100 0101	capital E	E
70	46	106	0100 0110	capital F	F
71	47	107	0100 0111	capital G	G
72	48	110	0100 1000	capital H	H
73	49	111	0100 1001	capital I	I
74	4A	112	0100 1010	capital J	J
75	4B	113	0100 1011	capital K	K
76	4C	114	0100 1100	capital L	L
77	4D	115	0100 1101	capital M	M
78	4E	116	0100 1110	capital N	N
79	4F	117	0100 1111	capital O	O
80	50	120	0101 0000	capital P	P
81	51	121	0101 0001	capital Q	Q
82	52	122	0101 0010	capital R	R
83	53	123	0101 0011	capital S	S
84	54	124	0101 0100	capital T	T
85	55	125	0101 0101	capital U	U
86	56	126	0101 0110	capital V	V
87	57	127	0101 0111	capital W	W
88	58	130	0101 1000	capital X	X
89	59	131	0101 1001	capital Y	Y
90	5A	132	0101 1010	capital Z	Z
91	5B	133	0101 1011	opening bracket	[
92	5C	134	0101 1100	backward slash	\
93	5D	135	0101 1101	closing bracket	]
94	5E	136	0101 1110	caret	^
95	5F	137	0101 1111	underscore	_
96	60	140	0110 0000	grave	`
97	61	141	0110 0001	lowercase A	a
98	62	142	0110 0010	lowercase B	b
99	63	143	0110 0011	lowercase C	c
100	64	144	0110 0100	lowercase D	d
101	65	145	0110 0101	lowercase E	e
102	66	146	0110 0110	lowercase F	f
103	67	147	0110 0111	lowercase G	g
104	68	150	0110 1000	lowercase H	h
105	69	151	0110 1001	lowercase I	i
106	6A	152	0110 1010	lowercase J	j
107	6B	153	0110 1011	lowercase K	k
108	6C	154	0110 1100	lowercase L	l
109	6D	155	0110 1101	lowercase M	m
110	6E	156	0110 1110	lowercase N	n
111	6F	157	0110 1111	lowercase O	o
112	70	160	0111 0000	lowercase P	p
113	71	161	0111 0001	lowercase Q	q
114	72	162	0111 0010	lowercase R	r
115	73	163	0111 0011	lowercase S	s
116	74	164	0111 0100	lowercase T	t
117	75	165	0111 0101	lowercase U	u
118	76	166	0111 0110	lowercase V	v
119	77	167	0111 0111	lowercase W	w
120	78	170	0111 1000	lowercase X	x
121	79	171	0111 1001	lowercase Y	y
122	7A	172	0111 1010	lowercase Z	z
123	7B	173	0111 1011	opening brace	{
124	7C	174	0111 1100	vertical line		
125	7D	175	0111 1101	closing brace	}
126	7E	176	0111 1110	tilde	~
127	7F	177	0111 1111	DEL	Delete

Notes:

•IBM does not use the ASCII codes for all characters, using, for example, the lower 32 characters for graphics (See 1.22. IBM ASCII Character Set)

•*ASCII defines characters 0-31 to be control characters (or nonprinting characters). On many systems the characters will display as shown and you can use the control sequence shown to enter these values from most systems' keyboards.

See Also:

1.20. ASCII Control Codes

1.22. IBM ASCII Character Set

1.22. IBM ASCII CHARACTER SET

Dec	Hex	Octal	Binary	Name	Character
0	00	0	0000 0000	blank	
1	01	1	0000 0001	happy face	☺
2	02	2	0000 0010	inverse happy face	☻
3	03	3	0000 0011	heart	♥
4	04	4	0000 0100	diamond	♦
5	05	5	0000 0101	club	♣
6	06	6	0000 0110	spade	♠
7	07	7	0000 0111	bullet	•
8	08	10	0000 1000	inverse bullet	◘
9	09	11	0000 1001	circle	○
10	0A	12	0000 1010	inverse circle	◙
11	0B	13	0000 1011	male sign	♂
12	0C	14	0000 1100	female sign	♀
13	0D	15	0000 1101	single note	♪
14	0E	16	0000 1110	double note	♫
15	0F	17	0000 1111	sun	☼
16	10	20	0001 0000	right triangle	▶
17	11	21	0001 0001	left triangle	◀
18	12	22	0001 0010	up/down arrow	↕
19	13	23	0001 0011	double exclamation	‼
20	14	24	0001 0100	paragraph sign	¶
21	15	25	0001 0101	section sign	§
22	16	26	0001 0110	rectangular bullet	▬
23	17	27	0001 0111	up/down to line	↨
24	18	30	0001 1000	up arrow	↑
25	19	31	0001 1001	down arrow	↓
26	1A	32	0001 1010	right arrow	→
27	1B	33	0001 1011	left arrow	←
28	1C	34	0001 1100	lower left box	└
29	1D	35	0001 1101	left/right arrow	↔
30	1E	36	0001 1110	up triangle	▲
31	1F	37	0001 1111	down triangle	▼
32	20	40	0010 0000	space	Space
33	21	41	0010 0001	exclamation point	!
34	22	42	0010 0010	quotation mark	"
35	23	43	0010 0011	number sign	#
36	24	44	0010 0100	dollar sign	$
37	25	45	0010 0101	percent sign	%
38	26	46	0010 0110	ampersand	&
39	27	47	0010 0111	apostrophe	'
40	28	50	0010 1000	opening parenthesis	(
41	29	51	0010 1001	closing parenthesis	)
42	2A	52	0010 1010	asterisk	*
43	2B	53	0010 1011	plus sign	+
44	2C	54	0010 1100	comma	,
45	2D	55	0010 1101	hyphen or minus sign	-
46	2E	56	0010 1110	period	.
47	2F	57	0010 1111	slash	/
48	30	60	0011 0000	zero	0
49	31	61	0011 0001	one	1
50	32	62	0011 0010	two	2
51	33	63	0011 0011	three	3
52	34	64	0011 0100	four	4
53	35	65	0011 0101	five	5
54	36	66	0011 0110	six	6
55	37	67	0011 0111	seven	7
56	38	70	0011 1000	eight	8
57	39	71	0011 1001	nine	9
58	3A	72	0011 1010	colon	:
59	3B	73	0011 1011	semicolon	;
60	3C	74	0011 1100	less than sign	<
61	3D	75	0011 1101	equal sign	=
62	3E	76	0011 1110	greater than sign	>
63	3F	77	0011 1111	question mark	?

Dec	Hex	Octal	Binary	Name	Character
64	40	100	0100 0000	at sign	@
65	41	101	0100 0001	capital A	A
66	42	102	0100 0010	capital B	B
67	43	103	0100 0011	capital C	C
68	44	104	0100 0100	capital D	D
69	45	105	0100 0101	capital E	E
70	46	106	0100 0110	capital F	F
71	47	107	0100 0111	capital G	G
72	48	110	0100 1000	capital H	H
73	49	111	0100 1001	capital I	I
74	4A	112	0100 1010	capital J	J
75	4B	113	0100 1011	capital K	K
76	4C	114	0100 1100	capital L	L
77	4D	115	0100 1101	capital M	M
78	4E	116	0100 1110	capital N	N
79	4F	117	0100 1111	capital O	O
80	50	120	0101 0000	capital P	P
81	51	121	0101 0001	capital Q	Q
82	52	122	0101 0010	capital R	R
83	53	123	0101 0011	capital S	S
84	54	124	0101 0100	capital T	T
85	55	125	0101 0101	capital U	U
86	56	126	0101 0110	capital V	V
87	57	127	0101 0111	capital W	W
88	58	130	0101 1000	capital X	X
89	59	131	0101 1001	capital Y	Y
90	5A	132	0101 1010	capital Z	Z
91	5B	133	0101 1011	opening bracket	[
92	5C	134	0101 1100	backward slash	\
93	5D	135	0101 1101	closing bracket	]
94	5E	136	0101 1110	caret	^
95	5F	137	0101 1111	underscore	_
96	60	140	0110 0000	grave	`
97	61	141	0110 0001	lowercase A	a
98	62	142	0110 0010	lowercase B	b
99	63	143	0110 0011	lowercase C	c
100	64	144	0110 0100	lowercase D	d
101	65	145	0110 0101	lowercase E	e
102	66	146	0110 0110	lowercase F	f
103	67	147	0110 0111	lowercase G	g
104	68	150	0110 1000	lowercase H	h
105	69	151	0110 1001	lowercase I	i
106	6A	152	0110 1010	lowercase J	j
107	6B	153	0110 1011	lowercase K	k
108	6C	154	0110 1100	lowercase L	l
109	6D	155	0110 1101	lowercase M	m
110	6E	156	0110 1110	lowercase N	n
111	6F	157	0110 1111	lowercase O	o
112	70	160	0111 0000	lowercase P	p
113	71	161	0111 0001	lowercase Q	q
114	72	162	0111 0010	lowercase R	r
115	73	163	0111 0011	lowercase S	s
116	74	164	0111 0100	lowercase T	t
117	75	165	0111 0101	lowercase U	u
118	76	166	0111 0110	lowercase V	v
119	77	167	0111 0111	lowercase W	w
120	78	170	0111 1000	lowercase X	x
121	79	171	0111 1001	lowercase Y	y
122	7A	172	0111 1010	lowercase Z	z
123	7B	173	0111 1011	opening brace	{
124	7C	174	0111 1100	vertical line		
125	7D	175	0111 1101	closing brace	}
126	7E	176	0111 1110	tilde	~
127	7F	177	0111 1111	small house	⌂

(Continued)

Table 1.22. Continued

Dec	Hex	Octal	Binary	Name	Character
128	80	200	1000 0000	C cedilla	Ç
129	81	201	1000 0001	u umlaut	ü
130	82	202	1000 0010	e acute	é
131	83	203	1000 0011	a circumflex	â
132	84	204	1000 0100	a umlaut	ä
133	85	205	1000 0101	a grave	à
134	86	206	1000 0110	a ring	å
135	87	207	1000 0111	c cedilla	ç
136	88	210	1000 1000	e circumflex	ê
137	89	211	1000 1001	e umlaut	ë
138	8A	212	1000 1010	e grave	è
139	8B	213	1000 1011	i umlaut	ï
140	8C	214	1000 1100	i circumflex	î
141	8D	215	1000 1101	i grave	ì
142	8E	216	1000 1110	A umlaut	Ä
143	8F	217	1000 1111	A ring	Å
144	90	220	1001 0000	E acute	É
145	91	221	1001 0001	ae ligature	æ
146	92	222	1001 0010	AE ligature	Æ
147	93	223	1001 0011	o circumflex	ô
148	94	224	1001 0100	o umlaut	ö
149	95	225	1001 0101	o grave	ò
150	96	226	1001 0110	u circumflex	û
151	97	227	1001 0111	u grave	ù
152	98	230	1001 1000	y umlaut	ÿ
153	99	231	1001 1001	O umlaut	Ö
154	9A	232	1001 1010	U umlaut	Ü
155	9B	233	1001 1011	cent sign	¢
156	9C	234	1001 1100	pound sign	£
157	9D	235	1001 1101	yen sign	¥
158	9E	236	1001 1110	Pt	₧
159	9F	237	1001 1111	function	ƒ
160	A0	240	1010 0000	a acute	á
161	A1	241	1010 0001	i acute	í
162	A2	242	1010 0010	o acute	ó
163	A3	243	1010 0011	u acute	ú
164	A4	244	1010 0100	n tilde	ñ
165	A5	245	1010 0101	N tilde	Ñ
166	A6	246	1010 0110	a macron	ª
167	A7	247	1010 0111	o macron	º
168	A8	250	1010 1000	opening question mark	¿
169	A9	251	1010 1001	upper left box	⌐
170	AA	252	1010 1010	upper right box	¬
171	AB	253	1010 1011	1 / 2	½
172	AC	254	1010 1100	1 / 4	¼
173	AD	255	1010 1101	opening exclamation	¡
174	AE	256	1010 1110	«	«
175	AF	257	1010 1111	»	»
176	B0	260	1011 0000	light block	░
177	B1	261	1011 0001	medium block	▒
178	B2	262	1011 0010	dark block	▓
179	B3	263	1011 0011	single vertical	│
180	B4	264	1011 0100	single right junction	┤
181	B5	265	1011 0101	2 to 1 right junction	╡
182	B6	266	1011 0110	1 to 2 right junction	╢
183	B7	267	1011 0111	1 to 2 upper right	╖
184	B8	270	1011 1000	2 to 1 upper right	╕
185	B9	271	1011 1001	double right junction	╣
186	BA	272	1011 1010	double vertical	║
187	BB	273	1011 1011	double upper right	╗
188	BC	274	1011 1100	double lower right	╝
189	BD	275	1011 1101	1 to 2 lower right	╜
190	BE	276	1011 1110	2 to 1 lower right	╛
191	BF	277	1011 1111	single upper right	┐

Dec	Hex	Octal	Binary	Name	Character
192	C0	300	1100 0000	single lower left	└
193	C1	301	1100 0001	single lower junction	┴
194	C2	302	1100 0010	single upper junction	┬
195	C3	303	1100 0011	single left junction	├
196	C4	304	1100 0100	single horizontal	─
197	C5	305	1100 0101	single intersection	┼
198	C6	306	1100 0110	2 to 1 left junction	╞
199	C7	307	1100 0111	1 to 2 left junction	╟
200	C8	310	1100 1000	double lower left	╚
201	C9	311	1100 1001	double upper left	╔
202	CA	312	1100 1010	double lower junction	╩
203	CB	313	1100 1011	double upper junction	╦
204	CC	314	1100 1100	double left junction	╠
205	CD	315	1100 1101	double horizontal	═
206	CE	316	1100 1110	double intersection	╬
207	CF	317	1100 1111	1 to 2 lower junction	╧
208	D0	320	1101 0000	2 to 1 lower junction	╨
209	D1	321	1101 0001	1 to 2 upper junction	╤
210	D2	322	1101 0010	2 to 1 upper junction	╥
211	D3	323	1101 0011	1 to 2 lower left	╙
212	D4	324	1101 0100	2 to 1 lower left	╘
213	D5	325	1101 0101	2 to 1 upper left	╒
214	D6	326	1101 0110	1 to 2 upper left	╓
215	D7	327	1101 0111	2 to 1 intersection	╫
216	D8	330	1101 1000	1 to 2 intersection	╪
217	D9	331	1101 1001	single lower right	┘
218	DA	332	1101 1010	single upper left	┌
219	DB	333	1101 1011	inverse space	█
220	DC	334	1101 1100	lower inverse	▄
221	DD	335	1101 1101	left inverse	▌
222	DE	336	1101 1110	right inverse	▐
223	DF	337	1101 1111	upper inverse	▀
224	E0	340	1110 0000	alpha	α
225	E1	341	1110 0001	beta	β
226	E2	342	1110 0010	gamma	Γ
227	E3	343	1110 0011	pi	π
228	E4	344	1110 0100	sigma	Σ
229	E5	345	1110 0101	sigma	σ
230	E6	346	1110 0110	mu	μ
231	E7	347	1110 0111	tau	τ
232	E8	350	1110 1000	phi	Φ
233	E9	351	1110 1001	theta	Θ
234	EA	352	1110 1010	omega	Ω
235	EB	353	1110 1011	delta	δ
236	EC	354	1110 1100	infinity	∞
237	ED	355	1110 1101	phi	φ
238	EE	356	1110 1110	epsilon	ε
239	EF	357	1110 1111	intersection of sets	∩
240	F0	360	1111 0000	is identical to	≡
241	F1	361	1111 0001	plus/minus sign	±
242	F2	362	1111 0010	greater/equal sign	≥
243	F3	363	1111 0011	less/equal sign	≤
244	F4	364	1111 0100	top half integral	⌠
245	F5	365	1111 0101	lower half integral	⌡
246	F6	366	1111 0110	divide by sign	÷
247	F7	367	1111 0111	approximately	≈
248	F8	370	1111 1000	degree	°
249	F9	371	1111 1001	filled in degree	∙
250	FA	372	1111 1010	small bullet	·
251	FB	373	1111 1011	square root	√
252	FC	374	1111 1100	superscript n	η
253	FD	375	1111 1101	superscript 2	²
254	FE	376	1111 1110	box	■
255	FF	377	1111 1111	phantom space	

Notes: The line drawing charaters are given arbitrary names in this table in this manner: the left-most component is named first, followed by the word "to," followed by the right-most component. Thus, if we were naming the upper left corner of a single-line box, it would be "1 to 1 upper left ." If the left side of the box were double lined, it would be "2 to 1 upper left."

Source: IBM PC/XT Technical Reference, pages C-12, 13

See Also: 1.21. ASCII Character Set
1.23. IBM Extended Character Codes
7.05. PC and XT Key Numbers and Scan Codes
7.06. AT 84-Key Key Numbers and Scan Codes
7.07. AT 101/102-Key Key Numbers and Scan Codes
7.08. PS/2 Key Numbers and Scan Codes

1.23. IBM EXTENDED CHARACTER CODES

Dec	Hex	Octal	Binary	Actual Keys Pressed
3	03	3	0000 0011	Null character (none)
15	0F	17	0000 1111	Shift Tab
16	10	20	0001 0000	Alt + Q
17	11	21	0001 0001	Alt + W
18	12	22	0001 0010	Alt + E
19	13	23	0001 0011	Alt + R
20	14	24	0001 0100	Alt + T
21	15	25	0001 0101	Alt + Y
22	16	26	0001 0110	Alt + U
23	17	27	0001 0111	Alt + I
24	18	30	0001 1000	Alt + O
25	19	31	0001 1001	Alt + P
30	1E	36	0001 1110	Alt + A
31	1F	37	0001 1111	Alt + S
32	20	40	0010 0000	Alt + D
33	21	41	0010 0001	Alt + F
34	22	42	0010 0010	Alt + G
35	23	43	0010 0011	Alt + H
36	24	44	0010 0100	Alt + J
37	25	45	0010 0101	Alt + K
38	26	46	0010 0110	Alt + L
44	2C	54	0010 1100	Alt + Z
45	2D	55	0010 1101	Alt + X
46	2E	56	0010 1110	Alt + C
47	2F	57	0010 1111	Alt + V
48	30	60	0011 0000	Alt + B
49	31	61	0011 0001	Alt + N
50	32	62	0011 0010	Alt + M
59	3B	73	0011 1011	Function key 1
60	3C	74	0011 1100	Function key 2
61	3D	75	0011 1101	Function key 3
62	3E	76	0011 1110	Function key 4
63	3F	77	0011 1111	Function key 5
64	40	100	0100 0000	Function key 6
65	41	101	0100 0001	Function key 7
66	42	102	0100 0010	Function key 8
67	43	103	0100 0011	Function key 9
68	44	104	0100 0100	Function key 10
71	47	107	0100 0111	Home
72	48	110	0100 1000	Up arrow
73	49	111	0100 1001	Page Up
75	4B	113	0100 1011	Left arrow
77	4D	115	0100 1101	Right arrow
79	4F	117	0100 1111	End
80	50	120	0101 0000	Down arrow
81	51	121	0101 0001	Page Down
82	52	122	0101 0010	Insert
83	53	123	0101 0011	Delete
84	54	124	0101 0100	Shift + F1

Dec	Hex	Octal	Binary	Actual Keys Pressed
85	55	125	0101 0101	Shift + F2
86	56	126	0101 0110	Shift + F3
87	57	127	0101 0111	Shift + F4
88	58	130	0101 1000	Shift + F5
89	59	131	0101 1001	Shift + F6
90	5A	132	0101 1010	Shift + F7
91	5B	133	0101 1011	Shift + F8
92	5C	134	0101 1100	Shift + F9
93	5D	135	0101 1101	Shift + F10
94	5E	136	0101 1110	Control + F1
95	5F	137	0101 1111	Control + F2
96	60	140	0110 0000	Control + F3
97	61	141	0110 0001	Control + F4
98	62	142	0110 0010	Control + F5
99	63	143	0110 0011	Control + F6
100	64	144	0110 0100	Control + F7
101	65	145	0110 0101	Control + F8
102	66	146	0110 0110	Control + F9
103	67	147	0110 0111	Control + F10
104	68	150	0110 1000	Alt + F1
105	69	151	0110 1001	Alt + F2
106	6A	152	0110 1010	Alt + F3
107	6B	153	0110 1011	Alt + F4
108	6C	154	0110 1100	Alt + F5
109	6D	155	0110 1101	Alt + F6
110	6E	156	0110 1110	Alt + F7
111	6F	157	0110 1111	Alt + F8
112	70	160	0111 0000	Alt + F9
113	71	161	0111 0001	Alt + F10
114	72	162	0111 0010	Control + PrtSc
115	73	163	0111 0011	Control + Left arrow
116	74	164	0111 0100	Control + Right arrow
117	75	165	0111 0101	Control + End
118	76	166	0111 0110	Control + PgDn
119	77	167	0111 0111	Control + Home
120	78	170	0111 1000	Alt + upper row 1
121	79	171	0111 1001	Alt + upper row 2
122	7A	172	0111 1010	Alt + upper row 3
123	7B	173	0111 1011	Alt + upper row 4
124	7C	174	0111 1100	Alt + upper row 5
125	7D	175	0111 1101	Alt + upper row 6
126	7E	176	0111 1110	Alt + upper row 7
127	7F	177	0111 1111	Alt + upper row 8
128	80	200	1000 0000	Alt + upper row 9
129	81	201	1000 0001	Alt + upper row 0
130	82	202	1000 0010	Alt + hyphen
131	83	203	1000 0011	Alt + equals
132	84	204	1000 0100	Control + PgUp

Notes: Extended codes are preceded by a byte of 00H;
(e.g., 00H, 81H means Alt and Zero were held down)

Source: IBM PC/XT Technical Reference, page 2-14

See Also: 1.21. ASCII Character Set
1.22. IBM ASCII Character Set
7.05. PC keyboard Key Numbers and Scan Codes
7.06. AT 84-key Key Numbers and Scan Codes
7.07. AT 101/102-key Key Numbers and Scan Codes
7.08. PS/2 Key Numbers and Scan Codes

1.24. LINE DRAWING CHARACTER SET

| 218 ┌ | 196 ─ | 194 ┬ | 191 ┐ | | 201 ╔ | 203 ╦ | 187 ╗ |

179 │

| 195 ├ | 197 ┼ | 180 ┤ | | 204 ╠ | 206 ╬ | 185 ╣ |

| 192 └ | 193 ┴ | 217 ┘ | | 200 ╚ | 202 ╩ | 188 ╝ |

| 213 ╒ | 205 ═ | 209 ╤ | 184 ╕ | | 214 ╓ | 210 ╖ | 183 ╖ |

186 ║

| 198 ╞ | 216 ╪ | 181 ╡ | | 199 ╟ | 215 ╫ | 182 ╢ |

| 212 ╘ | 207 ╧ | 190 ╛ | | 211 ╙ | 208 ╨ | 189 ╜ |

Notes: Line characters can be drawn by holding down the Alt key and typing the associated three-digit number on the number pad

Source: IBM PC/XT Technical Reference, page C-13

See Also: 1.22. IBM ASCII Character Set

1.25. EBCDIC CHARACTER SET

Dec	Hex	Octal	Binary	Name	Character
0	00	0	0000 0000	NUL	
1	01	1	0000 0001	SOH	
2	02	2	0000 0010	STX	
3	03	3	0000 0011	ETX	
4	04	4	0000 0100	PF	
5	05	5	0000 0101	HT	
6	06	6	0000 0110	LC	
7	07	7	0000 0111	DEL	
8	08	10	0000 1000	GE	
9	09	11	0000 1001	RLF	
10	0A	12	0000 1010	SMM	
11	0B	13	0000 1011	VT	
12	0C	14	0000 1100	FF	
13	0D	15	0000 1101	CR	
14	0E	16	0000 1110	SO	
15	0F	17	0000 1111	SI	
16	10	20	0001 0000	DLE	
17	11	21	0001 0001	DC1	
18	12	22	0001 0010	DC2	
19	13	23	0001 0011	TM	
20	14	24	0001 0100	RES	
21	15	25	0001 0101	NL	
22	16	26	0001 0110	BS	
23	17	27	0001 0111	IL	
24	18	30	0001 1000	CAN	
25	19	31	0001 1001	EM	
26	1A	32	0001 1010	CC	
27	1B	33	0001 1011	CU1	
28	1C	34	0001 1100	IFS	
29	1D	35	0001 1101	IGS	
30	1E	36	0001 1110	IRS	
31	1F	37	0001 1111	IUS	
32	20	40	0010 0000	DS	
33	21	41	0010 0001	SOS	
34	22	42	0010 0010	FS	
35	23	43	0010 0011		
36	24	44	0010 0100	BYP	
37	25	45	0010 0101	LF	
38	26	46	0010 0110	ETB	
39	27	47	0010 0111	ESC	
40	28	50	0010 1000		
41	29	51	0010 1001		
42	2A	52	0010 1010	SM	
43	2B	53	0010 1011	CU2	
44	2C	54	0010 1100		
45	2D	55	0010 1101	ENQ	
46	2E	56	0010 1110	ACK	
47	2F	57	0010 1111	BEL	
48	30	60	0011 0000		
49	31	61	0011 0001		
50	32	62	0011 0010	SYN	
51	33	63	0011 0011		
52	34	64	0011 0100	PN	
53	35	65	0011 0101	RS	
54	36	66	0011 0110	UC	
55	37	67	0011 0111	EOT	
56	38	70	0011 1000		
57	39	71	0011 1001		
58	3A	72	0011 1010		
59	3B	73	0011 1011	CU3	
60	3C	74	0011 1100	DC4	
61	3D	75	0011 1101	NAK	
62	3E	76	0011 1110		
63	3F	77	0011 1111	SUB	
64	40	100	0100 0000	SP	
65	41	101	0100 0001		
66	42	102	0100 0010		
67	43	103	0100 0011		
68	44	104	0100 0100		
69	45	105	0100 0101		
70	46	106	0100 0110		
71	47	107	0100 0111		
72	48	110	0100 1000		
73	49	111	0100 1001		
74	4A	112	0100 1010	¢	
75	4B	113	0100 1011	.	
76	4C	114	0100 1100	<	
77	4D	115	0100 1101	(	
78	4E	116	0100 1110	+	
79	4F	117	0100 1111			
80	50	120	0101 0000	&	
81	51	121	0101 0001		
82	52	122	0101 0010		
83	53	123	0101 0011		
84	54	124	0101 0100		
85	55	125	0101 0101		
86	56	126	0101 0110		
87	57	127	0101 0111		
88	58	130	0101 1000		
89	59	131	0101 1001		
90	5A	132	0101 1010	!	
91	5B	133	0101 1011	$	
92	5C	134	0101 1100	*	
93	5D	135	0101 1101	)	
94	5E	136	0101 1110	;	
95	5F	137	0101 1111	¬	
96	60	140	0110 0000	-	
97	61	141	0110 0001	/	
98	62	142	0110 0010		
99	63	143	0110 0011		
100	64	144	0110 0100		
101	65	145	0110 0101		
102	66	146	0110 0110		
103	67	147	0110 0111		
104	68	150	0110 1000		
105	69	151	0110 1001		
106	6A	152	0110 1010	¦	
107	6B	153	0110 1011	,	
108	6C	154	0110 1100	%	
109	6D	155	0110 1101	_	
110	6E	156	0110 1110	>	
111	6F	157	0110 1111	?	
112	70	160	0111 0000		
113	71	161	0111 0001		
114	72	162	0111 0010		
115	73	163	0111 0011		
116	74	164	0111 0100		
117	75	165	0111 0101		
118	76	166	0111 0110		
119	77	167	0111 0111		
120	78	170	0111 1000		
121	79	171	0111 1001		
122	7A	172	0111 1010	:	
123	7B	173	0111 1011	#	
124	7C	174	0111 1100	@	
125	7D	175	0111 1101	'	
126	7E	176	0111 1110	=	
127	7F	177	0111 1111	"	

(Continued)

Table 1.25. Continued

Dec	Hex	Octal	Binary	Name	Character
128	80	200	1000 0000		
129	81	201	1000 0001		a
130	82	202	1000 0010		b
131	83	203	1000 0011		c
132	84	204	1000 0100		d
133	85	205	1000 0101		e
134	86	206	1000 0110		f
135	87	207	1000 0111		g
136	88	210	1000 1000		h
137	89	211	1000 1001		i
138	8A	212	1000 1010		
139	8B	213	1000 1011		
140	8C	214	1000 1100		
141	8D	215	1000 1101		
142	8E	216	1000 1110		
143	8F	217	1000 1111		
144	90	220	1001 0000		
145	91	221	1001 0001		j
146	92	222	1001 0010		k
147	93	223	1001 0011		l
148	94	224	1001 0100		m
149	95	225	1001 0101		n
150	96	226	1001 0110		o
151	97	227	1001 0111		p
152	98	230	1001 1000		q
153	99	231	1001 1001		r
154	9A	232	1001 1010		
155	9B	233	1001 1011		
156	9C	234	1001 1100		
157	9D	235	1001 1101		
158	9E	236	1001 1110		
159	9F	237	1001 1111		
160	A0	240	1010 0000		
161	A1	241	1010 0001		~
162	A2	242	1010 0010		s
163	A3	243	1010 0011		t
164	A4	244	1010 0100		u
165	A5	245	1010 0101		v
166	A6	246	1010 0110		w
167	A7	247	1010 0111		x
168	A8	250	1010 1000		y
169	A9	251	1010 1001		z
170	AA	252	1010 1010		
171	AB	253	1010 1011		
172	AC	254	1010 1100		
173	AD	255	1010 1101		
174	AE	256	1010 1110		
175	AF	257	1010 1111		
176	B0	260	1011 0000		
177	B1	261	1011 0001		
178	B2	262	1011 0010		
179	B3	263	1011 0011		
180	B4	264	1011 0100		
181	B5	265	1011 0101		
182	B6	266	1011 0110		
183	B7	267	1011 0111		
184	B8	270	1011 1000		
185	B9	271	1011 1001		
186	BA	272	1011 1010		
187	BB	273	1011 1011		
188	BC	274	1011 1100		
189	BD	275	1011 1101		
190	BE	276	1011 1110		
191	BF	277	1011 1111		
192	C0	300	1100 0000		{
193	C1	301	1100 0001		A
194	C2	302	1100 0010		B
195	C3	303	1100 0011		C
196	C4	304	1100 0100		D
197	C5	305	1100 0101		E
198	C6	306	1100 0110		F
199	C7	307	1100 0111		G
200	C8	310	1100 1000		H
201	C9	311	1100 1001		I
202	CA	312	1100 1010		
203	CB	313	1100 1011		
204	CC	314	1100 1100		∫
205	CD	315	1100 1101		
206	CE	316	1100 1110		Ψ
207	CF	317	1100 1111		
208	D0	320	1101 0000		}
209	D1	321	1101 0001		J
210	D2	322	1101 0010		K
211	D3	323	1101 0011		L
212	D4	324	1101 0100		M
213	D5	325	1101 0101		N
214	D6	326	1101 0110		O
215	D7	327	1101 0111		P
216	D8	330	1101 1000		Q
217	D9	331	1101 1001		R
218	DA	332	1101 1010		
219	DB	333	1101 1011		
220	DC	334	1101 1100		
221	DD	335	1101 1101		
222	DE	336	1101 1110		
223	DF	337	1101 1111		
224	E0	340	1110 0000		\
225	E1	341	1110 0001		
226	E2	342	1110 0010		S
227	E3	343	1110 0011		T
228	E4	344	1110 0100		U
229	E5	345	1110 0101		V
230	E6	346	1110 0110		W
231	E7	347	1110 0111		X
232	E8	350	1110 1000		Y
233	E9	351	1110 1001		Z
234	EA	352	1110 1010		
235	EB	353	1110 1011		
236	EC	354	1110 1100		н
237	ED	355	1110 1101		
238	EE	356	1110 1110		
239	EF	357	1110 1111		
240	F0	360	1111 0000		0
241	F1	361	1111 0001		1
242	F2	362	1111 0010		2
243	F3	363	1111 0011		3
244	F4	364	1111 0100		4
245	F5	365	1111 0101		5
246	F6	366	1111 0110		6
247	F7	367	1111 0111		7
248	F8	370	1111 1000		8
249	F9	371	1111 1001		9
250	FA	372	1111 1010			
251	FB	373	1111 1011		
252	FC	374	1111 1100		
253	FD	375	1111 1101		
254	FE	376	1111 1110		
255	FF	377	1111 1111		EO

See Also: 1.21. ASCII Character Set

1.26. DIGIT POSITIONS IN COMMON BASES

Digit Position Value

Base	Name	6th Pos.	5th Pos.	4th Pos.	3rd Pos.	2nd Pos.	1st Pos.
2	binary	3 2	1 6	8	4	2	1
8	octal	32768	4096	5 1 2	6 4	8	1
1 0	decimal	100000	10000	1000	100	1 0	1
1 6	hexadecimal	1048576	65536	4096	256	1 6	1

Notes: The first digit position is the least significant

See Also: 1.11. Decimal to Binary Number Conversion
1.12. Decimal to Hexadecimal Number Conversion
1.13. Decimal to Octal Number Conversion

1.27. POWERS OF TWO

Power	Value	Common Definitions and Usage
2^1	2	(1 bit may have 2 possible values) (2 bytes = word)
2^2	4	(4 bits = nibble, BCD Digit) (4 bytes = double word)
2^3	8	(8 bits = byte, ASCII Character)
2^4	1 6	(16 bits = word, Near Address) (16 bytes = paragraph)
2^5	3 2	(32 bits = double word, Far Address)
2^6	6 4	
2^7	128	
2^8	256	(1 byte may have 256 possible values) (256 bytes = page)
2^9	512	
2^{10}	1,024	(1,024 bytes = kilobyte)
2^{11}	2,048	
2^{12}	4,096	
2^{13}	8,192	
2^{14}	16,384	
2^{15}	32,768	
2^{16}	65,536	(65,536 bytes = segment)
2^{17}	131,072	
2^{18}	262,144	
2^{19}	524,288	
2^{20}	1,048,576	(1,048,576 bytes = megabyte)
2^{21}	2,097,152	
2^{22}	4,194,304	
2^{23}	8,388,608	
2^{24}	16,777,216	
2^{25}	33,554,432	

Notes: 2^{15} means "2 raised to the 15th power"

See Also: 1.15. Common 8086 Family Data Formats
1.18. Common Memory Area Terminology

1.28. INTERNATIONAL SORT ORDERING

In ASCII sort ordering, characters are sorted as follows:
-Lower numbered ASCII characters appear before higher numbered ones, thus:
-All uppercase characters appear before lowercase ones
-Characters with diacritical marks come after all other letters

ASCII sort ordering would treat the alphabet like this:

ASCII Code	Character		ASCII Code	Character
65	A		114	r
66	B		115	s
67	C		116	t
68	D		117	u
69	E		118	v
70	F		119	w
71	G		120	x
72	H		121	y
73	I		122	z
74	J		128	Ç
75	K		129	ü
76	L		130	é
77	M		131	â
78	N		132	ä
79	O		133	à
80	P		134	å
81	Q		135	ç
82	R		136	ê
83	S		137	ë
84	T		138	è
85	U		139	ï
86	V		140	î
87	W		141	ì
88	X		142	Ä
89	Y		143	Å
90	Z		144	É
97	a		145	æ
98	b		146	Æ
99	c		147	ô
100	d		148	ö
101	e		149	ò
102	f		150	û
103	g		151	ù
104	h		152	ÿ
105	i		153	Ö
106	j		154	Ü
107	k		160	á
108	l		161	í
109	m		162	ó
110	n		163	ú
111	o		164	ñ
112	p		165	Ñ
113	q		225	ß

Table 1.28. Continued

In International sort ordering, ASCII sort order is changed, as follows:
-Characters are sorted by alphabetical position: A and a are equal and come before B
-Characters with diacritical marks are expanded accordingly: umlauted a becomes
ae for sort ordering, ß becomes ss, etc.
-Lowercase characters are applied first, for example, deJesus appears before DeJesus
-Norwegian, Danish, Swedish, and Finnish å, Å and umlauted characters are placed at
the end of the regular alphabet for those countries

International sort ordering would treat the alphabet like this:

ASCII Code	Character	ASCII Code	Character	ASCII Code	Character
97	a	139	ï	82	R
132	ä	161	í	115	s
160	á	141	ì	225	ß
133	à	140	î	83	S
131	â	73	I	116	t
65	A	106	j	84	T
142	Ä	74	J	117	u
98	b	107	k	129	ü
66	B	75	K	163	ú
99	c	108	l	151	ù
135	ç	76	L	150	û
67	C	109	m	85	U
128	Ç	77	M	154	Ü
100	d	110	n	118	v
68	D	164	ñ	86	V
101	e	78	N	119	w
137	ë	165	Ñ	87	W
130	é	111	o	120	x
138	è	148	ö	88	X
136	ê	162	ó	121	y
69	E	149	ò	152	ÿ
144	É	147	ô	89	Y
102	f	79	O	122	z
70	F	153	Ö	90	Z
103	g	112	p	134	å
71	G	80	P	143	Å
104	h	113	q	145	æ
72	H	81	Q	146	Æ
105	i	114	r		

Source: Paradox 2.0 User's Guide, pages 519 to 521

1.29. TRUTH TABLES FOR LOGICAL OPERATIONS

AND

Condition 1	Condition 2	Result
TRUE	TRUE	TRUE
TRUE	FALSE	FALSE
FALSE	TRUE	FALSE
FALSE	FALSE	FALSE

OR

Condition 1	Condition 2	Result
TRUE	TRUE	TRUE
TRUE	FALSE	TRUE
FALSE	TRUE	TRUE
FALSE	FALSE	FALSE

EXCLUSIVE OR

Condition 1	Condition 2	Result
TRUE	TRUE	FALSE
TRUE	FALSE	FALSE
FALSE	TRUE	FALSE
FALSE	FALSE	TRUE

EXCLUSIVE AND

Condition 1	Condition 2	Result
TRUE	TRUE	FALSE
TRUE	FALSE	TRUE
FALSE	TRUE	TRUE
FALSE	FALSE	TRUE

NOT

Condition	Result
TRUE	FALSE
FALSE	TRUE

Notes: The resulting value is read by finding a row in which the conditions you are looking up are met and by reading the result in the right-most column of that row

PART

II

SOFTWARE

— SECTION —

2

DOS Commands, Utilities, and Summaries

2.01. DOS COMMAND SUMMARY

Command Syntax	Function	Example	Comments
APPEND d:path[;d:path...]	Locates files outside current directory	APPEND c:\dbfiles	See 2.02. APPEND Parameters
ASSIGN [x[=]y [...]]	Routes disk I/O to another drive	ASSIGN a=c b=c	
ATTRIB [±parms] [d:][path][filespec/parms]	Modifies file attributes	ATTRIB -r myfile.doc /s	See 2.03. ATTRIB Parameters
BACKUP d:[path][filespec] d:[/parms]	Backs up one disk to another	BACKUP c:*.* a:/S/F	See 2.04. BACKUP Parameters
BREAK [ON|OFF]	Defines status of control break	BREAK ON	
CHCP [number]	Selects code page DOS uses	CHCP 850	Must execute NLSFUNC first
CHDIR [d:][path]	Sets or displays current path	CD c:\wp\word\data	May be abbreviated to CD
CHKDSK [d:][path][filespec][/parms]	Analyzes disk and FAT	CHKDSK c:/F	See 2.05. CHKDSK Parameters
CLS	Clears display screen	CLS	
COMMAND [d:][path][/parms]	Starts a secondary command processor	COMMAND c:\ut /p	See 2.06. COMMAND Parameters
COMP [d:][path][filespec][c:][path][filespec]	Compares contents of files	COMP *.BAT A:*.BAT	
COPY [/parms][d:][path][filespec][/parms] [d:][path][filespec][/parms]	Copies a file or set of files	COPY *.* c:	See 2.07. COPY Parameters
CTTY devicename	Changes stdin and stdout to auxiliary console	CTTY COM1	
DATE [date]	Enters, changes, or displays date	DATE 1-12-87	
DEL [d:][path][filespec]	Deletes specified file or files	DEL *.bak	See also ERASE below
DIR [d:][path][filespec][/parms]	Lists directory entries	DIR c:/w	See 2.08. DIR Parameters
DISKCOMP [d: [d:]][/parms]	Compares contents of two disks	DISKCOMP a: b:	See 2.09. DISKCOMP Parameters
DISKCOPY [d: [d:]][/parms]	Copies a disk	DISKCOPY a: b:	See 2.10. DISKCOPY Parameters
ERASE [d:][path][filespec]	Deletes specified file or files	ERASE *.bak	See also DEL above
FASTOPEN d:[=number]...	Stores location of opened files in memory	FASTOPEN c:=100	
FDISK	Creates, changes, or displays DOS partitions	FDISK	
FIND [/parms] "string" [[d:][path]filespec...]	Finds lines in files with matching "string"	FIND /N "Thom" c:m./file.dat	See 2.11. FIND Parameters
FORMAT d:[/parms]	Formats disk for use	FORMAT a:/s	See 2.12. FORMAT Parameters
GRAFTABL [437|860|863|865|/STATUS]	Loads additional character data into memory	GRAFTABLE 437	See 2.13. GRAFTABL Parameters
GRAPHICS [printer][/parms]	Sets system to print graphic displays	GRAPHICS COLOR1 /R	See 2.14. GRAPHICS Parameters
JOIN or JOIN d: d: \directory or JOIN d: /D	Logically connects drives	JOIN b: /d	
KEYB[xx[,[yyy]],[[d:][path]filespec]]]	Loads keyboard driver to replace BIOS routines	KEYBUK	
LABEL [d:][label]	Creates, changes, or displays volume label	LABEL c:thomhogan	
MKDIR [d:]path	Creates subdirectory	MKDIR c:\ss\excel\data	May be abbreviated to MD
MODE LPT#[:][n][,m[,p]]	Sets printer specifications	MODE lpt1:132,8,p	See 2.15. MODE Parameters
MODE n	Sets video display mode	MODE CO80	See 2.15. MODE Parameters
MODE [n,m[,T]	Sets video display mode	MODE 80,r,t	See 2.15. MODE Parameters
MODE COM#[:baud[,parity[,databits][,stopbits][,P]]]	Sets serial port specifications	MODE com1:12,n,8,1,p	See 2.15. MODE Parameters
MODE LPT#[:]=COM#	Redirects parallel printer output	MODE lpt1:=com1	See 2.15. MODE Parameters
MODE device CODEPAGE PREPARE=((cp) [d:][path]filespec)	Prepares code pages	MODE lpt1 cp prep=((850,,863)4201.cpi)	See 2.15. MODE Parameters
MODE device CODEPAGE PREPARE=((cplist)[d:][path]filespec)	Prepares code pages	MODE lpt1 cp prep=((850) 4201.cpi)	See 2.15. MODE Parameters
MODE device CODEPAGE SELECT=cp	Selects or activates code pages	MODE lpt1 cp select=863	See 2.15. MODE Parameters
MODE device CODEPAGE [STATUS]	Displays active code page	MODE lpt1 cp	See 2.15. MODE Parameters
MODE device CODEPAGE REFRESH	Refreshes a code page	MODE lpt1 cp refresh	See 2.15. MODE Parameters
MORE	Reads data from stdin, sends paged to stdout	MORE <screen.doc	
NLSFUNC [[d:][path]filespec]	Provides extended country support	NLSFUNC c:\ut\country.sys	
PATH [/parms][[d:][path]|;]	Sets search path for commands	PATH c:;c:\ut;c:\dos	See 2.16. PRINT Parameters
PRINT [/parms][[d:][path]filespec;...]	Puts selected files in print queue	PRINT c:*.asm	See 2.17. PROMPT Special Characters
PROMPT [prompt]	Sets new DOS prompt	PROMPT pg	
RECOVER [d:][path]filespec or RECOVER d:	Recovers files from defective disk	RECOVER c:	
RENAME [d:][path]filespec1 filespec2	Renames a file	RENAME b:tom thom	May be abbreviated to REN
REPLACE [d:][path]filespec [d:][path][/parms]	Selectively replaces matching files on target	REPLACE a:*.doc c:\ /s/p	See 2.20. REPLACE Parameters
RESTORE d: [d:][path][filespec][/parms]	Restores backed up files to disk	RESTORE a: c:*.* /s	See 2.21. RESTORE Parameters
RMDIR [d:]path	Deletes a subdirectory from disk	RD c:\lotus\123	May be abbreviated to RD
SELECT [[A:|B:][d: [path]] xxx yy	Installs DOS on new disk	SELECT a: 001	
SET [name=[value]]	Installs string with value in environment	SET sidekickin = YES	
SHARE [/parms]	Loads file sharing support	SHARE /F:4048	See 2.22. SHARE Parameters
SORT [/parms]	Sorts data read from stdin, sends to stdout	dir | SORT /+14	See 2.23. SORT Parameters
SUBST d: d:path or SUBST d: /D or SUBST	Sets up different drive specifier for drive or path	SUBST a: c:\wp\ws	
SYS d:	Copies DOS onto disk	SYS a:	
TIME [time]	Sets, changes, or displays time	TIME 15:10	
TREE [d:][/F]	Displays directory paths	TREE c:/f	

(Continued)

Table 2.01. Continued

Command Syntax	Function	Example	Comments
TYPE [d:][path]filespec	Displays contents of file on stdout	TYPE myfile.asm	
VER	Displays DOS version number	VER	
VERIFY [ON|OFF]	Sets verify after write setting	VERIFY OFF	
VOL [d:]	Displays volume label	VOL c:	
XCOPY [d:][path]filespec [d:][path][filespec][/parms]	Selectively copies groups of files to disk	XCOPY *.dat c:/E/S	See 2.24. XCOPY Parameters
XCOPY [d:]path]filespec[d:][path][filespec][/parms]	Selectively copies groups of files to disk	XCOPY \wp c:\wp\wp	See 2.24. XCOPY Parameters
XCOPY d:[path][filespec][d:][path][filespec][/parms]	Selectively copies groups of files to disk	XCOPY c: a:\copy /S	See 2.24. XCOPY Parameters

Notes:
•Some of the above commands may not be in all versions of DOS (See 2.47. Included Command Files Summary)
•IBM syntax specifications are followed except this table uses "filespec" for "filename[.ext]"

Source: IBM DOS 3.3 Reference, section 7

See Also:
2.25. Editing Command Lines
2.26. Batch File Commands and Default Settings
2.27. CONFIG.SYS Commands and Default Settings

2.02. APPEND PARAMETERS

APPEND general command form: *APPEND d:path[;d:path...]*   or   *APPEND [/X][/E]*

Parameter	Function	Comments
/X	Processes SEARCH FIRST, FIND FIRST, and EXEC functions	must issue APPEND ; before using BACKUP or RESTORE!
/E	Keeps APPEND paths in the DOS environment	

Version Info: Applies to all versions of DOS beginning with 3.3

Notes:
•Parameters may be used only on the first invocation of APPEND in each session
•Each subsequent APPEND command takes the place of the previous one

Source: IBM DOS 3.3 Reference, pages 7-13 to 7-17

See Also: The description of PATH in the IBM DOS 3.3 Reference

2.03. ATTRIB PARAMETERS

ATTRIB general command form: ATTRIB [+R/-R][+A/-A]filespec[/S]

Parameter	Function	Comments
+R	Set read-only attribute for file	
-R	Set read/write attribute for file (normal file)	Default state
+A	Set archive attribute bit for file	Means file needs to be backed up
-A	Cancel archive attribute bit for file	
/S	Process files in the specified directory and all its subdirectories	

Version Info: Attrib has been enhanced with each minor release of DOS:
           Version 3.0 supports +R and -R only
           Version 3.2 supports +R, -R, +A, -A
           Version 3.3 supports all listed parameters

Notes: The archive attribute bit is cleared by BACKUP and RESTORE
(and most backup programs)

Source: IBM DOS 3.3 Reference, pages 7-22 to 7-24

2.04. BACKUP PARAMETERS

BACKUP general command form: BACKUP d:[path][sourcefilespec] d: [parameters]

Parameter	Function	Comments
/A	Add files to those already present on backup disk	
/D:mm-dd-yy	Back up only files modified on or after date specified	Date specified in format consistent with country code
/F	Format target disk if it is not already formatted*	
/L[filespec]	Create log file naming disk number of each file backed up	If no name specified, uses BACKUP.LOG in root directory
/M	Back up only files modified since last backup	i.e., files with Archive attribute bit set
/S	Back up files in the specified directory and all its subdirectories	
/T:hh:mm:ss	Back up only files modified on or after time specified	Time specified in format consistent with country code

Version Info: •Applies to all versions of DOS beginning with 2.0
•*Added beginning with DOS 3.0

Notes: The archive attribute bit is cleared by BACKUP for files that are backed up

Source: IBM DOS 3.3 Reference, pages 7-25 to 7-30

See Also: 2.21. RESTORE Parameters

2.05. CHKDSK PARAMETERS

CHKDSK general command form: CHKDSK [d:][path][filespec][parameters]

Parameter	Function	Comments
/F	Fix errors found in directory or FAT	Lost allocation units are stored in files named FILE####.CHK
/V	Display all files and paths found on drive	

Notes: CHKDSK filespec with no parameters checks for file fragmentation

Source: IBM DOS 3.3 Reference, pages 7-63 to 7-66

2.06. COMMAND PARAMETERS

COMMAND general command form: COMMAND [d:][path][parameters]

Parameter	Function	Comments
/Cstring	Passes string to the new command processor	
/E:#	Sets size of the environment	Must be in range 160 to 32768 in bytes*
/P	Makes command processor permanent in memory	Must restart DOS to remove command processor

Notes: •Unless /P parameter used, command processor is unloaded by typing EXIT
•*Earlier versions (3.0, for example) express this number in paragraphs

Source: IBM DOS 3.3 Reference, pages 7-68 to 7-69

2.07. COPY PARAMETERS

COPY general command form: *COPY [/A][/B]filespec1[/A][/B] [filespec2][parameters]*

Parameter	Function	Comments
/A	Treats file as ASCII text	For source file: copies up to first 1AH; for dest: adds 1AH to end
/B	Treats file as binary file (based on size in directory)	For source file: copies entire file; for dest: does not add 1AH
/V	Turns verify check ON during copy operation	Verify may already be set to ON by DOS

Notes: /A and /B may be used prior to source or dest filespec, or at end of command

Source: IBM DOS 3.3 Reference, pages 7-75 to 7-85

See Also: 2.24. XCOPY Parameters

2.08. DIR PARAMETERS

DIR general command form: *DIR [d:][path][filespec][parameters]*

Parameter	Function	Comments
/P	Pause when screen is full	General 23 lines; any key displays next page of directory
/W	Display names only in wide format	

Source: IBM DOS 3.3 Reference, pages 7-94 to 7-98

2.09. DISKCOMP PARAMETERS

DISKCOMP general command form: *DISKCOMP [d:[d:]][parameter]*

Parameter	Function	Comments
/1	Compare only first side of disk	
/8	Compare only first 8 sectors/track	Applies even if disk is formatted 9 sectors/track

Source: IBM DOS 3.3 Reference, pages 7-99 to 7-104

2.10. DISKCOPY PARAMETERS

DISKCOPY general command form: *DISKCOPY [d: [d:]][/1]*

Parameter	Function	Comments
/1	Copy only first side of disk	

Source: IBM DOS 3.3 Reference, pages 7-105 to 7-111

See Also: 2.07. COPY Parameters
                    2.24. XCOPY Parameters

2.11. FIND PARAMETERS

FIND general command form: *FIND [parameters] "string" [d:][path]filespec...*

Parameter	Function	Comments
/C	Display number of lines containing "string"	
/N	Display relative line number of each match	Ignored if /C is also specified
/V	Display all lines NOT containing "string"	

Notes: •File is searched only until first end-of-file marker (1AH byte)
                    •Double quotes (") are required around string
                    •FIND is case sensitive; "B" does not match "b"

Source: IBM DOS 3.3 Reference, pages 7-120 to 7-122

2.12. FORMAT PARAMETERS

FORMAT general command form: FORMAT d:[parameters]

Parameter	Function	Comments
/1	Format disk for single-sided use	Only for 5.25 inch disks
/4	Format 360 KB disk in 1.2 MB drive	Disk reliable only for use with 1.2 MB drives
/8	Format 8 sectors per track	Only for floppy drives
/B	Format 8 sectors/track, space for DOS	
/N:#	Format # sectors/track	Must be used with /T; must be less than maximum for disk
/S	Copy operating system files to formatted disk	DOS copied from default drive; makes disk "bootable"
/T:#	Format # tracks on disk	Must be used with /N; must be less than maximum for disk
/V	Request volume name for disk after format	

Source: IBM DOS 3.3 Reference, pages 7-123 to 7-132

2.13. GRAFTABL PARAMETERS

GRAFTABL general command form: GRAFTABL [parameters]

Parameter	Function	Comments
437	Use United States character data	Default value
860	Use Portugal character data	
863	Use French Canadian character data	
865	Use Norwegian and Danish character data	
/STATUS	Display number of selected code page	

Version Info: Parameters were added beginning with DOS 3.3

Notes: GRAFTABL returns errorlevel values as follows:
                     0 = no previously defined char table; code page already resident
                     1 = previously loaded table exists; new table replaced old
                     2 = no previously loaded char table exists; no new table was loaded
                     3 = unrecognized parameter
                     4 = incorrect DOS version (3.3 required)

Source: IBM DOS 3.3 Reference, pages 7-133 to 7-134

See Also: 3.146. Code Page Parameter Blocks
                     3.147. Code Page Assignments

2.14. GRAPHICS PARAMETERS

GRAPHICS general command form: GRAPHICS [parameters]

Parameter	Function	Comments
printertype	Specifies type of printer being used	COLOR1 = IBM Color printer; black ribbon; uses four shades of grey COLOR4 = IBM Color printer; RGB ribbon; prints using red, green, blue, black COLOR8 = IBM Color printer; CMY ribbon; prints using black, cyan, mag.,yellow COMPACT = IBM Compact printer; prints black and white only GRAPHICS = IBM Graphics or Proprinter; prints black and white only (default) THERMAL = IBM Convertible printer; prints black and white only*
/B	Print background color	Applicable to COLOR4 and COLOR8 types only
/LCD*	Print as displayed on LCD display	Applicable to IBM Convertible computer only
/R	Print as displayed on monitor	Default is to print white pixels as black, and to not print black pixels

Version Info: *Parameter was added beginning with DOS 3.3

Source: IBM DOS 3.3 Reference, pages 7-135 to 7-137

See Also: 7.48. IBM Printer Control Codes

2.15. MODE PARAMETERS

Using MODE to Switch Display Modes:

Parameter	Function	Comments
40	Set display width to 40 characters	CGA, PCJr, and EGA only
80	Set display width to 80 characters	CGA, PCJr, and EGA only (default)
BW40	Set display width to 40 chars on CGA; disable color	CGA, PCJr, and EGA only
BW80	Set display width to 80 chars on CGA; disable color	CGA, PCJr, and EGA only
CO40	Set display width to 40 chars on CGA; enable color	CGA, PCJr, and EGA only
CO80	Set display width to 80 chars on CGA; enable color	CGA, PCJr, and EGA only
MONO	Set display to MDA	MDA only
R	Shift display slightly to right	CGA, PCJr, and EGA only
L	Shift display slightly to left	CGA, PCJr, and EGA only
T	Display test pattern	CGA, PCJr, and EGA only

General Form: MODE displaywidth [,[shiftparm][,T]]

Examples: MODE BW40   Sets CGA to 40 column width, disables color
                MODE CO80,R,T   Sets CGA to 80 column width, enables color, shifts display right 2 chars,
                                                shows test pattern
                MODE ,L,T   Shifts display left 1 or 2 chars, shows test pattern

Using MODE to Set Printer:

Parameter	Function	Comments
n	Set page print width	Must be 80 or 132 only (default=80)
m	Set vertical spacing	Must be 6 or 8 only (default=6)
P	Set continuous retry on time-out errors	

General Form: MODE LPT#[:][n][,[m][,P]]

Examples: MODE LPT1:132,8,P   Sets 132 column page width, 8 lines per inch, and continuous retry
                MODE LPT2:,,P   Leaves page width and lines per inch intact, sets continuous retry
                MODE LPT1 ,8   Sets 8 line per inch, page width left intact, no continuous retry

Using MODE to Set Async Port:

Parameter	Function	Comments
baud	Set baud rate for communications	Must be 110,150,300,600,1200,2400,4800,9600, or 19200; default=1200
parity	Set parity type for transmissions	Must be one of N (none), O (odd), or E (even); default=E
databits	Set number of databits per byte transmitted	Must be either 7 or 8; default=7
stopbits	Set number of bits between transmitted bytes	Must be either 1 or 2; default=2 for 110, 1 for all other baud rates)
P	Set continuous retry on time-out errors	

General Form: MODE COM#[:]baud[,[parity][,[databits][,[stopbits][,P]]]]

Examples: MODE COM1:1200,e,7,1,p   (default setting plus continuous retry on timeouts)
                MODE COM1:,,7,,p   Resets databits to 7 (others left unchanged) and sets continuous retries
                MODE COM1 19200,,,2   Resets baud to 19200, stopbits to 2 (others left unchanged), no retries

Using Mode to Redirect Output:
General Form: MODE LPT#[:]=COM#

Examples: MODE LPT1:=COM2   Redirects printer output to COM2
                MODE LPT1=COM1   Redirects printer output to COM1

(Continued)

Table 2.15. Continued

Using MODE to prepare Code Page:

Parameter	Function	Comments
device	Set device for code page use	Must be one of CON, PRN, LPT1, LPT2, or LPT3
cp	Set code page number	May be a list in parentheses; must be 437, 850, 860, 863, or 865

General Form: MODE device CODEPAGE PREPARE = ((cp)[d:][path]filespec)

Examples: MODE LPT1 CODEPAGE PREPARE = (437)4201.CPI Prepares US code page for IBM Proprinter
MODE LPT1 CP PREP = (437)4201.CPI Same, only uses abbreviations for CODEPAGE PREPARE

Using MODE to Select Code Page:

Parameter	Function	Comments
device	Set device for code page use	Must be one of CON, PRN, LPT1, LPT2, or LPT3
cp	Set code page number	Must be one of 437, 850, 860, 863, or 865

General Form: MODE device CODEPAGE SELECT = cp

Examples: MODE LPT1 CODEPAGE SELECT = 437 Selects US code page for use
MODE LPT1 CP SELECT = 437 Same, only uses abbreviation for CODEPAGE

Using MODE to Identify Code Page:

Parameter	Function	Comments
device	Set device for code page use	Must be one of CON, PRN, LPT1, LPT2, or LPT3
/STATUS	Display status for code pages	

General Form: MODE device CODEPAGE [/STATUS]

Examples: MODE LPT1 CODEPAGE Identifies current code page
MODE LPT1 CP /STATUS Same, only uses abbreviation and shows status of all code page possibilities

Using MODE to Refresh a Code Page:

Parameter	Function	Comments
device	Set device for code page use	Must be one of CON, PRN, LPT1, LPT2, or LPT3

General Form: MODE device CODEPAGE REFRESH

Examples: MODE LPT1 CODEPAGE REFRESH Reestablishes active code page for LPT1
MODE LPT1 CP REFRESH Same, only uses abbreviation

Version Info: Code page options apply to DOS 3.3 only

Source: IBM DOS 3.3 Reference, pages 7-153 to 7-164

See Also: 3.146. Code Page Parameter Blocks
3.147. Code Page Assignments

2.16. PRINT PARAMETERS

PRINT general command form: PRINT [parameters][d:][path][filespec...]

Parameter	Function	Comments
/B:buffersize*	Sets size of internal print buffer to buffersize; in bytes	Default is 512
/C	Cancels list of files from print queue	
/D:device*	Specifies print device to use	Default is PRN; if used, must be first parameter
/M:maxtick*	Sets number of clock ticks print device gets	Default is 2; range is from 1 to 255
/P	Sets print mode	
/Q:queuesize*	Sets number of files that can be in queue at once	Default is 10; range is from 1 to 32
/S:timeslice*	Specifies time slice value	Default is 8; range is from 1 to 255
/T	Cancels all queued files; printing stops	Sounds printer's alarm, prints cancellation message if file being printed
/U:busytick*	Sets number of clock ticks to wait for print device availability	Default is 1

Version Info: PRINT added to DOS beginning with version 2.0

Notes: *Can only be specified the first time PRINT is used

Source: IBM DOS 3.3 Reference, pages 7-171 to 7-176

2.17. PROMPT SPECIAL CHARACTERS

Character	Displays As		Example	Example Displays As
$b	Vertical slash (|)	ASCII 124	pb	C:\MYDIR|
$d	Current system date		$d ng	Mon 9-5-1986 C>
$e	Escape character	ASCII 27	See 2.18. PROMPT ANSI Control Strings	
$g	Greater than sign (>)	ASCII 62	pg	C:\MYDIR>
$h	Destructive backspace	ASCII 8	thhh pg	09:30:26 C:\MYDIR>
$l	Less than sign (<)	ASCII 60	ln$g	<C>
$n	Current drive letter		Drive is ng	Drive is C>
$p	Current pathname directory		Path is pg	Path is C:\MYDIR>
$q	Equals sign (=)	ASCII 61	Drive $q ng	Drive = C>
$t	Current system time		Time is $t	Time is 09:30:25.93
$v	DOS version number		$v	IBM Personal Computer DOS Version 3.20
$_	Carriage return/line feed	ASCII 13,10	thhh$_ pg	9:30:25 C:\MYDIR>
$$	Dollar sign ($)	ASCII 36	Time is $$$g	Time is $>
Any other	Treated as character typed		This is a prompt	This is a prompt

Version Info: Applies to all versions of DOS beginning with version 2.0

Notes: Examples assume that the current system date is September 5, 1986, the current time is 9:30:26, and the current logged drive and directory are C:\MYDIR

Source: IBM DOS 3.3 Reference, page 7-177

See Also: 2.18. PROMPT ANSI Control Strings
2.19. PROMPT ANSI Display Attribute Strings

2.18. PROMPT ANSI CONTROL STRINGS

String	Function	
$e[#;# f	Moves to row (first number), column (second #)	
$e[=# h	Sets display mode according to number (#):	0 = 40x25 monochrome 1 = 40x25 color 2 = 80x25 monochrome 3 = 80x25 color 4 = 320x200 color graphics 5 = 320x200 monochrome graphics 6 = 640x200 monochrome graphics 7 = wrap at end of line
$e[#;# j	Moves cursor to line (first #) and row (second #) position	
$e[K	Clears line from cursor to end of line	
$e[=# l	Resets display mode according to number (#):	0 = 40x25 monochrome 1 = 40x25 color 2 = 80x25 monochrome 3 = 80x25 color 4 = 320x200 color graphics 5 = 320x200 monochrome graphics 6 = 640x200 monochrome graphics 7 = wrap at end of line
$e[#;...;#m	Sets display attributes (see 2.19. PROMPT ANSI Display Attribute Strings	
$e[#;# p	Reassigns first key (first #) to second (second #) or remap key (first#) to ASCII string	
$e[s	Saves current cursor position	
$e[u	Restores cursor to saved position	
$e[#A	Moves cursor up number of rows indicated by #	(ignored if cursor on top line)
$e[#B	Moves cursor down number of rows indicated by #	(ignored if cursor on bottom line)
$e[#C	Moves cursor right number of columns indicated by #	(ignored if cursor in last column)
$e[#D	Moves cursor left number of columns indicated by #	(ignored if cursor in first column)
$e[H	Moves cursor to the Home position (row 1, column 1)	
$e[#;# H	Moves cursor to row (first #) and column (second #) position	
$e[2J	Clears display screen (see also $e[#;#f)	
$e[K	Erases from cursor to end of line, including cursor position	
$e[#;# R	Reports cursor position through standard input	
Esc [6n	Console driver outputs cursor position report sequence	(cannot be used as part of prompt)

Version Info: Applies to all versions of DOS beginning with version 2.0

Notes: There should be no spaces shown in the ANSI control strings shown

Source: IBM DOS 3.3 Technical Reference, pages 3-1 to 3-20

See Also: 2.17. PROMPT Special Characters
2.19. PROMPT ANSI Display Attribute Strings

2.19. PROMPT ANSI DISPLAY ATTRIBUTE STRINGS

String	Sets Display Attributes to	Video Adapter			
		MDA	CGA	EGA	VGA
$e[0 m	Normal text	X	X	X	X
$e[1 m	Bright text (intensity bit set)	X	X	X	X
$e[4 m	Underscored text	X			
$e[5 m	Blinking text	X			
$e[7 m	Reversed text	X	X	X	X
$e[8 m	Canceled (invisible) text	X			
$e[30 m	Black text		X	X	X
$e[31 m	Red text		X	X	X
$e[32 m	Green text		X	X	X
$e[33 m	Yellow text		X	X	X
$e[34 m	Blue text		X	X	X
$e[35 m	Magenta text		X	X	X
$e[36 m	Cyan text		X	X	X
$e[37 m	White text		X	X	X
$e[40 m	Black background		X	X	X
$e[41 m	Red background		X	X	X
$e[42 m	Green background		X	X	X
$e[43 m	Yellow background		X	X	X
$e[44 m	Blue background		X	X	X
$e[45 m	Magenta background		X	X	X
$e[46 m	Cyan background		X	X	X
$e[47 m	White background		X	X	X

Version Info: Applies to all versions of DOS beginning with version 2.0

Source: IBM DOS 3.3 Technical Reference, page 3-15

See Also: 2.17. PROMPT Special Characters
2.18. PROMPT ANSI Control Strings

2.20. REPLACE PARAMETERS

REPLACE general command form: REPLACE [d:][path]filespec[d:][path][parameters]

Parameter	Function	Comments
/A	Copies all files in source that do not exist on target	Cannot be used with /S
/P	Prompts when source file also found on target	Copy proceeds only if user presses Y
/R	Replaces files that have read-only attribute bit set on target	
/S	Searches all directories of target for source file match	Cannot be used with /A;
/W	Prompts for disk change before REPLACE continues	

Version Info: REPLACE added to DOS beginning with version 3.0

Notes: REPLACE sets errorlevel on completion as follows:
   2 = no source file(s) were found
   3 = the source or target path was invalid (not found)
   5 = the access code was incorrect; try repeating command using /R
   8 = insufficient memory to perform operation
   11 = invalid parameter or format of REPLACE command
   15 = invalid drive specified in source or target path
   22 = incorrect version of DOS being used with REPLACE
   (For complete error code list see 3.128. Extended Error Codes)

Source: IBM DOS 3.3 Reference, pages 7-185 to 7-188

2.21. RESTORE PARAMETERS

RESTORE general command form: RESTORE d: [d:][path]filespec[parameters]

Parameter	Function	Comments
/A:mm-dd-yy	Restore files modified on or after date mm-dd-yy	Date entered in format appropriate for current country code
/B:mm-dd-yy	Restore files modified on or before date mm-dd-yy	Date entered in format appropriate for current country code
/E:hh:mm	Restore files modified on or before time hh:mm	Time entered in format appropriate for current country code
/L:hh:mm	Restore files modified on or after time hh:mm	Time entered in format appropriate for current country code
/M	Restore files modified or deleted since last backup	
/N	Restore files that no longer exist on target	Should not be used with /B or /A
/P	Prompt for each file to restore	
/S	Restore files to proper subdirectories	

Version Info: RESTORE added to DOS beginning with version 2.0

Notes: RESTORE sets errorlevel on completion as follows:
                      0 = normal completion; no errors
                      1 = no files were found to restore
                      2 = some files not restored due to sharing conflicts
                      3 = operation terminated due to Ctrl-Break or Esc key pressed by user
                      4 = other error caused termination

Source: IBM DOS 3.3 Reference, pages 7-189 to 7-192

See Also: 2.04. BACKUP Parameters

2.22. SHARE PARAMETERS

SHARE general command form: SHARE [parameters]

Parameter	Function	Comments
/F:filespace	Allocates filespace bytes to record sharing info	Default is 2048; must be 25 bytes per shared file
/L:locks	Allocates space for number of locks to maintain	Default is 20

Version Info: SHARE added to DOS beginning with version 3.1

Source: IBM DOS 3.3 Reference, pages 7-200 to 7-201

2.23. SORT PARAMETERS

SORT general command form: SORT [parameters]

Parameter	Function	Comments
/R	Sort in reverse order (Z before A)	
/+#	Sort starting with column # specified	Default is column 1

Version Info: SORT added to DOS beginning with version 2.0

Notes: Sort equates lower and uppercase letters; characters with ASCII values
                      above 127 are sorted according to rules based on current country code.

Source: IBM DOS 3.3 Reference, pages 7-202 to 7-203

2.24. XCOPY PARAMETERS

XCOPY general command form: XCOPY [d:][path][filespec] [d:][path][filespec][parameters]

Parameter	Function	Comments
/A	Copy only files that have archive bit set	Source file archive bit is not changed
/D:mm-dd-yy	Copy files whose date is the same or later than specified	Date is in format appropriate to current country code
/E	Create subdirectories, even if empty, on target	
/M	Copy only files that have archive bit set	Source file archive bit is cleared
/P	Prompt before copying each file	Only files which are responded to by a Y by user are copied
/S	Copy files in directory and all its subdirectories	
/V	Verifies that target disk was recorded correctly	
/W	Causes XCOPY to wait until user presses key to start copying	

Version Info: XCOPY added to DOS beginning with version 3.2

Source: IBM DOS 3.3 Reference, pages 7-222 to 7-229

2.25 EDITING COMMAND LINES

Key	Function
F1	Supplies next character from the command buffer
F2	Supplies all characters from the command buffer up to the next character you type (e.g., [F2][r] is up to r)
F3	Supplies all remaining characters from the command buffer
F4	Skips all characters from the command buffer up to next character typed (e.g., [F4][r] skips to r)
F5	Erases previous command buffer and replaces it with current command line
Esc	Erases current command line
-->	Supplies next character from the command buffer
Ins	Inserts a character at current spot in the command buffer
Del	Deletes the character at the current spot in the command buffer

Notes: DOS keeps the last command typed in a buffer, and it is available even after the execution of a program, e.g., BASICA "myprog" runs a BASIC program named "myprog." After the program has finished, the DOS command line buffer still contains BASICA "myprog."

Source: IBM DOS 3.3 Reference, page 2-5

2.26. BATCH FILE COMMANDS AND DEFAULT SETTINGS

Command	Function	Syntax	Allowable Settings	Default	Example
:label	Label (destination of a GOTO statement)	:string	Colon followed by any characters		:ENDOFBATCHFILE
@command*	Does not echo command on display	@string	Any valid DOS or batch command		@ECHO OFF
%#	Substitutes command line parameter	%number	0-9 (0=command name)		DIR %1,%2
%string%	Substitutes environment variable (SET)	%string%	Any variable created with SET		IF NOT %OKAY% == "DONE" SET OKAY=DONE
CALL	Calls another batch file as a subroutine	CALL filename	Filename may include path		CALL DOINST
ECHO	Sets echo status or displays string	ECHO state, ECHO string	ON, OFF, message string	ON	ECHO This is a message.
FOR	Controls execution of commands	FOR %%var IN (set) DO command	%%variable string		FOR %%file IN (DOS,WRITE) DO DEL %%file.DAT
GOTO	Branches execution to new location in batch file	GOTO label	Any valid label		GOTO ENDOFBATCHFILE
IF ERRORLEVEL	Controls execution based upon error level	IF ERRORLEVEL number command	0-255		IF ERRORLEVEL 65 GOTO ENDOFBATCHFILE
IF EXIST	Controls execution based upon existence of file	IF EXIST filename command	Any DOS filename		IF EXIST hogan.%1 ERASE hogan.%1
IF s1 == s2	Controls execution based upon string comparison	IF string==string command	Any string or %parameter		IF %1="hogan" GOTO DEALWITHHOGAN
PAUSE	Pauses execution until key pressed	PAUSE string	Any message string		PAUSE Press a key to continue.
REM	Non-executable remark	REM string	Any message string		REM This won't display if echo is off
SHIFT	Shifts command line parameters down one number	SHIFT	NA		SHIFT

Version Info:
- @ is only available in DOS 3.3
- CALL is only available in DOS 3.3
- %string% and SET are not documented in all versions of DOS but appear starting in DOS 2.x
- ECHO and REM should be followed by at least one non-space character in DOS 3.x

Notes: *Command may be any valid DOS command

Source: IBM DOS 3.3 Reference, pages 7-31 to 7-55

2.27. CONFIG.SYS COMMANDS AND DEFAULT SETTINGS

Command	Allowable Settings	Default Settings	Example
AVAILDEV=state	TRUE,FALSE	TRUE	AVAILDEV=FALSE
BREAK=state	OFF, ON	OFF	BREAK=ON
BUFFERS=#	1-99	2 (XT), 3 (AT)*	BUFFERS=20
COUNTRY=#	See 3.144. Country Codes	001	COUNTRY=044
COUNTRY=#,#,filename	Country code, code page, file containing country info	001,437,\country.sys	COUNTRY=044,850,c:\dos\country.sys
DEVICE=name	Any DOS path and file name	None	DEVICE=DRIVER.SYS
DRIVPARM	See 2.28. DRIVPARM and DRIVER.SYS Parameter Settings	/F:0 /T:80 /H:2 /S:9	DRIVPARM /D:1 /F:1
FCBS=#,#	1-255, 0-255 (first number must be >= second)	4,0	FCBS=20,20
FILES=#	8-255	8	FILES=20
LASTDRIVE=letter	A-Z	E	LASTDRIVE=H
SHELL=name	Any DOS pathname	SHELL=COMMAND.COM	SHELL=C:\DOS\COMMAND.COM
STACKS=#,#	8-64, 32-512 (0,0=no dynamic stacks)	9,128	STACKS=12,256
SWITCHAR=char	Any character	\	SWITCHAR=/

Version Info: •*For DOS 2.0-3.2. Beginning with DOS 3.3, if RAM >128K, BUFFERS=5; if RAM >256K, BUFFERS=10:
if RAM >512K, BUFFERS=15.
•AVAILDEV and SWITCHAR are undocumented, and work only in DOS version 2.x
•COUNTRY, FCBS, and LASTDRIVE are available only in DOS 3.0 and later
•STACKS is available only in DOS 3.2 and later
•DRIVPARM available only in DOS 3.2

Source: IBM DOS 3.3 Reference, pages 4-1 to 4-44

See Also: 2.28. DRIVPARM and DRIVER.SYS Parameter Settings
3.144. Country Codes

2.28. DRIVPARM AND DRIVER.SYS PARAMETER SETTINGS

Parameter	Function	Allowable Settings	Default
/C	Changeline support required	None	None
/D:#	Drive number	0-255 (A=0, B=1, etc.)*	None
/F:#	Form factor	0=160/180K or 320/360K floppy 1=1.2M floppy (AT) 2=720K microfloppy (3.5") 7=1.4MB microfloppy (3.5")	2
/H:#	Max # of heads	1-99	2
/N	Nonremovable media	None	None
/S:#	Sectors per track	1-99	9
/T:#	Tracks per side	1-999	80

Version Info: •DRIVER:SYS information applies to all versions of DOS beginning with
version 3.0 (DRIVPARM version 3.2 only)
•DRIVPARM information applies only to DOS version 3.2

Notes: *2-127 reference external floppy drives; 128-255 reference fixed drives

Source: IBM DOS 3.3 Reference, pages 4-21 to 4-27

See Also: 2.27. CONFIG.SYS Commands and Default Settings

2.29. DEBUG COMMAND SUMMARY

Command Syntax	Function	Example	Example Explanation	Comments
A	Assemble statements into memory immediately following last assembly entry	A	Assemble statements at current pointer	Entry continues until ENTER pressed at start of line
A address	Assemble statements into memory beginning at address	A100	Assemble statements at 100H	Entry continues until ENTER pressed at start of line
C range address	Compare two blocks of memory	C100 L20 200	Compare 32 bytes at 100H to 32 bytes at 200H	
D	Dump (display) contents of memory starting at last position displayed	D	Display memory at current pointer	
D address	Dump (display) contents of memory starting at address	D208	Display memory at current pointer	
D range	Dump (display) contents of memory of entire range specified	D 100 L600	Display 600H bytes of memory	
E address	Enter hex bytes of data beginning at address specified	E DS:50	Enter data beginning at 50H in Data Segment	Entry continues until ENTER pressed; SPACE skips entry for a byte
E address list	Enter list of bytes beginning at address specified	E 100 20 20	Enter two spaces at 100 H in current segment	
F range list	Fill memory range with sequence of bytes in list	F DS:00 L0F "TEH"	Enter five repetitions of TEH at start of Data Seg.	Extra items in list that would fill beyond end of range are ignored
G	Go (begins execution) at current instruction (CS:IP)	G	Execute instructions at CS:IP	
G =address	Go (begins execution) at address	G =100	Start execution at 0100H in current CS	
G =address addresslist	Go (begins execution) at address with breakpoints specified in addresslist	G =100 10A 213	Same as above, but break if 10AH or 213H reached	
H value1 value2	Hex math performed (add 2 to 1, subtract 2 from 1) on value1 and value2	H 0F 8	Add 8 to 0F, subtract 8 from 0F	Results displayed on next line
I portaddress	Input one byte from portaddress	I 2E6	Get input from port 2E6H	Results displayed on next line
L	Load file (whose file specification is at CS:80)	L	File loaded beginning at CS:100	File loaded beginning at CS:100
L address	Load file (whose file name and type are at CS:80) beginning at address indicated	L 506	Load file beginning at 506H in memory	COM and EXE files are always loaded at CS:100, however
L address drive sector1 sector2	Load sector2 disk sectors from drive, beginning with sector1, into address	L DS:100 2 0 3	Load first three sectors of drive C beginning at DS:100	
M range address	Move memory from range to new address	M 100 L10 500	Move 16 bytes from 100H to 500H	Moves always performed without loss of memory during transfer
N [filespec]	Name file to place at CS:81 and in FCBs	N c:debug.com	Prepare debug.com for use by debugger	
O portaddress byte	Send a byte to specified port	O 2E6 FF	Send FFH to port 2E6H	
P	Proceed to end of call, loop, interrupt, or repeat string instruction	P	Execution starts at CS:IP	P uses same syntax a T(race) instruction
P =address	Proceed from address to end of call, loop, interrupt, or repeat instruction	P =1044	Execution starts at CS:1044	P uses same syntax a T(race) instruction
P =address value	Proceed from address to end of call, loop, int, or repeat, or value instructions	P =1044 10	Execution starts at CS:1044 for no more than 16 bytes	P uses same syntax a T(race) instruction
Q	Quit DEBUG	Q	DEBUG is terminated immediately	Working memory is NOT saved by this command
R	Display all registers	R	Display current contents of all registers	
R registername	Display contents of registername and allow entry of new value	RAX	Display AX contents and waits for new value	Pressing ENTER only leaves contents unchanged
S range list	Search the range of memory for the contents in list	R 100 L100 "TEH"	Search for pattern "TEH" in 100H bytes at CS:100H	
T	Trace a single instruction	T	Trace instructions from CS:IP, display registers	
T =address	Trace a single instruction at address	T CS:106	Trace instructions from CS:106H, display registers	
T =address value	Trace value instructions beginning at address	T 100 10	Trace 16 instructions from CS:100H	0=trace forever (same as G)
U	Unassemble instructions at CS:IP	U	Display disassembly of instructions at CS:IP	
U address	Unassemble instructions at address	U 100	Display disassembly of instructions at 100H	
U range	Unassemble instructions at CS:IP for range bytes	U 100 108	Display disassembly of instructions from 100H to 108H	
W	Write file (named at CS:80H) to disk	W	Write file in memory to disk	May display slightly more bytes than requested
W address	Write file (named at CS:80H) to disk beginning with byte at address	W 108	Write file beginning at 108H in memory to disk	BX:CX must contain number of bytes to write
W address drive sector1 sector2	Write data at address to drive starting with sector1 for sector2 sectors	W 108 2 0 3	Write first three sectors to drive C from memory at 108H	BX:CX must contain number of bytes to write

Notes: Lowercase names in command syntax indicate items you replace with values

Source: IBM DOS 3.3 Technical Reference, pages 13-15 to 13-58

See Also: 6.83. SYMDEB Command Summary

2.30. EDLIN COMMAND SUMMARY

Command Syntax	Function	Example	Example Explanation	Comments
A	Append lines from file to memory	A	Append lines from file until 75% of memory is full	Applies only if file is too large to fit into memory
#A	Append # lines from file to memory	5A	Append 5 lines from file	Applies only if file is too large to fit into memory
line C	Copy current line to line	10C	Copy current line to line 10	
line1,line2,line3 C	Copy range of line 1 to line 2 to area beginning with line 3	1,2,3C	Copy lines 1 and 2 to lines 3 and 4	
line1,line2,line3,count C	Copy range of line 1 to line 2 count times to area starting at line 3	1,2,3,2C	Copy lines 1 and 2 to lines 3 and 4, 5 and 6	
D	Delete current line from memory	D	Delete current line	
line1,line2 D	Delete range of lines between line 1 and line 2 from memory	1,3D	Delete lines 1 through 3	
.	Edit current line	.	Edit current line	
line	Edit line number specified	10	Edit line number 10	
E	End EDLIN and save file	E	End EDLIN and saves changes to file	Saves original as file .BAK
line I	Insert line at current line	10 I	Insert new line in front of line 10	
	Insert line before line specified		Insert new line in front of current line	
L	List 23 lines (11 before current, current, 11 after current)	L	Show current line in context	
line1,line2 L	List lines from line 1 to line 2	1,10L	Show lines 1 through 10	
line M	Move current line to line specified	10M	Move current line to line 10	
line1,line2,line3 M	Move range from line 1 to line 2 to area beginning at line 3	1,5,10M	Move lines 1 through 5 to line 10 (through 14)	
P	List 23 lines and move current line to last one displayed	P	Page through lines in file	
line1,line2 P	List lines from line 1 to line 2, move current line to line 2	1,10P	List first 10 lines and makes line 10 the current one	
Q	Quit EDLIN without saving changes	Q	Immediately leaves EDLIN	User is prompted before leaving EDLIN
R string1^Zstring2	Replace string 1 with string 2 from current line to last line	Rteh^ZTEH	Replace "teh" with "TEH" from current line to EOF	
line1,line2 R string1^Zstring2	Replace string 1 with string 2 in lines from line 1 to line 2	1,7Rmy^Zour	Replace "my" with "our" in lines 1 through 7	
S string	Search for string in current line through last line in memory	SIBM	Search for "IBM" in lines starting with current one	If no string specified, uses last string searched for
line1,line2S string	Search for string in range of lines from line 1 to line 2	1,10SIBM	Search for "IBM" in lines 1 through 10	If no string specified, uses last string searched for
T filespec	Transfer contents of file into memory starting before current line	TAUTOEXEC.BAT	Transfer contents of AUTOEXEC.BAT to file	
line T filespec	Transfer contents of file into memory starting before line	10TCONFIG.SYS	Transfer contents of CONFIG.SYS to area before line 10	
W	Write lines from memory to file until 75% of memory is available	W	Write lines to file until 75% of memory is free	Applies only if file is too large to fit into memory
#W	Writes # lines from memory to file	10W	Write 10 lines to file	Applies only if file is too large to fit into memory

Notes:

•Lowercase names in command syntax indicate items you replace with values

•In general, if a line number is omitted from a command, the current line number is used

Source:

IBM DOS 3.3 Reference, pages 8-11 to 8-36

2.31. LIB OPERATORS SUMMARY

LIB general command form: **LIB [libfile [pagesize] operators [,[listfile][[,[newlib][[:]]**

Operator	Function	Example	Example Explanation
+	Add contents of object or library file to the library	LIB YOUR.LIB+NEW.OBJ	Add NEW.OBJ code to YOUR.LIB library
-	Delete a module from the library	LIB YO-JR-MINE	Delete module MINE.OBJ from YOUR.LIB library
*	Extract object module from library, place in new file	LIB YOUR.LIB*MY.OBJ	Delete module MY.OBJ from YOUR.LIB and places it in file MY.OBJ
-+	Delete existing module and replace with new one	LIB YOUR-+MY	Delete module MY.OBJ from YOUR.LIB, then adds new MY.OBJ to library
-*	Extract object module from library and delete it	LIB YCUR.LIB-*MINE	Delete module MINE.OBJ from YOUR.LIB and saves it in file MINE.OBJ

Notes:
- Operations are performed in the order: 1) erasures and removals, 2) additions
- Library files have assumed type of LIB if not explicitly referenced; object files have an assumed type of OBJ

Source: IBM DOS 3.3 Technical Reference, pages A-3 to A-8

2.32. LINK PARAMETERS SUMMARY

LINK general command form: **LINK objlist, runfile, mapffile, liblist[;parameters]...;**

Parameter	Function	Comments
/DSALLOCATION	Defines data to be at high end of DGROUP	Default is to load data at the low end of DGROUP
/HIGH	Causes run image to be placed as high in memory as possible	Default is to place the file as low in memory as possible
/LINE	Causes line numbers and addresses in input modules to be included in list file	
/MAP	Lists all public symbols defined in input modules and their run file locations	The public symbols are listed at end of the list file
/PAUSE	Directs LINK to pause before creation of EXE file	Message is displayed to change diskettes prior to creating EXE file
/STACK:size	Overrides stack directive in source	Maximum is 65536; if an odd number, 1 is subtracted for even boundary
/X	Sets number of segments EXE file can contain	Default is 256 segments; limits are 0 to 1024 segments
/O	Links object modules created by version 1 of Pascal or FORTRAN compilers	

Notes:
- Parameters may be added to your responses to the four prompts LINK displays when invoked as LINK <Enter>
- Only the forward slash and first letter are required for the parameters

Source: IBM DOS 3.3 Technical Reference, pages 12-14 to 12-18

2.33. DIRECTORY ENTRIES

Offset	Length	Description	Format	Comments
0 (0)	8 bytes	File name**	ASCII chars.	Must be padded with spaces to fill field
8 (8)	3 bytes	File type (Extension)	ASCII chars.	Must be padded with spaces to fill field
B (11)	byte	File attribute byte	Bit codes: Bit 0 = read-only Bit 1 = hidden Bit 2 = system Bit 3 = volume label Bit 4 = directory Bit 5 = archive Bit 6 = RESERVED Bit 7 = RESERVED	See 2.34. File Attribute Byte
C (12)	10 bytes	RESERVED		
16 (22)	word	Time file last updated*	Coded word: (unsigned 16-bit integer) Time = Hr*2048+Min*32+Sec÷2	See 2.35. Date/Time Formats
18 (24)	word	Date file last updated*	Coded word: (see above) Date = (Yr-1980)*512+Mon*32+Day	See 2.35. Date/Time Formats
1A (26)	word	Starting cluster number*	Word binary integer*	See 1.15. Common 8086 Family Data Formats
1C (28)	dbl word	File size*	Double word binary integer*	See 1.15. Common 8086 Family Data Formats

Notes: •There is no period separating the file name and type fields
•*Least significant byte first
•**The first byte of the file name indicates status of directory entry, as follows:
   00H = name never used
   05H = first character of name is really E5H (sigma)
   E5H = file was used, but has been erased
   2EH = entry is a directory (if second byte also 2EH, cluster field contains cluster # of parent directory)

Source: IBM DOS 3.3 Technical Reference, pages 5-10 to 5-13

See Also: 1.15. Common 8086 Family Data Formats
2.34. File Attribute Byte
2.35. Date/Time Formats
2.50. Allowable Characters in Filenames
2.51. File Separator Characters

2.34. FILE ATTRIBUTE BYTE

Bit Number

7	6	5	4	3	2	1	0	Meaning if Set to 1	Meaning if Set to 0
							X	Read-only file	Read/write file
						X		Hidden file	Visible file
					X			System file	Regular file
				X				Volume name	Regular file
			X					Directory name	Regular file
		X						File changed since last backup	File unchanged since last backup
X	X							RESERVED	RESERVED

Version Info: DOS 1.x used only bits 0-3

Notes: •Bits 3 and 4 are mutually exclusive; you may set none, one or the other one, but not both
•Only one file (in the root directory) may have Bit 3 set

Source: IBM DOS Technical Reference, pages 5-11 to 5-12

See Also: 2.33. Directory Entries

2.35. DATE/TIME FORMATS

In DOS Functions 2AH, 2BH, 2CH, and 2DH, the
Date and Time are Passed Using Registers, as Follows:

Element	Register	Format	Allowable Values
Day of Week	AL	Coded value	0=Sunday 1=Monday 2=Tuesday 3=Wednesday 4=Thursday 5=Friday 6=Saturday
Day	DL	Binary value	1-31 (corresponds to date)
Month	DH	Binary value	1-12 (corresponds to month number)
Year	CX	Binary value	1980-2099 (must be in this range)
Hundredths	DL	Binary value	0-99 (corresponds to hundredths of a second)
Seconds	DH	Binary value	0-59 (corresponds to seconds)
Minutes	CL	Binary value	0-59 (corresponds to minutes)
Hour	CH	Binary value	0-23 (hour in military 24-hour style)

In Directory Entries and Function 57H the Date and Time are Kept
as Separate 16-bit Values (Least Significant Byte First), as Follows:

Element	Bits Used	Format	Allowable Values
Day	0 - 4	5-bit binary value	1-31 (corresponds to date)
Month	5 - 8	4-bit binary value	1-12 (corresponds to month number)
Year	9 - 15	7-bit binary value	0-119 (year biased by 1980)
Seconds	0 - 4	5-bit binary value	0-29 (multiply by 2 to get seconds)
Minutes	5 - 10	6-bit binary value	0-60 (corresponds to minutes)
Hours	11 - 15	5-bit binary value	0-24 (corresponds to military hours)

Notes: Note unusual format of seconds in directory entries

Source: IBM DOS 3.3 Technical Reference, pages 5-12 to 5-13, 6-98, 6-100

See Also: 3.006. System Functions
3.046. Function 2AH -- Get System Date
3.047. Function 2BH -- Set System Date
3.048. Function 2CH -- Get System Time
3.049. Function 2DH -- Set System Time
3.101. Function 57H,00H -- Get Date/Time of File
3.102. Function 57H,01H -- Set Date/Time of File

2.36. FAT LAYOUTS

12-bit FAT Layout

Reserved for DOS
From Directory Entry's
Starting Cluster Number

Entry #	Example Value	Use	
0	FF8	Disk ID byte	
1	FFF	Filler	
2	003	Cluster value:	000 = unused cluster
3	004		001-FEF = next cluster number
4	005		FF0-FF6 = reserved cluster
5	FFF		FF7 = cluster marked bad
6	000		FF8-FFF = last cluster in file

Note: In this example FAT, the first entry indicates that it is a FAT for a hard disk (FF8). The first directory entry in the directory for that disk has a starting cluster of 2, thus pointing to cluster number two in this table. The second cluster points to the third, the third to the fourth, the fourth to the fifth. The fifth cluster is the last cluster in the file, thus has a value of FFFH.

(Continued)

Table 2.36. Continued

16-bit FAT Layout

	Entry #	Example Value	Use	
Reserved for DOS {	0	FFF8	Disk ID byte	
{	1	FFFF	Filler	
From Directory Entry's → Starting Cluster Number	2	0003	Cluster value:	0000 = unused cluster
	3	0004		0001-FFEF = next cluster number
	4	0005		FFF0-FFF6 = reserved cluster
	5	FFFF		FFF7 = cluster marked bad
	6	0000		FFF8-FFFF = last cluster in file

Note: In this example FAT, the first entry indicates that it is a FAT for a hard disk (FFF8H). The first directory entry in the directory for that disk has a starting cluster of 2, thus pointing to cluster number two in this table. The second cluster points to the third, the third to the fourth, the fourth to the fifth. The fifth cluster is the last cluster in the file, thus has a value of FFFFH. Remember, words in the FAT are byte swapped (i.e., least significant byte first).

Source: IBM DOS 3.3 Technical Reference, pages 5-5 to 5-9

See Also: 2.37. Disk ID Bytes

2.37. DISK ID BYTE

ID Byte	Tracks/side	Sectors	Sides	Format
FFH	40	8	2	5.25-inch floppy disk
FEH	40	8	1	5.25-inch floppy disk
	77	2, 6,or 8	1	8-inch floppy disk
FDH	40	9	2	5.25-inch floppy disk
	77	26	2	8-inch floppy disk
FCH	40	9	1	5.25-inch floppy disk
FBH	80	8	2	5.25-inch floppy disk
	80	8	2	3.5-inch microfloppy disk
FAH	80	8	1	5.25-inch floppy disk
	80	8	1	3.5-inch microfloppy disk
F0H	80	18	2	3.5-inch high-density microfloppy disk
F9H	80	9	2	3.5-inch microfloppy disk
	80	15	2	5.25-inch high-density floppy disk
F8H	-	-	-	Fixed disk

Version Info: Beginning with DOS 2.x, the usefulness of the disk ID byte in the FAT was reduced, and it is now considered meaningless, since multiple formats may have the same ID. Microsoft recommends that you use the information in the media descriptor table to determine the type of disk being used.

Notes: The disk ID byte is the low-order byte of the first cluster indicator in the FAT (e.g., a first cluster value of FFF8H yields a disk ID byte of F8H)

Source: IBM DOS 3.3 Technical Reference, page 5-6

See Also: 2.39. Disk Partition Table Layout
3.165. Media Descriptor Table

2.38. DISK BOOT RECORD LAYOUT

Offset	Length	Description
0 (0)	3 bytes	JMP to boot code*
3 (3)	8 bytes	OEM name and version
B (11)	word	Bytes per sector
D (13)	byte	Sectors per cluster (must be a power of 2)
E (14)	word	Reserved sectors (for Dir, FAT, etc.)
10 (16)	byte	Number of copies of FAT
11 (17)	word	Maximum number of root directory entries
13 (19)	word	Total number of sectors in logical image
15 (21)	byte	Media descriptor byte
16 (22)	word	Number of sectors in FAT
18 (24)	word	Number of sectors per track
1A (26)	word	Number of heads
1C (28)	word	Number of hidden sectors

Version Info: •Note that media descriptor bytes are not necessarily valid beginning with DOS 2.x
•*For DOS 2.x = 3-byte near jump
  For DOS 3.x = 2-byte short jump + NOP

Notes: OEM name and version are not always present
(IBM does not use)

Source: IBM DOS 3.3 Technical Reference, page 2-31

See Also: 1.27. Powers of Two

2.39. DISK PARTITION TABLE LAYOUT

Offset	Length	Name	Contents
0 (0)	byte	Partition status	0=inactive; 80H=bootable, active
1 (1)	byte	Starting head	Binary value
2 (2)	word	Starting sector and cylinder	See note *
4 (4)	byte	Partition type	1=DOS with 12-bit FAT 4=DOS with 16-bit FAT 5=extended DOS 6=reserved for future use DBH=concurrent DOS
5 (5)	byte	Ending head	Binary value
6 (6)	word	Ending sector and cylinder	See note *
8 (8)	dbl word	Starting absolute sector	Binary value (least significant word first and byte swapped in each word)
C (12)	dbl word	Number of sectors	Binary value (least significant word first and byte swapped in each word)

16-byte Block Repeats, as Above, for Each Partition, and Is Followed By:

01FEH	word	Signature	55AAH (indicates valid boot record)

Notes: •Some manufacturers allow additional partition types in order to divide large capacity hard disks into several drives.
•The partition tables begin at an offset of 1BEH in the boot record. The actual boot record is defined by the starting head, cylinder, and sector number, and that sector is loaded to location 7C00H.
•*Cylinder and sector are stored in bit-position-coded notation. This applies to the starting cylinder and head and the ending cylinder and head. See below.

			byte n								byte n+1					
c	c	s	s	s	s	s	s	c	c	c	c	c	c	c	c
M		M					L								L
S		S					S								S
B		B					B								B

The two most significant bits of byte n precede the eight bits of byte n+1 to form the ten-bit cylinder number. The six least significant bits of byte n form the sector number.

Source: IBM DOS 3.3 Technical Reference, pages 9-6 to 9-16

See Also: 2.38. Disk Boot Record Layout

2.40. FLOPPY DISK FORMAT SUMMARY

System That Commonly Uses This Format	Obsolete	Obsolete	Obsolete	PC/XT	AT	Convert.	PS/2
Disk size	5.25	5.25	5.25	5.25	5.25	3.5	3.5
Disk ID byte (in FAT)*	FE	FF	FC	FD	F9	F9	F0
Number of heads	1	2	1	2	2	2	2
Tracks per side	40	40	40	40	80	80	80
Sectors per track	8	8	9	9	15	9	18
Bytes per sector	512	512	512	512	512	512	512
Sectors per cluster	1	2	1	2	1	2	1
Number of reserved sectors	1	1	1	1	1	1	1
Number of sectors per FAT	1	1	2	2	7	3	9
Number of FATs per disk	2	2	2	2	2	2	2
Number of root directory sectors	4	7	4	7	14	7	14
Maximum number of root directory entries allowed	64	112	64	112	224	112	224
Total number of sectors on disk	320	640	360	720	2400	1440	2880
Total number of usable sectors on disk	313	630	351	708	2371	1426	2847
Total number of usable clusters on disk	313	315	351	354	2371	713	2847
Capacity of disk	160 KB	320KB	180 KB	360 KB	1.2 MB	720 KB	1.5 MB
Format introduced with DOS version	1	1.1	2	2	3	3	3.3

Notes:
•Total usable sectors and total usable clusters will change if bad sectors are found during formatting.
•*FAT disk ID bytes are unreliable. Use disk parameter block to determine media type.

Source:
MS-DOS 3.2 Programmer's Reference, pages 3-9, 3-10

See Also:
2.41. Hard Disk Format Summary

2.41. HARD DISK FORMAT SUMMARY

System That Commonly Uses This Format	XT	AT	Model 50	Model 60	Model 80
Disk size	5.25	5.25	3.5	3.5	3.5
Disk ID byte (in FAT)*	F8	F8	F8	F8	F8
Interleave	6 to 1	3 to 1	1 to 1	1 to 1	1 to 1
Heads per disk	4	4			
Cylinders	306	615			
Sectors per track	17	17			
Bytes per sector	512	512	512	512	512
Sectors per cluster	8	4			
Number of reserved sectors	1	1			
Number of sectors per FAT	8	40			
Number of FATs per disk	2	2			
Number of root directory sectors	32	32			
Maximum number of root directory entries allowed	512	512			
Total number of sectors on disk	20808	41820			
Total number of usable sectors on disk	20759	41707			
Total number of usable clusters on disk	2595	10427			
Capacity of disk in kilobytes	10MB	20MB	20MB	44MB	70MB
Format introduced with DOS version	2	2	3.3	3.3	3.3

Notes:
•All numbers assume that the entire hard disk is formatted as a DOS partition (i.e., no non-DOS partitions on disk).
•*FAT disk ID bytes are unreliable. Use disk parameter block to determine media type.

Source:
IBM PC/XT Technical Reference, pages 1-151 to 1-152.

See Also:
2.40. Floppy Disk Format Summary

2.42. EXE FILE HEADER

Offset	Length	Usual Contents	Description	Comments
0 (0)	word	4D5AH	EXE file signature	
2 (2)	word		Length of last used sector in file	Modulo 512
4 (4)	word		Size of file, including header	In 512-byte pages
6 (6)	word		Number of relocation table items	
8 (8)	word		Size of header	In 16-byte paragraphs
A (10)	word		Minimum paragraphs needed above program	In 16-byte paragraphs
C (12)	word		Maximum paragraphs desired above program	In 16-byte paragraphs
E (14)	word		Displacement of stack segment in module	Relative to start of program, in paragraphs
10 (16)	word		Contents of SP register at entry	
12 (18)	word		Checksum	Two's complement
14 (20)	word		Contents of IP register at entry	
16 (22)	word		Displacement of code module	Relative to start of program (in paragraphs)
18 (24)	word		Offset to first relocation item in file	Relative to start of file (in bytes)
1A (26)	word		Overlay number	0 for resident part of program
1C (28)	varies		Variable RESERVED space	
varies	varies		Relocation table	
varies	varies		Variable RESERVED space	
varies	varies		Program and data segments	
varies	varies		Stack segment	

Notes: EXE files created for use with Microsoft Windows use a different format (See 6.10. Windows EXE File Format)

Sources: IBM DOS 3.3 Technical Reference, pages 10-3 to 10-6

See Also: 2.43. COM Program Layout
6.10. Windows EXE File Format

2.43. COM PROGRAM LAYOUT

Offset	Length	Description	Comments
0 (0)	256 bytes	Program segment prefix	Values filled in by DOS
100 (256)	varies	Code and data segment	Only one segment allowed
varies	varies	Stack	Usually at top of segment

Notes: The program segment prefix is not usually part of the actual file.
It is created and filled in by DOS at program load time. COM files
must have code segment ORGed at 100H.

Source: IBM DOS 3.3 Technical Reference, page 7-9

See Also: 2.42. EXE File Header
2.44. COM versus EXE File Differences
3.136. Program Segment Prefix Layout

2.44. COM VERSUS EXE FILE DIFFERENCES

Item	COM Programs	EXE Programs
Max. program size	65278*	No limit
Segment use	One segment only	Multiple segments allowed
Entry point	PSP:0100H	Defined by END Segment
CS at entry	PSP	Segment containing module with entry point
IP at entry	0100H	Offset of entry point within its segment
DS at entry	PSP	PSP
ES at entry	PSP	PSP
SS at entry	PSP	Segment with STACK attribute
SP at entry	0FFFEH or top word, whichever is lower	Size of segment defined with STACK attribute
Stack at entry	Zero word on stack	Initialized or unitialized
Stack size	65536 - (ProgramSize+256)	Defined in segment with STACK attribute (up to 65536 bytes)
Memory allocation	All free memory allocated to program	May be set to allocate portion of memory (offset 0CH in EXE header)
Subroutine calls	NEAR CALLs only	NEAR or FAR CALLS allowed
Size of file	Exact size of program (might not include PSP)	Size of program plus EXE header (which is multiple of 512 bytes)

Notes: *65536 - 256-byte PSP - 2-byte STACK

Sources: *Advanced MS-DOS* (Microsoft Press), Ray Duncan

See Also: 2.42. EXE File Header
2.43. COM Program Layout
3.136. Program Segment Prefix Layout

2.45. FONT FILE (CODE PAGE) LAYOUT

Offset	Length	Name	Contents
0 (0)	8 bytes	File tag	FFH followed by "font," followed by three spaces
8 (8)	8 bytes	RESERVED	
10 (16)	word	Number of pointers in header	1 for DOS 3.3
12 (18)	byte	Type of pointer	1 for DOS 3.3
13(19)	dbl word	Offset to info from start of file	Binary value
17(23)	word	Number of entries	Binary value
19(25)	word	Size of code	Binary value
1B(27)	dbl word	Pointer to header of next entry	0000H for last header
1F(31)	word	Device type	1=display, 2=printer
21(33)	8 bytes	Device name (ID)	ASCII text padded with spaces
29(41)	word	Code page ID	437
2B(43)	3 words	RESERVED	
31(49)	dbl word	Pointer to font info	Binary value
35(53)	word	RESERVED	Must be 1
37(55)	word	Number of fonts	Binary value
39(57)	word	Length of font data	Binary value

For Display Font:

Offset	Length	Name	Contents
3B(59)	byte	Rows in character box	Binary value
3C(60)	byte	Columns in character box	Binary value
3D(61)	2 bytes	Aspect ratio	Currently not used, = 0,0
3F(63)	word	Number of characters in font	Usually 256
41(65)	varies	Font data	Stored as pixel descriptions

For Printer Font:

Offset	Length	Name	Contents
3B(59)	word	Printer selection type	1=4201, 2=5202
3D(61)	word	Total bytes in control sequences	Binary value
3F(63)	varies	Hardware code page	Maximum length of 31
varies	varies	Downloadable code page	Maximum length of 31
varies	varies	Downloadable character definitions	See Printer Technical Reference

Version Info: Applies to DOS 3.3 only

Source: IBM DOS 3.3 Technical Reference, pages 7-17 to 7-20

See Also: 3.147. Code Page Assignments

2.46. OPERATING SYSTEM FILES SUMMARY

IBM PC-DOS Version

File	1	1.1	2	2.1	3	3.1	3.2	3.3
IBMBIO.COM	1920	1920	4608	4736	8964	9564	16369	22100
IBMDOS.COM	6400	6400	17152	17024	27920	27760	28477	30159
COMMAND.COM	3231	4959	17664	17792	22042	23210	23791	25307
Total file sizes	11551	13279	39424	39552	58926	60534	68637	77566

Microsoft MS-DOS Version

File	1	1.1	2	2.1	3	3.1	3.2	3.3
IO.SYS	*	*	*	*	*	*	16138	22357
MS-DOS.SYS	*	*	*	*	*	*	28480	30128
COMMAND.COM	*	*	*	*	*	*	23612	25276
Total file sizes	*	*	*	*	*	*	68230	77761

Notes: •The first total shown is for the entire operating system files only.
The actual amount of memory used by the operating system is dependent upon the environment size, device drivers that have been loaded, and the settings of the BUFFERS and FILES parameters.
•*MS-DOS released only through OEMs, so file sizes vary.

Source: DOS Disks

See Also: 2.47. Included System Files Summary
2.49. Typical DOS Memory Usage

INCLUDED COMMANDS (BUILT-IN)

DOS Version Number

Command Name	1	1.1	2	2.1	3	3.1	3.2	3.3
CD/CHDIR			X	X	X	X	X	X
CLS			X	X	X	X	X	X
COPY	X	X	X	X	X	X	X	X
CTTY			X	X	X	X	X	X
DATE	X	X	X	X	X	X	X	X
DEL/ERASE	X	X	X	X	X	X	X	X
DIR	X	X	X	X	X	X	X	X
MD/MKDIR			X	X	X	X	X	X
PATH			X	X	X	X	X	X
PROMPT			X	X	X	X	X	X
REN/RENAME	X	X	X	X	X	X	X	X
RM/RMDIR			X	X	X	X	X	X
SET			X	X	X	X	X	X
TIME	X	X	X	X	X	X	X	X
TYPE	X	X	X	X	X	X	X	X
VER			X	X	X	X	X	X
VERIFY			X	X	X	X	X	X
VOL			X	X	X	X	X	X

BATCH FILE COMMANDS (BUILT-IN)

DOS Version Number

Command	1	1.1	2	2.1	3	3.1	3.2	3.3
CALL								X
ECHO			X	X	X	X	X	X
FOR			X	X	X	X	X	X
GOTO			X	X	X	X	X	X
IF			X	X	X	X	X	X
PAUSE	X	X	X	X	X	X	X	X
REM	X	X	X	X	X	X	X	X
SHIFT			X	X	X	X	X	X

See Also: 2.46. Operating System Files Summary

2.47. INCLUDED COMMAND FILES SUMMARY*

DOS Version Number

Command File	1	1.1	2	2.1	3	3.1	3.2	3.3
APPEND								X
ASSIGN			X	X	X	X	X	X
ATTRIB			X	X	X	X	X	X
BACKUP			X	X	X	X	X	X
BASIC	X	X	X	X	X	X	X	
BASICA	X	X	X	X	X	X	X	X
CHCP								X
CHKDSK	X	X	X	X	X	X	X	X
COMP	X	X	X	X	X	X	X	X
DEBUG	X	X	X	X	X	X	X	**
DISKCOMP	X	X	X	X	X	X	X	X
DISKCOPY	X	X	X	X	X	X	X	X
EDLIN	X	X	X	X	X	X	X	X
EXE2BIN			X	X	X	X	**	**
FASTOPEN								X
FDISK			X	X	X	X	X	X
FIND			X	X	X	X	X	X
FORMAT	X	X	X	X	X	X	X	X
GRAFTABL			X	X	X	X	X	X
GRAPHICS			X	X	X	X	X	X
JOIN					X	X	X	X
KEYBUK					X	X	X	X
KEYBGR					X	X	X	X
KEYBFR					X	X	X	X
KEYBIT					X	X	X	X
KEYBSP					X	X	X	X
LABEL					X	X	X	X
LINK	X	X	X	X	X	X	X	**
MODE	X	X	X	X	X	X	X	X
MORE			X	X	X	X	X	X
NLSFUNC								X
PRINT			X	X	X	X	X	X
RECOVER			X	X	X	X	X	X
REPLACE							X	X
RESTORE			X	X	X	X	X	X
SELECT					X	X	X	X
SHARE					X	X	X	X
SORT			X	X	X	X	X	X
SUBST						X	X	X
SYS	X	X	X	X	X	X	X	X
TREE			X	X	X	X	X	X
XCOPY							X	X

Notes:
- *These COM and EXE files are from the IBM PC-DOS versions. The MS-DOS versions may differ slightly.
- **Supplied with Technical Reference manual

(Continued)

2.48. COMMON FILE TYPES (EXTENSIONS)

File Type	Program	Description
$$$	DOS	A "pipe" file created by using the redirection flag (|) in a DOS command
@@@	CodeviewDisk	
ACT	BITCOM	Communications account data file
ACT	Actor	Source code file for Actor programming language
AIO	APL	APL file transfer format file
AMG	Actor	System image file for Actor programming language
APL	APL	APL work space format file
APP	SQL Windows	Application file
ARF	BASCOM	Automatic response file created by the BM series of compilers; similar to batch files
ARF	FORTRAN	Automatic response file created by the BM series of compilers; similar to batch files
ARF	COBOL	Automatic response file created by the BM series of compilers; similar to batch files
ASC	Many	ASCII text file; may be typed to the screen
ASM	MASM	Assembly language source code file
AUX	Paradox	
BAK	Many	A backup file; contains a previous version of the information in the file
BAS	BASIC	A file containing BASIC program code; may not be in ASCII format!
BAS	BASICA	A file containing BASIC program code; may not be in ASCII format!
BAS	MS-QuickBASIC	A file containing BASIC program code; may not be in ASCII format!
BAS	Turbo BASIC	A file containing BASIC program code; may not be in ASCII format!
BAT	DOS	Batch file; contains commands to be executed by DOS, in order
BIN	Many	Binary file; often same as an OBJ file; contains 8-bit information (i.e., not ASCII)
BLK	ShowPartner	Block file; contains information about a block manipulated by ShowPartner
BMP	MS-Windows	Bitmap file; contains data for a Windows bitmap structure
C	C compilers	Contains C source code
CAL	SuperCalc	Spreadsheet file; contains contents of a spreadsheet
CCL	Intalk	Communication command language file
CFG	Many	A configuration file; contains information about machine and environment
CHK	CHKDSK	Recovered data file; contains data recovered when using the /F option in CHKDSK
CLR	ShowPartner	Color palette file
CLS	Actor	Class library file for Actor programming language
CMD	dBASE	Command file; used for file that contains dBASE programs
CMD	CP/M-86	Transient command file (similar to DOS EXE and COM files)
CMP	MS-Word	Compare file; contains dictionary of words to compare for spelling
CNF	Many	A configuration file; contains information about machine environment
COB	COBOL	COBOL program source code
COD	FORTRAN	FORTRAN program compiled code file
COL	MS-Multiplan	Spreadsheet data file; contains contents of a spreadsheet
COM	DOS	Command (program) file
CRF	MASM	Cross reference file; listing produced by MASM compiler
CRS	World Tour Golf	Course data file
CTX	Microsoft	Course text file; contains information for on-line tutorials
CUR	MS-Windows	Cursor file; contains data for a Windows cursor
DAT	Many	Data file; usually contains ASCII or specifically-formatted data
DB	Paradox	Data file; contains data for a Paradox table
DBD	Bricklin's DEMO	Demonstration data file
DBF	dBASE	Data file; contains data for a dBASE database
DBS	SQL Windows	Data file; contains data for a SQL Windows database
DBT	dBASE	Data file; contains dBASE textual database information
DBT	SQL Windows	Temporary data file
DCT	SpellStar	Dictionary file; contains spelling dictionary
DEF	MS-Windows	Module definition file
DEF	Access	
DES	Access	
DEV	Many	Device driver file; contains code needed by CONFIG.SYS to install a new device
DFM	Palantir Filer	Data entry form file
DGS	PC-DOS	Diagnostics file
DIC	Many	Dictionary file; contains spelling dictionary
DIF	Many	Data interchange format file; used to interchange data between programs
DIR	Sidekick	Directory file; used with dialing options
DIS	Q&A	Startup file used by Q&A
DOC	Many	Document file; may be in ASCII or word processor-specific format
DOC	MS-Word	Document file; contains formatted document in non-ASCII form
DRV	Many	Device driver file; contains information to drive a specific device
DTF	Q&A, PFS	Data file; contains data for a PFS or Q&A database
EMU	BITCOM	Terminal emulation file; contains definitions used to emulate a terminal
EPS	Pagemaker	Encapsulated postscript file; contains condensed postscript printer data
EXE	DOS	Executable program file
FMT	dBASE	Screen format file; contains information about how data is to be displayed on screen
F#	Paradox	Form file; contains form definition information

(Continued)

Table 2.48. Continued

File Type	Program	Description
FNT	Windows	Font file; contains description of what a font should look like
FNT	LaserFonts	Font file; contains description of what a font should look like
FNT	Paintbrush	Font file; contains description of what a font should look like
FON	Windows	GDI loadable font file
FOR	FORTRAN	FORTRAN source code file
FRM	dBASE	Report form file; contains information about how a dBASE report should be formatted
GRB	MS-Windows	
GX1	ShowPartner	Graphics screen capture file
H	C compilers	Header file; contains C source code definitions to be merged with other files
HEX	DEBUG	Hex file; contains ASCII only numbers formatted in Intel HEX format
HIN	Access	
HLP	Many	Help file; contains information to help user understand command or function
ICO	MS-Windows	Icon file; contains bit image of an icon
IDX	Q&A	Index file; contains indexing information for a database
IMG	MS-Windows	Hi-res scanned image file
IMP	Pascal	Implementation file for IBM Pascal
INC	Pascal	Include file for Microsoft Pascal
INC	Turbo BASIC	Include file for Borland Turbo BASIC
INI	MS-Windows	Initialization file; contains information about initial state of system
INI	MS-Word	Printer initialization file
INT	Pascal	Interface file for IBM Pascal
INT	Xywrite	Command file for Xywrite
IT	Intalk	Settings file
JOR	SQL Windows	Journal file
KBD	Xywrite	Keyboard configuration file
LAY	Superkey	Layout file; contains keyboard reconfiguration information
LBL	dBASE	Label file
LIB	Many	Library file; normally created by a compiler in one of several standard formats
LNK	MS-Windows/C	
LOD	Many	Load file; used by one copy-protection scheme
LST	MASM	Listing file; lists assembled source code
MAC	Prokey	Keyboard macro file; contains instructions to execute when certain keys are pressed
MAC	Superkey	Keyboard macro file; contains instructions to execute when certain keys are pressed
MAP	LINK	Map file; a list file created by LINK during the linking proces
MDM	Access	Modem file; contains information about modems
ME	Many	Usually a READ.ME file containing information about files on disk
MEM	dBASE	Memory file
MNU	Access	Menu file; contains menu definition
MSG	Multiplan	Message file
MSG	Sidekick	Message file; used with appointment calendar
MSP	MS-Windows	Windows Paint file; contains data for a picture drawn with Windows Paint
MOD	MS-Windows	
NDX	dBASE	Index file; contains indexing information for a database
NET	Paradox	Network configuration file
OBJ	LINK	Object code file; contains result of an assembly or compile in a specified format
OVD	Paradox	Overlay file
OVL	Many	Overlay file; contains part of program to be loaded at a later time
OVR	Many	Overlay file; contains part of program to be loaded at a later time
OV#	Many	Overlay file; contains part of program to be loaded at a later time
PAL	Paintbrush	Palette file
PAS	Pascal	Pascal source code file
PCX	Paintbrush	Picture file
PCC	Paintbrush	Cutout picture file

(Continued)

Table 2.48. Continued

File Type	Program	Description
PFM	MS-Windows	Printer font metric file
PGM	Many	Usually a program overlay file
PHB	Access	
PIC	Many	Picture file
PIX	Many	File containing one or more pictures
PIF	MS-Windows	Program information file; used by TopView and Windows to load program into memory
PJ	SuperProject	Project file; contains information about a scheduling project
PRD	MS-Word	Printer definition file; contains information about how to talk to printer
PRF	VisiCalc	Print format file (spreadsheet printed to disk)
PRG	dBASE	Procedure or program file
PRJ	Harvard TPM	Project data file
PRN	Many	Print format file (print to disk)
PRS	MS-Word	
PUB	Pagemaker	Publication file; contains data for page layout
PX	Paradox	Primary Index file
RC	MS-Windows	Resource Script file; contains a list of resource definitions used by MS-Windows
REF	CREF	Printable cross-reference file (see CRF)
R#	Paradox	Report format file; contains a report definition
SC	Paradox	Script file; contains a PAL script (program)
SCN	Microsoft	Screen file; contains screen displays for on-line tutorials
SCP	BITCOM	Script file; contains a macro script for communications session
SCR	Access	Script file
SET	Paradox	Settings file; contains information about settings for a form or table
SOB	Microsoft	Part of on-line tutorials
SOM	Paradox	Sort information file
SPL	SQL Windows	SQLTALK Spooler file
SPS	Mouse	
SQL	SQL Windows	Data file
STY	MS-Word	Style sheet; contains style formatting information
SYM	MS-Windows	Symbolic debugging definitions
SYN	Word Finder	Synonym file; contains information for thesaurus program
SYS	Many	Device driver file; contains information to create a device driver under CONFIG.SYS
TIF	Microsoft	Tagged info file format (see 6.11. Tag Image File Format)
TMP	Many	Temporary file
TPL	Access	
TXT	Many	Text file
VAL	Paradox	Validity check file
VC	VisiCalc	VisiCalc spreadsheet file
WK1	Lotus 1-2-3	1-2-3 spreadsheet file (version 2)
WKS	Lotus 1-2-3	1-2-3 spreadsheet file (version 1)
WMF	MS-Windows	Metafile picture (see 6.16. Metafile Format)
WRI	MS-Windows	Windows Write document file
X#	Paradox	Index file
XLC	MS-Excel	Chart file
XLS	MS-Excel	Spreadsheet file
Y#	Paradox	Index file
Z#	Paradox	Index file

Notes: •A # sign indicates a position held by a digit, 0-9
•MS-Windows can associate file types with a program. Registration of types is done in the MS-Windows programming SIG on Genie.

2.49. TYPICAL DOS MEMORY USAGE

Address	Memory Usage
0000:0000	Interrupt vector table (see 7.22. I/O Port Usage)
0000:0400	ROM BIOS parameter area
0000:0500	DOS parameter area
0000:0700	IBMBIO
0000:0E30	IBMDOS
0000:4DB9	Device drivers (includes ANSI.SYS, BUFFERS=, FILES=, etc.)
0000:53F0	Resident COMMAND.COM
0000:5FD0	Master environment for COMMAND.COM (see 3.141. Environment Blocks)
0000:6080	Environment for program (if any)
0000:60B0	Application program (if any) (see 3.136. Program Segment Prefix Layout) (see 2.44. COM versus EXE File Differences)
0009:C9E0	Stack (expands towards beginning of memory)
0009:CBE0	Transient COMMAND.COM (error messages, command table, last command)
000A:0000	Hardware RESERVED (video adapters, ROM, ROM expansion) (see 7.02. IBM Reserved Memory Layout)
0010:0000	

Notes: Memory addresses are for PC-DOS 2.1 only. Other
               DOS versions will use the same ordering, but the
               memory addresses may vary.

Source: IBM DOS 3.3 Technical Reference, pages 7-4, 7-5

See Also: 2.44. COM versus EXE File Differences
               3.136. Program Segment Prefix Layout
               3.141. Environment Blocks
               7.02. PC Memory Use
               7.22. I/O Port Usage

2.50. ALLOWABLE CHARACTERS IN FILENAMES

ASCII Codes	Character(s)	Allowed	Illegal
00H-1FH	Control codes		X
20H	Space		X
21H	Exclamation point	X	
22H	Quotation mark		X
23H-29H	Misc. punctuation	X	
2AH	Asterisk		X**
2BH	Plus sign		X
2CH	Comma		X
2DH	Hyphen	X	
2EH	Period		X**
2FH	Slash		X
30H-39H	Numbers	X	
3AH	Colon		X**
3BH	Semicolon		X
3CH	Less than sign		X
3DH	Equals sign		X
3EH	Greater than sign		X
3FH	Question mark		X**
40H	At sign	X	
41H-5AH	Capital letters	X	
5BH	Opening bracket		X
5CH	Backslash		X**
5DH	Closing bracket		X
5EH-60H	Misc. punctuation	X	
61H-7AH	Lowercase letters	X*	
7BH	Opening brace	X	
7CH	Vertical line		X
7DH	Closing brace	X	
7EH	Tilde	X	
7FH	DEL	X*	
80H-FFH	IBM extended ASCII	X*	

Notes: •This same table applies to file types, volume, and directory names
•*Cannot necessarily be entered directly from keyboard
•**Has special meaning in filenames

Source: IBM DOS 3.3 Reference, page 2-4

See Also: 2.51. Filename Separator Characters

2.51. FILENAME SEPARATOR CHARACTERS

ASCII Codes	Character(s)	Separator	Terminator
00H-1FH	Control codes		X
09H	Tab	X	X
20H	Space	X	X
22H	Quotation mark	X	X
2BH	Plus sign	X	X
2CH	Comma	X	X
2EH	Period	X	X
2FH	Forward slash	X	X
3AH	Colon	X	X
3BH	Semicolon	X	X
3CH	Less than sign	X	X
3DH	Equals sign	X	X
3EH	Greater than sign	X	X
5BH	Opening bracket	X	X
5CH	Backslash	X	X
5DH	Closing bracket	X	X
7CH	Vertical line	X	X

Notes: Filename separators and terminators are used in parsing filenames

Source: Microsoft DOS 3.2 Programmer's Reference, page 1-107

See Also: 2.50. Allowable Characters in Filenames
3.045. Function 29H -- Parse Filename

— SECTION —

3

DOS Function Calls and Support Tables

3.001. INT 21H FUNCTIONS BY DOS VERSION SUMMARY

DOS Versions That Support the Function

Func.Number	Function Name	1	1.1	2	2.1	3	3.1	3.2	3.3
0 (0)	Terminate program	X	X	O	O	O	O	O	O
1 (1)	Read keyboard and echo	X	X	X	X	X	X	X	X
2 (2)	Display character	X	X	X	X	X	X	X	X
3 (3)	Auxiliary input	X	X	X	X	X	X	X	X
4 (4)	Auxiliary output	X	X	X	X	X	X	X	X
5 (5)	Print character	X	X	X	X	X	X	X	X
6 (6)	Direct console I/O	X	X	X	X	X	X	X	X
7 (7)	Direct console input without echo	X	X	X	X	X	X	X	X
8 (8)	Read keyboard without echo	X	X	X	X	X	X	X	X
9 (9)	Display string	X	X	X	X	X	X	X	X
A (10)	Buffered keyboard input	X	X	X	X	X	X	X	X
B (11)	Check keyboard status	X	X	X	X	X	X	X	X
C (12)	Flush buffer, do function	X	X	X	X	X	X	X	X
D (13)	Reset disk	X	X	X	X	X	X	X	X
E (14)	Select disk	X	X	X	X	X	X	X	X
F (15)	Open file	X	X	O	O	O	O	O	O
10 (16)	Close file	X	X	O	O	O	O	O	O
11 (17)	Search for first entry	X	X	O	O	O	O	O	O
12 (18)	Search for next entry	X	X	O	O	O	O	O	O
13 (19)	Delete file	X	X	O	O	O	O	O	O
14 (20)	Sequential read	X	X	O	O	O	O	O	O
15 (21)	Sequential write	X	X	O	O	O	O	O	O
16 (22)	Create file	X	X	O	O	O	O	O	O
17 (23)	Rename file	X	X	O	O	O	O	O	O
18 (24)	RESERVED	R	R	R	R	R	R	R	R
19 (25)	Get current disk	X	X	O	O	O	O	O	O
1A (26)	Set disk transfer address	X	X	X	X	X	X	X	X
1B (27)	Get default drive data	X	X	O	O	O	O	O	O
1C (28)	Get drive data	X	X	O	O	O	O	O	O
1D (29)	RESERVED	R	R	R	R	R	R	R	R
1E (30)	RESERVED	R	R	R	R	R	R	R	R
1F (31)	RESERVED	R	R	R	R	R	R	R	R
20 (32)	RESERVED	R	R	R	R	R	R	R	R
21 (33)	Random read	X	X	O	O	O	O	O	O
22 (34)	Random write	X	X	O	O	O	O	O	O
23 (35)	Get file size	X	X	O	O	O	O	O	O
24 (36)	Set random record field	X	X	O	O	O	O	O	O
25 (37)	Set interrupt vector	X	X	X	X	X	X	X	X
26 (38)	Create new program segment	X	X	X	X	X	X	X	X
27 (39)	Random block read	X	X	O	O	O	O	O	O
28 (40)	Random block write	X	X	O	O	O	O	O	O
29 (41)	Parse file name	X	X	O	O	O	O	O	O
2A (42)	Get date	X	X	X	X	X	X	X	X
2B (43)	Set date	X	X	X	X	X	X	X	X
2C (44)	Get time	X	X	X	X	X	X	X	X
2D (45)	Set time	X	X	X	X	X	X	X	X
2E (46)	Set/reset verify flag	X	X	X	X	X	X	X	X
2F (47)	Get DTA			X	X	X	X	X	X
30 (48)	Get DOS version number			X	X	X	X	X	X
31 (49)	Terminate but stay resident			X	X	X	X	X	X
32 (50)	RESERVED	R	R	R	R	R	R	R	R
33 (51)	Control-C check			X	X	X	X	X	X
34 (52)	RESERVED	R	R	R	R	R	R	R	R
35 (53)	Get interrupt vector			X	X	X	X	X	X
36 (54)	Get disk free space			X	X	X	X	X	X
37 (55)	RESERVED	R	R	R	R	R	R	R	R
38,0(56,0)	Get country			X	X	X	X	X	X
38,X(56,X)	Set country (X=country code)					X	X	X	X
39 (57)	Create directory			X	X	X	X	X	X
3A (58)	Removed directory			X	X	X	X	X	X
3B (59)	Change current directory			X	X	X	X	X	X
3C (60)	Create file			X	X	X	X	X	X
3D (61)	Open file			X	X	E	E	E	E
3E (62)	Close file			X	X	X	X	X	X
3F (63)	Read file or device			X	X	X	X	X	X
40 (64)	Write file or device			X	X	X	X	X	X
41 (65)	Delete file			X	X	X	X	X	X
42 (66)	Move file pointer			X	X	X	X	X	X
43 (67)	Get/set file attributes			X	X	X	X	X	X
44,0(68,0)	IOCTL get data			X	X	X	X	X	X
44,1(68,1)	IOCTL set data			X	X	X	X	X	X
44,2(68,2)	IOCTL read character			X	X	X	X	X	X
44,3(68,3)	IOCTL write character			X	X	X	X	X	X

(Continued)

Table 3.001. Continued

Func.Number	Function Name	DOS Versions That Support the Function							
		1	1.1	2	2.1	3	3.1	3.2	3.3
44,4(68,4)	IOCTL read block			X	X	X	X	X	X
44,5(68,5)	IOCTL write block			X	X	X	X	X	X
44,6(68,6)	IOCTL get input status			X	X	X	X	X	X
44,7(68,7)	IOCTL get output status			X	X	X	X	X	X
44,8(68,8)	IOCTL is changeable?					X	X	X	X
44,9(68,9)	IOCTL is redirected block?						X	X	X
44,A(68,10)	IOCTL is redirected handle?						X	X	X
44,B(68,11)	IOCTL change retry count					X	X	X	X
44,C(68,12)	Generic IOCTL for handles							X	X
44,D(68,13)	Generic IOCTL for devices							X	X
44,E(68,14)	Get drive							X	X
44,F(68,15)	Set drive							X	X
45 (69)	Duplicate file handle			X	X	X	X	X	X
46 (70)	Force duplicate file handle			X	X	X	X	X	X
47 (71)	Get current directory			X	X	X	X	X	X
48 (72)	Allocate memory			X	X	X	X	X	X
49 (73)	Free allocated memory			X	X	X	X	X	X
4A (74)	SETBLOCK			X	X	X	X	X	X
4B,0(75,0)	Load and execute program			X	X	X	X	X	X
4B,3(75,3)	Load overlay			X	X	X	X	X	X
4C (76)	End process			X	X	X	X	X	X
4D (77)	Get return code of subprocess			X	X	X	X	X	X
4E (78)	Find first file			X	X	X	X	X	X
4F (79)	Find next file			X	X	X	X	X	X
50 (80)	RESERVED	R	R	R	R	R	R	R	R
51 (81)	RESERVED	R	R	R	R	R	R	R	R
52 (82)	RESERVED	R	R	R	R	R	R	R	R
53 (83)	RESERVED	R	R	R	R	R	R	R	R
54 (84)	Get verify state			X	X	X	X	X	X
55 (85)	RESERVED	R	R	R	R	R	R	R	R
56 (86)	Rename file			X	X	X	X	X	X
57 (87)	Get/set date/time of file			X	X	X	X	X	X
58 (88)	Get/set allocation strategy					X	X	X	X
59 (89)	Get extended error					X	X	X	X
5A (90)	Create temporary file					X	X	X	X
5B (91)	Create new file					X	X	X	X
5C,0(92,0)	Lock					X	X	X	X
5C,1(92,1)	Unlock					X	X	X	X
5D (93)	RESERVED	R	R	R	R	R	R	R	R
5E,0(94,0)	Get machine name						X	X	X
5E,2(94,2)	Printer setup						X	X	X
5F,2(95,2)	Get assign list entry						X	X	X
5F,3(95,3)	Make assign list entry						X	X	X
5F,4(95,4)	Cancel assign list entry						X	X	X
60 (96)	RESERVED	R	R	R	R	R	R	R	R
61 (97)	RESERVED	R	R	R	R	R	R	R	R
62 (98)	Get PSP address					X	X	X	X
63 (99)	Get lead byte table				2.25*				
65 (101)	Get extended country information								X
66 (102)	Get/set global code page								X
67 (103)	Set handle count								X
68 (104)	Commit file								X

Legend: X=supported, O=supported but considered obsolete, E=extended from previous versions, R=reserved

Version Info: *Note that function 63 (99) is available only in DOS 2.25

Notes: Function numbers with multiple values indicate that the AL register is also used to specify function (e.g. 5EH,1 represents function 5EH with the AL register set to 1)

Source: IBM DOS 3.3 Technical Reference, pages 6-6 to 6-7

See Also: 3.009.-3.122. Individual INT 21H Functions

3.002. INT 21H KEYBOARD FUNCTIONS SUMMARY

INT 21H Function #	Waits for Character	Echos Character	Interrupt on Ctrl-C	Buffer Register Used
01 (1)	Yes	Yes	Yes	AL
06 (6)	No	No	No	AL
07 (7)	Yes	No	No	AL
08 (8)	Yes	No	Yes	AL
0A (10)	Yes	No	Yes	DS:DX=buffer address
0B (11)	Keyboard status only			
0C (12)	Varies upon function requested			
3F (63)	Yes	No	Yes	DS:DX=buffer address

Notes: Control-C checking can be turned off completely using function 33H

Source: IBM DOS 3.3 Technical Reference, pages 6-35, 6-52, 6-57 to 6-60, 6-62 to 6-64, 6-137 to 6-138

See Also: 3.010. Function 01H -- Read Keyboard and Echo
3.015. Function 06H -- Direct Console I/O
3.016. Function 07H -- Direct Console Input Without Echo
3.017. Function 08H -- Read Keyboard Without Echo
3.019. Function 0AH -- Buffered Keyboard Input
3.020. Function 0BH -- Check Keyboard Status
3.021. Function 0CH -- Flush Buffer, Read Keyboard
3.065. Function 3FH -- Read Using Handle

3.003. INT 21H FCB-ORIENTED FUNCTIONS SUMMARY

INT 21H Function #	Function Name	Type of FCB Used*	Replaced by Function #
F (15)	Open file	Unopened FCB	3DH -- open handle
10 (16)	Close file	Opened FCB	3EH -- close handle
11 (17)	Search for first entry	Unopened FCB	4EH -- find first file
12 (18)	Search for next entry	Unopened FCB**	4FH -- find next file
13 (19)	Delete file	Unopened FCB	41H -- delete file
14 (20)	Sequential read	Opened FCB	3FH -- read handle
15 (21)	Sequential write	Opened FCB	40H -- write handle
16 (22)	Create file	Unopened FCB	3CH -- create handle 5AH -- create temp file 5BH -- create new file
17 (23)	Rename file	Rename FCB	56H -- change dir entry
21 (33)	Random read	Opened FCB	3FH -- read handle
22 (34)	Random write	Opened FCB	40H -- write handle
23 (35)	Get file size	Unopened FCB	42H -- move file pointer
24 (36)	Set relative record	Opened FCB	42H -- move file pointer
27 (39)	Random block read	Opened FCB	3FH -- read handle
28 (40)	Random block write	Opened FCB	40H -- write handle

Notes: •*Opened and unopened FCBs may also be extended if you need to set or are using the file attribute byte
•**Must be unchanged from use of function 11H -- search for first entry

Source: IBM DOS 3.3 Technical Reference, pages 6-35, 6-36, 6-67 to 6-80,6-85 to 6-88, 6-91 to 6-94

See Also:
3.004. INT 21H Handle-oriented Functions Summary
3.024. Function 0FH -- Open File With FCB
3.025. Function 10H -- Close File With FCB
3.026. Function 11H -- Find First Entry With FCB
3.027. Function 12H -- Find Next Entry With FCB
3.028. Function 13H -- Delete File With FCB
3.029. Function 14H -- Sequential Read With FCB
3.030. Function 15H -- Sequential Write With FCB
3.031. Function 16H -- Create File With FCB
3.032. Function 17H -- Rename File With FCB
3.037. Function 21H -- Random Read With FCB
3.038. Function 22H -- Random Write With FCB
3.039. Function 23H -- Get File Size With FCB
3.040. Function 24H -- Set Relative Record With FCB
3.043. Function 27H -- Random Block Read With FCB
3.044. Function 28H -- Random Block Write With FCB
3.062. Function 3CH -- Create File
3.063. Function 3DH -- Open File
3.064. Function 3EH -- Close File
3.065. Function 3FH -- Read Using Handle
3.066. Function 40H -- Write Using Handle
3.067. Function 41H -- Delete File
3.068. Function 42H -- Move File Pointer
3.097. Function 4EH -- Find First File
3.098. Function 4FH -- Find Next File
3.106. Function 5AH -- Create Temporary File
3.107. Function 5BH -- Create New File
3.123. Unopened FCB Format
3.124. Opened FCB Format
3.126. Rename FCB Format

3.004. INT 21H HANDLE-ORIENTED FUNCTIONS SUMMARY

INT 21H Function #	Function Name	Use
3C (60)	Create handle	Creates file for subsequent I/O; erases existing file, if any
3D (61)	Open handle	Readies file for I/O; assigns handle number
3E (62)	Close handle	Closes handle; frees handle number
3F (63)	Read handle	Reads from file at current pointer location
40 (64)	Write handle	Writes to file at current pointer location
41 (65)	Delete file	Deletes file
42 (66)	Move file pointer	Moves location of pointer in file
43 (67)	Get/set file attributes	Changes or retrieves attribute byte for file
45 (69)	Duplicate file handle	Assigns additional handle number to existing handle
46 (70)	Force duplicate file handle	Forces existing handle to refer to file that has a different handle
56 (86)	Rename file	Renames file
57 (87)	Get/set file date/time	Changes or retrieves Last Update time and date associated with file
5A (90)	Create temporary file	Creates file with unique name for subsequent I/O
5B (91)	Create new file	Creates file for subsequent I/O only if it does not already exist
67 (103)	Set handle count	Allows you to specify more than 20 handles (default maximum)
68 (104)	Commit file	Insures file is written to disk (flushes buffer)

Notes: The first five handle numbers are preassigned by DOS (See 3.130. Predefined Handles)

Source: IBM DOS 3.3 Technical Reference, pages 6-36, 6-37, 6-122 to 6-146, 6-186 to 6-187, 6-206 to 6-209, 6-213 to 6-215, 6-239 to 6-240

See Also: 3.003. INT 21H FCB-oriented Functions Summary
3.062. Function 3CH -- Create File
3.063. Function 3DH -- Open File
3.064. Function 3EH -- Close File
3.065. Function 3FH -- Read Using Handle
3.066. Function 40H -- Write Using Handle
3.067. Function 41H -- Delete File
3.068. Function 42H -- Move File Pointer
3.069. Function 43H, 00H -- Get File Attributes
3.070. Function 43H, 01H -- Set File Attributes
3.087. Function 45H -- Duplicate File Handle
3.088. Function 46H -- Force Duplicate File Handle
3.097. Function 4EH -- Find First File
3.098. Function 4FH -- Find Next File
3.100. Function 56H -- Rename File
3.101. Function 57H, 00H -- Get Date/Time of File
3.102. Function 57H, 01H -- Set Date/Time of File
3.106. Function 5AH -- Create Temporary File
3.107. Function 5BH -- Create New File
3.121. Function 67H -- Set Handle Count
3.122. Function 68H -- Commit File

3.005. INT 21H IOCTL DEVICE-ORIENTED FUNCTIONS SUMMARY

INT 21H Func.Num.*	Function Name	Use
44H,00H	Get data	Gets the device data word used to control device
44H,01H	Set data	Sets the device data word used to control device
44H,02H	Read character	Receives a character from character-oriented device
44H,03H	Write character	Sends a character to character-oriented device
44H,04H	Read block	Receives a block of data from block-oriented device
44H,05H	Write block	Sends a block of data to block-oriented device
44H,06H	Get input status	Checks input device for readiness
44H,07H	Get output status	Checks output device for readiness
44H,08H	Is changeable?	Reports whether block device contains removable media
44H,09H	Is redirected block?	Reports whether block device is local or remote (network)
44H,0AH	Is redirected handle?	Reports whether handle referencing device is local or remote
44H,0BH	Change retry count	Sets number of retries and pause between them for a file-sharing device
44H,0CH	Generic IOCTL for handles	Sets or gets number of retries for printer devices
44H,0DH	Generic IOCTL for devices	Sets/gets block device parameters; writes/reads/formats/verifies tracks
44H,0EH	Get drive map	Reports logical drive mapping
44H,0FH	Set drive map	Sets logical to physical drive mapping

Notes: *The first number is the AH function number, the second the AL subfunction number

Source: IBM DOS 3.3 Technical Reference, pages 6-36, 6-147 to 6-184

See Also: 3.004. INT 21H Handle-oriented Functions Summary
3.069. Function 43H, 00H -- Get File Attributes
3.070. Function 43H, 01H -- Set File Attributes
3.073. Function 44H, 02H -- IOCTL Read String
3.074. Function 44H, 03H -- IOCTL Write String
3.075. Function 44H, 04H -- IOCTL Read Block
3.076. Function 44H, 05H -- IOCTL Write Block
3.077. Function 44H, 06H -- IOCTL Get Input Status
3.078. Function 44H, 07H -- IOCTL Get Output Status
3.079. Function 44H, 08H -- IOCTL Is Removable?
3.080. Function 44H, 09H -- IOCTL Is Redirected Block?
3.081. Function 44H, 0AH -- IOCTL Is Redirected Handle?
3.082. Function 44H, 0BH -- IOCTL Change Retry Count
3.083. Function 44H, 0CH -- Generic IOCTL For Handles
3.084. Function 44H, 0DH -- Generic IOCTL For Devices
3.085. Function 44H, 0EH -- Get Logical Drive Map
3.086. Function 44H, 0FH -- Set Logical Drive Map
3.148. Reserved Device Names and Chain Order

3.006. INT 21H SYSTEM FUNCTIONS SUMMARY

INT 21H Function #	Function Name	Use
1A (26)	Set DTA	Make new disk transfer address
25 (37)	Set interrupt vector	Replace interrupt vector address in low memory
26 (38)	Create program segment	Make new program segment
2A (42)	Get system date	Retrieve current system date
2B (43)	Set system date	Store new system date
2C (44)	Get system time	Retrieve current system time
2D (45)	Set system time	Store new system time
2E (46)	Set/reset verify flag	Report or set verify flag state
2F (47)	Get DTA	Report current disk transfer address
30 (48)	Get DOS version number	Report DOS version being used
31 (49)	Keep process	End program execution but keep resident
33 (51)	Control-C check	Report or change Control-C check status
35 (53)	Get interrupt vector	Report address associated with Interrupt
36 (54)	Get disk free space	Report information about disk status
38 (56)	Get/set country code	Report or change country information
39 (57)	Create directory	Make a new directory on disk
3A (58)	Remove directory	Remove an existing directory from disk
3B (59)	Change current directory	Change to specified directory on disk
47 (71)	Get current directory	Report current directory on disk
48 (72)	Allocate memory	Get specified memory amount for use by program
49 (73)	Free allocated memory	Free memory currently being used by program
4A (74)	SETBLOCK	Change size of memory block being used
4B (75)	Load program or overlay	Load program and execute it, or load overlay
4C (76)	End process	End program execution and report errorlevel
4D (77)	Get return code	Get errorlevel report from child process
54 (84)	Get verify state	Report current verify flag setting
58 (88)	Get/set allocation strategy	Report or change memory allocation strategy used
59 (89)	Get extended error	Report details about last DOS function error
62 (98)	Get PSP address	Report current location of program segment prefix
65 (101)	Get/set extended country	Report or change country information
66 (102)	Get/set global code page	Report or change memory area used for country font info

Source: IBM DOS 3.3 Technical Reference, pages 6-35 to 6-37, 6-82, 6-89 to 6-90, 6-98 to 6-121, 6-188 to 6-201, 6-205, 6-210 to 6-212, 6-232 to 6-238

See Also:
3.034. Function 1AH -- Set Disk Transfer Address
3.041. Function 25H -- Set Interrupt Vector
3.042. Function 26H -- Create New Program Segment
3.046. Function 2AH -- Get System Date
3.047. Function 2BH -- Set System Date
3.048. Function 2CH -- Get System Time
3.049. Function 2DH -- Set System Time
3.050. Function 2EH -- Set/Reset Verify Flag
3.051. Function 2FH -- Get Disk Transfer Address
3.052. Function 30H -- Get DOS Version
3.053. Function 31H -- Keep Process
3.054. Function 33H -- Control-C Check
3.055. Function 35H -- Get Interrupt Vector
3.056. Function 36H -- Get Disk Free Space
3.057. Function 38H, 00H -- Get Country Data
3.058. Function 38H, xxH -- Set Country Data
3.059. Function 39H -- Create Subdirectory
3.060. Function 3AH -- Remove Subdirectory
3.061. Function 3BH -- Change Current Directory
3.089. Function 47H -- Get Current Directory
3.090. Function 48H -- Allocate Memory
3.091. Function 49H -- Free Allocated Memory
3.092. Function 4AH -- Set Block
3.093. Function 4BH, 00H -- Load and Execute Program
3.095. Function 4CH -- End Process
3.096. Function 4DH -- Get Return Code
3.099. Function 54H -- Get Verify State
3.103. Function 58H, 00H -- Get Allocation Strategy
3.104. Function 58H, 01H -- Set Allocation Strategy
3.105. Function 59H -- Get Extended Error
3.116. Function 62H -- Get Program Segment Prefix
3.118. Function 65H -- Get Extended Country Info
3.119. Function 66H, 01H -- Get Global Code Page
3.120. Function 66H, 02H -- Set Global Code Page

3.007. INT 21H NETWORK FUNCTIONS SUMMARY

INT 21H Function #	Function Name	Use
44H,09H	Is redirected block?	Reports whether drive letter is local or remote (network)
44H,0AH	Is redirected handle?	Reports whether device name is local or remote (network)
5CH,00H	Lock file	Locks region of file from use by others
5CH,01H	Unlock file	Unlocks locked region of file (restores to public use)
5EH,00H	Get machine name	Reports network name of the workstation
5EH,02H	Printer setup	Defines string of characters to be sent with each file to printer
5FH,02H	Get assign list entry	Reports IDs and names of drives/devices reassigned to network
5FH,03H	Make assign list entry	Redirects local drive/device to a network directory/device
5FH,04H	Cancel assign list entry	Cancels redirection created with function 5F,03

Version Info: Network functions require DOS 3.1 or later

Source: IBM DOS 3.3 Technical Reference, pages 6-36, 6-37, 6-155 to 6-156, 6-216 to 6-231

See Also: 3.080. Function 44H, 09H -- IOCTL Is Redirected Block?
3.081. Function 44H, 0AH -- IOCTL Is Redirected Handle?
3.108. Function 5CH, 00H -- Lock File
3.109. Function 5CH, 01H -- Unlock File
3.110. Function 5EH, 00H -- Get Machine Name
3.111. Function 5EH, 02H -- Set Printer String
3.113. Function 5FH, 02H -- Get Assignment List Entry
3.114. Function 5FH, 03H -- Make Assignment List Entry
3.115. Function 5FH, 04H -- Cancel Assignment List Entry

3.008. TYPICAL DOS REGISTER USE

Register	Standard Usage	# Bits	Comments
AX	General purpose data register	16	Passes MS-DOS parameters, returns error
AH	Function request register	8	Contains function number on call (INT 21H)
AL	Error return register	8	Returns error if carry flag set
BX	Data segment base register	16	Also returns data (e.g. handle number)
CX	Loop counter	16	Sometimes used for data passing
DX	General purpose data register	16	Often used as offset to DS for pointer to data
SP	Stack register	16	
IP	Instruction pointer register	16	
BP	Stack segment base register	16	
DS	Data segment of pointer	16	Normally used with DX
SS	Stack segment of pointer	16	Normally used with BX or CX
SI	Source index in string operations	16	
DI	Destination index in string ops	16	
Flags	Carry flag set=error; carry flag clear=no error	1	Used primarily by DOS 2.1 and later

Source: IBM DOS 3.3 Technical Reference, pages 6-8 to 6-9

3.009. FUNCTION 00H -- TERMINATE PROGRAM

Prior to Calling Function

	High	Low
AX	00H	
BX		
CX		
DX		
SP		
BP		
SI		
DI		
IP		
flags		
CS	Segment address of PSP*	
DS		
SS		
ES		

Upon Return From Function

Function does not return:
- •File buffers flushed
- •Termination handler address restored from PSP:000AH
- •Ctrl-C exit address restored from PSP:000EH
- •Critical error handler address restored from PSP:0012H**
- •Control passes to termination handler address

Notes:
- •Obsolete function; in DOS 2.x or later use function 31H or 4CH instead
- •*See 3.136. Program Segment Prefix Layout
- •**DOS versions 2.x and later only

Source: IBM DOS 3.3 Technical Reference, page 6-51

See Also: 3.001. INT 21H Functions by DOS Version Summary
3.053. Function 31H -- Keep Process
3.095. Function 4CH -- End Process

3.010. FUNCTION 01H -- READ KEYBOARD AND ECHO

Prior to Calling Function

	High	Low
AX	01H	
BX		
CX		
DX		
SP		
BP		
SI		
DI		
IP		
flags		
CS		
DS		
SS		
ES		

Upon Return From Function

	High	Low
AX		8-bit char code*
BX		
CX		
DX		
SP		
BP		
SI		
DI		
IP		
flags		
CS		
DS		
SS		
ES		

Notes:
- •Function echoes characters to display; Control-C is enabled; waits for character to be input from standard input device
- •Function is obsolete; in DOS 2.x or later use function 3FH instead
- •*Either 8-bit IBM ASCII code, or one of two bytes of an IBM Extended ASCII code

Source: MS-DOS 3.3 Programmer's Reference, page 6-52

See Also: 3.001. INT 21H Functions by DOS Version Summary
1.21. ASCII Character Set
1.22. IBM ASCII Character Set
1.23. IBM Extended Character Codes
3.015. Function 06H -- Direct Console I/O
3.016. Function 07H -- Direct Console Input Without Echo
3.017. Function 08H -- Read Keyboard Without Echo
3.019. Function 0AH -- Buffered Keyboard Input
3.021. Function 0CH -- Flush Buffer, Read Keyboard
3.065. Function 3FH -- Read Using Handle

3.011. FUNCTION 02H -- DISPLAY CHARACTER

Prior to Calling Function			*Upon Return From Function*

	High	Low
AX	02H	
BX		
CX		
DX		8-bit char to display

Function does not return any values

SP	
BP	
SI	
DI	

IP	
flags	

CS	
DS	
SS	
ES	

Notes: •Obsolete function; in DOS 2.x or later use function 40H instead
•Cursor position updated; if character is a backspace (08H),
the cursor is moved to the left one position, but the character there
is not erased

Source: MS-DOS 3.3 Programmer's Reference, page 6-53

See Also: 1.22. IBM ASCII Character Set
1.23. IBM Extended Character Set
3.001. INT 21H Functions by DOS Version Summary
3.015. Function 06H -- Direct Console I/O
3.018. Function 09H -- Display String
3.066. Function 40H -- Write Using Handle

3.012. FUNCTION 03H -- AUXILIARY INPUT

Prior to Calling Function			*Upon Return From Function*

	High	Low			High	Low
AX	03H			AX		8-bit char from AUX
BX				BX		
CX				CX		
DX				DX		

SP			SP	
BP			BP	
SI			SI	
DI			DI	

IP			IP	
flags			flags	

CS			CS	
DS			DS	
SS			SS	
ES			ES	

Notes: •This function does not check status of AUX port, buffer input, or return
error codes
•Obsolete function; in DOS 2.x or later use function 3FH instead
•DOS initializes the standard auxiliary device to 2400 baud, no parity,
one stop bit, and 8-bit words

Source: IBM DOS 3.3 Technical Reference, page 6-54

See Also: 1.21. ASCII Character Set
3.001. INT 21H Functions by DOS Version Summary
3.013. Function 04H -- Auxiliary Output
3.065. Function 3FH -- Read Using Handle

3.013. FUNCTION 04H -- AUXILIARY OUTPUT

Prior to Calling Function   *Upon Return From Function*

	High	Low
AX	04H	
BX		
CX		
DX		8-bit char to AUX

SP	
BP	
SI	
DI	

IP	
flags	

CS	
DS	
SS	
ES	

Function does not return any values

Notes: •This function does not check status of AUX port, buffer output, or return error codes
•Obsolete function; in DOS 2.x or later use function 40H instead

Source: IBM DOS 3.3 Technical Reference, page 6-55

See Also: 3.001. INT 21H Functions by DOS Version Summary
3.012. Function 03H -- Auxiliary Input
3.066. Function 40H -- Write Using Handle

3.014. FUNCTION 05H -- PRINT CHARACTER

Prior to Calling Function   *Upon Return From Function*

	High	Low
AX	05H	
BX		
CX		
DX		8-bit char to print

SP	
BP	
SI	
DI	

IP	
flags	

CS	
DS	
SS	
ES	

Function returns no values

Notes: •This function does not check status of printer port, buffer output, or return error codes
•Obsolete function; in DOS 2.x or later use function 40H instead

Source: IBM DOS 3.3 Technical Reference, page 6-56

See Also: 3.001. INT 21H Functions by DOS Version Summary
3.066. Function 40H -- Write Using Handle

3.015. FUNCTION 06H -- DIRECT CONSOLE I/O

		Prior to Calling Function				*Upon Return From Function*

Prior to Calling Function

	High	Low
AX	06H	
BX		
CX		
DX		8-bit char or FFH*

SP		
BP		
SI		
DI		

IP		
flags		

CS		
DS		
SS		
ES		

Upon Return From Function

	High	Low
AX		8-bit char or 00H**
BX		
CX		
DX		

SP		
BP		
SI		
DI		

IP		
flags	ZeroFlag set	

CS		
DS		
SS		
ES		

Notes:
- Obsolete function; in DOS 2.x and later use functions 3FH and 40H
- *If DL=FFH, console input is performed; otherwise DL is sent to console
- **If ZeroFlag is clear, AL contains character from console; otherwise AL = 0

Source: IBM DOS 3.3 Technical Reference, pages 6-57 to 6-58

See Also:
3.001. INT 21H Functions by DOS Version Summary
3.002. INT 21H Keyboard Functions Summary
3.010. Function 01H -- Read Keyboard and Echo
3.011. Function 02H -- Display Character
3.016. Function 07H -- Direct Console Input Without Echo
3.017. Function 08H -- Read Keyboard Without Echo
3.018. Function 09H -- Display String
3.019. Function 0AH -- Buffered Keyboard Input
3.021. Function 0CH -- Flush Buffer, Read Keyboard
3.065. Function 3FH -- Read Using Handle
3.066. Function 40H -- Write Using Handle

3.016. FUNCTION 07H -- DIRECT CONSOLE INPUT WITHOUT ECHO

Prior to Calling Function   *Upon Return From Function*

	High	Low			High	Low
AX	07H			AX		8-bit char from CON
BX				BX		
CX				CX		
DX				DX		
SP				SP		
BP				BP		
SI				SI		
DI				DI		
IP				IP		
flags				flags		
CS				CS		
DS				DS		
SS				SS		
ES				ES		

Notes: •Function does not echo character or check for Control-C
•Obsolete function; in DOS 2.x and later use function 3FH instead

Source: IBM DOS 3.3 Technical Reference, page 6-59

See Also: 3.001. INT 21H Functions by DOS Version Summary
3.002. INT 21H Keyboard Functions Summary
3.010. Function 01H -- Read Keyboard and Echo
3.015. Function 06H -- Direct Console I/O
3.017. Function 08H -- Read Keyboard Without Echo
3.019. Function 0AH -- Buffered Keyboard Input
3.021. Function 0CH -- Flush Buffer, Read Keyboard
3.065. Function 3FH -- Read Using Handle

3.017. FUNCTION 08H -- READ KEYBOARD WITHOUT ECHO

Prior to Calling Function   *Upon Return From Function*

	High	Low			High	Low
AX	08H			AX		8-bit char from CON
BX				BX		
CX				CX		
DX				DX		
SP				SP		
BP				BP		
SI				SI		
DI				DI		
IP				IP		
flags				flags		
CS				CS		
DS				DS		
SS				SS		
ES				ES		

Notes: •Function waits for and does not echo character
•Obsolete function; in DOS 2.x and later use function 3FH instead

Source: IBM DOS 3.3 Technical Reference, page 6-60

See Also: 3.001. INT 21H Functions by DOS Version Summary
3.002. INT 21H Keyboard Functions Summary
3.010. Function 01H -- Read Keyboard and Echo
3.015. Function 06H -- Direct Console I/O
3.016. Function 07H -- Direct Console Input Without Echo
3.019. Function 0AH -- Buffered Keyboard Input
3.021. Function 0CH -- Flush Buffer, Read Keyboard
3.065. Function 3FH -- Read Using Handle

3.018. FUNCTION 09H -- DISPLAY STRING

Prior to Calling Function   *Upon Return From Function*

	High	Low
AX	09H	
BX		
CX		
DX	Offset of pointer to $-terminated string	

Function does not return a value

SP	
BP	
SI	
DI	

IP	
flags	

CS	
DS	Segment of pointer to $-terminated string
SS	
ES	

Notes: Obsolete function; in DOS 2.x and later use function
                 40H instead

Source: IBM DOS 3.3 Technical Reference, page 6-61

See Also: 1.17. Common String Formats
                 3.001. INT 21H Functions by DOS Version Summary
                 3.011. Function 02H -- Display Character
                 3.066. Function 40H -- Write Using Handle

3.019. FUNCTION 0AH -- BUFFERED KEYBOARD INPUT

Prior to Calling Function   *Upon Return From Function*

	High	Low
AX	0AH	
BX		
CX		
DX	Offset of pointer to input buffer	

	High	Low
AX		
BX		
CX		
DX		

SP	
BP	
SI	
DI	

SP	
BP	
SI	
DI	

IP	
flags	

IP	
flags	

CS	
DS	Segment of pointer to input buffer
SS	
ES	

CS	
DS	
SS	
ES	

Buffer | Max. length byte (non-zero), empty string |

Buffer | Contains max. length, actual length, string typed |

Notes: Obsolete function; in DOS 2.x or later use function 3FH instead

Source: IBM DOS 3.3 Technical Reference, page 6-62

See Also: 3.001. INT 21H Functions by DOS Version Summary
                 3.010. Function 01H -- Read Keyboard and Echo
                 3.015. Function 06H -- Direct Console I/O
                 3.016. Function 07H -- Direct Console Input Without Echo
                 3.017. Function 08H -- Read Keyboard Without Echo
                 3.019. Function 0AH -- Buffered Keyboard Input
                 3.021. Function 0CH -- Flush Buffer, Read Keyboard
                 3.065. Function 3FH -- Read Using Handle

3.020. FUNCTION 0BH -- CHECK KEYBOARD STATUS

Prior to Calling Function

	High	Low
AX	0BH	
BX		
CX		
DX		

SP	
BP	
SI	
DI	

IP	
flags	

CS	
DS	
SS	
ES	

Upon Return From Function

	High	Low
AX		Buffer status*
BX		
CX		
DX		

SP	
BP	
SI	
DI	

IP	
flags	

CS	
DS	
SS	
ES	

Notes: •Obsolete function; in DOS 2.x and later use function 44H,6H instead
                 •*00=no character in buffer; FFH=character pending in buffer

Source: IBM DOS 3.3 Technical Reference, page 6-63

See Also: 3.001. INT 21H Functions by DOS Version Summary
                 3.002. INT 21H Keyboard Functions Summary
                 3.077. Function 44H, 06H -- IOCTL Get Input Status

3.021. FUNCTION 0CH -- FLUSH BUFFER, READ KEYBOARD

Prior to Calling Function

	High	Low
AX	0CH	Keyboard function*
BX		
CX		
DX	Offset of pointer to buffer (if AL=0AH)	

SP	
BP	
SI	
DI	

IP	
flags	

CS	
DS	Segment of pointer to buffer (if AL=0AH)
SS	
ES	

Buffer | Max. length, empty string (if AL=0AH) |

Upon Return From Function

	High	Low
AX		Varies**
BX		
CX		
DX		

SP	
BP	
SI	
DI	

IP	
flags	

CS	
DS	
SS	
ES	

Buffer | Max. length, actual length, string (if AL=0AH) |

Notes: •Obsolete function; in DOS 2.x or later use function 3FH instead
                 •*1, 6, 7, 8, or A are allowable keyboard functions and act just as do the INT 21H
                 functions with the same number
                 •**0=buffer was flushed, but no other processing was done. Otherwise, will be the
                 same as for the INT21H function called by value in AL.

Source: IBM DOS 3.3 Technical Reference, page 6-64

See Also: 3.001. INT 21H Functions by DOS Version Summary
                 3.002. INT 21H Keyboard Functions Summary
                 3.010. Function 01H -- Read Keyboard and Echo
                 3.015. Function 06H -- Direct Console I/O
                 3.016. Function 07H -- Direct Console Input Without Echo
                 3.017. Function 08H -- Read Keyboard Without Echo
                 3.019. Function 0AH -- Buffered Keyboard Input
                 3.065. Function 3FH -- Read Using Handle

3.022. FUNCTION 0DH -- RESET DISK

Prior to Calling Function

	High	Low
AX	0DH	
BX		
CX		
DX		

SP	
BP	
SI	
DI	

IP	
flags	

CS	
DS	
SS	
ES	

Upon Return From Function

Function returns no values

Notes:
- Obsolete function; in DOS 2.x and later, effects on default drive and DTA are undocumented
- Function flushes all file buffers to disk
- Close all files first to update directory

Source: IBM DOS 3.3 Technical Reference, page 6-65

See Also:
3.001. INT 21H Functions by DOS Version Summary
3.025. Function 10H -- Close File With FCB
3.064. Function 3EH -- Close File

3.023. FUNCTION 0EH -- SELECT DISK

Prior to Calling Function

	High	Low
AX	0EH	
BX		
CX		
DX		Drive number*

SP	
BP	
SI	
DI	

IP	
flags	

CS	
DS	
SS	
ES	

Upon Return From Function

	High	Low
AX		# Logical drives**
BX		
CX		
DX		

SP	
BP	
SI	
DI	

IP	
flags	

CS	
DS	
SS	
ES	

Notes:
- Note that the value returned in AL does not mean that all of the indicated logical drives are valid drives
- *0=A, 1=B, and so on. Note that this is different than logical drive number
- **Same value as LASTDRIVE= in CONFIG.SYS, or total number of devices, whichever is greater

Source: IBM DOS 3.3 Technical Reference, page 6-66

See Also:
3.001. INT 21H Functions by DOS Version Summary
3.033. Function 19H -- Get Current Disk
3.137. Logical Drive Numbers

3.024. FUNCTION 0FH -- OPEN FILE WITH FCB

Prior to Calling Function   **Upon Return From Function**

	High	Low
AX	0FH	
BX		
CX		
DX	Offset of pointer to unopened FCB	

	High	Low
AX		Status*
BX		
CX		
DX		

SP	
BP	
SI	
DI	

SP	
BP	
SI	
DI	

IP	
flags	

IP	
flags	

CS	
DS	Segment of pointer to unopened FCB
SS	
ES	

CS	
DS	
SS	
ES	

FCB

Drive Number	Logical drive number
File Name	ASCII file name
File Type	ASCII file extension
Current Block	0
Record Size	0
File Size	0
File Date	0
File Time	0
RESERVED	0
Current Record	0
Random Record #	0

FCB

Drive Number	Actual drive number
File Name	ASCII file name
File Type	ASCII file extension
Current Block	0
Record Size	80H (128)
File Size	Actual file size
File Date	Last change date
File Time	Last change time
RESERVED	RESERVED
Current Record	0
Random Record #	0

Version Info: On networks file is opened in compatibility mode only

Notes: •Obsolete function; in DOS 2.x or later use function 3DH instead
•*00=directory entry was found and opened; FFH=directory entry wasn't found

Source: IBM DOS 3.3 Technical Reference, pages 6-67 to 6-68

See Also: 3.001. INT 21H Functions by DOS Version Summary
3.003. INT 21H FCB-oriented Functions Summary
3.063. Function 3DH -- Open File
3.123. Unopened FCB Format
3.124. Opened FCB Format

3.025. FUNCTION 10H -- CLOSE FILE WITH FCB

	Prior to Calling Function			*Upon Return From Function*	
	High	*Low*		*High*	*Low*
AX	10H		AX		Status*
BX			BX		
CX			CX		
DX	Offset of pointer to opened FCB		DX		
SP			SP		
BP			BP		
SI			SI		
DI			DI		
IP			IP		
flags			flags		
CS			CS		
DS	Segment address of pointer to opened FCB		DS		
SS			SS		
ES			ES		

FCB		
	Drive Number	Do not change
	File Name	Do not change
	File Type	Do not change
	Current Block	Do not change
	Record Size	Do not change
	File Size	Do not change
	File Date	Do not change
	File Time	Do not change
	RESERVED	Do not change
	Current Record	Do not change
	Random Record #	Do not change

FCB | FCB no longer valid |

Notes:
•Obsolete function; in DOS 2.x or later use function 3EH instead
•*00=directory entry found and closed; FFH=entry not found

Source: IBM DOS 3.3 Technical Reference, page 6-69

See Also:
3.001. INT 21H Functions by DOS Version Summary
3.003. INT 21H FCB-oriented Functions Summary
3.064. Function 3EH -- Close File
3.124. Opened FCB Format

3.026. FUNCTION 11H -- FIND FIRST ENTRY WITH FCB

Prior to Calling Function				*Upon Return From Function*	

	High	Low			High	Low
AX	11H			AX		Status*
BX				BX		
CX				CX		
DX	Offset of pointer to unopened FCB			DX		

SP			SP		
BP			BP		
SI			SI		
DI			DI		

IP			IP		
flags			flags		

CS			CS		
DS	Segment of pointer to unopened FCB		DS		
SS			SS		
ES			ES		

DTA	Empty		DTA	Contains unopened FCB for file found

FCB	Drive Number	Logical drive number		FCB	Drive Number	Actual drive number
	File Name	ASCII file name**			File Name	ASCII file name**
	File Type	ASCII file type **			File Type	ASCII file type **
	Current Block	0			Current Block	0
	Record Size	0			Record Size	0
	File Size	0			File Size	0
	File Date	0			File Date	0
	File Time	0			File Time	0
	RESERVED	0			RESERVED	0
	Current Record	0			Current Record	0
	Random Record #	0			Random Record #	0

Version Info: **May contain ? wildcard character; may contain * wildcard character in DOS 3.x

Notes: •Obsolete function; with DOS 2.x or later use function 4EH instead
•You may use an extended FCB (unopened) to find files with a certain attribute
•*00=directory entry found; FFH=entry not found

Source: IBM DOS 3.3 Technical Reference, pages 6-70 to 6-71

See Also: 3.001. INT 21H Functions by DOS Version Summary
3.003. INT 21H FCB-oriented Functions Summary
3.027. Function 12H -- Find Next Entry With FCB
3.097. Function 4EH -- Find First File
3.098. Function 4FH -- Find Next File
3.123. Unopened FCB Format
3.125. Extended FCB Format

3.027. FUNCTION 12H -- FIND NEXT ENTRY WITH FCB

Prior to Calling Function   *Upon Return From Function*

	High	Low
AX	12H	
BX		
CX		
DX	Offset of pointer to unopened FCB**	

SP		
BP		
SI		
DI		

IP		
flags		

CS		
DS	Segment of pointer to unopened FCB**	
SS		
ES		

DTA	Empty

FCB		
Drive Number	Logical drive number
File Name	ASCII file name***
File Type	ASCII file type***
Current Block	0
Record Size	0
File Size	0
File Date	0
File Time	0
RESERVED	0
Current Record	0
Random Record #	0

	High	Low
AX		Status*
BX		
CX		
DX		

SP		
BP		
SI		
DI		

IP		
flags		

CS		
DS		
SS		
ES		

DTA	Unopened FCB of file found, if any

FCB		
Drive Number	Actual drive number
File Name	ASCII file name***
File Type	ASCII file type***
Current Block	0
Record Size	0
File Size	0
File Date	0
File Time	0
RESERVED	0
Current Record	0
Random Record #	0

Version Info:
- ***May contain ? wildcard characters; in DOS 3.x may also contain * wildcard characters

Notes:
- You may use extended FCBs (unopened) to search for file with a certain attribute
- Obsolete function; with DOS 2.x or later use function 4FH instead
- *00=directory entry found; FFH=entry not found
- **Must be unchanged FCB used previously with function 11H or function 12H

Source:
IBM DOS 3.3 Technical Reference, pages 6-72 to 6-73

See Also:
3.001. INT 21H Functions by DOS Version Summary
3.003. INT 21H FCB-oriented Functions Summary
3.026. Function 11H -- Find First Entry With FCB
3.097. Function 4EH -- Find First File
3.098. Function 4FH -- Find Next File
3.123. Unopened FCB Format
3.125. Extended FCB Format

3.028. FUNCTION 13H -- DELETE FILE WITH FCB

Prior to Calling Function

	High	Low
AX	13H	
BX		
CX		
DX	Offset of pointer to unopened FCB	

SP	
BP	
SI	
DI	

IP	
flags	

CS	
DS	Segment of pointer to unopened FCB
SS	
ES	

FCB	Drive Number	Logical drive number
	File Name	ASCII file name**
	File Type	ASCII file extension**
	Current Block	0
	Record Size	0
	File Size	0
	File Date	0
	File Time	0
	RESERVED	0
	Current Record	0
	Random Record #	0

Upon Return From Function

	High	Low
AX		Status*
BX		
CX		
DX		

SP	
BP	
SI	
DI	

IP	
flags	

CS	
DS	
SS	
ES	

FCB	No longer valid

Version Info: Requires create access rights on networks

Notes: •Obsolete function; in DOS 2.x or later use function 41H instead
•*00=at least one matching file found and deleted;
FFH=no matching files found
•**May contain ? wildcard characters

Source: IBM DOS 3.3 Technical Reference, page 6-74

See Also: 3.001. INT 21H Functions by DOS Version Summary
3.003. INT 21H FCB-oriented Functions Summary
3.060. Function 3AH -- Remove Subdirectory
3.067. Function 41H -- Delete File
3.123. Unopened FCB Format

3.029. FUNCTION 14H -- SEQUENTIAL READ WITH FCB

Prior to Calling Function

	High	Low
AX	14H	
BX		
CX		
DX	Offset of pointer to opened FCB	

SP	
BP	
SI	
DI	

IP	
flags	

CS	
DS	Segment of pointer to opened FCB
SS	
ES	

DTA	Blank (size=one record of data)

FCB		
	Drive Number	Actual drive number
	File Name	ASCII file name
	File Type	ASCII file extension
	Current Block	Current block**
	Record Size	128**
	File Size	Actual file size
	File Date	Last changed date
	File Time	Last changed time
	RESERVED	RESERVED
	Current Record	Current record**
	Random Record #	Not used

Upon Return From Function

	High	Low
AX		Status*
BX		
CX		
DX		

SP	
BP	
SI	
DI	

IP	
flags	

CS	
DS	
SS	
ES	

DTA	One record of data (size=record size)

FCB		
	Drive Number	Unchanged
	File Name	Unchanged
	File Type	Unchanged
	Current Block	Incremented
	Record Size	Unchanged
	File Size	Unchanged
	File Date	Unchanged
	File Time	Unchanged
	RESERVED	RESERVED
	Current Record	Incremented
	Random Record #	Unchanged

Version Info: Requires read access rights on networks

Notes:
• Obsolete function; with DOS 2.x or later use function 3FH instead
• *0=successful read; 1=end of file; 2=DTA too small; 3=partial record read
(See 3.127. FCB Error Codes)
• **You may change these fields prior to calling function

Source: IBM DOS 3.3 Technical Reference, page 6-75

See Also:
3.001. INT 21H Functions by DOS Version Summary
3.003. INT 21H FCB-oriented Functions Summary
3.037. Function 21H -- Random Read With FCB
3.043. Function 27H -- Random Block Read With FCB
3.065. Function 3FH -- Read Using Handle
3.124. Opened FCB Format

3.030. FUNCTION 15H -- SEQUENTIAL WRITE WITH FCB

Prior to Calling Function				*Upon Return From Function*		
	High	Low			High	Low
AX	15H			AX		Status*
BX				BX		
CX				CX		
DX	Offset of pointer to opened FCB			DX		
SP				SP		
BP				BP		
SI				SI		
DI				DI		
IP				IP		
flags				flags		
CS				CS		
DS	Segment of pointer to opened FCB			DS		
SS				SS		
ES				ES		

DTA	Record of data (size must match record size)		DTA	Unchanged data

FCB				FCB		
	Drive Number	Actual drive number			Drive Number	Unchanged
	File Name	ASCII file name			File Name	Unchanged
	File Type	ASCII file extension			File Type	Unchanged
	Current Block	May be set to new record**			Current Block	Incremented by call
	Record Size	128**			Record Size	Unchanged
	File Size	Actual file size			File Size	Unchanged
	File Date	Date last changed			File Date	Unchanged
	File Time	Time last changed			File Time	Unchanged
	RESERVED	RESERVED			RESERVED	RESERVED
	Current Record	May be set to new record**			Current Record	Incremented by call
	Random Record #	Not used			Random Record #	Unchanged

Version Info: Requires write access rights on networks

Notes: •Obsolete function; in DOS 2.x and later use function 40H instead
•*0=successful write; 1=disk full; 2=DTA too small
(See 3.127. FCB Error Codes)
•**You may change these values prior to calling function

Source: IBM DOS 3.3 Technical Reference, page 6-76

See Also: 3.001. INT 21H Functions by DOS Version Summary
3.003. INT 21H FCB-oriented Functions Summary
3.038. Function 22H -- Random Write With FCB
3.044. Function 28H -- Random Block Write With FCB
3.066. Function 40H -- Write Using Handle
3.124. Opened FCB Format

3.031. FUNCTION 16H -- CREATE FILE WITH FCB

	Prior to Calling Function	
	High	Low
AX	16H	
BX		
CX		
DX	Offset of pointer to unopened FCB	

SP		
BP		
SI		
DI		

IP		
flags		

CS		
DS	Segment of pointer to unopened FCB	
SS		
ES		

	Upon Return From Function	
	High	Low
AX		Status*
BX		
CX		
DX		

SP		
BP		
SI		
DI		

IP		
flags		

CS		
DS		
SS		
ES		

FCB		
Drive Number	Logical drive number
File Name	ASCII file name
File Type	ASCII file extension
Current Block	Must be 0
Record Size	Must be 0
File Size	Must be 0
File Date	Must be 0
File Time	Must be 0
RESERVED	Must be 0
Current Record	Must be 0
Random Record #	Must be 0

FCB		
Drive Number	Actual drive number
File Name	Unchanged
File Type	Unchanged
Current Block	Set to 0
Record Size	Set to 128
File Size	Set to 0
File Date	Set to current date
File Time	Set to current time
RESERVED	Set by call
Current Record	Set to 0
Random Record #	Set to 0

Version Info: Requires create access rights on networks

Notes:
•Obsolete function; in DOS 2.x and later use function 3CH, 5AH, or 5BH
•*00=file created; 0FFH=no more empty entries available
(See 3.127. FCB Error Codes)

Source: IBM DOS 3.3 Technical Reference, pages 6-77 to 6-78

See Also:
3.001. INT 21H Functions by DOS Version Summary
3.003. INT 21H FCB-oriented Functions Summary
3.024. Function 0FH -- Open File With FCB
3.062. Function 3CH -- Create File
3.063. Function 3DH -- Open File
3.106. Function 5AH -- Create Temporary File
3.107. Function 5BH -- Create New File
3.123. Unopened FCB Format
3.124. Opened FCB Format

3.032. FUNCTION 17H -- RENAME FILE WITH FCB

	Prior to Calling Function			*Upon Return From Function*	
	High	Low		High	Low
AX	17H		AX		Status*
BX			BX		
CX			CX		
DX	Offset of pointer to rename FCB		DX		
SP			SP		
BP			BP		
SI			SI		
DI			DI		
IP			IP		
flags			flags		
CS			CS		
DS	Segment of pointer to rename FCB		DS		
SS			SS		
ES			ES		

FCB			FCB		
Drive Number	Logical drive number		Drive Number	Actual drive number	
First File Name	ASCII file name**		First File Name	Unchanged	
First File Type	ASCII file type**		First File Type	Unchanged	
Second File Name	ASCII file name**		Second File Name	Unchanged	
Second File Type	ASCII file type**		Second File Type	Unchanged	

Version Info: Requires create access rights on networks

Notes: •Obsolete function; in DOS 2.x or later use function 56H instead.
                     •*00=at least one file renamed; FFH=no files renamed, or new name
                     already exists
                     •**May contain ? wildcard characters

Source: IBM DOS 3.3 Technical Reference, pages 6-79 to 6-80

See Also: 3.001. INT 21H Functions by DOS Version Summary
                     3.003. INT 21H FCB-oriented Functions Summary
                     3.100. Function 56H -- Rename File
                     3.126. Rename FCB Format

3.033. FUNCTION 19H -- GET CURRENT DISK

	Prior to Calling Function			*Upon Return From Function*	
	High	Low		High	Low
AX	19H		AX		Selected drive*
BX			BX		
CX			CX		
DX			DX		
SP			SP		
BP			BP		
SI			SI		
DI			DI		
IP			IP		
flags			flags		
CS			CS		
DS			DS		
SS			SS		
ES			ES		

Notes: *0=A drive, 1=B drive, and so on

Source: IBM DOS 3.3 Technical Reference, page 6-81

See Also: 3.001. INT 21H Functions by DOS Version Summary

3.034. FUNCTION 1AH -- SET DISK TRANSFER ADDRESS

Prior to Calling Function   *Upon Return From Function*

	High	Low
AX	1AH	
BX		
CX		
DX	Offset of pointer to disk transfer address	

SP	
BP	
SI	
DI	

IP	
flags	

CS	
DS	Segment of pointer to disk transfer address
SS	
ES	

Function returns no values

Notes: •DTA may not cross segment boundaries
•Default DTA is at 0080H in the PSP

Source: IBM DOS 3.3 Technical Reference, page 6-82

See Also: 3.001. INT 21H Functions by DOS Version Summary
3.051. Function 2FH -- Get Disk Transfer Address

3.035. FUNCTION 1BH -- GET DEFAULT DRIVE DATA

Prior to Calling Function   *Upon Return From Function*

	High	Low
AX	1BH	
BX		
CX		
DX		

SP	
BP	
SI	
DI	

IP	
flags	

CS	
DS	
SS	
ES	

	High	Low
AX		Sectors per cluster
BX	Offset of pointer to FAT ID byte	
CX	Number of bytes per sector	
DX	Number of clusters per drive	

SP	
BP	
SI	
DI	

IP	
flags	

CS	
DS	Segment of pointer to FAT ID byte
SS	
ES	

Notes: •The FAT ID byte is no longer adequate to identify the drive type
(beginning DOS 2.x)
•Obsolete function; in DOS 2.x or later use function 36H instead

Source: IBM DOS 3.3 Technical Reference, page 6-83

See Also: 2.37. Disk ID Byte
3.001. INT 21H Functions by DOS Version Summary
3.036. Function 1CH -- Get Drive Data
3.056. Function 36H -- Get Disk Free Space
3.128. Extended Error Codes Returned from Function 59H

3.036. FUNCTION 1CH -- GET DRIVE DATA

Prior to Calling Function   **Upon Return From Function**

	High	Low
AX	1CH	
BX		
CX		
DX		Logical drive number*

	High	Low
AX		Sectors per cluster**
BX	Offset of pointer to FAT ID byte	
CX	Number of bytes per sector	
DX	Number of clusters per drive	

SP	
BP	
SI	
DI	

SP	
BP	
SI	
DI	

IP	
flags	

IP	
flags	

CS	
DS	
SS	
ES	

CS	
DS	Segment of pointer to FAT ID byte
SS	
ES	

Notes:
•Obsolete function; in DOS 2.x or later use function 36H instead
•The FAT ID byte is no longer adequate to identify the drive type
(beginning DOS 2.x)
•*0=default, 1=A, 2=B, etc. (See 3.137. Logical Drive Numbers)
•**A value of FFH returned by call means the drive specified is invalid

Source:
IBM DOS 3.3 Technical Reference, page 6-84

See Also:
2.37. FAT ID Byte
3.001. INT 21H Functions by DOS Version Summary
3.035. Function 1BH -- Get Default Drive Data
3.056. Function 36H   Get Disk Free Space
3.137. Logical Drive Numbers

3.037. FUNCTION 21H -- RANDOM READ WITH FCB

Prior to Calling Function   **Upon Return From Function**

	High	Low
AX	21H	
BX		
CX		
DX	Offset of pointer to opened FCB	

	High	Low
AX		Status*
BX		
CX		
DX		

SP		
BP		
SI		
DI		

SP		
BP		
SI		
DI		

IP	
flags	

IP	
flags	

CS	
DS	Segment of pointer to opened FCB
SS	
ES	

CS	
DS	
SS	
ES	

DTA	Blank memory to hold one record of data

DTA	One record of data

FCB		
Drive Number	Actual drive number	
File Name	ASCII file name	
File Type	ASCII file extension	
Current Block	Will be set by call	
Record Size	128**	
File Size	As set by open file	
File Date	As set by open file	
File Time	As set by open file	
RESERVED	As set by open file	
Current Record	Will be set by call	
Random Record #	Record to read	

FCB		
Drive Number	Unchanged	
File Name	Unchanged	
File Type	Unchanged	
Current Block	Set by call	
Record Size	Unchanged	
File Size	Unchanged	
File Date	Unchanged	
File Time	Unchanged	
RESERVED	Unchanged	
Current Record	Set by call	
Random Record #	Incremented by call	

Version Info: Requires read access rights on networks

Notes:
- Random record # is usually set by using function 24H
- Obsolete function; in DOS 2.x or later use function 3FH instead
- *0=successful read; 1=end of file; 2=DTA too small; 3=partial record read (See 3.127. FCB Error Codes)
- **You may change these fields prior to calling function

Source: IBM DOS 3.3 Technical Reference, page 6-85

See Also:
3.001. INT 21H Functions by DOS Version Summary
3.003. INT 21H FCB-oriented Functions Summary
3.029. Function 14H -- Sequential Read With FCB
3.040. Function 24H -- Set Relative Record With FCB
3.043. Function 27H -- Random Block Read With FCB
3.065. Function 3FH -- Read Using Handle
3.124. Opened FCB Format

3.038. FUNCTION 22H -- RANDOM WRITE WITH FCB

	Prior to Calling Function			*Upon Return From Function*	
	High	*Low*		*High*	*Low*
AX	22H		AX		Status*
BX			BX		
CX			CX		
DX	Offset of pointer to opened FCB		DX		
SP			SP		
BP			BP		
SI			SI		
DI			DI		
IP			IP		
flags			flags		
CS			CS		
DS	Segment of pointer to opened FCB		DS		
SS			SS		
ES			ES		

DTA	One record of data to write to disk		DTA	Unchanged data

FCB			FCB		
	Drive Number	Actual drive number		Drive Number	Unchanged
	File Name	ASCII file name		File Name	Unchanged
	File Type	ASCII file extension		File Type	Unchanged
	Current Block	Will be set by call		Current Block	Set by call
	Record Size	128**		Record Size	Unchanged
	File Size	As set by open file		File Size	Updated if size changes
	File Date	As set by open file		File Date	Updated to current date
	File Time	As set by open file		File Time	Updated to current time
	RESERVED	As set by open file		RESERVED	RESERVED
	Current Record	Will be set by call		Current Record	Set by call
	Random Record #	Record to write**		Random Record #	Incremented by call

Version Info: Requires write access rights on networks

Notes: •Random record # is usually set with function 24H
•Obsolete function; in DOS 2.x or later use function 40H instead
•*0=successful write; 1=disk full; 2=DTA too small
(See 3.127. FCB Error Codes)
•**You may change these fields prior to calling function

Source: IBM DOS 3.3 Technical Reference, page 6-86

See Also: 3.001. INT 21H Functions by DOS Version Summary
3.003. INT 21H FCB-oriented Functions Summary
3.030. Function 15H -- Sequential Write With FCB
3.040. Function 24H -- Set Relative Record With FCB
3.044. Function 28H -- Random Block Write With FCB
3.066. Function 40H -- Write Using Handle
3.124. Opened FCB Format

3.039. FUNCTION 23H -- GET FILE SIZE WITH FCB

Prior to Calling Function   *Upon Return From Function*

	High	Low
AX	23H	
BX		
CX		
DX	Offset of pointer to unopened FCB	

SP	
BP	
SI	
DI	

IP	
flags	

CS	
DS	Segment of pointer to unopened FCB
SS	
ES	

	High	Low
AX		Status*
BX		
CX		
DX		

SP	
BP	
SI	
DI	

IP	
flags	

CS	
DS	
SS	
ES	

FCB		
	Drive Number	Actual drive number
	File Name	ASCII file name
	File Type	ASCII file extension
	Current Block	0
	Record Size	Set to 1 or record size***
	File Size	0
	File Date	0
	File Time	0
	RESERVED	0
	Current Record	0
	Random Record #	0

FCB		
	Drive Number	Unchanged
	File Name	Unchanged
	File Type	Unchanged
	Current Block	Unchanged
	Record Size	Unchanged
	File Size	Unchanged
	File Date	Unchanged
	File Time	Unchanged
	RESERVED	RESERVED
	Current Record	Unchanged
	Random Record #	Size of file in records**

Notes:
- Obsolete function; in DOS 2.x or later use function 42H instead
- *0=file found; 0FFH=file not found
- **Rounded up to next integer if partial record found
- ***Set to 1 to find file size in bytes

Source: IBM DOS 3.3 Technical Reference, page 6-87

See Also: 3.001. INT 21H Functions by DOS Version Summary
                 3.003. INT 21H FCB-oriented Functions Summary
                 3.068. Function 42H -- Move File Pointer
                 3.123. Unopened FCB Format

3.040. FUNCTION 24H -- SET RELATIVE RECORD WITH FCB

Prior to Calling Function

	High	Low
AX	24H	
BX		
CX		
DX	Offset of pointer to opened FCB	

SP	
BP	
SI	
DI	

IP	
flags	

CS	
DS	Segment of pointer to opened FCB
SS	
ES	

FCB		
	Drive Number	Actual drive number
	File Name	ASCII file name
	File Type	ASCII file extension
	Current Block	Set to block number*
	Record Size	Set to record size*
	File Size	Unchanged from open
	File Date	Unchanged from open
	File Time	Unchanged from open
	RESERVED	Unchanged from open
	Current Record	Set to record number*
	Random Record #	Set to 0

Upon Return From Function

	High	Low
AX		Always 00H
BX		
CX		
DX		

SP	
BP	
SI	
DI	

IP	
flags	

CS	
DS	
SS	
ES	

FCB		
	Drive Number	Unchanged
	File Name	Unchanged
	File Type	Unchanged
	Current Block	Unchanged
	Record Size	Unchanged
	File Size	Unchanged
	File Date	Unchanged
	File Time	Unchanged
	RESERVED	Unchanged
	Current Record	Unchanged
	Random Record #	Set to relative record

Notes:
- Obsolete function; in DOS 2.x or later use function 42H instead
- *You must set these fields prior to calling function

Source: IBM DOS 3.3 Technical Reference, page 6-88

See Also:
3.001. INT 21H Functions by DOS Version Summary
3.003. INT 21H FCB-oriented Functions Summary
3.068. Function 42H -- Move File Pointer
3.124. Opened FCB Format

3.041. FUNCTION 25H -- SET INTERRUPT VECTOR

Prior to Calling Function   *Upon Return From Function*

	High	Low
AX	25H	Interrupt number
BX		
CX		
DX	Offset of pointer to interrupt handler routine	

SP	
BP	
SI	
DI	

IP	
flags	

CS	
DS	Segment of pointer to interrupt handler routine
SS	
ES	

Function returns no values

Notes: The four byte address of DS:DX is placed at appropriate place in the interrupt vector table

Source: IBM DOS 3.3 Technical Reference, page 6-89

See Also: 3.001. INT 21H Functions by DOS Version Summary
3.055. Function 35H -- Get Interrupt Vector
7.04. PC Interrupt Usage

3.042. FUNCTION 26H -- CREATE NEW PROGRAM SEGMENT

Prior to Calling Function   *Upon Return From Function*

	High	Low
AX	26H	
BX		
CX		
DX	Segment address of new program segment	

SP	
BP	
SI	
DI	

IP	
flags	

CS	
DS	
SS	
ES	

Function returns no values

Notes: Obsolete function; in DOS 2.x or later use function 4BH instead

Source: IBM DOS 3.3 Technical Reference, page 6-90

See Also: 3.001. INT 21H Functions by DOS Version Summary
3.093. Function 4BH, 00H -- Load and Execute Program

3.043. FUNCTION 27H -- RANDOM BLOCK READ WITH FCB

Prior to Calling Function   **Upon Return From Function**

	High	Low
AX	27H	
BX		
CX	Number of blocks to read	
DX	Offset of pointer to opened FCB	

	High	Low
AX		Status*
BX		
CX	Number of blocks actually read	
DX		

SP	
BP	
SI	
DI	

SP	
BP	
SI	
DI	

IP	
flags	

IP	
flags	

CS	
DS	Segment of pointer to opened FCB
SS	
ES	

CS	
DS	
SS	
ES	

DTA	Blank memory to hold records of data

DTA	Data read

FCB		
	Drive Number	Actual drive number
	File Name	ASCII file name
	File Type	ASCII file extension
	Current Block	Will be set by call
	Record Size	128**
	File Size	As set by open file
	File Date	As set by open file
	File Time	As set by open file
	RESERVED	RESERVED
	Current Record	Will be set by call
	Random Record #	Starting record**

FCB		
	Drive Number	Unchanged
	File Name	Unchanged
	File Type	Unchanged
	Current Block	Set by call
	Record Size	Unchanged
	File Size	Unchanged
	File Date	Unchanged
	File Time	Unchanged
	RESERVED	RESERVED
	Current Record	Set by call
	Random Record #	Set to end block+1 by call

Version Info: Requires read access rights on networks

Notes:
- Obsolete function; in DOS 2.x or later use function 3FH instead
- Random record # is usually set by function 24H
- *0=successful read; 1=end of file; 2=DTA too small; 3=partial record read
(See 3.127. FCB Error Codes)
- **You may change these fields prior to calling function

Source: IBM DOS 3.3 Technical Reference, pages 6-91 to 6-92

See Also:
3.001. INT 21H Functions by DOS Version Summary
3.003. INT 21H FCB-oriented Functions Summary
3.029. Function 14H -- Sequential Read With FCB
3.037. Function 21H -- Random Read With FCB
3.040. Function 24H -- Set Relative Record With FCB
3.044. Function 28H -- Random Block Write With FCB
3.065. Function 3FH -- Read Using Handle
3.124. Opened FCB Format

3.044. FUNCTION 28H -- RANDOM BLOCK WRITE WITH FCB

Prior to Calling Function

	High	Low
AX	28H	
BX		
CX	Number of blocks to write	
DX	Offset of pointer to opened FCB	

SP	
BP	
SI	
DI	

| IP | |
| flags | |

CS	
DS	Segment of pointer to opened FCB
SS	
ES	

| DTA | Data to be written to disk |

FCB	Drive Number	Actual drive number
	File Name	ASCII file name
	File Type	ASCII file extension
	Current Block	Will be set by call
	Record Size	128**
	File Size	As set by open file
	File Date	As set by open file
	File Time	As set by open file
	RESERVED	RESERVED
	Current Record	Will be set by call
	Random Record #	Starting record #**

Upon Return From Function

	High	Low
AX		Status*
BX		
CX	Number of blocks actually written	
DX		

SP	
BP	
SI	
DI	

| IP | |
| flags | |

CS	
DS	
SS	
ES	

| DTA | Unchanged |

FCB	Drive Number	Unchanged
	File Name	Unchanged
	File Type	Unchanged
	Current Block	Set by call
	Record Size	Unchanged
	File Size	Set if file size changes
	File Date	Set to current date
	File Time	Set to current time
	RESERVED	RESERVED
	Current Record	Set by call
	Random Record #	Set to end block+1 by call

Version Info: Requires write access rights on networks

Notes:
- Obsolete function; in DOS 2.x or later use function 40H instead
- If CX=0 prior to call, file size is truncated to value in random record # field
- Random record # is usually set with function 24H
- *0=successful write; 1=disk full; 2=DTA too small
(See 3.127. FCB Error Codes)
- **You may change these fields prior to calling function

Source: IBM DOS 3.3 Technical Reference, pages 6-93 to 6-94

See Also:
3.001. INT 21H Functions by DOS Version Summary
3.003. INT 21H FCB-oriented Functions Summary
3.030. Function 15H -- Sequential Write With FCB
3.038. Function 22H -- Random Write With FCB
3.040. Function 24H -- Set Relative Record With FCB
3.043. Function 27H -- Random Block Read With FCB
3.066. Function 40H -- Write Using Handle
3.124. Opened FCB Format

3.045. FUNCTION 29H -- PARSE FILE NAME

Prior to Calling Function

	High	Low
AX	29H	Parse control byte
BX		
CX		
DX		

SP	
BP	
SI	Offset of pointer to string to parse
DI	Offset of pointer to buffer to contain unopened FCB

IP	
flags	

CS	
DS	Segment of pointer to string to parse
SS	
ES	Segment of pointer to buffer for unopened FCB

Buffer	Empty

Upon Return From Function

	High	Low
AX		Status*
BX		
CX		
DX		

SP	
BP	
SI	Offset of pointer 1 byte past parsed string
DI	Offset of pointer to unopened FCB

IP	
flags	

CS	
DS	Segment of pointer 1 byte past parsed string
SS	
ES	Segment of pointer to unopened FCB

Buffer (FCB)	
Drive Number	Logical drive number
File Name	ASCII file name
File Type	ASCII file type
Current Block	0
Record Size	0
File Size	0
File Date	0
File Time	0
RESERVED	0
Current Record	0
Random Record #	0

Notes: *00=FCB created, no wildcard characters; 01=FCB created, wildcard characters used in file name; FFH=drive letter invalid

Source: IBM DOS 3.3 Technical Reference, pages 6-95 to 6-97

See Also: 2.51. Filename Separator Characters
3.001. INT 21H Functions by DOS Version Summary
3.123. Unopened FCB Format
3.142. Parse Control Byte

3.046. FUNCTION 2AH -- GET SYSTEM DATE

Prior to Calling Function   *Upon Return From Function*

	High	Low			High	Low
AX	2AH			AX		Day of week*
BX				BX		
CX				CX	Year	
DX				DX	Month	Day

SP	
BP	
SI	
DI	

SP	
BP	
SI	
DI	

IP	
flags	

IP	
flags	

CS	
DS	
SS	
ES	

CS	
DS	
SS	
ES	

Notes: *0=Sunday, 1=Monday, etc. (See 2.35. Date/Time Formats)

Source: IBM DOS 3.3 Technical Reference, page 6-98

See Also: 2.35. Date/Time Formats
3.001. INT 21H Functions by DOS Version Summary
3.047. Function 2BH -- Set System Date
3.048. Function 2CH -- Get System Time

3.047. FUNCTION 2BH -- SET SYSTEM DATE

Prior to Calling Function

	High	Low
AX	2BH	
BX		
CX	Year	
DX	Month	Day

SP	
BP	
SI	
DI	

| IP | |
| flags | |

CS	
DS	
SS	
ES	

Upon Return From Function

	High	Low
AX		Status*
BX		
CX		
DX		

SP	
BP	
SI	
DI	

| IP | |
| flags | |

CS	
DS	
SS	
ES	

Notes: *00=valid date supplied; FFH=invalid date supplied

Source: IBM DOS 3.3 Technical Reference, page 6-99

See Also: 2.35. Date/Time Formats
3.001. INT 21H Functions by DOS Version Summary
3.046. Function 2AH -- Get System Date
3.049. Function 2DH -- Set System Time

3.048. FUNCTION 2CH -- GET SYSTEM TIME

Prior to Calling Function

	High	Low
AX	2CH	
BX		
CX		
DX		

SP	
BP	
SI	
DI	

| IP | |
| flags | |

CS	
DS	
SS	
ES	

Upon Return From Function

	High	Low
AX		
BX		
CX	Hour	Minutes
DX	Seconds	Hundredths

SP	
BP	
SI	
DI	

| IP | |
| flags | |

CS	
DS	
SS	
ES	

Notes: Hour is in 24-hour clock format

Source: IBM DOS 3.3 Technical Reference, page 6-100

See Also: 2.35. Date/Time Formats
3.001. INT 21H Functions by DOS Version Summary
3.046. Function 2AH -- Get System Date
3.049. Function 2DH -- Set System Time

3.049. FUNCTION 2DH -- SET SYSTEM TIME

Prior to Calling Function

	High	Low
AX	2DH	
BX		
CX	Hour	Minutes
DX	Seconds	Hundredths

SP	
BP	
SI	
DI	

IP	
flags	

CS	
DS	
SS	
ES	

Upon Return From Function

	High	Low
AX		Status*
BX		
CX		
DX		

SP	
BP	
SI	
DI	

IP	
flags	

CS	
DS	
SS	
ES	

Notes: *00=valid time supplied; FFH=invalid time supplied

Source: IBM DOS 3.3 Technical Reference, page 6-101

See Also:
2.35. Date/Time Formats
3.001. INT 21H Functions by DOS Version Summary
3.047. Function 2BH -- Set System Date
3.048. Function 2CH -- Get System Time

3.050. FUNCTION 2EH -- SET/RESET VERIFY FLAG

Prior to Calling Function

	High	Low
AX	2EH	Verify flag*
BX		
CX		
DX		00H**

SP	
BP	
SI	
DI	

IP	
flags	

CS	
DS	
SS	
ES	

Upon Return From Function

Function returns no values

Version Info: Verification is not supported for network disk writes in DOS 3.x

Notes:
•*00=do not verify after writes; 01=verify after writes
•**DOS 1.x and 2.x only

Source: IBM DOS 3.3 Technical Reference, page 6-102

See Also:
3.001. INT 21H Functions by DOS Version Summary
3.099. Function 54H -- Get Verify State

3.051. FUNCTION 2FH -- GET DISK TRANSFER ADDRESS

Prior to Calling Function   *Upon Return From Function*

	High	Low			High	Low
AX	2FH			AX		
BX				BX	Offset of pointer to disk transfer address	
CX				CX		
DX				DX		

SP				SP		
BP				BP		
SI				SI		
DI				DI		

IP			IP		
flags			flags		

CS			CS		
DS			DS		
SS			SS		
ES			ES	Segment of pointer to disk transfer address

Notes: Default DTA is at 0080H in the PSP.

Source: IBM DOS 3.3 Technical Reference, page 6-103

See Also: 3.001. INT 21H Functions by DOS Version Summary
3.034. Function 1AH -- Set Disk Transfer Address

3.052. FUNCTION 30H -- GET DOS VERSION

Prior to Calling Function   *Upon Return From Function*

	High	Low			High	Low
AX	30H			AX	Minor version #	Major version #
BX				BX	OEM number	High order serial #
CX				CX	Low order word of 24-bit serial number	
DX				DX		

SP				SP		
BP				BP		
SI				SI		
DI				DI		

IP			IP		
flags			flags		

CS			CS		
DS			DS		
SS			SS		
ES			ES		

Version Info: Applies only to versions of DOS 2.0 and later

Notes: •OEM and serial numbers may not be present (returns 0000H)
•If AL=0 on return, then version is assumed to be prior to 2.0

Source: IBM DOS 3.3 Technical Reference, page 6-104

See Also: 3.001. INT 21H Functions by DOS Version Summary

3.053. FUNCTION 31H -- KEEP PROCESS

Prior to Calling Function   *Upon Return From Function*

	High	Low
AX	31H	Return code*
BX		
CX		
DX	# of paragraphs of memory to keep resident

SP	
BP	
SI	
DI	

IP	
flags	

CS	
DS	
SS	
ES	

Function returns no values

Version Info: Applies to all versions of DOS beginning with 2.0

Notes: •Open files are not closed by this function
•*You establish return codes. By convention 00=no error.

Source: IBM DOS 3.3 Technical Reference, pages 6-105 to 6-106

See Also: 3.001. INT 21H Functions by DOS Version Summary
3.093. Function 4BH, 00H -- Load and Execute Program
3.095. Function 4CH -- End Process
3.096. Function 4DH -- Get Return Code

3.054. FUNCTION 33H -- CONTROL-C CHECK

Prior to Calling Function   *Upon Return From Function*

	High	Low
AX	33H	0=get, 1=set state, 2=exchange state with DL
BX		
CX		
DX		0=OFF, 1=ON (if AL=1,2)

SP	
BP	
SI	
DI	

IP	
flags	

CS	
DS	
SS	
ES	

	High	Low
AX		Status*
BX		
CX		
DX		0=OFF,1=ON (if AL=0,2)

SP	
BP	
SI	
DI	

IP	
flags	

CS	
DS	
SS	
ES	

Version Info: Applies to all versions of DOS beginning with 2.0

Notes: *FFH=error (AL did not contain 0, 1, or 2 on call)

Source: IBM DOS 3.3 Technical Reference, page 6-107

See Also: 3.001. INT 21H Functions by DOS Version Summary

3.055. FUNCTION 35H -- GET INTERRUPT VECTOR

Prior to Calling Function

	High	Low
AX	35H	Interrupt number
BX		
CX		
DX		

SP	
BP	
SI	
DI	

IP	
flags	

CS	
DS	
SS	
ES	

Upon Return From Function

	High	Low
AX		
BX	Offset of pointer to interrupt routine*	
CX		
DX		

SP	
BP	
SI	
DI	

IP	
flags	

CS	
DS	
SS	
ES	Segment of pointer to interrupt routine*

Version Info: Applies to all versions of DOS beginning with 2.0

Notes: *If ES:BX = 0 then no handler is associated with this interrupt

Source: IBM DOS 3.3 Technical Reference, page 6-108

See Also: 3.001. INT 21H Functions by DOS Version Summary
3.041. Function 25H -- Set Interrupt Vector
7.04. PC Interrupt Usage

3.056. FUNCTION 36H -- GET DISK FREE SPACE

Prior to Calling Function

	High	Low
AX	36H	
BX		
CX		
DX		Logical drive number**

SP	
BP	
SI	
DI	

IP	
flags	

CS	
DS	
SS	
ES	

Upon Return From Function

	High	Low
AX	Sectors per cluster*	
BX	Number of available clusters	
CX	Number of bytes per sector	
DX	Number of clusters per drive	

SP	
BP	
SI	
DI	

IP	
flags	

CS	
DS	
SS	
ES	

Version Info: Applies to all versions of DOS beginning with 2.0

Notes: *Or FFFFH if invalid drive was specified in DL
**0=default, 1=A, and so on

Source: IBM DOS 3.3 Technical Reference, page 6-109

See Also: 3.001. INT 21H Functions by DOS Version Summary
3.035. Function 1BH -- Get Default Drive Data
3.036. Function 1CH -- Get Drive Data
3.137. Logical Drive Numbers

3.057. FUNCTION 38H, 00H -- GET COUNTRY DATA

Prior to Calling Function   ### *Upon Return From Function*

	High	Low
AX	38H	0
BX		
CX		
DX	Offset of pointer to 32-byte buffer	

SP	
BP	
SI	
DI	

| IP | |
| flags | |

CS	
DS	Segment of pointer to 32-byte buffer
SS	
ES	

| Buffer | Empty |

	High	Low
AX	Error code (if carry flag set)	
BX	Country code (if carry flag clear)	
CX		
DX	Offset to country info buffer	

SP	
BP	
SI	
DI	

| IP | |
| flags | Carry* |

CS	
DS	Segment of country info buffer
SS	
ES	

| Buffer | Country data |

Version Info: Applies to all versions of DOS beginning with 2.0

Notes: *Carry flag set if error occurs

Source: IBM DOS 3.3 Technical Reference, pages 6-110 to 6-118

See Also: 3.001. INT 21H Functions by DOS Version Summary
                      3.058. Function 38H, xxH -- Set Country Data
                      3.105. Function 59H -- Get Extended Error
                      3.128. Extended Error Codes Returned from Function 59H
                      3.143. Country Code Buffer Layout
                      3.144. Country Codes

3.058. FUNCTION 38H, xxH -- SET COUNTRY DATA

Prior to Calling Function   ### *Upon Return From Function*

	High	Low
AX	38H	Country code or FFH
BX	Country code if AL=FFH	
CX		
DX	FFFFH	

SP	
BP	
SI	
DI	

| IP | |
| flags | |

CS	
DS	FFFFH
SS	
ES	

	High	Low
AX	Error code (if carry flag set)	
BX		
CX		
DX		

SP	
BP	
SI	
DI	

| IP | |
| flags | Carry* |

CS	
DS	
SS	
ES	

Version Info: Applies to all versions of DOS beginning with 3.0

Notes: *Carry flag set if error occurs

Source: IBM DOS 3.3 Technical Reference, pages 6-110 to 6-118

See Also: 3.001. INT 21H Functions by DOS Version Summary
                      3.057. Function 38H, 00H -- Get Country Data
                      3.105. Function 59H -- Get Extended Error
                      3.128. Extended Error Codes Returned from Function 59H
                      3.144. Country Codes

3.059. FUNCTION 39H -- CREATE SUBDIRECTORY

Prior to Calling Function

	High	Low
AX	39H	
BX		
CX		
DX	Offset of pointer to pathname string	

SP	
BP	
SI	
DI	

IP	
flags	

CS	
DS	Segment of pointer to pathname string
SS	
ES	

Upon Return From Function

	High	Low
AX	Error code (if carry flag set)	
BX		
CX		
DX		

SP	
BP	
SI	
DI	

IP	
flags	Carry*

CS	
DS	
SS	
ES	

Version Info: •Applies to all versions of DOS beginning with 2.0
                      •Requires create access rights on networks

Notes: •Pathname must be in ASCIIZ form
                     •*Carry flag set if error occurs

Source: IBM DOS 3.3 Technical Reference, page 6-119

See Also: 3.001. INT 21H Functions by DOS Version Summary
                     3.060. Function 3AH -- Remove Subdirectory
                     3.061. Function 3BH -- Change Current Directory
                     3.089. Function 47H -- Get Current Directory
                     3.105. Function 59H -- Get Extended Error
                     3.128. Extended Error Codes Returned from Function 59H

3.060. FUNCTION 3AH -- REMOVE SUBDIRECTORY

Prior to Calling Function *Upon Return From Function*

	High	Low
AX	3AH	
BX		
CX		
DX	Offset of pointer to pathname string	

SP	
BP	
SI	
DI	

IP	
flags	

CS	
DS	Segment of pointer to pathname string
SS	
ES	

	High	Low
AX	Error code (if carry flag set)	
BX		
CX		
DX		

SP	
BP	
SI	
DI	

IP	
flags	Carry*

CS	
DS	
SS	
ES	

Version Info: •Applies to all versions of DOS beginning with 2.0
•Requires create access rights on networks

Notes: •Pathname must be in ASCIIZ form
•*Carry flag set if error occurs

Source: IBM DOS 3.3 Technical Reference, page 6-120

See Also: 3.001. INT 21H Functions by DOS Version Summary
3.059. Function 39H -- Create Subdirectory
3.061. Function 3BH -- Change Current Directory
3.089. Function 47H -- Get Current Directory
3.105. Function 59H -- Get Extended Error
3.128. Extended Error Codes Returned from Function 59H

3.061. FUNCTION 3BH -- CHANGE CURRENT DIRECTORY

Prior to Calling Function   *Upon Return From Function*

	High	Low
AX	3BH	
BX		
CX		
DX	Offset of pointer to pathname string	

SP	
BP	
SI	
DI	

| IP | |
| flags | |

CS	
DS	Segment of pointer to pathname string
SS	
ES	

	High	Low
AX	Error code (if carry flag set)	
BX		
CX		
DX		

SP	
BP	
SI	
DI	

| IP | |
| flags | Carry* |

CS	
DS	
SS	
ES	

Version Info: Applies to all versions of DOS beginning with 2.0

Notes: •Pathname must be in ASCIIZ form
                      •Pathname string is limited to 64 characters and may not contain a network path
                      •*Carry flag set if error occurs

Source: IBM DOS 3.3 Technical Reference, page 6-121

See Also: 3.001. INT 21H Functions by DOS Version Summary
                      3.089. Function 47H -- Get Current Directory
                      3.105. Function 59H -- Get Extended Error
                      3.128. Extended Error Codes Returned from Function 59H

3.062. FUNCTION 3CH -- CREATE FILE

Prior to Calling Function   *Upon Return From Function*

	High	Low
AX	3CH	
BX		
CX	0	File attribute byte
DX	Offset of pointer to pathname string	
SP		
BP		
SI		
DI		
IP		
flags		
CS		
DS	Segment of pointer to pathname string	
SS		
ES		

	High	Low
AX	Handle or error code (if carry set)	
BX		
CX		
DX		
SP		
BP		
SI		
DI		
IP		
flags		Carry*
CS		
DS		
SS		
ES		

Version Info:	•Applies to all versions of DOS beginning with 2.0
	•Requires create access rights on networks
Notes:	•Pathname must be in ASCIIZ form
	•File is truncated if it already exists
	•Volume and subdirectory bits are ignored in attribute byte
	•*Carry flag set if error occurs
Source:	IBM DOS 3.3 Technical Reference, pages 6-122 to 6-123
See Also:	2.34. File Attribute Byte
	3.001. INT 21H Functions by DOS Version Summary
	3.031. Function 16H -- Create File With FCB
	3.069. Function 43H, 00H -- Get File Attributes
	3.070. Function 43H, 01H -- Set File Attributes
	3.105. Function 59H -- Get Extended Error
	3.106. Function 5AH -- Create Temporary File
	3.107. Function 5BH -- Create New File
	3.128. Extended Error Codes Returned from Function 59H

3.063. FUNCTION 3DH -- OPEN FILE

Prior to Calling Function   *Upon Return From Function*

	High	Low
AX	3DH	Access code**
BX		
CX		
DX	Offset of pointer to pathname string	

SP	
BP	
SI	
DI	

IP	
flags	

CS	
DS	Segment of pointer to pathname string
SS	
ES	

	High	Low
AX	Handle or error code (if carry set)	
BX		
CX		
DX		

SP	
BP	
SI	
DI	

IP	
flags	Carry*

CS	
DS	
SS	
ES	

Version Info: Applies to all versions of DOS beginning with 2.0

Notes: •Pathname must be in ASCIIZ form
•*Carry flag set if error occurs
•**AL=0 read only, AL=1 write only, AL=2 read/write

Source: IBM DOS 3.3 Technical Reference, pages 6-124 to 6-125

See Also: 3.001. INT 21H Functions by DOS Version Summary
3.024. Function 0FH -- Open File With FCB
3.105. Function 59H -- Get Extended Error
3.128. Extended Error Codes Returned from Function 59H
3.129. Handle Access Byte

3.064. FUNCTION 3EH -- CLOSE FILE

Prior to Calling Function   *Upon Return From Function*

	High	Low
AX	3EH	
BX	Handle	
CX		
DX		

SP	
BP	
SI	
DI	

IP	
flags	

CS	
DS	
SS	
ES	

	High	Low
AX	Error code (if carry flag set)	
BX		
CX		
DX		

SP	
BP	
SI	
DI	

IP	
flags	Carry*

CS	
DS	
SS	
ES	

Version Info: Applies to all versions of DOS beginning with 2.0

Notes: *Carry flag set if error occurs

Source: IBM DOS 3.3 Technical Reference, page 6-136

See Also: 3.001. INT 21H Functions by DOS Version Summary
3.025. Function 10H -- Close File With FCB
3.105. Function 59H -- Get Extended Error
3.128. Extended Error Codes Returned from Function 59H
3.130. Predefined Handles

3.065. FUNCTION 3FH -- READ USING HANDLE

	Prior to Calling Function	
	High	Low
AX	3FH	
BX	Handle	
CX	Number of bytes to read	
DX	Offset of pointer to empty buffer for data	

SP	
BP	
SI	
DI	

IP	
flags	

CS	
DS	Segment of pointer to empty buffer for data
SS	
ES	

Buffer | Empty

	Upon Return From Function	
	High	Low
AX	Bytes read** or error code (if carry set)	
BX		
CX		
DX		

SP	
BP	
SI	
DI	

IP	
flags	Carry*

CS	
DS	
SS	
ES	

Buffer | Data read

Version Info:	•Applies to all versions of DOS beginning with 2.0 •Requires read access rights on networks
Notes:	•*Carry flag set if error occurs •**A value of 0 indicates attempt to read at EOF
Source:	IBM DOS 3.3 Technical Reference, pages 6-137 to 6-138
See Also:	3.001. INT 21H Functions by DOS Version Summary 3.029. Function 14H -- Sequential Read With FCB 3.037. Function 21H -- Random Read With FCB 3.043. Function 27H -- Random Block Read With FCB 3.105. Function 59H -- Get Extended Error 3.128. Extended Error Codes Returned from Function 59H

3.066. FUNCTION 40H -- WRITE USING HANDLE

Prior to Calling Function   *Upon Return From Function*

	High	Low			High	Low
AX	40H			AX	Bytes written** or error code (if carry set)	
BX	Handle			BX		
CX	Number of bytes to write***			CX		
DX	Offset of pointer to buffer containing data			DX		

SP				SP		
BP				BP		
SI				SI		
DI				DI		

IP				IP		
flags				flags		Carry*

CS				CS		
DS	Segment of pointer to buffer containing data			DS		
SS				SS		
ES				ES		

Buffer | Data to write   Buffer | Unchanged data

Version Info:	•Applies to all versions of DOS beginning with 2.0
	•Requires write access rights on networks
Notes:	•*Carry flag set if error occurs
	•**A value of 0 indicates disk is full
	•***If 0, file is truncated at the pointer position
Source:	IBM DOS 3.3 Technical Reference, pages 6-139 to 6-140
See Also:	3.001. INT 21H Functions by DOS Version Summary
	3.030. Function 15H -- Sequential Write With FCB
	3.038. Function 22H -- Random Write With FCB
	3.044. Function 28H -- Random Block Write With FCB
	3.105. Function 59H -- Get Extended Error
	3.128. Extended Error Codes Returned from Function 59H

3.067. FUNCTION 41H -- DELETE FILE

Prior to Calling Function		*Upon Return From Function*	

Prior to Calling Function

	High	Low
AX	41H	
BX		
CX		
DX	Offset of pointer to pathname string	

SP		
BP		
SI		
DI		

IP		
flags		

CS		
DS	Segment of pointer to pathname string	
SS		
ES		

Upon Return From Function

	High	Low
AX	Error code (if carry set)	
BX		
CX		
DX		

SP		
BP		
SI		
DI		

IP		
flags		Carry*

CS		
DS		
SS		
ES		

Version Info: •Applies to all versions of DOS beginning with 2.0
•Requires create access rights on networks

Notes: •Pathname must be in ASCIIZ format
•*Carry flag set if error occurs

Source: IBM DOS 3.3 Technical Reference, pages 6-141 to 6-142

See Also: 1.17. Common String Formats
3.001. INT 21H Functions by DOS Version Summary
3.028. Function 13H -- Delete File with FCB
3.060. Function 3AH -- Remove Subdirectory
3.105. Function 59H -- Get Extended Error
3.128. Extended Error Codes Returned from Function 59H

3.068. FUNCTION 42H -- MOVE FILE POINTER

Prior to Calling Function

	High	Low
AX	42H	Movement method**
BX	Handle	
CX	High order of offset to move pointer (in bytes)	
DX	Low order of offset to move pointer	

SP	
BP	
SI	
DI	

IP	
flags	

CS	
DS	
SS	
ES	

Upon Return From Function

	High	Low
AX	LO position, or error code (if carry set)	
BX		
CX		
DX	High order position of pointer in file	

SP	
BP	
SI	
DI	

IP	
flags	Carry*

CS	
DS	
SS	
ES	

Version Info: Applies to all versions of DOS beginning with 2.0

Notes: •You can find the size of a file by setting AL=2 and CX:DX=0
•*Carry flag set if error occurs
•**0=move pointer to record CX:DX; 1=move pointer to current plus CX:DX;
2=move pointer to EOF plus CX:DX

Source: IBM DOS 3.3 Technical Reference, pages 6-143 to 6-144

See Also: 3.001. INT 21H Functions by DOS Version Summary
3.040. Function 24H -- Set Relative Record With FCB
3.105. Function 59H -- Get Extended Error
3.128. Extended Error Codes Returned from Function 59H
3.131. Handle Pointer Movement Methods

3.069. FUNCTION 43H,00H -- GET FILE ATTRIBUTES

Prior to Calling Function

	High	Low
AX	43H	0
BX		
CX		
DX	Offset of pointer to pathname string	

SP	
BP	
SI	
DI	

IP	
flags	

CS	
DS	Segment of pointer to pathname string
SS	
ES	

Upon Return From Function

	High	Low
AX	Error code (if carry set)	
BX		
CX	0	Attribute byte
DX		

SP	
BP	
SI	
DI	

IP	
flags	Carry*

CS	
DS	
SS	
ES	

Version Info: Applies to all versions of DOS beginning with 2.0

Notes: •Pathname must be in ASCIIZ format
•*Carry flag set if error occurs

Source: IBM DOS 3.3 Technical Reference, pages 6-145 to 6-146

See Also: 1.17. Common String Formats
2.34. File Attribute Byte
3.001. INT 21H Functions by DOS Version Summary
3.105. Function 59H -- Get Extended Error
3.128. Extended Error Codes Returned from Function 59H

3.070. FUNCTION 43H, 01H -- SET FILE ATTRIBUTES

Prior to Calling Function   *Upon Return From Function*

	High	Low
AX	43H	1
BX		
CX	0	Attribute byte
DX	Offset of pointer to pathname string	

SP	
BP	
SI	
DI	

IP	
flags	

CS	
DS	Segment of pointer to pathname string
SS	
ES	

	High	Low
AX	Error code (if carry set)	
BX		
CX		
DX		

SP	
BP	
SI	
DI	

IP	
flags	Carry*

CS	
DS	
SS	
ES	

Version Info: •Applies to all versions of DOS beginning with 2.0
•Requires Create access rights on networks to change any bit other than the archive bit (bit 5)

Notes: •Pathname must be in ASCIIZ format
•You can't change the volume or directory bits of an Attribute Byte
•*Carry flag set if error occurs

Source: IBM DOS 3.3 Technical Reference, pages 6-145 to 6-146

See Also: 1.17. Common String Formats
2.34. File Attribute Byte
3.001. INT 21H Functions by DOS Version Summary
3.105. Function 59H -- Get Extended Error
3.128. Extended Error Codes Returned from Function 59H

3.071. FUNCTION 44H,00H -- GET IOCTL DATA

Prior to Calling Function   *Upon Return From Function*

	High	Low
AX	44H	0
BX	Handle	
CX		
DX	0	0

SP	
BP	
SI	
DI	

IP	
flags	

CS	
DS	
SS	
ES	

	High	Low
AX	Error code (if carry set)	
BX		
CX		
DX	Device data word (if carry clear)	

SP	
BP	
SI	
DI	

IP	
flags	Carry*

CS	
DS	
SS	
ES	

Version Info: Applies to all versions of DOS beginning with 2.0

Notes: *Carry flag set if error occurs

Source: IBM DOS 3.3 Technical Reference, pages 6-148 to 6-150

See Also: 3.001. INT 21H Functions by DOS Version Summary
3.072. Function 44H, 01H -- Set IOCTL Data
3.105. Function 59H -- Get Extended Error
3.128. Extended Error Codes Returned from Function 59H
3.133. Device Data Word

3.072. FUNCTION 44H, 01H -- SET IOCTL DATA

Prior to Calling Function

	High	Low
AX	44H	1
BX	Handle	
CX		
DX	0	Device data

| SP |
| BP |
| SI |
| DI |

| IP | |
| flags | |

| CS |
| DS |
| SS |
| ES |

Upon Return From Function

	High	Low
AX	Error code (if carry set)	
BX		
CX		
DX		

| SP |
| BP |
| SI |
| DI |

| IP | |
| flags | Carry* |

| CS |
| DS |
| SS |
| ES |

Version Info: Applies to all versions of DOS beginning with 2.0

Notes: *Carry flag set if error occurs

Source: IBM DOS 3.3 Technical Reference, pages 6-148 to 6-150

See Also: 3.001. INT 21H Functions by DOS Version Summary
3.071. Function 44H, 00H -- Get IOCTL Data
3.105. Function 59H -- Get Extended Error
3.128. Extended Error Codes Returned from Function 59H
3.133. Device Data Word

3.073. FUNCTION 44H, 02H -- IOCTL READ STRING

Prior to Calling Function

	High	Low
AX	44H	2
BX	Handle	
CX	Number of bytes to read from handle	
DX	Offset of pointer to empty buffer	

| SP |
| BP |
| SI |
| DI |

| IP | |
| flags | |

CS	
DS	Segment of pointer to empty buffer
SS	
ES	

| Buffer | Empty |

Upon Return From Function

	High	Low
AX	Bytes read or error code (if carry set)	
BX		
CX		
DX		

| SP |
| BP |
| SI |
| DI |

| IP | |
| flags | Carry* |

| CS |
| DS |
| SS |
| ES |

| Buffer | Data read from device |

Version Info: Applies to all versions of DOS beginning with 2.0

Notes: *Carry flag set if error occurs

Source: IBM DOS 3.3 Technical Reference, page 6-151

See Also: 3.001. INT 21H Functions by DOS Version Summary
3.074. Function 44H, 03H -- IOCTL Write String
3.105. Function 59H -- Get Extended Error
3.128. Extended Error Codes Returned from Function 59H

3.074. FUNCTION 44H, 03H -- IOCTL WRITE STRING

Prior to Calling Function

	High	Low
AX	44H	3
BX	Handle	
CX	Number of bytes to write to handle	
DX	Offset of pointer to buffer of data to write	

SP	
BP	
SI	
DI	

| IP ||
| flags ||

CS	
DS	Segment of pointer to buffer of data to write	
SS	
ES	

| Buffer | Data to write |

Upon Return From Function

	High	Low
AX	Bytes written or error code (if carry set)	
BX		
CX		
DX		

SP	
BP	
SI	
DI	

| IP ||
| flags | Carry* |

CS	
DS	
SS	
ES	

| Buffer | Unchanged data |

Version Info: Applies to all versions of DOS beginning with 2.0

Notes: *Carry flag set if error occurs

Source: IBM DOS 3.3 Technical Reference, page 6-151

See Also:
3.001. INT 21H Functions by DOS Version Summary
3.073. Function 44H,02H -- IOCTL Read String
3.105. Function 59H -- Get Extended Error
3.128. Extended Error Codes Returned from Function 59H

3.075. FUNCTION 44H,04H -- IOCTL READ BLOCK

Prior to Calling Function

	High	Low
AX	44H	4
BX		Logical drive number**
CX	Number of bytes to read from drive	
DX	Offset of pointer to empty buffer	

SP	
BP	
SI	
DI	

| IP ||
| flags ||

CS	
DS	Segment of pointer to empty buffer	
SS	
ES	

| Buffer | Empty |

Upon Return From Function

	High	Low
AX	Bytes read or error code (if carry set)	
BX		
CX		
DX		

SP	
BP	
SI	
DI	

| IP ||
| flags | Carry* |

CS	
DS	
SS	
ES	

| Buffer | Data read from drive |

Version Info: Applies to all versions of DOS beginning with 2.0

Notes: •*Carry flag set if error occurs
•**Drive 0=default, drive 1=A, and so on

Source: IBM DOS 3.3 Technical Reference, page 152

See Also:
3.001. INT 21H Functions by DOS Version Summary
3.076. Function 44H,05H -- IOCTL Write Block
3.105. Function 59H -- Get Extended Error
3.128. Extended Error Codes Returned from Function 59H
3.137. Logical Drive Numbers

3.076. FUNCTION 44H, 05H -- IOCTL WRITE BLOCK

Prior to Calling Function

	High	Low
AX	44H	5
BX		Logical drive number**
CX	Number of bytes to write to drive	
DX	Offset of pointer to buffer of data to write	
SP		
BP		
SI		
DI		
IP		
flags		
CS		
DS	Segment of pointer to buffer of data to write	
SS		
ES		
Buffer	Data to write	

Upon Return From Function

	High	Low
AX	Bytes written or error code (if carry set)	
BX		
CX		
DX		
SP		
BP		
SI		
DI		
IP		
flags		Carry*
CS		
DS		
SS		
ES		
Buffer	Unchanged data	

Version Info:　　　Applies to all versions of DOS beginning with 2.0

Notes:　　　•*Carry flag set if error occurs
•**Drive 0=default, drive 1=A, and so on

Source:　　　IBM DOS 3.3 Technical Reference, page 6-152

See Also:　　　3.001. INT 21H Functions by DOS Version Summary
3.075. Function 44H,04H -- IOCTL Read Block
3.105. Function 59H -- Get Extended Error
3.128. Extended Error Codes Returned from Function 59H
3.137. Logical Drive Numbers

3.077. FUNCTION 44H, 06H -- IOCTL GET INPUT STATUS

Prior to Calling Function

	High	Low
AX	44H	6
BX	Handle	
CX		
DX		
SP		
BP		
SI		
DI		
IP		
flags		
CS		
DS		
SS		
ES		

Upon Return From Function

	High	Low
AX		Status*
BX		
CX		
DX		
SP		
BP		
SI		
DI		
IP		
flags		
CS		
DS		
SS		
ES		

Version Info:　　　Applies to all versions of DOS beginning with 2.0

Notes:　　　•*For character devices: 00=not ready, FF=ready
For block devices: 00=pointer at EOF, FF=ready

IBM DOS 3.3 Technical Reference, page 6-153

Source:

3.001. INT 21H Functions by DOS Version Summary

See Also:　　　3.078. Function 44H, 07H -- IOCTL Get Output Status
3.105. Function 59H -- Get Extended Error
3.128. Extended Error Codes Returned from Function 59H

3.078. FUNCTION 44H, 07H -- IOCTL GET OUTPUT STATUS

Prior to Calling Function

	High	Low
AX	44H	7
BX	Handle	
CX		
DX		

SP	
BP	
SI	
DI	

| IP | |
| flags | |

CS	
DS	
SS	
ES	

Upon Return From Function

	High	Low
AX		Status*
BX		
CX		
DX		

SP	
BP	
SI	
DI	

| IP | |
| flags | |

CS	
DS	
SS	
ES	

Version Info: Applies to all versions of DOS beginning with 2.0

Notes: •*For character devices: 00=not ready, FF=ready
For block devices: 00=not ready, FF=ready

Source: IBM DOS 3.3 Technical Reference, page 6-153

See Also:
3.001. INT 21H Functions by DOS Version Summary
3.077. Function 44H, 06H -- IOCTL Get Input Status
3.105. Function 59H -- Get Extended Error
3.128. Extended Error Codes Returned from Function 59H

3.079. FUNCTION 44H, 08H -- IOCTL IS REMOVABLE?

Prior to Calling Function

	High	Low
AX	44H	8
BX		Logical drive number
CX		
DX		

SP	
BP	
SI	
DI	

| IP | |
| flags | |

CS	
DS	
SS	
ES	

Upon Return From Function

	High	Low
AX	Status** or error code (if carry set)	
BX		
CX		
DX		

SP	
BP	
SI	
DI	

| IP | |
| flags | | Carry* |

CS	
DS	
SS	
ES	

Version Info: Applies to all versions of DOS beginning with 3.0

Notes: •*Carry flag set if error occurs
•**00=removable media; 01=media not removable; 0FH = invalid device

Source: IBM DOS 3.3 Technical Reference, page 6-154

See Also:
3.001. INT 21H Functions by DOS Version Summary
3.105. Function 59H -- Get Extended Error
3.128. Extended Error Codes Returned from Function 59H
3.137. Logical Drive Numbers

3.080. FUNCTION 44H, 09H -- IOCTL IS REDIRECTED BLOCK?

Prior to Calling Function

	High	Low
AX	44H	9
BX		Logical drive number
CX		
DX		

SP	
BP	
SI	
DI	

| IP | |
| flags | |

CS	
DS	
SS	
ES	

Upon Return From Function

	High	Low
AX	Error code (if carry set)	
BX		
CX		
DX	Device attribute code**	

SP	
BP	
SI	
DI	

| IP | |
| flags | Carry* |

CS	
DS	
SS	
ES	

Version Info: Applies to all versions of DOS beginning with 3.1

Notes: •*Carry flag set if error occurs
•**Bit 12 set=remote device; bit 12 clear=local device

Source: IBM DOS 3.3 Technical Reference, page 6-155

See Also: 3.001. INT 21H Functions by DOS Version Summary
3.081. Function 44H,0AH -- IOCTL Is Redirected Handle?
3.105. Function 59H -- Get Extended Error
3.128. Extended Error Codes Returned from Function 59H
3.137. Logical Drive Numbers
3.150. Device Attribute Codes

3.081. FUNCTION 44H, 0AH -- IOCTL IS REDIRECTED HANDLE?

Prior to Calling Function

	High	Low
AX	44H	0AH
BX	Handle	
CX		
DX		

SP	
BP	
SI	
DI	

| IP | |
| flags | |

CS	
DS	
SS	
ES	

Upon Return From Function

	High	Low
AX	Error code (if carry set)	
BX		
CX		
DX	Device attribute code**	

SP	
BP	
SI	
DI	

| IP | |
| flags | Carry* |

CS	
DS	
SS	
ES	

Version Info: Applies to all versions of DOS beginning with 3.1

Notes: •*Carry flag set if error occurs
•**Bit 15 set=remote device; bit 15 clear=local device

Source: IBM DOS 3.3 Technical Reference, page 6-156

See Also: 3.001. INT 21H Functions by DOS Version Summary
3.080. Function 44H, 09H -- IOCTL Is Redirected Block?
3.105. Function 59H -- Get Extended Error
3.128. Extended Error Codes Returned from Function 59H
3.137. Logical Drive Numbers
3.150. Device Attribute Codes

3.082. FUNCTION 44H, 0BH -- IOCTL CHANGE RETRY COUNT

Prior to Calling Function   *Upon Return From Function*

	High	Low
AX	44H	0BH
BX		
CX	Number of loops to wait between retries	
DX	Number of times to retry operation	
SP		
BP		
SI		
DI		
IP		
flags		
CS		
DS		
SS		
ES		

	High	Low
AX	Error code (if carry set)	
BX		
CX		
DX		
SP		
BP		
SI		
DI		
IP		
flags		Carry*
CS		
DS		
SS		
ES		

Version Info: •Applies to all versions of DOS beginning with 3.0

Notes: •*Carry flag set if error occurs
•A loop is 65,536 machine cycles, and is coded as follows:
  xor cx, cx
  loop $;loop 64K times
•Default is 1 loop, 3 retries

Source: IBM DOS 3.3 Technical Reference, pages 6-157 to 6-158

See Also: 3.001. INT 21H Functions by DOS Version Summary
3.105. Function 59H -- Get Extended Error
3.128. Extended Error Codes Returned from Function 59H

3.083. FUNCTION 44H, 0CH -- GENERIC IOCTL FOR HANDLES

Prior to Calling Function   **Upon Return From Function**

	High	Low
AX	44H	0CH
BX	Handle	
CX	Major code**	Minor code***
DX	Offset of pointer to data buffer	

SP	
BP	
SI	
DI	

IP	
flags	

CS	
DS	Segment of pointer to data buffer
SS	
ES	

Buffer	Code page parm block or iteration count

	High	Low
AX	Error code (if carry set)	
BX		
CX		
DX		

SP	
BP	
SI	
DI	

	High	Low
IP		
flags		Carry*

CS	
DS	
SS	
ES	

Buffer	Code page parm block or iteration count

Version Info:	•Applies to all versions of DOS beginning with 3.2 •Code page settings apply to DOS 3.3 only

Notes:	•*Carry flag set if error occurs
	•**Major code is one of: 0 = unknown
	                                             1 = COMx
	                                             3 = CON
	                                             5 = LPTx
	
	•***Minor code is one of: 45H = set iteration count
	                                             4AH = select
	                                             4CH = prepare start
	                                             4DH = prepare end
	                                             65H = get iteration count
	                                             6AH = query selected
	                                             6BH = query prepare list

Source:	IBM DOS 3.3 Technical Reference, pages 6-158 to 6-166
See Also:	3.001. INT 21H Functions by DOS Version Summary 3.105. Function 59H -- Get Extended Error 3.128. Extended Error Codes Returned from Function 59H 3.146. Code Page Parameter Blocks 3.151. Device Request Header Status Field & Error Codes

3.084. FUNCTION 44H, 0DH -- GENERIC IOCTL FOR DEVICES

Prior to Calling Function

	High	Low
AX	44H	0DH
BX		Logical drive number
CX	8	Function code**
DX	Offset of pointer to parameter block	

SP	
BP	
SI	
DI	

IP	
flags	

CS	
DS	Segment of pointer to parameter block
SS	
ES	

Buffer | Parameter block (if CL=40H,41H,42H,62H) |

Upon Return From Function

	High	Low
AX	Error code (if carry set)	
BX		
CX		
DX		

SP	
BP	
SI	
DI	

	High	Low
IP		
flags		Carry*

CS	
DS	
SS	
ES	

Buffer | Parameter block (if CL=60H,61H) |

Version Info:
• Applies to all versions of DOS beginning with 3.2

Notes:
• *Carry flag set if error occurs
• **Function code is one of:

- 40H =set device parameters
- 41H=write track on logical device
- 42H=format track on logical device
- 60H=get device parameters
- 61H=read track on logical device
- 62H=verify track on logical device

Source: IBM DOS 3.3 Technical Reference, pages 6-166 to 6-181

See Also:
3.001. INT 21H Functions by DOS Version Summary
3.105. Function 59H -- Get Extended Error
3.128. Extended Error Codes Returned from Function 59H
3.134. Block Device Function Codes
3.135. Device Parameter Blocks
3.167. Device BPB Layout

3.085. FUNCTION 44H, 0EH -- GET LOGICAL DRIVE MAP

Prior to Calling Function   *Upon Return From Function*

	High	Low
AX	44H	0EH
BX		Logical drive number
CX		
DX		
SP		
BP		
SI		
DI		
IP		
flags		
CS		
DS		
SS		
ES		

	High	Low
AX	Drive** or error code (if carry set)	
BX		
CX		
DX		
SP		
BP		
SI		
DI		
IP		
flags		Carry*
CS		
DS		
SS		
ES		

Version Info: Applies to all versions of DOS beginning with 3.2

Notes: •*Carry flag set if error occurs
•**AL returns physical drive data; 00=only one drive mapped to logical drive;
1-26(A-Z)=physical drive mapped to logical drive

Source: IBM DOS 3.3 Technical Reference, page 6-182

See Also: 3.001. INT 21H Functions by DOS Version Summary
3.086. Function 44H, 0FH -- Set Logical Drive Map
3.105. Function 59H -- Get Extended Error
3.128. Extended Error Codes Returned from Function 59H

3.086. FUNCTION 44H, 0FH -- SET LOGICAL DRIVE MAP

Prior to Calling Function   *Upon Return From Function*

	High	Low
AX	44H	0FH
BX		Logical drive number
CX		
DX		
SP		
BP		
SI		
DI		
IP		
flags		
CS		
DS		
SS		
ES		

	High	Low
AX	Logical drive used or error code** (if carry set)	
BX		
CX		
DX		
SP		
BP		
SI		
DI		
IP		
flags		Carry*
CS		
DS		
SS		
ES		

Version Info: •Applies to all versions of DOS beginning with 3.2

Notes: •*Carry flag set if error occurs
•**AL returns physical drive data; 00=only one drive mapped to logical drive;
1-26(A-Z)=physical drive mapped to logical drive

Source: IBM DOS 3.3 Technical Reference, pages 6-183 to 6-184

See Also: 3.001. INT 21H Functions by DOS Version Summary
3.085. Function 44H, 0EH -- Get Logical Drive Map
3.105. Function 59H -- Get Extended Error
3.128. Extended Error Codes Returned from Function 59H
3.137. Logical Drive Numbers

3.087. FUNCTION 45H -- DUPLICATE FILE HANDLE

Prior to Calling Function

	High	Low
AX	45H	
BX	Handle	
CX		
DX		
SP		
BP		
SI		
DI		
IP		
flags		
CS		
DS		
SS		
ES		

Upon Return From Function

	High	Low
AX	New handle or error code (if carry set)	
BX		
CX		
DX		
SP		
BP		
SI		
DI		
IP		
flags		Carry*
CS		
DS		
SS		
ES		

Version Info: Applies to all versions of DOS beginning with 2.0

Notes: *Carry flag set if error occurs

Source: IBM DOS 3.3 Technical Reference, page 6-185

See Also: 3.001. INT 21H Functions by DOS Version Summary
3.088. Function 46H -- Force Duplicate File Handle
3.105. Function 59H -- Get Extended Error
3.128. Extended Error Codes Returned from Function 59H

3.088. FUNCTION 46H -- FORCE DUPLICATE FILE HANDLE

Prior to Calling Function

	High	Low
AX	46H	
BX	Existing handle	
CX	Second handle	
DX		
SP		
BP		
SI		
DI		
IP		
flags		
CS		
DS		
SS		
ES		

Upon Return From Function

	High	Low
AX	Error code (if carry set)	
BX		
CX		
DX		
SP		
BP		
SI		
DI		
IP		
flags		Carry*
CS		
DS		
SS		
ES		

Version Info: Applies to all versions of DOS beginning with 2.0

Notes: •Almost always used immediately after Function 45H -- Duplicate File Handle
•*Carry flag set if error occurs

Source: IBM DOS 3.3 Technical Reference, pages 6-186 to 6-187

See Also: 3.001. INT 21H Functions by DOS Version Summary
3.087. Function 45H -- Duplicate File Handle
3.105. Function 59H -- Get Extended Error
3.128. Extended Error Codes Returned from Function 59H

3.089. FUNCTION 47H -- GET CURRENT DIRECTORY

Prior to Calling Function

	High	Low
AX	47H	
BX		
CX		
DX		Logical drive number

SP	
BP	
SI	Offset of pointer to 64-byte buffer
DI	

| IP | |
| flags | |

CS	
DS	Segment of pointer to 64-byte buffer
SS	
ES	

Buffer | Empty

Upon Return From Function

	High	Low
AX	Error code (if carry set)	
BX		
CX		
DX		

SP	
BP	
SI	
DI	

| IP | |
| flags | Carry* |

CS	
DS	
SS	
ES	

Buffer | ASCIIZ pathname (if carry flag clear)

Version Info: Applies to all versions of DOS beginning with 2.0

Notes: •Returned pathname does not begin with a backslash or drive ID
•*Carry flag set if error occurs

Source: IBM DOS 3.3 Technical Reference, pages 6-188 to 6-189

See Also: 3.001. INT 21H Functions by DOS Version Summary
3.061. Function 3BH -- Change Current Directory
3.105. Function 59H -- Get Extended Error
3.128. Extended Error Codes Returned from Function 59H

3.090. FUNCTION 48H -- ALLOCATE MEMORY

Prior to Calling Function

	High	Low
AX	48H	
BX	Number of paragraphs of memory	
CX		
DX		

SP	
BP	
SI	
DI	

| IP | |
| flags | |

CS	
DS	
SS	
ES	

Upon Return From Function

	High	Low
AX	Segment address** or error code (if carry set)	
BX	Paragraphs available (if carry set)	
CX		
DX		

SP	
BP	
SI	
DI	

| IP | |
| flags | Carry* |

CS	
DS	
SS	
ES	

Version Info: Applies to all versions of DOS beginning with 2.0

Notes: •*Carry flag set if error occurs
•**Segment address of allocated memory block

Source: IBM DOS 3.3 Technical Reference, pages 6-190 to 6-191

See Also: 3.001. INT 21H Functions by DOS Version Summary
3.091. Function 49H -- Free Allocated Memory
3.092. Function 4AH -- Set Block
3.103. Function 58H, 00H -- Get Allocation Strategy
3.104. Function 58H, 01H -- Set Allocation Strategy
3.105. Function 59H -- Get Extended Error
3.128. Extended Error Codes Returned from Function 59H
3.140. Memory Allocation Strategies

3.091. FUNCTION 49H -- FREE ALLOCATED MEMORY

Prior to Calling Function · *Upon Return From Function*

	High	Low		High	Low
AX	49H		AX	Error code (if carry set)	
BX			BX		
CX			CX		
DX			DX		
SP			SP		
BP			BP		
SI			SI		
DI			DI		
IP			IP		
flags			flags		Carry*
CS			CS		
DS			DS		
SS			SS		
ES	Segment address of allocated block to free		ES		

Version Info: Applies to all versions of DOS beginning with 2.0

Notes: *Carry flag set if error occurs

Source: IBM DOS 3.3 Technical Reference, page 6-192

See Also: 3.001. INT 21H Functions by DOS Version Summary
3.090. Function 48H -- Allocate Memory
3.092. Function 4AH -- Set Block
3.103. Function 58H, 00H -- Get Allocation Strategy
3.104. Function 58H, 01H -- Set Allocation Strategy
3.105. Function 59H -- Get Extended Error
3.128. Extended Error Codes Returned from Function 59H
3.140. Memory Allocation Strategies

3.092. FUNCTION 4AH -- SET BLOCK

Prior to Calling Function · *Upon Return From Function*

	High	Low		High	Low
AX	4AH		AX	Error code (if carry set)	
BX	Paragraphs of memory requested		BX	Paragraphs available (if carry set)	
CX			CX		
DX			DX		
SP			SP		
BP			BP		
SI			SI		
DI			DI		
IP			IP		
flags			flags		Carry*
CS			CS		
DS			DS		
SS			SS		
ES	Segment address of memory block to allocate		ES		

Version Info: Applies to all versions of DOS beginning with 2.0

Notes: *Carry flag set if error occurs

Source: IBM DOS 3.3 Technical Reference, pages 6-193 to 6-194

See Also: 3.001. INT 21H Functions by DOS Version Summary
3.090. Function 48H -- Allocate Memory
3.091. Function 49H -- Free Allocated Memory
3.103. Function 58H, 00H -- Get Allocation Strategy
3.104. Function 58H, 01H -- Set Allocation Strategy
3.105. Function 59H -- Get Extended Error
3.128. Extended Error Codes Returned from Function 59H
3.140. Memory Allocation Strategies

3.093. FUNCTION 4BH, 00H -- LOAD AND EXECUTE PROGRAM

Prior to Calling Function   *Upon Return From Function*

	High	Low			High	Low
AX	4BH	0		AX	Error code (if carry set)	
BX	Offset of pointer to parameter block			BX	Destroyed	Destroyed
CX				CX	Destroyed	Destroyed
DX	Offset of pointer to pathname			DX	Destroyed	Destroyed
SP				SP	Destroyed	
BP				BP	Destroyed	
SI				SI	Destroyed	
DI				DI	Destroyed	
IP				IP		
flags				flags		Carry*
CS				CS		
DS	Segment of pointer to pathname			DS	Destroyed	
SS				SS	Destroyed	
ES	Segment of pointer to parameter block			ES	Destroyed	

Version Info: Applies to all versions of DOS beginning with 2.0

Notes: *Carry flag set if error occurs

Source: IBM DOS 3.3 Technical Reference, pages 6-195 to 6-199

See Also: 3.001. INT 21H Functions by DOS Version Summary
3.053. Function 31H -- Keep Process
3.094. Function 4BH, 03H -- Load Overlay
3.105. Function 59H -- Get Extended Error
3.128. Extended Error Codes Returned from Function 59H
3.138. Execute Program Parameter Block

3.094. FUNCTION 4BH, 03H -- LOAD OVERLAY

Prior to Calling Function   *Upon Return From Function*

	High	Low			High	Low
AX	4BH	3		AX	Error code (if carry set)	
BX	Offset of pointer to parameter block			BX	Destroyed	Destroyed
CX				CX	Destroyed	Destroyed
DX	Offset of pointer to pathname			DX	Destroyed	Destroyed
SP				SP	Destroyed	
BP				BP	Destroyed	
SI				SI	Destroyed	
DI				DI	Destroyed	
IP				IP		
flags				flags		Carry*
CS				CS		
DS	Segment of pointer to pathname			DS	Destroyed	
SS				SS	Destroyed	
ES	Segment of pointer to parameter block			ES	Destroyed	

Version Info: Applies to all versions of DOS beginning with 2.0

Notes: *Carry flag set if error occurs

Source: IBM DOS 3.3 Technical Reference, pages 6-195 to 6-199

See Also: 3.001. INT 21H Functions by DOS Version Summary
3.053. Function 31H -- Keep Process
3.093. Function 4BH, 00H -- Load and Execute Program
3.105. Function 59H -- Get Extended Error
3.128. Extended Error Codes Returned from Function 59H
3.139. Overlay Program Parameter Block

3.095. FUNCTION 4CH -- END PROCESS

Prior to Calling Function   *Upon Return From Function*

	High	Low
AX	4CH	Return code
BX		
CX		
DX		
SP		
BP		
SI		
DI		
IP		
flags		
CS		
DS		
SS		
ES		

Function does not return any values

Version Info:	Applies to all versions of DOS beginning with 2.0
Notes:	All open files are closed by this function
Source:	IBM DOS 3.3 Technical Reference, page 6-200
See Also:	3.001. INT 21H Functions by DOS Version Summary 3.053. Function 31H -- Keep Process 3.096. Function 4DH -- Get Return Code

3.096. FUNCTION 4DH -- GET RETURN CODE

Prior to Calling Function

	High	Low
AX	4DH	
BX		
CX		
DX		
SP		
BP		
SI		
DI		
IP		
flags		
CS		
DS		
SS		
ES		

Upon Return From Function

	High	Low
AX	Termination code*	Return code
BX		
CX		
DX		
SP		
BP		
SI		
DI		
IP		
flags		
CS		
DS		
SS		
ES		

Version Info:	Applies to all versions of DOS beginning with 2.0
Notes:	*0=normal 4CH terminate; 1=Control-C pressed; 2=critical device error; 3=normal 31H terminate
Source:	IBM DOS 3.3 Technical Reference, page 6-201
See Also:	3.001. INT 21H Functions by DOS Version Summary 3.053. Function 31H -- Keep Process 3.095. Function 4CH -- End Process

3.097. FUNCTION 4EH -- FIND FIRST FILE

Prior to Calling Function

	High	Low
AX	4EH	
BX		
CX	0	Attribute byte
DX	Offset of pointer to pathname	

SP	
BP	
SI	
DI	

IP	
flags	

CS	
DS	Segment of pointer to pathname
SS	
ES	

DTA | Empty

Pathname | ASCIIZ string

Upon Return From Function

	High	Low
AX	Error code (if carry set)	
BX		
CX		
DX		

SP	
BP	
SI	
DI	

IP	
flags	Carry*

CS	
DS	
SS	
ES	

DTA | File info (See 3.132. Search First/Next Data Blocks)

Pathname | Unchanged

Version Info: Applies to all versions of DOS beginning with 2.0

Notes: *Carry flag set if error occurs

Source: IBM DOS 3.3 Technical Reference, pages 6-202 to 6-203

See Also: 2.34. File Attribute Byte
2.35. Date/Time Formats
3.001. INT 21H Functions by DOS Version Summary
3.026. Function 11H -- Find First Entry With FCB
3.027. Function 12H -- Find Next Entry With FCB
3.098. Function 4FH -- Find Next File
3.105. Function 59H -- Get Extended Error
3.128. Extended Error Codes Returned from Function 59H
3.132. Search First/Next Data Blocks

3.098. FUNCTION 4FH -- FIND NEXT FILE

Prior to Calling Function			*Upon Return From Function*		
	High	*Low*		*High*	*Low*
AX	4FH		AX	Error code (if carry set)	
BX			BX		
CX			CX		
DX			DX		
SP			SP		
BP			BP		
SI			SI		
DI			DI		
IP			IP		
flags			flags		Carry*
CS			CS		
DS			DS		
SS			SS		
ES			ES		
DTA	Data about previously found file		DTA	Data about next found file (if carry clear)	

Version Info: Applies to all versions of DOS beginning with 2.0

Notes: •Must be used after function 4EH
•*Carry flag set if error occurs

Source: IBM DOS 3.3 Technical Reference, page 6-204

See Also: 2.34. File Attribute Byte
2.35. Date/Time Formats
3.001. INT 21H Functions by DOS Version Summary
3.026. Function 11H -- Find First Entry With FCB
3.027. Function 12H -- Find Next Entry With FCB
3.097. Function 4EH -- Find First File
3.105. Function 59H -- Get Extended Error
3.128. Extended Error Codes Returned from Function 59H
3.132. Search First/Next Data Blocks

3.099. FUNCTION 54H -- GET VERIFY STATE

Prior to Calling Function				*Upon Return From Function*		
	High	Low			High	Low
AX	54H			AX		Verify state*
BX				BX		
CX				CX		
DX				DX		
SP				SP		
BP				BP		
SI				SI		
DI				DI		
IP				IP		
flags				flags		
CS				CS		
DS				DS		
SS				SS		
ES				ES		

Version Info: Applies to all versions of DOS beginning with 2.0

Notes: *0=no verify after write; 01=verify after write

Source: IBM DOS 3.3 Technical Reference, page 6-205

See Also: 3.001. INT 21H Functions by DOS Version Summary
3.050. Function 2EH -- Set/Reset Verify Flag

3.100. FUNCTION 56H -- RENAME FILE

Prior to Calling Function				*Upon Return From Function*		
	High	Low			High	Low
AX	56H			AX	Error code (if carry set)	
BX				BX		
CX				CX		
DX	Offset of pointer to old pathname			DX		
SP				SP		
BP				BP		
SI				SI		
DI	Offset of pointer to new pathname			DI		
IP				IP		
flags				flags		Carry*
CS				CS		
DS	Segment of pointer to old pathname			DS		
SS				SS		
ES	Segment of pointer to new pathname			ES		

Version Info: •Applies to all versions of DOS beginning with 2.0
•Requires create access rights on networks

Notes: •The ? wildcard character may not be used in the pathname
•If the directory path is not the same, but the file name and type specified are, the file is "moved" to the new directory
•*Carry flag set if error occurs

Source: IBM DOS 3.3 Technical Reference, pages 6-206 to 6-207

See Also: 3.001. INT 21H Functions by DOS Version Summary
3.032. Function 17H -- Rename File With FCB
3.105. Function 59H -- Get Extended Error
3.128. Extended Error Codes Returned from Function 59H

3.101. FUNCTION 57H, 00H -- GET DATE/TIME OF FILE

Prior to Calling Function

	High	Low
AX	57H	0
BX	Handle	
CX		
DX		

SP	
BP	
SI	
DI	

IP	
flags	

CS	
DS	
SS	
ES	

Upon Return From Function

	High	Low
AX	Error code (if carry set)	
BX		
CX	FCB format time file last changed	
DX	FCB format date file last changed	

SP	
BP	
SI	
DI	

IP	
flags	Carry*

CS	
DS	
SS	
ES	

Version Info: Applies to all versions of DOS beginning with 2.0

Notes: *Carry flag set if error occurs

Source: IBM DOS 3.3 Technical Reference, pages 6-208 to 6-209

See Also: 2.35. Date/Time Formats
3.001. INT 21H Functions by DOS Version Summary
3.105. Function 59H -- Get Extended Error
3.128. Extended Error Codes Returned from Function 59H

3.102. FUNCTION 57H, 01H -- SET DATE/TIME OF FILE

Prior to Calling Function

	High	Low
AX	57H	1
BX	Handle	
CX	FCB format time to be set	
DX	FCB format date to be set	

SP	
BP	
SI	
DI	

IP	
flags	

CS	
DS	
SS	
ES	

Upon Return From Function

	High	Low
AX	Error code (if carry set)	
BX		
CX		
DX		

SP	
BP	
SI	
DI	

IP	
flags	Carry*

CS	
DS	
SS	
ES	

Version Info: Applies to all versions of DOS beginning with 2.0

Notes: *Carry flag set if error occurs

Source: IBM DOS 3.3 Technical Reference, pages 6-208 to 6-209

See Also: 2.35. Date/Time Formats
3.001. INT 21H Functions by DOS Version Summary
3.105. Function 59H -- Get Extended Error
3.128. Extended Error Codes Returned from Function 59H

3.103. FUNCTION 58H, 00H -- GET ALLOCATION STRATEGY

	Prior to Calling Function	
	High	*Low*
AX	58H	0
BX		
CX		
DX		

SP	
BP	
SI	
DI	

IP	
flags	

CS	
DS	
SS	
ES	

	Upon Return From Function	
	High	*Low*
AX	Strategy** or error code (if carry set)	
BX		
CX		
DX		

SP	
BP	
SI	
DI	

IP	
flags	Carry*

CS	
DS	
SS	
ES	

Version Info: Applies to all versions of DOS beginning with 3.2

Notes:
- *Carry flag set if error occurs
- **AH returns 00=first fit; 01=best fit; 02=last fit

Source: MS-DOS 3.2 Programmer's Reference, page 1-212
Missing from IBM DOS 3.3 Technical Reference!

See Also: 3.001. INT 21H Functions by DOS Version Summary
3.090. Function 48H -- Allocate Memory
3.092. Function 4AH -- Set Block
3.105. Function 59H -- Get Extended Error
3.128. Extended Error Codes Returned from Function 59H
3.140. Memory Allocation Strategies

3.104. FUNCTION 58H, 01H -- SET ALLOCATION STRATEGY

	Prior to Calling Function			*Upon Return From Function*	
	High	*Low*		*High*	*Low*
AX	58H	1	AX	Error code (if carry set)	
BX	Allocation strategy**		BX		
CX			CX		
DX			DX		
SP			SP		
BP			BP		
SI			SI		
DI			DI		
IP			IP		
flags			flags		Carry*
CS			CS		
DS			DS		
SS			SS		
ES			ES		

Version Info: Applies to all versions of DOS beginning with 3.2

Notes: •*Carry flag set if error occurs
•**00=first fit; 01=best fit; 02=last fit

Source: MS-DOS 3.2 Programmer's Reference, page 1-212
Missing from IBM DOS 3.3 Technical Reference!

See Also: 3.001. INT 21H Functions by DOS Version Summary
3.090. Function 48H -- Allocate Memory
3.092. Function 4AH -- Set Block
3.105. Function 59H -- Get Extended Error
3.128. Extended Error Codes Returned from Function 59H
3.140. Memory Allocation Strategies

3.105. FUNCTION 59H -- GET EXTENDED ERROR

Prior to Calling Function

	High	Low
AX	59H	
BX	0	0
CX		
DX		

SP	
BP	
SI	
DI	

IP	
flags	

CS	
DS	
SS	
ES	

Upon Return From Function

	High	Low
AX	Extended error code (of last error)	
BX	Error class	Suggested action
CX	Location of error	Destroyed*
DX	Destroyed*	Destroyed*

SP	
BP	
SI	Destroyed*
DI	Destroyed*

IP	
flags	

CS	
DS	Destroyed*
SS	
ES	Destroyed*

Version Info: Applies to all versions of DOS beginning with 3.0

Notes: *These registers are not preserved by DOS

Source: IBM DOS 3.3 Technical Reference, pages 6-210 to 6-212

See Also: 3.001. INT 21H Functions by DOS Version Summary
3.128. Extended Error Codes Returned from Function 59H

3.106. FUNCTION 5AH -- CREATE TEMPORARY FILE

Prior to Calling Function

	High	Low
AX	5AH	
BX		
CX	0	Attribute byte
DX	Offset of pointer to special pathname**	

SP	
BP	
SI	
DI	

IP	
flags	

CS	
DS	Segment of pointer to special pathname**
SS	
ES	

Pathname	Pathname

Upon Return From Function

	High	Low
AX	Handle or error code (if carry set)	
BX		
CX		
DX		

SP	
BP	
SI	
DI	

	High	Low
IP		
flags		Carry*

CS	
DS	
SS	
ES	

Pathname	Pathname+filename

Version Info: •Applies to all versions of DOS beginning with 3.0
•Requires create access rights on network

Notes: •*Carry flag set if error occurs
•**Pathname, followed by backslash (\), followed by 14 bytes of 00H

Source: IBM DOS 3.3 Technical Reference, page 6-213

See Also: 2.34. File Attribute Byte
3.001. INT 21H Functions by DOS Version Summary
3.031. Function 16H -- Create File With FCB
3.062. Function 3CH -- Create File
3.105. Function 59H -- Get Extended Error
3.107. Function 5BH -- Create New File
3.128. Extended Error Codes Returned from Function 59H

3.107. FUNCTION 5BH -- CREATE NEW FILE

	Prior to Calling Function			*Upon Return From Function*	
	High	Low		High	Low
AX	5BH		AX	Handle or error code (if carry set)	
BX			BX		
CX	0	Attribute byte	CX		
DX	Offset of pointer to pathname		DX		
SP			SP		
BP			BP		
SI			SI		
DI			DI		
IP			IP		
flags			flags		Carry*
CS			CS		
DS	Segment of pointer to pathname		DS		
SS			SS		
ES			ES		

Version Info: •Applies to all versions of DOS beginning with 3.0
•Requires create access rights on networks

Notes: *Carry flag set if error occurs

Source: IBM DOS 3.3 Technical Reference, page 6-215

See Also: 2.34. File Attribute Byte
3.001. INT 21H Functions by DOS Version Summary
3.031. Function 16H -- Create File With FCB
3.062. Function 3CH -- Create File
3.105. Function 59H -- Get Extended Error
3.106. Function 5AH -- Create Temporary File
3.128. Extended Error Codes Returned from Function 59H

3.108. FUNCTION 5CH, 00H -- LOCK FILE

	Prior to Calling Function			*Upon Return From Function*	
	High	Low		High	Low
AX	5CH	0	AX	Error code (if carry set)	
BX	Handle		BX		
CX	High order of offset to region in file to lock		CX		
DX	Low order of offset to region in file to lock		DX		
SP			SP		
BP			BP		
SI	High order of length of region in file to lock		SI		
DI	Low order of length of region in file to lock		DI		
IP			IP		
flags			flags		Carry*
CS			CS		
DS			DS		
SS			SS		
ES			ES		

Version Info: Applies to all versions of DOS beginning with 3.0

Notes: •Should be used only if file was opened in deny read or deny none mode
•*Carry flag set if error occurs

Source: IBM DOS 3.3 Technical Reference, pages 6-216 to 6-218

See Also: 3.001. INT 21H Functions by DOS Version Summary
3.105. Function 59H -- Get Extended Error
3.128. Extended Error Codes Returned from Function 59H

3.109. FUNCTION 5CH, 01H -- UNLOCK FILE

Prior to Calling Function

	High	Low
AX	5CH	1
BX	Handle	
CX	High order of offset to region in file to unlock	
DX	Low order of offset to region in file to unlock	
SP		
BP		
SI	High order of length of region in file to unlock	
DI	Low order of length of region in file to unlock	
IP		
flags		
CS		
DS		
SS		
ES		

Upon Return From Function

	High	Low
AX	Error code (if carry set)	
BX		
CX		
DX		
SP		
BP		
SI		
DI		
IP		
flags		Carry*
CS		
DS		
SS		
ES		

Version Info: Applies to all versions of DOS beginning with 3.0

Notes: •Region must be same as one locked with function 5CH,0
•*Carry flag set if error occurs

Source: IBM DOS 3.3 Technical Reference, pages 6-216 to 6-218

See Also: 3.001. INT 21H Functions by DOS Version Summary
3.105. Function 59H -- Get Extended Error
3.108. Function 5CH,00H -- Lock File
3.128. Extended Error Codes Returned from Function 59H

3.110. FUNCTION 5EH, 00H -- GET MACHINE NAME

Prior to Calling Function

	High	Low
AX	5EH	0
BX		
CX		
DX	Offset of pointer to 16-byte buffer	
SP		
BP		
SI		
DI		
IP		
flags		
CS		
DS	Segment of pointer to 16-byte buffer	
SS		
ES		

Buffer | Empty |

Upon Return From Function

	High	Low
AX	Error code (if carry set)	
BX		
CX	Validity**	Netbios # for local
DX		
SP		
BP		
SI		
DI		
IP		
flags		Carry*
CS		
DS		
SS		
ES		

Buffer | Network name |

Version Info: Applies to all versions of DOS beginning with 3.1

Notes: •*Carry flag set if error occurs
•**0=invalid network device, 1=valid

Source: IBM DOS 3.3 Technical Reference, pages 6-219 to 6-220

See Also: 3.001. INT 21H Functions by DOS Version Summary
3.105. Function 59H -- Get Extended Error
3.128. Extended Error Codes Returned from Function 59H

3.111. FUNCTION 5EH, 02H -- SET PRINTER STRING

Prior to Calling Function

	High	Low
AX	5EH	2
BX	Assignment list index	
CX	Length of printer setup string	
DX		

SP	
BP	
SI	Offset of pointer to setup string
DI	

IP	
flags	

CS	
DS	Segment of pointer to setup string
SS	
ES	

String	Printer setup string

Upon Return From Function

	High	Low
AX	Error code (if carry set)	
BX		
CX		
DX		

SP	
BP	
SI	
DI	

IP	
flags	Carry*

CS	
DS	
SS	
ES	

Buffer	Unchanged string

Version Info: Applies to all versions of DOS beginning with 3.1

Notes:
•Printer setup string cannot be longer than 64 bytes
•*Carry flag set if error occurs

Source: IBM DOS 3.3 Technical Reference, pages 6-221 to 6-222

See Also:
3.001. INT 21H Functions by DOS Version Summary
3.105. Function 59H -- Get Extended Error
3.112. Function 5EH, 03H -- Get Printer String
3.128. Extended Error Codes Returned from Function 59H

3.112. FUNCTION 5EH, 03H -- GET PRINTER STRING

Prior to Calling Function

	High	Low
AX	5EH	3
BX	Assignment list index	
CX		
DX		

SP	
BP	
SI	
DI	Offset of pointer to 64-byte buffer

IP	
flags	

CS	
DS	
SS	
ES	Segment of pointer to 64-byte buffer

Buffer	Empty

Upon Return From Function

	High	Low
AX	Error code (if carry set)	
BX		
CX	Length of printer string	
DX		

SP	
BP	
SI	
DI	

IP	
flags	Carry*

CS	
DS	
SS	
ES	

Buffer	Setup string

Version Info: Applies to all versions of DOS beginning with 3.1

Notes: *Carry flag set if error occurs

Source: IBM DOS 3.3 Technical Reference, pages 6-223 to 6-224

See Also:
3.001. INT 21H Functions by DOS Version Summary
3.105. Function 59H -- Get Extended Error
3.111. Function 5EH,02H -- Set Printer String
3.128. Extended Error Codes Returned from Function 59H

3.113. FUNCTION 5FH, 02H -- GET ASSIGNMENT LIST ENTRY

Prior to Calling Function

	High	Low
AX	5FH	2
BX	Assignment list index	
CX		
DX		

SP	
BP	
SI	Offset of pointer to 16-byte local name buffer
DI	Offset of pointer to 128-byte remote name buffer

IP	
flags	

CS	
DS	Segment of pointer to 16-byte local name buffer
SS	
ES	Segment of pointer to 128-byte remote name buffer

16-byte buffer	Empty
128-byte buffer	Empty

Upon Return From Function

	High	Low
AX	Error code (if carry set)	
BX	Status***	Code** (if carry clear)
CX	Stored user value	
DX	Destroyed	Destroyed

SP		
BP	Destroyed	
SI		
DI		

IP		
flags		Carry*

CS	
DS	
SS	
ES	

16-byte buffer	Local name (ASCIIZ string)
128-byte buffer	Remote name (ASCIIZ string)

Version Info: Applies to all versions of DOS beginning with 3.1

Notes:
- •*Carry flag set if error occurs
- •**03=printer device; 04=drive device
- •***0=valid network device, 1=invalid device

Source: IBM DOS 3.3 Technical Reference, pages 6-225 to 6-226
MS-DOS 3.3 Programmer's Reference, pages 287, 289

See Also:
3.001. INT 21H Functions by DOS Version Summary
3.105. Function 59H -- Get Extended Error
3.110. Function 5EH,00H -- Get Machine Name
3.128. Extended Error Codes Returned from Function 59H

3.114. FUNCTION 5FH, 03H -- MAKE ASSIGNMENT LIST ENTRY

Prior to Calling Function   *Upon Return From Function*

	High	Low
AX	5FH	3
BX		Code**
CX	User value***	
DX		

SP	
BP	
SI	Offset of pointer to 16-byte source device name string
DI	Offset of pointer to 128-byte remote device name string

IP	
flags	

CS	
DS	Segment of pointer to 16-byte source device name string
SS	
ES	Segment of pointer to 128-byte remote device name string

	High	Low
AX	Error code (if carry set)	
BX		
CX		
DX		

SP	
BP	
SI	
DI	

IP	
flags	Carry*

CS	
DS	
SS	
ES	

Version Info:	Applies to all versions of DOS beginning with 3.1
Notes:	•Strings should be in ASCIIZ format •*Carry flag set if error occurs •**03=printer device; 04=drive device •***Should be zero to retain compatibility with IBM local area networks
Source:	IBM DOS 3.3 Technical Reference, pages 6-227 to 6-229
See Also:	3.001. INT 21H Functions by DOS Version Summary 3.105. Function 59H -- Get Extended Error 3.110. Function 5EH,00H -- Get Machine Name 3.128. Extended Error Codes Returned from Function 59H

3.115. FUNCTION 5FH, 04H -- CANCEL ASSIGNMENT LIST ENTRY

Prior to Calling Function

	High	Low
AX	5FH	4
BX		
CX		
DX		

SP	
BP	
SI	Offset of pointer to 16-byte source device name string
DI	

IP	
flags	

CS	
DS	Segment of pointer to 16-byte source device name string
SS	
ES	

Upon Return From Function

	High	Low
AX	Error code (if carry set)	
BX		
CX		
DX		

SP	
BP	
SI	
DI	

IP	
flags	Carry*

CS	
DS	
SS	
ES	

Version Info: Applies to all versions of DOS beginning with 3.1

Notes: •Strings should be ASCIIZ format
                      •*Carry flag set if error occurs

Source: IBM DOS 3.3 Technical Reference, pages 6-230 to 6-231

See Also: 3.001. INT 21H Functions by DOS Version Summary
                      3.105. Function 59H -- Get Extended Error
                      3.110. Function 5EH,00H -- Get Machine Name
                      3.128. Extended Error Codes Returned from Function 59H

3.116. FUNCTION 62H -- GET PROGRAM SEGMENT PREFIX

Prior to Calling Function

	High	Low
AX	62H	
BX		
CX		
DX		

SP	
BP	
SI	
DI	

IP	
flags	

CS	
DS	
SS	
ES	

Upon Return From Function

	High	Low
AX		
BX	Segment address of PSP for current process	
CX		
DX		

SP	
BP	
SI	
DI	

IP	
flags	

CS	
DS	
SS	
ES	

Version Info: Applies to all versions of DOS beginning with 3.0

Source: IBM DOS 3.3 Technical Reference, page 6-232

See Also: 3.001. INT 21H Functions by DOS Version Summary
                      3.136. Program Segment Prefix Layout

3.117. FUNCTION 63H -- GET LEAD BYTE TABLE

		Prior to Calling Function			*Upon Return From Function*	
	High	Low			High	Low
AX	63H	Function*		AX		
BX				BX		
CX				CX		
DX		Flag** (if AL=1)		DX		Flag (if AL=2)
SP				SP		
BP				BP		
SI				SI	Offset of pointer to lead byte table	
DI				DI		
IP				IP		
flags				flags		
CS				CS		
DS				DS	Segment of pointer to lead byte table	
SS				SS		
ES				ES		

Version Info: Function is available only in DOS 2.25

Notes: •*Function is one of:

0 = to get address of lead byte table
1 = to set or clear interim console flag
2 = to obtain interim console flag

•**Set/clear flag is one of:

0 = to clear interim console flag
1 = to set interim console flag

Source: *Advanced MS-DOS* (Microsoft Press), Ray Duncan, page 385

3.118. FUNCTION 65H -- GET EXTENDED COUNTRY INFO

		Prior to Calling Function			*Upon Return From Function*	
	High	Low			High	Low
AX	65H	Info wanted**		AX	Error code (if CF set)	
BX	Code page of interest (-1=CON)			BX		
CX	Number of bytes to return***			CX		
DX	Country code			DX		
SP				SP		
BP				BP		
SI				SI		
DI	Offset of pointer to country info table			DI		
IP				IP		
flags				flags		Carry*
CS				CS		
DS				DS		
SS				SS		
ES	Segment of pointer to country info table			ES		
Table	Empty			Table	Country info	

Version Info: Function is available only in DOS 3.3

Notes: •*Carry flag set if error occurs
•**Info wanted is one of:

1 = full country information table
2 = pointer to uppercase table
4 = pointer to filename uppercase table
6 = pointer to collating sequence

•***Must be at least 5

Source: IBM DOS 3.3 Technical Reference, pages 6-223 to 6-236

See Also: 3.057. Function 38H, 00H -- Get Country Data
3.058. Function 38H, xxH -- Set Country Data
3.143. Country Code Buffer Layout
3.144. Country Codes

3.119. FUNCTION 66H, 01H -- GET GLOBAL CODE PAGE

Prior to Calling Function

	High	Low
AX	66H	1
BX		
CX		
DX		

SP	
BP	
SI	
DI	

IP	
flags	

CS	
DS	
SS	
ES	

Upon Return From Function

	High	Low
AX	Error code (if carry set)	
BX	Active code page (set by user)	
CX		
DX	System code page (boot time)	

SP	
BP	
SI	
DI	

IP	
flags	Carry*

CS	
DS	
SS	
ES	

Version Info: Function is available only in DOS 3.3

Notes: *Carry flag set if error occurs

Source: IBM DOS 3.3 Technical Reference, pages 6-237 to 6-238

See Also: 3.120. Function 66H, 02H -- Set Global Code Page

3.120. FUNCTION 66H, 02H -- SET GLOBAL CODE PAGE

Prior to Calling Function

	High	Low
AX	66H	2
BX		
CX		
DX		

SP	
BP	
SI	
DI	

IP	
flags	

CS	
DS	
SS	
ES	

Upon Return From Function

	High	Low
AX	Error code (if carry set)	
BX		
CX		
DX		

SP	
BP	
SI	
DI	

IP	
flags	Carry*

CS	
DS	
SS	
ES	

Version Info: Function is available only in DOS 3.3

Notes: *Carry flag set if error occurs

Source: IBM DOS 3.3 Technical Reference, pages 6-237 to 6-238

See Also: 3.119. Function 66H, 01H -- Get Global Code Page

3.121. FUNCTION 67H -- SET HANDLE COUNT

Prior to Calling Function

	High	Low
AX	67H	
BX	Number of open handles allowed	
CX		
DX		

SP	
BP	
SI	
DI	

IP	
flags	

CS	
DS	
SS	
ES	

Upon Return From Function

	High	Low
AX	Error code (if carry set)	
BX		
CX		
DX		

SP	
BP	
SI	
DI	

IP	
flags	Carry*

CS	
DS	
SS	
ES	

Version Info: Function is available only in DOS 3.3

Notes: •Maximum is actually controlled by CONFIG.SYS FILES= setting
•You must release memory to DOS for the extended handle list
•*Carry flag set if error occurs

Source: IBM DOS 3.3 Technical Reference, page 6-239

See Also: 2.27. CONFIG.SYS Commands and Default Settings

3.122. FUNCTION 68H -- COMMIT FILE

Prior to Calling Function

	High	Low
AX	68H	
BX		
CX		
DX		

SP	
BP	
SI	
DI	

IP	
FLAGS	

CS	
DS	
SS	
ES	

Upon Return From Function

	High	Low
AX		
BX	File handle committed to disk	
CX		
DX		

SP	
BP	
SI	
DI	

IP	
FLAGS	Carry*

CS	
DS	
SS	
ES	

Version Info: Function is available only in DOS 3.3

Notes: *Carry flag set if error occurs

Source: IBM DOS 3.3 Technical Reference, page 6-240

3.123. UNOPENED FCB FORMAT

Offset	Length	Name	Contents
0 (0)	byte	Drive number	Logical drive number; 0=default, 1=A, 2=B, and so on
1 (1)	8 bytes	File name	ASCII characters, padded with spaces, if necessary
9 (9)	3 bytes	File type	ASCII characters, padded with spaces, if necessary
C (12)	25 bytes	RESERVED	(must be filled with zeros)

Source: IBM DOS 3.3 Technical Reference, pages 7-12 to 7-15

See Also: 3.003. INT 21H FCB-oriented Functions Summary
3.124. Opened FCB Format
3.125. Extended FCB Format
3.126. Rename FCB Format
3.137. Logical Drive Numbers

3.124. OPENED FCB FORMAT

Offset	Length	Name	Contents
0 (0)	byte	Drive number	Physical drive number; 0=A, 1=B, and so on
1 (1)	8 bytes	File name	ASCII characters, padded with spaces, if necessary
9 (9)	3 bytes	File type	ASCII characters, padded with spaces, if necessary
C (12)	word	Current block	Binary value indicating current block (set to 0 on File Open)
E (14)	word	Record size	Number of bytes per record (default=128)
10 (16)	dbl word	File size	Binary value indicating size of file, in bytes
14 (20)	word	File date	Packed word containing file last update date
16 (22)	word	File time	Packed word containing file last update time
18 (24)	8 bytes	RESERVED	Used internally by DOS
20 (32)	byte	Current record	Binary value indicating current record (set to 0 on File Open)
21 (33)	dbl word	Random record number	Binary value indicating next random block to read/write

Notes: In the PSP, an extended FCB starts 7 bytes prior to 5CH.
In your program (outside the PSP), your FCB pointer
probably points directly to the FFH byte of an extended FCB,
or to the drive number byte of a normal FCB. Thus, to insure
that you address items in an FCB correctly, you must first
know if it is extended or not (See 3.125. Extended FCB Format)

Source: IBM DOS 3.3 Technical Reference, pages 7-12 to 7-15

See Also: 3.003. INT 21H FCB-oriented Functions Summary
3.123. Unopened FCB Format
3.125. Extended FCB Format
3.126. Rename FCB Format

3.125. EXTENDED FCB FORMAT

Offset	Length	Name	Contents
0 (0)	byte	Extended FCB indicator	Always FF (255)
1 (1)	5 bytes	RESERVED	
6 (6)	byte	Attribute byte	See 2.34. File Attribute Byte
7 (7)	byte	Drive number	0=A,1=B, and so on
8 (8)	8 bytes	File name	ASCII characters, padded with spaces, if necessary
10 (16)	3 bytes	File type	ASCII characters, padded with spaces, if necessary
13 (19)	word	Current block	Binary value indicating current block (set to 0 on File Open)
15 (21)	word	Record size	Number of bytes per record; default=80 (128)
17 (23)	dbl word	File size	Binary value indicating size of file, in bytes
1B (27)	word	File date	Packed word containing file last update date
1D (29)	word	File time	Packed word containing file last update time
1F (31)	8 bytes	RESERVED	Used internally by DOS
27 (39)	byte	Current record	Binary value indicating current record (set to 0 on File Open)
28 (40)	dbl word	Random record number	Binary value indicating next random block to read/write

Notes: •A value other than FFH in the first byte of an FCB indicates it is not an Extended FCB
(See 3.124. Opened FCB Format)
•Values are in hexadecimal (decimal in parentheses)

Source: IBM DOS 3.3 Technical Reference, page 7-16

See Also: 2.34. File Attribute Byte
3.003. INT 21H FCB-oriented Functions Summary
3.123. Unopened FCB Format
3.124. Opened FCB Format
3.126. Rename FCB Format

3.126. RENAME FCB FORMAT

Offset	Length	Name	Contents
0 (0)	byte	Drive number	Logical drive number; 0=default, 1=A, 2=B, and so on
1 (1)	8 bytes	Original file name	ASCII characters, padded with spaces, if necessary
9 (9)	3 bytes	Original file type	ASCII characters, padded with spaces, if necessary
C (12)	5 bytes	RESERVED	
11 (17)	8 bytes	New file name	ASCII characters, padded with spaces, if necessary
19 (25)	3 bytes	New file type	ASCII characters, padded with spaces, if necessary
1C (28)	9 bytes	RESERVED	Set to zeros

Notes: Both file name and type fields may contain the DOS wildcard character ?
(match any character)

Source: IBM DOS 3.3 Technical Reference, page 6-79

See Also: 3.003. INT 21H FCB-oriented Functions Summary
3.123. Unopened FCB Format
3.124. Opened FCB Format
3.125. Extended FCB Format
3.137. Logical Drive Numbers

3.127. FCB ERROR CODES

For Read functions (14H, 21H, and 27H):

Code in AL	Meaning After Read
0	Read operation was completed successfully
1	Read attempted at end of file; no data was transferred
2	Not enough room in the DTA for record(s); read canceled
3	Read encountered end of file; partial record read, remainder padded with 0's

For Write functions (15H, 22H, and 28H):

Code in AL	Meaning After Write
0	Write operation was completed successfully
1	Disk full; write canceled
2	DTA does not contain enough data to write record(s); write canceled

Source: MS-DOS 3.2 Programmer's Reference, pages 1-75 to 1-103

See Also: 3.003. INT 21H FCB-oriented Functions Summary
3.029. Function 14H -- Sequential Read With FCB
3.030. Function 15H -- Sequential Write With FCB
3.037. Function 21H -- Random Read With FCB
3.038. Function 22H -- Random Write With FCB
3.043. Function 27H -- Random Block Read With FCB
3.044. Function 28H -- Random Block Write With FCB

3.128. EXTENDED ERROR CODES RETURNED FROM FUNCTION 59H

Error Class:

Value in BH	Description of Class	Example
1 (1)	Out of a resource	Storage or channels
2 (2)	Temporary situation	Locked region of file
3 (3)	Authorization problem	User doesn't have access rights
4 (4)	Internal error in system software	
5 (5)	Hardware failure	
6 (6)	System software failure	Missing configuration file
7 (7)	Application program failure	
8 (8)	Item not found	File couldn't be found
9 (9)	Invalid format or type	File in wrong format
A (10)	Interlocked item	File is interlocked
B (11)	Media problem	Wrong disk, bad spot on disk
C (12)	Already exists	Declared machine name that exists
D (13)	Unknown	

Suggested Action:

Value in BL	Description of Suggested Action
1 (1)	Retry, then prompt user
2 (2)	Retry after a brief pause
3 (3)	If user entered item, prompt for it again
4 (4)	Terminate after closing files
5 (5)	Terminate immediately; don't close files
6 (6)	No action; error was informational only
7 (7)	Prompt the user to perform an action (e.g., change disk)

Location:

Value in CH	Probable Location of Error	Example
1	Unknown to DOS	
2	Random access device	Disk drive
3	Network	Network software, hardware
4	Character device	Printer, communications
5	Memory	RAM

Error Code:

Value in AX	Description
1 (1)	Invalid function code
2 (2)	File not found
3 (3)	Path not found
4 (4)	Too many open files
5 (5)	Access denied
6 (6)	Invalid handle
7 (7)	Memory control blocks destroyed
8 (8)	Insufficient memory
9 (9)	Invalid memory block address
A (10)	Invalid environment
B (11)	Invalid format
C (12)	Invalid access code
D (13)	Invalid data
E (14)	NOT USED
F (15)	Invalid drive
10 (16)	Attempt to remove the current directory
11 (17)	Not same device
12 (18)	No more files
13 (19)	Disk is write-protected
14 (20)	Bad disk unit
15 (21)	Drive not ready
16 (22)	Invalid disk command
17 (23)	CRC error
18 (24)	Invalid length in disk operation
19 (25)	Seek error
1A (26)	Not a DOS disk
1B (27)	Sector not found
1C (28)	Out of paper
1D (29)	Write fault
1E (30)	Read fault
1F (31)	General failure
20 (32)	Sharing violation
21 (33)	Lock violation
22 (34)	Wrong disk

(Continued)

Table 3.128. Continued

Error Code:

Value in AX	Description
23 (35)	FCB unavailable
24 (36)	Sharing buffer overflow
25 (37)	RESERVED
26 (38)	RESERVED
27 (39)	RESERVED
28 (40)	RESERVED
29 (41)	RESERVED
3A (42)	RESERVED
3B (43)	RESERVED
3C (44)	RESERVED
3D (45)	RESERVED
3E (46)	RESERVED
3F (47)	RESERVED
40 (48)	RESERVED
41 (49)	RESERVED
42 (50)	Network request not supported
43 (51)	Remote computer not listening
44 (52)	Duplicate name on network
45 (53)	Network path not found
46 (54)	Network busy
47 (55)	Network device no longer exists
48 (56)	Net BIOS command limit exceeded
49 (57)	Network adapter hardware error
4A (58)	Incorrect response from network
4B (59)	Unexpected network error
4C (60)	Incompatible remote adapter
4D (61)	Print queue full
4E (62)	Not enough space for print file
4F (63)	Print file was canceled
50 (64)	Network name was deleted
51 (65)	Access denied
52 (66)	Network device type incorrect
53 (67)	Network name not found
54 (68)	Network name limit exceeded
55 (69)	Net BIOS session limit exceeded
56 (70)	Temporarily paused
57 (71)	Network request not accepted
58 (72)	Print or disk redirection is paused
59 (73)	RESERVED
5A (74)	RESERVED
5B (75)	RESERVED
5C (76)	RESERVED
5D (77)	RESERVED
5E (78)	RESERVED
5F (79)	RESERVED
60 (80)	File exists
61 (81)	NOT USED
62 (82)	Cannot make
63 (83)	Interrupt 24H failure
64 (84)	Out of structures
65 (85)	Already assigned
66 (86)	Invalid password
67 (87)	Invalid parameter
68 (88)	Net write fault

Version Info: •Error codes apply to all versions of DOS beginning with 2.0
•Error class, action, and location apply to all versions of DOS beginning with 3.0

Source: IBM DOS 3.3 Technical Reference, pages 6-40 to 6-46

See Also: 3.105. Function 59H -- Get Extended Error
3.127. FCB Error Codes

3.129. HANDLE ACCESS BYTE

Bit Numbers

7	6	5	4	3	2	1	0	Use
X								Inherit bit
	X	X	X					Sharing mode code
				X				Reserved; set to 0
					X	X	X	Access code

7	6	5	4	3	2	1	0	Allowable Values	Meaning
X								0=child inherits	If a child process is spawned, this file will be inherited
								1=child doesn't inherit	If a child process is spawned, it will not inherit this file
	X	X	X					000=compatibility mode	Fails if file has been opened in any of the other sharing modes
								001=deny read/write mode	Fails if file has been opened in any but deny none sharing mode
								010=deny write mode	Fails if file has been opened in compatibility or write sharing mode
								011=deny read mode	Fails if file has been opened in compatibility or read sharing mode
								100=deny none mode	Fails only if file has been opened in compatibility sharing mode
			X	X	X	X		0000=read access allowed	Fails if file has been opened in deny read or deny both sharing mode
								0001=write access allowed	Fails if file has been opened in deny write or deny both sharing mode
								0010=read/write access	Fails if file has been opened in deny read, write, or both sharing mode

Version Info: •Applies to all versions of DOS beginning with 2.0
•Fully implemented beginning with DOS 3.1. Normally access byte for all non-network workstations would be 02H (inherit, compatibility, read/write).

Source: IBM DOS 3.3 Technical Reference, pages 6-127 to 6-135

See Also: 3.063. Function 3DH -- Open File

3.130. PREDEFINED HANDLES

Handle Number	Device Assignment	Default Device
0	Standard input	Keyboard
1	Standard output	Display
2	Standard error	Display
3	Auxiliary device	COM1:
4	Printer output	LPT1:

Version Info: Applies to all versions of DOS beginning with 2.0

Notes: •The auxiliary device handle assumes that the proper parameters have been assigned to COM1: prior to start of communication
•Preopened handles may be redirected to devices other than the default by using DOS INT 21H functions 45H and 46H

Source: IBM DOS 3.3 Technical Reference, pages 4-8 to 4-9

See Also: 3.148. Reserved Device Names and Chain Order

3.131. HANDLE POINTER MOVEMENT METHODS

Value	Starting Location	Pointer is Moved To
0	From beginning	Offset bytes (in CX:DX) from beginning of the file
1	From current pointer	Offset bytes (in CX:DX) from current location
2	From end of file	Offset bytes (in CX:DX) from end of file

Version Info: Applies to all versions of DOS beginning with 2.0

Notes: CX:DX is considered a signed 32-bit integer, allowing offset values from -2,147,483,648 to 2,147,483,647

Source: IBM DOS 3.3 Technical Reference, page 6-144

See Also: 3.068. Function 42H -- Move File Pointer

3.132. SEARCH FIRST/NEXT DATA BLOCKS

Offset	Length	Name	Description
0 (0)	21 bytes	RESERVED	Used by subsequent Search Next Functions
15 (21)	byte	Attribute byte	See 2.34. File Attribute Byte
16 (22)	word	File last update time	See 2.35. Date/Time Formats
18 (24)	word	File last update date	See 2.35. Date/Time Formats
1A (26)	word	Low word of file size	
1C (28)	word	High word of file size	
1E (30)	13-byte ASCIIZ string	Full file name and type*	

Version Info: Applies to all versions of DOS beginning with 2.0

Notes: •Data block is stored in DTA
•*Filename string includes a period if a file type is present

Source: IBM DOS 3.3 Technical Reference, page 6-203

See Also: 3.097. Function 4EH -- Find First File
3.098. Function 4FH -- Find Next File

3.133. DEVICE DATA WORD

For Devices (Bit 7=1):

Bit Number

15	14	13	12	11	10	9	8	7	6	5	4	3	2	1	0	Function	Allowable Values
X			X		X	X	X				X					RESERVED*	
	X															Process control strings**	0=cannot process control strings / 1=can process control strings
		X														Output until busy**	0=no support for output until busy / 1=supports output until busy
				X												Understand open/close**	0=doesn't understand open/close / 1=understands open/close
								X								Device Type	1=device
									X							End of File	0=end of file on input / 1=not at end of file
										X						Control Char Check	0=check for control characters / 1=don't check for control chars
												X				Clock Device	0=is not clock device / 1=is a clock device
													X			Null Device	0=is not a null device / 1=is a null device
														X		Console Output Device	0=is not console output device / 1=is console output device
															X	Console Input Device	0=is not console input device / 1=is console input device

For Files (bit 7=0):

Bit Number

15	14	13	12	11	10	9	8	7	6	5	4	3	2	1	0	Function	Allowable Values
X	X	X	X	X	X	X	X									RESERVED	
								X								Device type	0=file
									X							File has been written	0=file has been written / 1=file has not been written
										X	X	X	X	X	X	Drive number	000000=A / 000001=B / and so on

Version Info: Applies to all versions of DOS beginning with 2.0

Notes: •Bit 14 may be read only; it cannot be set
•*RESERVED bits should be set to 0 when setting device data
•**DH must be 0, see page 6-147 of source

Source: IBM DOS 3.3 Technical Reference, pages 6-149 to 6-150

See Also: 3.071. Function 44H, 00H -- Get IOCTL Data
3.072. Function 44H, 01H -- Set IOCTL Data

3.134. BLOCK DEVICE FUNCTION CODES

Code	Function
40 (64)	Set device parameters
41 (65)	Write track on logical device
42 (66)	Format track on logical device
60 (96)	Get device parameters
61 (97)	Read track on logical device
62 (98)	Verify track on logical device

Version Info: Applies to all versions of DOS beginning with 3.0

Source: IBM DOS 3.3 Technical Reference, page 6-168

See Also: 3.084. Function 44H, 0DH -- Generic IOCTL For Devices

3.135. DEVICE PARAMETER BLOCKS

For Set Device (CL=40H):

Bit Numbers

Offset	Length	Name	7	6	5	4	3	2	1	0	Allowable Settings
0 (0)	byte	Special functions	X	X	X	X	X				Must be set to 0
								X			0=sectors different sizes
											1=sectors same size
									X		0=read all fields
											1=read only track layout field
										X	0=build new BPB
											1=use device BPB
1 (1)	byte	Device type	0	0	0	0	0	1	1	1	7=other device
			0	0	0	0	0	1	1	0	6=tape drive
			0	0	0	0	0	1	0	1	5=hard disk
			0	0	0	0	0	1	0	0	4=8" double density floppy
			0	0	0	0	0	0	1	1	3=8" single density floppy
			0	0	0	0	0	0	1	0	2=720K microfloppy
			0	0	0	0	0	0	0	1	1=1.2MB floppy
			0	0	0	0	0	0	0	0	0=320/360K floppy
2 (2)	word	Device attributes	X	X	X	X	X	X			Must be set to 0, RESERVED
									X		0=disk changeline not supported
											1=disk changeline supported
										X	0=media is removable
											1=media not removable
4 (4)	word	Number cylinders									Maximum # cylinders device supports
6 (6)	byte	Media type								X	0=1.2MB quad density
											1=320/360K dbl density
7 (7)	varies	Device BPB									See 3.167. Device BPB
varies	varies	Track layout									Word total # of sectors
											Word sector 1 sector #
											Word sector 1 sector size
											Word sector 2 sector #
											Word sector 2 sector size
											... and so on, up to...
											Word sector n sector #
											Word sector n sector size

For Get Device (CL=60H):

Bit Numbers

Offset	Length	Name	7	6	5	4	3	2	1	0	Allowable Settings
0 (0)	byte	Special functions	X	X	X	X	X	X	X		Must be set to 0
										X	0=return default BPB
											1=return BUILD BPB
1 (1)	byte	Device type	0	0	0	0	0	1	1	1	7=other device
			0	0	0	0	0	1	1	0	6=tape drive
			0	0	0	0	0	1	0	1	5=hard disk
			0	0	0	0	0	1	0	0	4=8" double density floppy
			0	0	0	0	0	0	1	1	3=8" single density floppy
			0	0	0	0	0	0	1	0	2=720K microfloppy
			0	0	0	0	0	0	0	1	1=1.2MB floppy
			0	0	0	0	0	0	0	0	0=320/360K floppy
2 (2)	word	Device attributes	X	X	X	X	X	X			Must be set to 0
									X		0=disk changeline not supported
											1=disk changeline supported
										X	0=media is removable
											1=media not removable
4 (4)	word	Number cylinders									Maximum # cylinders device supports
6 (6)	byte	Media type								X	0=1.2MB quad density
											1=320/360K dbl density
7 (7)	varies	Device BPB									See 3.167. Device BPB

For Read/Write Track (CL=61/41H):

Bit Numbers

Offset	Length	Name	7	6	5	4	3	2	1	0	Allowable Settings
0 (0)	byte	Special functions	X	X	X	X	X	X	X	X	Must be set to 0
1 (1)	word	Head									Head number to read/write
3 (3)	word	Cylinder									Cylinder number to read/write
5 (5)	word	First sector									First sector # to read/write
7 (7)	word	Number of sectors									Total # of sectors

(Continued)

Table 3.135. Continued

For Read/Write Track (CL=61/41H):

Offset	Length	Name	7	6	5	4	3	2	1	0	Allowable Settings
			Bit Numbers									
9 (9)	dbl word	Transfer address									Segment:Offset of transfer buffer

For Format/Verify Track (CL=42/62H):

Offset	Length	Name	7	6	5	4	3	2	1	0	Allowable Settings
			Bit Numbers									
0 (0)	byte	Special functions									
1 (1)	word	Head									Head number to format/verify
3 (3)	word	Cylinder									Cylinder number to format/verify

Version Info: Applies to all versions of DOS beginning with 2.0

Source: IBM DOS 3.3 Technical Reference, pages 6-169 to 6-180

See Also: 3.084. Function 44H, 0DH -- Generic IOCTL For Devices
3.134. Block Device Function Codes
3.167. Device BPB Layout

3.136. PROGRAM SEGMENT PREFIX LAYOUT

Offset	Length	Usual Contents	Description	Comments
0 (0)	word	CD20H	Int 20H termination address	
2 (2)	word		End of memory allocation block	Is a segment address
4 (4)	byte	00H	RESERVED	
5 (5)	5 bytes		CALL FAR to DOS function dispatcher	Obsolete
A (10)	dbl word		Int 22H terminate handler address	Restored at exit of program; stored as IP:CS
E (14)	dbl word		Int 23H Ctrl-Break handler address	Stored as IP:CS
12 (18)	dbl word		Int 24H Critical Error handler address	Stored as IP:CS
16 (22)	word		Parent process's PSP	Is a segment address
18 (24)	20 bytes	FF=available	Handle table	One byte per handle, bit 7=not inherited
2C (44)	word		Environment block address	Is a segment address
2E (46)	dbl word		RESERVED	
32 (50)	word	14H,00H	Handle table size	DOS 3.3 allows larger tables
34 (52)	dbl word	12H,00H	Handle table address (if not at 12H)	DOS 3.3 allows table address
38 (56)	23 bytes		RESERVED	
50 (80)	word	CD21H	Int 21H DOS CALL	
52 (82)	byte	CBH	RET FAR	
53 (83)	9 bytes		RESERVED	
5C (92)	36 bytes		Default unopened file control block #1	
6C (108)	20 bytes		Default unopened file control block #2	Overlays FCB #1
80 (128)	byte		Length of command line parameters	Also start of default DTA
81 (129)	127 bytes		Command line parameters	Starts with blank, ends with a CR

Notes: FCB's only useful information is drive number and filename

Sources: IBM DOS 3.3 Technical Reference, pages 7-10 to 7-11

See Also: 3.002. INT 21H Keyboard Functions Summary
3.006. INT 21H System Functions Summary
3.042. Function 26H -- Create New Program Segment
3.116. Function 62H -- Get Program Segment Prefix
3.123. Unopened FCB Format

3.137. LOGICAL DRIVE NUMBERS

In FCBs, Functions 1CH, 36H,
some 44H subfunctions, and 47H:

Value	Drive
0 (0)	Default
1 (1)	A
2 (2)	B
3 (3)	C
4 (4)	D
5 (5)	E
6 (6)	F
7 (7)	G
8 (8)	H
9 (9)	I
A (10)	J
B (11)	K
C (12)	L
D (13)	M
E (14)	N
F (15)	O
10 (16)	P
11 (17)	Q
12 (18)	R
13 (19)	S
14 (20)	T
15 (21)	U
16 (22)	V
17 (23)	W
18 (24)	X
19 (25)	Y
1A (26)	Z

In Functions 0EH and 19H:

Value	Drive
0 (0)	A
1 (1)	B
2 (2)	C
3 (3)	D
4 (4)	E
5 (5)	F
6 (6)	G
7 (7)	H
8 (8)	I
9 (9)	J
A (10)	K
B (11)	L
C (12)	M
D (13)	N
E (14)	O
F (15)	P
10 (16)	Q
11 (17)	R
12 (18)	S
13 (19)	T
14 (20)	U
15 (21)	V
16 (22)	W
17 (23)	X
18 (24)	Y
19 (25)	Z

Source: IBM DOS 3.3 Technical Reference,
page 6-66

See Also: 3.124. Opened FCB Format

3.138. EXECUTE PROGRAM PARAMETER BLOCK

Offset	Length	Name	Function
0 (0)	word	Environment address	Segment address of environment to be passed, or 00H to use parent process's environment
2 (2)	dbl word*	Command line	Segment:Offset address of a command line to be placed at 80H in child process's PSP
6 (6)	dbl word*	First FCB	Segment:Offset address of a FCB to be placed at 5CH of child process's PSP
A (10)	dbl word*	Second FCB	Segment:Offset address of a second FCB to be placed at 6CH of child process's PSP

Version Info: Applies to all versions of DOS beginning with 2.0

Notes: *dbl words are in Offset:Segment format (i.e., least significant word first)

Source: IBM DOS 3.3 Technical Reference, page 6-197

See Also: 3.093. Function 4BH, 00H -- Load and Execute Program
3.136. Program Segment Prefix Layout
3.141. Environment Blocks

3.139. OVERLAY PROGRAM PARAMETER BLOCK

Offset	Length	Name	Function
0 (0)	word	Load address	Segment address where overlay is to be loaded
2 (2)	word	Relocation factor	Segment offset where overlay is to be loaded (normally same as load address, but may be increased to overlay only higher portion of a program)

Version Info: Applies to all versions of DOS beginning with 2.0

Source: IBM DOS 3.3 Technical Reference, page 6-197

See Also: 3.094. Function 4BH, 03H -- Load Overlay
                      3.138. Execute Program Parameter Block

3.140. MEMORY ALLOCATION STRATEGIES

Value	Name	Description
0	First fit	Search beginning at lowest available memory and allocate first block large enough to accommodate request (default)
1	Best fit	Search all blocks and allocate smallest block that accommodates request
2	Last fit	Search beginning at highest available memory and allocate first block large enough to accommodate request

Version Info: Applies to all versions of DOS beginning with 3.0

Source: MS-DOS Programmer's Reference Version 3.3, page 262
                      Missing from the IBM DOS 3.3 Technical Reference!

See Also: 3.090. Function 48H -- Allocate Memory
                      3.091. Function 49H -- Free Allocated Memory
                      3.092. Function 4AH -- Set Block
                      3.103. Function 58H, 00H -- Get Allocation Strategy
                      3.104. Function 58H, 01H -- Set Allocation Strategy

3.141. ENVIRONMENT BLOCKS

Offset	Length	Name	Allowable Settings
0 (0)	varies	Environment string 1	ASCII string in form: PARAMETER=VALUE
varies	byte	String terminator	Must be a 0
varies	varies	Environment string 2	ASCII string in form: PARAMETER=VALUE
varies	byte	String terminator	Must be a 0

          and so on, until last string:

varies	varies	Environment string n	ASCII string in form: PARAMETER=VALUE
varies	byte	String terminator	Must be a 0
varies	byte	String terminator	Must be a 0
varies	word	Count	Number of other ASCIIZ strings following
varies	varies	Initial argument string	ASCIIZ path and file name of current process

Version Info: Applies to all versions of DOS beginning with 2.0

Notes: An environment may have no environment strings, in which case the first two
                      bytes are 00,00

Source: IBM DOS 3.3 Technical Reference, pages 6-198 to 2-199

3.142. PARSE CONTROL BYTE

Bit Position

7	6	5	4	3	2	1	0	Function	Allowable Settings
							X	Separator control	0=stop parsing if separator is encountered
									1=ignore leading file separators
						X		Drive # control	0=set FCB drive number to 0 if no drive in string
									1=leave FCB drive number unchanged if no drive in string
					X			File name control	0=set FCB filename to blanks if no name in string
									1=leave FCB filename unchanged if no file name in string
				X				Extension control	0=set FCB filetype to blanks if no type in string
									1=leave FCB filetype unchanged if no type in string
X	X	X	X					UNUSED	Must be 0

Notes: Filename separators are : . ; , = + / " [ ] \ < > | SPACE TAB

Source: IBM DOS 3.3 Technical Reference, pages 6-96 to 6-97

See Also: 2.51. File Separator Characters
3.045. Function 29H -- Parse File Name

3.143. COUNTRY CODE BUFFER LAYOUT

Offset	Length	Name	Contents	USA Value
0 (0)	word	Date format	0 = American (mm/dd/yy)	0
			1 = European (dd/mm/yy)	
			2 = Japanese (yy/mm/dd)	
2 (2)	5 byte	Currency symbol	ASCIIZ String	$
7 (7)	2 byte	Thousands separator	ASCIIZ String	,
9 (9)	2 byte	Decimal separator	ASCIIZ String	.
B (11)	2 byte	Date separator*	ASCIIZ String	/
D (13)	2 byte	Time separator*	ASCIIZ String	:
F (15)	byte	Currency Code*	0 = currency symbol before amount, no spaces between	0
			1 = currency symbol after amount, no spaces between	
			2 = currency symbol before amount, one space between	
			3 = currency symbol after amount, one space between	
			4 = currency symbol replaces decimal separator	
10 (16)	byte	Currency places*	Binary value	2
11 (17)	byte	Time format*	0 = 12-hour clock	1
			1 = 24-hour clock	
12 (18)	dbl word	Case-Map call address*	Segment:offset address of FAR procedure that performs lowercase to uppercase mapping on characters from 80H to FFH.	NA
16 (22)	2 bytes	Datalist separator*	ASCIIZ String	NA
18 (24)	10 bytes	RESERVED		NA

Version Info: •Applies to all versions of DOS beginning with 2.0
•*DOS 3.x only

Source: IBM DOS 3.3 Technical Reference, page 6-115

See Also: 3.057. Function 38, 00H -- Get Country Data
3.144. Country Codes

3.144. COUNTRY CODES

Numerical Order

Code	Country	Keyboard Code
001	United States	US
002	Canada (French)	CF
002	Canada (English)	US
003	Latin America	LA
031	Netherlands	NL
032	Belgium	BE
033	France	FR
034	Spain	SP
039	Italy	IT
041	Switzerland (French)	SF
041	Switzerland (German)	SG
044	Great Britain	UK
045	Denmark	DK
046	Sweden	SV
047	Norway	NO
049	West Germany	GR
061	Australia	US
351	Portugal	PO
358	Finland	SU
785	Middle East (Arabic)	-
972	Israel (Hebrew)	-

Alphabetic Order (by Country)

Code	Country	Keyboard Code
061	Australia	US
032	Belgium	BE
002	Canada (English)	US
002	Canada (French)	CF
045	Denmark	DK
358	Finland	SU
033	France	FR
044	Great Britain	UK
972	Israel (Hebrew)	-
039	Italy	IT
003	Latin America	LA
785	Middle East (Arabic)	-
031	Netherlands	NL
047	Norway	NO
351	Portugal	PO
034	Spain	SP
046	Sweden	SV
041	Switzerland (French)	SF
041	Switzerland (German)	SG
001	United States	US
049	West Germany	GR

Version Info: Applies to all version of DOS beginning with 2.0

Notes: Country codes are usually the international telephone prefix number for the country

Source: IBM DOS 3.3 Reference, page B-2

See Also: 3.143. Country Code Buffer Layout

3.145. DOS MEMORY CONTROL BLOCKS

Offset	Length	Name	Contents
0	byte	Location	4DH (M) if not last block; 5AH (Z) if last block
1	word	Process ID	PSP segment address
3	word	Allocation amount	Number of paragraphs allocated
5	11 bytes	RESERVED	RESERVED

Version Info: Applies to all version of DOS beginning with 2.0

Notes: Memory control block and memory controlled are adjacent in memory

Source: *Advanced MS-DOS* (Microsoft Press), Ray Duncan, page 179

See Also: 3.092. Function 4AH -- Set Block

3.146. CODE PAGE PARAMETER BLOCKS

When CL=4AH, 4DH, or 6BH

Offset	Length	Name	Contents
0	word	Packet length	Must be 2, the length of the packet
2	word	Packet ID	Code page ID

When CL=4CH

Offset	Length	Name	Contents
0	word	Packet flags	0
2	word	Packet length	Number of bytes in remainder of packet
4	word	Number pages	Number of code pages in following list
6	word	Code page 1	
8	word	Code page 2	

and so on, until:

varies	word	Code page n	

When CL=6AH

Offset	Length	Name	Contents
0	word	Packet length	((n+1)+(m+1))*2
2	word	Hrdw # pages	n
4	word	Hrdw page 1	
6	word	Hrdw page 2	

and so on, until:

varies	word	Hrdw page n	
varies	word	Prepd # pages	m
varies	word	Prepd page 1	
varies	word	Prepd page 2	

and so on, until:

varies	word	Prepd page m	

Version Info: Applies only to DOS 3.3

Source: IBM DOS 3.3 Technical Reference, pages 6-160 to 6-162

See Also: 3.120. Function 66H, 02H -- Set Global Code Page

3.147. CODE PAGE ASSIGNMENTS

Code Pages

Code Page	Language
437	USA English
850	multilingual
860	Portuguese
863	Canadian French
865	Norwegian and Danish

Use Code Page	Country	Prev Code Page	Keyboard Code
850	Australia	437	US
850	Belgium	437	BE
850	Canada (English)	437	US
850	Canada (French)	863	CF
850	Denmark	865	DK
850	Finland	437	SU
850	France	437	FR
850	Germany	437	GR
850	Italy	437	IT
850	Latin America	437	LA
850	Netherlands	437	NL
850	Norway	865	NO
850	Portugal	860	PO
850	Spain	437	SP
850	Sweden	437	SV
850	Switzerland (French)	437	SF
850	Switzerland (German)	437	SG
850	United Kingdom	437	UK
850	United States	437	US

Version Info: Applies to DOS 3.3 only

Source: IBM DOS 3.3 Reference, pages 9-5 to 9-7

See Also: 3.120. Function 66H, 02H -- Set Global Code Page

3.148. RESERVED DEVICE NAMES AND CHAIN ORDER

Name	Description
NUL	Null device
---	Drivers established in CONFIG.SYS, in order encountered
CON	Console keyboard and display
AUX	Auxiliary device (COM1:)
PRN	Printer device (LPT1:)
CLOCK	Timer device (system clock 18.2 ticks/second)

Version Info: Applies to all versions of DOS beginning with 2.0

Notes: •You may substitute your own device drivers for CON, AUX,
PRN, and CLOCK (by redirecting their handles), but you
may not redirect NUL
•Devices are "chained" in the order presented in the above
table (i.e., NUL is the first entry in the device chain, the
CONFIG.SYS drivers are next, and so on)

Source: *Advanced MS-DOS* (Microsoft Press), Ray Duncan, page 254

See Also: 3.130. Predefined Handles

3.149. DEVICE DRIVER HEADERS

Offset	Length	Name	Function
0 (0)	dbl word	Next device pointer	Offset:segment* address of next device in file, or FFFF FFFFH if last driver
4 (4)	word	Device attribute code	See 3.150. Device Attribute Codes
6 (6)	word	Device strategy pointer	Offset address to device strategy routine
8 (8)	word	Device interrupt pointer	Offset address to device interrupt routine
A (10)	8-bytes	Device name	ASCII device name; for block devices, first byte is number of units

Version Info: Applies to all versions of DOS beginning with 2.0

Notes: *Note that first word is offset within segment, second word is segment address

Source: IBM DOS 3.3 Technical Reference, page 2-6

See Also: 3.150. Device Attribute Codes

3.150. DEVICE ATTRIBUTE CODES

For Character-oriented Devices:

Bit Numbers

15	14	13	12	11	10	9	8	7	6	5	4	3	2	1	0	Name	Allowable Settings
X																Device type	1=device is character oriented
	X															Control string support	0=doesn't support control strings 1=supports IOCTL control strings
		X														Output until busy support	0=doesn't support output until busy 1=supports output until busy
			X		X	X	X	X		X	X					RESERVED	
				X												Understands open/close	0=doesn't understand open/close 1=understands open/close
									X							Supports IOCTL functions	0=doesn't support IOCTL functions 1=supports IOTCL functions
												X				Clock device	0=is not a clock device 1=is a clock device
													X			Null device	0=is not a null device 1=is a null device
														X		Console output device	0=is not console output device 1=is console output device
															X	Console input device	0=is not console input device 1=is console input device

For Block-oriented Devices:

Bit Numbers

15	14	13	12	11	10	9	8	7	6	5	4	3	2	1	0	Name	Allowable Settings
X																Device type	0=block-oriented device
	X															Control string support	0=doesn't support control strings 1=supports IOCTL control strings
		X														Media type determiner	0=doesn't use FAT ID byte 1=uses FAT ID byte to find type*
			X		X	X	X	X		X	X	X	X	X	X	RESERVED	
				X												Understands open/close Removable media	0=doesn't understand open/close 1=understands open/close
									X							Supports IOCTL functions	0=doesn't support IOCTL functions 1=supports IOCTL functions

Version Info: Applies to all versions of DOS beginning with 2.0

Notes: *If FAT ID byte used, the first sector of the FAT must always be in the same physical location

Source: IBM DOS 3.3 Technical Reference, pages 2-7 to 2-10

See Also: 3.149. Device Driver Headers

3.151. DEVICE REQUEST HEADER STATUS FIELD & ERROR CODES

Status Field

Bit Numbers

15	14	13	12	11	10	9	8	7	6	5	4	3	2	1	0	Name	Allowable Values
X																Error	0=no error 1=error
	X	X	X	X	X											RESERVED	
						X										Busy	0=not busy 1=busy
							X									Done	0=operation in progress 1=operation complete
								X	X	X	X	X	X	X	X	Error code	See table below

Error Codes

Bit Numbers

15	14	13	12	11	10	9	8	7	6	5	4	3	2	1	0	Error Name
X																0=write-protect violation
X															X	1=unknown unit
X														X		2=drive not ready
X														X	X	3=unknown command
X													X			4=CRC error
X													X		X	5=bad drive request structure length
X													X	X		6=seek error
X													X	X	X	7=unknown media
X												X				8=sector not found
X												X			X	9=printer out of paper
X												X		X		A=write fault
X												X		X	X	B=read fault
X												X	X			C=general failure
X												X	X		X	D=RESERVED
X												X	X	X		E=RESERVED
X												X	X	X	X	F=invalid disk change

Version Info: Applies to all versions of DOS beginning with 2.0

Source: IBM DOS 3.3 Technical Reference, pages 2-18 to 2-19

See Also: 3.152. Device Request Header

3.152. DEVICE REQUEST HEADER

Offset	Length	Name	Function
0 (0)	byte	Length of record	Length, in bytes, of the entire request header (including code specific items)
1 (1)	byte	Unit code	Subunit (minor device within a block device) that request is intended for
2 (2)	byte	Command code	0 = init
			1 = media check (block devices only)
			2 = build BPB (block devices only)
			3 = IOCTL input
			4 = input (read from device)
			5 = non-destructive input, no wait (character devices only)
			6 = input status (character devices only)
			7 = flush input (character devices only)
			8 = output (write to device)
			9 = output with verify (write to device)
			10 = output status (character devices only)
			11 = flush output (character devices only)
			12 = IOCTL output
			13 = open device
			14 = close device
			15 = removable media (block devices only)
			16 = output until busy
			19 = generic IOCTL request (block devices only)
			23 = get drive map (block devices only)
			24 = set drive map (block devices only)
3 (3)	word	Status	0 before call; set by device routine on return
5 (5)	8-bytes	RESERVED	

Version Info: Applies to all versions of DOS beginning with 2.0

Notes: •All unused command codes are reserved
•Many of the command codes require that the appropriate bit be set in the device attribute code

Source: IBM DOS 3.3 Technical Reference, pages 2-16 to 2-17

See Also: 3.150. Device Attribute Codes
3.153. Init Device Request
3.154. Media Check Request
3.155. Build BIOS Parameter Block Request
3.156. Read Device Request
3.157. Write Device Request
3.158. Non-Destructive Read with No Wait Request
3.159. Open or Close Request
3.160. Removable Media Request
3.161. Status Request
3.162. Flush Request

3.153. INIT DEVICE REQUEST

Offset	Length	Name	Function
0 (0)	byte	Length of request record	Number of bytes in request; should be 23
1 (1)	byte	Unit code	Subunit (for block devices)
2 (2)	byte	Command code	0 = INIT request
3 (3)	word	Status	See 3.152. Device Request Header
5 (5)	8-bytes	RESERVED	
D (13)	byte	Number of units	Number of units in block device
E (14)	dbl word	End address pointer	Segment:offset of resident portion of driver (returned by Init)
12 (18)	dbl word	BPB array pointer	Segment:offset of BPB for block devices (name returned by Init)*
16 (22)	byte	Block device number	Logical drive assignment for first unit (0=A, 1=B, etc.)

Version Info: Applies to all versions of DOS beginning with 2.0

Notes: •Note that double words are formatted as offset first, segment second
•*On return, BPB array pointer will point to the first character following the equal sign (=) on the line of the CONFIG.SYS that created the device

Source: IBM DOS 3.3 Technical Reference, pages 2-21 to 2-22

See Also: 3.152. Device Request Header

3.154. MEDIA CHECK REQUEST

Offset	Length	Name	Function
0 (0)	byte	Length of request record	Number of bytes in request; should be 19
1 (1)	byte	Unit code	Subunit (for block devices)
2 (2)	byte	Command code	1 = media check
3 (3)	word	Status	See 3.151. Device Request Header Status Field & Error Codes
5 (5)	8-bytes	RESERVED	
D (13)	byte	Media descriptor	Type of drive
E (14)	byte	Check status	Returned by function 1=not changed, 0=don't know, -1=changed
10 (16)	dbl word	Previous volume ID	Returned by function if bit 11 of attributes set and media changed

Version Info: Applies to all versions of DOS beginning with 2.0

Notes: Double words are formatted as offset first, segment second

Source: IBM DOS 3.3 Technical Reference, pages 2-23 to 2-25

See Also: 3.150. Device Attribute Codes
3.152. Device Request Header

3.155. BUILD BIOS PARAMETER BLOCK REQUEST

Offset	Length	Name	Function
0 (0)	byte	Length of request record	Number of bytes in request; should be 22
1 (1)	byte	Unit code	Subunit (for block devices)
2 (2)	byte	Command code	2 = build BPB
3 (3)	word	Status	See 3.151. Device Request Header Status Field & Error Codes
5 (5)	8-bytes	RESERVED	
D (13)	byte	Media descriptor	Type of drive
E (14)	dbl word	Transfer address pointer	Offset:segment of buffer address
12 (18)	dbl word	BPB pointer	Offset:segment of BPB

Version Info: Applies to all versions of DOS beginning with 2.0

Notes: Double words are formatted as offset first, segment second

Source: IBM DOS 3.3 Technical Reference, pages 2-29 to 2-30

See Also: 3.150. Device Attribute Codes
3.152. Device Request Header

3.156. READ DEVICE REQUEST

Offset	Length	Name	Function
0 (0)	byte	Length of request record	Number of bytes in request; should be 26
1 (1)	byte	Unit code	Subunit (for block devices)
2 (2)	byte	Command code	3 = read device (IOCTL); 4 = read device
3 (3)	word	Status	See 3.151. Device Request Header Status Field & Error Codes
5 (5)	8-bytes	RESERVED	
D (13)	byte	Media descriptor	Type of drive
E (14)	dbl word	Transfer address pointer	Offset:segment pointer to blank area to transfer data to
12 (18)	word	Byte/sector count	Number of bytes (character) or sectors (block) to read
14 (20)	word	Starting sector number	First sector to read (block devices only)
16 (22)	dbl word	Volume ID pointer	Returned offset:segment pointer to volume ID if error 0FH

Version Info: Applies to all versions of DOS beginning with 2.0

Notes: Double words are formatted as offset first, segment second

Source: IBM DOS 3.3 Technical Reference, pages 2-32 to 2-33

See Also: 3.150. Device Attribute Codes
                       3.152. Device Request Header

3.157. WRITE DEVICE REQUEST

Offset	Length	Name	Function
0 (0)	byte	Length of request record	Number of bytes in request; should be 26
1 (1)	byte	Unit code	Subunit (for block devices)
2 (2)	byte	Command code	8=write, 9=write w/verify, 12=IOCTL write, 16=output til busy
3 (3)	word	Status	See 3.151. Device Request Header Status Field & Error Codes
5 (5)	8-bytes	RESERVED	
D (13)	byte	Media descriptor	Type of drive
E (14)	dbl word	Transfer address pointer	Offset:segment pointer to data area to transfer data from
12 (18)	word	Byte/sector count	Number of bytes (character) or sectors (block) to write
14 (20)	word	Starting sector number	First sector to write (block devices only)
16 (22)	dbl word	Volume ID pointer	Returned Offset:segment pointer to volume ID if error 0FH

Version Info: Applies to all versions of DOS beginning with 2.0

Notes: Double words are formatted as offset first, segment second

Source: IBM DOS 3.3 Technical Reference, pages 2-32 to 2-33

See Also: 3.150. Device Attribute Codes
                       3.152. Device Request Header

3.158. NON-DESTRUCTIVE READ WITH NO WAIT REQUEST

Offset	Length	Name	Function
0 (0)	byte	Length of request record	Number of bytes in request; should be 14
1 (1)	byte	Unit code	Subunit (for block devices)
2 (2)	byte	Command code	5 = non destructive read with no wait function
3 (3)	word	Status	See 3.151. Device Request Header Status Field & Error Codes
5 (5)	8-bytes	RESERVED	
D (13)	byte	Character	Returned character from device

Version Info: Applies to all versions of DOS beginning with 2.0

Source: IBM DOS 3.3 Technical Reference, page 2-34

See Also: 3.150. Device Attribute Codes
                       3.152. Device Request Header

3.159. OPEN OR CLOSE REQUEST

Offset	Length	Name	Function
0 (0)	byte	Length of request record	Number of bytes in request; should be 13
1 (1)	byte	Unit code	Subunit (for block devices)
2 (2)	byte	Command code	13 = open, 14 = close
3 (3)	word	Status	See 3.151. Device Request Header Status Field & Error Codes
5 (5)	8-bytes	RESERVED	

Version Info: Applies to all versions of DOS beginning with 2.0

Source: IBM DOS 3.3 Technical Reference, pages 2-37 to 2-38

See Also: 3.150. Device Attribute Codes
3.152. Device Request Header

3.160. REMOVABLE MEDIA REQUEST

Offset	Length	Name	Function
0 (0)	byte	Length of request record	Number of bytes in request; should be 13
1 (1)	byte	Unit code	Subunit (for block devices)
2 (2)	byte	Command code	15 = removable media
3 (3)	word	Status	See 3.151. Device Request Header Status Field & Error Codes
5 (5)	8-bytes	RESERVED	

Version Info: DOS 3.x only, and only if the open/close/removable media bit is set in the device attribute code

Source: IBM DOS 3.3 Technical Reference, page 2-39

See Also: 3.150. Device Attribute Codes
3.152. Device Request Header

3.161. STATUS REQUEST

Offset	Length	Name	Function
0 (0)	byte	Length of request record	Number of bytes in request; should be 13
1 (1)	byte	Unit code	Subunit (for block devices)
2 (2)	byte	Command code	6 = input status, 10 = output status
3 (3)	word	Status	See 3.151. Device Request Header Status Field & Error Codes
5 (5)	8-bytes	RESERVED	

Version Info: Applies to all versions of DOS beginning with 2.0

Notes: Character devices only. Sets status word.

Source: IBM DOS 3.3 Technical Reference, page 2-35

See Also: 3.150. Device Attribute Codes
3.152. Device Request Header

3.162. FLUSH REQUEST

Offset	Length	Name	Function
0 (0)	byte	Length of request record	Number of bytes in request; should be 13
1 (1)	byte	Unit code	Subunit (for block devices)
2 (2)	byte	Command code	7 = flush input, 11 = flush output
3 (3)	word	Status	See 3.151. Device Request Header Status Field & Error Codes
5 (5)	8-bytes	RESERVED	

Version Info: Applies to all versions of DOS beginning with 2.0

Notes: Character devices only; sets the status word

Source: IBM DOS 3.3 Technical Reference, page 2-36

See Also: 3.150. Device Attribute Codes
3.152. Device Request Header

3.163. GENERIC IOCTL REQUEST

Offset	Length	Name	Function
0 (0)	byte	Length of request record	Number of bytes in request; should be 23
1 (1)	byte	Unit code	Subunit (for block devices)
2 (2)	byte	Command code	19 = generic IOCTRL request
3 (3)	word	Status	See 3.151. Device Request Header Status Field & Error Codes
5 (5)	8-bytes	RESERVED	
D (13)	byte	Category code	See 3.083. Function 44H, 0CH Generic IOCTL for Handles
E (14)	byte	Function code	See 3.083. Function 44H, 0CH Generic IOCTL for Handles
F (15)	word	SI contents	?
11 (17)	word	DI contents	?
13 (19)	dbl word	Data buffer pointer	Offset:segment of pointer to a data buffer

Version Info: Applies to all versions of DOS beginning with 2.0

Source: IBM DOS 3.3 Technical Reference, page 2-40

See Also: 3.150. Device Attribute Codes
3.152. Device Request Header

3.164. LOGICAL DRIVE MAP REQUEST

Offset	Length	Name	Function
0 (0)	byte	Length of request record	Number of bytes in request; should be 21
1 (1)	byte	Unit code	Subunit (for block devices)
2 (2)	byte	Command code	23 = get map, 24 = set map
3 (3)	word	Status	See 3.151. Device Request Header Status Field & Error Codes
5 (5)	8-bytes	RESERVED	
D (13)	byte	Unit code	Logical drive
E (14)	byte	Command code	See 3.134. Block Device Function Codes
F (15)	word	Status	
11 (17)	dbl word	RESERVED	

Version Info: Applies to all versions of DOS beginning with 2.0

Source: IBM DOS 3.3 Technical Reference, page 2-41

See Also: 3.150. Device Attribute Codes
3.152. Device Request Header

3.165. MEDIA DESCRIPTOR TABLE LAYOUT

Offset	Length	Name
0 (0)	3 bytes	JUMP to boot code
3 (3)	8 bytes	OEM name/version
B(11)	word	Number of bytes per sector
D(13)	byte	Number of sectors per allocation unit
E(14)	word	Number of reserved sectors
10(16)	byte	Number of FATs
11(17)	word	Number of root directory entries
13(19)	word	Number of sectors in logical image
15(21)	byte	Media descriptor
16(22)	word	Number of sectors in each FAT
18(24)	word	Number of sectors per track
1A(26)	word	Number of heads
1C(28)	word	Number of hidden sectors
1E(30)	word	High order number of hidden sectors
20(32)	dbl word	Total number of logical sectors

Version Info: Applies to all versions of DOS beginning with 2.0

Source: IBM DOS 3.3 Technical Reference, page 2-31
MS-DOS 3.3 Programmer's Reference, page 352

See Also: 3.167. Device BPB Layout

3.166. CLOCK DEVICE TABLE LAYOUT

Offset	Length	Name
0 (0)	word	Days since Jan. 1, 1980 (low byte, high byte)
2 (2)	byte	Minutes
3 (3)	byte	Hours
4 (4)	byte	Hundredths of seconds
5 (5)	byte	Seconds

Version Info: Applies to all versions of DOS beginning with 2.0

Source: IBM DOS 3.3 Technical Reference, page 2-42

See Also: 2.35. Date/Time Formats

3.167. DEVICE BPB LAYOUT

Offset	Length	Name
0 (0)	word	Bytes per sector
2 (2)	byte	Sectors per cluster
3 (3)	word	Reserved sectors
5 (5)	byte	Number of FATs
6 (6)	word	Number of root directory entries
8 (8)	word	Total number of sectors
A (10)	byte	Media descriptor
B (11)	word	Sectors per FAT
D (13)	word	Sectors per track
F (15)	word	Number of heads
11 (17)	dbl word	Number of hidden sectors
15 (21)	dbl word	RESERVED-1
19 (25)	6 bytes	RESERVED-2

Version Info: Applies to all versions of DOS beginning with 2.0

Source: IBM DOS 3.3 Technical Reference, page 6-175

SECTION

4

DOS BIOS
Calls and
Support Tables

4.001. BIOS SERVICES SUMMARY

Models Supporting Function (columns PC through PS/2-80)

Interrupt	Function*	Description	PC	XT	PCjr	AT	Conv.	PS/2-30	PS/2-50	PS/2-60	PS/2-80	Comments
0	NA	Divide by zero trap	X	X	X	X	X	X	X	X	X	
1	NA	Single-step (Debug mode)	X	X	X	X	X	X	X	X	X	
2 (NMI)	NA	Parity check routine	X	X		X	X	X	X	X	X	
	NA	Coprocessor interrupt direct	X	X				X				
	NA	Coprocessor interrupt via Int 75, IRQ 13			X	X			X	X	X	
	NA	Keyboard interrupt routine					X					
	NA	I/O channel check					X					
	NA	Disk controller power on request					X					
	NA	System suspend					X					
	NA	Real time clock (alarm interrupt)						X	X	X	X	
	NA	System watchdog timer (IRQ0 missed)						X	X	X	X	
	NA	Microchannel DMA timer time-out interrupt							X	X	X	
3	NA	Breakpoint (Debug mode)	X	X	X	X	X	X	X	X	X	
4	NA	Overflow trap	X	X	X	X	X	X	X	X	X	
5	NA	Print screen	X	X	X	X	X	X	X	X	X	Address 500 indicates status
6		RESERVED										
7		RESERVED										
8 (IRQ 0)	NA	Timer interrupt handler	X	X	X	X	X	X	X	X	X	18.2 times per second
9 (IRQ 1)	NA	Keyboard interrupt handler	X	X	X	X	X	X	X	X	X	
0AH (IRQ 2)	NA	Cascade IRQ8 to IRQ15				X	X	X	X	X	X	Also vertical retrace for EGA/VGA on PS/2 models
0BH (IRQ 3)	NA	COM2 controller interrupt entry	X	X		X	X	X	X	X	X	
0CH (IRQ 4)	NA	COM1 controller interrupt entry	X	X	X	X	X	X	X	X	X	
0DH (IRQ 5)	NA	LPT2: controller interrupt entry	X	X	X	X	X	X	X	X	X	Also 80287 entry on AT, hard disk on XT, Model 30, vertical retrace on PCjr
0EH (IRQ 6)	NA	Disk controller interrupt entry	X	X	X	X	X	X	X	X	X	
0FH (IRQ 7)	NA	LPT1: controller interrupt entry	X	X	X	X	X	X	X	X	X	

(Continued)

Table 4.001. Continued

Interrupt	Function*	Description	Models Supporting Function									Comments
			PC	XT	PCjr	AT	Conv.	PS/2-30	PS/2-50	PS/2-60	PS/2-80	
10H	0	VIDEO set mode	X	X	P	X	X	X	X	X	X	
	1	VIDEO set cursor type	X	X	X	X	X	X	X	X	X	
	2	VIDEO set cursor position	X	X	X	X	X	X	X	X	X	
	3	VIDEO read cursor position	X	X	X	X	X	X	X	X	X	
	4	VIDEO read light pen position	X	X	P	X	X					Not implemented on PS/2
	5	VIDEO select display page	X	X	P	X	X	X	X	X	X	
	6	VIDEO init window, or scroll contents up	X	X	X	X	X	X	X	X	X	
	7	VIDEO init window, or scroll contents down	X	X	X	X	X	X	X	X	X	
	8	VIDEO read attribute and char at cursor	X	X	X	X	X	X	X	X	X	
	9	VIDEO write attribute and char at cursor	X	X	X	X	X	X	X	X	X	
	0A	VIDEO write character only at cursor	X	X	P	X	X	X	X	X	X	Valid only for mode 4 CGA, modes 6-8 and 0A on PCjr
	0B	VIDEO set color palette	X	X	P	X	X	X	X	X	X	Not valid for MDA
	0C	VIDEO write graphics pixel	X	X	X	X	X	X	X	X	X	Not valid for MDA
	0D	VIDEO read graphics pixel	X	X	X	X	X	X	X	X	X	
	0E	VIDEO write text in teletype mode	X	X	X	X	X	X	X	X	X	
	0F	VIDEO get mode	X	X	X	X	X	X	X	X	X	
	10	VIDEO set palette registers			X			X	X	X	X	EGA and PCjr only
	11	VIDEO character generator						X	X	X	X	EGA only
	12	VIDEO alternate select						X	X	X	X	EGA and VGA only
	13	VIDEO write character string				X		X	X	X	X	
	14	VIDEO load LCD char font					X					Convertible only
	15	VIDEO return physical parameters					X					Convertible only
	16	RESERVED										
	17	RESERVED										
	18	RESERVED										
	19	RESERVED										
	1A	VIDEO read/write display combo code						X	X	X	X	
	1B	VIDEO return state information						X	X	X	X	
	1C	VIDEO save/restore video state						X	X	X	X	
	1D-FF	RESERVED										
11H	-	EQUIPMENT LIST	X	X	X	X	X	X	X	X	X	Returns EQUIP_FLAG from BIOS data area (See 4.002.)
12H	-	MEMORY SIZE	X	X	X	X	X	X	X	X	X	

(Continued)

Table 4.001. Continued

Interrupt	Function*	Description	PC	XT	PCjr	AT	Conv.	PS/2-30	PS/2-50	PS/2-60	PS/2-80	Comments
								Models Supporting Function				
13H	0	FLOPPY DISK reset system	X	X	X	X	X	X	X	X	X	
	1	FLOPPY DISK get system status	X	X	X	X	X	X	X	X	X	
	2	FLOPPY DISK read disk	X	X	X	X	X	X	X	X	X	
	3	FLOPPY DISK write disk	X	X	X	X	X	X	X	X	X	
	4	FLOPPY DISK verify disk sectors	X	X	X	X	X	X	X	X	X	
	5	FLOPPY DISK format diskette track	X	X	X	X	X	X	X	X	X	
	6	DISK format cylinder set bad sector flags				O		O	O	O	O	Considered obsolete except on original XT
	7	DISK format drive starting at cylinder				O		O	O	O	O	Considered obsolete except on original XT
	8	DISK get current drive parameters		X		X		X	X	X	X	Only model 319 and 339 ATs
	9	DISK init drive pair characteristics				X		X	X	X	X	
	0A	DISK read long				O		D	D	D	D	Diagnostics only on PS/2s
	0B	DISK write long				O		D	D	D	D	Diagnostics only on PS/2s
	0C	DISK seek to cylinder		X		X		X	X	X	X	
	0D	DISK alternate disk reset				X		D	D	D	D	Not on ESDI controllers
	0E	DISK read sector buffer				O		D	D	D	D	Diagnostics only on PS/2s
	0F	DISK write sector buffer				O		D	D	D	D	Diagnostics only on PS/2s
	10	DISK test for drive ready status				X		X	X	X	X	
	11	DISK recalibrate drive				X		X	X	X	X	
	12	DISK controller RAM diagnostic		X		O		D	D	D	D	Diagnostics only on PS/2s
	13	DISK drive diagnostic		X		O		D	D	D	D	Diagnostics only on PS/2s
	14	DISK controller diagnostics				X		D	D	D	D	Diagnostics only on PS/2s
	15	DISK get disk type				X		X	X	X	X	
	16	FLOPPY DISK change disk status				X	X	X	X	X	X	
	17	FLOPPY DISK set disk type				X	X	X	X	X	X	
	18	FLOPPY DISK set media type				X	X	X	X	X	X	Added beginning with XT BIOS dated 1/10/86; only model 319/339 ATs
	19	DISK park heads						X	X	X	X	
	1A	DISK format unit							X	X	X	Only on ESDI controllers
	1B-FF	RESERVED										
14H	0	SERIAL init port	X	X	X	X	X	X	X	X	X	2 ports on PCs, 4 ports on PS/2s
	1	SERIAL write character to port	X	X	X	X	X	X	X	X	X	2 ports on PCs, 4 ports on PS/2s
	2	SERIAL read character from port	X	X	X	X	X	X	X	X	X	2 ports on PCs, 4 ports on PS/2s
	3	SERIAL return port status	X	X	X	X	X	X	X	X	X	2 ports on PCs, 4 ports on PS/2s
	4	SERIAL extended initialize						X	X	X	X	4 ports on PS/2s
	5	SERIAL extended port control						X	X	X	X	4 ports on PS/2s
	6-FF	RESERVED										

(Continued)

Table 4.001. Continued

Interrupt	Function*	Description	Models Supporting Function									Comments
			PC	XT	PCjr	AT	Conv.	PS/2-30	PS/2-50	PS/2-60	PS/2-80	
15H	0	CASSETTE motor ON	X		X							Original PC only, later models didn't have port
	1	CASSETTE motor OFF	X		X							Original PC only, later models didn't have port
	2	CASSETTE read data blocks	X		X							Original PC only, later models didn't have port
	3	CASSETTE write data blocks	X		X							Original PC only, later models didn't have port
	4-0E	RESERVED										
	0F	DISK format periodic interrupt							X	X	X	ESDI controllers only
	10-1F	RESERVED										
	20	AL=10 SYSREQ setup; AL=11 SYSREQ completion				X			X	X	X	
	21	DEVICE power-on self-test error log							X	X	X	
	22-3F	RESERVED										
	40	DEVICE read/modify profiles					X					
	41	DEVICE wait for external event					X					
	42	DEVICE request system power OFF					X					
	43	DEVICE read system status					X					
	44	DEVICE activate internal modem power					X					
	45-4E	RESERVED										
	4F	KEYBOARD intercept				X	X	X	X	X	X	Model 319/339 ATs only
	50-7F	RESERVED										
	80	DEVICE open device				X		X	X	X	X	
	81	DEVICE close device				X		X	X	X	X	
	82	DEVICE program termination				X		X	X	X	X	
	83	DEVICE event wait				X	X	X	X	X	X	
	84	JOYSTICK				X		X	X	X	X	
	85	SYSTEM system request key press				X	X	X	X	X	X	
	86	DEVICE wait				X	X	X	X	X	X	
	87	DEVICE move block				X		X	X	X	X	
	88	MEMORY get extended memory size				X		X	X	X	X	
	89	MEMORY switch to protected mode				X		X	X	X	X	
	90	DEVICE busy loop				X	X	X	X	X	X	
	91	DEVICE set flag and complete interrupt				X	X	X	X	X	X	
	92-BF	RESERVED										
	C0	DEVICE return system parameters				X	X	X	X	X	X	Model 319/339 ATs only
	C1	DEVICE return extended BIOS seg.addr.						X	X	X	X	
	C2	DEVICE pointing device BIOS interface							X	X	X	
	C3	DEVICE enable watchdog time-out							X	X	X	
	C4	DEVICE programmable option select							X	X	X	
	C5-FF	RESERVED										

(Continued)

Table 4.001. Continued

			Models Supporting Function									
Interrupt	Function*	Description	PC	XT	PCjr	AT	Conv.	PS/2-30	PS/2-50	PS/2-60	PS/2-80	Comments
16H	0	KEYBOARD read char from keyboard	X	X	X	X	X	X	X	X	X	
	1	KEYBOARD read keyboard status	X	X	X	X	X	X	X	X	X	
	2	KEYBOARD return keyboard flags	X	X	X	X	X	X	X	X	X	Model 339 ATs only
	3	KEYBOARD typematic and delay			X							
	4	KEYBOARD click ON/OFF			X		X					
	5	KEYBOARD write		X		X		X	X	X	X	XT after 1/10/86, AT after 6/10/85
	6-0F	RESERVED										
	10	KEYBOARD extended keyboard read		X		X		X	X	X	X	XT after 1/10/86, AT after 6/10/85
	11	KEYBOARD extended keystroke status		X		X		X	X	X	X	XT after 1/10/86, AT after 6/10/85
	12	KEYBOARD extended shift status		X		X		X	X	X	X	XT after 1/10/86, AT after 6/10/85
	13-FF	RESERVED										
17H	0	PRINTER write char to printer	X	X	X	X	X	X	X	X	X	3 ports on PCs, 2 on PS/2s
	1	PRINTER init printer port	X	X	X	X	X	X	X	X	X	3 ports on PCs, 2 on PS/2s
	2	PRINTER return printer status	X	X	X	X	X	X	X	X	X	3 ports on PCs, 2 on PS/2s
	3-FF	RESERVED										
18H	-	BASIC load BASIC	X	X	X	X	X	X	X	X	X	
19H	-	BOOTSTRAP loader	X	X	X	X	X	X	X	X	X	PC loads system from disk, PCjr from cartridge or disk, others from any disk
1AH	0	TIME OF DAY read clock count	X	X	X	X	X	X	X	X	X	
	1	TIME OF DAY set clock count	X	X	X	X	X	X	X	X	X	
	2	TIME OF DAY read real time clock				X	X	X	X	X	X	
	3	TIME OF DAY set real time clock				X	X	X	X	X	X	
	4	TIME OF DAY read date from RT clock				X	X	X	X	X	X	
	5	TIME OF DAY set date in RT clock				X	X	X	X	X	X	
	6	TIME OF DAY set alarm				X	X	X	X	X	X	
	7	TIME OF DAY reset alarm				X	X	X	X	X	X	
	8	TIME OF DAY set RTC-activated power ON					X	X	X	X	X	
	9	TIME OF DAY read RTC alarm time & status						X	X	X	X	
	0A	TIME OF DAY read system timer day count		X				X	X	X	X	XT after 1/10/86
	0B	TIME OF DAY set system timer day count		X				X	X	X	X	XT after 1/10/86
	0C-7F	RESERVED										
	80	SOUND set up multiplexer			X							
	81-FF	RESERVED										

Legend: X = supported
O = obsolete (implemented but not normally used)
P = partial or peculiar support, see comments
D = diagnostic call only

Notes: *Usually value in AH register; values in hexadecimal

Source: Programmer's Guide to the IBM PC (Microsoft Press), Peter Norton, chapters 8 to 13
IBM PC/XT Technical Reference BIOS Listings
IBM PC/AT Technical Reference BIOS Listings
IBM PS/2 and PC BIOS Interface Technical Reference, pages 2-10 to 2-122

See Also: 5.01. DOS Interrupt Usage by Version
5.08. INT 33H Mouse Functions Summary
5.29. INT 67H Expanded Memory Manager Functions Summary
7.04. PC Interrupt Usage Summary

4.002. BIOS MEMORY USAGE SUMMARY

Location	Length	Description	7	6	5	4	3	2	1	0	Comments
							Bit Numbers				
40:00	Word	COM1 base address									
40:02	Word	COM2 base address									
40:04	Word	COM3 base address									Supported only by PS/2 BIOS
40:06	Word	COM4 base address									Supported only by PS/2 BIOS
40:08	Word	LPT1 base address									
40:0A	Word	LPT2 base address									
40:0C	Word	LPT3 base address									
40:0E	Word	LPT4 base address									PC, XT, AT & Convertible only
40:10	Byte	Installed hardware 1	X	X							Number of floppy drives (0-based)
					X	X					Video mode (01=40x25 color, 10=80x25 color, 11=80x25 mono)
							X	X			RESERVED (old PC and PCJr bits 2-3 indicate memory installed)
									X		Pointing device installed (PS/2 only)
									X		Math coprocessor installed (not on PCjr or Convertible)
										X	Floppy drives installed
40:11	Byte	Installed hardware 2	X	X							Number of printer adapters
					X						Internal modem (Convertible only)
						X					Joystick installed
							X	X	X		Number of RS-232 Adapters
										X	RESERVED (PCJr=DMA device installed)
40:12	Byte	Power-on self test status									
40:13	Word	Memory size									Convertible only
											in KBytes (0 to 640)
40:15	Word	RESERVED									
40:17	Byte	Keyboard control 1	X								Insert mode active
				X							Caps lock mode active
					X						Num lock mode active
						X					Scroll lock mode active
							X				Alt key held down
								X			Ctrl key held down
									X		Left Shift key held down
										X	Right Shift key held down
40:18	Byte	Keyboard control 2	X								Insert key held down
				X							Caps Lock key held down
					X						Num Lock key held down
						X					Scroll Lock key held down
							X				Pause mode active
								X			System Request key held down
									X		Left Alt key held down
										X	Left Ctrl key held down
40:19	Byte	Alternate keypad entry									
40:1A	Word	Keyboard buffer head pointer									Points to first character in typeahead buffer
40:1C	Word	Keyboard buffer tail pointer									Points to last character in typeahead buffer
40:1E	32 bytes	Keyboard buffer									

(Continued)

Table 4.002. Continued

Location	Length	Description	7	6	5	4	3	2	1	0	Comments
40:3E	Byte	Floppy recalibrate status	X								Interrupt flag
				X	X	X					RESERVED
							X				Recalibrate drive 3
								X			Recalibrate drive 2
									X		Recalibrate drive 1
										X	Recalibrate drive 0
40:3F	Byte	Floppy motor status	X								Write/read operation
				X							RESERVED
					X	X					Drive selected (binary value equals drive number)
							X				Drive 3 motor ON status
								X			Drive 2 motor ON status
									X		Drive 1 motor ON status
										X	Drive 0 motor ON status
40:40	Byte	Motor off counter									
40:41	Byte	Floppy previous operation status	X								Drive not ready
				X							Seek operation failed
					X						General controller failure
						X					CRC error on diskette read
							X				DMA overrun on operation
								X			Requested sector not found
									X		Address mark not found
										X	Invalid drive parameter
											No error
									X	X	Write-protect error
								X	X		Disk changed
							X			X	DMA attempt across 64K segment boundary
							X	X			Media type not found
40:42	7 bytes	Floppy controller status bytes									
40:49	Byte	Display mode									
40:4A	Word	Number of columns									
40:4C	Word	Length of regen buffer in bytes									
40:4E	Word	Address of regen buffer									
40:50	Word	Cursor position page 1									
40:52	Word	Cursor position page 2									
40:54	Word	Cursor position page 3									
40:56	Word	Cursor position page 4									
40:58	Word	Cursor position page 5									
40:5A	Word	Cursor position page 6									
40:5C	Word	Cursor position page 7									
40:5E	Word	Cursor position page 8									
40:60	Word	Cursor type									
40:62	Byte	Current display page									
40:63	Word	Video controller base address									
40:65	Byte	Current 3x8 register setting									
40:66	Byte	Current 3x9 register setting									

(Continued)

Table 4.002. Continued

Location	Length	Description	Bit Numbers 7	6	5	4	3	2	1	0	Comments
40:67	Dbl word	Pointer to reset code									PS/2 only (except Model 30)
40:6B	Byte	RESERVED									
40:6C	Dbl word	Timer counter									
40:70	Byte	Timer overflow flag									Non-zero means timer passed 24 hours
40:71	Byte	Break key state									
40:72	Word	Reset flag									1234H=bypass mem test; 4321H=preserve mem (PS/2) 5678H=system suspended (Convert.); 9ABCH=mfg test (Convert.) ABCDH=system post loop (Convertible only)
40:74	Byte	Fixed disk previous operation status									See 4.041. INT 13H, Disk System Status Byte Layout (not used PS/2)
40:75	Byte	Number of fixed drives									
40:76	Byte	Fixed disk drive control									
40:77	Byte	Fixed disk controller port									XT only
40:78	Byte	Printer 1 time-out value									XT only
40:79	Byte	Printer 2 time-out value									
40:7A	Byte	Printer 3 time-out value									
40:7B	Byte	Printer 4 time-out value									PC, XT, and AT only
40:7C	Byte	COM1 time-out value									
40:7D	Byte	COM2 time-out value									
40:7E	Byte	COM3 time-out value									
40:7F	Byte	COM4 time-out value									
40:80	Word	Keyboard buffer start offset pointer									
40:82	Word	Keyboard buffer end offset pointer									
40:84	Byte	Video rows (minus one)									
40:85	Word	Char height (bytes/char)									
40:87	Byte	Video control states 1									
40:88	Byte	Video control states 2									
40:89	Word	RESERVED									
40:8B	Byte	Media control	X	X	X	X	X	X	X	X	Last floppy drive data rate* (AT, XT after 1/10/85, PS/2) / Last floppy drive step rate (AT, XT after 1/10/85, PS/2) / RESERVED
40:8C	Byte	Fixed disk controller status									AT, XT after 1/10/85, PS/2 only
40:8D	Byte	Fixed disk controller error status									AT, XT after 1/10/85, PS/2 only
40:8E	Byte	Fixed disk interrupt control									AT, XT after 1/10/85, PS/2 only
40:8F	Byte	RESERVED									
40:90	Byte	Drive 0 media state	X	X	X	X	X	X	X	X	Drive data rate* (AT, XT after 1/10/85, PS/2) / Double stepping required (AT, XT after 1/10/85, PS/2) / Media established (AT, XT after 1/10/85, PS/2) / RESERVED / Drive/media state** (AT, XT after 1/10/85, PS/2)
40:91	Byte	Drive 1 media state	X	X	X	X	X	X	X	X	Drive data rate* (AT, XT after 1/10/85, PS/2) / Double stepping required (AT, XT after 1/10/85, PS/2) / Media established (AT, XT after 1/10/85, PS/2) / RESERVED / Drive/media state** (AT, XT after 1/10/85, PS/2)

(Continued)

Table 4.002. Continued

Bit Numbers

Location	Length	Description	7	6	5	4	3	2	1	0	Comments
40:92	Word	RESERVED									
40:94	Byte	Drive 0 current cylinder									
40:95	Byte	Drive 1 current cylinder									
40:96	Byte	Keyboard mode state, type flags	X								Read ID in progress
				X							Last character was first ID character
					X						Force Num Lock if read ID and KBX
						X					101/102-key keyboard installed
							X				Right Alt key held down
								X			Right Ctrl key held down
									X		Last code was E0 hidden code
										X	Last code was E1 hidden code
40:97	Byte	Keyboard LED flags	X								Keyboard transmit error flag
				X							Mode indicator update
					X						Resend receive flag
						X					Acknowledgment received
							X				RESERVED (must be 0)
								X	X	X	LED state bits
40:98	Word	Offset address to user wait complete flag									
40:9A	Word	Segment address to user wait complete									
40:9C	Word	User wait count (low word)									In microseconds
40:9E	Word	User wait count (high word)									In microseconds
40:A0	Byte	Wait active flag	X								Wait time elapsed and post
				X	X	X	X	X	X		RESERVED
										X	Int 15H Function 86H (Wait) has occurred
40:A1	7 bytes	RESERVED									
40:A8	Dbl word	Video parameter table pointer									EGA and PS/2 only
40:AC	Dbl word	Dynamic save area pointer									EGA and PS/2 only
40:B0	Dbl word	Alpha mode aux char gen pointer									EGA and PS/2 only
40:B4	Dbl word	Graphics mode aux char gen pointer									EGA and PS/2 only
40:B8	Dbl word	Secondary save pointer									PS/2 only (not Model 30)
40:BC	8 bytes	RESERVED									
40:C0	64 bytes	RESERVED									Set to zeros only
50:00	Byte	Print screen status byte									

Version Info: PS/2 Extended BIOS uses space at top of memory for an Extended BIOS data area

Notes: • *Drive data notes: 00 = 500 KB/second
                              01 = 300 KB/second
                              10 = 250 KB/second
                              11 = RESERVED

             • **Drive media state values not currently documented in IBM BIOS references

Source: IBM PS/2 and PC BIOS Interface Technical Reference, pages 3-3 to 3-15

See Also: 4.003. Extended BIOS Data Area Layout
                7.02. PC, AT, and PS/2 Memory Use Summary

4.003. EXTENDED BIOS DATA AREA LAYOUT

Location	Function
40:13	KB value below 640KB limit at which extended BIOS data area begins

Offset	Function
0	Single byte containing length of extended BIOS data area in KB
1	Beginning of extended BIOS data area

Source: IBM PS/2 and PC BIOS Technical Reference, page 3-15

See Also: 4.090. INT 15H, AH=C0H -- Return System Config Parameters
4.092. INT 15H, AH=C1H -- Return Ext BIOS Segment Address

4.004. MODEL NUMBER BYTES

Model Byte*	Submodel**	Revision**	BIOS Version	Machine
FF (255)	Not used	Not used	All	IBM PC
FE (254)	Not used	Not used	11/8/82	IBM PC/XT and Portable PC
FD (253)	Not used	Not used	All	IBM PCJr
FC (252)	Not used	Not used	1/10/84	IBM PC/AT
	00	01	6/10/85	IBM PC/AT
	01	00	11/15/85	IBM PC/AT
	04	00	Initial	IBM PS/2 Model 50
	05	00	Initial	IBM PS/2 Model 60
	02	00	All	IBM PC/XT286
FB (251)	00	01	1/10/86	IBM PC/XT
	00	02	5/9/86	IBM PC/XT
FA (250)	00	00	9/2/86	IBM PS/2 Model 30
F9 (249)	00	00	9/13/85	IBM PC Convertible
F8 (248)	00	00	Initial	IBM PS/2 Model 80
	01	00	Initial	IBM PS/2 Model 80
FE (254)	Not supported	Not supported		Compaq DeskPro
2D (45)	Not supported	Not supported		Compaq Portable
9A (154)	Not supported	Not supported		Compaq Portable Plus
4B (75)	Not supported	Not supported		MegaBIOS ROM (Display Telecom)
B6 (182)	Not supported	Not supported		HP110 Portable (original model)

Notes: •Many non-IBM machines use the same Machine ID Byte as the IBM machine they emulate
•*The model number byte is located at F000:FFFE.
•**Submodel and revision numbers are returned by BIOS service INT 15H, AH=C0H (Return System Config Parameters)

Source: IBM PS/2 and PC BIOS Technical Reference, page 4-18
Manufacturer's information (Compaq, et. al.)

See Also: 4.002. BIOS Memory Usage Summary

4.005 INT 10H, AH=00H -- SET MODE

Prior to Issuing INT 10H   *Upon Return from INT 10H*

	High	Low
AX	00H	Video mode*
BX		
CX		
DX		

SP	
BP	
SI	
DI	

IP	
flags	

CS	
DS	
SS	
ES	

Interrupt returns no values

Notes: *See 4.006. INT 10H, Display Modes

Source: IBM PS/2 and PC BIOS Interface Technical Reference, page 2-11

See Also: 4.001. BIOS Services Summary
                 4.022. INT 10H, AH=0FH -- Get Current Display Mode

4.006. INT 10H, DISPLAY MODES

Mode Number	Type	Max Colors	Text Format	Graphics Size			Max Pages	Buffer Start
0 (0)	Text	16	40x25	320x200*	320x350¥		8	B8000
1 (1)	Text	16	40x25	320x400§	360x400∞		8	B8000
2 (2)	Text	16	80x25	640x200*¥	640x350¥		4* 8** 8***	B8000
3 (3)	Text	16	80x25	640x400§	720x400∞		4* 8** 8***	B8000
4 (4)	Graphics	4	40x25	320x200			1	B8000
5 (5)	Graphics	4	40x25				1	B8000
6 (6)	Graphics	2	80x25	640x200			1	B8000
7 (7)	Text	Mono	80x25	720x350****¥	720x400∞	640x200†	1**** 8¥ 4†	B0000
8 (8)	Graphics	16	20x25	160x200	PCjr only		1	B0000
9 (9)	Graphics	16	40x25	320x200	PCjr only		1	B0000
A (10)	Graphics	4	80x25	640x200	PCjr only		1	B0000
B (11)	RESERVED							
C (12)	RESERVED							
D (13)	Graphics	16	40x25	320x200¥			8 ¥	A0000
E (14)	Graphics	16	80x25	640x200¥			4 ¥	A0000
F (15)	Graphics	Mono	80x25	640x350¥			2 ¥	A0000
10 (16)	Graphics	16	80x25				2 ¥	A0000
11 (17)	Graphics	2	80x30	640x480***			1***	A0000
12 (18)	Graphics	16	80x30	640x480∞			1***	A0000
13 (19)	Graphics	256	40x25	320x200***			1***	A0000

Notes:
- *CGA, PCJr, Convertible
- **EGA
- ***PS/2
- ****MDA
- † Convertible
- ¥ EGA and PS/2 (except Model 30)
- § PS/2 Model 30
- ∞ PS/2 models except Model 30

Source: IBM PS/2 and PC BIOS Interface Technical Reference, pages 2-10 to 2-12

See Also: 4.005. INT 10H, AH=00H -- Set Mode
                 4.022. INT 10H, AH=0FH -- Get Current Display Mode

4.007. INT 10H, AH=01H -- SET CURSOR TYPE

Prior to Issuing INT 10H   **Upon Return from INT 10H**

	High	Low
AX	01H	
BX		
CX	Starting scan line	Ending scan line
DX		

SP	
BP	
SI	
DI	

| IP | |
| flags | |

CS	
DS	
SS	
ES	

Interrupt returns no values

Notes: •CGA allowable scan lines=0 - 7; MDA = 0 -13
                    •Note that setting bits 5 or 6 in CH may cause erratic behavior

Source: IBM PS/2 and PC BIOS Interface Technical Reference,
                    pages 2-14 to 2-15

See Also: 4.001. BIOS Services Summary
                    4.008. INT 10H, AH=02H -- Set Cursor Position
                    4.009. INT 10H, AH=03H -- Read Cursor Position

4.008. INT 10H, AH=02H -- SET CURSOR POSITION

Prior to Issuing INT 10H   **Upon Return from INT 10H**

	High	Low
AX	02H	
BX	Display page	
CX		
DX	Row	Column

SP	
BP	
SI	
DI	

| IP | |
| flags | |

CS	
DS	
SS	
ES	

Interrupt returns no values

Notes: Page numbers, rows, and columns are 0-based
                    (start with 0)

Source: IBM PS/2 and PC BIOS Interface Technical Reference,
                    page 2-15

See Also: 4.001. BIOS Services Summary
                    4.007. INT 10H, AH=01H -- Set Cursor Type
                    4.009. INT 10H, AH=03H -- Read Cursor Position

4.009. INT 10H, AH=03H -- READ CURSOR POSITION

Prior to Issuing INT 10H   **Upon Return from INT 10H**

	High	Low
AX	03H	
BX	Display page	
CX		
DX		

SP	
BP	
SI	
DI	

IP	
flags	

CS	
DS	
SS	
ES	

	High	Low
AX		
BX		
CX	Starting scan line	Ending scan line
DX	Row	Column

SP	
BP	
SI	
DI	

IP	
flags	

CS	
DS	
SS	
ES	

Notes: •Page numbers, rows, and columns are 0-based (start with 0)
                  •CX returns current cursor type

Source: IBM PS/2 and PC BIOS Interface Technical Reference, page 2-15

See Also: 4.001. BIOS Services Summary
                  4.007. INT 10H, AH=01H -- Set Cursor Type
                  4.008. INT 10H, AH=02H -- Set Cursor Position

4.010. INT 10H, AH=04H -- READ LIGHT PEN POSITION

Prior to Issuing INT 10H   **Upon Return from INT 10H**

	High	Low
AX	04H	
BX		
CX		
DX		

SP	
BP	
SI	
DI	

IP	
flags	

CS	
DS	
SS	
ES	

	High	Low
AX	Pen trigger signal	
BX	Pixel column	
CX	Pixel row*	
DX	Character row	Character column

SP	
BP	
SI	
DI	

IP	
flags	

CS	
DS	
SS	
ES	

Version Info: Light pen is not supported for Convertible or PS/2 models

Notes: *May be extended to CX for some graphics modes

Source: IBM PS/2 and PC BIOS Interface Technical Reference, page 2-15

See Also: 4.001. BIOS Services Summary

4.011. INT 10H, AH=05H -- SELECT DISPLAY PAGE

Prior to Issuing INT 10H   *Upon Return from INT 10H*

	High	Low			High	Low
AX	05H	Page number*		AX		
BX	**	**		BX	CRT **	microprocessor **
CX				CX		
DX				DX		

SP			SP	
BP			BP	
SI			SI	
DI			DI	

IP			IP	
flags			flags	

CS			CS	
DS			DS	
SS			SS	
ES			ES	

Notes: *Page numbers are 0-based; PCjr uses AL to set function:
   80H = Read CRT/microprocessor page registers
   81H = Set microprocessor page register
      (page register in BL)
   82H = Set CRT page register (page register in BH)
   83H = Set both page registers
      (CRT in BH, microprocessor in BL)

** Used by PCjr only

Source: IBM PS/2 and PC BIOS Interface Technical Reference, page 2-16

See Also: 4.001. BIOS Services Summary

4.012. INT 10H, AH=06H -- INIT WINDOW, SCROLL WINDOW UP

Prior to Issuing INT 10H   *Upon Return from INT 10H*

	High	Low
AX	06H	Lines to scroll up*
BX	Blank line attribute	
CX	Upper row	Left column
DX	Lower row	Right column

Interrupt returns no values

SP	
BP	
SI	
DI	

IP	
flags	

CS	
DS	
SS	
ES	

Notes: •BH contains attribute to use for all new blank lines created
by function
•*0=blank entire window (Init Window)

Source: IBM PS/2 and PC BIOS Interface Technical Reference,
page 2-16

See Also: 4.001. BIOS Services Summary
4.013. INT 10H, AH=07H -- Init Window, Scroll Window Down

4.013. INT 10H, AH=07H -- INIT WINDOW, SCROLL WINDOW DOWN

	Prior to Issuing INT 10H		*Upon Return from INT 10H*

	High	Low
AX	07H	Lines to scroll down*
BX	Blank line attribute	
CX	Upper row	Left column
DX	Lower row	Right column

SP		
BP		
SI		
DI		

IP		
flags		

CS		
DS		
SS		
ES		

Interrupt returns no values

Notes:	•BH contains attribute to use for all new blank lines created by function •*0=blank entire window (Init window)
Source:	IBM PS/2 and PC BIOS Interface Technical Reference, page 2-16
See Also:	4.001. BIOS Services Summary 4.012. INT 10H, AH=06H -- Init Window, Scroll Window Up

4.014. INT 10H, AH=08H -- READ CHARACTER AND ATTRIBUTE

	Prior to Issuing INT 10H		*Upon Return from INT 10H*

	High	Low
AX	08H	
BX	Page number	
CX		
DX		

SP		
BP		
SI		
DI		

IP		
flags		

CS		
DS		
SS		
ES		

	High	Low
AX	Attribute*	Character
BX		
CX		
DX		

SP		
BP		
SI		
DI		

IP		
flags		

CS		
DS		
SS		
ES		

Notes:	*Text modes only
Source:	IBM PS/2 and PC BIOS Interface Technical Reference, page 2-17
See Also:	4.001. BIOS Services Summary 4.015. INT 10H, AH=09H -- Write Character and Attribute 4.016. INT 10H, AH=0AH -- Write Character only at Cursor 4.020. INT 10H, AH=0DH -- Read Pixel

4.015. INT 10H, AH=09H -- WRITE CHARACTER AND ATTRIBUTE

Prior to Issuing INT 10H ***Upon Return from INT 10H***

	High	Low
AX	09H	Character
BX	Page number	Attribute
CX	Number of characters to write*	
DX		
SP		
BP		
SI		
DI		
IP		
flags		
CS		
DS		
SS		
ES		

Interrupt returns no values

Notes: *Does not wrap to next line (i.e., characters all on same row, up to limit)

Source: IBM PS/2 and PC BIOS Interface Technical Reference, page 2-17

See Also: 4.001. BIOS Services Summary
4.014. INT 10H, AH=08H -- Read Character and Attribute
4.016. INT 10H, AH=0AH -- Write Character Only at Cursor
4.019. INT 10H, AH=0CH -- Write Pixel

4.016. INT 10H, AH=0AH -- WRITE CHARACTER ONLY AT CURSOR

Prior to Issuing INT 10H ***Upon Return from INT 10H***

	High	Low
AX	0AH	Character
BX	Page number	
CX	Number of characters to write*	
DX		
SP		
BP		
SI		
DI		
IP		
flags		
CS		
DS		
SS		
ES		

Interrupt returns no values

Notes: *Does not wrap to next line (i.e., characters all on same row, up to limit)

Source: IBM PS/2 and PC BIOS Interface Technical Reference, page 2-17

See Also: 4.001. BIOS Services Summary
4.014. INT 10H, AH=08H -- Read Character and Attribute
4.015. INT 10H, AH=09H -- Write Character and Attribute
4.019. INT 10H, AH=0CH -- Write Pixel

4.017. INT 10H, AH=0BH -- SET COLOR PALETTE

Prior to Issuing INT 10H   *Upon Return from INT 10H*

	High	Low
AX	0BH	
BX	Palette ID*	Color ID**
CX		
DX		

Interrupt returns no values

SP	
BP	
SI	
DI	

IP	
flags	

CS	
DS	
SS	
ES	

Notes: •*0=red/green/brown, 1=cyan/magenta/white on CGA
•**See 4.018. INT 10H, Palette and Color Values

Source: IBM PS/2 and PC BIOS Interface Technical Reference, page 2-18

See Also: 4.001. BIOS Services Summary

4.018. INT 10H, PALETTE AND COLOR VALUES

If BH=0, then BL register
contains two nibble color values
(foreground, background) as follows:

Value	Color
0 (0)	Black
1 (1)	Blue
2 (2)	Green
3 (3)	Cyan
4 (4)	Red
5 (5)	Magenta
6 (6)	Brown
7 (7)	White
8 (8)	Gray
9 (9)	Light blue
A (10)	Light green
B (11)	Light cyan
C (12)	Light red
D (13)	Light magenta
E (14)	Yellow
F (15)	Bright white

if BH=1, then BL register
contains palette number, as follows:

Value	Palette
0	Green/red/brown
1	Cyan/magenta/white

Source: IBM Technical Reference Options and Adapters, CGA 8
Microsoft QuickBASIC, page 453

See Also: 4.017. INT 10H, AH=0BH -- Set Color Palette

4.019. INT 10H, AH=0CH -- WRITE PIXEL

Prior to Issuing INT 10H   *Upon Return from INT 10H*

	High	Low
AX	0CH	Color*
BX	Page number	
CX	Pixel column	
DX	Pixel row	

SP	
BP	
SI	
DI	

| IP | |
| flags | |

CS	
DS	
SS	
ES	

Interrupt returns no values

Notes: *If bit 7 is set, the color value is XORed with current contents
(except display mode 13H)

Source: IBM PS/2 and PC BIOS Interface Technical Reference,
page 2-18 to 2-19

See Also: 4.001. BIOS Services Summary
4.015. INT 10H, AH=09H -- Write Character and Attribute
4.016. INT 10H, AH=0AH -- Write Character Only at Cursor
4.020. INT 10H, AH=0DH -- Read Pixel

4.020. INT 10H, AH=0DH -- READ PIXEL

Prior to Issuing INT 10H   *Upon Return from INT 10H*

	High	Low
AX	0DH	
BX	Page number*	
CX	Pixel column	
DX	Pixel row	

SP	
BP	
SI	
DI	

| IP | |
| flags | |

CS	
DS	
SS	
ES	

	High	Low
AX		Color
BX		
CX		
DX		

SP	
BP	
SI	
DI	

| IP | |
| flags | |

CS	
DS	
SS	
ES	

Notes: *Only if display mode supports more than one page

Source: IBM PS/2 and PC BIOS Interface Technical Reference, page 2-19

See Also: 4.001. BIOS Services Summary
4.014. INT 10H, AH=08H -- Read Character and Attribute
4.019. INT 10H, AH=0CH -- Write Pixel

4.021. INT 10H, AH=0EH -- WRITE TEXT IN TELETYPE MODE

Prior to Issuing INT 10H

	High	Low
AX	0EH	Character**
BX	Page number***	Foreground color*
CX		
DX		
SP		
BP		
SI		
DI		
IP		
flags		
CS		
DS		
SS		
ES		

Upon Return from INT 10H

Interrupt returns no values

Notes:
- *If in a graphics display mode
- **Carriage Return, Linefeed, Backspace, and Bell are treated as commands instead of displayable characters
- ***For PC BIOS dated 4/24/81 and 10/19/81 only

Source: IBM PS/2 and PC BIOS Interface Technical Reference, page 2-19

See Also:
4.001. BIOS Services Summary
4.015. INT 10H, AH=09H -- Write Character and Attribute
4.016. INT 10H, AH=0AH -- Write Character Only at Cursor
4.019. INT 10H, AH=0CH -- Write Pixel

4.022. INT 10H, AH=0FH -- GET CURRENT DISPLAY MODE

Prior to Issuing INT 10H

	High	Low
AX	0FH	
BX		
CX		
DX		
SP		
BP		
SI		
DI		
IP		
flags		
CS		
DS		
SS		
ES		

Upon Return from INT 10H

	High	Low
AX	Columns	Display mode
BX	Page number	
CX		
DX		
SP		
BP		
SI		
DI		
IP		
flags		
CS		
DS		
SS		
ES		

Source: IBM PS/2 and PC BIOS Interface Technical Reference, page 2-19

See Also:
4.001. BIOS Services Summary
4.005. INT 10H, AH=00H -- Set Mode
4.006. INT 10H, Display Modes

4.023. INT 10H, AH=10H -- SET PALETTE REGISTERS

Prior to Issuing INT 10H   *Upon Return from INT 10H*

	High	Low
AX	10H	Command*
BX	Value**	Palette reg***
CX		
DX	Offset of pointer to 17-byte table****	
SP		
BP		
SI		
DI		
IP		
flags		
CS		
DS		
SS		
ES	Segment of pointer to 17-byte table****	

Interrupt returns no values

Version Info: •Applies to PCJr and EGA-equipped systems only (includes PS/2 emulating EGA)

Notes: •*0=set individual palette register; 1=set overscan register; 2=set all registers; 3=toggle intensify/blinking bit
•**only if AL=0 or 1
•***only if AL=0
•****only if AL=2; table contains 16=byte palette registers, 1 byte overscan register

Source: IBM PS/2 and PC BIOS Interface Technical Reference, pages 2-20 to 2-24

See Also: 4.001. BIOS Services Summary

4.024. INT 10H, AH=11H -- CHARACTER GENERATOR

Prior to Issuing INT 10H   *Upon Return from INT 10H*

	High	Low
AX	11H	Command*
BX	# Bytes/character**	Block to load***
CX	Count to store**	
DX	Character offset into table**	
SP		
BP	Pointer to user table**	
SI		
DI		
IP		
flags		
CS		
DS		
SS		
ES	Pointer to user table**	

Interrupt returns no values

Version Info: Applies to EGA-equipped systems only (includes PS/2 emulating EGA)

Notes:
•*0=user alpha load; 1=ROM monochrome set; 2=ROM 8x8 double dot; 3=set block specifier; other commands available, see Tech Ref
•**only if AL=0
•***only if AL=0, 1 or 2; if AL=3 BL=character block selection

Source: IBM PS/2 and PC BIOS Interface Technical Reference, pages 2-24 to 2-32

See Also: 4.001. BIOS Services Summary

4.025. INT 10H, AH=12H -- ALTERNATE SELECT

Prior to Issuing INT 10H

	High	Low
AX	12H	Value**
BX	***	Command*
CX	***	***
DX		
SP		
BP		
SI		
DI		
IP		
flags		
CS		
DS		
SS		
ES		

Upon Return from INT 10H

Varies, see Technical Reference manual

Version Info: Applies to EGA-equipped systems only (includes PS/2 emulating EGA)

Notes:
- •*10H = return EGA information
  - 20H = select alternate print screen routine
  - 30H = select scan lines for alphanumeric modes
  - 31H = default palette loading during set mode
  - 32H = enable/disable video
  - 33H = summing to gray shades
  - 34H = cursor emulation
- •**0=enable, 1=disable for commands 31H-34H
- •***Register used by some commands, see Technical Reference manual

Source: IBM PS/2 and PC BIOS Interface Technical Reference, pages 2-24 to 2-32

See Also: 4.001. BIOS Services Summary
4.024. INT 10H, AH=11H -- Character Generator

4.026. INT 10H, AH=13H -- WRITE STRING

Prior to Issuing INT 10H   *Upon Return from INT 10H*

	High	Low
AX	13H	Mode*
BX	Page number	Attribute*
CX	Character count	
DX	Start cursor position	

Interrupt returns no values

SP	
BP	Offset of pointer to string
SI	
DI	

IP	
flags	

CS	
DS	
SS	
ES	Segment of pointer to string

Version Info: Applies to AT and PS/2 only

Notes: •*If AL=00 then BL contains attribute, cursor is not moved
  AL=01 then BL contains attribute, cursor is updated
  AL=02 then string contains alternating character and attribute
    bytes and cursor is not moved (alpha modes only)
  AL=03 then string contains alternating character and attribute
    bytes and cursor is updated (alpha modes only)
  •CR, LF, Backspace, and Bell are treated as commands, not characters

Source: IBM PS/2 and PC BIOS Interface Technical Reference, pages 2-36 to 2-37

See Also: 4.001. BIOS Services Summary

4.027. INT 10H, AH=1AH, AL=00H -- READ DISPLAY CODES

Prior to Issuing INT 10H

	High	Low
AX	1AH	00H
BX		
CX		
DX		

SP		
BP		
SI		
DI		

IP		
flags		

CS		
DS		
SS		
ES		

Upon Return from INT 10H

	High	Low
AX		Status*
BX	Alternate disp code**	Active disp code**
CX		
DX		

SP		
BP		
SI		
DI		

IP		
flags		

CS		
DS		
SS		
ES		

Version Info: Applies to PS/2 models only

Notes:
- *1AH= function was supported (display codes are valid)
- **See 4.029. INT 10H, Display Codes

Source: IBM PS/2 and PC BIOS Interface Technical Reference, page 2-39

See Also: 4.001. BIOS Services Summary

4.028. INT 10H, AH=1AH, AL=01H -- WRITE DISPLAY CODES

Prior to Issuing INT 10H

	High	Low
AX	1AH	01H
BX	Alternate disp code**	Active disp code**
CX		
DX		

SP		
BP		
SI		
DI		

IP		
flags		

CS		
DS		
SS		
ES		

Upon Return from INT 10H

	High	Low
AX		Status*
BX		
CX		
DX		

SP		
BP		
SI		
DI		

IP		
flags		

CS		
DS		
SS		
ES		

Version Info: Applies to PS/2 models only

Notes:
- *1AH= function was supported (display codes were changed)
- **See 4.029. INT 10H, Display Codes

Source: IBM PS/2 and PC BIOS Interface Technical Reference, page 2-39

See Also: 4.001. BIOS Services Summary
4.027. INT 10H, AH=1AH, AL=00H -- Read Display Codes

4.029. INT 10H, DISPLAY CODES

Value	Function
0 (0)	No display
1 (1)	Monochrome with 5151 (monochrome) monitor
2 (2)	CGA with 5153/4 (color) monitor
3 (3)	RESERVED
4 (4)	EGA with 5153/4 (color) monitor
5 (5)	EGA with 5151 (monochrome) monitor
6 (6)	*PGS with 5175 (color) monitor
7 (7)	VGA with analog monochrome monitor (except Model 30)
8 (8)	VGA with analog color monitor (except Model 30)
9 (9)- A(10)	RESERVED
B (11)	Model 30 with analog monochrome monitor (MCGA)
C (12)	Model 30 with analog color monitor (MCGA)
D (13)-FE(254)	RESERVED
FF (255)	Unknown monitor type

Notes: *PGS refers to Professional Graphics System

Source: IBM PS/2 and PC BIOS Technical Reference, page 2-39

See Also: 4.027. INT 10H, AH=1AH, AL=00H -- Read Display Codes
4.028. INT 10H, AH=1AH, AL=01H -- Write Display Codes

4.030. INT 10H, AH=1BH -- RETURN STATE

Prior to Issuing INT 10H   *Upon Return from INT 10H*

	High	Low			High	Low
AX	1BH			AX		Status*
BX	Implementation type***			BX		
CX				CX		
DX				DX		

SP			SP		
BP			BP		
SI			SI		
DI	Offset of pointer to empty buffer		DI	Offset of pointer to video state buffer**	

IP			IP		
flags			flags		

CS			CS		
DS			DS		
SS			SS		
ES	Segment of pointer to empty buffer		ES	Segment of pointer to video state buffer**	

Version Info: Applies to PS/2 models only

Notes: •*1BH= function was supported (buffer contains valid info)
•**See 4.031. INT 10H, Video State Buffer Layout
•***Currently only 00 is supported

Source: IBM PS/2 and PC BIOS Interface Technical Reference, pages 2-40 to 2-44

See Also: 4.001. BIOS Services Summary

4.031. INT 10H, VIDEO STATE BUFFER LAYOUT

Offset	Size	Function	Allowable Values
0 (0)	word	Offset to static functionality info	
2 (2)	word	Segment of static functionality info	
4 (4)	byte	Video mode	See 4.006. INT 10H, Display Modes
5 (5)	word	Character columns in display	
7 (7)	word	Length of regenerator buffer	In bytes
9 (9)	word	Start address in regeneration buffer	
B (11)	word	Cursor position for page 0	Row, column
D (13)	word	Cursor position for page 1	Row, column
F (15)	word	Cursor position for page 2	Row, column
11 (17)	word	Cursor position for page 3	Row, column
13 (19)	word	Cursor position for page 4	Row, column
15 (21)	word	Cursor position for page 5	Row, column
17 (23)	word	Cursor position for page 6	Row, column
19 (25)	word	Cursor position for page 7	Row, column
1B (27)	word	Cursor type	Start, end values
1D (29)	byte	Active display page	
1E (30)	word	CRT controller address	e.g., 3Bx for monochrome, 3Dx for color
20 (32)	byte	3x8 register setting	
21 (33)	byte	3x9 register setting	
22 (34)	byte	Character rows in display	
23 (35)	word	Character height	In scan lines per character
25 (37)	byte	Active display combination code	
26 (38)	byte	Alternate display combination code	
27 (39)	word	# colors supported in current mode	
29 (41)	byte	# pages supported in current mode	
2A (42)	byte	# scan lines supported in current mode	0=200, 1=350, 2=400, 3=480, 4-255=RESERVED
2B (43)	byte	Primary character block	0=block 0, 1=block 1, and so on/(RESERVED on PS/2 Model 30)
2C (44)	byte	Secondary character block	0=block 0, 1=block 1, and so on/(RESERVED on PS/2 Model 30)
2D (45)	byte	Miscellaneous Information	Bits 6,7=RESERVED Bit 5; 0=background intensity ON, 1=blinking Bit 4; 0=no emulation, 1=cursor emulation ON Bit 3; 1=mode set default palette loading DISABLED Bit 2; 1=monochrome display attached Bit 1; 1=summing is active Bit 0; 1=all modes on all displays are active
2E (46)	3 bytes	RESERVED	
31 (49)	byte	Amt of available video memory	0=64K, 1=128K, 2=192K, 3=256K, 4-255=RESERVED
32 (50)	byte	Save pointer state information	Bits 6,7=RESERVED Bit 5; 1=DCC extension is active Bit 4; 1=palette override is active Bit 3; 1=graphics font override is active Bit 2; 1=alpha font override is active Bit 1; 1=dynamic save area is active Bit 0; 1=512-character set is active
33 (51)	13 bytes	RESERVED	

Source: IBM PS/2 and PC BIOS Technical Reference, pages 2-40 to 2-42

See Also: 4.030. INT 10H, AH=1BH -- Return State

4.032. INT 10H, AH=1CH, AL=00H -- RETURN SAVE/RESTORE BUFFER SIZE

	Prior to Issuing INT 10H			*Upon Return from INT 10H*	
	High	Low		High	Low
AX	1CH	00H	AX		Status*
BX			BX	Number 64-byte blocks for state	
CX	Requested states**		CX		
DX			DX		
SP			SP		
BP			BP		
SI			SI		
DI			DI		
IP			IP		
flags			flags		
CS			CS		
DS			DS		
SS			SS		
ES			ES		

Version Info: Applies to PS/2 Models 50, 60 and 80 only

Notes:
- *1CH= function was supported (BX is valid value)
- **Bit 0 set = save/restore video hardware state
   Bit 1 set = save/restore video BIOS data area
   Bit 2 set = save/restore video DAC state and color registers
   Bits 3-15 should be set to 0 only

Source: IBM PS/2 and PC BIOS Interface Technical Reference, pages 2-44 to 2-45

See Also: 4.001. BIOS Services Summary

4.033. INT 10H, AH=1CH, AL=01H -- SAVE STATE

	Prior to Issuing INT 10H			*Upon Return from INT 10H*	
	High	Low		High	Low
AX	1CH	01H	AX		Status*
BX	Offset of pointer to video state buffer		BX		
CX	Requested states**		CX		
DX			DX		
SP			SP		
BP			BP		
SI			SI		
DI			DI		
IP			IP		
flags			flags		
CS			CS		
DS			DS		
SS			SS		
ES	Segment of pointer to video state buffer		ES		

Version Info: Applies to PS/2 models 50, 60 and 80 only

Notes:
- *1CH= function was supported (states were saved)
- **Bit 0 set = save/restore video hardware state
   Bit 1 set = save/restore video BIOS data area
   Bit 2 set = save/restore video DAC state and color registers
   Bits 3-15 should be set to 0 only

Source: IBM PS/2 and PC BIOS Interface Technical Reference, pages 2-44 to 2-45

See Also: 4.001. BIOS Services Summary
4.031. INT 10H, Video State Buffer Layout

4.034. INT 10H, AH=1CH, AL=02H -- RESTORE STATE

Prior to Issuing INT 10H   *Upon Return from INT 10H*

	High	Low
AX	1CH	02H
BX	Offset of pointer to video state buffer	
CX	Requested states**	
DX		

SP	
BP	
SI	
DI	

IP	
flags	

CS	
DS	
SS	
ES	Segment of pointer to video state buffer

	High	Low
AX		Status*
BX		
CX		
DX		

SP	
BP	
SI	
DI	

IP	
flags	

CS	
DS	
SS	
ES	

Version Info: Applies to PS/2 models 50, 60 and 80 only

Notes: •*1CH= function was supported (states were restored)
•**Bit 0 set = save/restore video hardware state
Bit 1 set = save/restore video BIOS data area
Bit 2 set = save/restore video DAC state and color registers
Bits 3-15 should be set to 0 only

Source: IBM PS/2 and PC BIOS Interface Technical Reference, pages 2-44 to 2-45

See Also: 4.001. BIOS Services Summary
4.031. INT 10H, Video State Buffer Layout

4.035. INT 10H, AH=FEH -- GET VIDEO BUFFER (TOPVIEW)

Prior to Issuing INT 10H   *Upon Return from INT 10H*

	High	Low
AX	FEH	
BX		
CX		
DX		

SP	
BP	
SI	
DI	Offset of physical video buffer

IP	
flags	

CS	
DS	
SS	
ES	Segment of physical video buffer

	High	Low
AX		
BX		
CX		
DX		

SP	
BP	
SI	
DI	Offset of logical video buffer

IP	
flags	

CS	
DS	
SS	
ES	Segment of logical video buffer

Notes: •Physical address is B000:0000H for MDA
B800:0000H for CGA and EGA
•Logical address is memory assigned to video buffer by Topview
•Function is ignored if Topview is not running

Source: *Advanced MS-DOS* (Microsoft Press), Ray Duncan, pages 418 to 419

See Also: 4.001. BIOS Function Summary
4.036. INT 10H, AH=FFH -- Update Video Buffer (Topview)

4.036. INT 10H, AH=FFH -- UPDATE VIDEO BUFFER (TOPVIEW)

Prior to Calling INT 10H   *Upon Return from INT 10H*

	High	Low
AX	FFH	
BX		
CX	Number of chars modified*	
DX		

SP	
BP	
SI	
DI	Offset to first char modified

IP	
FLAGS	

CS	
DS	
SS	
ES	Segment of logical video buffer

Function returns no values

Notes:
- •Logical video buffer is obtained using Function FEH
- •Function is ignored if Topview is not running
- •*Characters must be in sequence (i.e., contiguous)

Source: *Advanced MS-DOS* (Microsoft Press), Ray Duncan, pages 419 to 420

See Also: 4.001. BIOS Services Summary
4.035. INT 10H, AH=FEH -- Get Video Buffer (Topview)

4.037. INT 11H: GET EQUIPMENT LIST SERVICE

Prior to Issuing INT 11H   *Upon Return from INT 11H*

	High	Low
AX		
BX		
CX		
DX		

SP	
BP	
SI	
DI	

IP	
flags	

CS	
DS	
SS	
ES	

	High	Low
AX	Equipment flag word*	
BX		
CX		
DX		

SP	
BP	
SI	
DI	

IP	
flags	

CS	
DS	
SS	
ES	

Notes:
- •*Bit 0 = floppy drive installed
- Bit 1 = math coprocessor installed
- Bits 2-3 = 16K blocks RAM installed on system board**
- Bits 4-5 = video mode (1=40x25 color, 2=80x25 color, 3=80x25 mono)
- Bits 6-7 = number of floppy drives - 1
- Bit 8 = DMA present**
- Bits 9-11 = number of RS-232 cards attached
- Bit 12 = game port adapter attached**
- Bit 13 = serial printer attached (PCJr only)
- Bit 13 = internal modem installed for all others
- Bits 14-15 = number of printers attached
- •**These bits have different meanings for AT and PS/2

Source: IBM PS/2 and PC BIOS Interface Technical Reference, page 2-46

See Also: 4.001. BIOS Services Summary

4.038. INT 12H: GET MEMORY SIZE SERVICE

Prior to Issuing INT 12H

	High	Low
AX		
BX		
CX		
DX		

SP	
BP	
SI	
DI	

IP	
flags	

CS	
DS	
SS	
ES	

Upon Return from INT 12H

	High	Low
AX	Memory size*	
BX		
CX		
DX		

SP	
BP	
SI	
DI	

IP	
flags	

CS	
DS	
SS	
ES	

Version Info: On PS/2, value in AX is total memory minus that allocated to the Extended BIOS data area

Notes:
- All memory is assumed to be functional
- *In 1K bytes

Source: IBM PS/2 and PC BIOS Interface Technical Reference, page 2-47

See Also: 4.001. BIOS Services Summary

4.039. INT 13H, AH=00H -- RESET DISK SYSTEM

Prior to Issuing INT 13H

	High	Low
AX	00H	
BX		
CX		
DX		Drive*

SP	
BP	
SI	
DI	

IP	
flags	

CS	
DS	
SS	
ES	

Upon Return from INT 13H

	High	Low
AX	Status**	
BX		
CX		
DX		

SP	
BP	
SI	
DI	

IP	
flags	Carry set on error*

CS	
DS	
SS	
ES	

Version Info:
- *On PS/2 only
- **On PS/2 only, see 4.041. INT 13H, Disk System Status Byte Layout

Source: IBM PS/2 and PC BIOS Interface Technical Reference, pages 2-48 to 2-49

See Also:
4.001. BIOS Services Summary
4.041. Disk System Status Byte Layout

4.040. INT 13H, AH=01H -- GET DISK SYSTEM STATUS

Prior to Issuing INT 13H

	High	Low
AX	01H	
BX		
CX		
DX		Drive**

SP	
BP	
SI	
DI	

IP	
flags	

CS	
DS	
SS	
ES	

Upon Return from INT 13H

	High	Low
AX	Status*	
BX		
CX		
DX		

SP	
BP	
SI	
DI	

IP	
flags	Carry set on error**

CS	
DS	
SS	
ES	

Version Info: **On PS/2 and Extended BIOS only

Notes: *Status of previous call; See 4.041. INT 13H, Disk System Status Byte Layout

Source: IBM PS/2 and PC BIOS Interface Technical Reference, page 2-49

See Also: 4.001. BIOS Services Summary
4.041. Disk System Status Byte Layout

4.041. INT 13H, DISK SYSTEM STATUS BYTE LAYOUT

Value	Floppy/Fixed	Description
0 (0)	Both	No error
1 (1)	Both	Invalid diskette parameter (bad command)
2 (2)	Both	Address mark was not found
3 (3)	Floppy	Attempted write on protected diskette
4 (4)	Both	Sector was not found
5 (5)	Fixed	Reset failed
6 (6)	Floppy	Diskette was removed
7 (7)	Fixed	Bad parameter table
8 (8)	Floppy	DMA overrun on previous operation
9 (9)	Both	Attempted to cross 64k segment boundary on DMA operation
A (10)	Fixed	Bad sector flag
B (11)	Fixed	Bad cylinder detected*
C (12)	Floppy	Media type requested was not found*
D (13)	Fixed	Invalid number of sectors in format*
E (14)	Fixed	Control data address mark detected*
F (15)	Fixed	DMA arbitration level out of allowable range*
10 (16)	Both	CRC or ECC error on disk read
11 (17)	Fixed	ECC corrected data error
20 (32)	Both	Controller failed
40 (64)	Both	Seek operation failed
80 (128)	Both	Drive timed out, assumed not ready
AA (170)	Fixed	Drive not ready
BB (187)	Fixed	Undefined error
CC (204)	Fixed	Write fault
EO (224)	Fixed	Status error
FF (255)	Fixed	Sense operation failed*

Version Info: *Documented for PS/2 and Extended BIOS only

Notes: Fixed disk status byte applies to XT and AT hard disks; floppy applies to all models of IBM PCs

Source: IBM PS/2 and PC BIOS Interface Technical Reference, pages 2-49 and 2-59

See Also: 4.040. INT 13H, AH=01H -- Get Disk System Status

4.042. INT 13H, AH=02H -- READ DISK

Prior to Issuing INT 13H

	High	Low
AX	02H	# Sectors to read
BX	Offset of pointer to read buffer	
CX	Cylinder number	Sector number**
DX	Head number	Drive number***

SP	
BP	
SI	
DI	

IP	
flags	

CS	
DS	
SS	
ES	Segment of pointer to read buffer

Upon Return from INT 13H

	High	Low
AX	Status*	# Sectors read
BX		
CX		
DX		

SP	
BP	
SI	
DI	

IP	
flags	Carry set on error

CS	
DS	
SS	
ES	

Notes:
- Only value in DL is checked for an appropriate value
- *See 4.041. INT 13H, Disk System Status Byte Layout
- **For fixed drives, top 2 bits are HO bits of 10-bit cylinder number, bottom 6 bits are sector number
- ***Bit 7=0 for floppy drive, 1 for fixed drive

Source: IBM PS/2 and PC BIOS Interface Technical Reference, pages 2-50 and 2-60

See Also:
4.001. BIOS Services Summary
4.041. Disk System Status Byte Layout
4.043. INT 13H, AH=03H -- Write Disk

4.043. INT 13H, AH=03H -- WRITE DISK

Prior to Issuing INT 13H

	High	Low
AX	03H	# Sectors to write
BX	Offset of pointer to buffer with data	
CX	Cylinder number	Sector number**
DX	Head number	Drive number***

SP	
BP	
SI	
DI	

IP	
flags	

CS	
DS	
SS	
ES	Segment of pointer to buffer with data

Upon Return from INT 13H

	High	Low
AX	Status*	# Sectors written
BX		
CX		
DX		

SP	
BP	
SI	
DI	

IP	
flags	Carry set on error

CS	
DS	
SS	
ES	

Notes:
- Only value in DL is checked for an appropriate value
- *See 4.041. INT 13H, Disk System Status Byte Layout
- **For fixed drives, top 2 bits are HO bits of 10-bit cylinder number, bottom 6 bits are sector number
- ***bit 7=0 for floppy drive, 1 for fixed drive

Source: IBM PS/2 and PC BIOS Interface Technical Reference, pages 2-50 and 2-61

See Also:
4.001. BIOS Services Summary
4.041. Disk System Status Byte Layout
4.042. INT 13H, AH=02H -- Read Disk

4.044. INT 13H, AH=04H -- VERIFY SECTORS

	Prior to Issuing INT 13H			*Upon Return from INT 13H*	
	High	*Low*		*High*	*Low*
AX	04H	# Sectors to verify	AX	Status*	# Sectors verified
BX	Offset of pointer to data buffer****		BX		
CX	Cylinder number	Sector number**	CX		
DX	Head number	Drive number***	DX		
SP			SP		
BP			BP		
SI			SI		
DI			DI		
IP			IP		
flags			flags	Carry set on error	
CS			CS		
DS			DS		
SS			SS		
ES	Segment of pointer to buffer with data****		ES		

Version Info: ****Not required for AT BIOS after 11/15/85, or for XT286, Convertible, or PS/2

Notes:
•Only value in DL is checked for an appropriate value
•*See 4.041. INT 13H, Disk System Status Byte Layout
•**For fixed drives, top 2 bits are HO bits of 10-bit cylinder number, bottom 6 bits are sector number
•***Bit 7=0 for floppy drive, 1 for fixed drive

Source: IBM PS/2 and PC BIOS Interface Technical Reference, pages 2-51 and 2-61 to 2-62

See Also:
4.001. BIOS Services Summary
4.041. Disk System Status Byte Layout
4.042. INT 13H, AH=02H -- Read Disk

4.045. INT 13H, AH=05H -- FORMAT TRACK/CYLINDER

Prior to Issuing INT 13H

	High	Low
AX	05H	Number of sectors†
BX	Offset of pointer to address fields****	
CX	Cylinder number	Sector number**
DX	Head number	Drive number***

SP	
BP	
SI	
DI	

IP	
flags	

CS	
DS	
SS	
ES	Segment of pointer to address fields****

Upon Return from INT 13H

	High	Low
AX	Status*	
BX		
CX		
DX		

SP	
BP	
SI	
DI	

IP	
flags	Carry set on error

CS	
DS	
SS	
ES	

Notes:
- Only value in DL is checked for an appropriate value
- *See 4.041. INT 13H, Disk System Status Byte Layout
- **For fixed drives, top 2 bits are HO bits of 10-bit cylinder number, bottom 6 bits are sector number (sector number is ignored)
- ***Bit 7=0 for floppy drive, 1 for fixed drive
- ****For floppy controller only: Must be one address field for every sector on the track. For AT, XT286 and PS/2 hard disk controller, ES:BX points to 512-byte buffer, which contains 00H (good sector) or 80H (bad sector) bytes followed by the sector number for each sector on a cylinder.

Address field:

Byte	Meaning	Allowable Values
1	Cylinder number	
2	Head number	
3	Sector number	
4	Number bytes/sector	0=128, 1=256, 2=512, 3=1024

- † Ignored on hard disk controller, except for XT, where AL should contain interleave value

Source: IBM PS/2 and PC BIOS Interface Technical Reference, pages 2-51 to 2-52 and 2-62 to 2-63

See Also: 4.001. BIOS Services Summary
4.041. Disk System Status Byte Layout
4.046. INT 13H, AH=06H -- Format Cylinder Set Bad Sector Flags
4.047. INT 13H, AH=07H -- Format Drive Starting at Cylinder

4.046. INT 13H, AH=06H -- FORMAT CYLINDER SET BAD SECTOR FLAGS

Prior to Issuing INT 13H   *Upon Return from INT 13H*

	High	Low
AX	06H	Interleave
BX		
CX	Cylinder number	Sector number**
DX	Head number	Drive number***

	High	Low
AX	Status*	
BX		
CX		
DX		

SP	
BP	
SI	
DI	

SP	
BP	
SI	
DI	

IP	
flags	

IP	
flags	Carry set on error

CS	
DS	
SS	
ES	

CS	
DS	
SS	
ES	

Version Info: Applies to XT, AT, XT286 and PS/2 with fixed disk drives only

Notes: •Only value in DL is checked for an appropriate value
•*See 4.041. INT 13H, Disk System Status Byte Layout
•**Top 2 bits are HO bits of 10-bit cylinder number, bottom 6 bits
are sector number (sector number is ignored)
•***Bit 7= 1 for fixed drive

Source: IBM PS/2 and PC BIOS Interface Technical Reference, page 2-63

See Also: 4.001. BIOS Services Summary
4.041. Disk System Status Byte Layout
4.045. INT 13H, AH=05H -- Format Cylinder
4.047. INT 13H, AH=07H -- Format Drive Starting at Cylinder

4.047. INT 13H, AH=07H -- FORMAT DRIVE STARTING AT CYLINDER

Prior to Issuing INT 13H   *Upon Return from INT 13H*

	High	Low			High	Low
AX	07H	Interleave		AX	Status*	
BX				BX		
CX	Cylinder number	Sector number**		CX		
DX		Drive number***		DX		
SP				SP		
BP				BP		
SI				SI		
DI				DI		
IP				IP		
flags				flags	Carry set on error	
CS				CS		
DS				DS		
SS				SS		
ES				ES		

Version Info: Applies to XT with fixed disk drives only

Notes: •Only value in DL is checked for an appropriate value
•*See 4.041. INT 13H, Disk System Status Byte Layout
•**Top 2 bits are HO bits of 10-bit cylinder number, bottom 6 bits
are sector number (sector number is ignored)
•***Bit 7= 1 for fixed drive

Source: IBM PS/2 and PC BIOS Interface Technical Reference, page 2-64

See Also: 4.001. BIOS Services Summary
4.041. Disk System Status Byte Layout
4.045. INT 13H, AH=05H -- Format Cylinder
4.046. INT 13H, AH=06H -- Format Cylinder Set Bad Sector Flags

4.048. INT 13H, AH=08H -- READ DRIVE PARAMETERS

Prior to Issuing INT 13H   *Upon Return from INT 13H*

	High	Low			High	Low
AX	08H			AX	0	
BX				BX	0	Drive type**
CX				CX	Max cylinders	Max sectors/track***
DX		Drive number*		DX	Max heads	Number drives
SP				SP		
BP				BP		
SI				SI		
DI				DI	Offset of pointer to 11-byte parm table	
IP				IP		
flags				flags	Carry set on error	
CS				CS		
DS				DS		
SS				SS		
ES				ES	Segment of pointer to 11-byte parm table	

Version Info: Applies to XT, AT and PS/2 only

Notes: •*0-based; bit 7=0 indicates floppy drive
•**01=360K, 02=1.2Mb, 03=720K, 04=1.44Mb
•***Top 2 bits are HO bits of 10-bit max cylinders, bits 0-5 are
max sectors per track

Source: IBM PS/2 and PC BIOS Interface Technical Reference, pages 2-53 to 2-54

See Also: 4.001. BIOS Services Summary

4.049. INT 13H, AH=09H -- INIT DRIVE PAIR CHARACTERISTICS

	Prior to Issuing INT 13H			*Upon Return from INT 13H*	
	High	Low		High	Low
AX	09H		AX	Status**	
BX			BX		
CX			CX		
DX		Drive number*	DX		
SP			SP		
BP			BP		
SI			SI		
DI			DI		
IP			IP		
flags			flags	Carry flag set if status is non-zero	
CS			CS		
DS			DS		
SS			SS		
ES			ES		

Version Info: Applies to XT, AT and PS/2 only

Notes: •*0-based; bit 7 indicates fixed drive
•**See 4.041. INT 13H, Disk System Status Byte Layout

Source: IBM PS/2 and PC BIOS Interface Technical Reference, page 2-65

See Also: 4.001. BIOS Services Summary
4.041. Disk System Status Byte Layout

4.050. INT 13H, AH=0CH -- SEEK

	Prior to Issuing INT 13H			*Upon Return from INT 13H*	
	High	Low		High	Low
AX	0CH		AX	Status**	
BX			BX		
CX	Cylinder number***		CX		
DX	Head number	Drive number*	DX		
SP			SP		
BP			BP		
SI			SI		
DI			DI		
IP			IP		
flags			flags	Carry set if status is non-zero	
CS			CS		
DS			DS		
SS			SS		
ES			ES		

Version Info: Applies to XT, AT and PS/2 only

Notes: •*0-based; bit 7 set indicates fixed disk
•**See 4.041. INT 13H, Disk System Status Byte Layout
•***Bits 7-6 of CL are 2 HO bits of 10-bit cylinder number; CH=8 LO bits of
10-bit cylinder number

Source: IBM PS/2 and PC BIOS Interface Technical Reference, page 2-66

See Also: 4.001. BIOS Services Summary
4.041. Disk System Status Byte Layout

4.051. INT 13H, AH=0DH -- ALTERNATE DISK RESET

Prior to Issuing INT 13H   *Upon Return from INT 13H*

	High	Low			High	Low
AX	0DH			AX	Status**	
BX				BX		
CX				CX		
DX		Drive number*		DX		

SP				SP		
BP				BP		
SI				SI		
DI				DI		

| IP | | | | IP | | |
| flags | | | | flags | Carry set if status is non-zero | |

CS				CS		
DS				DS		
SS				SS		
ES				ES		

Version Info: Applies to XT, AT and PS/2 fixed disks only

Notes: •*0-based; bit 7 set indicates fixed disk
                      •**See 4.041. INT 13H, Disk System Status Byte Layout

Source: IBM PS/2 and PC BIOS Interface Technical Reference, page 2-66

See Also: 4.001. BIOS Services Summary
                      4.041. Disk System Status Byte Layout

4.052. INT 13H, AH=10H -- TEST DRIVE READY

Prior to Issuing INT 13H   *Upon Return from INT 13H*

	High	Low			High	Low
AX	10H			AX	Status**	
BX				BX		
CX				CX		
DX		Drive number*		DX		

SP				SP		
BP				BP		
SI				SI		
DI				DI		

| IP | | | | IP | | |
| flags | | | | flags | Carry set if status is non-zero | |

CS				CS		
DS				DS		
SS				SS		
ES				ES		

Version Info: Applies to XT, AT and PS/2 fixed disks only

Notes: •*0-based;bit 7 set indicates fixed drive
                      •**See 4.041. INT 13H, Disk System Status Byte Layout

Source: IBM PS/2 and PC BIOS Interface Technical Reference, pages 2-66 to 2-67

See Also: 4.001. BIOS Services Summary
                      4.041. Disk System Status Byte Layout

4.053. INT 13H, AH=11H -- RECALIBRATE DRIVE

Prior to Issuing INT 13H   *Upon Return from INT 13H*

	High	Low
AX	11H	
BX		
CX		
DX		Drive number*

SP	
BP	
SI	
DI	

IP	
flags	

CS	
DS	
SS	
ES	

	High	Low
AX	Status**	
BX		
CX		
DX		

SP	
BP	
SI	
DI	

IP	
flags	Carry set if status is non-zero

CS	
DS	
SS	
ES	

Version Info: Applies to XT, AT and PS/2 fixed disks only

Notes: •*0-based; bit 7 set indicates fixed drive
•**See 4.041. INT 13H, Disk System Status Byte Layout

Source: IBM PS/2 and PC BIOS Interface Technical Reference, page 2-67

See Also: 4.001. BIOS Services Summary
4.041. Disk System Status Byte Layout

4.054. INT 13H, AH=15H -- READ DASD TYPE

Prior to Issuing INT 13H   *Upon Return from INT 13H*

	High	Low
AX	15H	
BX		
CX		
DX		Drive number*

SP	
BP	
SI	
DI	

IP	
flags	

CS	
DS	
SS	
ES	

	High	Low
AX	Type**	
BX		
CX	HO number 512-byte blocks	
DX	LO number 512-byte blocks	

SP	
BP	
SI	
DI	

IP	
flags	Carry set if operation unsuccessful

CS	
DS	
SS	
ES	

Version Info: Applies to AT, Convertible, and PS/2 only

Notes: •DASD (Direct Access Storage Device)
•*0-based; bit 7 set indicates fixed disk
•**00=drive not present or invalid
  01=no change line support
  02=change line supported
  03=fixed disk

Source: IBM PS/2 and PC BIOS Interface Technical Reference, page 2-67

See Also: 4.001. BIOS Services Summary

4.055. INT 13H, AH=16H -- DISKETTE CHANGE LINE STATUS

Prior to Issuing INT 13H

	High	Low
AX	16H	
BX		
CX		
DX		Drive number*

SP	
BP	
SI	
DI	

IP	
flags	

CS	
DS	
SS	
ES	

Upon Return from INT 13H

	High	Low
AX	Status**	
BX		
CX		
DX		

SP	
BP	
SI	
DI	

IP	
flags	Carry set if status is non-zero

CS	
DS	
SS	
ES	

Version Info: Applies to AT, Convertible, and PS/2 only

Notes: •*0-based; bit 7 set indicates fixed disk
•**00=diskette change signal not active
01= invalid diskette parameter
06= diskette change signal active
80H=diskette drive not ready

Source: IBM PS/2 and PC BIOS Interface Technical Reference, page 2-55

See Also: 4.001. BIOS Services Summary

4.056. INT 13H, AH=17H -- SET DASD TYPE FOR FORMAT

Prior to Issuing INT 13H

	High	Low
AX	17H	DASD Type*
BX		
CX		
DX		Drive number**

SP	
BP	
SI	
DI	

IP	
flags	

CS	
DS	
SS	
ES	

Upon Return from INT 13H

	High	Low
AX	Status***	
BX		
CX		
DX		

SP	
BP	
SI	
DI	

IP	
flags	Carry set if status is non-zero

CS	
DS	
SS	
ES	

Version Info: Applies to AT, Convertible, and PS/2 only

Notes: •*00, 05-FFH=invalid request
01=320/360K diskette in 360K drive
02=360K diskette in 1.2Mb drive
03=1.2Mb diskette in 1.2Mb drive
04=720Kb disk in 720K drive (only for BIOS 6/10/85 and later)
•**0-based; bit 7 set indicates fixed drive
•***See 4.041. INT 13H, Disk System Status Byte Layout

Source: IBM PS/2 and PC BIOS Interface Technical Reference, pages 2-55 to 2-56

See Also: 4.001. BIOS Services Summary
4.041. Disk System Status Byte Layout

4.057. INT 13H, AH=18H -- SET MEDIA TYPE FOR FORMAT

	Prior to Issuing INT 13H			*Upon Return from INT 13H*	
	High	*Low*		*High*	*Low*
AX	18H		AX	Status*	
BX			BX		
CX	Number of tracks	Number of sectors**	CX		
DX		Drive number***	DX		
SP			SP		
BP			BP		
SI			SI		
DI			DI	Offset of pointer to 11-byte media parm table****
IP			IP		
flags			flags	Carry set on error
CS			CS		
DS			DS		
SS			SS		
ES			ES	Segment of pointer to 11-byte media parm table****

Version Info: Applies to AT after 11/15/85, XT after 1/10/86, XT286, and PS/2

Notes:
- Only value in DL is checked for an appropriate value
- *See 4.041. INT 13H, Disk System Status Byte Layout
- **Top 2 bits are HO bits of 10-bit number of tracks, bottom 6 bits are number of sectors
- ***Bit 7=0 for floppy disk drives
- ****See 4.058. INT 13H, Media Descriptor Table

Source: IBM PS/2 and PC BIOS Interface Technical Reference, pages 2-56 to 2-57

See Also:
4.001. BIOS Services Summary
4.041. Disk System Status Byte Layout
4.045. INT 13H, AH=05H -- Format Cylinder
4.046. INT 13H, AH=06H --Format Cylinder Set Bad Sector Flags
4.058. Media Descriptor Table

4.058. MEDIA DESCRIPTOR TABLE

Offset	Length	Description	Allowable Values
0 (0)	Byte	First specify byte	
1 (1)	Byte	Second specify byte	
2 (2)	Byte	Timer ticks to wait until motor OFF	
3 (3)	Byte	Number of bytes/sector	0=128, 1=256, 2=512, 3=1024
4 (4)	Byte	Number of sectors/track	
5 (5)	Byte	Gap length, in bytes	
6 (6)	Byte	Data length, in bytes	
7 (7)	Byte	Gap length for format	
8 (8)	Byte	Fill byte for formatting	
9 (9)	Byte	Head settle time, in milliseconds	
A (10)	Byte	Motor startup time, in 1/8 seconds	

Version Info: Applies to AT after 11/15/85, XT after 1/10/86, XT286, and PS/2

Notes: Sometimes referred to as MPT (Media Parameter Table)

Source: IBM PS/2 and PC BIOS Interface Technical Reference, page 3-23

See Also: 4.057. INT 13H, AH=18H -- Set Media Type For Format

4.059. INT 13H, AH=19H -- PARK HEADS

Prior to Issuing INT 13H

	High	Low
AX	19H	
BX		
CX		
DX		Drive**

SP	
BP	
SI	
DI	

IP	
flags	

CS	
DS	
SS	
ES	

Upon Return from INT 13H

	High	Low
AX	Status*	
BX		
CX		
DX		

SP	
BP	
SI	
DI	

IP	
flags	Carry set on error

CS	
DS	
SS	
ES	

Version Info: Applies to AT, XT, XT286, and PS/2

Notes: •*See 4.041. INT 13H, Disk System Status Byte Layout
•**For PS/2 products only; bit 7=1 for fixed disk

Source: IBM PS/2 and PC BIOS Interface Technical Reference, page 2-68

See Also: 4.001. BIOS Services Summary
4.041. Disk System Status Byte Layout

4.060. INT 13H, AH=1AH -- FORMAT UNIT

Prior to Issuing INT 13H

	High	Low
AX	1AH	Defect table count*
BX	Offset of pointer to defect table	
CX		Modifier bits**
DX		Drive***

SP	
BP	
SI	
DI	

IP	
flags	

CS	
DS	
SS	
ES	Segment of pointer to defect table

Upon Return from INT 13H

Interrupt returns no values

Version Info: Applies to PS/2 models 50, 60 and 80 only

Notes: •*0=no defect table used; >0 means use defect table.
Defect table consists of relative block addresses of
defective sectors.
•**See 4.061. INT 13H, Format Unit Modifier Bits
•***Bit 7=1 for fixed disk

Source: IBM PS/2 and PC BIOS Interface Technical Reference,
pages 2-68 to 2-69

See Also: 4.001. BIOS Services Summary
4.061. Format Unit Modifier Bits

4.061. INT 13H, FORMAT UNIT MODIFIER BITS

Bit Number	Function
5-7	RESERVED
4	Periodic interrupt status (1=ON, 0=OFF)
3	Extended surface analysis (1=perform, 0=don't perform)
2	Secondary defect map (1=update, 0=don't update)
1	Use secondary defect map (1=ignore it, 0=use it)
0	Use primary defect map (1=ignore it, 0=use it)

Source: IBM PS/2 and PC BIOS Technical Reference, pages 2-68 to 2-69

See Also: 4.060. INT 13H, AH=1AH -- Format Unit

4.062. INT 14H, AH=00H -- INIT COMMUNICATIONS PORT

Prior to Issuing INT 14H

	High	Low
AX	00H	Comm parm byte*
BX		
CX		
DX	Comm port number	

SP		
BP		
SI		
DI		

| IP | | |
| flags | | |

CS		
DS		
SS		
ES		

Upon Return from INT 14H

	High	Low
AX	Line status**	Modem status**
BX		
CX		
DX		

SP		
BP		
SI		
DI		

| IP | | |
| flags | | |

CS		
DS		
SS		
ES		

Notes:
- *See 4.064. INT 14H, Com Port Parameter Byte
- **See 4.063. Modem Status Byte

Source: IBM PS/2 and PC BIOS Interface Technical Reference, pages 2-70 to 2-71

See Also:
4.001. BIOS Services Summary
4.063. Modem Status Byte
4.064. Com Port Parameter Byte

4.063. MODEM AND LINE STATUS BYTES

Modem Status Byte:

Bit Numbers

7	6	5	4	3	2	1	0	Description
X								Received line signal detect
	X							Ring indicator
		X						Data set ready
			X					Clear to send
				X				Delta receive line signal detect
					X			Trailing edge ring detector
						X		Delta data set ready
							X	Delta clear to send

Line Status Byte:

Bit Numbers

7	6	5	4	3	2	1	0	Description
X								Time-out*
	X							Transmitter shift register empty
		X						Transmitter holding register empty
			X					Break detect
				X				Framing error
					X			Parity error
						X		Overrun error
							X	Data ready

Notes: *Unpredictable results in other bits when this bit is set

Source: IBM PS/2 and PC BIOS Interface Technical Reference,
                 pages 2-70 to 2-71

See Also: 4.062. INT 14H, AH=00H -- Init Communications Port
                 4.065. INT 14H, AH=01H -- Write Character
                 4.066. INT 14H, AH=02H -- Read Character
                 4.067. INT 14H, AH=03H -- Status Request

4.064. COM PORT PARAMETER BYTE

Bit Numbers

7	6	5	4	3	2	1	0	Description	Allowable Values
X	X	X						Baud rate	000 = 110 baud 001 = 150 010 = 300 011 = 600 100 = 1200 (default) 101 = 2400 110 = 4800 111 = 9600
			X	X				Parity	00 = No parity 01 = Odd parity 10 = No parity 11 = Even parity
					X			Stop bits	0=1 stop bit, 1=2 stop bits
						X	X	Word length	10 = 7 bits 11 = 8 bits

Notes: On PS/2, baud rates higher than 9600 are set using functions 4 and 5

Source: IBM PS/2 and PC BIOS Interface Technical Reference, pages 2-70 to 2-71

See Also: 4.062. INT 14H, AH=00H -- Init Communications Port

4.065. INT 14H, AH=01H -- WRITE CHARACTER

Prior to Issuing INT 14H

	High	Low
AX	01H	Character
BX		
CX		
DX	Comm port number	

SP	
BP	
SI	
DI	

IP	
flags	

CS	
DS	
SS	
ES	

Upon Return from INT 14H

	High	Low
AX	Line status*	Character
BX		
CX		
DX		

SP	
BP	
SI	
DI	

IP	
flags	

CS	
DS	
SS	
ES	

Notes: *See 4.063. Modem and Line Status Bytes

Source: IBM PS/2 and PC BIOS Interface Technical Reference, page 2-71

See Also: 4.001. BIOS Services Summary
4.063. Modem and Line Status Bytes
4.066. INT 14H, AH=02H -- Read Character

4.066. INT 14H, AH=02H -- READ CHARACTER

Prior to Issuing INT 14H

	High	Low
AX	02H	
BX		
CX		
DX	Comm port number	

SP	
BP	
SI	
DI	

IP	
flags	

CS	
DS	
SS	
ES	

Upon Return from INT 14H

	High	Low
AX	Line status*	Character
BX		
CX		
DX		

SP	
BP	
SI	
DI	

IP	
flags	

CS	
DS	
SS	
ES	

Notes: *See 4.063. Modem and Line Status Bytes

Source: IBM PS/2 and PC BIOS Interface Technical Reference, page 2-71

See Also: 4.001. BIOS Services Summary
4.063. Modem and Line Status Bytes
4.065. INT 14H, AH=01H -- Write Character

4.067. INT 14H, AH=03H -- STATUS REQUEST

Prior to Issuing INT 14H

	High	Low
AX	03H	
BX		
CX		
DX	Comm port number	

SP	
BP	
SI	
DI	

IP	
flags	

CS	
DS	
SS	
ES	

Upon Return from INT 14H

	High	Low
AX	Line status*	Modem status*
BX		
CX		
DX		

SP	
BP	
SI	
DI	

IP	
flags	

CS	
DS	
SS	
ES	

Notes: *See 4.063. Modem and Line Status Bytes

Source: IBM PS/2 and PC BIOS Interface Technical Reference, page 2-72

See Also: 4.001. BIOS Services Summary
                4.063. Modem and Line Status Bytes

4.068. INT 14H, AH=04H -- EXTENDED INIT

Prior to Issuing INT 14H

	High	Low
AX	04H	Break setting *
BX	Parity setting **	Stop bit setting ***
CX	Word length ****	Baud rate †
DX	Port number ¥	

SP	
BP	
SI	
DI	

IP	
flags	

CS	
DS	
SS	
ES	

Upon Return from INT 14H

	High	Low
AX	Line status §	Modem status §
BX		
CX		
DX		

SP	
BP	
SI	
DI	

IP	
flags	

CS	
DS	
SS	
ES	

Version Info: Applies to PS/2 models only

Notes:
- * 00=no break, 01=break
- ** 00=no parity, 01=odd parity, 02=even parity, 03=stick parity odd, 04=stick parity even
- *** 00=one, 01=two (one and a half for 5-bit word lengths)
- **** 00=5 bits, 01=6 bits, 02=7 bits, 03=8 bits
- † 00=110 baud, 01=150 baud, 02=300 baud, 03=600 baud, 04=1200 baud, 05=2400 baud, 06=4800 baud, 07=9600 baud, 08=19,200 baud
- ¥ Must be 0, 1, 2, or 3
- § See 4.063. Modem and Line Status Bytes

Source: IBM PS/2 and PC BIOS Interface Technical Reference, pages 2-72 to 2-73

See Also: 4.001. BIOS Services Summary
                4.062. INT 14H, AH=00H -- Init Communications Port
                4.063. Modem and Line Status Bytes

4.069. INT 14H, AH=05H, AL=00H -- READ MODEM CONTROL REGISTER

Prior to Issuing INT 14H

	High	Low
AX	05H	00H
BX		
CX		
DX	Port number**	

SP		
BP		
SI		
DI		

IP		
flags		

CS		
DS		
SS		
ES		

Upon Return from INT 14H

	High	Low
AX		
BX		Modem control reg*
CX		
DX		

SP		
BP		
SI		
DI		

IP		
flags		

CS		
DS		
SS		
ES		

Version Info: Applies to PS/2 models only

Notes: •*Modem control register formatted as follows:

Bit	Meaning when set
5-7	RESERVED
4	Loop
3	Out2
2	Out1
1	Request to send
0	Data terminal ready

•**Serial port to use, must be 0, 1, 2, or 3

Source: IBM PS/2 and PC BIOS Interface Technical Reference, page 2-73

See Also: 4.001. BIOS Services Summary
4.070. INT 14H, AH=05H, AL=01H -- Write Modem Control Register

4.070. INT 14H, AH=05H, AL=01H -- WRITE MODEM CONTROL REGISTER

Prior to Issuing INT 14H   *Upon Return from INT 14H*

	High	Low			High	Low
AX	05H	01H		AX	Line status***	Modem status***
BX				BX		Modem control reg*
CX				CX		
DX	Port number**			DX		
SP				SP		
BP				BP		
SI				SI		
DI				DI		
IP				IP		
flags				flags		
CS				CS		
DS				DS		
SS				SS		
ES				ES		

Version Info: Applies to PS/2 models only

Notes: •*Modem control register formatted as follows:

Bit	Meaning when set
5-7	RESERVED
4	Loop
3	Out2
2	Out1
1	Request to send
0	Data terminal ready

•**Serial port to use, must be 0, 1, 2, or 3
•***See 4.063. Modem and Line Status Bytes

Source: IBM PS/2 and PC BIOS Interface Technical Reference, page 2-73

See Also: 4.001. BIOS Services Summary
4.063. Modem and Line Status Bytes
4.069. INT 14H, AH=05H, AL=00H -- Read Modem Control Register

4.071. INT 15H, AH=00H -- CASSETTE MOTOR ON

Prior to Issuing INT 15H   *Upon Return from INT 15H*

	High	Low			High	Low
AX	00H			AX	00H	
BX				BX		
CX				CX		
DX				DX		
SP				SP		
BP				BP		
SI				SI		
DI				DI		
IP				IP		
flags				flags	Carry clear	
CS				CS		
DS				DS		
SS				SS		
ES				ES		

Version Info: Applies to PC and PCJr only, all others set Carry and return 86H in AH

Notes: Obsolete function, no longer supported

Source: IBM PS/2 and PC BIOS Interface Technical Reference, pages 2-74 to 2-75

See Also: 4.001. BIOS Services Summary
4.072. INT 15H, AH=01H -- Cassette Motor OFF

4.072. INT 15H, AH=01H -- CASSETTE MOTOR OFF

Prior to Issuing INT 15H

	High	Low
AX	01H	
BX		
CX		
DX		

SP	
BP	
SI	
DI	

IP	
flags	

CS	
DS	
SS	
ES	

Upon Return from INT 15H

	High	Low
AX	00H	
BX		
CX		
DX		

SP	
BP	
SI	
DI	

IP	
flags	Carry clear

CS	
DS	
SS	
ES	

Version Info: Applies to PC and PCJr only, all others set Carry and return 86H in AH

Notes: Obsolete function, no longer supported

Source: IBM PS/2 and PC BIOS Interface Technical Reference, page 2-75

See Also: 4.001. BIOS Services Summary
4.071. INT 15H, AH=00H -- Cassette Motor ON

4.073. INT 15H, AH=02H -- CASSETTE READ DATA BLOCKS

Prior to Issuing INT 15H

	High	Low
AX	02H	
BX	Offset of pointer to data buffer	
CX	# Bytes to read	
DX		

SP	
BP	
SI	
DI	

IP	
flags	

CS	
DS	
SS	
ES	Segment of pointer to data buffer

Upon Return from INT 15H

	High	Low
AX	Error*	
BX	Offset of pointer to last byte read +1	
CX		
DX	# Bytes read	

SP	
BP	
SI	
DI	

IP	
flags	Carry set on error

CS	
DS	
SS	
ES	Segment of pointer to last byte read +1

Version Info: •PC and PCJr only, all others set Carry and return 86H in AH
•*For PCJr, 1=CRC error, 2=lost data transitions, 4=no data found

Notes: Obsolete function, no longer supported

Source: IBM PS/2 and PC BIOS Interface Technical Reference, page 2-75

See Also: 4.001. BIOS Services Summary
4.074. INT 15H, AH=03H -- Cassette Write Data Blocks

4.074. INT 15H, AH=03H -- CASSETTE WRITE DATA BLOCKS

Prior to Issuing INT 15H

	High	Low
AX	03H	
BX	Offset of pointer to data buffer	
CX	# Bytes to write	
DX		
SP		
BP		
SI		
DI		
IP		
flags		
CS		
DS		
SS		
ES	Segment of pointer to data buffer	

Upon Return from INT 15H

	High	Low
AX		
BX	Offset of pointer to last byte written +1	
CX	00H	00H
DX		
SP		
BP		
SI		
DI		
IP		
flags		
CS		
DS		
SS		
ES	Segment of pointer to last byte written +1	

Version Info: PC and PCJr only, all others set Carry and return 86H in AH

Notes: Obsolete function, no longer supported

Source: IBM PS/2 and PC BIOS Interface Technical Reference, page 2-76

See Also: 4.001. BIOS Services Summary
4.073. INT 15H, AH=02H -- Cassette Read Data Blocks

4.075. INT 15H, AH=0FH -- FORMAT PERIODIC INTERRUPT

Prior to Issuing INT 15H

	High	Low
AX	0FH	Phase code*
BX		
CX		
DX		
SP		
BP		
SI		
DI		
IP		
flags		
CS		
DS		
SS		
ES		

Upon Return from INT 15H

	High	Low
AX		
BX		
CX		
DX		
SP		
BP		
SI		
DI		
IP		
flags	Carry set if end formatting or scanning	
CS		
DS		
SS		
ES		

Version Info: Applies only to PS/2 machines using ESDI fixed disk drive adapter

Notes: *00=reserved, 01=surface analysis, 02=formatting

Source: IBM PS/2 and PC BIOS Interface Technical Reference, pages 2-76 to 2-77

See Also: 4.001. BIOS Services Summary

4.076. INT 15H, AH=4FH -- KEYBOARD INTERCEPT

Prior to Issuing INT 15H

	High	Low
AX	4FH	Scan code*
BX		
CX		
DX		

SP	
BP	
SI	
DI	

IP	
flags	Carry must be set

CS	
DS	
SS	
ES	

Upon Return from INT 15H

	High	Low
AX		Scan code**
BX		
CX		
DX		

SP	
BP	
SI	
DI	

IP	
flags	Carry clear if scan code to be ignored

CS	
DS	
SS	
ES	

Version Info: Applies to AT, Convertible, and PS/2 only

Notes: •*See 7.06. AT 84-key Key Numbers and Scan Codes
7.07. AT 101/102-key Key Numbers and Scan Codes
7.08. PS/2 Key Numbers and Scan Codes
•**May be changed by interrupt handler

Source: IBM PS/2 and PC BIOS Interface Technical Reference, page 2-82

See Also: 4.001. BIOS Services Summary
7.06. AT 84-key Key Numbers and Scan Codes
7.07. AT 101/102-key Key Numbers and Scan Codes
7.08. PS/2 Key Numbers and Scan Codes

4.077. INT 15H, AH=80H -- OPEN DEVICE

Prior to Issuing INT 15H

	High	Low
AX	80H	
BX	Device ID	
CX	Process ID	
DX		

SP	
BP	
SI	
DI	

IP	
flags	

CS	
DS	
SS	
ES	

Upon Return from INT 15H

Interrupt returns no values

Version Info: Applies to AT and PS/2 only

Source: IBM PS/2 and PC BIOS Interface Technical Reference, page 2-83

See Also: 4.001. BIOS Services Summary
4.078. INT 15H, AH=81H -- Close Device

4.078. INT 15H, AH=81H -- CLOSE DEVICE

Prior to Issuing INT 15H

Upon Return from INT 15H

	High	Low
AX	81H	
BX	Device ID	
CX	Process ID	
DX		

SP	
BP	
SI	
DI	

| IP | |
| flags | |

CS	
DS	
SS	
ES	

Interrupt returns no values

Version Info: Applies to AT and PS/2 only

Source: IBM PS/2 and PC BIOS Interface Technical Reference, page 2-83

See Also: 4.001. BIOS Services Summary
4.077. INT 15H, AH=80H -- Open Device

4.079. INT 15H, AH=82H -- PROGRAM TERMINATE

Prior to Issuing INT 15H

Upon Return from INT 15H

	High	Low
AX	82H	
BX	Device ID	
CX		
DX		

SP	
BP	
SI	
DI	

| IP | |
| flags | |

CS	
DS	
SS	
ES	

Interrupt returns no values

Version Info: Applies to AT and PS/2 only

Source: IBM PS/2 and PC BIOS Interface Technical Reference, page 2-84

See Also: 4.001. BIOS Services Summary

4.080. INT 15H, AH=83H -- EVENT WAIT

Prior to Issuing INT 15H

	High	Low
AX	83H	0 or 1*
BX	Offset of pointer to byte	
CX	HO microseconds to posting	
DX	LO microseconds to posting	

SP		
BP		
SI		
DI		

IP		
flags		

CS		
DS		
SS		
ES	Segment of pointer to byte	

Upon Return from INT 15H

	High	Low
AX		
BX		
CX		
DX		

SP		
BP		
SI		
DI		

IP		
flags	Carry set if set operation unsuccessful	

CS		
DS		
SS		
ES		

Version Info: Applies to AT, Convertible, and PS/2 only

Notes:
•Carry always set on PS/2 model 30
•*0=set interval, 1=cancel set interval; for all except AT BIOS 1/10/84

Source: IBM PS/2 and PC BIOS Interface Technical Reference, pages 2-84 to 2-85

See Also: 4.001. BIOS Services Summary

4.081. INT 15H, AH=84H -- JOYSTICK SUPPORT

Prior to Issuing INT 15H

	High	Low
AX	84H	
BX		
CX		
DX		0 or 1**

SP		
BP		
SI		
DI		

IP		
flags		

CS		
DS		
SS		
ES		

Upon Return from INT 15H

	High	Low
AX	A(x) value***	switch settings*
BX	A(y) value***	
CX	B(x) value***	
DX	B(y) value***	

SP		
BP		
SI		
DI		

IP		
flags	Carry set on error	

CS		
DS		
SS		
ES		

Version Info: Applies to AT and PS/2 only

Notes:
•*Bits 7 - 4 are used to represent switches; returned only if DX was 0 prior to interrupt
•**0=read switch settings, 1=read resistive inputs
•***Returned only if DX was 1 prior to interrupt

Source: IBM PS/2 and PC BIOS Interface Technical Reference, pages 2-85 to 2-86

See Also: 4.001. BIOS Services Summary

4.082. INT 15H, AH=85H -- SYSTEM REQUEST KEY PRESSED

Prior to Issuing INT 15H   *Upon Return from INT 15H*

	High	Low
AX	85H	Value*
BX		
CX		
DX		

SP		
BP		
SI		
DI		

IP	
flags	

CS	
DS	
SS	
ES	

	High	Low
AX		
BX		
CX		
DX		

SP		
BP		
SI		
DI		

IP	
flags	

CS	
DS	
SS	
ES	

Version Info: Applies to AT, Convertible, and PS/2 only

Notes: *0=key make, 1=key break

Source: IBM PS/2 and PC BIOS Interface Technical Reference, page 2-86

See Also: 4.001. BIOS Services Summary

4.083. INT 15H, AH=86H -- WAIT

Prior to Issuing INT 15H   *Upon Return from INT 15H*

	High	Low
AX	86H	
BX		
CX	HO microseconds before return	
DX	LO microseconds before return	

SP		
BP		
SI		
DI		

IP	
flags	

CS	
DS	
SS	
ES	

	High	Low
AX		
BX		
CX		
DX		

SP		
BP		
SI		
DI		

IP	
flags	Carry flag set if wait already in progress

CS	
DS	
SS	
ES	

Version Info: Applies to AT, Convertible, and PS/2 only

Source: IBM PS/2 and PC BIOS Interface Technical Reference, pages 2-86 to 2-87

See Also: 4.001. BIOS Services Summary

4.084. INT 15H, AH=87H -- MOVE BLOCK

Prior to Issuing INT 15H   *Upon Return from INT 15H*

	High	Low
AX	87H	
BX		
CX	Word count of block to move*	
DX		

SP	
BP	
SI	Offset of pointer to global desc. table***
DI	

IP	
flags	

CS	
DS	
SS	
ES	Segment of pointer to global desc. table***

	High	Low
AX	Status**	
BX		
CX		
DX		

SP	
BP	
SI	
DI	

IP	
flags	Carry, zero flags set on some errors

CS	
DS	
SS	
ES	

Version Info: Applies to AT and PS/2 only

Notes: •*Maximum of 8000H words (64K bytes)
•**00=successful, 01=RAM parity, 02=other exception error, 03=Gate address line 20H failed
•***Six 8-byte blocks: dummy, GDT location, source GDT, target GDT, BIOS CS, SS

Source: IBM PS/2 and PC BIOS Interface Technical Reference, pages 2-87 to 2-89

See Also: 4.001. BIOS Services Summary

4.085. INT 15H, AH=88H -- GET EXTENDED MEMORY SIZE

Prior to Issuing INT 15H   *Upon Return from INT 15H*

	High	Low
AX	88H	
BX		
CX		
DX		

SP	
BP	
SI	
DI	

IP	
flags	

CS	
DS	
SS	
ES	

	High	Low
AX	1k blocks*	
BX		
CX		
DX		

SP	
BP	
SI	
DI	

IP	
flags	

CS	
DS	
SS	
ES	

Version Info: Applies to AT and PS/2 only

Notes: *Contiguous memory beginning at 100000H (1 Mbyte)

Source: IBM PS/2 and PC BIOS Interface Technical Reference, pages 2-89 to 2-90

See Also: 4.001. BIOS Services Summary

4.086. INT 15H, AH=89H -- SWITCH TO PROTECTED MODE

	Prior to Issuing INT 15H			*Upon Return from INT 15H*	
	High	*Low*		*High*	*Low*
AX	89H		AX	00 if successful	
BX	Index to Int Level 1	Index to Int Level 2	BX	Destroyed	
CX			CX	Destroyed	
DX			DX	Destroyed	
SP			SP	Destroyed	
BP			BP	Destroyed	
SI	Offset of pointer to global desc. table		SI	Destroyed	
DI			DI	Destroyed	
IP			IP	Destroyed	
flags			flags	Destroyed	
CS			CS	Destroyed	
DS			DS	Destroyed	
SS			SS	Destroyed	
ES	Segment of pointer to global desc. table		ES	Destroyed	

Version Info: Applies to AT and PS/2 only

Source: IBM PS/2 and PC BIOS Interface Technical Reference, pages 2-90 to 2-92

See Also: 4.001. BIOS Services Summary
4.087. INT 15H, Global Descriptor Table

4.087. INT 15H, GLOBAL DESCRIPTOR TABLE

Offset	Length	Pointer To
0	8 bytes	Dummy
8	8 bytes	Global descriptor table
10 (16)	8 bytes	Interrupt descriptor table
18 (24)	8 bytes	User data segment
20 (32)	8 bytes	User extra segment
28 (40)	8 bytes	User stack segment
30 (48)	8 bytes	User code segment
38 (56)	8 bytes	Temporary BIOS code segment

Source: IBM PS/2 BIOS Technical Reference, pages 2-91 to 2-92

See Also: 4.086. INT 15H, AH=89H -- Switch to Protected Mode

4.088. INT 15H, AH=90H -- DEVICE BUSY

Prior to Issuing INT 15H

	High	Low
AX	90H	Type code*
BX	Offset of pointer to network control block**	
CX		
DX		

SP	
BP	
SI	
DI	

IP	
flags	

CS	
DS	
SS	
ES	Segment of pointer to network control block**

Upon Return from INT 15H

	High	Low
AX		
BX		
CX		
DX		

SP	
BP	
SI	
DI	

IP	
flags	Carry flag set if min. wait time satisfied

CS	
DS	
SS	
ES	

Version Info: Applies to AT, Convertible, and PS/2 only

Notes: •*Type codes are as follows:
00=fixed disk (time out)
01=floppy disk (time out)
02=keyboard (no time out)
03=pointing device (time out)
80H=network (no time out)
FCH=fixed disk reset for PS/2 products (time out)
FDH=floppy disk drive motor start (time out)
FEH=printer (time-out)
•**Only for type code of 80H

Source: IBM PS/2 and PC BIOS Interface Technical Reference, pages 2-93 to 2-94

See Also: 4.001. BIOS Services Summary

4.089. INT 15H, AH=91H -- INTERRUPT COMPLETE

Prior to Issuing INT 15H   *Upon Return from INT 15H*

	High	Low
AX	91H	Type code*
BX		
CX		
DX		

No values returned for this interrupt

SP	
BP	
SI	
DI	

IP	
flags	

CS	
DS	
SS	
ES	

Version Info: Applies to AT, Convertible, and PS/2 only

Notes: *Type codes are as follows:
00=fixed disk (time-out)
01=floppy disk (time-out)
02=keyboard (no time-out)
03=pointing device (time-out)
80H=network (no time-out)
FCH=fixed disk reset for PS/2 products (time-out)
FDH=floppy disk motor start (time-out)
FEH=printer (time-out)

Source: IBM PS/2 and PC BIOS Interface Technical Reference,
pages 2-94 and 2-93

See Also: 4.001. BIOS Services Summary

4.090. INT 15H, AH=C0H -- RETURN SYSTEM CONFIG PARAMETERS

Prior to Issuing INT 15H   *Upon Return from INT 15H*

	High	Low
AX	C0H	
BX		
CX		
DX		

	High	Low
AX	0	
BX	Offset of pointer to system descriptor table*	
CX		
DX		

SP	
BP	
SI	
DI	

SP	
BP	
SI	
DI	

IP	
flags	

IP	
flags	Carry clear

CS	
DS	
SS	
ES	

CS	
DS	
SS	
ES	Segment of pointer to system descriptor table*

Version Info: Appplies to AT after 6/10/85, XT after 1/10/86, XT286, Convertible, and PS/2 only

Notes: *See 4.091. INT 15H, System Descriptor Table

Source: IBM PS/2 and PC BIOS Interface Technical Reference, pages 2-94 to 2-96

See Also: 4.001. BIOS Services Summary
4.091. System Descriptor Table

4.091. INT 15H, SYSTEM DESCRIPTOR TABLE

Offset	Length	Description	Allowable Values
0	Word	Number of bytes in table	Minimum of 8
2	Byte	Model byte	See "Machine ID Byte"
3	Byte	Submodel byte	
4	Byte	BIOS revision level	00=first release
5	Byte	Feature information	bit 7 = fixed disk BIOS use DMA 3 bit 6 = 2nd interrupt chip present bit 5 = real-time clock present bit 4 = keyboard intercept called bit 3 = wait for ext event supported bit 2 = extended BIOS area allocated bit 1 = PS/2-type I/O channel bit 0 = RESERVED
6	Byte	Feature information RESERVED	
7	Byte	Feature information RESERVED	
8	Byte	Feature information RESERVED	
9	Byte	Feature information RESERVED	

Version Info: Applies to AT after 11/15/85, XT after 1/10/86, XT286, PC Convertible, and PS/2

Source: IBM PS/2 and PC BIOS Interface Technical Reference, pages 2-94 to 2-96

See Also: 4.090. INT 15H, AH=C0H -- Return System Config Parameters

4.092. INT 15H, AH=C1H -- RETURN EXT BIOS SEGMENT ADDRESS

Prior to Issuing INT 15H

	High	Low
AX	C1H	
BX		
CX		
DX		

SP	
BP	
SI	
DI	

IP	
flags	

CS	
DS	
SS	
ES	

Upon Return from INT 15H

	High	Low
AX		
BX		
CX		
DX		

SP	
BP	
SI	
DI	

IP	
flags	Carry set on error

CS	
DS	
SS	
ES	Segment address of extended BIOS data area

Version Info: Applies to PS/2 models only

Source: IBM PS/2 and PC BIOS Interface Technical Reference, pages 2-96 to 2-97

See Also: 4.001. BIOS Services Summary
4.003. Extended BIOS Data Area Layout

4.093. INT 15H, AH=C2H, AL=00H -- ENABLE/DISABLE POINTING DEVICE

	Prior to Issuing INT 15H			*Upon Return from INT 15H*	
	High	*Low*		*High*	*Low*
AX	C2H	00H	AX	Mouse status**	
BX	Enable/disable*		BX		
CX			CX		
DX			DX		
SP			SP		
BP			BP		
SI			SI		
DI			DI		
IP			IP		
flags			flags	Carry set on error	
CS			CS		
DS			DS		
SS			SS		
ES			ES		

Version Info: Applies to PS/2 models only

Notes: •*00=disable, 01=enable
•**See 4.101. Mouse Port Status Bytes

Source: IBM PS/2 and PC BIOS Interface Technical Reference, page 2-97

See Also: 4.001. BIOS Services Summary
4.101. Mouse Port Status Bytes

4.094. INT 15H, AH=C2H, AL=01H -- RESET POINTING DEVICE

	Prior to Issuing INT 15H			*Upon Return from INT 15H*	
	High	*Low*		*High*	*Low*
AX	C2H	01H	AX	Mouse status*	
BX			BX	Device ID**	(Destroyed)
CX			CX		
DX			DX		
SP			SP		
BP			BP		
SI			SI		
DI			DI		
IP			IP		
flags			flags	Carry set on error	
CS			CS		
DS			DS		
SS			SS		
ES			ES		

Version Info: Applies to PS/2 models only

Notes: •Pointing device state is set to: disabled, 100 reports/second sample rate,
4 count/mm resolution, 1 to 1 scaling, data package size unmodified
•*See 4.101. Mouse Port Status Bytes
•**Only if no error occurred; set to 00H

Source: IBM PS/2 and PC BIOS Interface Technical Reference, page 2-98

See Also: 4.001. BIOS Services Summary
4.101. Mouse Port Status Bytes

4.095. INT 15H, AH=C2H, AL=02H -- SET SAMPLE RATE

Prior to Issuing INT 15H *Upon Return from INT 15H*

	High	Low			High	Low
AX	C2H	02H		AX	Mouse status*	
BX	Sample rate**			BX		
CX				CX		
DX				DX		
SP				SP		
BP				BP		
SI				SI		
DI				DI		
IP				IP		
flags				flags	Carry set on error	
CS				CS		
DS				DS		
SS				SS		
ES				ES		

Version Info: Applies to PS/2 models only

Notes: •*See 4.101. Mouse Port Status Bytes
•**00=10 reports/second, 01=20 rpts/sec, 02=40 rpts/sec, 03=60 rpts/sec, 04=80 rpts/sec, 05=100 rpts/sec (default), 06=200 rpts/sec

Source: IBM PS/2 and PC BIOS Interface Technical Reference, page 2-98

See Also: 4.001. BIOS Services Summary
4.101. Mouse Port Status Bytes

4.096. INT 15H, AH=C2H, AL=03H -- SET RESOLUTION

Prior to Issuing INT 15H *Upon Return from INT 15H*

	High	Low			High	Low
AX	C2H	03H		AX	Mouse status*	
BX	Resolution**			BX		
CX				CX		
DX				DX		
SP				SP		
BP				BP		
SI				SI		
DI				DI		
IP				IP		
flags				flags	Carry set on error	
CS				CS		
DS				DS		
SS				SS		
ES				ES		

Version Info: Applies to PS/2 models only

Notes: •*See 4.101. Mouse Port Status Bytes
•**00=1 count/millimeter, 01=2 cnts/mm, 02=4 cnts/mm, 03=8 cnts/mm

Source: IBM PS/2 and PC BIOS Interface Technical Reference, page 2-98

See Also: 4.001. BIOS Services Summary
4.101. Mouse Port Status Bytes

4.097. INT 15H, AH=C2H, AL=04H -- READ DEVICE TYPE

Prior to Issuing INT 15H

	High	Low
AX	C2H	04H
BX		
CX		
DX		

SP	
BP	
SI	
DI	

IP	
flags	

CS	
DS	
SS	
ES	

Upon Return from INT 15H

	High	Low
AX	Mouse status*	
BX	Device ID**	
CX		
DX		

SP	
BP	
SI	
DI	

IP	
flags	Carry set on error

CS	
DS	
SS	
ES	

Version Info: Applies to PS/2 models only

Notes:
- *See 4.101. Mouse Port Status Bytes
- **Only if operation successful; set to 0

Source: IBM PS/2 and PC BIOS Interface Technical Reference, pages 2-98 to 2-99

See Also:
4.001. BIOS Services Summary
4.101. Mouse Port Status Bytes

4.098. INT 15H, AH=C2H, AL=05H -- INITIALIZE POINTING DEVICE

Prior to Issuing INT 15H

	High	Low
AX	C2H	05H
BX	Bytes in data package	
CX		
DX		

SP	
BP	
SI	
DI	

IP	
flags	

CS	
DS	
SS	
ES	

Upon Return from INT 15H

	High	Low
AX	Mouse status*	
BX		
CX		
DX		

SP	
BP	
SI	
DI	

IP	
flags	Carry set on error

CS	
DS	
SS	
ES	

Version Info: Applies to PS/2 models only

Notes:
- Device is initialized as: disabled state, 100 reports/second sampling rate, 4 count/millimeter resolution, 1 to 1 scaling
- *See 4.101. Mouse Port Status Bytes

Source: IBM PS/2 and PC BIOS Interface Technical Reference, page 2-99

See Also:
4.001. BIOS Services Summary
4.101. Mouse Port Status Bytes

4.099. INT 15H, AH=C2H, AL=06H -- EXTENDED COMMANDS

Prior to Issuing INT 15H

	High	Low
AX	C2H	06H
BX	Command**	
CX		
DX		

SP	
BP	
SI	
DI	

IP	
flags	

CS	
DS	
SS	
ES	

Upon Return from INT 15H

	High	Low
AX	Mouse status*	
BX		Status byte 1***
CX		Status byte 2***
DX		Status byte 3***

SP	
BP	
SI	
DI	

IP	
flags	Carry set on error

CS	
DS	
SS	
ES	

Version Info: Applies to PS/2 models only

Notes:
- *See 4.101. Mouse Port Status Bytes
- **0=get status, 1=set scaling to 1 to 1, 2=set scaling to 2 to 1
- ***For BH=0 only, successful operation returns:

Status byte 1

Bit	Meaning
7	RESERVED
6	0=stream mode, 1=remote mode
5	0=disable, 1=enable
4	0=1:1 scaling, 1=2:1 scaling
3	RESERVED
2	Left button pressed
1	RESERVED
0	Right button pressed

Status byte 2

Value	Meaning
0	1 count per millimeter
1	2 counts per millimeter
2	4 counts per millimeter
3	8 counts per millimeter

Status byte 3

Value	Meaning
0A	10 reports per second
14	20 reports per second
28	40 reports per second
3C	60 reports per second
50	80 reports per second
64	100 reports per second
C8	200 reports per second

Source: IBM PS/2 and PC BIOS Technical Reference, pages 2-99 to 2-100

See Also:
4.001. BIOS Services Summary
4.101. Mouse Port Status Bytes

4.100. INT 15H, AH=C2H, AL=07H -- DEVICE DRIVER INIT CALL

Prior to Issuing INT 15H

	High	Low
AX	C2H	07H
BX	Offset of pointer to device driver	
CX		
DX		

SP	
BP	
SI	
DI	

IP	
flags	

CS	
DS	
SS	
ES	Segment of pointer to device driver

Upon Return from INT 15H

	High	Low
AX	Mouse status*	
BX		
CX		
DX		

SP	
BP	
SI	
DI	

IP	
flags	Carry set on error

CS	
DS	
SS	
ES	

Version Info: Applies to PS/2 models only

Notes: *See 4.101. Mouse Port Status Bytes

Source: IBM PS/2 and PC BIOS Technical Reference, page 2-100

See Also: 4.001. BIOS Services Summary
4.101. Mouse Port Status Bytes

4.101. INT 15H MOUSE PORT STATUS BYTES

Value	Meaning
0	No error occurred
1	Invalid function call attempted
2	Invalid input to function call
3	Interface error
4	Resend
5	No far call installed for device

Source: IBM PS/2 and PC BIOS Technical Reference, page 2-97

See Also: 4.093. INT 15H, AH=C2H, AL=00H -- Enable/Disable Pointing Device
4.094. INT 15H, AH=C2H, AL=01H -- Reset Pointing Device
4.095. INT 15H, AH=C2H, AL=02H -- Set Sample Rate
4.096. INT 15H, AH=C2H, AL=03H -- Set Resolution
4.097. INT 15H, AH=C2H, AL=04H -- Read Device Type
4.098. INT 15H, AH=C2H, AL=05H -- Initialize Pointing Device
4.099. INT 15H, AH=C2H, AL=06H -- Extended Commands
4.100. INT 15H, AH=C2H, AL=07H -- Device Driver Init Call

4.102. INT 15H, AH=C3H -- WATCHDOG TIMEOUT

Prior to Issuing INT 15H

	High	Low
AX	C3H	1=enable, 0=disable
BX	Watchdog timer count (1-255)	
CX		
DX		

SP	
BP	
SI	
DI	

IP	
flags	

CS	
DS	
SS	
ES	

Upon Return from INT 15H

	High	Low
AX		
BX		
CX		
DX		

SP	
BP	
SI	
DI	

IP	
flags	Carry set on error

CS	
DS	
SS	
ES	

Version Info: Applies to PS/2 products only except Model 30

Source: IBM PS/2 and PC BIOS Technical Reference, page 2-102

See Also: 4.001. BIOS Services Summary

4.103. INT 15H, AH=C4H -- PROG OPTION SELECT

Prior to Issuing INT 15H

	High	Low
AX	C4H	Option*
BX		Slot number**
CX		
DX		

SP	
BP	
SI	
DI	

IP	
flags	

CS	
DS	
SS	
ES	

Upon Return from INT 15H

	High	Low
AX		Option*
BX		Slot number**
CX		
DX	Base POS adapter register address***	

SP	
BP	
SI	
DI	

IP	
flags	Carry set on error

CS	
DS	
SS	
ES	

Version Info: Applies to PS/2 products only except Model 30

Notes:
- *0=get base POS adapter register address, 1=enable slot, 2=enable adapter
- **Only if AL=1
- ***Only AL=0

Source: IBM PS/2 and PC BIOS Technical Reference, pages 2-102 to 2-103

See Also: 4.001. BIOS Services Summary

4.104. INT 16H, AH=00H -- READ CHARACTER

Prior to Issuing INT 16H

	High	Low
AX	00H	
BX		
CX		
DX		
SP		
BP		
SI		
DI		
IP		
flags		
CS		
DS		
SS		
ES		

Upon Return from INT 16H

	High	Low
AX	Scan code	ASCII character
BX		
CX		
DX		
SP		
BP		
SI		
DI		
IP		
flags		
CS		
DS		
SS		
ES		

Notes: Character is extracted from keyboard buffer

Source: IBM PS/2 and PC BIOS Interface Technical Reference, page 2-106

See Also:
1.21. ASCII Character Set
1.22. IBM ASCII Character Set
4.001. BIOS Services Summary
7.05. PC Keyboard Key Numbers and Scan Codes
7.06. AT 84-key Key Numbers and Scan Codes
7.07. AT 101/102-key Key Numbers and Scan Codes
7.08. PS/2 Key Numbers and Scan Codes
7.09. PC & XT Typeahead Buffer Layout

4.105. INT 16H, AH=01H -- READ STATUS

Prior to Issuing INT 16H

	High	Low
AX	01H	
BX		
CX		
DX		
SP		
BP		
SI		
DI		
IP		
flags		
CS		
DS		
SS		
ES		

Upon Return from INT 16H

	High	Low
AX	Scan code (if zero flag clear)	ASCII char (if zero flag clear)
BX		
CX		
DX		
SP		
BP		
SI		
DI		
IP		
flags	Zero flag set if no character available	
CS		
DS		
SS		
ES		

Notes: Character is not removed from keyboard buffer

Source: IBM PS/2 and PC BIOS Interface Technical Reference, page 2-106

See Also:
1.21. ASCII Character Set
1.22. IBM ASCII Character Set
4.001. BIOS Services Summary
7.05. PC Keyboard Key Numbers and Scan Codes
7.06. AT 84-key Key Numbers and Scan Codes
7.07. AT 101/102-key Key Numbers and Scan Codes
7.08. PS/2 Key Numbers and Scan Codes
7.09. PC & XT Typeahead Buffer Layout

4.106. INT 16H, AH=02H -- READ FLAGS

Prior to Issuing INT 16H   *Upon Return from INT 16H*

	High	Low
AX	02H	
BX		
CX		
DX		

SP	
BP	
SI	
DI	

| IP | |
| flags | |

CS	
DS	
SS	
ES	

	High	Low
AX	RESERVED	Shift status byte*
BX		
CX		
DX		

SP	
BP	
SI	
DI	

| IP | |
| flags | |

CS	
DS	
SS	
ES	

Notes: *See 4.107. Keyboard Flags Byte

Source: IBM PS/2 and PC BIOS Interface Technical Reference, page 2-107

See Also: 4.001. BIOS Services Summary
                 4.107. Keyboard Flags Byte

4.107. KEYBOARD FLAGS BYTE

Bit Numbers:

7	6	5	4	3	2	1	0	Description
X								Insert state locked active
	X							Caps lock key active
		X						Num lock key active
			X					Scroll lock key active
				X				Alt key held down
					X			Ctrl key held down
						X		Left shift key held down
							X	Right shift key held down

Source: IBM PS/2 and PC BIOS Interface Technical Reference,
                 page 2-107

See Also: 4.106. INT 16H, AH=02H -- Read Flags
                 4.112. INT 16H, Extended Keyboard Flags Byte

4.108. INT 16H, AH=05H -- KEYBOARD WRITE

Prior to Issuing INT 16H   *Upon Return from INT 16H*

	High	Low			High	Low
AX	05H			AX		Status*
BX				BX		
CX	Scan code	ASCII char		CX		
DX				DX		
SP				SP		
BP				BP		
SI				SI		
DI				DI		
IP				IP		
flags				flags		
CS				CS		
DS				DS		
SS				SS		
ES				ES		

Version Info: Applies to AT after 11/15/85, XT after 1/10/86, XT286, and PS/2 only

Notes: •Function places key in typeahead buffer as if typed from keyboard
                       •*0=successful, 1=buffer full

Source: IBM PS/2 and PC BIOS Interface Technical Reference, pages 2-108 to 2-109

See Also: 4.001. BIOS Services Summary
                       7.09. PC& XT Typeahead Buffer Layout

4.109. INT 16H, AH=10H -- EXTENDED KEYBOARD READ

Prior to Issuing INT 16H   *Upon Return from INT 16H*

	High	Low			High	Low
AX	10H			AX	Scan code	ASCII character
BX				BX		
CX				CX		
DX				DX		
SP				SP		
BP				BP		
SI				SI		
DI				DI		
IP				IP		
flags				flags		
CS				CS		
DS				DS		
SS				SS		
ES				ES		

Version Info: Applies to AT after 11/15/85, XT after 1/10/86, XT286, and PS/2 only

Notes: Key is removed from typeahead buffer

Source: IBM PS/2 and PC BIOS Interface Technical Reference, page 2-109

See Also: 4.001. BIOS Services Summary
                       4.104. INT 16H, AH=00H -- Read Character
                       7.09. PC & XT Typeahead Buffer Layout

4.110. INT 16H, AH=11H -- EXTENDED KEYSTROKE STATUS

	Prior to Issuing INT 16H				*Upon Return from INT 16H*	

	High	Low
AX	11H	
BX		
CX		
DX		

SP	
BP	
SI	
DI	

IP	
flags	

CS	
DS	
SS	
ES	

	High	Low
AX	Scan code (if Z flag 0)	ASCII char (if Z flag 0)
BX		
CX		
DX		

SP	
BP	
SI	
DI	

IP	
flags	Zero flag set if no character is available

CS	
DS	
SS	
ES	

Version Info: Applies to AT after 11/15/85, XT after 1/10/86, XT286, and PS/2 only

Notes: Key is NOT removed from typeahead buffer

Source: IBM PS/2 and PC BIOS Interface Technical Reference, page 2-109

See Also: 4.001. BIOS Services Summary
4.105. INT 16H, AH=01H -- Read Status
7.09. PC & XT Typeahead Buffer Layout

4.111. INT 16H, AH=12H -- EXTENDED SHIFT STATUS

	Prior to Issuing INT 16H				*Upon Return from INT 16H*	

	High	Low
AX	12H	
BX		
CX		
DX		

SP	
BP	
SI	
DI	

IP	
flags	

CS	
DS	
SS	
ES	

	High	Low
AX	Ext shift status*	Shift status**
BX		
CX		
DX		

SP	
BP	
SI	
DI	

IP	
flags	

CS	
DS	
SS	
ES	

Version Info: Applies to AT after 11/15/85, XT after 1/10/86, XT286, and PS/2 only

Notes: •*See 4.112. Extended Keyboard Flags Byte
•**See 4.107. Keyboard Flags Byte

Source: IBM PS/2 and PC BIOS Interface Technical Reference, page 2-110

See Also: 4.001. BIOS Services Summary
4.106. INT 16H, AH=02H -- Read Flags
7.09. PC & XT Typeahead Buffer Layout
4.112. Extended Keyboard Flags Byte
4.107. Keyboard Flags Byte

4.112. INT 16H, EXTENDED KEYBOARD FLAGS BYTE

Bit Numbers:

7	6	5	4	3	2	1	0	Description
X								SysRq key held down
	X							Caps Lock key held down
		X						Num Lock key held down
			X					Scroll Lock key held down
				X				Right Alt key held down
					X			Right Ctrl key held down
						X		Left Alt key held down
							X	Left Ctrl key held down

Source: IBM PS/2 and PC BIOS Interface Technical Reference,
                 page 2-110

See Also: 4.107. INT 16H, Keyboard Flags Byte
                 4.111. INT 16H, AH=12H -- Extended Shift Status

4.113. INT 17H, AH=00H -- WRITE CHARACTER

Prior to Issuing INT 17H

	High	Low
AX	00H	Character
BX		
CX		
DX	Printer number	
SP		
BP		
SI		
DI		
IP		
flags		
CS		
DS		
SS		
ES		

Upon Return from INT 17H

	High	Low
AX	Status*	
BX		
CX		
DX		
SP		
BP		
SI		
DI		
IP		
flags		
CS		
DS		
SS		
ES		

Notes: *See 4.114. INT 17H, Printer Status Byte

Source: IBM PS/2 and PC BIOS Interface Technical Reference, page 2-111

4.114. INT 17H, PRINTER STATUS BYTE

Bit Numbers:

7	6	5	4	3	2	1	0	Description
X								Not Busy
	X							Acknowledge
		X						Out of Paper
			X					Selected
				X				I/O Error
					X			RESERVED
						X		RESERVED
							X	Time-Out

Source: IBM PS/2 and PC BIOS Interface Technical Reference,
                 page 2-111

See Also: 4.113. INT 17H, AH=00H -- Write Character

4.115. INT 17H, AH=01H -- INITIALIZE PRINTER PORT

Prior to Issuing INT 17H   *Upon Return from INT 17H*

	High	Low			High	Low
AX	01H			AX	Status*	
BX				BX		
CX				CX		
DX	Printer number			DX		
SP				SP		
BP				BP		
SI				SI		
DI				DI		
IP				IP		
flags				flags		
CS				CS		
DS				DS		
SS				SS		
ES				ES		

Notes: *See 4.114. INT 17H, Printer Status Byte

Source: IBM PS/2 and PC BIOS Interface Technical Reference, page 2-111

4.116. INT 17H, AH=02H -- STATUS REQUEST

Prior to Issuing INT 17H   *Upon Return from INT 17H*

	High	Low			High	Low
AX	02H			AX	Status*	
BX				BX		
CX				CX		
DX	Printer number			DX		
SP				SP		
BP				BP		
SI				SI		
DI				DI		
IP				IP		
flags				flags		
CS				CS		
DS				DS		
SS				SS		
ES				ES		

Notes: *See 4.114. INT 17H, Printer Status Byte

Source: IBM PS/2 and PC BIOS Interface Technical Reference, page 2-112

4.117. INT 18H: BASIC LOADER

Prior to Issuing INT 18H   *Upon Return from INT 18H*

	High	Low
AX		
BX		
CX		
DX		

SP	
BP	
SI	
DI	

IP	
flags	

CS	
DS	
SS	
ES	

Interrupt does not return

Notes: •Interrupt switches control to ROM BASIC
                   •Not documented in IBM BIOS reference

Source: *Programmer's Guide to the IBM PC* (Microsoft Press),
                   Peter Norton, page 239

See Also: 4.001. BIOS Services Summary

4.118. INT 19H: BOOTSTRAP LOADER

Prior to Issuing INT 19H   *Upon Return from INT 19H*

	High	Low
AX		
BX		
CX		
DX		

SP	
BP	
SI	
DI	

IP	
flags	

CS	
DS	
SS	
ES	

Interrupt does not return

Notes: Interrupt reboots computer by reading cylinder 0, sector 1 into
                   segment 0, offset 7C00H. Control is transferred to that location.

Source: IBM PS/2 and PC BIOS Interface Technical Reference,
                   page 2-114

See Also: 4.001. BIOS Services Summary

4.119. INT 1AH, AH=00H -- READ CLOCK COUNT

Prior to Issuing INT 1AH

	High	Low
AX	00H	
BX		
CX		
DX		

SP	
BP	
SI	
DI	

IP	
flags	

CS	
DS	
SS	
ES	

Upon Return from INT 1AH

	High	Low
AX		24-hour check*
BX		
CX	HO Count	
DX	LO Count	

SP	
BP	
SI	
DI	

IP	
flags	

CS	
DS	
SS	
ES	

Notes: •Timer overflow flag is reset to 0
•*0=hasn't been 24 hours since power-on; >0=has been 24 hours or more

Source: IBM PS/2 and PC BIOS Interface Technical Reference, page 2-115

See Also: 4.001. BIOS Services Summary
4.002. BIOS Memory Usage Summary
4.120. INT 1AH, AH=01H -- Set Clock Count

4.120. INT 1AH, AH=01H -- SET CLOCK COUNT

Prior to Issuing INT 1AH

	High	Low
AX	01H	
BX		
CX	HO Count	
DX	LO Count	

SP	
BP	
SI	
DI	

IP	
flags	

CS	
DS	
SS	
ES	

Upon Return from INT 1AH

Interrupt returns no values

Notes: Timer overflow flag is set to 0

Source: IBM PS/2 and PC BIOS Interface Technical Reference,
page 2-116

See Also: 4.001. BIOS Services Summary
4.002. BIOS Memory Usage Summary
4.119. INT 1AH, AH=00H -- Read Clock Count

4.121. INT 1AH, AH=02H -- READ REAL TIME CLOCK TIME

Prior to Issuing INT 1AH   *Upon Return from INT 1AH*

	High	Low
AX	02H	
BX		
CX		
DX		

	High	Low
AX		
BX		
CX	BCD Hours	BCD Minutes
DX	BCD Seconds	DST Option*

SP		
BP		
SI		
DI		

SP		
BP		
SI		
DI		

IP		
flags		

IP	
flags	Carry set if clock not operating

CS		
DS		
SS		
ES		

CS		
DS		
SS		
ES		

Version Info: Applies to AT with BIOS dated 6/10/85 and after, XT286, Convertible, and PS/2 products

Notes: *Daylight savings time option, 0=not used 1=operative

Source: IBM PS/2 and PC BIOS Interface Technical Reference, page 2-116

See Also: 4.001. BIOS Services Summary
4.122. INT 1AH, AH=03H -- Set Real Time Clock Time
4.123. INT 1AH, AH=04H -- Read Real Time Clock Date

4.122. INT 1AH, AH=03H -- SET REAL TIME CLOCK TIME

Prior to Issuing INT 1AH   *Upon Return from INT 1AH*

	High	Low
AX	03H	
BX		
CX	BCD Hours	BCD Minutes
DX	BCD Seconds	DST Option*

Interrupt returns no values

SP		
BP		
SI		
DI		

IP		
flags		

CS		
DS		
SS		
ES		

Version Info: This option works only on AT with BIOS dated 6/10/85 and after, XT286, and PS/2 products

Notes: *Daylight savings time option, 0=not used 1=operative

Source: IBM PS/2 and PC BIOS Interface Technical Reference, page 2-117

See Also: 4.001. BIOS Services Summary
4.121. INT 1AH, AH=02H -- Read Real Time Clock Time
4.124. INT 1AH, AH=05H -- Set Real Time Clock Date

4.123. INT 1AH, AH=04H -- READ REAL TIME CLOCK DATE

Prior to Issuing INT 1AH

	High	Low
AX	04H	
BX		
CX		
DX		

SP	
BP	
SI	
DI	

IP	
flags	

CS	
DS	
SS	
ES	

Upon Return from INT 1AH

	High	Low
AX		
BX		
CX	BCD Century*	BCD Year
DX	BCD Month	BCD Day

SP	
BP	
SI	
DI	

IP	
flags	Carry set if clock not operating

CS	
DS	
SS	
ES	

Version Info:	Applies to AT, Convertible and PS/2 only
Notes:	*Century is binary coded decimal 19 or 20 only
Source:	IBM PS/2 and PC BIOS Interface Technical Reference, page 2-117
See Also:	4.001. BIOS Services Summary
	4.121. INT 1AH, AH=02H -- Read Real Time Clock Time
	4.124. INT 1AH, AH=05H -- Set Real Time Clock Date

4.124. INT 1AH, AH=05H -- SET REAL TIME CLOCK DATE

Prior to Issuing INT 1AH

	High	Low
AX	05H	
BX		
CX	BCD Century*	BCD Year
DX	BCD Month	BCD Day

SP	
BP	
SI	
DI	

IP	
flags	

CS	
DS	
SS	
ES	

Upon Return from INT 1AH

Interrupt returns no values

Version Info:	Applies to AT, Convertible and PS/2 only
Notes:	*Century is binary coded decimal 19 or 20 only
Source:	IBM PS/2 and PC BIOS Interface Technical Reference, page 2-117
See Also:	4.001. BIOS Services Summary
	4.122. INT 1AH, AH=03H -- Set Real Time Clock Time
	4.123. INT 1AH, AH=04H -- Read Real Time Clock Date

4.125. INT 1AH, AH=06H -- SET REAL TIME CLOCK ALARM

Prior to Issuing INT 1AH

	High	Low
AX	06H	
BX		
CX	BCD Hours	BCD Minutes
DX	BCD Seconds	

SP	
BP	
SI	
DI	

IP	
flags	

CS	
DS	
SS	
ES	

Upon Return from INT 1AH

	High	Low
AX		
BX		
CX		
DX		

SP	
BP	
SI	
DI	

IP	
flags	Carry set if alarm not ready or no clock

CS	
DS	
SS	
ES	

Version Info: Applies to AT, Convertible and PS/2 only

Source: IBM PS/2 and PC BIOS Interface Technical Reference, page 2-118

See Also: 4.001. BIOS Services Summary
4.126. INT 1AH, AH=07H -- Turn Off Real Time Clock Alarm

4.126. INT 1AH, AH=07H -- TURN OFF REAL TIME CLOCK ALARM

Prior to Issuing INT 1AH

	High	Low
AX	07H	
BX		
CX		
DX		

SP	
BP	
SI	
DI	

IP	
flags	

CS	
DS	
SS	
ES	

Upon Return from INT 1AH

Interrupt returns no values

Version Info: Applies to AT, Convertible and PS/2 only

Source: IBM PS/2 and PC BIOS Interface Technical Reference, page 2-118

See Also: 4.001. BIOS Services Summary
4.125. INT 1AH, AH=06H -- Set Real Time Clock Alarm

4.127. INT 1AH, AH=09H -- READ REAL TIME CLOCK ALARM

Prior to Issuing INT 1AH

	High	Low
AX	09H	
BX		
CX		
DX		

SP	
BP	
SI	
DI	

IP	
flags	

CS	
DS	
SS	
ES	

Upon Return from INT 1AH

	High	Low
AX		
BX		
CX	BCD hours	BCD minutes
DX	BCD seconds	Alarm Status*

SP	
BP	
SI	
DI	

IP	
flags	

CS	
DS	
SS	
ES	

Version Info: Applies only to Model 30 and PC Convertible

Notes: *0=alarm not enabled, 1=alarm enabled, no power on
2=alarm enabled, will power on system (Convertible only)

Source: IBM PS/2 and PC BIOS Technical Reference, page 2-119

See Also: 4.001. BIOS Services Summary

4.128. INT 1AH, AH=0AH -- READ SYSTEM TIMER DAY COUNT

Prior to Issuing INT 1AH

	High	Low
AX	0AH	
BX		
CX		
DX		

SP	
BP	
SI	
DI	

IP	
flags	

CS	
DS	
SS	
ES	

Upon Return from INT 1AH

	High	Low
AX		
BX		
CX	Count of days after 1/1/80	
DX		

SP	
BP	
SI	
DI	

IP	
flags	

CS	
DS	
SS	
ES	

Version Info: Applies to XT after 1/10/86 and PS/2 only

Source: IBM PS/2 and PC BIOS Interface Technical Reference, page 2-120

See Also: 4.001. BIOS Services Summary
4.002. BIOS Memory Usage Summary
4.129. INT 1AH, AH=0BH -- Set System Timer Day Count

4.129. INT 1AH, AH=0BH -- SET SYSTEM TIMER DAY COUNT

	Prior to Issuing INT 1AH		*Upon Return from INT 1AH*

	High	Low
AX	0BH	
BX		
CX	Count of days after 1/1/80	
DX		

Interrupt returns no values

SP		
BP		
SI		
DI		

IP		
flags		

CS		
DS		
SS		
ES		

Version Info: Applies to XT after 1/10/86 and PS/2 only

Source: IBM PS/2 and PC BIOS Interface Technical Reference, page 2-120

See Also: 4.001. BIOS Services Summary
4.002. BIOS Memory Usage Summary
4.128. INT 1AH, AH=0AH -- Read System Timer Day Count

— SECTION —

5

Other Interrupts, Mouse, and EMS Support

5.01. DOS INTERRUPT USAGE BY VERSION

DOS Versions that Support Interrupt

Int. Number	Interrupt Name	1	1.1	2	2.1	3	3.1	3.2	3.3
20 (32)	Program terminate	X	X	O	O	O	O	O	O
21 (33)	Function request	X	X	X	X	X	X	X	X
22 (34)	Terminate address	X	X	X	X	X	X	X	X
23 (35)	Control-Break exit address	X	X	X	X	X	X	X	X
24 (36)	Critical error handler vector	X	X	X	X	X	X	X	X
25 (37)	Absolute disk read	X	X	X	X	X	X	X	X
26 (38)	Absolute disk write	X	X	X	X	X	X	X	X
27 (39)	Terminate & stay resident	X	X	O	O	O	O	O	O
28 (40)	RESERVED	R	R	R	R	R	R	R	R
29 (41)	RESERVED	R	R	R	R	R	R	R	R
2A (42)	MS-Net access						X	X	X
2B (43)	RESERVED	R	R	R	R	R	R	R	R
2C (44)	RESERVED	R	R	R	R	R	R	R	R
2D (45)	RESERVED	R	R	R	R	R	R	R	R
2E (46)	RESERVED	R	R	R	R	R	R	R	R
2F (47)	Printer					X			
2F (47)	Multiplex						X	X	X
30 (48)	RESERVED	R	R	R	R	R	R	R	R
31 (49)	RESERVED	R	R	R	R	R	R	R	R
32 (50)	RESERVED	R	R	R	R	R	R	R	R
33 (51)	RESERVED	R	R	R	R	R	R	R	R
34 (52)	RESERVED	R	R	R	R	R	R	R	R
35 (53)	RESERVED	R	R	R	R	R	R	R	R
36 (54)	RESERVED	R	R	R	R	R	R	R	R
37 (55)	RESERVED	R	R	R	R	R	R	R	R
38 (56)	RESERVED	R	R	R	R	R	R	R	R
39 (57)	RESERVED	R	R	R	R	R	R	R	R
3A (58)	RESERVED	R	R	R	R	R	R	R	R
3B (59)	RESERVED	R	R	R	R	R	R	R	R
3C (60)	RESERVED	R	R	R	R	R	R	R	R
3D (61)	RESERVED	R	R	R	R	R	R	R	R
3E (62)	RESERVED	R	R	R	R	R	R	R	R
3F (63)	RESERVED	R	R	R	R	R	R	R	R

Legend: X=supported, O=supported but considered obsolete, R=reserved for future use

Notes: Interrupt 2FH changed name beginning with DOS 3.1.

Source: IBM DOS 3.3 Technical Reference, pages 6-1 to 6-33

See Also: 3.001. INT 21H Functions by DOS Version Summary
                5.02. INT 24H Error Codes
                5.03. INT 25H Absolute Disk Read
                5.04. INT 26H Absolute Disk Write
                5.06. INT 2FH Multiplex
                7.04. PC Interrupt Usage Summary

5.02. INT 24H ERROR CODES

For Error Codes Returned in AH Register:

Bit Numbers

7	6	5	4	3	2	1	0	Name	Allowable Values
							X	Type of operation	0=read operation; 1=write operation
					X	X		Location of error	00 = DOS Area 01 = FAT 10 = directory 11 = data area
				X				Fail response	0 = fail not allowed, 1 = fail allowed
			X					Retry response	0 = retry not allowed, 1 = retry allowed
		X						Ignore response	0 = can't be ignored, 1 = can be ignored
	X							NOT USED	NOT USED
X								Device type	0 = disk drive device,** 1 = other device type*

Notes: •*If bit 7=1, then either the memory image of the FAT is bad, or the error occurred on a character device. To determine the type of error, examine bit 15 of the fifth byte in the device header (attribute bits). If it is 0, the error is a bad memory image of the FAT. Otherwise, bits 0-3 will tell you what character device failed, as follows:

Bit Number

3	2	1	0	Character Device that Failed
			X	Current standard input
		X		Current standard output
	X			Current NULL device
X				Current clock device

•**If bit 7=0, then AL contains the failing drive number.

Error Code Returned in Low Byte of DI Register:

Error Code	Error Name	DOS versions		
		1.x	2.x	3.x
0 (0)	Write attempt on write-protected media	X	X	X
1 (1)	Unknown unit		X	X
2 (2)	Drive not ready	X	X	X
3 (3)	Unknown command		X	X
4 (4)	Data error (CRC error)	X	X	X
5 (5)	Bad request structure length		X	X
6 (6)	Seek error	X	X	X
7 (7)	Unknown media type		X	X
8 (8)	Sector not found	X	X	X
9 (9)	Printer is out of paper		X	X
A (10)	Write fault	X	X	X
B (11)	Read fault		X	X
C (12)	General failure	X	X	X
D (13)	UNDEFINED	R	R	R
E (14)	UNDEFINED	R	R	R
F (15)	Invalid disk change			X

Legend: X=supported, R=reserved

Notes: These are the same error codes returned by a device driver in its request header

Source: IBM DOS 3.3 Technical Reference, pages 6-15 to 6-16, 6-19 to 6-23

See Also: 5.01. DOS Interrupt Usage by Version

5.03. INT 25H ABSOLUTE DISK READ

Prior to Interrupt

	High	Low
AX		Drive number*
BX	Offset of transfer address	
CX	Number of sectors to read	
DX	Beginning logical sector #	

SP	
BP	
SI	
DI	

IP	
flags	

CS	
DS	Segment of transfer address
SS	
ES	

Upon Return from Interrupt

	High	Low	
AX	Destroyed	Destroyed	**
BX	Destroyed	Destroyed	
CX	Destroyed	Destroyed	
DX	Destroyed	Destroyed	

SP	Destroyed
BP	Destroyed
SI	Destroyed
DI	Destroyed

IP	Destroyed	
flags	Destroyed	**

CS	
DS	
SS	
ES	

Notes: •*0=A , 1=B, and so on
•**On error CF=1 and AX contains error data

Source: IBM DOS 3.3 Technical Reference, pages 6-24 to 6-25

See Also: 5.04. INT 26H Absolute Disk Write
5.05. INT 25H and 26H Error Codes

5.04. INT 26H ABSOLUTE DISK WRITE

Prior to Interrupt

	High	Low
AX		Drive number*
BX	Offset of transfer address	
CX	Number of sectors to write	
DX	Beginning logical sector #	

SP	
BP	
SI	
DI	

IP	
flags	

CS	
DS	Segment of transfer address
SS	
ES	

Upon Return from Interrupt

	High	Low	
AX	Destroyed	Destroyed	**
BX	Destroyed	Destroyed	
CX	Destroyed	Destroyed	
DX	Destroyed	Destroyed	

SP	Destroyed
BP	Destroyed
SI	Destroyed
DI	Destroyed

IP	Destroyed	
flags	Destroyed	**

CS	
DS	
SS	
ES	

Notes: •*0=A , 1=B, and so on
•**On error CF=1 and AX contains error data

Source: IBM DOS 3.3 Technical Reference, page 6-25

See Also: 5.03. INT 25H Absolute Disk Read
5.05. INT 25H and 26H Error Codes

5.05. INT 25H AND 26H ERROR CODES

Error Code	Error Name	1.x	2.x	3.x
02 (2)	Error (other than those listed below)	X	X	X
03 (3)	Write attempt on write-protected device	X	X	X
04 (4)	Requested sector not found	X	X	X
08 (8)	Bad CRC on disk read	X	X	X
40 (64)	SEEK operation failed	X	X	X
80 (128)	Attachment failed to respond	X	X	X

Legend: X=supported

Source: IBM DOS 3.3 Technical Reference, page 6-25

See Also: 5.03. INT 25H Absolute Disk Read
5.04. INT 26H Absolute Disk Write

5.06. INT 2FH MULTIPLEX

Prior to Interrupt

	High	Low
AX	Process*	Function**
BX		
CX		
DX	Offset of pointer to ASCIIZ string***	

SP	
BP	
SI	
DI	

IP	
flags	

CS	
DS	Segment of pointer to ASCIIZ string***
SS	
ES	

Upon Return from Interrupt

	High	Low
AX	Print error codes¥	State****
BX		
CX		
DX	Error count†	

SP	
BP	
SI	Offset of pointer to queue†
DI	

IP	
flags	

CS	
DS	Segment of pointer to queue†
SS	
ES	

Version Info: Interrupt used in DOS 3.x only

Notes:

•*Process is one of the following:
1 = resident portion of PRINT
2 = resident portion of ASSIGN
10H = resident portion of SHARE
B7H = resident portion of APPEND
C0H-FFH = reserved for user applications

•**Function is one of the following:
0 = get installed state
1 = submit file
2 = cancel file
3 = cancel all files
4 = status
5 = end of status

•***Functions 1 and 2 only
•****Function 0 only; one of the following:
0 = not installed, OK to install
1 = not installed, do not install
FFH = installed

•†Function 4 only
•¥Function 5 only (See 5.07. INT 2FH Error Codes)

Source: IBM DOS 3.3 Technical Reference, pages 6-28 to 6-33

See Also: 5.07. INT 2FH Error Codes

5.07. INT 2FH ERROR CODES

Error Code	Error Name	1.x	2.x	3.x
1	Invalid function			X
2	File not found			X
3	Path not found			X
4	Too many open files			X
5	Access denied			X
8	Queue full			X
9	Busy			X
12	Name too long			X

Legend: X=supported

Source: IBM DOS 3.3 Technical Reference, page 6-29

See Also: 5.06. INT 2FH Multiplex

5.08. INT 33H: MOUSE FUNCTIONS SUMMARY

Interrupt	Function*	Description	Comments
33H	00H	Mouse installed flag	Also resets mouse to default driver values
	01H	Show cursor	
	02H	Hide cursor	
	03H	Get mouse position and button status	
	04H	Set mouse cursor position	
	05H	Get button press information	
	06H	Get button release information	
	07H	Set min/max horizontal position	Restricts mouse movement to window
	08H	Set min/max vertical position	Restricts mouse movement to window
	09H	Set graphics cursor block	
	0AH	Set text cursor	
	0BH	Read mouse motion counters	
	0CH	Set user-defined subroutine input mask	
	0DH	Light pen emulation ON	
	0EH	Light pen emulation OFF	
	0FH	Set mickey/pixel ratio	
	10H	Conditional OFF	
	13H	Set doublespeed threshold	

Notes: *Value entered in AX register

Source: Microsoft Mouse User's Guide, page 175

5.09. INT 33H, AX=00H -- MOUSE INSTALLED FLAG

Prior to Issuing INT 33H   *Upon Return from INT 33H*

	High	Low
AX	00H	
BX		
CX		
DX		

SP	
BP	
SI	
DI	

IP	
flags	

CS	
DS	
SS	
ES	

	High	Low
AX	Status*	
BX	Buttons**	
CX		
DX		

SP	
BP	
SI	
DI	

IP	
flags	

CS	
DS	
SS	
ES	

Notes: •Function also resets mouse driver to default parameters
•*0=mouse not installed; -1=mouse installed
•**Always 2 for Microsoft Mouse

Source: Microsoft Mouse User's Guide, pages 176 to 177

See Also: 5.28. INT 33H, Mouse Driver Default Parameters

5.10. INT 33H, AX=01H -- SHOW CURSOR

Prior to Issuing INT 33H   *Upon Return from INT 33H*

	High	Low
AX	01H	
BX		
CX		
DX		

SP	
BP	
SI	
DI	

IP	
flags	

CS	
DS	
SS	
ES	

Interrupt returns no values

Notes: Cursor flag is incremented by this function; cursor is displayed
if the cursor flag has a value of 0 (default is -1)

Source: Microsoft Mouse User's Guide, page 178

See Also: 5.28. INT 33H, Mouse Driver Default Parameters

5.11. INT 33H, AX=02H -- HIDE CURSOR

Prior to Issuing INT 33H

	High	Low
AX		02H
BX		
CX		
DX		
SP		
BP		
SI		
DI		
IP		
flags		
CS		
DS		
SS		
ES		

Upon Return from INT 33H

Interrupt returns no values

Notes: Cursor flag is decremented by this function; cursor is removed from screen

Source: Microsoft Mouse User's Guide, pages 178 to 179

See Also: 5.28. INT 33H, Mouse Driver Default Parameters

5.12. INT 33H, AX=03H -- GET POSITION AND BUTTON STATUS

Prior to Issuing INT 33H

	High	Low
AX		03H
BX		
CX		
DX		
SP		
BP		
SI		
DI		
IP		
flags		
CS		
DS		
SS		
ES		

Upon Return from INT 33H

	High	Low
AX		
BX	Button status*	
CX	Horiz position	
DX	Vert position	
SP		
BP		
SI		
DI		
IP		
flags		
CS		
DS		
SS		
ES		

Notes: •A bit value of 1 represents a button held down (0=button up)
•*Bit 0 represents left button, bit 1 represents right button

Source: Microsoft Mouse User's Guide, page 179

See Also: 5.13. INT 33H, AX=04H -- Set Mouse Cursor Position
5.14. INT 33H, AX=05H -- Get Button Press Information
5.15. INT 33H, AX=06H -- Get Button Release Information

5.13. INT 33H, AX=04H -- SET MOUSE CURSOR POSITION

Prior to Issuing INT 33H   *Upon Return from INT 33H*

	High	Low
AX	04H	
BX		
CX	Horz position	
DX	Vert position	
SP		
BP		
SI		
DI		
IP		
flags		
CS		
DS		
SS		
ES		

Interrupt returns no values

Notes: •Position may be rounded to nearest values if screen is not in high resolution mode
•Position must be within range for current video mode

Source: Microsoft Mouse User's Guide, page 180

See Also: 5.12. INT 33H, AX=03H -- Get Position and Button Status
5.14. INT 33H, AX=05H -- Get Button Press Information
5.15. INT 33H, AX=06H -- Get Button Release Information

5.14. INT 33H, AX=05H -- GET BUTTON PRESS INFORMATION

Prior to Issuing INT 33H   *Upon Return from INT 33H*

	High	Low
AX	05H	
BX	Button*	
CX		
DX		
SP		
BP		
SI		
DI		
IP		
flags		
CS		
DS		
SS		
ES		

	High	Low
AX	Status**	
BX	Count***	
CX	Horz position at last press	
DX	Vert position at last press	
SP		
BP		
SI		
DI		
IP		
flags		
CS		
DS		
SS		
ES		

Notes: •*0=left button, 1=right button
•**Bit 0 represents left button, bit 1 is right button; 1=button down, 0=button up
•***Count of button presses, in range of 0 to 32767, set to 0 after call

Source: Microsoft Mouse User's Guide, page 181

See Also: 5.12. INT 33H, AX=03H -- Get Position and Button Status
5.13. INT 33H, AX=04H -- Set Mouse Cursor Position
5.15. INT 33H, AX=06H -- Get Button Release Information

5.15. INT 33H, AX=06H -- GET BUTTON RELEASE INFORMATION

Prior to Issuing INT 33H

	High	Low
AX	06H	
BX	Button*	
CX		
DX		

SP	
BP	
SI	
DI	

IP	
flags	

CS	
DS	
SS	
ES	

Upon Return from INT 33H

	High	Low
AX	Status**	
BX	Count***	
CX	Horz position at last release	
DX	Vert position at last release	

SP	
BP	
SI	
DI	

IP	
flags	

CS	
DS	
SS	
ES	

Notes:
- *0=left button, 1=right button
- **Bit 0 represents left button, bit 1 is right button; 1=button down, 0=button up
- ***Count of button releases, in range of 0 to 32767, set to 0 after call

Source: Microsoft Mouse User's Guide, page 182

See Also:
5.12. INT 33H, AX=03H -- Get Position and Button Status
5.13. INT 33H, AX=04H -- Set Mouse Cursor Position
5.14. INT 33H, AX=05H -- Get Button Press Information

5.16. INT 33H, AX=07H -- SET MIN AND MAX HORIZONTAL POSITION

Prior to Issuing INT 33H

	High	Low
AX	07H	
BX		
CX	Minimum position	
DX	Maximum position	

SP	
BP	
SI	
DI	

IP	
flags	

CS	
DS	
SS	
ES	

Upon Return from INT 33H

Interrupt returns no values

Notes:
- Function restricts mouse movement to horizontal coordinates specified
- If min value is greater than max, the two values are swapped

Source: Microsoft Mouse User's Guide, page 183

See Also:
5.17. INT 33H, AX=08H -- Set Min and Max Vertical Position

5.17. INT 33H, AX=08H -- SET MIN AND MAX VERTICAL POSITION

Prior to Issuing INT 33H   *Upon Return from INT 33H*

	High	Low
AX	08H	
BX		
CX	Minimum position	
DX	Maximum position	

SP	
BP	
SI	
DI	

IP	
flags	

CS	
DS	
SS	
ES	

Interrupt returns no values

Notes: •Function restricts mouse movement to vertical coordinates specified
•If min value is greater than max, the two values are swapped

Source: Microsoft Mouse User's Guide, page 184

See Also: 5.16. INT 33H, AX=07H -- Set Min and Max Horizontal Position

5.18. INT 33H, AX=09H -- SET GRAPHICS CURSOR BLOCK

Prior to Issuing INT 33H   *Upon Return from INT 33H*

	High	Low
AX	09H	
BX	Horz hot spot	
CX	Vert hot spot	
DX	Offset of pointer to screen/cursor masks	

SP	
BP	
SI	
DI	

IP	
flags	

CS	
DS	
SS	
ES	Segment of pointer to screen/cursor masks

Interrupt returns no values

Notes: Hot spot values must be within the range -16 to 16

Source: Microsoft Mouse User's Guide, page 185

See Also: 5.19. INT 33H, AX=0AH -- Set Text Cursor
5.27. INT 33H, Screen and Cursor Masks

5.19. INT 33H, AX=0AH -- SET TEXT CURSOR

Prior to Issuing INT 33H   *Upon Return from INT 33H*

	High	Low
AX	0AH	
BX	Cursor type*	
CX	Screen mask**	
DX	Cursor mask***	

Interrupt returns no values

SP	
BP	
SI	
DI	

IP	
flags	

CS	
DS	
SS	
ES	

Notes:
- •*0=software cursor, 1=hardware cursor
- •**Screen mask if software cursor, otherwise scan line start for hardware cursor
- •***Cursor mask if software cursor, otherwise scan line end for hardware cursor

Source: Microsoft Mouse User's Guide, page 187

See Also: 5.18. INT 33H, AX=O9H -- Set Graphics Cursor Block
5.27. INT 33H, Screen and Cursor Masks

5.20. INT 33H, AX=0BH -- READ MOUSE MOTION COUNTERS

Prior to Issuing INT 33H   *Upon Return from INT 33H*

	High	Low
AX	0BH	
BX		
CX		
DX		

	High	Low
AX		
BX		
CX	Horizontal count	
DX	Vertical count	

SP	
BP	
SI	
DI	

SP	
BP	
SI	
DI	

IP	
flags	

IP	
flags	

CS	
DS	
SS	
ES	

CS	
DS	
SS	
ES	

Notes:
- •Count values returned are the number of mickeys moved since the last call to this function. A mickey is 1/200 of an inch.
- •Count values are in range -32768 to 32767

Source: Microsoft Mouse User's Guide, page 188

5.21. INT 33H, AX=0CH -- SET USER-DEFINED SUBROUTINE INPUT MASK

Prior to Issuing INT 33H   *Upon Return from INT 33H*

	High	Low
AX		0CH
BX		
CX		Call mask*
DX		Offset of pointer to subroutine
SP		
BP		
SI		
DI		
IP		
flags		
CS		
DS		
SS		
ES		Segment of pointer to subroutine

Interrupt returns no values

Notes: •Subroutine is called when any of the conditions whose bit is 1 is met:

Bit	Condition
0	Cursor position changes
1	Left button pressed
2	Left button released
3	Right button pressed
4	Right button released
5-15	NOT USED

•Subroutine is passed information as follows:

Reg	Information
AX	Mask with condition bit set that triggered call
BX	Button state (bit 0=left, 1=right)
CX	Horizontal cursor position
DX	Vertical cursor position

Source: Microsoft Mouse User's Guide, pages 189 to 190

5.22. INT 33H, AX=0DH -- SET LIGHT PEN EMULATION ON

Prior to Issuing INT 33H   *Upon Return from INT 33H*

	High	Low
AX		0DH
BX		
CX		
DX		
SP		
BP		
SI		
DI		
IP		
flags		
CS		
DS		
SS		
ES		

Interrupt returns no values

Notes: Function causes mouse to emulate light pen, as follows:
Pen is down when both buttons are down
Pen is off screen when both buttons are up

Source: Microsoft Mouse User's Guide, page 191

See Also: 5.23. INT 33H, AX=0EH -- Set Light Pen Emulation OFF

5.23. INT 33H, AX=0EH -- SET LIGHT PEN EMULATION OFF

Prior to Issuing INT 33H   **Upon Return from INT 33H**

High   Low

AX	0EH
BX	
CX	
DX	

SP	
BP	
SI	
DI	

IP	
flags	

CS	
DS	
SS	
ES	

Interrupt returns no values

Notes: Function disables light pen emulation

Source: Microsoft Mouse User's Guide, page 192

See Also: 5.22. INT 33H, AX=0DH -- Set Light Pen Emulation ON

5.24. INT 33H, AX=0FH -- SET MICKEY TO PIXEL RATIO

Prior to Issuing INT 33H   **Upon Return from INT 33H**

High   Low

AX	0FH
BX	
CX	Horizontal ratio
DX	Vertical ratio

SP	
BP	
SI	
DI	

IP	
flags	

CS	
DS	
SS	
ES	

Interrupt returns no values

Notes: •Ratio values must be in range 1 to 32767
                 •Default horizontal value is 8
                 •Default vertical value is 16

Source: Microsoft Mouse User's Guide, page 193

5.25. INT 33H, AX=10H -- CONDITIONAL OFF

	Prior to Issuing INT 33H	*Upon Return from INT 33H*

	High	Low
AX	10H	
BX		
CX	Upper x screen coord	
DX	Upper y screen coord	
SP		
BP		
SI	Lower x screen coord	
DI	Lower y screen coord	
IP		
flags		
CS		
DS		
SS		
ES		

Interrupt returns no values

Notes: Function defines region for updating; mouse cursor hidden when in this region, and you must use INT 33H, AX=01H to turn it back on

Source: Microsoft Mouse User's Guide, page 193

See Also: 5.10. INT 33H, AX=01H -- Show Cursor

5.26. INT 33H, AX=13H -- SET DOUBLE SPEED THRESHOLD

	Prior to Issuing INT 33H	*Upon Return from INT 33H*

	High	Low
AX	13H	
BX		
CX		
DX	Threshold speed*	
SP		
BP		
SI		
DI		
IP		
flags		
CS		
DS		
SS		
ES		

Interrupt returns no values

Notes: *Speed defined in Mickeys per second; default is 64

Source: Microsoft Mouse User's Guide, page 194

5.27. INT 33H, SCREEN AND CURSOR MASKS

Effect of Screen and Cursor Mask Combinations:

Screen mask bit	Cursor mask bit	Resulting screen bit
0	0	0
0	1	1
1	0	Unchanged
1	1	Inverted

Screen Data for Character:

Bit Number*	Description	Comments
15	Blink control	1=blinking character
12-14	Background color	
11	Intensity control	1=high intensity
8-10	Foreground color	
0-7	Character	

Notes: *Bytes are stored in reverse order

Source: Microsoft Mouse User's Guide, pages 165 to 166

See Also: 7.25. CGA Character Attributes

5.28. INT 33H, MOUSE DRIVER DEFAULT PARAMETERS

Function	Parameter	Comments
Cursor position	Screen center	e.g., 100,320 for CGA in 640x200 mono mode
Internal cursor flag	-1	Means not displayed
Graphics cursor	-1,-1	Arrow
Text cursor		Inverting box
Interrupt call mask	All 0	No interrupts
Light pen emulation mode	Enabled	
Mickey/pixel ratio (horz)	8 to 8	
Mickey/pixel ratio (vert)	16 to 8	
Min/max cursor pos (horz)	Varies	Set to maximum width of video mode
Min/max cursor pos (vert)	Varies	Set to maximum height of video mode

Source: Microsoft Mouse User's Guide, pages 176 to 177

See Also: 5.09. INT 33H, AX=00H -- Mouse Installed Flag

5.29. INT 67H: EXPANDED MEMORY MANAGER FUNCTIONS SUMMARY

Interrupt	Function*	Description	Comments
67H	40H	Get status	
	41H	Get page frame address	
	42H	Get page count	
	43H	Allocate pages	
	44H	Map memory	
	45H	Deallocate pages	
	46H	Get version	
	47H	Save page map	
	48H	Restore page map	
	4BH	Get handle count	
	4CH	Get page count for a handle	
	4DH	Get page counts for all handles	
	4EH,0	Get map	
	4EH,1	Set map	
	4EH,2	Swap map	
	4EH,3	Get size	
	60H	Get physical window array	EEMS only
	68H	Get system physical window array	EEMS only
	69H	Map page into window	EEMS only
	6AH,0	Get system map	EEMS only
	6AH,1	Set system map	EEMS only
	6AH,2	Swap system map	EEMS only
	6AH,3	Get map size	EEMS only
	6AH,4	Set standard mapping	EEMS only
	6AH,5	Set alternate mapping	EEMS only
	6AH,6	Deallocate initial pages	EEMS only

Notes: •These functions work only if an Expanded Memory Manager (EMM) is active in the system. To check for EMM, see *Advanced MS-DOS,* pages 182 to 185.
•*First number is AH, second number (if any) is AL

Source: *Advanced MS-DOS* (Microsoft Press), Ray Duncan, pages 442 to 443
AST Rampage Technical Reference

5.30. INT 67H, AH=40H -- GET STATUS

Prior to Issuing INT 67H

	High	Low
AX	40H	
BX		
CX		
DX		

SP	
BP	
SI	
DI	

IP	
flags	

CS	
DS	
SS	
ES	

Upon Return from INT 67H

	High	Low
AX	Status*	
BX		
CX		
DX		

SP	
BP	
SI	
DI	

IP	
flags	

CS	
DS	
SS	
ES	

Notes: *00=no error (Otherwise see 5.56. INT 67H, Expanded Memory Manager Error Codes)

Source: *Advanced MS-DOS* (Microsoft Press), Ray Duncan, pages 441 to 442

See Also: 5.29. INT 67H: Expanded Memory Manager Functions Summary
5.56. INT 67H, Expanded Memory Manager Error Codes

5.31. INT 67H, AH=41H -- GET PAGE FRAME ADDRESS

Prior to Issuing INT 67H

	High	Low
AX	41H	
BX		
CX		
DX		

SP	
BP	
SI	
DI	

IP	
flags	

CS	
DS	
SS	
ES	

Upon Return from INT 67H

	High	Low
AX	Status*	
BX	Segment address of page frame	
CX		
DX		

SP	
BP	
SI	
DI	

IP	
flags	

CS	
DS	
SS	
ES	

Notes: *00=no error (Otherwise see 5.56. INT 67H, Expanded Memory Manager Error Codes)

Source: *Advanced MS-DOS* (Microsoft Press), Ray Duncan, pages 442 to 443

See Also: 5.29. INT 67H: Expanded Memory Manager Functions Summary
5.56. INT 67H, Expanded Memory Manager Error Codes

5.32. INT 67H, AH=42H -- GET PAGE COUNT

Prior to Issuing INT 67H

	High	Low
AX	42H	
BX		
CX		
DX		

SP	
BP	
SI	
DI	

| IP | |
| flags | |

CS	
DS	
SS	
ES	

Upon Return from INT 67H

	High	Low
AX	Status*	
BX	Unallocated pages	
CX		
DX	Total page count	

SP	
BP	
SI	
DI	

| IP | |
| flags | |

CS	
DS	
SS	
ES	

Notes: *00=no error (Otherwise see 5.56. INT 67H, Expanded Memory Manager Error Codes)

Source: *Advanced MS-DOS* (Microsoft Press), Ray Duncan, page 443

See Also: 5.29. INT 67H: Expanded Memory Manager Functions Summary
5.56. INT 67H, Expanded Memory Manager Error Codes

5.33. INT 67H, AH=43H -- ALLOCATE PAGES

Prior to Issuing INT 67H

	High	Low
AX	43H	
BX	Pages to allocate	
CX		
DX		

SP	
BP	
SI	
DI	

| IP | |
| flags | |

CS	
DS	
SS	
ES	

Upon Return from INT 67H

	High	Low
AX	Status*	
BX		
CX		
DX	EMM page handle	

SP	
BP	
SI	
DI	

| IP | |
| flags | |

CS	
DS	
SS	
ES	

Notes: *00=no error (Otherwise see 5.56. INT 67H, Expanded Memory Manager Error Codes)

Source: *Advanced MS-DOS* (Microsoft Press), Ray Duncan, pages 444 to 445

See Also: 5.29. INT 67H: Expanded Memory Manager Functions Summary
5.56. INT 67H, Expanded Memory Manager Error Codes

5.34. INT 67H, AH=44H -- MAP MEMORY

Prior to Issuing INT 67H

	High	Low
AX	44H	Phys Page #**
BX	Logical page #	
CX		
DX	EMM page handle	

SP	
BP	
SI	
DI	

IP	
flags	

CS	
DS	
SS	
ES	

Upon Return from INT 67H

	High	Low
AX	Status*	
BX		
CX		
DX		

SP	
BP	
SI	
DI	

IP	
flags	

CS	
DS	
SS	
ES	

Notes:
- *00=no error (Otherwise see 5.56. INT 67H, Expanded Memory Manager Error Codes)
- **Must be in range 0-3

Source: *Advanced MS-DOS* (Microsoft Press), Ray Duncan, pages 445 to 446

See Also:
5.29. INT 67H: Expanded Memory Manager Functions Summary
5.33. INT 67H, AH=43H -- Allocate Pages
5.56. INT 67H, Expanded Memory Manager Error Codes

5.35. INT 67H, AH=45H -- DEALLOCATE PAGES

Prior to Issuing INT 67H

	High	Low
AX	45H	
BX		
CX		
DX	EMM page handle	

SP	
BP	
SI	
DI	

IP	
flags	

CS	
DS	
SS	
ES	

Upon Return from INT 67H

	High	Low
AX	Status*	
BX		
CX		
DX		

SP	
BP	
SI	
DI	

IP	
flags	

CS	
DS	
SS	
ES	

Notes: *00=no error (Otherwise see 5.56. INT 67H, Expanded Memory Manager Error Codes)

Source: *Advanced MS-DOS* (Microsoft Press), Ray Duncan, pages 446 to 447

See Also:
5.29. INT 67H: Expanded Memory Manager Functions Summary
5.33. INT 67H, AH=43H -- Allocate Pages
5.56. INT 67H, Expanded Memory Manager Error Codes

5.36. INT 67H, AH=46H -- GET EMM VERSION

Prior to Issuing INT 67H

	High	Low
AX	46H	
BX		
CX		
DX		
SP		
BP		
SI		
DI		
IP		
flags		
CS		
DS		
SS		
ES		

Upon Return from INT 67H

	High	Low
AX	Status*	Version**
BX		
CX		
DX		
SP		
BP		
SI		
DI		
IP		
flags		
CS		
DS		
SS		
ES		

Notes: •*00=no error (Otherwise see 5.56. INT 67H, Expanded Memory Manager Error Codes)
•**HO nibble is BCD-coded major version number, LO nibble is BCD-coded minor version number

Source: *Advanced MS-DOS* (Microsoft Press), Ray Duncan, pages 447 to 448

See Also: 5.29. INT 67H: Expanded Memory Manager Functions Summary
5.56. INT 67H, Expanded Memory Manager Error Codes

5.37. INT 67H, AH=47H -- SAVE PAGE MAP

Prior to Issuing INT 67H

	High	Low
AX	47H	
BX		
CX		
DX	EMM Page Handle	
SP		
BP		
SI		
DI		
IP		
flags		
CS		
DS		
SS		
ES		

Upon Return from INT 67H

	High	Low
AX	Status*	
BX		
CX		
DX		
SP		
BP		
SI		
DI		
IP		
flags		
CS		
DS		
SS		
ES		

Notes: *00=no error (Otherwise see 5.56. INT 67H, Expanded Memory Manager Error Codes)

Source: *Advanced MS-DOS* (Microsoft Press), Ray Duncan, pages 448 to 449

See Also: 5.29. INT 67H: Expanded Memory Manager Functions Summary
5.33. INT 67H, AH=43H -- Allocate Pages
5.56. INT 67H, Expanded Memory Manager Error Codes

5.38. INT 67H, AH=48H -- RESTORE PAGE MAP

Prior to Issuing INT 67H

	High	Low
AX	48H	
BX		
CX		
DX	EMM page handle	

SP	
BP	
SI	
DI	

IP	
flags	

CS	
DS	
SS	
ES	

Upon Return from INT 67H

	High	Low
AX	Status*	
BX		
CX		
DX		

SP	
BP	
SI	
DI	

IP	
flags	

CS	
DS	
SS	
ES	

Notes:
- •Function is used after an INT 67H, AH=47H call
- •*00=no error (Otherwise see 5.56. INT 67H, Expanded Memory Manager Error Codes)

Source: *Advanced MS-DOS* (Microsoft Press), Ray Duncan, page 449

See Also:
5.29. INT 67H: Expanded Memory Manager Functions Summary
5.33. INT 67H, AH=43H -- Allocate Pages
5.37. INT 67H, AH=47H -- Save Page Map
5.56. INT 67H, Expanded Memory Manager Error Codes

5.39. INT 67H, AH=4BH -- GET HANDLE COUNT

Prior to Issuing INT 67H

	High	Low
AX	4BH	
BX		
CX		
DX		

SP	
BP	
SI	
DI	

IP	
flags	

CS	
DS	
SS	
ES	

Upon Return from INT 67H

	High	Low
AX	Status*	
BX	Number of handles	
CX		
DX		

SP	
BP	
SI	
DI	

IP	
flags	

CS	
DS	
SS	
ES	

Notes: *00=no error (Otherwise see 5.56. INT 67H, Expanded Memory Manager Error Codes)

Source: *Advanced MS-DOS* (Microsoft Press), Ray Duncan, pages 450 to 451

See Also:
5.29. INT 67H: Expanded Memory Manager Functions Summary
5.56. INT 67H, Expanded Memory Manager Error Codes

5.40. INT 67H, AH=4CH -- GET PAGE COUNT FOR HANDLE

Prior to Issuing INT 67H

	High	Low
AX	4CH	
BX		
CX		
DX	EMM page handle	

SP	
BP	
SI	
DI	

IP	
flags	

CS	
DS	
SS	
ES	

Upon Return from INT 67H

	High	Low
AX	Status*	
BX	Number of pages**	
CX		
DX		

SP	
BP	
SI	
DI	

IP	
flags	

CS	
DS	
SS	
ES	

Notes:
- *00=no error (Otherwise see 5.56. INT 67H, Expanded Memory Manager Error Codes)
- **Logical pages in range of 1 to 512

Source: *Advanced MS-DOS* (Microsoft Press), Ray Duncan, pages 451 to 452

See Also:
5.29. INT 67H: Expanded Memory Manager Functions Summary
5.56. INT 67H, Expanded Memory Manager Error Codes

5.41. INT 67H, AH=4DH -- GET PAGE COUNTS FOR ALL HANDLES

Prior to Issuing INT 67H

	High	Low
AX	4DH	
BX		
CX		
DX		

SP	
BP	
SI	
DI	Offset of pointer to empty array

IP	
flags	

CS	
DS	
SS	
ES	Segment of pointer to empty array

Upon Return from INT 67H

	High	Low
AX	Status*	
BX	Number of handles	
CX		
DX		

SP	
BP	
SI	
DI	Offset of pointer to filled array

IP	
flags	

CS	
DS	
SS	
ES	Segment of pointer to filled array

Notes:
- Array is a 1024-byte area which will be filled with two words for each handle being used (first word is handle number, second is number of pages associated with it)
- *00=no error (Otherwise see 5.56. INT 67H, Expanded Memory Manager Error Codes)

Source: *Advanced MS-DOS* (Microsoft Press), Ray Duncan, pages 452 to 453

See Also:
5.29. INT 67H: Expanded Memory Manager Functions Summary
5.40. INT 67H, AH=4CH -- Get Page Count for Handle
5.56. INT 67H, Expanded Memory Manager Error Codes

5.42. INT 67H, AH=4EH, AL=00H -- GET PAGE MAP

Prior to Issuing INT 67H

	High	Low
AX	4EH	00H
BX		
CX		
DX		

SP	
BP	
SI	
DI	Offset of pointer to empty array

IP	
flags	

CS	
DS	
SS	
ES	Segment of pointer to empty array

Upon Return from INT 67H

	High	Low
AX	Status*	
BX	Number of handles	
CX		
DX		

SP	
BP	
SI	
DI	Offset of pointer to filled array

IP	
flags	

CS	
DS	
SS	
ES	Segment of pointer to filled array

Notes:

•Array is a 1024-byte area which will be filled with two words for each handle being used (first word is handle number, second is number of pages associated with it)

•*00=no error (Otherwise see 5.56. INT 67H, Expanded Memory Manager Error Codes)

Source: *Advanced MS-DOS* (Microsoft Press), Ray Duncan, pages 453 to 454

See Also: 5.29. INT 67H: Expanded Memory Manager Functions Summary
5.56. INT 67H, Expanded Memory Manager Error Codes

5.43. INT 67H, AH=4EH, AL=01H -- SET PAGE MAP

Prior to Issuing INT 67H

	High	Low
AX	4EH	01H
BX		
CX		
DX		

SP	
BP	
SI	Offset of pointer to page map array
DI	

IP	
flags	

CS	
DS	Segment of pointer to page map array
SS	
ES	

Upon Return from INT 67H

	High	Low
AX	Status*	
BX		
CX		
DX		

SP	
BP	
SI	
DI	

IP	
flags	

CS	
DS	
SS	
ES	

Notes:

•Array is a 1024-byte area which will be filled with two words for each handle being used (first word is handle number, second is number of pages associated with it)

•*00=no error (Otherwise see 5.56. INT 67H, Expanded Memory Manager Error Codes)

Source: *Advanced MS-DOS* (Microsoft Press), Ray Duncan, pages 453 to 454

See Also: 5.29. INT 67H: Expanded Memory Manager Functions Summary
5.56. INT 67H, Expanded Memory Manager Error Codes

5.44. INT 67H, AH=4EH, AL=02H -- SWAP PAGE MAP

Prior to Issuing INT 67H

	High	Low
AX	4EH	02H
BX		
CX		
DX		

SP	
BP	
SI	Offset of pointer to page map array
DI	

IP	
flags	

CS	
DS	Segment of pointer to page map array
SS	
ES	

Upon Return from INT 67H

	High	Low
AX	Status*	
BX		
CX		
DX		

SP	
BP	
SI	
DI	Offset of pointer to previous page map array

IP	
flags	

CS	
DS	
SS	
ES	Segment of pointer to previous page map array

Notes: •Array is a 1024-byte area which will be filled with two words for each handle being used (first word is handle number, second is number of pages associated with it)
•*00=no error (Otherwise see 5.56. INT 67H, Expanded Memory Manager Error Codes)

Source: *Advanced MS-DOS* (Microsoft Press), Ray Duncan, pages 453 to 454

See Also: 5.29. INT 67H: Expanded Memory Manager Functions Summary
5.56. INT 67H, Expanded Memory Manager Error Codes

5.45. INT 67H, AH=4EH, AL=03H -- GET PAGE MAP ARRAY SIZE

Prior to Issuing INT 67H

	High	Low
AX	4EH	03H
BX		
CX		
DX		

SP	
BP	
SI	
DI	

IP	
flags	

CS	
DS	
SS	
ES	

Upon Return from INT 67H

	High	Low
AX	Status*	Size**
BX		
CX		
DX		

SP	
BP	
SI	
DI	

IP	
flags	

CS	
DS	
SS	
ES	

Notes: •*00=no error (Otherwise see 5.56. INT 67H, Expanded Memory Manager Error Codes)
•**Size is in bytes and represents size of current page map array

Source: *Advanced MS-DOS* (Microsoft Press), Ray Duncan, pages 453 to 454

See Also: 5.29. INT 67H: Expanded Memory Manager Functions Summary
5.56. INT 67H, Expanded Memory Manager Error Codes

5.46. INT 67H, AH=60H -- GET PHYSICAL WINDOW ARRAY

Prior to Issuing INT 67H

	High	Low
AX	60H	
BX		
CX		
DX		

SP	
BP	
SI	
DI	Offset of pointer to empty array

| IP | |
| flags | |

CS	
DS	
SS	
ES	Segment of pointer to empty array

Upon Return from INT 67H

	High	Low
AX	Status*	Number entries**
BX		
CX		
DX		

SP	
BP	
SI	
DI	Offset of pointer to filled array

| IP | |
| flags | |

CS	
DS	
SS	
ES	Segment of pointer to filled array

Notes: •*00=no error (Otherwise see 5.56. INT 67H, Expanded Memory Manager Error Codes)
•**Size is in entries (four bytes per entry in array)

Source: AST Rampage Technical Reference

See Also: 5.29. INT 67H: Expanded Memory Manager Functions Summary
5.56. INT 67H, Expanded Memory Manager Error Codes

5.47. INT 67H, AH=68H -- GET SYSTEM PHYSICAL WINDOW ARRAY

Prior to Issuing INT 67H

	High	Low
AX	68H	
BX		
CX		
DX		

SP	
BP	
SI	
DI	Offset of pointer to empty array

| IP | |
| flags | |

CS	
DS	
SS	
ES	Segment of pointer to empty array

Upon Return from INT 67H

	High	Low
AX	Status*	Number entries**
BX		
CX		
DX		

SP	
BP	
SI	
DI	Offset of pointer to filled array

| IP | |
| flags | |

CS	
DS	
SS	
ES	Segment of pointer to filled array

Notes: •*00=no error (Otherwise see 5.56. INT 67H, Expanded Memory Manager Error Codes)
•**Size is in entries (four bytes per entry in array)

Source: AST Rampage Technical Reference

See Also: 5.29. INT 67H: Expanded Memory Manager Functions Summary
5.56. INT 67H, Expanded Memory Manager Error Codes

5.48. INT 67H, AH=69H -- MAP PAGE TO WINDOW

Prior to Issuing INT 67H

	High	Low
AX	69H	
BX	Page number	
CX		
DX	EMM page handle	
SP		
BP		
SI		
DI		
IP		
flags		
CS		
DS		
SS		
ES		

Upon Return from INT 67H

	High	Low
AX	Status*	
BX		
CX		
DX		
SP		
BP		
SI		
DI		
IP		
flags		
CS		
DS		
SS		
ES		

Notes: *00=no error (Otherwise see 5.56. INT 67H, Expanded Memory Manager Error Codes)

Source: AST Rampage Technical Reference

See Also: 5.29. INT 67H: Expanded Memory Manager Functions Summary
5.56. INT 67H, Expanded Memory Manager Error Codes

5.49. INT 67H, AH=6AH, AL=00H -- GET SYSTEM MAP

Prior to Issuing INT 67H

	High	Low
AX	6AH	00H
BX		
CX	First window	Window count
DX		
SP		
BP		
SI		
DI	Offset of pointer to empty array	
IP		
flags		
CS		
DS		
SS		
ES	Segment of pointer to empty array	

Upon Return from INT 67H

	High	Low
AX	Status*	
BX		
CX		
DX		
SP		
BP		
SI		
DI	Offset of pointer to saved page map array	
IP		
flags		
CS		
DS		
SS		
ES	Segment of pointer to saved page map array	

Notes: *00=no error (Otherwise see 5.56. INT 67H, Expanded Memory Manager Error Codes)

Source: AST Rampage Technical Reference

See Also: 5.29. INT 67H: Expanded Memory Manager Functions Summary
5.56. INT 67H, Expanded Memory Manager Error Codes

5.50. INT 67H, AH=6AH, AL=01H -- SET SYSTEM MAP

Prior to Issuing INT 67H

	High	Low
AX	6AH	01H
BX		
CX	1st window	Window count
DX		

SP	
BP	
SI	
DI	Offset of pointer to saved page map array

IP	
flags	

CS	
DS	
SS	
ES	Segment of pointer to saved page map array

Upon Return from INT 67H

	High	Low
AX	Status*	
BX		
CX		
DX		

SP	
BP	
SI	
DI	

IP	
flags	

CS	
DS	
SS	
ES	

Notes: *00=no error (Otherwise see 5.56. INT 67H, Expanded Memory Manager
Error Codes)

Source: AST Rampage Technical Reference

See Also: 5.29. INT 67H: Expanded Memory Manager Functions Summary
5.56. INT 67H, Expanded Memory Manager Error Codes

5.51. INT 67H, AH=6AH, AL=02H -- SWAP SYSTEM MAP

Prior to Issuing INT 67H

	High	Low
AX	6AH	02H
BX		
CX	1st window	Window count
DX		

SP	
BP	
SI	Offset of pointer to next page map
DI	Offset of pointer to empty array

IP	
flags	

CS	
DS	Segment of pointer to next page map
SS	
ES	Segment of pointer to empty array

Upon Return from INT 67H

	High	Low
AX	Status*	
BX		
CX		
DX		

SP	
BP	
SI	
DI	Offset of pointer to previous page map

IP	
flags	

CS	
DS	
SS	
ES	Segment of pointer to previous page map

Notes: *00=no error (Otherwise see 5.56. INT 67H, Expanded Memory Manager
Error Codes)

Source: AST Rampage Technical Reference

See Also: 5.29. INT 67H: Expanded Memory Manager Functions Summary
5.56. INT 67H, Expanded Memory Manager Error Codes

5.52. INT 67H, AH=6AH, AL=03H -- GET MAP SIZE

	Prior to Issuing INT 67H			*Upon Return from INT 67H*	
	High	*Low*		*High*	*Low*
AX	6AH	03H	AX	Status*	Size**
BX			BX		
CX	1st window	Window count	CX		
DX			DX		
SP			SP		
BP			BP		
SI			SI		
DI			DI		
IP			IP		
flags			flags		
CS			CS		
DS			DS		
SS			SS		
ES			ES		

Notes: •*00=no error (Otherwise see 5.56. INT 67H, Expanded Memory Manager Error Codes)
•**Size of page map array in bytes

Source: AST Rampage Technical Reference

See Also: 5.29. INT 67H: Expanded Memory Manager Functions Summary
5.56. INT 67H, Expanded Memory Manager Error Codes

5.53. INT 67H, AH=6AH, AL=O4H -- SET STANDARD MAPPING

	Prior to Issuing INT 67H			*Upon Return from INT 67H*	
	High	*Low*		*High*	*Low*
AX	6AH	04H	AX	Status*	
BX			BX		
CX			CX		
DX			DX		
SP			SP		
BP			BP		
SI			SI		
DI			DI		
IP			IP		
flags			flags		
CS			CS		
DS			DS		
SS			SS		
ES			ES		

Notes: *00=no error (Otherwise see 5.56. INT 67H, Expanded Memory Manager Error Codes)

Source: AST Rampage Technical Reference

See Also: 5.29. INT 67H: Expanded Memory Manager Functions Summary
5.56. INT 67H, Expanded Memory Manager Error Codes

5.54. INT 67H, AH=6AH, AL=05H -- SET ALTERNATE MAPPING

Prior to Issuing INT 67H   *Upon Return from INT 67H*

	High	Low			High	Low
AX	6AH	05H		AX	Status*	
BX				BX		
CX				CX		
DX				DX		
SP				SP		
BP				BP		
SI				SI		
DI				DI		
IP				IP		
flags				flags		
CS				CS		
DS				DS		
SS				SS		
ES				ES		

Notes: *00=no error (Otherwise see 5.56. INT 67H, Expanded Memory Manager Error Codes)

Source: AST Rampage Technical Reference

See Also: 5.29. INT 67H: Expanded Memory Manager Functions Summary
5.56. INT 67H, Expanded Memory Manager Error Codes

5.55. INT 67H, AH=6AH, AL=O6H -- DEALLOCATE INITIAL SYSTEM PAGES

Prior to Issuing INT 67H   *Upon Return from INT 67H*

	High	Low		High	Low
AX	6AH	06H	AX	Status*	
BX			BX		
CX	1st window	Window count	CX		
DX			DX		
SP			SP		
BP			BP		
SI			SI		
DI			DI		
IP			IP		
flags			flags		
CS			CS		
DS			DS		
SS			SS		
ES			ES		

Notes: *00=no error (Otherwise see 5.56. INT 67H, Expanded Memory Manager Error Codes)

Source: AST Rampage Technical Reference

See Also: 5.29. INT 67H: Expanded Memory Manager Functions Summary
5.56. INT 67H, Expanded Memory Manager Error Codes

5.56. INT 67H -- EXPANDED MEMORY MANAGER ERROR CODES

Code	Description	Comments
00H	Normal return code	No error occurred
80H	Software error	
81H	Hardware error	
83H	Unallocated or invalid handle	
84H	Undefined function code	
85H	Out of handles	
87H	Page count error	> total pages
88H	Page count error	
89H	Requested zero pages	
8AH	No logical page for this handle	
8BH	Physical page outside valid range	
8CH	Context stack out of memory	
8DH	Handle already has context stack	
8EH	No context stack for that handle	
8FH	Undefined subfunction code	

Source: *Advanced MS-DOS* (Microsoft Press), Ray Duncan, pages 441 to 454

— SECTION —

6

Microsoft
Windows

6.01. RESERVED SYSTEM KEYS

Key Code	Key Name	Windows Action	Never Redefine Used by System	Reserved for Use in Menus	Reserved for Use in Dialogs
No equivalent	Alt + Tab	Selects active window from top down	X		
No equivalent	Alt + Shft + Tab	Selects active window from bottom up	X		
No equivalent	Alt + Spacebar	Selects System menu of active window	X		
0,10H to 0,32H	Alt + letter	Selects menu from active menu bar			
0,6BH	Alt+F4**	Closes window	X		
0,6CH	Alt+F5**	Restores window	X		
0,6EH	Alt+F7**	Moves window	X		
0,6FH	Alt+F8**	Sizes window	X		
0,70H	Alt+F9**	Shrinks window	X		
0,71H	Alt+F10**	Enlarges window	X		
No equivalent	Alt+Escape**	Selects next application	X		
No equivalent	Ctrl+Escape**	RESERVED	X		
No equivalent	Shft+Escape**	Selects system menu of active window	X		
0,44H	F10**	Selects system menu of active window	X		
0,4BH	Left*	Selects menu to left of current one		X	
0,4DH	Right*	Selects menu to right of current one		X	
0,48H	Up*	Selects command above current one		X	
0,50H	Down*	Selects command below current one		X	
13H	Enter	Invokes selected command or action		X	X
1BH	Escape	Cancels menu or dialog box		X	X
09H	Tab	Selects active control from top down			X
No equivalent	Shift + Tab	Selects active control from bottom up			X
20H	Spacebar	Invokes default action (default push button)			X

Version Info: **Applies only to versions of Windows beginning with 2.0

Notes: *Any direction key of this type should not be redefined

Source: Microsoft Windows SDK Application Style Guide 2.0, pages 44 to 45

See Also: 1.23. IBM Extended Character Codes
6.02. Recommended Keyboard Actions
6.05. Recommended Mouse Usage

6.02. RECOMMENDED KEYBOARD ACTIONS

Key Code	Key Name	Recommended Windows Action In General Selections	In Text/Graphics Selections
09H	Tab	Move to next item (left to right, top to bottom)	Move to next tab stop to the right
No equivalent	Shift+Tab	Move to previous item (right to left, bottom to top)	Move to next tab stop to the left
13H	Enter	Confirm or execute default or highlighted item	Create an empty line
Varies	Left*	Move left one item	Move left one character
Varies	Right*	Move right one item	Move right one character
Varies	Up*	Move up one item	Move up one line
Varies	Down*	Move down one item	Move down one line
0,49H	PgUp	Move up one screen	Move up one screen
0,51H	PgDn	Move down one screen	Move down one screen
0,52H	Insert	Insert contents of Clipboard at cursor position	
0,53H	Delete	Move selected item to Clipboard	
No equivalent	Shft + Up*	Extend selection up from current item	Extend current selection up
No equivalent	Shft + Down*	Extend selection down from current item	Extend current selection down
No equivalent	Shft + Left*	Extend selection left from current item	Extend current selection left
No equivalent	Shft + Right*	Extend selection right from current item	Extend current selection right
No equivalent	Shft + Delete	Delete selected item (do not move to clipboard)	Delete selected item
Varies	Control + Direction	Leave selection intact, move in indicated direction	
No equivalent	Control + Shft + Direction	Add to discontinuous selection moving in direction	
No equivalent	Shft + Backspace		Delete character to right
08H	Backspace		Delete character to left
0,3BH	F1**	Help	
0,40H	F6**	Next section (pane) within application	
0,59H	Shft+F6**	Previous section (pane) within application	
0,63H	Ctrl+F6**	Next child or document window within application	
No equivalent	Shft+Ctrl+F6**	Previous child or document window within application	
0,68H	Alt+F1**	F11	
0,69H	Alt+F2**	F12	
No equivalent	Shft+Insert**	Insert contents of clipboard	
0,84H	Ctrl+PgUp**	Move left one screen	
0,76H	Ctrl+PgDn**	Move right one screen	

(Continued)

Table 6.02. Continued

Recommended Windows Action

Key Code	Key Name	In General Selections	In Text/Graphics Selections
No equivalent	Shft+PgUp**		Move selection up one screen
No equivalent	Shft+PgDn**		Move selection down one screen
No equivalent	Alt+Backspace**	Undo last action	
No equivalent	Ctrl+Delete**	Clear to end of line	
0,47H	Home		Move to top of current screen
0,4FH	End		Move to bottom of current screen

Version Info: **Applies to versions of Windows beginning with 2.0 only

Notes: *Any direction key of this type should not be redefined

Source: Microsoft Windows SDK Application Style Guide 2.0, pages 46 to 49

See Also: 1.23. IBM Extended Character Codes
6.01. Reserved System Keys
6.05. Recommended Mouse Usage

6.03. VIRTUAL KEYS

Key Name	Description	Key Name	Description
VK_ADD	Add key	VK_INSERT	Insert key
VK_BACK	Backspace key	VK_LBUTTON	Left mouse button
VK_CANCEL	Cancel key	VK_LEFT	Left arrow key
VK_CAPITAL	Caps lock key	VK_MBUTTON	Middle mouse button
VK_CLEAR	Clear key	VK_MENU	Alt key
VK_CONTROL	Control key	VK_MULTIPLY	Multiply key
VK_DECIMAL	Decimal point key (.)	VK_NEXT	Next screen key (PgDn)
VK_DELETE	Delete key	VK_NUMPAD0	Numeric keypad 0 key
VK_DIVIDE	Divide key	VK_NUMPAD1	Numeric keypad 1 key
VK_DOWN	Down arrow key	VK_NUMPAD2	Numeric keypad 2 key
VK_END	End of document key (End)	VK_NUMPAD3	Numeric keypad 3 key
VK_ESCAPE	Escape key (Esc)	VK_NUMPAD4	Numeric keypad 4 key
VK_F1	Function key 1	VK_NUMPAD5	Numeric keypad 5 key
VK_F2	Function key 2	VK_NUMPAD6	Numeric keypad 6 key
VK_F3	Function key 3	VK_NUMPAD7	Numeric keypad 7 key
VK_F4	Function key 4	VK_NUMPAD8	Numeric keypad 8 key
VK_F5	Function key 5	VK_NUMPAD9	Numeric keypad 9 key
VK_F6	Function key 6	VK_PAUSE	Pause key
VK_F7	Function key 7	VK_PRINT	Print key
VK_F8	Function key 8	VK_PRIOR	Prior screen key (PgUp)
VK_F9	Function key 9	VK_RBUTTON	Right mouse button
VK_F10	Function key 10	VK_RETURN	Carriage return key (Enter key)
VK_F11	Function key 11	VK_RIGHT	Right arrow key
VK_F12	Function key 12	VK_SELECT	Select key
VK_F13	Function key 13	VK_SEPARATOR	Separator key
VK_F14	Function key 14	VK_SHIFT	Shift key
VK_F15	Function key 15	VK_SPACE	Spacebar
VK_F16	Function key 16	VK_SUBTRACT	Subtract key
VK_HELP	Help key	VK_TAB	Tab key
VK_HOME	Beginning of document key (Home)	VK_UP	Up arrow key

Source: Microsoft Windows SDK Programmer's Reference 2.0,
pages 280 to 281

See Also: 6.01. Reserved System Keys
6.02. Recommended Keyboard Actions
6.05. Recommended Mouse Usage

6.04. WINDOWS TERMINAL -- VT52 KEY EMULATIONS

ANSI VT52 Key	Windows Key Equivalent	Numlock Status
0	Numeric keypad 0 (insert)	ON
1	Numeric keypad 1 (end)	ON
2	Numeric keypad 2 (down)	ON
3	Numeric keypad 3 (PgDn)	ON
4	Numeric keypad 4 (left)	ON
5	Numeric keypad 5	ON
6	Numeric keypad 6 (right)	ON
7	Numeric keypad 7 (home)	ON
8	Numeric keypad 8 (up)	ON
9	Numeric keypad 9 (PgUp)	ON
-	Numeric keypad -	ON
,	Numeric keypad * (prtscr)	ON
.	Numeric keypad . (delete)	ON
Enter	Numeric keypad plus	ON
Insert char mode	Insert	OFF
Insert line	End	OFF
Cursor down	Down arrow	OFF
Delete line	PgDn	OFF
Cursor left	Left arrow	OFF
Cursor right	Right arrow	OFF
Home	Home	OFF
Cursor up	Up arrow	OFF
Delete char	PgUp	OFF
PF1	F1	NA
PF2	F2	NA
PF3	F3	NA
PF4	F4	NA

Notes: Keys listed are for IBM PC compatible keyboards only

Source: Microsoft Windows Desktop Applications User's Guide 2.0,
                  pages 89 to 90

See Also: 6.01. Reserved System Keys
                  6.02. Recommended Keyboard Actions

6.05. RECOMMENDED MOUSE USAGE

Recommended Usage

Mouse Action	In Text Selection	In Item Selection
Click	Move insertion point to mouse pointer	Select item at pointer position
Double-click	Select word at mouse pointer position	Confirm or execute item at pointer position
Drag	Extend selection from pointer to release point	Extend selection from pointer to release point
Shift + drag	Extend current selection to new position	Move left one character
Shift + click	Extend current selection to new release point	Extend current selection to new release point
Control + drag		Allow discontinuous selection; add addition selection
Control + click		Toggle: delete or restore selection

Source: Microsoft Windows SDK Application Style Guide 2.0, pages 53 to 55

See Also: 1.23. IBM Extended Character Codes
                  6.01. Reserved System Keys
                  6.02. Recommended Keyboard Actions

6.06. WINDOWS OPERATING ENVIRONMENT FILES

File Name	Function	1	2
MSDOS.EXE	DOS Executive	X	X
SPOOLER.EXE	Print spooler	X	X
WIN.COM	Windows loader file	X	X
WIN.INI	Windows initialization file	X	X
WIN#.BIN	Windows code file (for 2.0, #=200)	X	X
WIN#.OVL	Windows overlay file (for 2.0, #=200)	X	X
WINOLDAP.GRB	Windows old applications support	X	X
WINOLDAP.MOD	Windows old applications support	X	X

Optional Files:

File Name	Function	1	2
CALC.EXE	Windows calculator program	X	X
CALENDAR.EXE	Windows calendar program	X	X
CARDFILE.EXE	Windows cardfile program	X	X
CLIPBRD.EXE	Windows clipboard program	X	X
CLOCK.EXE	Windows clock program	X	X
CONTROL.EXE	Windows control panel program	X	X
COUR*.FON	Courier font file (* is letter)	X	X
HELV*.FON	Helvetica font file (* is letter)	X	X
*.DRV	Printer driver file (* is printer name)	X	X
*.PCL	Printer control file (* is port name)	X	X
NOTEPAD.EXE	Windows notepad program	X	X
PAINT.EXE	Windows paint program	X	X
REVERSI.EXE	Windows game program	X	X
TERMINAL.EXE	Windows terminal emulation program	X	X
TMSR*.FON	Times Roman font file (* is letter)	X	X
WRITE.EXE	Windows write program	X	X

Source: Microsoft Windows 2.03 disks

See Also: 6.07. Windows C Programming Library Files
6.08. Windows Development Utilities

6.07. WINDOWS C PROGRAMMING LIBRARY FILES

File Name	Function	1	2
CLIBW.LIB	Standard library, compact memory model	X	X
CLIBC.LIB	Startup library, compact memory model	X	X
LLIBW.LIB	Standard library, large memory model	X	X
LLIBC.LIB	Startup library, large memory model	X	X
MLIBW.LIB	Standard library, medium memory model	X	X
MLIBC.LIB	Startup library, medium memory model	X	X
SLIBW.LIB	Standard library, small memory model	X	X
SLIBC.LIB	Startup library, small memory model	X	X
WIN87EM.LIB	8087, extended memory library		X
WINDOWS.H	Windows include file for C-language applications	X	X

Source: Microsoft Windows SDK Programming Tools 2.0, page 17

See Also: 6.06. Windows Operating Environment Files
6.08. Windows Development Utilities

6.08. WINDOWS DEVELOPMENT UTILITIES

File Name	Function	1	2
DIALOG.EXE	Creates and edits Windows dialog boxes	X	
DLGEDIT.EXE	Creates and edits Windows dialog boxes		X
EXEHDR.EXE	Displays EXE file header information	X	
NEWFON.EXE	Converts version 1.03 fonts to 2.01 or later style		X
FONTEDIT.EXE	Creates and edits Windows fonts	X	X
GDI.EXE	Debugging executable for GDI library	X	X
GDI.SYM	Symbolic debugging information for GDI library	X	X
HEAPWALK.EXE	Displays allocated blocks in Windows global heap	X	
ICONEDIT.EXE	Creates and edits Windows icons	X	X
IMPLIB.EXE	Creates linkable, dynamic library files	X	
KERNEL.EXE	Debugging executable for kernel library	X	X
KERNEL.SYM	Symbolic debugging information for kernel library	X	X
LIB.EXE	Creates and maintains library files	X	
LINK4.EXE	Creates executable Windows applications	X	
MAKE.EXE	Automated file maintenance utility	X	
MAPSYM.EXE	Creates symbol files for symbolic debugger	X	
RC.EXE	Resource compiler	X	X
RCPP.EXE	Preprocessor for resource compiler	X	X
SHAKER.EXE	Randomly allocates memory in global heap	X	X
WINTOOL.EXE			X
WIN87EM.EXE	80X87 support		X
SLAPJR.EXE	Sends screen to file or printer	X	
SYMDEB.EXE	Symbolic debugger for Windows applications	X	
USER.EXE	Debugging executable for user library	X	X
USER.SYM	Symbolic debugging information for user library	X	X
WINSTUB.EXE	Warning message for non-Windows environs.	X	X

Notes: Additional utilities are available directly from Microsoft and the
Microsoft-supported conference on Genie

Source: Microsoft Windows SDK 2.0 disks

See Also: 6.06. Windows Operating Environment Files
6.07. Windows C Programming Library Files

6.09. EXTENDED ANSI CHARACTER CODES

Dec	Hex	Octal	Binary	Name	Character
8	08	10	0000 1000	Backspace	
9	09	11	0000 1001	Tab	
13	0D	15	0000 1101	Carriage return	
32	20	40	0010 0000	Space	Space
33	21	41	0010 0001	Exclamation point	!
34	22	42	0010 0010	Quotation mark	"
35	23	43	0010 0011	Number sign	#
36	24	44	0010 0100	Dollar sign	$
37	25	45	0010 0101	Percent sign	%
38	26	46	0010 0110	Ampersand	&
39	27	47	0010 0111	Apostrophe	'
40	28	50	0010 1000	Opening parentheses	(
41	29	51	0010 1001	Closing parentheses	)
42	2A	52	0010 1010	Asterisk	*
43	2B	53	0010 1011	Plus sign	+
44	2C	54	0010 1100	Comma	,
45	2D	55	0010 1101	Hyphen	-
46	2E	56	0010 1110	Period	.
47	2F	57	0010 1111	Forward slash	/
48	30	60	0011 0000	Zero	0
49	31	61	0011 0001	One	1
50	32	62	0011 0010	Two	2
51	33	63	0011 0011	Three	3
52	34	64	0011 0100	Four	4
53	35	65	0011 0101	Five	5
54	36	66	0011 0110	Six	6
55	37	67	0011 0111	Seven	7
56	38	70	0011 1000	Eight	8
57	39	71	0011 1001	Nine	9
58	3A	72	0011 1010	Colon	:

(Continued)

Table 6.09. Continued

Dec	Hex	Octal	Binary	Name	Character
59	3B	73	0011 1011	Semicolon	;
60	3C	74	0011 1100	Less than sign	<
61	3D	75	0011 1101	Equal sign	=
62	3E	76	0011 1110	Greater than sign	>
63	3F	77	0011 1111	Question mark	?
64	40	100	0100 0000	Commercial at sign	@
65	41	101	0100 0001	Capital A	A
66	42	102	0100 0010	Capital B	B
67	43	103	0100 0011	Capital C	C
68	44	104	0100 0100	Capital D	D
69	45	105	0100 0101	Capital E	E
70	46	106	0100 0110	Capital F	F
71	47	107	0100 0111	Capital G	G
72	48	110	0100 1000	Capital H	H
73	49	111	0100 1001	Capital I	I
74	4A	112	0100 1010	Capital J	J
75	4B	113	0100 1011	Capital K	K
76	4C	114	0100 1100	Capital L	L
77	4D	115	0100 1101	Capital M	M
78	4E	116	0100 1110	Capital N	N
79	4F	117	0100 1111	Capital O	O
80	50	120	0101 0000	Capital P	P
81	51	121	0101 0001	Capital Q	Q
82	52	122	0101 0010	Capital R	R
83	53	123	0101 0011	Capital S	S
84	54	124	0101 0100	Capital T	T
85	55	125	0101 0101	Capital U	U
86	56	126	0101 0110	Capital V	V
87	57	127	0101 0111	Capital W	W
88	58	130	0101 1000	Capital X	X
89	59	131	0101 1001	Capital Y	Y
90	5A	132	0101 1010	Capital Z	Z
91	5B	133	0101 1011	Opening bracket	[
92	5C	134	0101 1100	Backward slash	\
93	5D	135	0101 1101	Closing bracket	]
94	5E	136	0101 1110	Caret	^
95	5F	137	0101 1111	Underscore	_
96	60	140	0110 0000	Grave	`
97	61	141	0110 0001	Lowercase A	a
98	62	142	0110 0010	Lowercase B	b
99	63	143	0110 0011	Lowercase C	c
100	64	144	0110 0100	Lowercase D	d
101	65	145	0110 0101	Lowercase E	e
102	66	146	0110 0110	Lowercase F	f
103	67	147	0110 0111	Lowercase G	g
104	68	150	0110 1000	Lowercase H	h
105	69	151	0110 1001	Lowercase I	i
106	6A	152	0110 1010	Lowercase J	j
107	6B	153	0110 1011	Lowercase K	k
108	6C	154	0110 1100	Lowercase L	l
109	6D	155	0110 1101	Lowercase M	m
110	6E	156	0110 1110	Lowercase N	n
111	6F	157	0110 1111	Lowercase O	o
112	70	160	0111 0000	Lowercase P	p
113	71	161	0111 0001	Lowercase Q	q
114	72	162	0111 0010	Lowercase R	r
115	73	163	0111 0011	Lowercase S	s
116	74	164	0111 0100	Lowercase T	t
117	75	165	0111 0101	Lowercase U	u
118	76	166	0111 0110	Lowercase V	v
119	77	167	0111 0111	Lowercase W	w
120	78	170	0111 1000	Lowercase X	x
121	79	171	0111 1001	Lowercase Y	y
122	7A	172	0111 1010	Lowercase Z	z
123	7B	173	0111 1011	Opening brace	{
124	7C	174	0111 1100	Vertical line		
125	7D	175	0111 1101	Closing brace	}
126	7E	176	0111 1110	Tilde	~
127	7F	177	0111 1111	DEL	Delete
128	80	200	1000 0000	Box	
129	81	201	1000 0001	Box	

(Continued)

Table 6.09. Continued

Dec	Hex	Octal	Binary	Name	Character
130	82	202	1000 0010	Box	
131	83	203	1000 0011	Box	
132	84	204	1000 0100	Box	
133	85	205	1000 0101	Box	
134	86	206	1000 0110	Box	
135	87	207	1000 0111	Box	
136	88	210	1000 1000	Box	
137	89	211	1000 1001	Box	
138	8A	212	1000 1010	Box	
139	8B	213	1000 1011	Box	
140	8C	214	1000 1100	Box	
141	8D	215	1000 1101	Box	
142	8E	216	1000 1110	Box	
143	8F	217	1000 1111	Box	
144	90	220	1001 0000	Box	
145	91	221	1001 0001	Box	
146	92	222	1001 0010	Box	
147	93	223	1001 0011	Box	
148	94	224	1001 0100	Box	
149	95	225	1001 0101	Box	
150	96	226	1001 0110	Box	
151	97	227	1001 0111	Box	
152	98	230	1001 1000	Box	
153	99	231	1001 1001	Box	
154	9A	232	1001 1010	Box	
155	9B	233	1001 1011	Box	
156	9C	234	1001 1100	Box	
157	9D	235	1001 1101	Box	
158	9E	236	1001 1110	Box	
159	9F	237	1001 1111	Box	
160	A0	240	1010 0000	Blank	
161	A1	241	1010 0001	Opening exclamation	
162	A2	242	1010 0010	Cent sign	
163	A3	243	1010 0011	Pound sign	
164	A4	244	1010 0100		
165	A5	245	1010 0101	Yen sign	
166	A6	246	1010 0110	Vertical line	
167	A7	247	1010 0111	Section symbol	
168	A8	250	1010 1000	Diaeresis symbol	
169	A9	251	1010 1001	Copyright symbol	
170	AA	252	1010 1010	Underlined a	
171	AB	253	1010 1011	Much less than	
172	AC	254	1010 1100		
173	AD	255	1010 1101	Hyphen	
174	AE	256	1010 1110	Registered symbol	
175	AF	257	1010 1111	Macron symbol	
176	B0	260	1011 0000	Degree symbol	
177	B1	261	1011 0001	Plus/minus symbol	
178	B2	262	1011 0010	Superscript 2	
179	B3	263	1011 0011	Superscript 3	
180	B4	264	1011 0100	Acute accent	
181	B5	265	1011 0101	Mu	
182	B6	266	1011 0110	Paragraph symbol	
183	B7	267	1011 0111	1 to 2 upper right	
184	B8	270	1011 1000	Cedilla symbol	
185	B9	271	1011 1001	Superscript 1	
186	BA	272	1011 1010	Superscript 0	
187	BB	273	1011 1011	Much greater than	
188	BC	274	1011 1100	One-quarter	
189	BD	275	1011 1101	One-half	
190	BE	276	1011 1110	Three-quarters	
191	BF	277	1011 1111	Opening question mark	
192	C0	300	1100 0000	Grave A	
193	C1	301	1100 0001	Acute A	
194	C2	302	1100 0010	Circumflex A	
195	C3	303	1100 0011	Circumflex A	
196	C4	304	1100 0100	Umlaut A	
197	C5	305	1100 0101	A	
198	C6	306	1100 0110	Dipthong AE	
199	C7	307	1100 0111	C cedilla	

(Continued)

Table 6.09. Continued

Dec	Hex	Octal	Binary	Name	Character
200	C8	310	1100 1000	Grave E	
201	C9	311	1100 1001	Acute E	
202	CA	312	1100 1010	Circumflex E	
203	CB	313	1100 1011	Umlaut E	
204	CC	314	1100 1100	Grave I	
205	CD	315	1100 1101	Acute I	
206	CE	316	1100 1110	Circumflex I	
207	CF	317	1100 1111	Umlaut I	
208	D0	320	1101 0000		
209	D1	321	1101 0001	Circumflex N	
210	D2	322	1101 0010	Grave O	
211	D3	323	1101 0011	Acute O	
212	D4	324	1101 0100	Circumflex O	
213	D5	325	1101 0101	Circumflex O	
214	D6	326	1101 0110	Umlaut O	
215	D7	327	1101 0111	Box	
216	D8	330	1101 1000	Slashed zero (0)	
217	D9	331	1101 1001	Grave U	
218	DA	332	1101 1010	Acute U	
219	DB	333	1101 1011	Circumflex u	
220	DC	334	1101 1100	Umlaut U	
221	DD	335	1101 1101	Acute Y	
222	DE	336	1101 1110		
223	DF	337	1101 1111	Beta	
224	E0	340	1110 0000	Grave a	
225	E1	341	1110 0001	Acute a	
226	E2	342	1110 0010	Circumflex a	
227	E3	343	1110 0011	Circumflex a	
228	E4	344	1110 0100	Umlaut a	
229	E5	345	1110 0101	a	
230	E6	346	1110 0110	Dipthong ae	
231	E7	347	1110 0111	c cedilla	
232	E8	350	1110 1000	Grave e	
233	E9	351	1110 1001	Acute e	
234	EA	352	1110 1010	Circumflex e	
235	EB	353	1110 1011	Umlaut e	
236	EC	354	1110 1100	Grave i	
237	ED	355	1110 1101	Acute i	
238	EE	356	1110 1110	Circumflex i	
239	EF	357	1110 1111	Umlaut i	
240	F0	360	1111 0000		
241	F1	361	1111 0001	Circumflex n	
242	F2	362	1111 0010	Grave o	
243	F3	363	1111 0011	Acute o	
244	F4	364	1111 0100	Circumflex o	
245	F5	365	1111 0101	Circumflex o	
246	F6	366	1111 0110	Umlaut o	
247	F7	367	1111 0111	Box	
248	F8	370	1111 1000	Slashed zero (0)	
249	F9	371	1111 1001	Grave u	
250	FA	372	1111 1010	Acute u	
251	FB	373	1111 1011	Circumflex u	
252	FC	374	1111 1100	Umlaut U	
253	FD	375	1111 1101	Acute y	
254	FE	376	1111 1110		
255	FF	377	1111 1111	Umlaut y	

Source: Microsoft Windows SDK Programmer's Reference 2.0, page 121

See Also: 1.21. ASCII Character Set
                  1.22. IBM ASCII Character Set

6.10. WINDOWS EXE FILE FORMAT

The Overall Layout of the File Looks Like This:

Offset	Size	Function
0 (0)	32 bytes	Old-style EXE header info
20 (32)	29 bytes	RESERVED
3C (60)	4 bytes	New-style offset
40 (64)	Varies	Relocation table for DOS stub program
varies	Varies	New-style EXE information

The Layout of the New-Style EXE Information Section Looks Like This:

Offset	Size	Function	Allowable Values
0 (0)	Word	Signature word	"EN"
2 (2)	Byte	Version number of linker	
3 (3)	Byte	Revision number of linker	
4 (4)	Word	Offset of entry table	(Relative to beginning of this section of header)
6 (6)	Word	Number of bytes in entry table	
8 (8)	Dbl word	32-bit CRC of entire file	
C (12)	Word	Keyword	0000H = NOAUTODATA 0001H = SINGLEDATA (solo) 0002H = MULTIPLEDATA (instance) 2000H = Errors detected at link time 8000H = Library module
E (14)	Word	Segment # of automatic data segment	
10 (16)	Word	Initial size of dynamic heap added to DS	(In bytes) 0=no local allocation
12 (18)	Word	Initial size of stack added to DS	(In bytes) 0=SS does not equal DS
14 (20)	Dbl word	CS:IP	
18 (24)	Dbl word	SS:SP	
1C (28)	Word	# entries in segment table	
1E (30)	Word	# bytes in nonresident-name table	
20 (32)	Word	Offset of segment table	(Relative to beginning of this section of header)
22 (34)	Word	Offset of resource table	(Relative to beginning of this section of header)
24 (36)	Word	Offset of resident-name table	(Relative to beginning of this section of header)
26 (38)	Word	Offset of module-reference table	(Relative to beginning of this section of header)
28 (40)	Word	Offset of imported-names table	(Relative to beginning of this section of header)
2A (42)	Dbl word	Offset of nonresident-name table	(Relative to beginning of file)
2E (46)	Word	# of movable entry points	
30 (48)	Word	Shift count of logical sector alignment	(Log [base 2] of the segment sector size)
32 (50)	Word	# of reserved segments	
34 (52)	10 bytes	RESERVED	Must be 0

Version Info: Applies to Windows 2.0 and Windows 386

Source: Microsoft Windows SDK Programmer's Reference 2.0, pages 645 to 648

See Also: 2.42. EXE File Header
      2.43. COM Program Layout

6.11. TAG IMAGE FILE FORMAT (TIFF)

Header and Directory Format:

Offset	Size	Description	Field Size	Field Description	Comments
0 (0)	8 bytes	Header	Word	Byte order	4949H=least to most; 4D4DH=most to least
			Word	Version	2AH (version 42)
			Dbl word	Pointer to first IFD	
A (10)	Varies	Image file directory	Word	Number of directory entries	Must begin on word boundary
			12 bytes	First directory entry	See below for format
			12 bytes each	Additional directory entries	
			Dbl word	Pointer to next IFD	
Varies	Varies	Values (tags)			See table below

Directory Entry Format (in Image File Directory):

Offset	Size	Description	Allowable Values, Comments
0 (0)	Word	Tag	See Tag table, below
2 (2)	Word	Type	1=bytes 2=ASCIIZ string 3=short (16-bit unsigned integers) 4=long (32-bit unsigned integers) 5=rational (2 longs: first is numerator, second is denominator)
4 (4)	Word	Length	Specified in terms of the data type (1 short=2 bytes)
8 (8)	Dbl word	Pointer to value	If value fits in four bytes or less, it is stored here

(Continued)

Table 6.11. Continued

Tags:

Tag	Type	Name	Allowable Values, Comments
FF (255)	Short	Subfile type	1=full resolution image data (requires image width, image length, strip offset)
			2=reduced resolution data (requires image width, image length, strip offset)
100 (256)	Short	Image width	Width of image, in pixels
101 (257)	Short	Image length	Length of image, in pixels (rows)
102 (258)	Short	Bits per sample	(default=1)
103 (259)	Short	Compression	1=no compression, but tightly packed (default)
			2=CCITT Group 3 compression
			3=1-dimensional modified Huffman run length encoding
106 (262)	Short	Photometric interp.	0=min sample value is white, max sample value is black, all other grey
			1=min sample value is black, max sample value is white, all other grey
			2=RGB; min and max sample values control intensity
			(planar configuration affects stored order)
			3=hue, saturation, brightness
107 (263)	Short	Thresholding	1=bilevel 'line art' scan (default)
			2='halftone' or 'dithered' scan (bits per sample must be 1)
108 (264)	Short	Cell width	If thresholding=2, this is width of dithering matrix in 1-bit samples
109 (265)	Short	Cell length	If thresholding=2, this is length of dithering matrix in 1-bit samples
10A (266)	Short	Order of data values	1=most significant bits of byte filled first (default)
			2=least significant bits of byte filled first
10D (269)	ASCIIZ	Name of document	
10E (270)	ASCIIZ	Image description	
10F (271)	ASCIIZ	Maker of scanner	
110 (272)	ASCIIZ	Model # of scanner	
111 (273)	Long	Strip offset	For each strip, the byte offset of that strip
112 (274)	Short	Orientation	1=first row at top, first column at left (default)
			2=first row at top, first column at right
			3=first row at bottom, first column at right
			4=first row at bottom, first column at left
			5=first row at left, first column at top
			6=first row at right, first column at top
			7=first row at right, first column at bottom
			8=first row at left, first column at bottom
115 (277)	Short	Samples per pixel	1=monochrome (default)
			3=color (other values allowed)
116 (278)	Long	Rows per strip	Number of rows per data strip (default=2**32-1)
117 (279)	Long	Strip byte counts	For each strip, the number of bytes it contains
118 (280)	Short	Min sample value	(Default=0)
119 (281)	Short	Max sample value	(Default= 2**(bitspersample)-1)
11A (282)	Rational	Width resolution	Number of pixels per inch
11B (283)	Rational	Length resolution	Number of pixels per inch
11C (284)	Short	Planar configuration	1=samples stored contiguously; single image plane
			2=samples stored in separate sample planes
11D (285)	ASCIIZ	Name of page	
11E (286)	Rational	X position	Offset to left side of image on page, in inches
11F (287)	Rational	Y position	Offset to top side of image on page, in inches
120 (288)	Long	Free offsets	For each 'free' block in file, pointer to it, in bytes
121 (289)	Long	Free byte count	For each 'free' block in file, number of bytes in block

Notes: •Tags with a value of 8000H (32768) or higher are reserved for user-defined information
•The entries for image file directories must be sorted in ascending order by value of the tag

Source: Tag Image File Format Draft (22 October 86), pages 2 to13

See Also: 6.13. Windows Paint File Format

6.12. DYNAMIC DATA EXCHANGE PROTOCOL

Message Type	Purpose	Parameters	
WM_DDE_INITIATE	Request start of conversation	sparam = not used	
		lparam = aDDEServerID (atom specifying application class name)	LO
		aDDETopicID (atom specifying desired topic)	HO
WM_DDE_TERMINATE	End conversation	None	
WM_DDE_ACK	Acceptance of prev. message	sparam = not used	
		For WM_DDE_INITIATE:	
		lparam = aDDEID (atom specifying data item or topic involved)	HO
		wStatus (high bit set specifies acceptance)	LO
		For WM_DDE_EXECUTE:	
		lparam = hCommands (handle to data item containing commands)	HO
		wStatus (high bit set specifies acceptance)	LO
WM_DDE_REQUEST	Request for data item	lparam = aDataID (atom identifying data item)	HO
		cfFormat (valid clipboard format)	LO
WM_DDE_DATA	Publication of data	lparam = aDDEID (atom specifying data item)	HO
		hDDEData (handle to shared memory containing data)*	LO
WM_DDE_POKE	Place data at destination	lparam = aDataID (destination for data item)	HO
		hDDEData (handle to shared memory containing data)*	LO
WM_DDE_ADVISE	Request for data	lparam = aDDEID (atom specifying data item)	HO
		hOptions (handle to shared memory object)**	LO
WM_DDE_UNADVISE	Cancel request for data	lparam = aDDEID (atom specifying data item no longer needed)	HO
		(null atom cancels all requests)	LO
WM_DD_EXECUTE	Request to process commands	lparam = hCommands (handle to shared memory containing	HO
		command string [as if typed from keyboard])	LO

Notes:

•*Data items are stored in shared memory in this format:
Word   fACKRequired   bit 15 set to 1 requires acknowledgement
          fClientRelease   bit 13 set to 1 client should free data object after examining
Word   wFormat   clipboard type of data object
Varies Data   in clipboard format
•**Options are stored in a shared memory object in this format:
Word   fACKRequired   bit 15 set to 1 requires acknowledgement
          fNoData   bit 14 set to 1 indicates server should send null hDDEData 'alarms'
Word   wFormat   clipboard data type preferred by client

Source:

DDE-Protocol Definition (15 Oct 86) pages 1-8 to 8-8.
Microsoft Systems Journal,
2 (5), page 16

6.13. WINDOWS PAINT FILE FORMAT

Offset	Length	Usual Contents	Description
0 (0)	Word	6144H	Key#1 (version of paint program used to create file)
2 (2)	Word	4D6EH	Key#2 (version of paint program used to create file)
4 (4)	Word		Width of bitmap (in pixels)
6 (6)	Word		Height of bitmap (in pixels)
8 (8)	Word		X aspect ratio of bitmap
A (10)	Word		Y aspect ratio of bitmap
C (12)	Word		X aspect ratio of printer at creation time
E (14)	Word		Y aspect ratio of printer at creation time
10 (16)	Word		Width of printer in pixels
12 (18)	Word		Height of printer in pixels
14 (20)	Word		Used for checksum calculations
16 (22)	Word		Used for checksum calculations
18 (24)	Word		Checksum of header
1A (26)	Word		RESERVED
1C (28)	Word		RESERVED
1E (30)	Word		RESERVED
20 (32)	Varies		Bitmap

Notes:

•A paint file (version 1.01) consists of a 32-byte header, as described above,
followed by bitmap organized as scan lines. The total size of the bitmap will be
=WidthOfBitmap x HeightOfBitmap/8.
•The third through tenth fields in the header are determined by calling
GetDeviceCaps().
•Paint files in Windows 2.03 use a different format

Source: Unpublished document from Microsoft University Windows Seminar

See Also: 6.15. Clipboard Formats
                   6.52. METAFILEPICT Structure Format

6.14. FONT FILE FORMAT (VERSION 1)

Field	Size	Description	Allowable Values
dfVersion	Word	Version of the file	Currently must be 100 (256)
dfSize	Dbl word	Total file size (in bytes)	Unsigned 32-bit integer
dfCopyright	60 bytes	Copyright information	ASCIIZ string
dfType	Word	Font file type	LObit0=0 (raster type file)
			LObit0=1 (vector type file)
			LObit3=1 (bitmap in memory)
			HO=0 (GDI realized standard font)
dfPoints	Word	Nominal point size for best look	
dfVertRes	Word	Nominal vert resolution dots per inch	Size at which font was digitized
dfHorizRes	Word	Nominal horiz resolution dots per inch	Size at which font was digitized
dfAscent	Word	Dist from top of char to baseline	
dfInternalLeading	Word	Area inside dfPixHeight for accent marks	
dfExternalLeading	Word	Extra leading requested between rows	
dfItalic	Byte	Is font an italic font?	0=no, 1=yes
dfUnderline	Byte	Is font underlined?	0=no, 1=yes
dfStrikeOut	Byte	Is font over stricken?	0=no, 1=yes
dfWeight	Word	Weight of character	Value 1-1000 (200 is normal)
dfCharSet	Byte	Character set used	FF (255) = IBM PC char set
dfPixWidth	Word	Width of grid for vector fonts	Size at which font was digitized
		Width of all chars for raster fonts	0=variable width
dfPixHeight	Word	Height of grid for vector fonts	Size at which font was digitized
		Height of the char bitmap for raster fonts	
dfPitchAndFamily	Byte	Pitch and family of font	LObit=1 (variable pitch)
			LObit=0 (fixed pitch)
			HO4bits=0000 (FF_DONTCARE)
			HO4bits=0001 (FF_ROMAN)
			HO4bits=0010 (FF_SWISS)
			HO4bits=0011 (FF_MODERN)
			HO4bits=0100 (FF_SCRIPT)
			HO4bits=0101 (FF_DECORATIVE)
dfAvgWidth	Word	Average width of chars in font	Usually 'X'
dfMaxWidth	Word	Maximum pixel width of any char in font	
dfFirstChar	Byte	Character code of first char defined	
dfLastChar	Byte	Character code of last char defined	
dfDefaultChar	Byte	Character to substitute for missing chars	
dfBreakChar	Byte	Character used to define word breaks	
dfWidthBytes	Word	# bytes in each row of bitmap	(Raster fonts only)
dfDevice	Dbl word	Offset in file to device name string	0=generic device
dfFace	Dbl word	Offset in file to face name string	
dfBitsPointer	Dbl word	Absolute address of bitmap	(Set by GDI at load time)
dfBitsOffset	Dbl word	Offset in file to beginning of bitmap	
dfCharOffset	Word each	Offset in bitmap rows to each char in set	For variable spaced raster fonts
	0 bytes	Not used	For fixed spaced raster fonts
	Word each	Offset in bitmap to string for each char in set	For fixed spaced vector fonts
	Word	Offset in bitmap to char strokes for each char	For variable spaced vector fonts
	Word	Pixel width of the character	
(facename)	String	Name of typeface	ASCIIZ string
(devicename)	String	Name of device font was designed for	ASCIIZ string
(bitmap)	Bytes	Bitmap containing font data	Each row must start on word boundary

Source: Microsoft Windows SDK Programmer's Reference 2.0, pages 639 to 645

6.15. CLIPBOARD FORMATS

Format Name	Description
CF_BITMAP	Bitmap
CF_DIF	Data interchange format
CF_DSPBITMAP	Bitmap display associated with a private format
CF_DSPMETAFILEPICT	Metafile picture display associated with a private format
CF_DSPTEXT	Text display associated with a private format
CF_METAFILEPICT	Metafile picture structure (See 6.52. METAFILEPICT Structure Format)
CF_OWNERDISPLAY	Owner display format (clipboard owner must display and update clipboard)
CF_PRIVATEFIRST	Private format begin with this value
CF_SYLK	Microsoft SYLK data interchange format
CF_TEXT	Null-terminated text (ASCIIZ string)

Source: Microsoft Windows SDK Programmer's Reference 2.0, page 423

See Also: 1.17. Common String Formats
6.16. MetaFile Format

6.16. METAFILE FORMAT

MetaFile Header:

Field	Size	Description	Allowable Values
mtType	Dbl word	Location indicator	
mtHeaderSize	Dbl word	Header size	
mtVersion	Dbl word	Version number	
mtSize	Dbl word	Size	Size of the MetaFile in words
mtNoObjects	Dbl word	Total number of objects	
mtMaxRecord	Dbl word	Size of largest record	
mtNoParameters	Dbl word	Number of parameters	Field not currently used

MetaFile GDI Function Records:

Field	Size	Description	Allowable Values	
rdSize	Dbl word	Size of this Record	Size in words	
rdFunction	Dbl word	Magic Number of Function	0817H	Arc
			0418H	Ellipse
			0415H	ExcludeClipRect
			0419H	FloodFill
			0416H	IntersectClipRect
			0213H	LineTo
			0214H	MoveTo
			0220H	OffsetClipRgn
			0211H	OffsetViewportOrg
			020FH	OffsetWindowOrg
			061DH	PatBlt
			081AH	Pie
			041BH	Rectangle
			0127H	RestoreDC
			061CH	RoundRect
			001EH	SaveDC
			0201H	SetBkColor
			0102H	SetBkMode
			0103H	SetMapMode
			041FH	SetPixel
			0106H	SetPolyFillMode
			0105H	SetRelAbs
			0104H	SetROP2
			0107H	SetStrectchBltMode
			0108H	SetTextCharExtra
			0209H	SetTextColor
			020AH	SetTextJustification
			020CH	SetWindowExt
			020BH	SetWindowOrg
			020EH	SetViewportExt
			020DH	SetViewportOrg
rdParm#	Var. words	Parameter(s) for function	Variable number of words, each containing a parameter	

MetaFile Object-Creation Records:

Field	Size	Description	Allowable Values
rdSize	Dbl word	Size of this record	Size in bytes
rdFunction	Dbl word	Object creation ID	012DH
Index	Varies	Index into table to location of object	

MetaFile CreatePen Records:

Field	Size	Description	Allowable Values
rdSize	Dbl word	Size of this record	5 (size in words)
rdFunction	Dbl word	CreatePen ID	0230H
rdParm		LOGPEN structure	See 6.50. LOGPEN Structure Format

MetaFile CreateFont Records:

Field	Size	Description	Allowable Values
rdSize	Dbl word	Size of this record	28 (size in words)
rdFunction	Dbl word	CreateFont ID	0231H
rdParm		LOGFONT structure	See 6.49. LOGFONT Structure Format

MetaFile CreateBrush Records:

Field	Size	Description	Allowable Values
rdSize	Dbl word	Size of this record	7 (size in words)
rdFunction	Dbl word	CreateBrush ID	0232H
rdParm		LOGBRUSH structure	See 6.48. LOGBRUSH Structure Format

(Continued)

Table 6.16. Continued

MetaFile CreatePatternBrush Records:

Field	Size	Description	Allowable Values
rdSize	Dbl word	Size of this record	Size of this record in words
rdFunction	Dbl word	CreatePatternBrush ID	012FH
rdParm	Varies	Bitmap	Bitmap consists of: bitmap header, 9 unused words, then bmType — Bitmap type bmWidth — Bitmap width bmHeight — Bitmap height bmWidthBytes — Bytes per raster line bmPlanes — Number of color planes bmBitsPixel — Number adjacent color bits per pixel bmBits — Pointer to bit values bits — Actual bits of pattern

MetaFile CreateRegion Records:

Field	Size	Description	Allowable Values
rdSize	Dbl word	Size of this record	Size of this record in words
rdFunction	Dbl word	CreateRegion ID	0635H
rdParm		Region	

MetaFile TextOut Records:

Field	Size	Description	Allowable Values
rdSize	Dbl word	Size of this record	Size of this record in words
rdFunction	Dbl word	TextOut ID	0521H
rdParm	Varies	TextOut info	TextOut info consists of: count — Length of string flstring — The string flylocation — The y value of string's starting point flxlocation — The x value of string's starting point

MetaFile Polygon Records:

Field	Size	Description	Allowable Values
rdSize	Dbl word	Size of this record	Size of this record in words
rdFunction	Dbl word	Polygon ID	0324H
rdParm	Varies	Polygon info	Polygon info consists of: count — Number of points in polygon ptlist — A list of the individual points

MetaFile Polyline Records:

Field	Size	Description	Allowable Values
rdSize	Dbl word	Size of this record	Size of this record in words
rdFunction	Dbl word	Polyline ID	0325H
rdParm	Varies	Polyline info	Polyline info consists of: count — Number of points in polygon ptlist — A list of the individual points

MetaFile Escape Records:

Field	Size	Description	Allowable Values
rdSize	Dbl word	Size of this record	Size of this record in words
rdFunction	Dbl word	Escape ID	0626H
rdParm	Varies	Escape info	Escape info consists of: escape# — Number of escape count — Number of bytes of escape data escapedata

MetaFile InvertRegion Records:

Field	Size	Description	Allowable Values
rdSize	Dbl word	Size of this record	Size of this record in words
rdFunction	Dbl word	InvertRegion ID	012AH
rdParm		Region	Index to region in metafile table

MetaFile PaintRegion Records:

Field	Size	Description	Allowable Values
rdSize	Dbl word	Size of this record	Size of this record in words
rdFunction	Dbl word	PaintRegion ID	012BH
rdParm		Region	Index to region in metafile table

(Continued)

Table 6.16. Continued

MetaFile FillRegion Records:

Field	Size	Description	Allowable Values
rdSize	Dbl word	Size of this record	Size of this record in words
rdFunction	Dbl word	FillRegion ID	0228H
rdParm		Region	Index to region in metafile table

MetaFile FrameRegion Records:

Field	Size	Description	Allowable Values
rdSize	Dbl word	Size of this record	Size of this record in words
rdFunction	Dbl word	FrameRegion ID	0429H
rdParm		Region	Index to region in metafile table

MetaFile BitBlt Records:

Field	Size	Description	Allowable Values
rdSize	Dbl word	Size of this record	Size of this record in words
rdFunction	Dbl word	BitBlt ID	0922H
rdParm	Varies	BitBlt info	BitBlt info consists of:
			raster op — LO word, HO word of raster operation
			SY — The y coordinate of source origin
			SX — The x coordinate of source origin
			DYE — The destination y extent
			DXE — The destination x extent
			DY — The y coordinate of the dest origin
			DX — The x coordinate of the dest origin
			bmWidth — The width of the bitmap, in pixels
			bmHeight — The height of the bitmap, in raster lines
			bmWidthBytes — The number of bytes per raster line
			bmPlanes — The number of color planes per raster line
			bmBitsPixel — The number of adjacent color bits/pixel
			bits — The actual bitmap

MetaFile StretchBlt Records:

Field	Size	Description	Allowable Values
rdSize	Dbl word	Size of this record	Size of this record in words
rdFunction	Dbl word	StretchBlt ID	0B23H
rdParm	Varies	StretchBlt info	StretchBlt info consists of:
			raster op — LO word, HO word of raster operation
			SYE — The source y extent
			SXE — The source x extent
			SY — The y coordinate of source origin
			SX — The x coordinate of source origin
			DYE — The destination y extent
			DXE — The destination x extent
			DY — The y coordinate of the dest origin
			DX — The x coordinate of the dest origin
			bmWidth — The width of the bitmap, in pixels
			bmHeight — The height of the bitmap, in raster lines
			bmWidthBytes — The number of bytes per raster line
			bmPlanes — The number of color planes per raster line
			bmBitsPixel — The number of adjacent color bits/pixel
			bits — The actual bitmap

Notes: The actual MetaFile format is comprised of:
-A MetaFile header
-A variable number of MetaFile GDI or other function records
-A table of any objects referenced by function records

Source: Microsoft Windows SDK Programmer's Reference 2.0, pages 127 to 129
Microsoft Windows Beta2 Documentation 2.0, pages 646 to 655

See Also: 6.48. LOGBRUSH Structure Format
6.49. LOGFONT Structure Format
6.50. LOGPEN Structure Format
6.79. Binary Raster Operation Codes (ROP2)

6.17. RESOURCE SCRIPT FILE DIRECTIVES

Directive	Function	Syntax	Comments
#include	Copies contents of file into resource script	#include filename	Filename is a string (e.g., "windows.h")
#define	Assigns a value to a name	#define name value	Name=letters,digits,punc.;value=int,char,string
#undef	Removes definition assigned to name	#undef name	Name=letters,digits,punctuation
#ifdef	Compiles up to #endif if name is defined	#ifdef name STATEMENT(s)	See #endif (see example 1, below)
#ifndef	Compiles up to #endif if name not defined	#ifndef name STATEMENT(S)	See #endif (see example 1, below)
#if	Compiles up to #endif if constant is non-zero	#if constant STATEMENT(S)	See #endif
#elif	Compiles block within #if- if constant is non-zero	#ifil constant STATEMENT(S)	Used within #if,#ifndef, & #ifdef (see example 2)
#else	Optional clause within #if- construct	#else STATEMENT(S)	Used within #if,#ifndef, & #ifdef (see example 3)
#endif	Ends conditional compilation	#endif	Ends #if, #ifndef, #ifdef compilation

Example 1: #ifdef Debug
    errbox BITMAP errbox.bmp
    #endif

Example 2: #if Version<3
    errbox BITMAP errbox.bmp
    #elif Version<7
    errbox BITMAP userbox.bmp
    #endif

Example 3: #ifdef Debug
    errbox BITMAP errbox.bmp
    #else
    errbox BITMAP userbox.bmp
    #endif

Source: Microsoft Windows SDK Programming Tools 2.0, pages 25 to 27

See Also: 6.18. Single-line Resource Statements (ICON, CURSOR, BITMAP, FONT)
    6.19. Menu Resource Script Definitions
    6.20. Dialog Resource Script Definitions
    6.21. Dialog Box Control Definitions
    6.22. Accelerator Resource Script Definitions
    6.24. STRINGTABLE Resource Script Definitions

6.18. SINGLE-LINE RESOURCE STATEMENTS (ICON, CURSOR, BITMAP, FONT)

General Single Statement Resource Script Format:
nameID resourcetype [loadoption] [memoryoption] filespec

Item	Description	Allowable Values
nameID	Name or number used to identify resource	For FONT resource, must be an integer number

resourcetype	Type of resource being defined	One of: CURSOR
		    ICON
		    BITMAP
		    FONT

loadoption	When the resource should be loaded	One of: PRELOAD (loaded immediately) LOADONCALL (loaded only when called)default

memoryoption	How resource should be handled in memory	One of: FIXED (always remains at fixed location)
		    MOVEABLE (may be moved in memory)
		    DISCARDABLE (may be discarded from memory)

filespec	Name and extension of file containing resource	ASCII string, which may contain pathname

Source: Microsoft Windows SDK Programming Tools 2.0, pages 30 to 31

See Also: 6.17. Resource Script File Directives
    6.19. Menu Resource Script Definitions
    6.20. Dialog Resource Script Definitions
    6.21. Dialog Box Control Definitions
    6.22. Accelerator Resource Script Definitions
    6.24. STRINGTABLE Resource Script Definitions

6.19. MENU RESOURCE SCRIPT DEFINITIONS

General MENU Resource Script Format:
menuID MENU [load-option] [mem-option]
BEGIN
menuitems
END

Item	Description	Allowable Values
menuID	Name or number used to identify the menu resource	
load-option	Specifies when the resource is to be loaded	PRELOAD (resource loaded immediately)
		LOADONCALL (default: resource loaded when called)
mem-option	Determines how resource is treated in memory	FIXED (remains in fixed location)
		MOVEABLE (may be moved to compact memory)
		DISCARDABLE (may be discarded when not needed)

Allowable Menuitems:

Menuitem Name	Syntax	Description
MENUITEM	MENUITEM text, result, optionlist1	Defines a menu item
POPUP	POPUP text, optionlist2 BEGIN definitions END	Defines a popup menu definition
MENUITEM SEPARATOR	MENUITEM SEPARATOR	Special 'dividing' menu item, usually a horiz. bar

optionlist1: MENUBREAK   Item is immediately preceded by a new line
CHECKED   Item has a checkmark next to it
INACTIVE   Item is displayed, but cannot be selected
GRAYED   Item is inactive and displayed 'grayed' (disabled)

optionlist2: MENUBREAK   Item is placed in new column
CHECKED   Item has a checkmark next to it
INACTIVE   Item is displayed, but cannot be selected
GRAYED   Item is inactive and displayed 'grayed' (disabled)
MENUBARBREAK   Item is placed in new column separated by vert. bar

text: ASCII string (in quotes)

result: Integer number of result to return when user selects item

Source: Microsoft Windows SDK Programming Tools 2.0, pages 36 to 40

See Also:
6.17. Resource Script File Directives
6.18. Single-line Resource Statements
6.21. Dialog Box Control Definitions
6.22. Accelerator Resource Script Definitions
6.24. STRINGTABLE Resource Script Definitions

6.20. DIALOG RESOURCE SCRIPT DEFINITIONS

General DIALOG Resource Script Format:
nameID DIALOG [loadoption] [memoryoption] x,y,width,height
optionstatements
BEGIN
controlstatements
END

Item	Description	Allowable Values
nameID	Name or number used to identify the dialog	
loadoption	Specifies when the resource is to be loaded	PRELOAD (resource loaded immediately)
		LOADONCALL (default: resource loaded when called)
memoryoption	Determines how resource is treated in memory	FIXED (remains in fixed location)
		MOVEABLE (may be moved to compact memory)
		DISCARDABLE (may be discarded when not needed)
optionstatements	Define special attributes of dialog box	STYLE (defines style of dialog box)
		CAPTION text (defines dialog box's title)
		MENU name (defines dialog box's menu)
		CLASS class (defines dialog box's class)
controlstatements	Define attributes of controls within dialog box	See 6.21. Dialog Box Control Definitions

Notes:
Default STYLE is:
WS_POPUP
WS_BORDER
WS_SYSMENU

Source: Microsoft Windows SDK Programming Tools 2.0, pages 40 to 46

See Also: 6.21. Dialog Box Control Definitions

6.21. DIALOG BOX CONTROL DEFINITIONS

Resource Script Format:
general form: CONTROLNAME text, id, xposition, yposition, width, height, [style]

Control Name	Class	Appears As	Syntax	Default Style
LTEXT	Static	Left-justified text	LTEXT text,id,x,y,w,h[,style]	ES_LEFT, WS_GROUP
RTEXT	Static	Right-justified text	RTEXT text,id,x,y,w,h[,style]	ES_RIGHT, WS_GROUP
CTEXT	Static	Centered text	CTEXT text,id,x,y,w,h[,style]	ES_CENTER, WS_GROUP
CHECKBOX	Button	Check box with text	CHECKBOX text,id,x,y,w,h[,style]	BS_CHECKBOX, WS_TABSTOP
PUSHBUTTON	Button	Push button with text	PUSHBUTTON text,id,x,y,w,h[,style]	BS_PUSHBUTTON, WS_TABSTOP
LISTBOX	List box	Boxed list of strings	LISTBOX id,x,y,w,h[,style]	LBS_NOTIFY,LBS_SORT,WS_VSCROLL,WS_BORDER
GROUPBOX	Button	Group of buttons	GROUPBOX text,id,x,y,w,h[,style]	BS_GROUPBOX, WS_TABSTOP
DEFPUSHBUTTON	Button	Default push button	DEFPUSHBUTTON text,id,x,y,w,h[,style]	BS_DEFPUSHBUTTON, WS_TABSTOP
RADIOBUTTON	Button	Radio button with text	RADIOBUTTON text,id,x,y,w,h[,style]	BS_RADIOBUTTON, WS_TABSTOP
EDITTEXT	Edit	Boxed text	EDITTEXT id,x,y,w,h[,style]	WS_TABSTOP, ES_LEFT, WS_BORDER
ICON	Static	Icon	ICON iconname,id,x,y,0,0[,style]	SS_ICON
CONTROL	Varies	User-defined window	CONTROL text,id,class,style,x,y,w,h	none

Control Styles:

Style Name	Class	Description
BS_PUSHBUTTON	Button	Same as PUSHBUTTON
BS_DEFPUSHBUTTON	Button	Same as DEFPUSHBUTTON
BS_CHECKBOX	Button	Same as CHECKBOX
BS_AUTOCHECKBOX	Button	Button automatically toggles state when user clicks on it
BS_AUTORADIOBUTTON*	Button	Button checked, application notified, all other radio buttons in group unchecked
BS_PUSHBOX*	Button	Same as PUSHBUTTON, but no border drawn
BS_LEFTTEXT*	Button	Causes text to appear to left of button (used with CHECKBOX, 3STATE, or RADIOBUTTON)
BS_RADIOBUTTON	Button	Same as RADIOBUTTON
BS_3STATE	Button	Same as BS_CHECKBOX except button can be 'grayed'
BS_AUTO3STATE	Button	Same as BS_3STATE except that button automatically toggles state when user clicks on it
BS_GROUPBOX	Button	Same as GROUPBOX
BS_USERBUTTON	Button	User-defined button; parent notified when clicked
ES_LEFT	Edit	Left-justified text
ES_RIGHT	Edit	Right-justified text
ES_CENTER	Edit	Centered text
ES_MULTILINE	Edit	Multiline edit control
ES_AUTOVSCROLL	Edit	Text scrolled up one 'page' when user presses CR on last line
ES_AUTOHSCROLL	Edit	Text scrolled 10 chars right at end of line, to 0 when CR pressed
ES_NOHIDESEL	Edit	Overrides hiding and inverting of text as focus moves to and from text
SS_LEFT	Static	Same as LTEXT
SS_RIGHT	Static	Same as RTEXT
SS_CENTER	Static	Same as CTEXT
SS_ICON	Static	Same as ICON
SS_BLACKRECT	Static	Black filled rectangle
SS_GRAYRECT	Static	Gray filled rectangle
SS_WHITERECT	Static	White filled rectangle
SS_BLACKFRAME	Static	Box with black frame
SS_GRAYFRAME	Static	Box with gray frame
SS_WHITEFRAME	Static	Box with white frame
SS_USERITEM	Static	User-defined static item
LBS_NOTIFY	Listbox	Parent receives message when user clicks or doubleclicks string

(Continued)

Table 6.21. Continued

Control Styles:

Style Name	Class	Description
LBS_MULTIPLESEL	Listbox	String selection toggled when user clicks or double clicks
LBS_SORT	Listbox	Strings are listed in box alphabetically
LBS_NOREDRAW	Listbox	List box display not updated when changes are made
SBS_VERT	Scrollbar	Vertical scroll bar
SBS_RIGHTALIGN	Scrollbar	Used with SBS_VERT, right edge is right edge of rectangle
SBS_LEFTALIGN	Scrollbar	Used with SBS_VERT, left edge is left edge of rectangle
SBS_HORZ	Scrollbar	Horizontal scroll bar
SBS_TOPALIGN	Scrollbar	Used with SBS_HORZ, top edge is top edge of rectangle
SBS_BOTTOMALIGN	Scrollbar	Used with SBS_HORZ, bottom edge is bottom edge of rectangle
SBS_SIZEBOX	Scrollbar	Size box
SBS_SIZEBOXTOPLEFTALIGN	Scrollbar	Used with SBS_SIZEBOX, aligns sizebox to top left corner of rectangle
SBS_SIZEBOXBOTTOMRIGHTALIGN	Scrollbar	Used with SBS_SIZEBOX, aligns sizebox to bottom right corner of rectangle
WS_GROUP	All	First control of group in which user may move using cursor keys
WS_TOPLEVEL*	All	Creates top-level window
WS_POPUP*	All	Creates pop-up window (cannot be used with WS_CHILD)
WS_CHILD*	All	Creates child window (cannot be used with WS_POPUP)
WS_ICONIC*	All	Creates window that is initially iconic (use with WS_TOPLEVEL only)
WS_ICONICPOPUP*	All	Creates iconic pop-up window
WS_MAXIMIZE*	All	Creates window of maximum size
WS_BORDER*	All	Creates window that has a border
WS_CAPTION*	All	Creates window that has a title bar (implies WS_BORDER)
WS_DLGFRAME*	All	Creates window with a double border but no title
WS_SYSMENU*	All	Creates window that has a system menu box in its title bar
WS_SIZEBOX*	All	Creates window that has a size box (must have title bar or scroll bars)
WS_VSCROLL*	All	Creates window with vertical scroll bar
WS_HSCROLL*	All	Creates window with horizontal scroll bar
WS_CLIPCHILDREN*	All	Excludes the area occupied by child window when drawing parent window
WS_CLIPSIBLINGS*	All	Clips child windows relative to each other
WS_VISIBLE*	All	Creates window that is initially visible (applies to toplevel and popup windows)
WS_DISABLED*	All	Creates window that is initially disabled
WS_TOPLEVELWINDOW*	All	Creates window with: WS_TOPLEVEL, WS_CAPTION, WS_SYSMENU, WS_SIZEBOX
WS_POPUPWINDOW*	All	Creates window with: WS_POPUP, WS_BORDER, WS_SYSMENU
WS_CHILDWINDOW*	All	Creates child window
WS_TABSTOP	All	Control in which user may move using Tab key
WS_OVERLAPPED	All	Creates overlapping window
WS_OVERLAPPEDWINDOW	All	Creates overlapped window having the styles WS_OVERLAPPED, WS_CAPTION, WS_SYSMENU, and WS_SIZEBOX
WS_MINIMIZE	All	Creates window of minimum size
WS_MINIMIZEBOX	All	Creates window that has a Minimize box
WS_MAXIMIZEBOX	All	Creates window that has a Maximize box

*First defined in Windows 2.0

Version Info:

Source: Microsoft Windows SDK Programming Tools 2.0, pages 44 to 65.

See Also:
6.17. Resource Script File Directives
6.18. Single-line Resource Statements
6.19. Menu Resource Script Definitions
6.22. Accelerator Resource Script Definitions
6.24. STRINGTABLE Resource Script Definitions

6.22. ACCELERATOR RESOURCE SCRIPT DEFINITIONS

General ACCELERATOR Resource Script Format:
tablename ACCELERATORS
BEGIN
event, idvalue [,type][,NOINVERT][,SHIFT][,CONTROL]
END

Item	Description	Allowable Values
tablename	Name of the accelerator table	
event	Keystroke to be used as accelerator	"char" or "^char" (single character, control char) ASCII character code Virtual key character
idvalue	ID of accelerator keystroke	Integer value
type	Defines keytype of accelerator	Not used if using quoted chars (e.g., "^C") ASCII (if ASCII character code) VIRTKEY (if Virtual key character)
NOINVERT	Defines whether top-level menu is highlighted on ke	If omitted, top-level menu is highlighted If included, top-level menu is not highlighted
SHIFT	Defines if accelerator requires shift key down	If omitted, shift key need not be down If included, shift key must be down
CONTROL	Defines if accelerator requires control key down	If omitted, control key shouldn't be down If included, control key must also be down

Notes: More than one key may be defined at once by including additional 'event' statements between the BEGIN and END statements

Source: Microsoft Windows SDK Programming Tools 2.0, pages 35 to 36

See Also: 6.17. Resource Script File Directives
6.18. Single-line Resource Statements
6.19. Menu Resource Script Definitions
6.21. Dialog Box Control Definitions
6.24. STRINGTABLE Resource Script Definitions

6.23. COMMON EDIT MENU ACCELERATOR KEY DEFINITIONS

Key Name	Action Performed in Windows 1	Action Performed in Windows 2
Shift + Escape	Invokes the Edit menu's Undo command	Selects system menu of active window
Alt+Backspace	Not defined	Invokes the Edit menu's Undo command
Delete	Invokes the Edit menu's Cut command	Invokes the Edit menu's Clear command
F2	Invokes the Edit menu's Copy command	Not defined
Insert + Control	Invokes the Edit menu's Paste command	Invokes the Edit menu's Copy command
Shift + Delete	Invokes the Edit menu's Clear command	Invokes the Edit menu's Cut command
Shift + Insert	Not defined	Invokes the Edit menu's Paste command

Source: Microsoft Windows SDK Application Style Guide 2.0, page 30

See Also: 6.01. Reserved System Keys
6.02. Recommended Keyboard Actions
6.22. Accelerator Resource Script Definitions

6.24. STRINGTABLE RESOURCE SCRIPT DEFINITIONS

General STRINGTABLE Resource Script Format:
```
STRINGTABLE [loadoption] [memoryoption]
BEGIN
ID string
END
```

Item	Description	Allowable Values
loadoption	Specifies when the resource is to be loaded	PRELOAD (resource loaded immediately)
		LOADONCALL (default: resource loaded when called)
memoryoption	Determines how resource is treated in memory	FIXED (remains in fixed location)
		MOVEABLE (may be moved to compact memory)
		DISCARDABLE (may be discarded when not needed)
ID	Identifier used to name string	Must be an integer value
string	Text comprising string	ASCII string in quotes

Notes: Multiple strings may be defined at once by including multiple ID string statements between the BEGIN and END statements

Source: Microsoft Windows SDK Programming Tools 2.0, pages 34 to 35

See Also:
6.17. Resource Script File Directives
6.18. Single-line Resource Statements
6.19. Menu Resource Script Definitions
6.21. Dialog Box Control Definitions
6.22. Accelerator Resource Script Definitions

6.25. WIN.INI EXTENSION SETTINGS

Section Header: [extensions]

Option	Function	Syntax	Allowable values
Extension setting	Associates extension with application	ext = apname.typ ^.ext	'ext' is the extension to associate with application

Source: Microsoft Windows User's Guide 2.0, page 207

See Also:
6.26. WIN.INI Windows Settings
6.27. WIN.INI Devices Settings
6.28. WIN.INI Colors Settings
6.29. WIN.INI PIF Settings
6.31. WIN.INI Ports Settings
6.32. WIN.INI International Settings
6.33. WIN.INI Fonts Settings

6.26. WIN.INI WINDOWS SETTINGS

Section Header: [windows]

Option	Function	Syntax	Example
Beep	Defines whether system beeps on errors	Beep=boolean	Beep=yes
BorderWidth	Sets area to display outside window	BorderWidth=integer	BorderWidth=5
CursorBlinkRate	Sets system's cursor blink rate	CursorBlinkRate=milliseconds	CursorBlinkRate=817
Device	Defines default output device	Device=name,drivermodule,portname	Device=PCL/LaserJet,HPPCL,LPT1:
DeviceNotSelectedTimeout	Sets device timeout value	DeviceNotSelectedTimeout=seconds	DeviceNotSelectedTimeout=15
DoubleClickSpeed	Sets system's double click speed	DoubleClickSpeed=milliseconds	DoubleClickSpeed=500
Load	Programs made into icons at startup	Load=list	Load clock notepad
MouseSpeed	Sets mouse acceleration rate	MouseSpeed=integer	MouseSpeed=1
NullPort	Defines null port	NullPort=portname	NullPort=none
Programs	Programs listed by MS-DOS Executive	Programs=list	Programs=com exe bat
Run	Programs run at startup	Run=list	Run excel
Spooler	Defines whether spooler is used	Spooler=boolean	Spooler=yes
SwapMouseButtons	Allows mouse buttons to be reversed	SwapMouseButtons=boolean	SwapMouseButtons=no
TransmissionRetryTimeout	Sets timeout value for communications	TransmissionRetryTimeout=seconds	TransmissionRetryTimeout=45
xMouseThreshold	Sets horizontal mouse threshold level	xMouseThreshold=integer	xMouseThreshold=2
yMouseThreshold	Sets vertical mouse threshold level	yMouseThreshold=integer	yMouseThreshold=2

Notes: Values in lists may be separated by commas or white space

Source: Microsoft Windows User's Guide 2.0, pages 201 to 202

See Also:
6.25. WIN.INI Extension Settings
6.27. WIN.INI Devices Settings
6.28. WIN.INI Colors Settings
6.29. WIN.INI PIF Settings
6.31. WIN.INI Ports Settings
6.32. WIN.INI International Settings

6.27. WIN.INI DEVICES SETTINGS

Section Header: [devices]

Option	Function	Syntax	Allowable values
devicename	Names output devices and their port	devicename=drivername,portname*	Portname: See 6.31. WIN.INI Ports Settings

Notes: •*Additional port names may be specified (separated by commas)
•If device not connected, 'portname' should be the NullPort device defined in the Ports section

Source: Microsoft Windows User's Guide 2.0, page 214

See Also: 6.25. WIN.INI Extension Settings
6.26. WIN.INI Windows Settings
6.28. WIN.INI Colors Settings
6.29. WIN.INI PIF Settings
6.31. WIN.INI Ports Settings
6.32. WIN.INI International Settings

6.28. WIN.INI COLORS SETTINGS

Section Header [colors]

Option	Function	Syntax	Allowable values
Component	Defines Windows background colors	Component = redval greenval blueval	Component is one of: ActiveBorder (active window border) ActiveTitle (active caption bar) AppWorkSpace (application work space) Background (icon area, screen back) Inactive Title (inactive caption bar) InactiveBorder (inactive window border) Menu (menu background) MenuText (menu text) Scrollbar (scroll bars) TitleText (title text) Window (Window client area back) WindowFrame (Title back, frame) WindowText (window text) Color vals: 0 (black) to 255 (white)(integer only)

Notes: Windows expects a solid color for MenuText, WindowText, Title Text and Window

Source: Microsoft Windows User's Guide 2.0, pages 207 to 208

See Also: 6.25. WIN.INI Extension Settings
6.26. WIN.INI Windows Settings
6.27. WIN.INI Devices Settings
6.29. WIN.INI PIF Settings
6.31. WIN.INI Ports Settings
6.32. WIN.INI International Settings

6.29. WIN.INI PIF SETTINGS

Section Header: [pif]

Option	Function	Syntax	Allowable values
Program Setting*	Sets memory setting for program	pgmname.typ=value	Value=amount of memory in KBytes
SwapDisk	Sets swap area for applications	SwapDisk=value	Value=? (swap to first fixed disk) Value=letter (swap to that letter drive) Value=0 (do not swap)
SwapSize	Sets amount of memory to swap	SwapSize=value	Value=min amt of memory in KBytes or 0 (set swap to first app size)

Notes: •All disk swapping is done to the root directory unless the [environment] section specifies
a temporary directory
•*Multiple Program Settings may appear in [pif] section

Source: Microsoft Windows User's Guide 2.0, pages 208 to 211

See Also: 6.25. WIN.INI Extension Settings
6.26. WIN.INI Windows Settings
6.27. WIN.INI Devices Settings
6.30. Default PIF Settings
6.31. WIN.INI Ports Settings
6.32. WIN.INI International Settings
6.33. WIN.INI Fonts Settings

6.30. DEFAULT PIF SETTINGS

Item	Default Setting
Program title	Ignored
Initial directory	Ignored
Memory required	52KBytes
Memory desired	All available memory
Directly modifies	Screen
Program switch	Prevent program switch
Screen exchange	Text only
Close window on exit	Does not close

Notes: These settings are only used if no
                    PIF file exists for the application

Source: Microsoft Windows User's Guide 2.0, page 188

See Also: 6.29. WIN.INI PIF Settings

6.31. WIN.INI PORTS SETTINGS

Section Header: [ports]

Option	Function	Syntax	Allowable values
Portname	Defines port settings	Portname:=baud,parity,wordlen,stopbits	Baud: actual baud rate (e.g. 300)
			Parity: o, e, n (odd, even, none)
			Wordlen: # of bits (e.g. 8)
			Stopbits: # of bits (e.g. 2)

Notes: 'Portname' must be one of the recognized DOS ports (e.g. COM1).
                    Alternatively, 'portname' may be a filename, in which case output may be sent directly to a file.

Source: Microsoft Windows User's Guide 2.0, pages 212 to 213

See Also: 6.25. WIN.INI Extension Settings
                    6.26. WIN.INI Windows Settings
                    6.27. WIN.INI Devices Settings
                    6.28. WIN.INI Colors Settings
                    6.29. WIN.INI PIF Settings
                    6.32. WIN.INI International Settings

6.32. WIN.INI INTERNATIONAL SETTINGS

Section Header: [intl]

Option	Function	Syntax	Allowable values
Country	Sets country code	iCountry=country code	See 3.144. Country Codes
Date format	Sets format for date	iDate=value	Value of 0=month-day-year
			Value of 1=day-month-year
			Value of 2=year-month-day
Currency format	Sets format for currency	iCurrency=value	Value of 0=currency prefix, no space
			Value of 1=currency suffix, no space
			Value of 2=currency prefix, 1 space
			Value of 3=currency suffix, 1 space
Decimal digits	Sets # of decimal digits in currency	iDigits=value	Value=# of significant digits
Time format	Sets format of time	iTime=value	Value of 0=12 hour clock
			Value of 1=24 hour clock
Leading zeros	Allows for leading zeros in currency	iLzero=value	0=none, 1=use leading zeroes
AM string	Sets trailing string for morning times	s1159=string	
PM string	Sets trailing string for afternoon times	s2359=string	
Currency symbol	Defines currency symbol	sCurrency=string	
Thousands separator	Defines thousands separator symbol	sThousands=string	
Decimal separator	Defines decimal separator symbol	sDecimal=string	
Date separator	Defines date separator symbol	sDate=string	
Time separator	Defines time separator symbol	sTime=string	
List separator	Defines list separator symbol	sList=string	
Preferences menu	Defines if Country Settings appear	dialog=yes	Always set to yes

Notes: The US version of Windows does
             not require the intl section

Source: Microsoft Windows User's Guide 2.0,
             pages 211 to 212

See Also: 6.25. WIN.INI Extension Settings
                6.26. WIN.INI Windows Settings
                6.27. WIN.INI Devices Settings
                6.28. WIN.INI Colors Settings
                6.29. WIN.INI PIF Settings
                6.31. WIN.INI Ports Settings
                6.33. WIN.INI Fonts Settings

6.33. WIN.INI FONTS SETTINGS

Section Header: [fonts]

Option	Function	Syntax	Allowable values
Fontname	Names font files to load at startup	Fontname ptsize(s) (set #number) =fontfile	Fontname=description font name ptsize=1 or more point sizes to load Number=set number Fontfile=filename, no extension

Notes: Windows 1.xx used the FNT extension for fontfiles, while Windows 2.xx uses the FON extension. The file formats are different.

Source: Microsoft Windows User's Guide 2.0, page 214

See Also:
- 6.25. WIN.INI Extension Settings
- 6.26. WIN.INI Windows Settings
- 6.27. WIN.INI Devices Settings
- 6.28. WIN.INI Colors Settings
- 6.29. WIN.INI PIF Settings
- 6.31. WIN.INI Ports Settings
- 6.32. WIN.INI International Settings

6.34. DATA TYPES USED IN WINDOWS ARGUMENT NAMES

Prefix Used	Meaning	Size	Comments
c	Character	Byte	See 6.09. Extended ANSI Character Codes
b	Boolean value	Word	0=false; non-zero=true
f	Bit flag value	Word	16 individual flags
n	Short integer value	Word	Signed values
l	Long integer value	Dbl word	Signed values
w	Short unsigned integer value	Word	Unsigned values
dw	Long unsigned integer value	Dbl word	Unsigned values
h	Handle	Word	Handle is an index into a table
p	Short pointer	Word	Near pointer
lp	Long pointer	Dbl word	Far pointer
pt	x,y coordinate point	Dbl word	Unsigned, 2 word values
rgb	RGB color value	Dbl word	Unsigned

Notes: The letters in the lefthand column are used as prefixes to an argument name, as in lpMinPos (e.g., MinPos is a long pointer argument).

Source: Microsoft Windows SDK Programmer's Reference 2.0, page 9

See Also:
- 1.16. Common Numeric Data Formats
- 6.09. Extended ANSI Character Codes
- 6.35. Data Types Available as C Keywords

6.35. DATA TYPES AVAILABLE AS C KEYWORDS

Keyword	Meaning	Size	Signed	Comments
char	ASCII character	Byte	Y	See 6.09. Extended ANSI Character Codes
BYTE	Unsigned byte integer	Byte	N	
int	Signed word integer	Word	Y	
short	Signed word integer	Word	Y	
WORD	Unsigned word integer	Word	N	
long	Signed dbl word integer	Dbl word	Y	
LONG	Signed dbl word integer	Dbl word	Y	
DWORD	Unsigned dbl word integer	Dbl word	N	May also be Segment:Offset address
BOOL	Unsigned word	Word	N	0=false, non-zero=true
void	Empty value		N	
PSTR	Pointer to character string	Word	N	Data is assumed within current segment
PINT	Pointer to integer	Word	N	Data is assumed within current segment
LPSTR	Long pointer to char string	Dbl word	N	Data may be in another segment
LPINT	Long pointer to integer	Dbl word	N	Data may be in another segment
LPRECT	Long pointer to RECT struct.	Dbl word	N	Data may be in another segment
LPMSG	Long pointer to MSG struct.	Dbl word	N	Data may be in another segment
FARPROC	Long pointer to function	Dbl word	N	Function may be in another segment
FAR	Pointer	Word	N	Cast as a long pointer (data in any segment)
NEAR	Pointer	Word	N	Cast as a short pointer (data in current segment)
HANDLE	General handle	Word	N	

(Continued)

Table 6.35. Continued

Keyword	Meaning	Size	Signed	Comments
HSTR	String resource handle	Word	N	
HCURSOR	Cursor resource handle	Word	N	
HICON	Icon resource handle	Word	N	
HMENU	Menu resource handle	Word	N	
HDC	Display context handle	Word	N	
HPEN	Physical pen handle	Word	N	
HFONT	Physical font handle	Word	N	
HBRUSH	Physical brush handle	Word	N	
HBITMAP	Physical bitmap handle	Word	N	
HRGN	Physical region handle	Word	N	
GLOBALHANDLE	Global memory handle	Word	N	
LOCALHANDLE	Local memory handle	Word	N	

Notes: Microsoft C is case sensitive

Source: Microsoft Windows SDK Programmer's Reference 2.0, pages 607 to 608

See Also: 1.16. Common Numeric Data Formats
                    6.09. Extended ANSI Character Codes
                    6.34. Data Types Used in Windows Argument Names

6.36. WINDOWS HANDLE AND POINTER TYPES

Name	Function
FAR	Data type attribute that can be used to create a long pointer
FARPROC	Long pointer to a function
GLOBALHANDLE	Global memory handle; index to memory block in system's global heap
HANDLE	General handle; index to table entry identifying program data
HBITMAP	Physical bitmap handle; index to GDI's physical drawing objects
HBRUSH	Physical brush handle; index to GDI's physical drawing objects
HCURSOR	Cursor resource handle; index to a resource table entry
HDC	Display context handle; index to GDI's display context tables
HFONT	Physical font handle; index to GDI's physical drawing objects
HICON	Icon resource handle; index to a resource table entry
HMENU	Menu resource handle; index to a resource table entry
HPEN	Physical pen handle; index to GDI's physical drawing objects
HRGN	Physical region handle; index to GDI's physical drawing objects
HSTR	String resource handle; index to a resource table entry
LOCALHANDLE	Local memory handle; index to memory block in application's local heap
LPINT	Long pointer to a signed 16-bit integer
LPMSG	Long pointer to MSG data structure
LPRECT	Long pointer to RECT data structure
LPSTR	Long pointer to a character string
NEAR	Data type attribute that can be used to create a short pointer
PINT	Pointer to a signed 16-bit integer
PSTR	Pointer to a character string

Notes: All handles are 16-bit values.

Source: Microsoft Windows SDK Programmer's Reference 2.0, pages 607 to 608

See Also: 6.34. Data Types Used in Windows Argument Names
                    6.35. Data Types Available as C Keywords
                    6.53. MSG Structure Format
                    6.57. RECT Structure Format

6.37. INCLUDE FILE CONSTANTS DEFINITIONS BY NAME

Defined Name	Used As	Hex Value	Decimal Value	Comments
ABORTDOC	GDI escape	2	2	
ABSOLUTE	GDI coordinate mode	1	1	
ALTERNATE	Polyfill mode	1	1	
ANSI_CHARSET	Logical font constant	0	0	
ANSI_FIXED_FONT	Stock logical object	B	11	
ANSI_VAR_FONT	Stock logical object	C	12	
ASPECT_FILTERING		1	1	
ASPECTX	Getdevicecaps device parameter	28	40	
ASPECTXY	Getdevicecaps device parameter	2C	44	
ASPECTY	Getdevicecaps device parameter	2A	42	
BANDINFO*	GDI escape code	18	24	
BITSPIXEL	Getdevicecaps device parameter	C	12	
BLACKNESS	Ternary raster op	0000 0042H	66	Dest = BLACK
BLACKONWHITE	Stretchblt mode	1	1	
BLACK_BRUSH	Stock logical object	4	4	
BLACK_PEN	Stock logical object	7	7	
BM_GETCHECK*	Control message	400	1024	
BM_GETSTATE*	Control message	402	1026	
BM_SETCHECK*	Control message	401	1025	
BM_SETSTATE*	Control message	403	1027	
BM_SETSTYLE*	Control message	404	1208	
BN_CLICKED	User button notification code	0	0	
BN_DISABLE	User button notification code	4	4	
BN_DOUBLECLICKED*	Control message	5	5	
BN_HILITE	User button notification code	2	2	
BN_PAINT	User button notification code	1	1	
BN_UNHILITE	User button notification code	3	3	
BS_3STATE	Button control style	5	5	
BS_AUTO3STATE	Button control style	6	6	
BS_AUTOCHECKBOX	Button control style	3	3	
BS_AUTORADIOBUTTON*	Button style	9	9	
BS_CHECKBOX	Button control style	2	2	
BS_DEFPUSHBUTTON	Button control style	1	1	
BS_GROUPBOX	Button control style	7	7	
BS_HATCHED	Brush style	2	2	
BS_HOLLOW	Brush style	1	1	Defined as BS_NULL
BS_INDEXED*	Button control style	4	4	
BS_LEFTTEXT*	Button style	20	32	
BS_NULL	Brush style	1	1	
BS_PATTERN	Brush style	3	3	
BS_PUSHBOX*	Button style	A	10	
BS_PUSHBUTTON	Button control style	0	0	
BS_RADIOBUTTON	Button control style	4	4	
BS_SOLID	Brush style	0	0	
BS_USERBUTTON	Button control style	8	8	
CC_CHORD	Device capability mask	4	4	
CC_CIRCLES	Device capability mask	1	1	
CC_ELLIPSES	Device capability mask	8	8	
CC_INTERIORS	Device capability mask	80	128	
CC_NONE	Device capability mask	0	0	
CC_PIE	Device capability mask	2	2	
CC_STYLED	Device capability mask	20	32	
CC_WIDE	Device capability mask	10	16	
CC_WIDESTYLED	Device capability mask	40	64	
CE_BREAK	Comm device driver error	10	16	
CE_CTSTO	Comm device driver error	20	32	
CE_DNS	Comm device driver error	800	2048	
CE_DSRTO	Comm device driver error	40	64	
CE_FRAME	Comm device driver error	8	8	
CE_IOE	Comm device driver error	400	1024	
CE_MODE	Comm device driver error	8000	32768	
CE_OOP	Comm device driver error	1000	4096	
CE_OVERRUN	Comm device driver error	2	2	
CE_PTO	Comm device driver error	200	512	
CE_RLSDTO	Comm device driver error	80	128	
CE_RXOVER	Comm device driver error	1	1	
CE_RXPARITY	Comm device driver error	4	4	
CE_TXFULL	Comm device driver error	100	256	
CF_BITMAP	Clipboard format	2	2	
CF_DIF	Clipboard format	5	5	
CF_DSPBITMAP	Clipboard format	82	130	
CF_DSPMETAFILEPICT	Clipboard format	83	131	
CF_DSPTEXT	Clipboard format	81	129	

(Continued)

Table 6.37. Continued

Defined Name	Used As	Hex Value	Decimal Value	Comments
CF_GDIOBJFIRST	Clipboard format	300	768	
CF_GDIOBJLAST	Clipboard format	3FF	1023	
CF_METAFILEPICT	Clipboard format	3	3	
CF_OEMTEXT*	Clipboard format	7	7	
CF_OWNERDISPLAY	Clipboard format	80	128	
CF_PRIVATEFIRST	Clipboard format	200	512	
CF_PRIVATELAST	Clipboard format	2FF	767	
CF_SYLK	Clipboard format	4	4	
CF_TEXT	Clipboard format	1	1	
CF_TIFF*	Clipboard format	6	6	
CLIPCAPS	Getdevicecaps device parameter	24	36	
CLIP_CHARACTER_PRECIS	Logical font constant	1	1	
CLIP_DEFAULT_PRECIS	Logical font constant	0	0	
CLIP_STROKE_PRECIS	Logical font constant	2	2	
CLRDTR	Comm escape function	6	6	
CLRRTS	Comm escape function	4	4	
COLORONCOLOR	Stretchblt mode	3	3	
COLOR_ACTIVEBORDER*	Color type index	A	10	
COLOR_ACTIVECAPTION	Color type index	2	2	
COLOR_APPWORKSPACE*	Color type index	C	12	
COLOR_BACKGROUND	Color type index	1	1	
COLOR_CAPTIONTEXT	Color type index	9	9	
COLOR_INACTIVEBORDER*	Color type index	B	11	
COLOR_INACTIVECAPTION	Color type index	3	3	
COLOR_MENU	Color type index	4	4	
COLOR_MENUTEXT	Color type index	7	7	
COLOR_SCROLLBAR	Color type index	0	0	
COLOR_WINDOW	Color type index	5	5	
COLOR_WINDOWFRAME	Color type index	6	6	
COLOR_WINDOWTEXT	Color type index	8	8	
COMPLEXREGION	Region flag	3	3	
CP_DIRECT*	Device capability mode	2	2	
CP_GETBEEP*	Control panel info	1	1	
CP_GETBORDER*	Control panel info	5	5	
CP_GETMOUSE*	Control panel info	3	3	
CP_HWND*	Device capability mode	0	0	
CP_KANJIMENU*	Control panel info	8	8	
CP_NONE	Device capability mask	0	0	
CP_OPEN*	Device capability mode	1	1	
CP_RECTANGLE	Device capability mask	1	1	
CP_SETBEEP*	Control panel info	2	2	
CP_SETBORDER*	Control panel info	6	6	
CP_SETMOUSE*	Control panel info	4	4	
CP_TIMEOUTS*	Control panel info	7	7	
CS_KEYCUTWINDOW	Class style	4	4	
CS_BYTEALIGNCLIENT*	Class style	1000	4096	
CS_BYTEALIGNWINDOW*	Class style	2000	8192	
CS_CLASSDC	Class style	40	64	
CS_DBLCLKS	Class style	8	8	
CS_HREDRAW	Class style	2	2	
CS_MENUPOPUP	Class style	80	128	
CS_NOCLOSE*	Class style	200	512	
CS_NOKEYCUT	Class style	100	512	
CS_OEMCHARS	Class style	10	16	
CS_OWNDC	Class style	20	32	
CS_PARENTDC*	Class style	80	128	
CS_SAVEBITS*	Class style	800	2048	
CS_VREDRAW	Class style	1	1	
CTLCOLOR_BTN	Color type index	3	3	
CTLCOLOR_DLG	Color type index	4	4	
CTLCOLOR_EDIT	Color type index	1	1	
CTLCOLOR_LISTBOX	Color type index	2	2	
CTLCOLOR_MAX	Color type index	8	8	
CTLCOLOR_MSGBOX	Color type index	0	0	
CTLCOLOR_SCROLLBAR	Color type index	5	5	
CTLCOLOR_STATIC	Color type index	6	6	
CURVECAPS	Getdevicecaps device parameter	1C	28	
DEFAULT_PITCH	Logical font constant	0	0	
DEFAULT_QUALITY	Logical font constant	0	0	
DEVICEDATA	MetaFile comment esc.	13	19	
DEVICEDEFAULT_FONT	Stock logical object	E	14	
DEVICE_FONTTYPE	Enumfont mask	2	2	
DF_ACTIVEBORDER*	DrawFrame index			COLOR_ACTIVEBORDER+1<<3
DF_ACTIVECAPTION*	DrawFrame index			COLOR_ACTIVECAPTION+1<<3
DF_APPWORKSPACE*	DrawFrame index			COLOR_APPWORKSPACE+1<<3
DF_BACKGROUND*	DrawFrame index			COLOR_BACKGROUND+1<<3
DF_CAPTIONTEXT*	DrawFrame index			COLOR_CAPTIONTEXT+1<<3

(Continued)

Table 6.37. Continued

Defined Name	Used As	Hex Value	Decimal Value	Comments
DF_GRAY*	DrawFrame index			COLOR_APPWORKSPACE+(1<<3)
DF_INACTIVEBORDER*	DrawFrame index			COLOR_INACTIVEBORDER+1<<3
DF_INACTIVECAPTION*	DrawFrame index			COLOR_INACTIVECAPTION+1<<3
DF_MENU*	DrawFrame index			COLOR_MENU+1<<3
DF_MENUTEXT*	DrawFrame index			COLOR_MENUTEXT+1<<3
DF_PATCOPY*	DrawFrame index	0	0	
DF_PATINVERT*	DrawFrame index	4	4	
DF_SCROLLBAR*	DrawFrame index			COLOR_SCROLLBAR+1<<3
DF_SHIFT0*	DrawFrame index	0	0	
DF_SHIFT1*	DrawFrame index	1	1	
DF_SHIFT2*	DrawFrame index	2	2	
DF_SHIFT3*	DrawFrame index	3	3	
DF_WINDOW*	DrawFrame index			COLOR_WINDOW+1<<3
DF_WINDOWFRAME*	DrawFrame index			COLOR_WINDOWFRAME+1<<3
DF_WINDOWTEXT*	DrawFrame index			COLOR_WINDOWTEXT+1<<3
DKGRAY_BRUSH	Stock logical object	3	3	
DLGC_BUTTON*	Dialog code	2000	8192	
DLGC_DEFPUSHBUTTON*	Dialog code	10	16	
DLGC_HASSETSEL	Dialog code	8	8	
DLGC_RADIOBUTTON*	Dialog code	40	64	
DLGC_STATIC*	Dialog code	100	256	
DLGC_UNDEFPUSHBUTTON*	Dialog code	20	32	
DLGC_WANTALLKEYS	Dialog code	4	4	
DLGC_WANTARROWS	Dialog code	1	1	
DLGC_WANTCHARS*	Dialog code	80	128	
DLGC_WANTMESSAGE*	Dialog code	4	4	
DLGC_WANTTAB	Dialog code	2	2	
DM_GETDEFID	Dialog style bits	400	1024	WM_USER+0
DM_SETDEFID	Dialog style bits	401	1025	WM_USER+1
DM_HASDEFID	Dialog style bits	534B	21323	
DRAFTMODE	GDI escape	7	7	
DRAFT_QUALITY	Logical font constant	1	1	
DRAWPATTERNRECT*	GDI escape code	19	25	
DRIVERVERSION	Getdevicecaps device parameter	0	0	
DSTINVERT	Ternary raster op	0055 0009H	5570569	Dest = (not dest)
DS_ABSALIGN	Dialog style	1	1	
DS_LOCALEDIT*	Dialog style	20	32	
DS_SYSMODAL	Dialog style	2	2	
DT_BOTTOM	DrawText format flag	8	8	
DT_CALCRECT*	DrawText format flag	400	1024	
DT_CENTER	DrawText format flag	1	1	
DT_CHARSTREAM	Device capability mask	4	4	
DT_DISPFILE	Device capability mask	6	6	
DT_EXPANDTABS	DrawText format flag	40	64	
DT_EXTERNALLEADING	DrawText format flag	200	512	
DT_INTERNAL	DrawText format flag	1000	4096	
DT_LEFT	DrawText format flag	0	0	
DT_METAFILE	Device capability mask	5	5	
DT_NOCLIP	DrawText format flag	100	256	
DT_NOPREFIX*	DrawText format flag	800	2048	
DT_PLOTTER	Device capability mask	0	0	
DT_RASCAMERA	Device capability mask	3	3	
DT_RASDISPLAY	Device capability mask	1	1	
DT_RASPRINTER	Device capability mask	2	2	
DT_RIGHT	DrawText format flag	2	2	
DT_SINGLELINE	DrawText format flag	20	32	
DT_TABSTOP	DrawText format flag	80	128	
DT_TOP	DrawText format flag	0	0	
DT_VCENTER	DrawText format flag	4	4	
DT_WORDBREAK	DrawText format flag	10	16	
EM_CANUNDO*	Edit control message	413	1043	
EM_FMTLINES*	Edit control message	415	1045	
EM_GETHANDLE*	Edit control message	40C	1036	
EM_GETLINE*	Edit control message	411	1041	
EM_GETLINECOUNT*	Edit control message	409	1033	
EM_GETMODIFY*	Edit control message	407	1031	
EM_GETRECT*	Edit control message	402	1026	
EM_GETSEL*	Edit control message	400	1024	
EM_GETTHUMB*	Edit control message	40D	1037	
EM_LIMITTEXT*	Edit control message	412	1042	
EM_LINEFROMCHAR*	Edit control message	416	1046	
EM_LINEINDEX*	Edit control message	40A	1034	
EM_LINELENGTH*	Edit control message	40E	1038	
EM_LINESCROLL*	Edit control message	406	1030	
EM_REPLACESEL*	Edit control message	40F	1039	
EM_SCROLL*	Edit control message	405	1029	
EM_SETFONT*	Edit control message	410	1040	

(Continued)

Table 6.37. Continued

Defined Name	Used As	Hex Value	Decimal Value	Comments
EM_SETHANDLE*	Edit control message	40B	1035	
EM_SETMODIFY*	Edit control message	408	1032	
EM_SETRECT*	Edit control message	403	1027	
EM_SETRECTNP*	Edit control message	404	1028	
EM_SETSEL*	Edit control message	401	1025	
EM_SETWORDBREAK*	Edit control message	417	1047	
EM_UNDO*	Edit control message	414	1044	
ENABLEDUPLEX*	GDI escape code	1C	28	
ENABLEMANUALFEED*	GDI escape code	1D	29	
ENABLEPAIRKERNING*	GDI escape code	301	769	
ENABLERELATIVEWIDTHS*	GDI escape code	300	768	
ENDDOC	GDI escape	B	11	
EN_CHANGE	Edit control notification code	300	768	
EN_ERRSPACE	Edit control notification code	500	1280	
EN_HSCROLL	Edit control notification code	601	1537	
EN_KILLFOCUS	Edit control notification code	200	512	
EN_SETFOCUS	Edit control notification code	100	256	
EN_UPDATE*	Edit control notification code	400	1024	
EN_VSCROLL	Edit control notification code	602	1538	
ERROR	Region flag	0	0	
ES_AUTOHSCROLL	Edit control style	80	128	
ES_AUTOVSCROLL	Edit control style	40	64	
ES_CENTER	Edit control style	1	1	
ES_LEFT	Edit control style	0	0	
ES_MULTILINE	Edit control style	4	4	
ES_NOHIDESEL	Edit control style	100	256	
ES_RIGHT	Edit control style	2	2	
ETO_CLIPPED*	Edit text option	4	4	
ETO_GRAYED*	Edit text option	1	1	
ETO_OPAQUE*	Edit text option	2	2	
EVENPARITY	Dcb field definition	2	2	
EV_BREAK	Comm event definition	40	64	
EV_CTS	Comm event definition	8	8	
EV_DSR	Comm event definition	10	16	
EV_ERR	Comm event definition	80	128	
EV_PERR	Comm event definition	200	512	
EV_RING	Comm event definition	100	256	
EV_RLSD	Comm event definition	20	32	
EV_RXCHAR	Comm event definition	1	1	
EV_RXFLAG	Comm event definition	2	2	
EV_TXEMPTY	Comm event definition	4	4	
EXTTEXTOUT*	GDI escape code	200	512	
FALSE	Standard definitions	0	0	
FF_DECORATIVE	Font family ID	5*	5*	*Shifted left four bits
FF_DONTCARE	Font family ID	0*	0*	*Shifted left four bits
FF_MODERN	Font family ID	3*	3*	*Shifted left four bits
FF_ROMAN	Font family ID	1*	1*	*Shifted left four bits
FF_SCRIPT	Font family ID	4*	4*	*Shifted left four bits
FF_SWISS	Font family ID	2*	2*	*Shifted left four bits
FIXED_PITCH	Logical font constant	1	1	
FLUSHOUTPUT	GDI escape	6	6	
FW_BLACK	Font weight constant	384	900	Defined as FW_HEAVY
FW_BOLD	Font weight constant	26C	700	
FW_DEMIBOLD	Font weight constant	258	600	Defined as FW_SEMIBOLD
FW_DONTCARE	Font weight constant	0	0	
FW_EXTRABOLD	Font weight constant	320	800	
FW_EXTRALIGHT	Font weight constant	C8	200	
FW_HEAVY	Font weight constant	384	900	
FW_LIGHT	Font weight constant	12C	300	
FW_MEDIUM	Font weight constant	1F4	500	
FW_NORMAL	Font weight constant	190	400	
FW_REGULAR*	Font weight	190	400	
FW_SEMIBOLD	Font weight constant	258	600	
FW_THIN	Font weight constant	64	100	
FW_ULTRABOLD	Font weight constant	320	800	Defined as FW_EXTRABOLD
FW_ULTRALIGHT	Font weight constant	C8	200	Defined as FW_EXTRALIGHT
GCL_MENUNAME	Class field offset	FFF8	-8	
GCL_WNDPROC	Class field offset	FFEA	-24	
GCW_CBCLSEXTRA	Class field offset	FFEC	-22	
GCW_CBWNDEXTRA	Class field offset	FFEE	-20	
GCW_HBRBACKGROUND	Class field offset	FFF6	-10	
GCW_HCURSOR	Class field offset	FFF4	-12	
GCW_HICON	Class field offset	FFF2	-14	
GCW_HMODULE	Class field offset	FFF0	-16	
GCW_STYLE	Class field offset	FFE8	-26	
GETCOLORTABLE	GDI escape	5	5	
GETEXTENDEDTEXTMETRICS*	GDI escape code	100	256	
GETEXTENTTABLE*	GDI escape code	101	257	

(Continued)

Table 6.37. Continued

Defined Name	Used As	Hex Value	Decimal Value	Comments
GETPAIRKERNTABLE*	GDI escape code	102	258	
GETPENWIDTH*	GDI escape code	10	16	
GETPHYSPAGESIZE	GDI escape	C	12	
GETPRINTINGOFFSET	GDI escape	D	13	
GETSCALINGFACTOR	GDI escape	E	14	
GETTECHNOLOGY*	GDI escape code	14	20	
GETTRACKKERNTABLE*	GDI escape code	103	259	
GETVECTORBRUSHSIZE*	GDI escape code	1B	27	
GETVECTORPENSIZE*	GDI escape code	1A	26	
GHND*	Global memory management	42	66	
GMEM_DDESHARE*	Global memory management	2000	8192	
GMEM_DISCARDABLE	Global memory management	F00	3840	
GMEM_DISCARDED	GlobalFlag flag	4000	16384	
GMEM_FIXED	Global memory management	0	0	
GMEM_LOCKCOUNT	GlobalFlag flag	FF	255	
GMEM_LOWER*	Global memory management	1000	4096	
GMEM_MODIFY	Global memory management	80	128	
GMEM_MOVEABLE	Global memory management	2	2	
GMEM_NOCOMPACT	Global memory management	10	16	
GMEM_NODISCARD	Global memory management	20	32	
GMEM_NOTBANKED*	Global memory management	1000	4096	
GMEM_NOTIFY*	Global memory management	4000	16384	
GMEM_SHARE*	Global memory management	2000	8196	
GMEM_SWAPPED	GlobalFlag flag	8000	32768	
GMEM_ZEROINIT	Global memory management	40	64	
GPTR*	Global memory management	2	2	
GRAY_BRUSH	Stock logical object	2	2	
GWL_STYLE	Window field offset	FFF0	-16	
GWL_WNDPROC	Window field offset	FFFC	-4	
GWW_HINSTANCE	Window field offset	FFFA	-6	
GWW_HWNDPARENT	Window field offset	FFF8	-8	
GWW_HWNDTEXT	Window field offset	FFF6	-10	
GWW_ID	Window field offset	FFF4	-12	
GW_CHILD*	GetWindow constant	5	5	
GW_HWNDFIRST*	GetWindow constant	0	0	
GW_HWNDLAST*	GetWindow constant	1	1	
GW_HWNDNEXT*	GetWindow constant	2	2	
GW_HWNDPREV*	GetWindow constant	3	3	
GW_OWNER*	GetWindow constant	4	4	
HCBT_MINMAX*	Hook code	1	1	
HCBT_MOVESIZE*	Hook code	0	0	
HCBT_QS	Hook code	2	2	
HC_ACTION*	Hook code	0	0	
HC_GETNEXT*	Hook code	1	1	
HC_LPFNNEXT*	Hook code	FFFF	-1	
HC_LPLPFNNEXT*	Hook code	FFFE	-2	
HC_NOREM*	Hook code	3	3	
HC_SKIP*	Hook code	2	2	
HIDE_WINDOW	Showwindow command	0	0	
HOLLOW_BRUSH	Stock logical object	5	5	Defined as NULL_BRUSH
HORZRES	Getdevicecaps device parameter	8	8	
HORZSIZE	Getdevicecaps device parameter	4	4	
HS_BDIAGONAL	Hatch style	3	3	
HS_CROSS	Hatch style	4	4	
HS_DIAGCROSS	Hatch style	5	5	
HS_FDIAGONAL	Hatch style	2	2	
HS_HORIZONTAL	Hatch style	0	0	
HS_VERTICAL	Hatch style	1	1	
HTCAPTION	Winwhere area code	2	2	
HTCLIENT	Winwhere area code	1	1	
HTERROR	Winwhere area code	FFFE	-2	
HTGROWBOX	Winwhere area code	4	4	
HTHSCROLL	Winwhere area code	6	6	
HTMENU	Winwhere area code	5	5	
HTNOWHERE	Winwhere area code	0	0	
HTSYSMENU	Winwhere area code	3	3	
HTTRANSPARENT	Winwhere area code	FFFF	-1	
HTVSCROLL	Winwhere area code	7	7	
HTBOTTOM*	Winwhere area code	F	15	
HTBOTTOMLEFT*	Winwhere area code	10	16	
HTBOTTOMRIGHT*	Winwhere area code	11	17	
HTLEFT*	Winwhere area code	A	10	
HTREDUCE*	Winwhere area code	8	8	
HTRIGHT*	Winwhere area code	B	11	
HTSIZE*	Winwhere area code	4	4	
HTSIZEFIRST*	Winwhere area code	A	10	
HTSIZELAST*	Winwhere area code	11	17	

(Continued)

Table 6.37. Continued

Defined Name	Used As	Hex Value	Decimal Value	Comments
HTTOP*	Winwhere area code	C	12	
HTTOPLEFT*	Winwhere area code	D	13	
HTTOPRIGHT*	Winwhere area code	E	14	
HTZOOM*	Winwhere area code	9	9	
IDABORT	Dialog/message box command ID	3	3	
IDCANCEL	Dialog/message box command ID	2	2	
IDC_ARROW	Standard cursor ID	7F00	32512	MAKEINTRESOURCE(32512)
IDC_CROSS	Standard cursor ID	7F03	32515	MAKEINTRESOURCE(32515)
IDC_IBEAM	Standard cursor ID	7F01	32513	MAKEINTRESOURCE(32513)
IDC_ICON	Standard cursor ID	7F81	32641	MAKEINTRESOURCE(32641)
IDC_SIZENWSE	Standard cursor ID	7F82	32642	
IDC_SIZENESW	Standard cursor ID	7F83	32643	
IDC_SIZEWE	Standard cursor ID	7F84	32644	
IDC_SIZENS	Standard cursor ID	7F85	32645	
IDC_SIZE	Standard cursor ID	7F80	32640	MAKEINTRESOURCE(32640)
IDC_UPARROW	Standard cursor ID	7F04	32516	MAKEINTRESOURCE(32516)
IDC_WAIT	Standard cursor ID	7F02	32514	MAKEINTRESOURCE(32514
IDIGNORE	Dialog/message box command ID	5	5	
IDI_APPLICATION	Standard icon ID	7F00	32512	MAKEINTRESOURCE(32512)
IDI_ASTERISK	Standard icon ID	7F04	32516	MAKEINTRESOURCE(32516)
IDI_EXCLAMATION	Standard icon ID	7F03	32515	MAKEINTRESOURCE(32515)
IDI_HAND	Standard icon ID	7F01	32513	MAKEINTRESOURCE(32513)
IDI_QUESTION	Standard icon ID	7F02	32514	MAKEINTRESOURCE(32514)
IDNO	Dialog/message box command ID	7	7	
IDOK	Dialog/message box command ID	1	1	
IDRETRY	Dialog/message box command ID	4	4	
IDYES	Dialog/message box command ID	6	6	
IE_BADID	Comm init error	FFFF	-1	
IE_BAUDRATE	Comm init error	FFF4	-12	
IE_BYTESIZE	Comm init error	FFF5	-11	
IE_DEFAULT	Comm init error	FFFB	-5	
IE_HARDWARE	Comm init error	FFF6	-10	
IE_MEMORY	Comm init error	FFFC	-4	
IE_NOPEN	Comm init error	FFFD	-3	
IE_OPEN	Comm init error	FFFE	-2	
IGNORE	Dcb field definition	0	0	
INFINITE	Dcb field definition	FFFF	-1	
KNJ_START	Conversion function	1	1	
KNJ_END	Conversion function	2	2	
KNJ_QUERY	Conversion function	3	3	
KNJ_LEARN_MODE	Conversion function	10	16	
KNJ_GETMODE	Conversion function	11	17	
KNJ_SETMODE	Conversion function	12	18	
KNJ_CODECONVERT	Conversion function	20	32	
KNJ_CONVERT	Conversion function	21	33	
KNJ_NEXT	Conversion function	22	34	
KNJ_PREVIOUS	Conversion function	23	35	
KNJ_ACCEPT	Conversion function	24	36	
KNJ_LEARN	Conversion function	30	48	
KNJ_REGISTER	Conversion function	31	49	
KNJ_REMOVE	Conversion function	32	50	
KNJ_CHANGE_UDIC	Conversion function	33	51	
KNJ_JIS1 to JIS1 KATAKANA	Conversion function	14	20	
KNJ_JIS1 to JIS2	Conversion function	13	19	
KNJ_JIS1 to JIS2 HIRAGANA	Conversion function	15	21	
KNJ_JIS1 to JIS2 KATAKANA	Conversion function	16	22	
KNJ_JIS1 to DEFAULT	Conversion function	10	16	
KNJ_JIS1 to JIS2 OEM	Conversion function	1F	31	
KNJ_JIS2 to JIS2	Conversion function	23	35	
KNJ_SJIS2 to JIS2	Conversion function	32	50	
KNJ_MD_ALPHA	Conversion function	1	1	
KNJ_MD_HIRAGANA	Conversion function	2	2	
KNJ_MD_HALF	Conversion function	4	4	
KNJ_MD_JIS	Conversion function	8	8	
KNJ_MD_SPECIAL	Conversion function	10	16	
KNJ_CUT_NEXT	Conversion function	1	1	
KNJ_CUT_PREV	Conversion function	2	2	
KNJ_CUT_KATAKANA	Conversion function	3	3	
KNJ_CUT_HIRAGANA	Conversion function	4	4	
KNJ_CUT_JIS1	Conversion function	5	5	
KNJ_CUT_JIS2	Conversion function	6	6	
KNJ_CUT_DEFAULT	Conversion function	7	7	
KNJ_CUT_TYPED	Conversion function	8	8	
LBN_DBLCLK	Listbox notification code	2	2	
LBN_ERRSPACE	Listbox notification code	FFFE	-2	
LBN_SELCHANGE	Listbox notification code	1	1	
LBS_MULTIPLESEL	Listbox style	8	8	

(Continued)

Table 6.37. Continued

Defined Name	Used As	Hex Value	Decimal Value	Comments
LBS_NOREDRAW	Listbox style	4	4	
LBS_NOTIFY	Listbox style	1	1	
LBS_SORT	Listbox style	2	2	
LBS_STANDARD*	Listbox style	F	15	
LB_ADDSTRING*	Listbox message	400	1024	
LB_CTLCODE	Listbox control	0	0	
LB_DELETESTRING*	Listbox message	402	1	
LB_DIR*	Listbox message	40D	2	
LB_ERR	Listbox control	FFFF	-1	
LB_ERRSPACE	Listbox control	FFFE	-2	
LB_GETCOUNT*	Listbox message	40B	-1	
LB_GETCURSEL*	Listbox message	409	0	
LB_GETSEL*	Listbox message	408	1	
LB_GETTEXT*	Listbox message	407	2	
LB_GETTEXTLEN*	Listbox message	40A	3	
LB_GETTOPINDEX*	Listbox message	40E	4	
LB_INSERTSTRING*	Listbox message	401	5	
LB_MSGMAX*	Listbox message	40F	6	
LB_OKAY	Listbox control	0	0	
LB_RESETCONTENT*	Listbox message	404	1	
LB_SELECTSTRING*	Listbox message	40C	2	
LB_SETCURSEL*	Listbox message	406	3	
LB_SETSEL*	Listbox message	405	4	
LC_INTERIORS	Device capability mask	80	128	
LC_MARKER	Device capability mask	4	4	
LC_NONE	Device capability mask	0	0	
LC_POLYLINE	Device capability mask	2	2	
LC_POLYMARKER	Device capability mask	8	8	
LC_STYLED	Device capability mask	20	32	
LC_WIDE	Device capability mask	10	16	
LC_WIDESTYLED	Device capability mask	40	64	
LF_FACESIZE	Logical font constant	20	32	
LHND*	Global memory management	42	66	
LINECAPS	Getdevicecaps device parameter	1E	30	
LMEM_DISCARDABLE	Local memory management	F00	3840	
LMEM_DISCARDED*	Local memory management	4000	16384	
LMEM_FIXED	Local memory management	0	0	
LMEM_LOCKCOUNT	Local memory management	FF	255	
LMEM_MODIFY	Local memory management	80	128	
LMEM_MOVEABLE	Local memory management	2	2	
LMEM_NOCOMPACT	Local memory management	10	16	
LMEM_NODISCARD	Local memory management	20	32	
LMEM_ZEROINIT	Local memory management	40	64	
LNOTIFY_DISCARD	Local memory management	2	2	
LNOTIFY_MOVE	Local memory management	1	1	
LNOTIFY_OUTOFMEM	Local memory management	0	0	
LOGPIXELSX	Getdevicecaps device parameter	58	88	
LOGPIXELSY	Getdevicecaps device parameter	5A	90	
LPTR*	Global memory management	2	2	
LPTx*	Device description	80	128	
LTGRAY_BRUSH	Stock logical object	1	1	
MARKPARITY	Dcb field definition	3	3	
MA_ACTIVATE*	Mouse activate return code	1	1	
MA_ACTIVATEANDEAT*	Mouse activate return code	2	2	
MA_NOACTIVATE*	Mouse activate return code	3	3	
MB_ABORTRETRYIGNORE	MessageBox type flag	2	2	
MB_APPLMODAL	MessageBox type flag	0	0	
MB_DEFBUTTON1	MessageBox type flag	0	0	
MB_DEFBUTTON2	MessageBox type flag	100	256	
MB_DEFBUTTON3	MessageBox type flag	200	512	
MB_DEFMASK	MessageBox type flag	F00	3840	
MB_ICONASTERISK	MessageBox type flag	40	64	
MB_ICONEXCLAMATION	MessageBox type flag	30	48	
MB_ICONHAND	MessageBox type flag	10	16	
MB_ICONMASK	MessageBox type flag	F0	240	
MB_ICONQUESTION	MessageBox type flag	20	32	
MB_MISCMASK	MessageBox type flag	C000	49152	
MB_MODEMASK	MessageBox type flag	3000	12288	
MB_NOFOCUS	MessageBox type flag	8000	32768	
MB_OK	MessageBox type flag	0	0	
MB_OKCANCEL	MessageBox type flag	1	1	
MB_RETRYCANCEL	MessageBox type flag	5	5	
MB_SYSTEMMODAL	MessageBox type flag	1000	4096	
MB_TYPEMASK	MessageBox type flag	F	15	
MB_YESNO	MessageBox type flag	4	4	
MB_YESNOCANCEL	MessageBox type flag	3	3	
MERGECOPY	Ternary raster op	00C0 00CA	12583114	Dest = (source AND pattern)

(Continued)

Table 6.37. Continued

Defined Name	Used As	Hex Value	Decimal Value	Comments
MERGEPAINT	Ternary raster op	00BB 0226	12255782	Dest = (not source) OR dest
META_ARC*	Metafile function	817	2071	
META_BITBLT*	Metafile function	922	2338	
META_CHORD*	Metafile function	630	1584	
META_CREATEBITMAP*	Metafile function	6FE	1790	
META_CREATEBITMAPINDIRECT*	Metafile function	2FD	765	
META_CREATEBRUSH*	Metafile function	F8	248	
META_CREATEBRUSHINDIRECT*	Metafile function	2FC	764	
META_CREATEFONTINDIRECT*	Metafile function	2FB	763	
META_CREATEPATTERNBRUSH*	Metafile function	1F9	505	
META_CREATEPENDIRECT*	Metafile function	2FA	762	
META_CREATEREGION*	Metafile function	6FF	1791	
META_DRAWTEXT*	Metafile function	62F	1583	
META_ELLIPSE*	Metafile function	418	1048	
META_ESCAPE*	Metafile function	626	1574	
META_EXCLUDECLIPRECT*	Metafile function	415	1045	
META_FILLREGION*	Metafile function	228	552	
META_FLOODFILL*	Metafile function	419	1049	
META_FRAMEREGION*	Metafile function	429	1065	
META_INTERSECTCLIPRECT*	Metafile function	416	1046	
META_INVERTREGION*	Metafile function	12A	298	
META_LINETO*	Metafile function	213	531	
META_MOVETO*	Metafile function	214	532	
META_OFFSETCLIPRGN*	Metafile function	220	544	
META_OFFSETVIEWPORTORG*	Metafile function	211	529	
META_OFFSETWINDOWORG*	Metafile function	20F	527	
META_PAINTREGION*	Metafile function	12B	299	
META_PATBLT*	Metafile function	61D	1565	
META_PIE*	Metafile function	81A	2074	
META_POLYGON*	Metafile function	324	804	
META_POLYLINE*	Metafile function	325	805	
META_RECTANGLE*	Metafile function	41B	1051	
META_RESTOREDC*	Metafile function	127	295	
META_ROUNDRECT*	Metafile function	61C	1564	
META_SAVEDC*	Metafile function	1E	30	
META_SCALEVIEWPORTEXT*	Metafile function	412	1042	
META_SCALEWINDOWEXT*	Metafile function	400	1024	
META_SELECTCLIPREGION*	Metafile function	12C	300	
META_SELECTOBJECT*	Metafile function	12D	301	
META_SETBKCOLOR*	Metafile function	201	513	
META_SETBKMODE*	Metafile function	102	258	
META_SETMAPMODE*	Metafile function	103	259	
META_SETPIXEL*	Metafile function	41F	1055	
META_SETPOLYFILLMODE*	Metafile function	106	262	
META_SETRELABS*	Metafile function	105	261	
META_SETROP2*	Metafile function	104	260	
META_SETSTRECTCHBLTMODE*	Metafile function	107	263	
META_SETTEXTALIGN*	Metafile function	12E	302	
META_SETTEXTCHAREXTRA*	Metafile function	108	264	
META_SETTEXTCOLOR*	Metafile function	209	521	
META_SETTEXTJUSTIFICATION*	Metafile function	20A	522	
META_SETVIEWPORTEXT*	Metafile function	20E	526	
META_SETVIEWPORTORG*	Metafile function	20D	525	
META_SETWINDOWEXT*	Metafile function	20C	524	
META_SETWINDOWORG*	Metafile function	20B	523	
META_STRETCHBLT*	Metafile function	B23	2851	
META_TEXTOUT*	Metafile function	521	1313	
MFCOMMENT*	GDI escape code	F	15	
MF_APPEND	MenuItem menu flag	100	256	
MF_BITMAP	MenuItem menu flag	4	4	
MF_BYCOMMAND	MenuItem menu flag	0	0	
MF_BYPOSITION	MenuItem menu flag	400	1024	
MF_CHANGE	MenuItem menu flag	80	128	
MF_CHECKED	MenuItem menu flag	8	8	
MF_DELETE	MenuItem menu flag	200	512	
MF_DISABLED	MenuItem menu flag	2	2	
MF_ENABLED	MenuItem menu flag	0	0	
MF_GRAYED	MenuItem menu flag	1	1	
MF_HELP*	MenuItem menu flag	4000	16384	
MF_HILITE	MenuItem menu flag	80	128	
MF_INSERT	MenuItem menu flag	0	0	
MF_MENUBARBREAK	MenuItem menu flag	20	32	
MF_MENUBREAK	MenuItem menu flag	40	64	
MF_MOUSESELECT*	MenuItem menu flag	8000	32768	
MF_POPUP	MenuItem menu flag	10	16	
MF_REMOVE*	MenuItem menu flag	1000	4096	
MF_SEPARATOR	MenuItem menu flag	800	2048	

(Continued)

Table 6.37. Continued

Defined Name	Used As	Hex Value	Decimal Value	Comments
MF_STRING	MenuItem menu flag	0	0	
MF_SYSMENU*	MenuItem menu flag	2000	8192	
MF_UNCHECKED	MenuItem menu flag	0	0	
MF_UNHILITE	MenuItem menu flag	0	0	
MK_CONTROL	Key state mask f/mouse msg.	8	8	
MK_LBUTTON	Key state mask f/mouse msg.	1	1	
MK_MBUTTON	Key state mask f/mouse msg.	10	16	
MK_RBUTTON	Key state mask f/mouse msg.	2	2	
MK_SHIFT	Key state mask f/mouse msg.	4	4	
MM_ANISOTROPIC	GDI map mode	8	8	
MM_HIENGLISH	GDI map mode	5	5	
MM_HIMETRIC	GDI map mode	3	3	
MM_ISOTROPIC	GDI map mode	7	7	
MM_LOENGLISH	GDI map mode	4	4	
MM_LOMETRIC	GDI map mode	2	2	
MM_TEXT	GDI map mode	1	1	
MM_TWIPS	GDI map mode	6	6	
MSGF_DIALOGBOX	Filter procedure code	0	0	
MSGF_MENU	Filter procedure code	2	2	
MSGF_MESSAGEBOX	Filter procedure code	1	1	
MSGF_MOVE*	Filter procedure code	3	3	
MSGF_NEXTWINDOW*	Filter procedure code	6	6	
MSGF_SCROLLBAR*	Filter procedure code	5	5	
MSGF_SIZE*	Filter procedure code	4	4	
NEWFRAME	GDI escape	1	1	
NEXTBAND	GDI escape	3	3	
NONZEROLHND*	Global memory management	2	2	
NONZEROLPTR*	Global memory management	0	0	
NOPARITY	Dcb field definition	0	0	
NOTSRCCOPY	Ternary raster op	0033 0008	3342344	Dest = (not source)
NOTSRCERASE	Ternary raster op	0011 00A6	1114278	Dest = (not source) AND (not dest)
NULL	Standard definitions	0	0	
NULLREGION	Region flag	1	1	
NULL_BRUSH	Stock logical object	5	5	
NULL_PEN	Stock logical object	8	8	
NUMBRUSHES	Getdevicecaps device parameter	10	16	
NUMCOLORS	Getdevicecaps device parameter	18	24	
NUMFONTS	Getdevicecaps device parameter	16	22	
NUMMARKERS	Getdevicecaps device parameter	14	20	
NUMPENS	Getdevicecaps device parameter	12	18	
OBJ_BRUSH	Object definition	2	2	
OBJ_PEN	Object definition	1	1	
OBM_BTNCORNERS	OEM definition	7FF6	32758	
OBM_BTSIZE	OEM definition	7FF9	32761	
OBM_CHECK	OEM definition	7FF8	32760	
OBM_CHECKBOXES	OEM definition	7FF7	32759	
OBM_CLOSE	OEM definition	7FFF	32767	
OBM_DNARROW	OEM definition	7FFC	32764	
OBM_LFARROW	OEM definition	7FFA	32762	
OBM_REDUCE*	OEM definition	7FF5	32757	
OBM_RESTORE*	OEM definition	7FF3	32755	
OBM_RGARROW	OEM definition	7FFB	32763	
OBM_SIZE	OEM definition	7FFE	32766	
OBM_UPARROW	OEM definition	7FFD	32765	
OBM_ZOOM*	OEM definition	7FF4	32756	
OCR_CROSS	OEM definition	7F03	32515	
OCR_IBEAM	OEM definition	7F01	32513	
OCR_ICON	OEM definition	7F81	32641	
OCR_NORMAL	OEM definition	7F00	32512	
OCR_SIZE	OEM definition	7F80	32640	
OCR_SIZEALL*	OEM definition	7F86	32646	
OCR_SIZENESW*	OEM definition	7F83	32643	
OCR_SIZENS*	OEM definition	7F85	32645	
OCR_SIZENWSE*	OEM definition	7F82	32642	
OCR_SIZEWE*	OEM definition	7F84	32644	
OCR_UP	OEM definition	7F04	32516	
OCR_WAIT	OEM definition	7F02	32514	
ODDPARITY	Dcb field definition	1	1	
OEM_CHARSET	Logical font constant	FF	255	
OEM_FIXED_FONT	Stock logical object	A	10	
OF_CANCEL	OpenFile flag	800	2048	
OF_CREATE	OpenFile flag	1000	4096	
OF_DELETE	OpenFile flag	200	512	
OF_EXIST	OpenFile flag	4000	16384	
OF_PARSE	OpenFile flag	100	256	
OF_PROMPT	OpenFile flag	2000	8192	
OF_READ	OpenFile flag	0	0	

(Continued)

Table 6.37. Continued

Defined Name	Used As	Hex Value	Decimal Value	Comments
OF_READWRITE	OpenFile flag	2	2	
OF_REOPEN	OpenFile flag	8000	32768	
OF_VERIFY	OpenFile flag	400	1024	
OF_WRITE	OpenFile flag	1	1	
OIC_BANG	OEM definition	7F03	32515	
OIC_HAND	OEM definition	7F01	32513	
OIC_NOTE	OEM definition	7F04	32516	
OIC_QUES	OEM definition	7F02	32514	
OIC_SAMPLE	OEM definition	7F00	32512	
ONE5STOPBITS	Dcb field definition	1	1	
ONESTOPBIT	Dcb field definition	0	0	
OPAQUE	GDI background mode	2	2	
OUT_CHARACTER_PRECIS	Logical font constant	2	2	
OUT_DEFAULT_PRECIS	Logical font constant	0	0	
OUT_STRING_PRECIS	Logical font constant	1	1	
OUT_STROKE_PRECIS	Logical font constant	3	3	
PASSTHROUGH*	GDI escape code	13	19	
PATCOPY	Ternary raster op	00F0 0021	15728673	Dest = pattern
PATINVERT	Ternary raster op	005A 0049	5898313	Dest = pattern XOR dest
PATPAINT	Ternary raster op	00FB 0A09	16452105	Dest = DPSnoo
PC_INTERIORS	Device capability mask	80	128	
PC_NONE	Device capability mask	0	0	
PC_POLYGON	Device capability mask	1	1	
PC_RECTANGLE	Device capability mask	2	2	
PC_SCANLINE	Device capability mask	8	8	
PC_STYLED	Device capability mask	20	32	
PC_TRAPEZOID	Device capability mask	4	4	
PC_WIDE	Device capability mask	10	16	
PC_WIDESTYLED	Device capability mask	40	64	
PDEVICESIZE	Getdevicecaps device parameter	1A	26	
PLANES	Getdevicecaps device parameter	E	14	
PM_NOREMOVE*	Peekmessage options	0	0	
PM_NOYIELD*	Peekmessage options	2	2	
PM_REMOVE*	Peekmessage options	1	1	
POLYGONALCAPS	Getdevicecaps device parameter	20	32	
PR_JOBSTATUS	Spooler wparm class	0	0	
PROOF_QUALITY	Logical font constant	2	2	
PS_DASH	Pen style	1	1	
PS_DASHDOT	Pen style	3	3	
PS_DASHDOTDOT	Pen style	4	4	
PS_DOT	Pen style	2	2	
PS_NULL	Pen style	5	5	
PS_SOLID	Pen style	0	0	
QUERYESCSUPPORT	GDI escape	8	8	
R2_BLACK	Binary raster op	1	1	O
R2_COPYPEN	Binary raster op	13	13	P
R2_MASKNOTPEN	Binary raster op	3	3	DPna
R2_MASKPEN	Binary raster op	9	9	DPa
R2_MASKPENNOT	Binary raster op	5	5	PDna
R2_MERGENOTPEN	Binary raster op	12	12	DPno
R2_MERGEPEN	Binary raster op	15	15	DPo
R2_MERGEPENNOT	Binary raster op	14	14	PDno
R2_NOP	Binary raster op	11	11	D
R2_NOT	Binary raster op	6	6	Dn
R2_NOTCOPYPEN	Binary raster op	4	4	PN
R2_NOTMASKPEN	Binary raster op	8	8	DPan
R2_NOTMERGEPEN	Binary raster op	2	2	DPon
R2_NOTXORPEN	Binary raster op	10	10	DPxn
R2_WHITE	Binary raster op	16	16	1
R2_XORPEN	Binary raster op	7	7	DPx
RASTERCAPS	Getdevicecaps device parameter	26	38	
RASTER_FONTTYPE	Enumfont mask	1	1	
RC_BANDING	Device capability mask	2	2	
RC_BITBLT	Device capability mask	1	1	
RC_BITMAP64*	Device capability mask	8	8	
RC_SCALING	Device capability mask	4	4	
RELATIVE	GDI coordinate mode	2	2	
RESETDEV	Comm escape function	7	7	
RGN_AND	Combinergn style	1	1	
RGN_COPY	Combinergn style	5	5	
RGN_DIFF	Combinergn style	4	4	
RGN_OR	Combinergn style	2	2	
RGN_XOR	Combinergn style	3	3	
RT_ACCELERATOR	Predefined resource type	9	9	MAKEINTRESOURCE (9)
RT_BITMAP	Predefined resource type	2	2	MAKEINTRESOURCE (2)
RT_CURSOR	Predefined resource type	1	1	MAKEINTRESOURCE (1)

(Continued)

Table 6.37. Continued

Defined Name	Used As	Hex Value	Decimal Value	Comments
RT_DIALOG	Predefined resource type	5	5	MAKEINTRESOURCE (5)
RT_FONT	Predefined resource type	8	8	MAKEINTRESOURCE (8)
RT_FONTDIR	Predefined resource type	7	7	MAKEINTRESOURCE (7)
RT_ICON	Predefined resource type	3	3	MAKEINTRESOURCE (3)
RT_MENU	Predefined resource type	4	4	MAKEINTRESOURCE (4)
RT_RCDATA*	Predefined resource type	A	10	MAKEINTRESOURCE(10)
RT_STRING	Predefined resource type	6	6	MAKEINTRESOURCE (6)
SBS_BOTTOMALIGN*	Scroll bar style	4	4	
SBS_HORZ*	Scroll bar style	0	0	
SBS_LEFTALIGN*	Scroll bar style	2	2	
SBS_RIGHTALIGN*	Scroll bar style	4	4	
SBS_SIZEBOX*	Scroll bar style	8	8	
SBS_SIZEBOXBOTTOMRIGHTALIGN*	Scroll bar style	4	4	
SBS_SIZEBOXTOPLEFTALIGN*	Scroll bar style	2	2	
SBS_TOPALIGN*	Scroll bar style	2	2	
SBS_VERT*	Scroll bar style	1	1	
SB_BOTH*	Scroll bar constant	3	3	
SB_BOTTOM	Scroll bar constant	7	7	
SB_CTL	Scroll bar constant	2	2	
SB_ENDSCROLL	Scroll bar constant	8	8	
SB_HORZ	Scroll bar constant	0	0	
SB_LINEDOWN	Scroll bar constant	1	1	
SB_LINEUP	Scroll bar constant	0	0	
SB_PAGEDOWN	Scroll bar constant	3	3	
SB_PAGEUP	Scroll bar constant	2	2	
SB_THUMBPOSITION	Scroll bar constant	4	4	
SB_THUMBTRACK	Scroll bar constant	5	5	
SB_TOP	Scroll bar constant	6	6	
SB_VERT	Scroll bar constant	1	1	
SC_ARRANGE*	System menu command	F110	61712	
SC_CLOSE	System menu command	F060	61536	
SC_HSCROLL	System menu command	F080	61568	
SC_ICON	System menu command	F020	61472	
SC_KEYMENU	System menu command	F100	61696	
SC_MAXIMIZE*	System menu command	F030	61488	
SC_MINIMIZE*	System menu command	F020	61472	
SC_MOUSEMENU	System menu command	F090	61584	
SC_MOVE	System menu command	F010	61456	
SC_NEXTWINDOW	System menu command	F040	61504	
SC_PREVWINDOW	System menu command	F050	61520	
SC_RESTORE*	System menu command	F120	61728	
SC_SIZE	System menu command	F000	61440	
SC_VSCROLL	System menu command	F070	61552	
SC_ZOOM	System menu command	F030	61488	
SELECTPAPERSOURCE*	GDI escape code	12	18	
SETABORTPROC	GDI escape	9	9	
SETCOLORTABLE	GDI escape	4	4	
SETCOPYCOUNT*	GDI escape code	11	17	
SETDTR	Comm escape function	5	5	
SETENDCAP	Metafile comment esc.	15	21	
SETKERNTRACK*	GDI escape code	302	770	
SETLINEJOIN*	GDI escape code	16	22	
SETMITERLIMIT*	GDI escape code	17	23	
SETRTS	Comm escape function	3	3	
SETXOFF	Comm escape function	1	1	
SETXON	Comm escape function	2	2	
SHIFTJIS_CHARSET*	Logical font constant	80	128	
SHOW_FULLSCREEN	Showwindow command	3	3	
SHOW_ICONWINDOW	Showwindow command	2	2	
SHOW_OPENNOACTIVATE	Showwindow command	4	4	
SHOW_OPENWINDOW	Showwindow command	1	1	
SIMPLEREGION	Region flag	2	2	
SIZEFULLSCREEN	Size message command	2	2	
SIZEICONIC	Size message command	1	1	
SIZENORMAL	Size message command	0	0	
SIZEZOOMHIDE	Size message command	4	4	
SIZEZOOMSHOW	Size message command	3	3	
SM_CMETRICS*	GetSystemMetrics code	24	36	
SM_CXBORDER	GetSystemMetrics code	5	5	
SM_CXCURSOR	GetSystemMetrics code	D	13	
SM_CXDLGFRAME	GetSystemMetrics code	7	7	
SM_CXFRAME*	GetSystemMetrics code	20	32	
SM_CXFULLSCREEN	GetSystemMetrics code	10	16	
SM_CXHSCROLL	GetSystemMetrics code	15	21	
SM_CXHTHUMB	GetSystemMetrics code	A	10	
SM_CXICON	GetSystemMetrics code	B	11	
SM_CXMIN*	GetSystemMetrics code	1C	28	

(Continued)

Table 6.37. Continued

Defined Name	Used As	Hex Value	Decimal Value	Comments
SM_CXMINTRACK*	GetSystemMetrics code	22	34	
SM_CXSCREEN	GetSystemMetrics code	0	0	
SM_CXSIZE*	GetSystemMetrics code	1E	30	
SM_CXVSCROLL	GetSystemMetrics code	2	2	
SM_CYBORDER	GetSystemMetrics code	6	6	
SM_CYCAPTION	GetSystemMetrics code	4	4	
SM_CYDLGFRAME	GetSystemMetrics code	8	8	
SM_CYFRAME*	GetSystemMetrics code	21	33	
SM_CYFULLSCREEN	GetSystemMetrics code	11	17	
SM_CYHSCROLL	GetSystemMetrics code	3	3	
SM_CYICON	GetSystemMetrics code	C	12	
SM_CYICONSLOT*	GetSystemMetrics code	1B	27	
SM_CYKANJIWINDOW	GetSystemMetrics code	12	18	
SM_CYMENU	GetSystemMetrics code	F	15	
SM_CYMIN*	GetSystemMetrics code	1D	29	
SM_CYMINTRACK*	GetSystemMetrics code	23	35	
SM_CYSCREEN	GetSystemMetrics code	1	1	
SM_CYSIZE*	GetSystemMetrics code	1F	31	
SM_CYVSCROLL	GetSystemMetrics code	14	20	
SM_CYVTHUMB	GetSystemMetrics code	9	9	
SM_DEBUG	GetSystemMetrics code	16	22	
SM_FULLSCREEN	GetSystemMetrics code	18	24	
SM_MOUSEPRESENT	GetSystemMetrics code	13	19	
SM_SWAPBUTTON	GetSystemMetrics code	17	23	
SM_CYCURSOR	GetSystemMetrics code	E	14	
SPACEPARITY	Dcb field definition	4	4	
SP_APPABORT	Spooler error code	FFFE	-2	
SP_ERROR	Spooler error code	FFFF	-1	
SP_NOTREPORTED	Spooler error code	4000	16384	
SP_OUTOFDISK	Spooler error code	FFFC	-4	
SP_OUTOFMEMORY	Spooler error code	FFFB	-5	
SP_USERABORT	Spooler error code	FFFD	-3	
SRCAND	Ternary raster op	0088 00C6	8913094	Dest = source AND dest
SRCCOPY	Ternary raster op	00CC 0020	13369376	Dest=source
SRCERASE	Ternary raster op	0044 0328	4457256	Dest = source AND (not dest)
SRCINVERT	Ternary raster op	0066 0046	6684742	Dest = source XOR dest
SRCPAINT	Ternary raster op	00EE 0086	15597702	Dest=source OR dest
SS_BLACKFRAME	Static control constant	7	7	
SS_BLACKRECT	Static control constant	4	4	
SS_CENTER	Static control constant	1	1	
SS_GRAYFRAME	Static control constant	8	8	
SS_GRAYRECT	Static control constant	5	5	
SS_ICON	Static control constant	3	3	
SS_LEFT	Static control constant	0	0	
SS_NOPREFIX*	Static control constant	80	128	
SS_RIGHT	Static control constant	2	2	
SS_SIMPLE*	Static control constant	13	11	
SS_USERITEM	Static control constant	A	10	
SS_WHITEFRAME	Static control constant	9	9	
SS_WHITERECT	Static control constant	6	6	
STARTDOC	GDI escape	A	10	
STRETCHBLT*	GDI escape code	800	2048	
ST_BEGINSWP*		0	0	
ST_ENDSWP*		1	1	
SWP_DRAWFRAME*	SetWindow position flag	20	32	
SWP_HIDEWINDOW*	SetWindow position flag	80	128	
SWP_NOACTIVATE*	SetWindow position flag	10	16	
SWP_NOCOPYBITS*	SetWindow position flag	100	256	
SWP_NOMOVE*	SetWindow position flag	2	2	
SWP_NOREDRAW*	SetWindow position flag	8	8	
SWP_NOREPOSITION*	SetWindow position flag	200	512	
SWP_NOSIZE*	SetWindow position flag	1	1	
SWP_NOZORDER*	SetWindow position flag	4	4	
SWP_SHOWWINDOW*	SetWindow position flag	40	64	
SW_HIDE*	Showwindow message ID	0	0	
SW_MAXIMIZE*	Showwindow message ID	3	3	
SW_MINIMIZE*	Showwindow message ID	6	6	
SW_NORMAL*	Showwindow message ID	1	1	
SW_OTHERUNZOOM	Showwindow message ID	4	4	
SW_OTHERZOOM	Showwindow message ID	2	2	
SW_PARENTCLOSING	Showwindow message ID	1	1	
SW_PARENTOPENING	Showwindow message ID	3	3	
SW_RESTORE*	Showwindow message ID	1	1	
SW_SHOW*	Showwindow message ID	5	5	
SW_SHOWMAXIMIZED*	Showwindow message ID	3	3	
SW_SHOWMINIMIZED*	Showwindow message ID	2	2	
SW_SHOWMINNOACTIVE*	Showwindow message ID	7	7	

(Continued)

Table 6.37. Continued

Defined Name	Used As	Hex Value	Decimal Value	Comments
SW_SHOWNA*	Showwindow message ID	8	8	
SW_SHOWNOACTIVE*	Showwindow message ID	4	4	
SW_SHOWNORMAL*	Showwindow message ID	1	1	
SYSTEM_FONT	Stock logical object	D	13	
S_ALLTHRESHOLD*	WaitSoundState constant	2	2	
S_LEGATO	Accent mode constant	1	1	
S_NORMAL	Accent mode constant	0	0	
S_PERIOD1024	SetSoundNoise source	1	1	
S_PERIOD2048	SetSoundNoise source	2	2	
S_PERIOD512	SetSoundNoise source	0	0	
S_PERIODVOICE	SetSoundNoise source	3	3	
S_QUEUEEMPTY	WaitSoundState constant	0	0	
S_SERBDNT	SetSoundNoise source	FFFB	-5	
S_SERDCC	SetSoundNoise source	FFF9	-7	
S_SERDDR	SetSoundNoise source	FFF2	-14	
S_SERDFQ	SetSoundNoise source	FFF3	-13	
S_SERDLN	SetSoundNoise source	FFFA	-6	
S_SERDMD	SetSoundNoise source	FFF6	-10	
S_SERDPT	SetSoundNoise source	FFF4	-12	
S_SERDSH	SetSoundNoise source	FFF5	-11	
S_SERDSR	SetSoundNoise source	FFF1	-15	
S_SERDST	SetSoundNoise source	FFF0	-16	
S_SERDTP	SetSoundNoise source	FFF8	-8	
S_SERDVL	SetSoundNoise source	FFF7	-9	
S_SERDVNA	SetSoundNoise source	FFFF	-1	
S_SERMACT	SetSoundNoise source	FFFD	-3	
S_SEROFM	SetSoundNoise source	FFFE	-2	
S_SERQFUL	SetSoundNoise source	FFFC	-4	
S_STACCATO	Accent mode constant	2	2	
S_THRESHOLD	WaitSoundState constant	1	1	
S_WHITE1024	SetSoundNoise source	5	5	
S_WHITE2048	SetSoundNoise source	6	6	
S_WHITE512	SetSoundNoise source	4	4	
S_WHITEVOICE	SetSoundNoise source	7	7	
TA_BASELINE*	Text alignment option	18	24	
TA_BOTTOM*	Text alignment option	8	8	
TA_CENTER*	Text alignment option	6	6	
TA_LEFT*	Text alignment option	0	0	
TA_NOUPDATECP*	Text alignment option	0	0	
TA_RIGHT*	Text alignment option	2	2	
TA_TOP*	Text alignment option	0	0	
TA_UPDATECP*	Text alignment option	1	1	
TC_CP_STROKE	Device capability mask	4	4	
TC_CR_90	Device capability mask	8	8	
TC_CR_ANY	Device capability mask	10	16	
TC_EA_DOUBLE	Device capability mask	200	512	
TC_IA_ABLE	Device capability mask	400	1024	
TC_OP_CHARACTER	Device capability mask	1	1	
TC_OP_STROKE	Device capability mask	2	2	
TC_RA_ABLE	Device capability mask	2000	8192	
TC_RESERVED	Device capability mask	8000	32768	
TC_SA_CONTIN	Device capability mask	100	256	
TC_SA_DOUBLE	Device capability mask	40	64	
TC_SA_INTEGER	Device capability mask	80	128	
TC_SF_X_YINDEP	Device capability mask	20	32	
TC_SO_ABLE	Device capability mask	1000	4096	
TC_UA_ABLE	Device capability mask	800	2048	
TC_VA_ABLE	Device capability mask	4000	16384	
TECHNOLOGY	Getdevicecaps device parameter	2	2	
TEXTCAPS	Getdevicecaps device parameter	22	34	
TRANSPARENT	GDI background mode	1	1	
TRUE	Standard definitions	1	1	
TWOSTOPBITS	Dcb field definition	2	2	
VARIABLE_PITCH	Logical font constant	2	2	
VERTRES	Getdevicecaps device parameter	A	10	
VERTSIZE	Getdevicecaps device parameter	6	6	
VK_ACCEPT*	Virtual key	1E	30	
VK_ADD	Standard set virtual key	6B	107	
VK_BACK	Standard set virtual key	8	8	
VK_CANCEL	Standard set virtual key	3	3	
VK_CAPITAL	Standard set virtual key	14	20	
VK_CLEAR	Standard set virtual key	C	12	
VK_CONTROL	Standard set virtual key	11	17	
VK_COPY	Standard set virtual key	2C	44	
VK_CONVERT*	Virtual key	1C	28	
VK_DECIMAL	Standard set virtual key	6E	110	
VK_DELETE	Standard set virtual key	2E	46	
VK_DIVIDE	Standard set virtual key	6F	111	

(Continued)

Table 6.37. Continued

Defined Name	Used As	Hex Value	Decimal Value	Comments
VK_DOWN	Standard set virtual key	28	40	
VK_END	Standard set virtual key	23	35	
VK_ESCAPE	Standard set virtual key	1B	27	
VK_EXECUTE	Standard set virtual key	2B	43	
VK_F1	Standard set virtual key	70	112	
VK_F10	Standard set virtual key	79	121	
VK_F11	Standard set virtual key	7A	122	
VK_F12	Standard set virtual key	7B	123	
VK_F13	Standard set virtual key	7C	124	
VK_F14	Standard set virtual key	7D	125	
VK_F15	Standard set virtual key	7E	126	
VK_F16	Standard set virtual key	7F	127	
VK_F2	Standard set virtual key	71	113	
VK_F3	Standard set virtual key	72	114	
VK_F4	Standard set virtual key	73	115	
VK_F5	Standard set virtual key	74	116	
VK_F6	Standard set virtual key	75	117	
VK_F7	Standard set virtual key	76	118	
VK_F8	Standard set virtual key	77	119	
VK_F9	Standard set virtual key	78	120	
VK_HELP	Standard set virtual key	2F	47	
VK_HIRAGANA*	Virtual key	18	24	
VK_HOME	Standard set virtual key	24	36	
VK_INSERT	Standard set virtual key	2D	45	
VK_KANA*	Virtual key	15	21	
VK_KANJI*	Virtual key	19	25	
VK_LBUTTON	Standard set virtual key	1	1	
VK_LEFT	Standard set virtual key	25	37	
VK_MBUTTON	Standard set virtual key	4	4	
VK_MENU	Standard set virtual key	12	18	
VK_MODECHANGE*	Virtual key	1F	31	
VK_MULTIPLY	Standard set virtual key	6A	106	
VK_NEXT	Standard set virtual key	22	34	
VK_NONCONVERT*	Virtual key	1D	29	
VK_NUMLOCK	Standard set virtual key	90	144	
VK_NUMPAD0	Standard set virtual key	60	96	
VK_NUMPAD1	Standard set virtual key	61	97	
VK_NUMPAD2	Standard set virtual key	62	98	
VK_NUMPAD3	Standard set virtual key	63	99	
VK_NUMPAD4	Standard set virtual key	64	100	
VK_NUMPAD5	Standard set virtual key	65	101	
VK_NUMPAD6	Standard set virtual key	66	102	
VK_NUMPAD7	Standard set virtual key	67	103	
VK_NUMPAD8	Standard set virtual key	68	104	
VK_NUMPAD9	Standard set virtual key	69	105	
VK_PAUSE	Standard set virtual key	13	19	
VK_PRINT	Standard set virtual key	2A	42	
VK_PRIOR	Standard set virtual key	21	33	
VK_RBUTTON	Standard set virtual key	2	2	
VK_RETURN	Standard set virtual key	D	13	
VK_RIGHT	Standard set virtual key	27	39	
VK_ROMAJI*	Virtual key	16	22	
VK_SELECT	Standard set virtual key	29	41	
VK_SEPARATOR	Standard set virtual key	6C	108	
VK_SHIFT	Standard set virtual key	10	16	
VK_SPACE	Standard set virtual key	20	32	
VK_SUBTRACT	Standard set virtual key	6D	109	
VK_TAB	Standard set virtual key	9	9	
VK_UP	Standard set virtual key	26	38	
VK_ZENKAKU*	Virtual key	17	23	
WC_DEFWINDOWPROC*	Window manager hook code	3	3	
WC_DRAWCAPTION*	Window manager hook code	7	7	
WC_INIT*	Window manager hook code	1	1	
WC_MINMAX*	Window manager hook code	4	4	
WC_MOVE*	Window manager hook code	5	5	
WC_SIZE*	Window manager hook code	6	6	
WC_SWP*	Window manager hook code	2	2	
WHITENESS	Ternary raster op	00FF 0062	16711778	Dest = WHITE
WHITEONBLACK	Stretchblt mode	2	2	
WHITE_BRUSH	Stock logical object	0	0	
WHITE_PEN	Stock logical object	6	6	
WH_CALLWNDPROC	Setwindowshook code	4	4	
WH_CBT*	Window hook	5	5	
WH_GETMESSAGE	Setwindowshook code	3	3	
WH_JOURNALPLAYBACK	Setwindowshook code	1	1	
WH_JOURNALRECORD	Setwindowshook code	0	0	
WH_KEYBOARD	Setwindowshook code	2	2	
WH_MSGFILTER	Setwindowshook code	FFFF	-1	

(Continued)

Table 6.37. Continued

Defined Name	Used As	Hex Value	Decimal Value	Comments
WH_SYSMSGFILTER*	Window hook	6	6	
WH_WINDOWMGR*	Window hook	7	7	
WINDING	Polyfill mode	2	2	
WM_ACTIVATE	Window procedure message ID	6	6	
WM_ACTIVATEAPP	Window procedure message ID	1C	28	
WM_ASKCBFORMATNAME	Window procedure message ID	30C	780	
WM_CANCELMODE	Window procedure message ID	1F	31	
WM_CHANGECBCHAIN	Window procedure message ID	30D	781	
WM_CHAR	Window procedure message ID	102	258	
WM_CHILDACTIVATE*	Window procedure message ID	22	34	
WM_CLEAR	Window procedure message ID	303	771	
WM_CLOSE	Window procedure message ID	10	16	
WM_COMMAND	Window procedure message ID	111	273	
WM_CONVERTREQUEST	Window procedure message ID	10A	266	
WM_CONVERTRESULT	Window procedure message ID	10B	267	
WM_COPY	Window procedure message ID	301	769	
WM_CREATE	Window procedure message ID	1	1	
WM_CTLCOLOR	Window procedure message ID	19	25	
WM_CUT	Window procedure message ID	300	768	
WM_DEADCHAR	Window procedure message ID	103	259	
WM_DESTROY	Window procedure message ID	2	2	
WM_DESTROYCLIPBOARD	Window procedure message ID	307	775	
WM_DEVMODECHANGE	Window procedure message ID	1B	27	
WM_DRAWCLIPBOARD	Window procedure message ID	308	776	
WM_ENABLE	Window procedure message ID	0A	10	
WM_ENDSESSION	Window procedure message ID	16	22	
WM_ENTERIDLE	Window procedure message ID	121	289	
WM_ERASEBKGND	Window procedure message ID	14	20	
WM_FONTCHANGE	Window procedure message ID	1D	29	
WM_GETDLGCODE	Window procedure message ID	87	135	
WM_GETMINMAXINFO*	Window procedure message ID	24	36	
WM_GETTEXT	Window procedure message ID	D	13	
WM_GETTEXTLENGTH	Window procedure message ID	E	14	
WM_HSCROLL	Window procedure message ID	114	276	
WM_HSCROLLCLIPBOARD	Window procedure message ID	30E	782	
WM_ICONERASEBKGND*	Window procedure message ID	27	39	
WM_INITDIALOG	Window procedure message ID	110	272	
WM_INITMENU	Window procedure message ID	116	278	
WM_INITMENUPOPUP	Window procedure message ID	117	279	
WM_KANJIFIRST	Window procedure message ID	280	640	
WM_KANJILAST	Window procedure message ID	29F	671	
WM_KEYDOWN	Window procedure message ID	100	256	
WM_KEYFIRST	Window procedure message ID	100	256	
WM_KEYLAST	Window procedure message ID	107	263	
WM_KEYUP	Window procedure message ID	101	257	
WM_KILLFOCUS	Window procedure message ID	8	8	
WM_LBUTTONDBLCLK	Window procedure message ID	203	515	
WM_LBUTTONDOWN	Window procedure message ID	201	513	
WM_LBUTTONUP	Window procedure message ID	202	514	
WM_MBUTTONDBLCLK	Window procedure message ID	209	521	
WM_MBUTTONDOWN	Window procedure message ID	207	519	
WM_MBUTTONUP	Window procedure message ID	208	520	
WM_MENUCHAR*	Window procedure message ID	120	521	
WM_MENUSELECT*	Window procedure message ID	11F	522	
WM_MOUSEACTIVATE*	Window procedure message ID	21	33	
WM_MOUSEFIRST	Window procedure message ID	200	512	
WM_MOUSELAST	Window procedure message ID	209	521	
WM_MOUSEMOVE	Window procedure message ID	200	512	
WM_MOVE	Window procedure message ID	3	3	
WM_NCACTIVATE	Window procedure message ID	86	134	
WM_NCCALCSIZE	Window procedure message ID	83	131	
WM_NCCREATE	Window procedure message ID	81	129	
WM_NCDESTROY	Window procedure message ID	82	130	
WM_NCHITTEST	Window procedure message ID	84	132	
WM_NCLBUTTONDBLCLK	Window procedure message ID	A3	163	
WM_NCLBUTTONDOWN	Window procedure message ID	A1	161	
WM_NCLBUTTONUP	Window procedure message ID	A2	162	
WM_NCMBUTTONDBLCLK	Window procedure message ID	A9	169	
WM_NCMBUTTONDOWN	Window procedure message ID	A7	167	
WM_NCMBUTTONUP	Window procedure message ID	A8	168	
WM_NCMOUSEMOVE	Window procedure message ID	A0	160	
WM_NCPAINT	Window procedure message ID	85	133	
WM_NCRBUTTONDBLCLK	Window procedure message ID	A6	166	
WM_NCRBUTTONDOWN	Window procedure message ID	A4	164	
WM_NCRBUTTONUP	Window procedure message ID	A5	165	
WM_NEXTDLGCTL*	Window procedure message ID	28	40	
WM_NULL	Window procedure message ID	0	0	
WM_PAINT	Window procedure message ID	F	15	

(Continued)

Table 6.37. Continued

Defined Name	Used As	Hex Value	Decimal Value	Comments
WM_PAINTCLIPBOARD	Window procedure message ID	309	777	
WM_PAINTICON*	Window procedure message ID	26	38	
WM_PASTE	Window procedure message ID	302	770	
WM_QUERYENDSESSION	Window procedure message ID	11	17	
WM_QUERYOPEN	Window procedure message ID	13	19	
WM_QUEUESYNC*	Window procedure message ID	23	35	
WM_QUIT	Window procedure message ID	12	18	
WM_RBUTTONDBLCKL	Window procedure message ID	206	518	
WM_RBUTTONDOWN	Window procedure message ID	204	516	
WM_RBUTTONUP	Window procedure message ID	205	517	
WM_RENDERALLFORMATS	Window procedure message ID	306	774	
WM_RENDERFORMAT	Window procedure message ID	305	773	
WM_SETCURSOR*	Window procedure message ID	20	32	
WM_SETFOCUS	Window procedure message ID	7	7	
WM_SETREDRAW	Window procedure message ID	B	11	
WM_SETTEXT	Window procedure message ID	C	12	
WM_SETVISIBLE	Window procedure message ID	9	9	
WM_SHOWWINDOW	Window procedure message ID	18	24	
WM_SIZE	Window procedure message ID	5	5	
WM_SIZECLIPBOARD	Window procedure message ID	30B	779	
WM_SIZEWAIT	Window procedure message ID	4	4	
WM_SPOOLERSTATUS	Window procedure message ID	2A	42	
WM_SYNCPAINT*	Window procedure message ID	88	136	
WM_SYNCTASK*	Window procedure message ID	89	137	
WM_SYSCHAR	Window procedure message ID	106	262	
WM_SYSCOLORCHANGE	Window procedure message ID	15	21	
WM_SYSCOMMAND	Window procedure message ID	112	274	
WM_SYSDEADCHAR	Window procedure message ID	107	263	
WM_SYSKEYDOWN	Window procedure message ID	104	260	
WM_SYSKEYUP	Window procedure message ID	105	261	
WM_SYSTEMERROR	Window procedure message ID	17	23	
WM_SYSTIMER	Window procedure message ID	118	280	
WM_TIMECHANGE	Window procedure message ID	1E	30	
WM_TIMER	Window procedure message ID	113	275	
WM_UNDO	Window procedure message ID	304	772	
WM_USER	Window procedure message ID	400	1024	First application window message
WM_VSCROLL	Window procedure message ID	115	277	
WM_VSCROLLCLIPBOARD	Window procedure message ID	30A	778	
WM_WININICHANGE	Window procedure message ID	1A	26	
WM_YOMICHAR	Window procedure message ID	108	264	
WS_BORDER	Window style	0080 0000	8388608	
WS_CAPTION	Window style	00C0 0000	12582912	
WS_CHILD	Window style	4000 0000	1073741824	
WS_CHILDWINDOW*	Window style	4000 0000	1073741824	
WS_CLIPCHILDREN	Window style	0200 0000	33554432	
WS_CLIPSIBLINGS	Window style	0400 0000	67108864	
WS_DISABLED	Window style	0800 0000	134217728	
WS_DLGFRAME	Window style	0040 0000	4194304	
WS_GROUP	Window style	0002 0000	131072	
WS_HSCROLL	Window style	0010 0000	1048576	
WS_ICONIC	Window style	2000 0000	536870912	Defined as WS_MINIMIZE
WS_ICONICPOPUP*	Window style	C000 0000	3221225472	
WS_MAXIMIZE*	Window style	0100 0000	16777216	
WS_MAXIMIZEBOX*	Window style	0001 0000	65536	
WS_MINIMIZE	Window style	2000 0000	536870912	
WS_MINIMIZEBOX*	Window style	0002 0000	131072	
WS_OVERLAPPED*	Window style	0	0	
WS_OVERLAPPEDWINDOW*	Window style	00CC 0000	13369344	
WS_POPUP	Window style	8000 0000	-2147483648	
WS_POPUPWINDOW*	Window style	8088 0000	2156396544	
WS_SIZEBOX	Window style	0004 0000	262144	
WS_SYSMENU	Window style	0008 0000	524288	
WS_TABSTOP	Window style	0001 0000	65536	
WS_THICKFRAME*	Window style	0004 0000	262144	
WS_TILED	Window style	0	0	
WS_TILEDWINDOW*	Window style	00CC 0000	13369344	
WS_VISIBLE	Window style	1000 0000	268435456	
WS_VSCROLL	Window style	0020 0000	2097152	

Version Info: *Applies to all versions of Windows beginning with 2.0

Source: WINDOWS.H file in development kit

See Also: 6.38. Include File Constants Definitions by Use

6.38. INCLUDE FILE CONSTANTS DEFINITIONS BY USE

Defined Name	Used As	Hex Value	Decimal Value	Comments
S_LEGATO	Accent mode constant	1	1	
S_NORMAL	Accent mode constant	0	0	
S_STACCATO	Accent mode constant	2	2	
R2_BLACK	Binary raster op	1	1	O
R2_COPYPEN	Binary raster op	13	13	P
R2_MASKNOTPEN	Binary raster op	3	3	DPna
R2_MASKPEN	Binary raster op	9	9	DPa
R2_MASKPENNOT	Binary raster op	5	5	PDna
R2_MERGENOTPEN	Binary raster op	12	12	DPno
R2_MERGEPEN	Binary raster op	15	15	DPo
R2_MERGEPENNOT	Binary raster op	14	14	PDno
R2_NOP	Binary raster op	11	11	D
R2_NOT	Binary raster op	6	6	Dn
R2_NOTCOPYPEN	Binary raster op	4	4	PN
R2_NOTMASKPEN	Binary raster op	8	8	DPan
R2_NOTMERGEPEN	Binary raster op	2	2	DPon
R2_NOTXORPEN	Binary raster op	10	10	DPxn
R2_WHITE	Binary raster op	16	16	1
R2_XORPEN	Binary raster op	7	7	DPx
BS_HATCHED	Brush style	2	2	
BS_HOLLOW	Brush style	1	1	Defined as BS_NULL
BS_NULL	Brush style	1	1	
BS_PATTERN	Brush style	3	3	
BS_SOLID	Brush style	0	0	
BS_3STATE	Button control style	5	5	
BS_AUTO3STATE	Button control style	6	6	
BS_AUTOCHECKBOX	Button control style	3	3	
BS_CHECKBOX	Button control style	2	2	
BS_DEFPUSHBUTTON	Button control style	1	1	
BS_GROUPBOX	Button control style	7	7	
BS_INDEXED*	Button control style	4	4	
BS_PUSHBUTTON	Button control style	0	0	
BS_RADIOBUTTON	Button control style	4	4	
BS_USERBUTTON	Button control style	8	8	
BS_AUTORADIOBUTTON*	Button style	9	9	
BS_LEFTTEXT*	Button style	20	32	
BS_PUSHBOX*	Button style	A	10	
GCL_MENUNAME	Class field offset	FFF8	-8	
GCL_WNDPROC	Class field offset	FFEA	-24	
GCW_CBCLSEXTRA	Class field offset	FFEC	-22	
GCW_CBWNDEXTRA	Class field offset	FFEE	-20	
GCW_HBRBACKGROUND	Class field offset	FFF6	-10	
GCW_HCURSOR	Class field offset	FFF4	-12	
GCW_HICON	Class field offset	FFF2	-14	
GCW_HMODULE	Class field offset	FFF0	-16	
GCW_STYLE	Class field offset	FFE8	-26	
CS_BYTEALIGNCLIENT*	Class style	1000	4096	
CS_BYTEALIGNWINDOW*	Class style	2000	8192	
CS_CLASSDC	Class style	40	64	
CS_DBLCLKS	Class style	8	8	
CS_HREDRAW	Class style	2	2	
CS_KEYCUTWINDOW	Class style	4	4	
CS_MENUPOPUP	Class style	80	128	
CS_NOCLOSE*	Class style	200	512	
CS_NOKEYCUT	Class style	100	512	
CS_OEMCHARS	Class style	10	16	
CS_OWNDC	Class style	20	32	
CS_PARENTDC*	Class style	80	128	
CS_SAVEBITS*	Class style	800	2048	
CS_VREDRAW	Class style	1	1	
CF_BITMAP	Clipboard format	2	2	
CF_DIF	Clipboard format	5	5	
CF_DSPBITMAP	Clipboard format	82	130	
CF_DSPMETAFILEPICT	Clipboard format	83	131	
CF_DSPTEXT	Clipboard format	81	129	
CF_GDIOBJFIRST	Clipboard format	300	768	
CF_GDIOBJLAST	Clipboard format	3FF	1023	
CF_METAFILEPICT	Clipboard format	3	3	
CF_OEMTEXT*	Clipboard format	7	7	
CF_OWNERDISPLAY	Clipboard format	80	128	
CF_PRIVATEFIRST	Clipboard format	200	512	
CF_PRIVATELAST	Clipboard format	2FF	767	
CF_SYLK	Clipboard format	4	4	
CF_TEXT	Clipboard format	1	1	

(Continued)

Table 6.38. Continued

Defined Name	Used As	Hex Value	Decimal Value	Comments
CF_TIFF*	Clipboard format	6	6	
COLOR_ACTIVEBORDER*	Color type index	A	10	
COLOR_ACTIVECAPTION	Color type index	2	2	
COLOR_APPWORKSPACE*	Color type index	C	12	
COLOR_BACKGROUND	Color type index	1	1	
COLOR_CAPTIONTEXT	Color type index	9	9	
COLOR_INACTIVEBORDER*	Color type index	B	11	
COLOR_INACTIVECAPTION	Color type index	3	3	
COLOR_MENU	Color type index	4	4	
COLOR_MENUTEXT	Color type index	7	7	
COLOR_SCROLLBAR	Color type index	0	0	
COLOR_WINDOW	Color type index	5	5	
COLOR_WINDOWFRAME	Color type index	6	6	
COLOR_WINDOWTEXT	Color type index	8	8	
CTLCOLOR_BTN	Color type index	3	3	
CTLCOLOR_DLG	Color type index	4	4	
CTLCOLOR_EDIT	Color type index	1	1	
CTLCOLOR_LISTBOX	Color type index	2	2	
CTLCOLOR_MAX	Color type index	8	8	
CTLCOLOR_MSGBOX	Color type index	0	0	
CTLCOLOR_SCROLLBAR	Color type index	5	5	
CTLCOLOR_STATIC	Color type index	6	6	
RGN_AND	Combinergn style	1	1	
RGN_COPY	Combinergn style	5	5	
RGN_DIFF	Combinergn style	4	4	
RGN_OR	Combinergn style	2	2	
RGN_XOR	Combinergn style	3	3	
CE_BREAK	Comm device driver error	10	16	
CE_CTSTO	Comm device driver error	20	32	
CE_DNS	Comm device driver error	800	2048	
CE_DSRTO	Comm device driver error	40	64	
CE_FRAME	Comm device driver error	8	8	
CE_IOE	Comm device driver error	400	1024	
CE_MODE	Comm device driver error	8000	32768	
CE_OOP	Comm device driver error	1000	4096	
CE_OVERRUN	Comm device driver error	2	2	
CE_PTO	Comm device driver error	200	512	
CE_RLSDTO	Comm device driver error	80	128	
CE_RXOVER	Comm device driver error	1	1	
CE_RXPARITY	Comm device driver error	4	4	
CE_TXFULL	Comm device driver error	100	256	
CLRDTR	Comm escape function	6	6	
CLRRTS	Comm escape function	4	4	
RESETDEV	Comm escape function	7	7	
SETDTR	Comm escape function	5	5	
SETRTS	Comm escape function	3	3	
SETXOFF	Comm escape function	1	1	
SETXON	Comm escape function	2	2	
EV_BREAK	Comm event definition	40	64	
EV_CTS	Comm event definition	8	8	
EV_DSR	Comm event definition	10	16	
EV_ERR	Comm event definition	80	128	
EV_PERR	Comm event definition	200	512	
EV_RING	Comm event definition	100	256	
EV_RLSD	Comm event definition	20	32	
EV_RXCHAR	Comm event definition	1	1	
EV_RXFLAG	Comm event definition	2	2	
EV_TXEMPTY	Comm event definition	4	4	
IE_BADID	Comm init error	FFFF	-1	
IE_BAUDRATE	Comm init error	FFF4	-12	
IE_BYTESIZE	Comm init error	FFF5	-11	
IE_DEFAULT	Comm init error	FFFB	-5	
IE_HARDWARE	Comm init error	FFF6	-10	
IE_MEMORY	Comm init error	FFFC	-4	
IE_NOPEN	Comm init error	FFFD	-3	
IE_OPEN	Comm init error	FFFE	-2	
BM_GETCHECK*	Control message	400	1024	
BM_GETSTATE*	Control message	402	1026	
BM_SETCHECK*	Control message	401	1025	
BM_SETSTATE*	Control message	403	1027	
BM_SETSTYLE*	Control message	404	1208	
BN_DOUBLECLICKED*	Control message	5	5	
CP_GETBEEP*	Control panel info	1	1	
CP_GETBORDER*	Control panel info	5	5	
CP_GETMOUSE*	Control panel info	3	3	
CP_KANJIMENU*	Control panel info	8	8	
CP_SETBEEP*	Control panel info	2	2	

(Continued)

Table 6.38. Continued

Defined Name	Used As	Hex Value	Decimal Value	Comments
CP_SETBORDER*	Control panel info	6	6	
CP_SETMOUSE*	Control panel info	4	4	
CP_TIMEOUTS*	Control panel info	7	7	
KNJ_ACCEPT	Conversion function	24	36	
KNJ_CHANGE_UDIC	Conversion function	33	51	
KNJ_CODECONVERT	Conversion function	20	32	
KNJ_CONVERT	Conversion function	21	33	
KNJ_CUT_DEFAULT	Conversion function	7	7	
KNJ_CUT_HIRAGANA	Conversion function	4	4	
KNJ_CUT_JIS1	Conversion function	5	5	
KNJ_CUT_JIS2	Conversion function	6	6	
KNJ_CUT_KATAKANA	Conversion function	3	3	
KNJ_CUT_NEXT	Conversion function	1	1	
KNJ_CUT_PREV	Conversion function	2	2	
KNJ_CUT_TYPED	Conversion function	8	8	
KNJ_END	Conversion function	2	2	
KNJ_GETMODE	Conversion function	11	17	
KNJ_JIS1 to DEFAULT	Conversion function	10	16	
KNJ_JIS1 to JIS1 KATAKANA	Conversion function	14	20	
KNJ_JIS1 to JIS2	Conversion function	13	19	
KNJ_JIS1 to JIS2 HIRAGANA	Conversion function	15	21	
KNJ_JIS1 to JIS2 KATAKANA	Conversion function	16	22	
KNJ_JIS1 to JIS2 OEM	Conversion function	1F	31	
KNJ_JIS2 to JIS2	Conversion function	23	35	
KNJ_LEARN	Conversion function	30	48	
KNJ_LEARN_MODE	Conversion function	10	16	
KNJ_MD_ALPHA	Conversion function	1	1	
KNJ_MD_HALF	Conversion function	4	4	
KNJ_MD_HIRAGANA	Conversion function	2	2	
KNJ_MD_JIS	Conversion function	8	8	
KNJ_MD_SPECIAL	Conversion function	10	16	
KNJ_NEXT	Conversion function	22	34	
KNJ_PREVIOUS	Conversion function	23	35	
KNJ_QUERY	Conversion function	3	3	
KNJ_REGISTER	Conversion function	31	49	
KNJ_REMOVE	Conversion function	32	50	
KNJ_SETMODE	Conversion function	12	18	
KNJ_SJIS2 to JIS2	Conversion function	32	50	
KNJ_START	Conversion function	1	1	
EVENPARITY	Dcb field definition	2	2	
IGNORE	Dcb field definition	0	0	
INFINITE	Dcb field definition	FFFF	-1	
MARKPARITY	Dcb field definition	3	3	
NOPARITY	Dcb field definition	0	0	
ODDPARITY	Dcb field definition	1	1	
ONE5STOPBITS	Dcb field definition	1	1	
ONESTOPBIT	Dcb field definition	0	0	
SPACEPARITY	Dcb field definition	4	4	
TWOSTOPBITS	Dcb field definition	2	2	
CC_CHORD	Device capability mask	4	4	
CC_CIRCLES	Device capability mask	1	1	
CC_ELLIPSES	Device capability mask	8	8	
CC_INTERIORS	Device capability mask	80	128	
CC_NONE	Device capability mask	0	0	
CC_PIE	Device capability mask	2	2	
CC_STYLED	Device capability mask	20	32	
CC_WIDE	Device capability mask	10	16	
CC_WIDESTYLED	Device capability mask	40	64	
CP_NONE	Device capability mask	0	0	
CP_RECTANGLE	Device capability mask	1	1	
DT_CHARSTREAM	Device capability mask	4	4	
DT_DISPFILE	Device capability mask	6	6	
DT_METAFILE	Device capability mask	5	5	
DT_PLOTTER	Device capability mask	0	0	
DT_RASCAMERA	Device capability mask	3	3	
DT_RASDISPLAY	Device capability mask	1	1	
DT_RASPRINTER	Device capability mask	2	2	
LC_INTERIORS	Device capability mask	80	128	
LC_MARKER	Device capability mask	4	4	
LC_NONE	Device capability mask	0	0	
LC_POLYLINE	Device capability mask	2	2	
LC_POLYMARKER	Device capability mask	8	8	
LC_STYLED	Device capability mask	20	32	
LC_WIDE	Device capability mask	10	16	
LC_WIDESTYLED	Device capability mask	40	64	
PC_INTERIORS	Device capability mask	80	128	
PC_NONE	Device capability mask	0	0	

(Continued)

Table 6.38. Continued

Defined Name	Used As	Hex Value	Decimal Value	Comments
PC_POLYGON	Device capability mask	1	1	
PC_RECTANGLE	Device capability mask	2	2	
PC_SCANLINE	Device capability mask	8	8	
PC_STYLED	Device capability mask	20	32	
PC_TRAPEZOID	Device capability mask	4	4	
PC_WIDE	Device capability mask	10	16	
PC_WIDESTYLED	Device capability mask	40	64	
RC_BANDING	Device capability mask	2	2	
RC_BITBLT	Device capability mask	1	1	
RC_BITMAP64*	Device capability mask	8	8	
RC_SCALING	Device capability mask	4	4	
TC_CP_STROKE	Device capability mask	4	4	
TC_CR_90	Device capability mask	8	8	
TC_CR_ANY	Device capability mask	10	16	
TC_EA_DOUBLE	Device capability mask	200	512	
TC_IA_ABLE	Device capability mask	400	1024	
TC_OP_CHARACTER	Device capability mask	1	1	
TC_OP_STROKE	Device capability mask	2	2	
TC_RA_ABLE	Device capability mask	2000	8192	
TC_RESERVED	Device capability mask	8000	32768	
TC_SA_CONTIN	Device capability mask	100	256	
TC_SA_DOUBLE	Device capability mask	40	64	
TC_SA_INTEGER	Device capability mask	80	128	
TC_SF_X_YINDEP	Device capability mask	20	32	
TC_SO_ABLE	Device capability mask	1000	4096	
TC_UA_ABLE	Device capability mask	800	2048	
TC_VA_ABLE	Device capability mask	4000	16384	
CP_DIRECT*	Device capability mode	2	2	
CP_HWND*	Device capability mode	0	0	
CP_OPEN*	Device capability mode	1	1	
LPTx*	Device description	80	128	
DLGC_BUTTON*	Dialog code	2000	8192	
DLGC_DEFPUSHBUTTON*	Dialog code	10	16	
DLGC_HASSETSEL	Dialog code	8	8	
DLGC_RADIOBUTTON*	Dialog code	40	64	
DLGC_STATIC*	Dialog code	100	256	
DLGC_UNDEFPUSHBUTTON*	Dialog code	20	32	
DLGC_WANTALLKEYS	Dialog code	4	4	
DLGC_WANTARROWS	Dialog code	1	1	
DLGC_WANTCHARS*	Dialog code	80	128	
DLGC_WANTMESSAGE*	Dialog code	4	4	
DLGC_WANTTAB	Dialog code	2	2	
DS_ABSALIGN	Dialog style	1	1	
DS_LOCALEDIT*	Dialog style	20	32	
DS_SYSMODAL	Dialog style	2	2	
DM_GETDEFID	Dialog style bits	400	1024	WM_USER+0
DM_HASDEFID	Dialog style bits	534B	21323	
DM_SETDEFID	Dialog style bits	401	1025	WM_USER+1
IDABORT	Dialog/message box command ID	3	3	
IDCANCEL	Dialog/message box command ID	2	2	
IDIGNORE	Dialog/message box command ID	5	5	
IDNO	Dialog/message box command ID	7	7	
IDOK	Dialog/message box command ID	1	1	
IDRETRY	Dialog/message box command ID	4	4	
IDYES	Dialog/message box command ID	6	6	
DF_ACTIVEBORDER*	DrawFrame index			COLOR_ACTIVEBORDER+1<<3
DF_ACTIVECAPTION*	DrawFrame index			COLOR_ACTIVECAPTION+1<<3
DF_APPWORKSPACE*	DrawFrame index			COLOR_APPWORKSPACE+1<<3
DF_BACKGROUND*	DrawFrame index			COLOR_BACKGROUND+1<<3
DF_CAPTIONTEXT*	DrawFrame index			COLOR_CAPTIONTEXT+1<<3
DF_GRAY*	DrawFrame index			COLOR_APPWORKSPACE(+1<<3)
DF_INACTIVEBORDER*	DrawFrame index			COLOR_INACTIVEBORDER+1<<3
DF_INACTIVECAPTION*	DrawFrame index			COLOR_INACTIVECAPTION+1<<3
DF_MENU*	DrawFrame index			COLOR_MENU+1<<3
DF_MENUTEXT*	DrawFrame index			COLOR_MENUTEXT+1<<3
DF_PATCOPY*	DrawFrame index	0	0	
DF_PATINVERT*	DrawFrame index	4	4	
DF_SCROLLBAR*	DrawFrame index			COLOR_SCROLLBAR+1<<3
DF_SHIFT0*	DrawFrame index	0	0	
DF_SHIFT1*	DrawFrame index	1	1	
DF_SHIFT2*	DrawFrame index	2	2	
DF_SHIFT3*	DrawFrame index	3	3	
DF_WINDOW*	DrawFrame index			COLOR_WINDOW+1<<3
DF_WINDOWFRAME*	DrawFrame index			COLOR_WINDOWFRAME+1<<3
DF_WINDOWTEXT*	DrawFrame index			COLOR_WINDOWTEXT+1<<3
DT_BOTTOM	DrawText format flag	8	8	
DT_CENTER	DrawText format flag	1	1	

(Continued)

Table 6.38. Continued

Defined Name	Used As	Hex Value	Decimal Value	Comments
DT_EXPANDTABS	DrawText format flag	40	64	
DT_EXTERNALLEADING	DrawText format flag	200	512	
DT_INTERNAL	DrawText format flag	1000	4096	
DT_LEFT	DrawText format flag	0	0	
DT_NOCLIP	DrawText format flag	100	256	
DT_RIGHT	DrawText format flag	2	2	
DT_SINGLELINE	DrawText format flag	20	32	
DT_TABSTOP	DrawText format flag	80	128	
DT_TOP	DrawText format flag	0	0	
DT_VCENTER	DrawText format flag	4	4	
DT_WORDBREAK	DrawText format flag	10	16	
DT_CALCRECT*	DrawText format flag	400	1024	
DT_NOPREFIX*	DrawText format flag	800	2048	
EM_CANUNDO*	Edit control message	413	1043	
EM_FMTLINES*	Edit control message	415	1045	
EM_GETHANDLE*	Edit control message	40C	1036	
EM_GETLINE*	Edit control message	411	1041	
EM_GETLINECOUNT*	Edit control message	409	1033	
EM_GETMODIFY*	Edit control message	407	1031	
EM_GETRECT*	Edit control message	402	1026	
EM_GETSEL*	Edit control message	400	1024	
EM_GETTHUMB*	Edit control message	40D	1037	
EM_LIMITTEXT*	Edit control message	412	1042	
EM_LINEFROMCHAR*	Edit control message	416	1046	
EM_LINEINDEX*	Edit control message	40A	1034	
EM_LINELENGTH*	Edit control message	40E	1038	
EM_LINESCROLL*	Edit control message	406	1030	
EM_REPLACESEL*	Edit control message	40F	1039	
EM_SCROLL*	Edit control message	405	1029	
EM_SETFONT*	Edit control message	410	1040	
EM_SETHANDLE*	Edit control message	40B	1035	
EM_SETMODIFY*	Edit control message	408	1032	
EM_SETRECT*	Edit control message	403	1027	
EM_SETRECTNP*	Edit control message	404	1028	
EM_SETSEL*	Edit control message	401	1025	
EM_SETWORDBREAK*	Edit control message	417	1047	
EM_UNDO*	Edit control message	414	1044	
EN_CHANGE	Edit control notification code	300	768	
EN_ERRSPACE	Edit control notification code	500	1280	
EN_HSCROLL	Edit control notification code	601	1537	
EN_KILLFOCUS	Edit control notification code	200	512	
EN_SETFOCUS	Edit control notification code	100	256	
EN_UPDATE*	Edit control notification code	400	1024	
EN_VSCROLL	Edit control notification code	602	1538	
ES_AUTOHSCROLL	Edit control style	80	128	
ES_AUTOVSCROLL	Edit control style	40	64	
ES_CENTER	Edit control style	1	1	
ES_LEFT	Edit control style	0	0	
ES_MULTILINE	Edit control style	4	4	
ES_NOHIDESEL	Edit control style	100	256	
ES_RIGHT	Edit control style	2	2	
ETO_CLIPPED*	Edit text option	4	4	
ETO_GRAYED*	Edit text option	1	1	
ETO_OPAQUE*	Edit text option	2	2	
DEVICE_FONTTYPE	Enumfont mask	2	2	
RASTER_FONTTYPE	Enumfont mask	1	1	
MSGF_DIALOGBOX	Filter procedure code	0	0	
MSGF_MENU	Filter procedure code	2	2	
MSGF_MESSAGEBOX	Filter procedure code	1	1	
MSGF_MOVE*	Filter procedure code	3	3	
MSGF_NEXTWINDOW*	Filter procedure code	6	6	
MSGF_SCROLLBAR*	Filter procedure code	5	5	
MSGF_SIZE*	Filter procedure code	4	4	
FF_DECORATIVE	Font family ID	5*	5*	*Shifted left four bits
FF_DONTCARE	Font family ID	0*	0*	*Shifted left four bits
FF_MODERN	Font family ID	3*	3*	*Shifted left four bits
FF_ROMAN	Font family ID	1*	1*	*Shifted left four bits
FF_SCRIPT	Font family ID	4*	4*	*Shifted left four bits
FF_SWISS	Font family ID	2*	2*	*Shifted left four bits
FW_REGULAR*	Font weight	190	400	
FW_BLACK	Font weight constant	384	900	Defined as FW_HEAVY
FW_BOLD	Font weight constant	26C	700	
FW_DEMIBOLD	Font weight constant	258	600	Defined as FW_SEMIBOLD
FW_DONTCARE	Font weight constant	0	0	
FW_EXTRABOLD	Font weight constant	320	800	
FW_EXTRALIGHT	Font weight constant	C8	200	
FW_HEAVY	Font weight constant	384	900	

(Continued)

Table 6.38. Continued

Defined Name	Used As	Hex Value	Decimal Value	Comments
FW_LIGHT	Font weight constant	12C	300	
FW_MEDIUM	Font weight constant	1F4	500	
FW_NORMAL	Font weight constant	190	400	
FW_SEMIBOLD	Font weight constant	258	600	
FW_THIN	Font weight constant	64	100	
FW_ULTRABOLD	Font weight constant	320	800	Defined as FW_EXTRABOLD
FW_ULTRALIGHT	Font weight constant	C8	200	Defined as FW_EXTRALIGHT
OPAQUE	GDI background mode	2	2	
TRANSPARENT	GDI background mode	1	1	
ABSOLUTE	GDI coordinate mode	1	1	
RELATIVE	GDI coordinate mode	2	2	
ABORTDOC	GDI escape	2	2	
DRAFTMODE	GDI escape	7	7	
ENDDOC	GDI escape	B	11	
FLUSHOUTPUT	GDI escape	6	6	
GETCOLORTABLE	GDI escape	5	5	
GETPHYSPAGESIZE	GDI escape	C	12	
GETPRINTINGOFFSET	GDI escape	D	13	
GETSCALINGFACTOR	GDI escape	E	14	
NEWFRAME	GDI escape	1	1	
NEXTBAND	GDI escape	3	3	
QUERYESCSUPPORT	GDI escape	8	8	
SETABORTPROC	GDI escape	9	9	
SETCOLORTABLE	GDI escape	4	4	
STARTDOC	GDI escape	A	10	
BANDINFO*	GDI escape code	18	24	
DRAWPATTERNRECT*	GDI escape code	19	25	
ENABLEDUPLEX*	GDI escape code	1C	28	
ENABLEMANUALFEED*	GDI escape code	1D	29	
ENABLEPAIRKERNING*	GDI escape code	301	769	
ENABLERELATIVEWIDTHS*	GDI escape code	300	768	
EXTTEXTOUT*	GDI escape code	200	512	
GETEXTENDEDTEXTMETRICS*	GDI escape code	100	256	
GETEXTENTTABLE*	GDI escape code	101	257	
GETPAIRKERNTABLE*	GDI escape code	102	258	
GETPENWIDTH*	GDI escape code	10	16	
GETTECHNOLOGY*	GDI escape code	14	20	
GETTRACKKERNTABLE*	GDI escape code	103	259	
GETVECTORBRUSHSIZE*	GDI escape code	1B	27	
GETVECTORPENSIZE*	GDI escape code	1A	26	
MFCOMMENT*	GDI escape code	F	15	
PASSTHROUGH*	GDI escape code	13	19	
SELECTPAPERSOURCE*	GDI escape code	12	18	
SETCOPYCOUNT*	GDI escape code	11	17	
SETKERNTRACK*	GDI escape code	302	770	
SETLINEJOIN*	GDI escape code	16	22	
SETMITERLIMIT*	GDI escape code	17	23	
STRETCHBLT*	GDI escape code	800	2048	
MM_ANISOTROPIC	GDI map mode	8	8	
MM_HIENGLISH	GDI map mode	5	5	
MM_HIMETRIC	GDI map mode	3	3	
MM_ISOTROPIC	GDI map mode	7	7	
MM_LOENGLISH	GDI map mode	4	4	
MM_LOMETRIC	GDI map mode	2	2	
MM_TEXT	GDI map mode	1	1	
MM_TWIPS	GDI map mode	6	6	
ASPECTX	Getdevicecaps device parameter	28	40	
ASPECTXY	Getdevicecaps device parameter	2C	44	
ASPECTY	Getdevicecaps device parameter	2A	42	
BITSPIXEL	Getdevicecaps device parameter	C	12	
CLIPCAPS	Getdevicecaps device parameter	24	36	
CURVECAPS	Getdevicecaps device parameter	1C	28	
DRIVERVERSION	Getdevicecaps device parameter	0	0	
HORZRES	Getdevicecaps device parameter	8	8	
HORZSIZE	Getdevicecaps device parameter	4	4	
LINECAPS	Getdevicecaps device parameter	1E	30	
LOGPIXELSX	Getdevicecaps device parameter	58	88	
LOGPIXELSY	Getdevicecaps device parameter	5A	90	
NUMBRUSHES	Getdevicecaps device parameter	10	16	
NUMCOLORS	Getdevicecaps device parameter	18	24	
NUMFONTS	Getdevicecaps device parameter	16	22	
NUMMARKERS	Getdevicecaps device parameter	14	20	
NUMPENS	Getdevicecaps device parameter	12	18	
PDEVICESIZE	Getdevicecaps device parameter	1A	26	
PLANES	Getdevicecaps device parameter	E	14	
POLYGONALCAPS	Getdevicecaps device parameter	20	32	
RASTERCAPS	Getdevicecaps device parameter	26	38	

(Continued)

Table 6.38. Continued

Defined Name	Used As	Hex Value	Decimal Value	Comments
TECHNOLOGY	Getdevicecaps device parameter	2	2	
TEXTCAPS	Getdevicecaps device parameter	22	34	
VERTRES	Getdevicecaps device parameter	A	10	
VERTSIZE	Getdevicecaps device parameter	6	6	
SM_CMETRICS*	GetSystemMetrics code	24	36	
SM_CXBORDER	GetSystemMetrics code	5	5	
SM_CXCURSOR	GetSystemMetrics code	D	13	
SM_CXDLGFRAME	GetSystemMetrics code	7	7	
SM_CXFRAME*	GetSystemMetrics code	20	32	
SM_CXFULLSCREEN	GetSystemMetrics code	10	16	
SM_CXHSCROLL	GetSystemMetrics code	15	21	
SM_CXHTHUMB	GetSystemMetrics code	A	10	
SM_CXICON	GetSystemMetrics code	B	11	
SM_CXMIN*	GetSystemMetrics code	1C	28	
SM_CXMINTRACK*	GetSystemMetrics code	22	34	
SM_CXSCREEN	GetSystemMetrics code	0	0	
SM_CXSIZE*	GetSystemMetrics code	1E	30	
SM_CXVSCROLL	GetSystemMetrics code	2	2	
SM_CYBORDER	GetSystemMetrics code	6	6	
SM_CYCAPTION	GetSystemMetrics code	4	4	
SM_CYCURSOR	GetSystemMetrics code	E	14	
SM_CYDLGFRAME	GetSystemMetrics code	8	8	
SM_CYFRAME*	GetSystemMetrics code	21	33	
SM_CYFULLSCREEN	GetSystemMetrics code	11	17	
SM_CYHSCROLL	GetSystemMetrics code	3	3	
SM_CYICON	GetSystemMetrics code	C	12	
SM_CYICONSLOT*	GetSystemMetrics code	1B	27	
SM_CYKANJIWINDOW	GetSystemMetrics code	12	18	
SM_CYMENU	GetSystemMetrics code	F	15	
SM_CYMIN*	GetSystemMetrics code	1D	29	
SM_CYMINTRACK*	GetSystemMetrics code	23	35	
SM_CYSCREEN	GetSystemMetrics code	1	1	
SM_CYSIZE*	GetSystemMetrics code	1F	31	
SM_CYVSCROLL	GetSystemMetrics code	14	20	
SM_CYVTHUMB	GetSystemMetrics code	9	9	
SM_DEBUG	GetSystemMetrics code	16	22	
SM_FULLSCREEN	GetSystemMetrics code	18	24	
SM_MOUSEPRESENT	GetSystemMetrics code	13	19	
SM_SWAPBUTTON	GetSystemMetrics code	17	23	
GW_CHILD*	GetWindow constant	5	5	
GW_HWNDFIRST*	GetWindow constant	0	0	
GW_HWNDLAST*	GetWindow constant	1	1	
GW_HWNDNEXT*	GetWindow constant	2	2	
GW_HWNDPREV*	GetWindow constant	3	3	
GW_OWNER*	GetWindow constant	4	4	
GHND*	Global memory management	42	66	
GMEM_DDESHARE*	Global memory management	2000	8192	
GMEM_DISCARDABLE	Global memory management	F00	3840	
GMEM_FIXED	Global memory management	0	0	
GMEM_LOWER*	Global memory management	1000	4096	
GMEM_MODIFY	Global memory management	80	128	
GMEM_MOVEABLE	Global memory management	2	2	
GMEM_NOCOMPACT	Global memory management	10	16	
GMEM_NODISCARD	Global memory management	20	32	
GMEM_NOTBANKED*	Global memory management	1000	4096	
GMEM_NOTIFY*	Global memory management	4000	16384	
GMEM_SHARE*	Global memory management	2000	8196	
GMEM_ZEROINIT	Global memory management	40	64	
GPTR*	Global memory management	2	2	
LHND*	Global memory management	42	66	
LPTR*	Global memory management	2	2	
NONZEROLHND*	Global memory management	2	2	
NONZEROLPTR*	Global memory management	0	0	
GMEM_DISCARDED	GlobalFlag flag	4000	16384	
GMEM_LOCKCOUNT	GlobalFlag flag	FF	255	
GMEM_SWAPPED	GlobalFlag flag	8000	32768	
HS_BDIAGONAL	Hatch style	3	3	
HS_CROSS	Hatch style	4	4	
HS_DIAGCROSS	Hatch style	5	5	
HS_FDIAGONAL	Hatch style	2	2	
HS_HORIZONTAL	Hatch style	0	0	
HS_VERTICAL	Hatch style	1	1	
HCBT_MINMAX*	Hook code	1	1	
HCBT_MOVESIZE*	Hook code	0	0	
HCBT_QS	Hook code	2	2	
HC_ACTION*	Hook code	0	0	
HC_GETNEXT*	Hook code	1	1	

(Continued)

Table 6.38. Continued

Defined Name	Used As	Hex Value	Decimal Value	Comments
HC_LPFNNEXT*	Hook code	FFFF	-1	
HC_LPLPFNNEXT*	Hook code	FFFE	-2	
HC_NOREM*	Hook code	3	3	
HC_SKIP*	Hook code	2	2	
MK_CONTROL	Key state mask f/mouse msg.	8	8	
MK_LBUTTON	Key state mask f/mouse msg.	1	1	
MK_MBUTTON	Key state mask f/mouse msg.	10	16	
MK_RBUTTON	Key state mask f/mouse msg.	2	2	
MK_SHIFT	Key state mask f/mouse msg.	4	4	
LB_CTLCODE	Listbox control	0	0	
LB_ERR	Listbox control	FFFF	-1	
LB_ERRSPACE	Listbox control	FFFE	-2	
LB_OKAY	Listbox control	0	0	
LB_ADDSTRING*	Listbox message	400	1024	
LB_DELETESTRING*	Listbox message	402	1025	
LB_DIR*	Listbox message	40D	1026	
LB_GETCOUNT*	Listbox message	40B	1027	
LB_GETCURSEL*	Listbox message	409	1028	
LB_GETSEL*	Listbox message	408	1029	
LB_GETTEXT*	Listbox message	407	1030	
LB_GETTEXTLEN*	Listbox message	40A	1031	
LB_GETTOPINDEX*	Listbox message	40E	1032	
LB_INSERTSTRING*	Listbox message	401	1033	
LB_MSGMAX*	Listbox message	40F	1034	
LB_RESETCONTENT*	Listbox message	404	1	
LB_SELECTSTRING*	Listbox message	40C	2	
LB_SETCURSEL*	Listbox message	406	3	
LB_SETSEL*	Listbox message	405	4	
LBN_DBLCLK	Listbox notification code	2	2	
LBN_ERRSPACE	Listbox notification code	FFFE	-2	
LBN_SELCHANGE	Listbox notification code	1	1	
LBS_MULTIPLESEL	Listbox style	8	8	
LBS_NOREDRAW	Listbox style	4	4	
LBS_NOTIFY	Listbox style	1	1	
LBS_SORT	Listbox style	2	2	
LBS_STANDARD*	Listbox style	F	15	
LMEM_DISCARDABLE	Local memory management	F00	3840	
LMEM_DISCARDED*	Local memory management	4000	16384	
LMEM_FIXED	Local memory management	0	0	
LMEM_LOCKCOUNT	Local memory management	FF	255	
LMEM_MODIFY	Local memory management	80	128	
LMEM_MOVEABLE	Local memory management	2	2	
LMEM_NOCOMPACT	Local memory management	10	16	
LMEM_NODISCARD	Local memory management	20	32	
LMEM_ZEROINIT	Local memory management	40	64	
LNOTIFY_DISCARD	Local memory management	2	2	
LNOTIFY_MOVE	Local memory management	1	1	
LNOTIFY_OUTOFMEM	Local memory management	0	0	
ANSI_CHARSET	Logical font constant	0	0	
CLIP_CHARACTER_PRECIS	Logical font constant	1	1	
CLIP_DEFAULT_PRECIS	Logical font constant	0	0	
CLIP_STROKE_PRECIS	Logical font constant	2	2	
DEFAULT_PITCH	Logical font constant	0	0	
DEFAULT_QUALITY	Logical font constant	0	0	
DRAFT_QUALITY	Logical font constant	1	1	
FIXED_PITCH	Logical font constant	1	1	
LF_FACESIZE	Logical font constant	20	32	
OEM_CHARSET	Logical font constant	FF	255	
OUT_CHARACTER_PRECIS	Logical font constant	2	2	
OUT_DEFAULT_PRECIS	Logical font constant	0	0	
OUT_STRING_PRECIS	Logical font constant	1	1	
OUT_STROKE_PRECIS	Logical font constant	3	3	
PROOF_QUALITY	Logical font constant	2	2	
SHIFTJIS_CHARSET*	Logical font constant	80	128	
VARIABLE_PITCH	Logical font constant	2	2	
MF_APPEND	MenuItem menu flag	100	256	
MF_BITMAP	MenuItem menu flag	4	4	
MF_BYCOMMAND	MenuItem menu flag	0	0	
MF_BYPOSITION	MenuItem menu flag	400	1024	
MF_CHANGE	MenuItem menu flag	80	128	
MF_CHECKED	MenuItem menu flag	8	8	
MF_DELETE	MenuItem menu flag	200	512	
MF_DISABLED	MenuItem menu flag	2	2	
MF_ENABLED	MenuItem menu flag	0	0	
MF_GRAYED	MenuItem menu flag	1	1	
MF_HELP*	MenuItem menu flag	4000	16384	
MF_HILITE	MenuItem menu flag	80	128	

(Continued)

Table 6.38. Continued

Defined Name	Used As	Hex Value	Decimal Value	Comments
MF_INSERT	MenuItem menu flag	0	0	
MF_MENUBARBREAK	MenuItem menu flag	20	32	
MF_MENUBREAK	MenuItem menu flag	40	64	
MF_MOUSESELECT*	MenuItem menu flag	8000	32768	
MF_POPUP	MenuItem menu flag	10	16	
MF_REMOVE*	MenuItem menu flag	1000	4096	
MF_SEPARATOR	MenuItem menu flag	800	2048	
MF_STRING	MenuItem menu flag	0	0	
MF_SYSMENU*	MenuItem menu flag	2000	8192	
MF_UNCHECKED	MenuItem menu flag	0	0	
MF_UNHILITE	MenuItem menu flag	0	0	
MB_ABORTRETRYIGNORE	MessageBox type flag	2	2	
MB_APPLMODAL	MessageBox type flag	0	0	
MB_DEFBUTTON1	MessageBox type flag	0	0	
MB_DEFBUTTON2	MessageBox type flag	100	256	
MB_DEFBUTTON3	MessageBox type flag	200	512	
MB_DEFMASK	MessageBox type flag	F00	3840	
MB_ICONASTERISK	MessageBox type flag	40	64	
MB_ICONEXCLAMATION	MessageBox type flag	30	48	
MB_ICONHAND	MessageBox type flag	10	16	
MB_ICONMASK	MessageBox type flag	F0	240	
MB_ICONQUESTION	MessageBox type flag	20	32	
MB_MISCMASK	MessageBox type flag	C000	49152	
MB_MODEMASK	MessageBox type flag	3000	12288	
MB_NOFOCUS	MessageBox type flag	8000	32768	
MB_OK	MessageBox type flag	0	0	
MB_OKCANCEL	MessageBox type flag	1	1	
MB_RETRYCANCEL	MessageBox type flag	5	5	
MB_SYSTEMMODAL	MessageBox type flag	1000	4096	
MB_TYPEMASK	MessageBox type flag	F	15	
MB_YESNO	MessageBox type flag	4	4	
MB_YESNOCANCEL	MessageBox type flag	3	3	
DEVICEDATA	Metafile comment esc.	13	19	
SETENDCAP	Metafile comment esc.	15	21	
META_ARC*	Metafile function	817	2071	
META_BITBLT*	Metafile function	922	2338	
META_CHORD*	Metafile function	630	1584	
META_CREATEBITMAP*	Metafile function	6FE	1790	
META_CREATEBITMAPINDIRECT*	Metafile function	2FD	765	
META_CREATEBRUSH*	Metafile function	F8	248	
META_CREATEBRUSHINDIRECT*	Metafile function	2FC	764	
META_CREATEFONTINDIRECT*	Metafile function	2FB	763	
META_CREATEPATTERNBRUSH*	Metafile function	1F9	505	
META_CREATEPENDIRECT*	Metafile function	2FA	762	
META_CREATEREGION*	Metafile function	6FF	1791	
META_DRAWTEXT*	Metafile function	62F	1583	
META_ELLIPSE*	Metafile function	418	1048	
META_ESCAPE*	Metafile function	626	1574	
META_EXCLUDECLIPRECT*	Metafile function	415	1045	
META_FILLREGION*	Metafile function	228	552	
META_FLOODFILL*	Metafile function	419	1049	
META_FRAMEREGION*	Metafile function	429	1065	
META_INTERSECTCLIPRECT*	Metafile function	416	1046	
META_INVERTREGION*	Metafile function	12A	298	
META_LINETO*	Metafile function	213	531	
META_MOVETO*	Metafile function	214	532	
META_OFFSETCLIPRGN*	Metafile function	220	544	
META_OFFSETVIEWPORTORG*	Metafile function	211	529	
META_OFFSETWINDOWORG*	Metafile function	20F	527	
META_PAINTREGION*	Metafile function	12B	299	
META_PATBLT*	Metafile function	61D	1565	
META_PIE*	Metafile function	81A	2074	
META_POLYGON*	Metafile function	324	804	
META_POLYLINE*	Metafile function	325	805	
META_RECTANGLE*	Metafile function	41B	1051	
META_RESTOREDC*	Metafile function	127	295	
META_ROUNDRECT*	Metafile function	61C	1564	
META_SAVEDC*	Metafile function	1E	30	
META_SCALEVIEWPORTEXT*	Metafile function	412	1042	
META_SCALEWINDOWEXT*	Metafile function	400	1024	
META_SELECTCLIPREGION*	Metafile function	12C	300	
META_SELECTOBJECT*	Metafile function	12D	301	
META_SETBKCOLOR*	Metafile function	201	513	
META_SETBKMODE*	Metafile function	102	258	
META_SETMAPMODE*	Metafile function	103	259	
META_SETPIXEL*	Metafile function	41F	1055	
META_SETPOLYFILLMODE*	Metafile function	106	262	

(Continued)

Table 6.38. Continued

Defined Name	Used As	Hex Value	Decimal Value	Comments
META_SETRELABS*	Metafile function	105	261	
META_SETROP2*	Metafile function	104	260	
META_SETSTRECTCHBLTMODE*	Metafile function	107	263	
META_SETTEXTALIGN*	Metafile function	12E	302	
META_SETTEXTCHAREXTRA*	Metafile function	108	264	
META_SETTEXTCOLOR*	Metafile function	209	521	
META_SETTEXTJUSTIFICATION*	Metafile function	20A	522	
META_SETVIEWPORTEXT*	Metafile function	20E	526	
META_SETVIEWPORTORG*	Metafile function	20D	525	
META_SETWINDOWEXT*	Metafile function	20C	524	
META_SETWINDOWORG*	Metafile function	20B	523	
META_STRETCHBLT*	Metafile function	B23	2851	
META_TEXTOUT*	Metafile function	521	1313	
MA_ACTIVATE*	Mouse activate return code	1	1	
MA_ACTIVATEANDEAT*	Mouse activate return code	2	2	
MA_NOACTIVATE*	Mouse activate return code	3	3	
OBJ_BRUSH	Object definition	2	2	
OBJ_PEN	Object definition	1	1	
OBM_BTNCORNERS	OEM definition	7FF6	32758	
OBM_BTSIZE	OEM definition	7FF9	32761	
OBM_CHECK	OEM definition	7FF8	32760	
OBM_CHECKBOXES	OEM definition	7FF7	32759	
OBM_CLOSE	OEM definition	7FFF	32767	
OBM_DNARROW	OEM definition	7FFC	32764	
OBM_LFARROW	OEM definition	7FFA	32762	
OBM_REDUCE*	OEM definition	7FF5	32757	
OBM_RESTORE*	OEM definition	7FF3	32755	
OBM_RGARROW	OEM definition	7FFB	32763	
OBM_SIZE	OEM definition	7FFE	32766	
OBM_UPARROW	OEM definition	7FFD	32765	
OBM_ZOOM*	OEM definition	7FF4	32756	
OCR_CROSS	OEM definition	7F03	32515	
OCR_IBEAM	OEM definition	7F01	32513	
OCR_ICON	OEM definition	7F81	32641	
OCR_NORMAL	OEM definition	7F00	32512	
OCR_SIZE	OEM definition	7F80	32640	
OCR_SIZEALL*	OEM definition	7F86	32646	
OCR_SIZENESW*	OEM definition	7F83	32643	
OCR_SIZENS*	OEM definition	7F85	32645	
OCR_SIZENWSE*	OEM definition	7F82	32642	
OCR_SIZEWE*	OEM definition	7F84	32644	
OCR_UP	OEM definition	7F04	32516	
OCR_WAIT	OEM definition	7F02	32514	
OIC_BANG	OEM definition	7F03	32515	
OIC_HAND	OEM definition	7F01	32513	
OIC_NOTE	OEM definition	7F04	32516	
OIC_QUES	OEM definition	7F02	32514	
OIC_SAMPLE	OEM definition	7F00	32512	
OF_CANCEL	OpenFile flag	800	2048	
OF_CREATE	OpenFile flag	1000	4096	
OF_DELETE	OpenFile flag	200	512	
OF_EXIST	OpenFile flag	4000	16384	
OF_PARSE	OpenFile flag	100	256	
OF_PROMPT	OpenFile flag	2000	8192	
OF_READ	OpenFile flag	0	0	
OF_READWRITE	OpenFile flag	2	2	
OF_REOPEN	OpenFile flag	8000	32768	
OF_VERIFY	OpenFile flag	400	1024	
OF_WRITE	OpenFile flag	1	1	
PM_NOREMOVE*	Peekmessage options	0	0	
PM_NOYIELD*	Peekmessage options	2	2	
PM_REMOVE*	Peekmessage options	1	1	
PS_DASH	Pen style	1	1	
PS_DASHDOT	Pen style	3	3	
PS_DASHDOTDOT	Pen style	4	4	
PS_DOT	Pen style	2	2	
PS_NULL	Pen style	5	5	
PS_SOLID	Pen style	0	0	
ALTERNATE	Polyfill mode	1	1	
WINDING	Polyfill mode	2	2	
RT_ACCELERATOR	Predefined resource type	9	9	MAKEINTRESOURCE (9)
RT_BITMAP	Predefined resource type	2	2	MAKEINTRESOURCE (2)
RT_CURSOR	Predefined resource type	1	1	MAKEINTRESOURCE (1)
RT_DIALOG	Predefined resource type	5	5	MAKEINTRESOURCE (5)
RT_FONT	Predefined resource type	8	8	MAKEINTRESOURCE (8)
RT_FONTDIR	Predefined resource type	7	7	MAKEINTRESOURCE (7)
RT_ICON	Predefined resource type	3	3	MAKEINTRESOURCE (3)

(Continued)

Table 6.38. Continued

Defined Name	Used As	Hex Value	Decimal Value	Comments
RT_MENU	Predefined resource type	4	4	MAKEINTRESOURCE (4)
RT_RCDATA*	Predefined resource type	A	10	MAKEINTRESOURCE(10)
RT_STRING	Predefined resource type	6	6	MAKEINTRESOURCE (6)
COMPLEXREGION	Region flag	3	3	
ERROR	Region flag	0	0	
NULLREGION	Region flag	1	1	
SIMPLEREGION	Region flag	2	2	
SB_BOTH*	Scroll bar constant	3	3	
SB_BOTTOM	Scroll bar constant	7	7	
SB_CTL	Scroll bar constant	2	2	
SB_ENDSCROLL	Scroll bar constant	8	8	
SB_HORZ	Scroll bar constant	0	0	
SB_LINEDOWN	Scroll bar constant	1	1	
SB_LINEUP	Scroll bar constant	0	0	
SB_PAGEDOWN	Scroll bar constant	3	3	
SB_PAGEUP	Scroll bar constant	2	2	
SB_THUMBPOSITION	Scroll bar constant	4	4	
SB_THUMBTRACK	Scroll bar constant	5	5	
SB_TOP	Scroll bar constant	6	6	
SB_VERT	Scroll bar constant	1	1	
SBS_BOTTOMALIGN*	Scroll bar style	4	4	
SBS_HORZ*	Scroll bar style	0	0	
SBS_LEFTALIGN*	Scroll bar style	2	2	
SBS_RIGHTALIGN*	Scroll bar style	4	4	
SBS_SIZEBOX*	Scroll bar style	8	8	
SBS_SIZEBOXBOTTOMRIGHTALIGN*	Scroll bar style	4	4	
SBS_SIZEBOXTOPLEFTALIGN*	Scroll bar style	2	2	
SBS_TOPALIGN*	Scroll bar style	2	2	
SBS_VERT*	Scroll bar style	1	1	
S_PERIOD1024	SetSoundNoise source	1	1	
S_PERIOD2048	SetSoundNoise source	2	2	
S_PERIOD512	SetSoundNoise source	0	0	
S_PERIODVOICE	SetSoundNoise source	3	3	
S_SERBDNT	SetSoundNoise source	FFFB	-5	
S_SERDCC	SetSoundNoise source	FFF9	-7	
S_SERDDR	SetSoundNoise source	FFF2	-14	
S_SERDFQ	SetSoundNoise source	FFF3	-13	
S_SERDLN	SetSoundNoise source	FFFA	-6	
S_SERDMD	SetSoundNoise source	FFF6	-10	
S_SERDPT	SetSoundNoise source	FFF4	-12	
S_SERDSH	SetSoundNoise source	FFF5	-11	
S_SERDSR	SetSoundNoise source	FFF1	-15	
S_SERDST	SetSoundNoise source	FFF0	-16	
S_SERDTP	SetSoundNoise source	FFF8	-8	
S_SERDVL	SetSoundNoise source	FFF7	-9	
S_SERDVNA	SetSoundNoise source	FFFF	-1	
S_SERMACT	SetSoundNoise source	FFFD	-3	
S_SEROFM	SetSoundNoise source	FFFE	-2	
S_SERQFUL	SetSoundNoise source	FFFC	-4	
S_WHITE1024	SetSoundNoise source	5	5	
S_WHITE2048	SetSoundNoise source	6	6	
S_WHITE512	SetSoundNoise source	4	4	
S_WHITEVOICE	SetSoundNoise source	7	7	
SWP_DRAWFRAME*	SetWindow position flag	20	32	
SWP_HIDEWINDOW*	SetWindow position flag	80	128	
SWP_NOACTIVATE*	SetWindow position flag	10	16	
SWP_NOCOPYBITS*	SetWindow position flag	100	256	
SWP_NOMOVE*	SetWindow position flag	2	2	
SWP_NOREDRAW*	SetWindow position flag	8	8	
SWP_NOREPOSITION*	SetWindow position flag	200	512	
SWP_NOSIZE*	SetWindow position flag	1	1	
SWP_NOZORDER*	SetWindow position flag	4	4	
SWP_SHOWWINDOW*	SetWindow position flag	40	64	
WH_CALLWNDPROC	Setwindowshook code	4	4	
WH_GETMESSAGE	Setwindowshook code	3	3	
WH_JOURNALPLAYBACK	Setwindowshook code	1	1	
WH_JOURNALRECORD	Setwindowshook code	0	0	
WH_KEYBOARD	Setwindowshook code	2	2	
WH_MSGFILTER	Setwindowshook code	FFFF	-1	
HIDE_WINDOW	Showwindow command	0	0	
SHOW_FULLSCREEN	Showwindow command	3	3	
SHOW_ICONWINDOW	Showwindow command	2	2	
SHOW_OPENNOACTIVATE	Showwindow command	4	4	
SHOW_OPENWINDOW	Showwindow command	1	1	
SW_HIDE*	Showwindow message ID	0	0	
SW_MAXIMIZE*	Showwindow message ID	3	3	
SW_MINIMIZE*	Showwindow message ID	6	6	

(Continued)

Table 6.38. Continued

Defined Name	Used As	Hex Value	Decimal Value	Comments
SW_NORMAL*	Showwindow message ID	1	1	
SW_OTHERUNZOOM	Showwindow message ID	4	4	
SW_OTHERZOOM	Showwindow message ID	2	2	
SW_PARENTCLOSING	Showwindow message ID	1	1	
SW_PARENTOPENING	Showwindow message ID	3	3	
SW_RESTORE*	Showwindow message ID	1	1	
SW_SHOW*	Showwindow message ID	5	5	
SW_SHOWMAXIMIZED*	Showwindow message ID	3	3	
SW_SHOWMINIMIZED*	Showwindow message ID	2	2	
SW_SHOWMINNOACTIVE*	Showwindow message ID	7	7	
SW_SHOWNA*	Showwindow message ID	8	8	
SW_SHOWNOACTIVE*	Showwindow message ID	4	4	
SW_SHOWNORMAL*	Showwindow message ID	1	1	
SIZEFULLSCREEN	Size message command	2	2	
SIZEICONIC	Size message command	1	1	
SIZENORMAL	Size message command	0	0	
SIZEZOOMHIDE	Size message command	4	4	
SIZEZOOMSHOW	Size message command	3	3	
SP_APPABORT	Spooler error code	FFFE	-2	
SP_ERROR	Spooler error code	FFFF	-1	
SP_NOTREPORTED	Spooler error code	4000	16384	
SP_OUTOFDISK	Spooler error code	FFFC	-4	
SP_OUTOFMEMORY	Spooler error code	FFFB	-5	
SP_USERABORT	Spooler error code	FFFD	-3	
PR_JOBSTATUS	Spooler wparm class	0	0	
IDC_ARROW	Standard cursor ID	7F00	32512	MAKEINTRESOURCE(32512)
IDC_CROSS	Standard cursor ID	7F03	32515	MAKEINTRESOURCE(32515)
IDC_IBEAM	Standard cursor ID	7F01	32513	MAKEINTRESOURCE(32513)
IDC_ICON	Standard cursor ID	7F81	32641	MAKEINTRESOURCE(32641)
IDC_SIZE	Standard cursor ID	7F80	32640	MAKEINTRESOURCE(32640)
IDC_SIZENESW	Standard cursor ID	7F83	32643	
IDC_SIZENS	Standard cursor ID	7F85	32645	
IDC_SIZENWSE	Standard cursor ID	7F82	32642	
IDC_SIZEWE	Standard cursor ID	7F84	32644	
IDC_UPARROW	Standard cursor ID	7F04	32516	MAKEINTRESOURCE(32516)
IDC_WAIT	Standard cursor ID	7F02	32514	MAKEINTRESOURCE(32514)
NULL	Standard definitions	0	0	
FALSE	Standard definitions	0	0	
TRUE	Standard definitions	1	1	
IDI_APPLICATION	Standard icon ID	7F00	32512	MAKEINTRESOURCE(32512)
IDI_ASTERISK	Standard icon ID	7F04	32516	MAKEINTRESOURCE(32516)
IDI_EXCLAMATION	Standard icon ID	7F03	32515	MAKEINTRESOURCE(32515)
IDI_HAND	Standard icon ID	7F01	32513	MAKEINTRESOURCE(32513)
IDI_QUESTION	Standard icon ID	7F02	32514	MAKEINTRESOURCE(32514)
VK_ADD	Standard set virtual key	6B	107	
VK_BACK	Standard set virtual key	8	8	
VK_CANCEL	Standard set virtual key	3	3	
VK_CAPITAL	Standard set virtual key	14	20	
VK_CLEAR	Standard set virtual key	C	12	
VK_CONTROL	Standard set virtual key	11	17	
VK_COPY	Standard set virtual key	2C	44	
VK_DECIMAL	Standard set virtual key	6E	110	
VK_DELETE	Standard set virtual key	2E	46	
VK_DIVIDE	Standard set virtual key	6F	111	
VK_DOWN	Standard set virtual key	28	40	
VK_END	Standard set virtual key	23	35	
VK_ESCAPE	Standard set virtual key	1B	27	
VK_EXECUTE	Standard set virtual key	2B	43	
VK_F1	Standard set virtual key	70	112	
VK_F10	Standard set virtual key	79	121	
VK_F11	Standard set virtual key	7A	122	
VK_F12	Standard set virtual key	7B	123	
VK_F13	Standard set virtual key	7C	124	
VK_F14	Standard set virtual key	7D	125	
VK_F15	Standard set virtual key	7E	126	
VK_F16	Standard set virtual key	7F	127	
VK_F2	Standard set virtual key	71	113	
VK_F3	Standard set virtual key	72	114	
VK_F4	Standard set virtual key	73	115	
VK_F5	Standard set virtual key	74	116	
VK_F6	Standard set virtual key	75	117	
VK_F7	Standard set virtual key	76	118	
VK_F8	Standard set virtual key	77	119	
VK_F9	Standard set virtual key	78	120	
VK_HELP	Standard set virtual key	2F	47	
VK_HOME	Standard set virtual key	24	36	
VK_INSERT	Standard set virtual key	2D	45	

(Continued)

Table 6.38. Continued

Defined Name	Used As	Hex Value	Decimal Value	Comments
VK_LBUTTON	Standard set virtual key	1	1	
VK_LEFT	Standard set virtual key	25	37	
VK_MBUTTON	Standard set virtual key	4	4	
VK_MENU	Standard set virtual key	12	18	
VK_MULTIPLY	Standard set virtual key	6A	106	
VK_NEXT	Standard set virtual key	22	34	
VK_NUMLOCK	Standard set virtual key	90	144	
VK_NUMPAD0	Standard set virtual key	60	96	
VK_NUMPAD1	Standard set virtual key	61	97	
VK_NUMPAD2	Standard set virtual key	62	98	
VK_NUMPAD3	Standard set virtual key	63	99	
VK_NUMPAD4	Standard set virtual key	64	100	
VK_NUMPAD5	Standard set virtual key	65	101	
VK_NUMPAD6	Standard set virtual key	66	102	
VK_NUMPAD7	Standard set virtual key	67	103	
VK_NUMPAD8	Standard set virtual key	68	104	
VK_NUMPAD9	Standard set virtual key	69	105	
VK_PAUSE	Standard set virtual key	13	19	
VK_PRINT	Standard set virtual key	2A	42	
VK_PRIOR	Standard set virtual key	21	33	
VK_RBUTTON	Standard set virtual key	2	2	
VK_RETURN	Standard set virtual key	D	13	
VK_RIGHT	Standard set virtual key	27	39	
VK_SELECT	Standard set virtual key	29	41	
VK_SEPARATOR	Standard set virtual key	6C	108	
VK_SHIFT	Standard set virtual key	10	16	
VK_SPACE	Standard set virtual key	20	32	
VK_SUBTRACT	Standard set virtual key	6D	109	
VK_TAB	Standard set virtual key	9	9	
VK_UP	Standard set virtual key	26	38	
SS_BLACKFRAME	Static control constant	7	7	
SS_BLACKRECT	Static control constant	4	4	
SS_CENTER	Static control constant	1	1	
SS_GRAYFRAME	Static control constant	8	8	
SS_GRAYRECT	Static control constant	5	5	
SS_ICON	Static control constant	3	3	
SS_LEFT	Static control constant	0	0	
SS_NOPREFIX*	Static control constant	80	128	
SS_RIGHT	Static control constant	2	2	
SS_SIMPLE*	Static control constant	13	11	
SS_USERITEM	Static control constant	A	10	
SS_WHITEFRAME	Static control constant	9	9	
SS_WHITERECT	Static control constant	6	6	
ANSI_FIXED_FONT	Stock logical object	B	11	
ANSI_VAR_FONT	Stock logical object	C	12	
BLACK_BRUSH	Stock logical object	4	4	
BLACK_PEN	Stock logical object	7	7	
DEVICEDEFAULT_FONT	Stock logical object	E	14	
DKGRAY_BRUSH	Stock logical object	3	3	
GRAY_BRUSH	Stock logical object	2	2	
HOLLOW_BRUSH	Stock logical object	5	5	Defined as NULL_BRUSH
LTGRAY_BRUSH	Stock logical object	1	1	
NULL_BRUSH	Stock logical object	5	5	
NULL_PEN	Stock logical object	8	8	
OEM_FIXED_FONT	Stock logical object	A	10	
SYSTEM_FONT	Stock logical object	D	13	
WHITE_BRUSH	Stock logical object	0	0	
WHITE_PEN	Stock logical object	6	6	
BLACKONWHITE	Stretchblt mode	1	1	
COLORONCOLOR	Stretchblt mode	3	3	
WHITEONBLACK	Stretchblt mode	2	2	
SC_ARRANGE*	System menu command	F110	61712	
SC_CLOSE	System menu command	F060	61536	
SC_HSCROLL	System menu command	F080	61568	
SC_ICON	System menu command	F020	61472	
SC_KEYMENU	System menu command	F100	61696	
SC_MAXIMIZE*	System menu command	F030	61488	
SC_MINIMIZE*	System menu command	F020	61472	
SC_MOUSEMENU	System menu command	F090	61584	
SC_MOVE	System menu command	F010	61456	
SC_NEXTWINDOW	System menu command	F040	61504	
SC_PREVWINDOW	System menu command	F050	61520	
SC_RESTORE*	System menu command	F120	61728	
SC_SIZE	System menu command	F000	61440	
SC_VSCROLL	System menu command	F070	61552	
SC_ZOOM	System menu command	F030	61488	
BLACKNESS	Ternary raster op	0000 0042H	66	Dest = BLACK

(Continued)

Table 6.38. Continued

Defined Name	Used As	Hex Value	Decimal Value	Comments
DSTINVERT	Ternary raster op	0055 0009H	5570569	Dest = (not dest)
MERGECOPY	Ternary raster op	00C0 00CA	12583114	Dest = (source AND pattern)
MERGEPAINT	Ternary raster op	00BB 0226	12255782	Dest = (not source) OR dest
NOTSRCCOPY	Ternary raster op	0033 0008	3342344	Dest = (not source)
NOTSRCERASE	Ternary raster op	0011 00A6	1114278	Dest = (not source) AND (not dest)
PATCOPY	Ternary raster op	00F0 0021	15728673	Dest = pattern
PATINVERT	Ternary raster op	005A 0049	5898313	Dest = pattern XOR dest
PATPAINT	Ternary raster op	00FB 0A09	16452105	Dest = DPSnoo
SRCAND	Ternary raster op	0088 00C6	8913094	Dest = source AND dest
SRCCOPY	Ternary raster op	00CC 0020	13369376	Dest=source
SRCERASE	Ternary raster op	0044 0328	4457256	Dest = source AND (not dest)
SRCINVERT	Ternary raster op	0066 0046	6684742	Dest = source XOR dest
SRCPAINT	Ternary raster op	00EE 0086	15597702	Dest=source OR dest
WHITENESS	Ternary raster op	00FF 0062	16711778	Dest = WHITE
TA_BASELINE*	Text alignment option	18	24	
TA_BOTTOM*	Text alignment option	8	8	
TA_CENTER*	Text alignment option	6	6	
TA_LEFT*	Text alignment option	0	0	
TA_NOUPDATECP*	Text alignment option	0	0	
TA_RIGHT*	Text alignment option	2	2	
TA_TOP*	Text alignment option	0	0	
TA_UPDATECP*	Text alignment option	1	1	
BN_CLICKED	User button notification code	0	0	
BN_DISABLE	User button notification code	4	4	
BN_HILITE	User button notification code	2	2	
BN_PAINT	User button notification code	1	1	
BN_UNHILITE	User button notification code	3	3	
VK_ACCEPT*	Virtual key	1E	30	
VK_CONVERT*	Virtual key	1C	28	
VK_HIRAGANA*	Virtual key	18	24	
VK_KANA*	Virtual key	15	21	
VK_KANJI*	Virtual key	19	25	
VK_MODECHANGE*	Virtual key	1F	31	
VK_NONCONVERT*	Virtual key	1D	29	
VK_ROMAJI*	Virtual key	16	22	
VK_ZENKAKU*	Virtual key	17	23	
S_ALLTHRESHOLD*	WaitSoundState constant	2	2	
S_QUEUEEMPTY	WaitSoundState constant	0	0	
S_THRESHOLD	WaitSoundState constant	1	1	
GWL_STYLE	Window field offset	FFF0	-16	
GWL_WNDPROC	Window field offset	FFFC	-4	
GWW_HINSTANCE	Window field offset	FFFA	-6	
GWW_HWNDPARENT	Window field offset	FFF8	-8	
GWW_HWNDTEXT	Window field offset	FFF6	-10	
GWW_ID	Window field offset	FFF4	-12	
WH_SYSMSGFILTER*	Window hook	6	6	
WH_WINDOWMGR*	Window hook	7	7	
WH_CBT*	Window hook	5	5	
WC_DEFWINDOWPROC*	Window manager hook code	3	3	
WC_DRAWCAPTION*	Window manager hook code	7	7	
WC_INIT*	Window manager hook code	1	1	
WC_MINMAX*	Window manager hook code	4	4	
WC_MOVE*	Window manager hook code	5	5	
WC_SIZE*	Window manager hook code	6	6	
WC_SWP*	Window manager hook code	2	2	
WM_ACTIVATE	Window procedure message ID	6	6	
WM_ACTIVATEAPP	Window procedure message ID	1C	28	
WM_ASKCBFORMATNAME	Window procedure message ID	30C	780	
WM_CANCELMODE	Window procedure message ID	1F	31	
WM_CHANGECBCHAIN	Window procedure message ID	30D	781	
WM_CHAR	Window procedure message ID	102	258	
WM_CHILDACTIVATE*	Window procedure message ID	22	34	
WM_CLEAR	Window procedure message ID	303	771	
WM_CLOSE	Window procedure message ID	10	16	
WM_COMMAND	Window procedure message ID	111	273	
WM_CONVERTREQUEST	Window procedure message ID	10A	266	
WM_CONVERTRESULT	Window procedure message ID	10B	267	
WM_COPY	Window procedure message ID	301	769	
WM_CREATE	Window procedure message ID	1	1	
WM_CTLCOLOR	Window procedure message ID	19	25	
WM_CUT	Window procedure message ID	300	768	
WM_DEADCHAR	Window procedure message ID	103	259	
WM_DESTROY	Window procedure message ID	2	2	
WM_DESTROYCLIPBOARD	Window procedure message ID	307	775	
WM_DEVMODECHANGE	Window procedure message ID	1B	27	
WM_DRAWCLIPBOARD	Window procedure message ID	308	776	
WM_ENABLE	Window procedure message ID	A	10	

(Continued)

Table 6.38. Continued

Defined Name	Used As	Hex Value	Decimal Value	Comments
WM_ENDSESSION	Window procedure message ID	16	22	
WM_ENTERIDLE	Window procedure message ID	121	289	
WM_ERASEBKGND	Window procedure message ID	14	20	
WM_FONTCHANGE	Window procedure message ID	1D	29	
WM_GETDLGCODE	Window procedure message ID	87	135	
WM_GETMINMAXINFO*	Window procedure message ID	24	36	
WM_GETTEXT	Window procedure message ID	D	13	
WM_GETTEXTLENGTH	Window procedure message ID	E	14	
WM_HSCROLL	Window procedure message ID	114	276	
WM_HSCROLLCLIPBOARD	Window procedure message ID	30E	782	
WM_ICONERASEBKGND*	Window procedure message ID	27	39	
WM_INITDIALOG	Window procedure message ID	110	272	
WM_INITMENU	Window procedure message ID	116	278	
WM_INITMENUPOPUP	Window procedure message ID	117	279	
WM_KANJIFIRST	Window procedure message ID	280	640	
WM_KANJILAST	Window procedure message ID	29F	671	
WM_KEYDOWN	Window procedure message ID	100	256	
WM_KEYFIRST	Window procedure message ID	100	256	
WM_KEYLAST	Window procedure message ID	107	263	
WM_KEYUP	Window procedure message ID	101	257	
WM_KILLFOCUS	Window procedure message ID	8	8	
WM_LBUTTONDBLCLK	Window procedure message ID	203	515	
WM_LBUTTONDOWN	Window procedure message ID	201	513	
WM_LBUTTONUP	Window procedure message ID	202	514	
WM_MBUTTONDBLCLK	Window procedure message ID	209	521	
WM_MBUTTONDOWN	Window procedure message ID	207	519	
WM_MBUTTONUP	Window procedure message ID	208	520	
WM_MENUCHAR*	Window procedure message ID	120	521	
WM_MENUSELECT*	Window procedure message ID	11F	522	
WM_MOUSEACTIVATE*	Window procedure message ID	21	33	
WM_MOUSEFIRST	Window procedure message ID	200	512	
WM_MOUSELAST	Window procedure message ID	209	521	
WM_MOUSEMOVE	Window procedure message ID	200	512	
WM_MOVE	Window procedure message ID	3	3	
WM_NCACTIVATE	Window procedure message ID	86	134	
WM_NCCALCSIZE	Window procedure message ID	83	131	
WM_NCCREATE	Window procedure message ID	81	129	
WM_NCDESTROY	Window procedure message ID	82	130	
WM_NCHITTEST	Window procedure message ID	84	132	
WM_NCLBUTTONDBLCLK	Window procedure message ID	A3	163	
WM_NCLBUTTONDOWN	Window procedure message ID	A1	161	
WM_NCLBUTTONUP	Window procedure message ID	A2	162	
WM_NCMBUTTONDBLCLK	Window procedure message ID	A9	169	
WM_NCMBUTTONDOWN	Window procedure message ID	A7	167	
WM_NCMBUTTONUP	Window procedure message ID	A8	168	
WM_NCMOUSEMOVE	Window procedure message ID	A0	160	
WM_NCPAINT	Window procedure message ID	85	133	
WM_NCRBUTTONDBLCLK	Window procedure message ID	A6	166	
WM_NCRBUTTONDOWN	Window procedure message ID	A4	164	
WM_NCRBUTTONUP	Window procedure message ID	A5	165	
WM_NEXTDLGCTL*	Window procedure message ID	28	40	
WM_NULL	Window procedure message ID	0	0	
WM_PAINT	Window procedure message ID	F	15	
WM_PAINTCLIPBOARD	Window procedure message ID	309	777	
WM_PAINTICON*	Window procedure message ID	26	38	
WM_PASTE	Window procedure message ID	302	770	
WM_QUERYENDSESSION	Window procedure message ID	11	17	
WM_QUERYOPEN	Window procedure message ID	13	19	
WM_QUEUESYNC*	Window procedure message ID	23	35	
WM_QUIT	Window procedure message ID	12	18	
WM_RBUTTONDBLCLKL	Window procedure message ID	206	518	
WM_RBUTTONDOWN	Window procedure message ID	204	516	
WM_RBUTTONUP	Window procedure message ID	205	517	
WM_RENDERALLFORMATS	Window procedure message ID	306	774	
WM_RENDERFORMAT	Window procedure message ID	305	773	
WM_SETCURSOR*	Window procedure message ID	20	32	
WM_SETFOCUS	Window procedure message ID	7	7	
WM_SETREDRAW	Window procedure message ID	B	11	
WM_SETTEXT	Window procedure message ID	C	12	
WM_SETVISIBLE	Window procedure message ID	9	9	
WM_SHOWWINDOW	Window procedure message ID	18	24	
WM_SIZE	Window procedure message ID	5	5	
WM_SIZECLIPBOARD	Window procedure message ID	30B	779	
WM_SIZEWAIT	Window procedure message ID	4	4	
WM_SPOOLERSTATUS	Window procedure message ID	2A	42	
WM_SYNCPAINT*	Window procedure message ID	88	136	
WM_SYNCTASK*	Window procedure message ID	89	137	

(Continued)

Table 6.38. Continued

Defined Name	Used As	Hex Value	Decimal Value	Comments
WM_SYSCHAR	Window procedure message ID	106	262	
WM_SYSCOLORCHANGE	Window procedure message ID	15	21	
WM_SYSCOMMAND	Window procedure message ID	112	274	
WM_SYSDEADCHAR	Window procedure message ID	107	263	
WM_SYSKEYDOWN	Window procedure message ID	104	260	
WM_SYSKEYUP	Window procedure message ID	105	261	
WM_SYSTEMERROR	Window procedure message ID	17	23	
WM_SYSTIMER	Window procedure message ID	118	280	
WM_TIMECHANGE	Window procedure message ID	1E	30	
WM_TIMER	Window procedure message ID	113	275	
WM_UNDO	Window procedure message ID	304	772	
WM_USER	Window procedure message ID	400	1024	First application window message
WM_VSCROLL	Window procedure message ID	115	277	
WM_VSCROLLCLIPBOARD	Window procedure message ID	30A	778	
WM_WININICHANGE	Window procedure message ID	1A	26	
WM_YOMICHAR	Window procedure message ID	108	264	
WS_BORDER	Window style	0080 0000	8388608	
WS_CAPTION	Window style	00C0 0000	12582912	
WS_CHILD	Window style	4000 0000	1073741824	
WS_CHILDWINDOW*	Window style	4000 0000	1073741824	
WS_CLIPCHILDREN	Window style	0200 0000	33554432	
WS_CLIPSIBLINGS	Window style	0400 0000	67108864	
WS_DISABLED	Window style	0800 0000	134217728	
WS_DLGFRAME	Window style	0040 0000	4194304	
WS_GROUP	Window style	0002 0000	131072	
WS_HSCROLL	Window style	0010 0000	1048576	
WS_ICONIC	Window style	2000 0000	536870912	Defined as WS_MINIMIZE
WS_ICONICPOPUP*	Window style	C000 0000	3221225472	
WS_MAXIMIZE*	Window style	0100 0000	16777216	
WS_MAXIMIZEBOX*	Window style	0001 0000	65536	
WS_MINIMIZE	Window style	2000 0000	536870912	
WS_MINIMIZEBOX*	Window style	0002 0000	131072	
WS_OVERLAPPED*	Window style	0	0	
WS_OVERLAPPEDWINDOW*	Window style	00CC 0000	13369344	
WS_POPUP	Window style	8000 0000	-2147483648	
WS_POPUPWINDOW*	Window style	8088 0000	2156396544	
WS_SIZEBOX	Window style	0004 0000	262144	
WS_SYSMENU	Window style	0008 0000	524288	
WS_TABSTOP	Window style	0001 0000	65536	
WS_THICKFRAME*	Window style	0004 0000	262144	
WS_TILED	Window style	0	0	
WS_TILEDWINDOW*	Window style	00CC 0000	13369344	
WS_VISIBLE	Window style	1000 0000	268435456	
WS_VSCROLL	Window style	0020 0000	2097152	
HTBOTTOM*	Winwhere area code	F	15	
HTBOTTOMLEFT*	Winwhere area code	10	16	
HTBOTTOMRIGHT*	Winwhere area code	11	17	
HTCAPTION	Winwhere area code	2	2	
HTCLIENT	Winwhere area code	1	1	
HTERROR	Winwhere area code	FFFE	-2	
HTGROWBOX	Winwhere area code	4	4	
HTHSCROLL	Winwhere area code	6	6	
HTLEFT*	Winwhere area code	A	10	
HTMENU	Winwhere area code	5	5	
HTNOWHERE	Winwhere area code	0	0	
HTREDUCE*	Winwhere area code	8	8	
HTRIGHT*	Winwhere area code	B	11	
HTSIZE*	Winwhere area code	4	4	
HTSIZEFIRST*	Winwhere area code	A	10	
HTSIZELAST*	Winwhere area code	11	17	
HTSYSMENU	Winwhere area code	3	3	
HTTOP*	Winwhere area code	C	12	
HTTOPLEFT*	Winwhere area code	D	13	
HTTOPRIGHT*	Winwhere area code	E	14	
HTTRANSPARENT	Winwhere area code	FFFF	-1	
HTVSCROLL	Winwhere area code	7	7	
HTZOOM*	Winwhere area code	9	9	
ASPECT_FILTERING		1	1	
ST_BEGINSWP*		0	0	
ST_ENDSWP*		1	1	

Version Info: *Applies to all versions of Windows beginning with 2.0

Source: WINDOWS.H file in development kit

See Also: 6.37. Include File Constants Definitions by Name

6.39. BITMAP STRUCTURE FORMAT

Field Type	Argument Type	Description	Restrictions on Allowable Values
Short	bmType	Bitmap type	Must be 0 for logical bitmaps
Short	bmWidth	Width of bitmap in pixels	Must be greater than 0
Short	bmHeight	Height of bitmap in raster lines	Must be greater than 0
Short	bmWidthBytes	Number of bytes per raster line	Must be an even number
BYTE	bmPlanes	Points to number of color planes in bitmap	
BYTE	bmBitsPixel	Points to number of adjacent color bits on each plane	
LPSTR	bmBits	Points to bitmap	Long pointer to array of BYTE values comprising bitmap

Notes: •C is case sensitive
              •Numbers in parentheses show actual values

Source: Microsoft Windows SDK Programmer's Reference 2.0, pages 609 to 611

See Also: 1.17. Common String Formats

6.40. COMSTAT STRUCTURE FORMAT

Field Type	Argument Type	Description
BYTE	fCtsHold	Waiting for CTS?
BYTE	fDsrHold	Waiting for DSR?
BYTE	fR1sdHold	Waiting for received signal detect?
BYTE	fXoffHold	Waiting due to received XOFF?
BYTE	fXoffSent	Waiting due to sent XOFF?
BYTE	fEof	Has EOF been received?
BYTE	fTxim	Send char immediately?
WORD	cbInQue	Number of characters in receive queue
WORD	cbOutQue	Number of characters in transmit queue

Notes: •C is case sensitive
              •Numbers in parentheses show actual values

Source: Microsoft Windows SDK Programmer's Reference 2.0, pages 611 to 612

6.41. CREATESTRUCT STRUCTURE FORMAT

Field Type	Argument Type	Description	Restrictions on Allowable Values
LPSTR	lpCreateParams	Pointer to data for window creation parameters	
HANDLE	hInstance	Module instance handle of module owning new window	
HANDLE	hMenu	Handle of menu to be used by new window	
HWND	hwndParent	Window handle of window opening the new window	NULL=top-level window
int	cy	Height of new window	
int	cx	Width column of new window (child and popup only)	
int	y	y coordinate of upper-left corner of new window	Relative to parent (if new is child)
int	x	x coordinate of upper-left corner of new window	Relative to parent (if new is child)
long	style	New window's style	
LPSTR	lpszName	New window's name	Pointer to ASCIIZ string
LPSTR	lpszClass	New window's class name	Pointer to ASCIIZ string

Notes: C is case sensitive

Source: Microsoft Windows SDK Programmer's Reference 2.0, pages 612 to 613

See Also: 1.17. Common String Formats

6.42. DCB STRUCTURE FORMAT

Field Type	Argument Type	Description	Restrictions on Allowable Values
BYTE	Id	Communication device ID	Set by device driver; sig. bit set=parallel device
WORD	BaudRate	Baud rate	
BYTE	ByteSize	Number of bits in transmitted char	Must in range 4 to 8
BYTE	Parity	Parity scheme to use	Must be one of: NOPARITY (0) ODDPARITY (1) EVENPARITY (2) MARKPARITY (3) SPACEPARITY (4)
BYTE	StopBits	Number of stop bits in transmitted char	Must be one of: ONESTOPBIT (0) ONE5STOPBITS (1) TWOSTOPBITS (2)
WORD	RlsTimeout	Milliseconds to wait for CD to go high	
WORD	CtsTimeout	Milliseconds to wait for CTS to go high	
WORD	DsrTimeout	Milliseconds to wait for DSR to go high	
BYTE	Bit 7:fBinary Bit 6:fRtsDisable Bit 5:fParity Bit 4:fOutxCtsFlow Bit 3:fOutxDsrFlow Bits 1-2: fDummy Bit 0:fDtrDisable	Is binary mode? Is RTS disabled? Is Parity checking enabled? Monitor CTS for output flow control? Monitor DSR for output flow control? Place holder only Is DTR enabled?	0=ASCII mode; 1=binary mode 0=RTS enabled; 1=RTS disabled 0=parity not checked; 1=parity enabled 0=don't monitor CTS; 1=monitor CTS 0=don't monitor DSR; 1=monitor DSR 0=DTR enabled; 1=DTR not enabled
BYTE	Bit 7:fOutX Bit 6:fInX Bit 5:fPeChar Bit 4:fNull Bit 3:fChEvt Bit 2:fDtrFlow Bit 1:fRtsFlow Bit 0:fDummy2	Use XON/XOFF during transmission? Use XON/XOFF during reception? Replace parity chars with PeChar? Discard NULL characters? Flag EvtChar as an event? Monitor DTR for input flow control? Monitor RTS for input flow control? Place holder only	0=don't use; 1=use XON/XOFF 0=don't use; 1=use XON/XOFF 0=don't replace; 1=replace chars with parity error 0=don't discard; 1=discard NULL characters 0=don't flag; 1=EvtChar indicates event 0=don't monitor DTR; 1=monitor DTR 0=don't monitor RTS; 1=monitor RTS
Char	XonChar	XON character for transmit & receive	ASCII value
Char	XoffChar	XOFF character for transmit & receive	ASCII value
WORD	XonLim	Min. chars in receive queue before XON	
WORD	XoffLim	Max. chars in receive queue before XOFF	
Char	PeChar	Character that replaces parity errors	ASCII value
Char	EofChar	Character that signals an event	ASCII value
Char	EvtChar	Character that signals end-of-data	ASCII value
WORD	TxDelay	Min. milliseconds between transmissions	

Notes: •C is case sensitive
•Numbers in parentheses show actual values

Source: Microsoft Windows SDK Programmer's Reference 2.0, pages 613 to 617

See Also: 1.17. Common String Formats

6.43. DLGTEMPLATE STRUCTURE FORMAT

DLGTEMPLATE Header:

Field Type	Argument Type	Description	Restrictions on Allowable Values
Long	dtStyle	Style of dialog box	
Byte	dtItemCount	Number of items in dialog box (controls)	
Int	dtX	x-coordinate of upper-left corner of box	
Int	dtY	y-coordinate of upper-left corner of box	
Int	dtCX	x-extent of the dialog box	
Int	dtCY	y-extent of the dialog box	
Char	dtResourceName[]	Name of application's resource file	ASCIIZ string
Char	dtClassName[]	Window's class name	ASCIIZ string
Char	dtCaptionText[]	Caption string for dialog box	ASCIIZ string

Item List (of Controls) Follows Header with Each Item Containing:

Field Type	Argument Type	Description	Restrictions on Allowable Values
Int	dtilX	x-coordinate of upper-left corner of item	(Relative to origin of box)
Int	dtilY	y-coordinate of upper-left corner of item	(Relative to origin of box)
Int	dtilCX	x-extent of item	
Int	dtilCY	y-extent of item	
Int	dtilID	Dialog item ID number	
Long	dtilStyle	Style of the dialog item	
Char	dtilText	Text for the item (if any)	ASCIIZ string
BYTE	dtilInfo	Number of bytes to next item in structure	

Version Info: First defined in Windows 2.0

Notes: C is case sensitive

Source: Microsoft Windows SDK Programmer's Reference 2.0, pages 617 to 618

6.44. EXTTEXTMETRIC STRUCTURE FORMAT

Field Type	Argument Type	Description	Restrictions on Allowable Values
Short	etmsize	Size of EXTTEXTMETRIC structure	
Short	etmPointSize	Font's point size in twips	
Short	etmOrientation	Font orientation	1=portrait, 2=landscape, 0=either
Short	etmMasterHeight	Font height in device units	
Short	etmMinScale	Mmin range of device units for font	
Short	etmMaxScale	Mmax range of device units for font	
Short	etmMasterUnits	Number of units per em	
Short	etmCapHeight	Height of uppercase letters	In font units, typically height of 'H'
Short	etmXHeight	Height of lowercase letters	In font units, typically height of 'x'
Short	etmLowerCaseAscent	Distance ascenders above baseline	In font units, typically ascent of 'd'
Short	etmUpperCaseDescent	Distance descenders below baseline	In font units, typically descent of 'p'
Short	etmSlant	Angle counterclockwise from vert.	In degrees
Short	etmSuperScript	Distance above baseline	Specified as negative offset
Short	etmSubScript	Distance below baseline	Specified as positive offset
Short	etmSuperScriptSize	Recommended size of superscripts	
Short	etmSubScriptSize	Recommended size of subscripts	
Short	etmUnderlineOffset	Distance below baseline to top of line	
Short	etmUnderlineWidth	Thickness of underline	
Short	etmDoubleUpperUnderlineOffset	Distance below baseline to top of line	
Short	etmDoubleLowerUnderlineOffset	Distance below baseline to top of line	
Short	etmDoubleUpperUnderlineWidth	Thickness of underline	
Short	etmDoubleLowerUnderlineWidth	Thickness of underline	
Short	etmStrikeOutOffset	Distance above baseline to strikeout	
Short	etmStrikeOutWidth	Thickness of strikeout line	
Short	etmNKernPairs	Number of kerned pairs in font	
Short	etmNKernTracks	Number of kerning tracks defined for font	

Notes: C is case sensitive

Source: Microsoft Windows Reference Update 1.0, pages 46 to 48
(Not documented in Microsoft Windows SDK Programmer's Reference 2.0)

6.45. HANDLETABLE STRUCTURE FORMAT

DLGTEMPLATE Header:

Field Type	Argument Type	Description	Restrictions on Allowable Values
HANDLE	objectHandle[1]	Array of handles	(Each handle contains address and description of GDI object)

Version Info: First defined in Windows 2.0

Notes: C is case sensitive

Source: Microsoft Windows SDK Programmer's Reference 2.0, page 619

6.46. KERNPAIR STRUCTURE FORMAT

Field Type	Argument Type	Description	Restrictions on Allowable Values
BYTE*	letter1	First letter of kerning pair	ASCII character code
BYTE*	letter2	Second letter of kerning pair	ASCII character code
short	kernAmount	Amount that pair will be kerned	Generally a negative value

Notes: •C is case sensitive
•Numbers in parentheses show actual values
•*Note that the first two bytes of KERNPAIR are defined as a union, which may contain either two individual bytes, as shown here, or a single WORD, in which case letters are reversed in byte order

Source: Microsoft Windows Reference Manual Update 1.0, page 49
(Not documented in Microsoft Windows Programmer's Reference 2.0)

See Also: 1.21. ASCII Character Set

6.47. KERNTRACK STRUCTURE FORMAT

Field Type	Argument Type	Description	Restrictions on Allowable Values
Short	degree	Controls amount of track kerning	Increasing negative increases track kerning
Short	minSize	Minimum font size to apply track kerning	
Short	minAmount	Amount of track kerning to apply to fonts smaller than min size	
Short	maxSize	Maximum font size to apply track kerning	
Short	maxAmount	Amount of track kerning to apply to fonts larger than max size	

Notes: C is case sensitive

Source: Microsoft Windows Reference Update 1.0, pages 50 to 51
(Not documented in Microsoft Windows SDK Programmer's Reference 2.0)

See Also: 1.17. Common String Formats

6.48. LOGBRUSH STRUCTURE FORMAT

Field Type	Argument Type	Description	Restrictions on Allowable Values
WORD	lbStyle	Brush style	Must be one of following: BS_SOLID (0) BS_HOLLOW (1) BS_HATCHED (2) BS_PATTERN (3) BS_INDEXED (4)
DWORD	lbColor	Brush color	Must be RGB color value*
Short int	lbHatch	Brush hatch style	If lbStyle=BS_PATTERN, must be handle to pattern bitmap If lbStyle=BS_SOLID or BS_HOLLOW, lbHatch is ignored Otherwise must be: HS_HORIZONTAL (0) ----- HS_VERTICAL (1) ||||| HS_FDIAGONAL (2) ///// HS_BDIAGONAL (3) \\\\\\ HS_CROSS (4) +++++ HS_DIAGCROSS (5) xxxxx

Notes: C is case sensitive

Source: Microsoft Windows SDK Programmer's Reference 2.0, pages 619 to 620

See Also: 1.17. Common String Formats

6.49. LOGFONT STRUCTURE FORMAT

Field Type	Argument Type	Description	Restrictions on Allowable Values
Short	lfHeight	Font height in user units	0=use reasonable size; <0 transform to device units
Short	lfWidth	Font width in user units	0=match aspect ratio against digitization aspect ratio
Short	lfEscapement	Angle between line origins and x-axis	In tenths of degree; measured counterclockwise from x-axis
Short	lfOrientation	Angle between char baseline and x-axis	In tenths of degree; measured counterclockwise from x-axis
Short	lfWeight	Font weight in inked pixels per 1000	400=normal, 700=bold, 0=use default weight
BYTE	lfItalic	Is font italic?	0=not italic; non-zero = italic
BYTE	lfUnderline	Is font underlined?	0=not underlined; non-zero = underlined
BYTE	lfStrikeOut	Is font striken out?	0=not stricken; non-zero = stricken out
BYTE	lfCharSet	Character set to use for font	Must be either ANSI-CHARSET (0) or OEM_CHARSET (255)
BYTE	lfOutPrecision	Font's output precision	Must be OUT_DEFAULT_PRECIS
BYTE	lfClipPrecision	Font's clipping precision	Must be OUT_DEFAULT_PRECIS
BYTE	lfQuality	Font's output quality	Must be one of: PROOF_QUALITY (2) DRAFT_QUALITY (1) DEFAULT_QUALITY (0)
BYTE	lfPitchAndFamily	Font's pitch and family type	Pitch is indicated by low-order two bits Pitch must be one of: DEFAULT_PITCH (0) FIXED_PITCH (1) VARIABLE_PITCH (2) Font family is indicated by high-order four bits Family must be one of: FF_DONTCARE (0) FF_ROMAN (1) FF_SWISS (2) FF_MODERN (3) FF_SCRIPT (4) FF_DECORATIVE (5)
BYTE	lfFaceName[LF_FACESIZE]	Font's typeface name	Points to ASCIIZ string; if NULL uses default typeface

Notes: •C is case sensitive
                  •Numbers in parentheses show actual values

Source: Microsoft Windows SDK Programmer's Reference 2.0, pages 620 to 624

See Also: 1.17. Common String Formats

6.50. LOGPEN STRUCTURE FORMAT

Field Type	Argument Type	Description	trictions on Allowable Values
WORD	lopnStyle	Pen type	Must be one of following: 0 (solid line) 1 (dashed line) 2 (dotted line) 3 (dash-dot line) 4 (dash-dot-dot line) 5 (null line; invisible)
POINT	lopnWidth	Pen width	In logical units; 0=one pixel on raster devices
DWORD	lopnColor	Pen color	Must be RGB color value

Notes: C is case sensitive

Source: Microsoft Windows SDK Programmer's Reference 2.0, page 624

6.51. MENUITEMTEMPLATE STRUCTURE FORMAT

DLGTEMPLATE Header:

Field Type	Argument Type	Description	Restrictions on Allowable Values
BYTE	mtOption	Predefined menu option	One of the following options: GRAYED INACTIVE HELP CHECKED POPUP MENUBREAKBAR MENUBREAK END
WORD	mtID	ID code for menu item	(Must be non-popup menu item)
LPSTR	mtString	Name of menu item	ASCIIZ string

Version Info: First defined in Windows 2.0

Notes: C is case sensitive

Source: Microsoft Windows SDK Programmer's Reference 2.0, pages 625 to 626

6.52. METAFILEPICT STRUCTURE FORMAT

Field Type	Argument Type	Description
Int	mm	Mapping mode picture was drawn in
Int	xExt	x width of rectangle for picture*
Int	yExt	y height of rectangle for picture*
HANDLE	hMF	Memory metafile handle

Notes: •C is case sensitive
•*Except MM_ISOTROPIC and MM_ANISOTROPIC mapping modes.
xExt and yExt are 0 or suggested size for MM_ANISOTROPIC.
xExt and yExt are negative values representing aspect ratio for
MM_ISOTROPIC (only ratio, not actual values, are used).

Source: Microsoft Windows SDK Programmer's Reference 2.0, pages 626 to 627

See Also: 6.16. MetaFile Format

6.53. MSG STRUCTURE FORMAT

Field Type	Argument Type	Description	Restrictions on Allowable Values
HWND	hwnd	Handle to window receiving message	
WORD	message	Message number	
WORD	wParam	Additional info about the message	Exact value depends on message value
LONG	lParam	Additional info about the message	Exact value depends on message value
DWORD	time	Time message posted	
POINT	pt	Position of mouse when message posted	In screen coordinates

Notes: C is case sensitive

Source: Microsoft Windows SDK Programmer's Reference 2.0, page 627

6.54. OFSTRUCT STRUCTURE FORMAT

Field Type	Argument Type	Description	Restrictions on Allowable Values
BYTE	cBytes	Length of OFSTRUCT	In bytes
BYTE	fFixedDisk	Is file on fixed disk?	0=not fixed; non-zero=on fixed disk
WORD	nErrCode	DOS error code if open failed	-1
4 BYTES	RESERVED	RESERVED	
128 BYTEs	szPathName	File pathname	ASCIIZ string

Notes: C is case sensitive

Source: Microsoft Windows SDK Programmer's Reference 2.0, page 628

See Also: 1.17. Common String Formats

6.55. PAINTSTRUCT STRUCTURE FORMAT

Field Type	Argument Type	Description	Restrictions on Allowable Values
HDC	hdc	Display context for painting	
BOOL	fErase	Must background be redrawn	0=no; non-zero=yes
RECT	rcPaint	Upper-left, lower-right corners of rectangle to paint	
BOOL	fRestore	USED INTERNALLY BY WINDOWS	
BOOL	fIncUpdate	USED INTERNALLY BY WINDOWS	
BYTE	rgbReserved[16]	Block of memory reserved for use by Windows	

Notes: C is case sensitive

Source: Microsoft Windows SDK Programmer's Reference 2.0, pages 628 to 629

6.56. POINT STRUCTURE FORMAT

Field Type	Argument Type	Description
Int	x	x coordinate value of a point
Int	y	y coordinate value of a point

Notes: C is case sensitive

Source: Microsoft Windows SDK Programmer's Reference 2.0, page 629

6.57. RECT STRUCTURE FORMAT

Field Type	Argument Type	Description
Int	Left	x coordinate of upper-left corner of rectangle
Int	Top	y coordinate of upper-left corner of rectangle
Int	Right	x coordinate of lower-right corner of rectangle
Int	Bottom	y coordinate of lower-right corner of rectangle

Notes: •C is case sensitive
•The width of a rectangle (right-left) must not exceed 32 KB units

Source: Microsoft Windows SDK Programmer's Reference 2.0, page 630

6.58. RGB STRUCTURE FORMAT*

Byte Number

3	2	1	0	Description	Allowable Values
X				NOT USED	Must be 00H
	X			Red intensity of color	0=no red; 0FFH=maximum red
		X		Green intensity of color	0=no green; 0FFH=maximum green
			X	Blue intensity of color	0=no blue; 0FFH=maximum blue

Notes: •Black is defined as 0000 0000H; white is defined as 00FF FFFFH
medium gray is defined as 007F 7F7FH
•*An RGB structure consists of a single long integer, which is formatted as
shown above

Source: Microsoft Windows SDK Programmer's Reference 2.0, page 630

6.59. TEXTMETRIC STRUCTURE FORMAT

Field Type	Argument Type	Description	Restrictions on Allowable Values
Short	tmHeight	Height of characters (ascent+descent)	
Short	tmAscent	Ascent of characters above baseline	
Short	tmDescent	Descent of characters below baseline	
Short	tmInternalLeading	Amount of leading within tmHeight	
Short	tmExternalLeading	Amount of leading outside char box	
Short	tmAveCharWidth	Average width of characters	Usually width of X character
Short	tmMaxCharWidth	Maximum width of characters	Must be actual maximum width
Short	tmWeight	Font weight	0=default weight; 400=normal; 700=bold
BYTE	tmItalic	Is font italic?	0=not italic; non-zero=italic
BYTE	tmUnderlined	Is font underlined?	0=not underlined; non-zero=underlined
BYTE	tmStruckOut	Is font stricken out?	0=not stricken; non-zero=stricken out
BYTE	tmFirstChar	Value of first character defined in font	
BYTE	tmLastChar	Value of last character defined in font	
BYTE	tmDefaultChar	Value of character substituted for missing chars	
BYTE	tmBreakChar	Value of character used for word breaks	Usually 20H
BYTE	tmPitchAndFamily	Font's pitch and family type	Pitch is indicated by low-order two bits Pitch must be one of: DEFAULT_PITCH (0) DRAFT_QUALITY (1) DEFAULT_QUALITY (2) Font family is indicated by high-order four bits Family must be one of: FF_DONTCARE (0) FF_ROMAN (1) FF_SWISS (2) FF_MODERN (3) FF_SCRIPT (4) FF_DECORATIVE (5)
BYTE	tmCharSet	Character set to use for font	Must be either ANSI_CHARSET (0) or OEM_CHARSET (255)
Short	tmOverhang	Extra width per string to add	Assumed to be top of char skew for italic fonts
Short	tmDigitizedAspectX	x aspect ratio of device font was designed for	
Short	tmDigitizedAspectY	y aspect ratio of device font was designed for	

Notes: •C is case sensitive
•Numbers in parentheses show actual values

Source: Microsoft Windows SDK Programmer's Reference 2.0, pages 631 to 633

6.60. WNDCLASS STRUCTURE FORMAT

Field Type	Argument Type	Description	Restrictions on Allowable Values
WORD	style	Class style	Must be one of: CS_VREDRAW (1) CS_HREDRAW (2) CS_DBLCKS (8) CS_OEMCHARS (10H) CS_OWNDC (20H) CS_CLASSDC (40H) CS_BYTEALIGNCLIENT (1000H)* CS_BYTEALIGNWINDOW (2000H)* CS_PARENTDC (80H)* CS_SAVEBITS (800H)* CS_NOCLOSE (200H)*
Long	lpfnWndProc	Window function	
Int	cbClsExtra	# Bytes to allocate after window class structure	
Int	cbWndExtra	# Bytes to allocate after window instance	
HANDLE	hInstance	Class module	Must not be NULL
HICON	hIcon	Class icon	If NULL, application must draw icon on close
HCURSOR	hCursor	Class cursor	If NULL, application must set cursor shape

(Continued)

Table 6.60. Continued

Field Type	Argument Type	Description	Restrictions on Allowable Values
HBRUSH	hbrBackground	Class background brush	Handle of physical brush; NULL; or one of: COLOR_SCROLLBAR+1 (1) COLOR_BACKGROUND+1 (2) COLOR_ACTIVECAPTION+1 (3) COLOR_INACTIVECAPTION+1 (4) COLOR_MENU+1 (5) COLOR_WINDOW+1 (6) COLOR_WINDOWFRAME+1 (7) COLOR_MENUTEXT+1 (8) COLOR_WINDOWTEXT+1 (9) COLOR_CAPTIONTEXT+1 (0AH) COLOR_ACTIVEBORDER+1* COLOR_APPWORKSPACE+1* COLOR_INACTIVEBORDER+1*
LPSTR	lpszMenuName	Resource name of class menu	Points to ASCIIZ string; if NULL, no default menu
LPSTR	lpszClassName	Name of window class	Points to ASCIIZ string

Version Info: *Applies only to version 2.0 and later

Notes: •C is case sensitive
•Numbers in parentheses show actual values

Source: Microsoft Windows SDK Programmer's Reference 2.0, pages 634 to 636

6.61. FORMAT OF A WINDOWS MESSAGE

Offset	Size	Function
0	Word	Message identifier (message number)
2	Word	Word parameter (set to 0 if not used)
4	Dbl word	Long parameter (set to 0 if not used)

Source: Microsoft Windows SDK Programmer's Reference 2.0, page 517

See Also: 6.62. Windows General Message Numbering

6.62. WINDOWS GENERAL MESSAGE NUMBERING

Number	Function
0 to (WM_USER-1)	RESERVED for use by Windows
WM_USER to 7FFFH	'Integer' messages for use within an application
8000 to BFFFH	RESERVED for future use by Windows
C000 to FFFFH	'String' messages for use by applications

Source: Microsoft Windows SDK Programmer's Reference 2.0, page 517

See Also: 6.61. Format of a Windows Message

6.63. WINDOW MANAGEMENT MESSAGES

Message Name	Purpose	wParam	lParam
WM_ACTIVATE	Occurs when window becomes active or inactive	State of window 0=inactive 1=active (not mouse click) 2=active via mouse click	HO=non-zero if window iconic; LO=handle to new active window HO=non-zero if window iconic; LO=handle of inactive window
WM_ACTIVATEAPP	Sent when window activation is another app	0=window going inactive Non-zero=window becoming active	LO=handle of task of application being activated LO=handle of task of previously active application
WM_CHILDACTIVE*	Occurs when child window has moved	Not used	Not used
WM_CLOSE	Occurs when a window is closed	Not used	Not used
WM_CREATE	Occurs when CreateWindow called	Not used	Long pointer to CREATESTRUCT data structure
WM_CTLCOLOR	Sent to parent of control just before drawing it	Handle of display context for child window	LO=handle to child window HO is one of: CTLCOLOR_MSGBOX CTLCOLOR_EDIT CTLCOLOR_LISTBOX CTLCOLOR_BTN CTLCOLOR_DLG CTLCOLOR_SCROLLBAR CTLCOLOR_STATIC
WM_DESTROY	Sent on call to DestroyWindow, after removal	Not used	Not used
WM_ENABLE	Occurs after window enabled or disabled	0=window disabled, non-zero=enabled	Not used
WM_ENDSESSION	Sent when application responds non-zero to WM_QUERYENDSESSION	0=not end of session, non-zero=session being ended	Not used
WM_ERASEBKGND	Occurs when background needs erasing	Handle of display context	Not used
WM_GETDLGCODE	Sent by Windows dialog manager to control	Not used	Not used
WM_GETMINMAXINFO*	Sent to determine size of window	Not used	Long pointer to an array of 5 points
WM_GETTEXT	Used to copy text corresponding to a window	Number of bytes to be copied (including ending null)	Long pointer to buffer to receive text
WM_GETTEXTLENGTH	Used to find length of text associated w/ window	Not used	Not used
WM_KILLFOCUS	Sent before a window loses input focus	Handle of window receiving input focus	Not used
WM_MOVE	Sent when a window is moved	Not used	New location of upper-left corner of client area of window
WM_PAINT	Occurs when request to repaint window occurs	Not used	Long pointer to PAINTSTRUCT data structure
WM_QUERYENDSESSION	Occurs when user invokes End Session command	Not used	Not used
WM_QUERYOPEN	Sent to icon when user requests it be opened	Not used	Not used
WM_QUIT	Indicates a request to terminate an application	Exit code in PostQuitMessage call	Not used
WM_SETFOCUS	Sent after a window gets the input focus	Handle of window losing input focus	Not used
WM_SETREDRAW	Sets or clears the redraw flag	If non-zero, redraw flag is set; otherwise cleared	Not used
WM_SETTEXT	Used to set the text of a window	Not used	Long pointer to ASCIIZ string containing window text
WM_SETVISIBLE	Sent before a window is made visible or hidden	Non-zero if window being visible; otherwise invisible	Not used
WM_SHOWWINDOW	Sent when a window is hidden or shown	Non-zero if window being shown; otherwise hidden	0 if message sent due to ShowWindow call Otherwise one of: SW_OTHERZOOM SW_OTHERUNZOOM SW_PARENTCLOSING SW_PARENTOPENING
WM_SIZE	Occurs after size of window has been changed	One of: SIZEICONIC SIZEFULLSCREEN SIZENORMAL SIZEZOOMSHOW SIZEZOOMHIDE	New width and height of client area (width=LO, height=HO)

Version Info: *Message available beginning with Windows 2.0

Source: Microsoft Windows SDK Programmer's Reference 2.0, pages 501 to 502 and 549 to 594

See Also:
6.61. Format of a Windows Message
6.62. Windows General Message Numbering
6.64. Initialization Messages
6.65. Input Messages
6.66. System Information Messages
6.67. Clipboard Messages
6.68. Control Messages
6.69. Notification Codes
6.70. Non-Client Area Messages

6.64. INITIALIZATION MESSAGES

Message Name	Purpose	wParam	lParam
WM_INITDIALOG	Sent before dialog box displayed	Handle to first control item that can take input focus	Not used
WM_INITMENU	Request to initialize a menu	Handle of the menu to be initialized	Not used
WM_INITMENUPOPUP	Sent before popup menu is displayed	Handle of the popup menu	HO=non-zero if popup is system menu LO=index of popup menu in the main menu

Source: Microsoft Windows SDK Programmer's Reference 2.0, pages 503 and 565 to 567

See Also: 6.61. Format of a Windows Message
                     6.62. Windows General Message Numbering
                     6.63. Window Management Messages
                     6.65. Input Messages
                     6.66. System Information Messages
                     6.67. Clipboard Messages
                     6.68. Control Messages
                     6.69. Notification Codes
                     6.70. Non-Client Area Messages

6.65. INPUT MESSAGES

Message Name	Purpose	wParm	lParam
WM_CHAR	Result of translated WM_KEYUP or WM_KEYDOWN	ASCII value of the key	Formatted as follows: Bits 1-16 = repeat count Bits 17-25 = scan code (OEM dependent value) Bit 29 = context code (1=ALT key down) Bit 30 = previous key state (1=key held down before message) Bit 31 = transition state (1=key is being released,0=pressed)
WM_COMMAND	Menu item selected, control passed message to Parent, or accelerator key translated	Either menu item, control ID, or accelerator ID	0=message f/menu or HO=1 if/accelerator otherwise HO=window handle of control; LO=control ID
WM_DEADCHAR	Result of translated WM_KEYUP or WM_KEYDOWN	Character value of dead key	Formatted as follows: Bits 1-16 = repeat count Bits 17-25 = scan code (OEM dependent value) Bit 29 = context code (1=ALT key down) Bit 30 = previous key state (1=key held down before message) Bit 31 = transition state (1=key is being released,0=pressed)
WM_HSCROLL	Occurs when user clicks mouse in scrollbar	One of following scrollbar codes: SB_LINEUP (scroll one line left) SB_LINEDOWN (scroll one line right) SB_PAGEUP (scroll one page left) SB_PAGEDOWN (scroll one page right) SB_THUMBPOSITION (scroll to absolute position) SB_THUMBTRACK (thumb dragged to specified pos) SB_TOP (scroll to far left) SB_BOTTOM (scroll to far right) SB_ENDSCROLL (end of scroll)	Not used Not used Not used Not used LO= current position of thumb LO= current position of thumb Not used Not used Not used
WM_KEYDOWN	Sent when nonsystem key pressed	Virtual key code of the key pressed	Formatted as follows: Bits 1-16 = repeat count Bits 17-25 = scan code (OEM dependent value) Bit 29 = context code (1=ALT key down) Bit 30 = previous key state (1=key held down before message) Bit 31 = transition state (1=key is being released,0=pressed)
WM_KEYUP	Sent when nonsystem key is released	Virtual key code of the key released	Formatted as follows: Bits 1-16 = repeat count Bits 17-25 = scan code (OEM dependent value) Bit 29 = context code (1=ALT key down) Bit 30 = previous key state (1=key held down before message) Bit 31 = transition state (1=key is being released,0=pressed)
WM_LBUTTONDBLCLK	Sent when user double clicks left mouse button	One of the following: MK_RBUTTON (right button down) MK_MBUTTON (middle button down) MK_LBUTTON (left button down) MK_SHIFT (shift key down) MK_CONTROL (control key down)	LO=x coordinate of mouse cursor HO=y coordinate of mouse cursor (Coordinates relative to top left corner of window)
WM_LBUTTONDOWN	Sent when left mouse button pressed	One of the following: MK_RBUTTON (right button down) MK_MBUTTON (middle button down) MK_LBUTTON (left button down) MK_SHIFT (shift key down) MK_CONTROL (control key down)	LO=x coordinate of mouse cursor HO=y coordinate of mouse cursor (Coordinates relative to top left corner of window)
WM_LBUTTONUP	Sent when left mouse button released	One of the following: MK_RBUTTON (right button down) MK_MBUTTON (middle button down) MK_LBUTTON (left button down) MK_SHIFT (shift key down) MK_CONTROL (control key down)	LO=x coordinate of mouse cursor HO=y coordinate of mouse cursor (Coordinates relative to top left corner of window)

(Continued)

Message Name	Purpose	wParm	lParam
WM_MBUTTONDBLCLK	Sent when user double clicks middle mouse button	One of the following: MK_RBUTTON (right button down) MK_MBUTTON (middle button down) MK_LBUTTON (left button down) MK_SHIFT (shift key down) MK_CONTROL (control key down)	LO=x coordinate of mouse cursor HO=y coordinate of mouse cursor (Coordinates relative to top left corner of window)
WM_MBUTTONDOWN	Sent when middle mouse button pressed	One of the following: MK_RBUTTON (right button down) MK_LBUTTON (left button down) MK_SHIFT (shift key down) MK_CONTROL (control key down)	LO=x coordinate of mouse cursor HO=y coordinate of mouse cursor (Coordinates relative to top left corner of window)
WM_MBUTTONUP	Sent when middle mouse button released	One of the following: MK_RBUTTON (right button down) MK_LBUTTON (left button down) MK_SHIFT (shift key down) MK_CONTROL (control key down)	LO=x coordinate of mouse cursor HO=y coordinate of mouse cursor (Coordinates relative to top left corner of window)
WM_MOUSEMOVE	Sent when mouse is moved	One of the following: MK_RBUTTON (right button down) MK_MBUTTON (middle button down) MK_LBUTTON (left button down) MK_SHIFT (shift key down) MK_CONTROL (control key down)	LO=x coordinate of mouse cursor HO=y coordinate of mouse cursor (Coordinates relative to top left corner of window)
WM_RBUTTONDBLCKL	Sent when right mouse button is doubled clicked	One of the following: MK_RBUTTON (right button down) MK_MBUTTON (middle button down) MK_LBUTTON (left button down) MK_SHIFT (shift key down) MK_CONTROL (control key down)	LO=x coordinate of mouse cursor HO=y coordinate of mouse cursor (Coordinates relative to top left corner of window)
WM_RBUTTONDOWN	Sent when right mouse button is pressed	One of the following: MK_MBUTTON (middle button down) MK_LBUTTON (left button down) MK_SHIFT (shift key down) MK_CONTROL (control key down)	LO=x coordinate of mouse cursor HO=y coordinate of mouse cursor (Coordinates relative to top left corner of window)
WM_RBUTTONUP	Sent when right mouse button is released	One of the following: MK_MBUTTON (middle button down) MK_LBUTTON (left button down) MK_SHIFT (shift key down) MK_CONTROL (control key down)	LO=x coordinate of mouse cursor HO=y coordinate of mouse cursor (Coordinates relative to top left corner of window)
WM_TIMER	Sent when time limit for timer is elapsed	Timer ID	Long pointer to function passed to SetTimer
WM_VSCROLL	Sent when user clicks mouse in vert scroll bar	One of following scrollbar codes: SB_LINEUP (scroll up one line) SB_LINEDOWN (scroll down one line) SB_PAGEUP (scroll up one page) SB_PAGEDOWN (scroll down one page) SB_THUMBPOSITION (scroll to absolute position) SB_THUMBTRACK (thumb dragged to specified pos) SB_TOP (scroll to top) SB_BOTTOM (scroll to bottom) SB_ENDSCROLL (end of scroll)	Not used Not used Not used Not used LO= current position of thumb LO= current position of thumb Not used Not used Not used

Source: Microsoft Windows SDK Programmer's Reference 2.0, pages 503 to 504 and 551 to 602

See Also: 6.61. Format of a Windows Message
6.62. Windows General Message Numbering
6.63. Window Management Messages
6.64. Initialization Messages
6.66. System Information Messages
6.67. Clipboard Messages
6.68. Control Messages
6.69. Notification Codes
6.70. Non-Client Area Messages

6.66. SYSTEM INFORMATION MESSAGES

Message Name	Purpose	wParam	lParam
WM_DEVMODECHANGE	Sent to top-level windows when device mode settings change	Not used	Long pointer to WIN.INI device name
WM_FONTCHANGE	Sent to top-level windows when pool of font resources changes	Not used	Not used
WM_SYSCOLORCHANGE	Sent to top-level windows when system color setting changes	Not used	Not used
WM_SYSTEMERROR	Sent to top-level windows when out-of-memory error occurs	8=out of memory error code	Not used
WM_TIMECHANGE	Sent to top-level windows when application changes system time	Not used	Not used
WM_WININICHANGE	Sent to top-level windows when WIN.INI is changed	Not used	Long pointer to string specifying section that changed; 0 if more than one change

Source: Microsoft Windows SDK Programmer's Reference 2.0, pages 507 and 558 to 604

See Also:
6.61. Format of a Windows Message
6.62. Windows General Message Numbering
6.63. Window Management Messages
6.64. Initialization Messages
6.65. Input Messages
6.67. Clipboard Messages
6.68. Control Messages
6.69. Notification Codes
6.70. Non-Client Area Messages

6.67. CLIPBOARD MESSAGES

Message Name	Purpose	wParam	lParam
WM_ASKCBFORMATNAME	Sent when clipboard needs handle for CF_OWNERDISPLAY format	Integer number of bytes to copy	Long pointer to buffer where copy of the format name is stored
WM_CHANGECBCHAIN	Sent to first window in viewer chain when window is removed from chain	Handle of window being removed from chain	LO=handle of window following one being removed (next wind)
WM_DESTROYCLIPBOARD	Sent to clipboard owner when clipboard is emptied by EmptyClipboard	Not used	Not used
WM_DRAWCLIPBOARD	Sent to first window in viewer chain when contents are changed	Not used	Not used
WM_HSCROLLCLIPBOARD	Sent when clipboard is CF_OWNERDISPLAY and horizontal scroll event occurs	Handle to clipboard application window	LO contains one of the following scrollbar codes: SB_LINEUP (scroll one line left), SB_LINEDOWN (scroll one line right), SB_PAGEUP (scroll one page left), SB_PAGEDOWN (scroll one page right), SB_THUMBPOSITION (scroll to absolute position), SB_TOP (scroll to far left), SB_BOTTOM (scroll to far right), SB_ENDSCROLL (end of scroll). HO contains thumb position if LO=SB_THUMBPOSITION
WM_PAINTCLIPBOARD	Sent when clipboard is CF_OWNERSHIP and clipboard app's client area needs repainting	Handle to clipboard application window	Long pointer to PAINTSTRUCT defining area to paint
WM_RENDERALLFORMATS	Sent to application that owns clipboard when application is being destroyed	Not used	Not used
WM_RENDERFORMAT	Sent to request clipboard owner format data in specified format	Data format to render	Not used
WM_SIZECLIPBOARD	Sent when clipboard is CF_OWNERSHIP and clipboard app window has changed size	Handle to clipboard application window	LO=pointer to RECT data structure defining area to paint
WM_VSCROLLCLIPBOARD	Sent when clipboard is CF_OWNERSHIP and vertical scroll event occurs	Handle to clipboard application window	LO contains one of the following scrollbar codes: SB_LINEUP (scroll one line left), SB_LINEDOWN (scroll one line right), SB_PAGEUP (scroll one page left), SB_PAGEDOWN (scroll one page right), SB_THUMBPOSITION (scroll to absolute position), SB_TOP (scroll to far left), SB_BOTTOM (scroll to far right), SB_ENDSCROLL (end of scroll). HO contains thumb position if LO=SB_THUMBPOSITION

See Also:
6.15. Clipboard Formats
6.61. Format of a Windows Message
6.62. Windows General Message Numbering
6.63. Window Management Messages
6.64. Initialization Messages
6.65. Input Messages
6.66. System Information Messages
6.68. Control Messages
6.69. Notification Codes
6.70. Non-Client Area Messages

Source: Microsoft Windows SDK Programmer's Reference 2.0, pages 506 to 507 and 550 to 603

6.68. CONTROL MESSAGES

Message Name	Purpose	wParam	lParam
BM_GETCHECK	Sent to determine status of check box or radio button	Not used	Not used
BM_GETSTATE	Sent to determine if cursor over button and moused clicked	Not used	Not used
BM_SETCHECK	Sent to check radio button or check box	0=remove check; non-zero=place check	Not used
BM_SETSTATE	Sent to highlight button or check box	0=highlight removed; non-zero=highlighted	Not used
BM_SETSTYLE*	Sent to alter button style	Style value	Not used
EM_CANUNDO	Sent to determine if edit control can undo last edit	Not used	Not used
EM_FMTLINES	Sent to add or remove EOL char from text lines	0=remove EOL, non-zero=add CR CR LF to lines	Not used
EM_GETHANDLE	Sent to determine handle of buffer holding control window contents	Not used	Not used
EM_GETLINE	Sent to copy a line from the edit control	Line number	Far pointer to buffer to store line (first word=max length allowed)
EM_GETLINECOUNT	Sent to determine number of lines of text in edit control	Not used	Not used
EM_GETRECT	Sent to determine formatting rectangle of control	Not used	Long pointer to RECT data structure
EM_GETSEL	Sent to determine start and end positions of selection	Not used	Not used
EM_LIMITTEXT	Sent to limit length of text the user may enter	Maximum number of bytes that can be entered	Not used
EM_LINEFROMCHAR*	Sent to determine which line contains a specific character	Index to character	Not used
EM_LINEINDEX	Sent to determine what char positions before first char on line	Line number or -1 for current line	Not used
EM_LINELENGTH	Sent to determine length of line in edit control's text buffer	Line number or -1 for current line	Not used
EM_LINESCROLL	Sent to scroll context of control by a number of lines	Not used	HO=number of lines, LO=number of horiz. char positions
EM_REPLACESEL	Sent to replace selection with new text	Not used	Far pointer to ASCIIZ string of replacement text
EM_SCROLL	Sent to direct edit control to scroll window vertically	One of the following values: SB_LINEUP (scroll one line up) SB_LINEDOWN (scroll one line down) SB_PAGEUP (scroll one page up) SB_PAGEDOWN (scroll one page down) SB_THUMBPOSITION (scroll to position) EM_GETTHUMB (retrieve thumb position)	Not used
EM_SETFONT	Sent to set edit control font being used	Font ID (must be fixed pitch)	Not used
EM_SETHANDLE	Sent to establish text buffer used to hold control window contents	Handle to buffer in application's data segment	Not used
EM_SETRECTNP	Sent to set formatting rect of control w/ no repainting	Not used	Long pointer to RECT data structure specifying new rectangle
EM_SETSEL	Sent to select chars between start and end position	LO=start pos. HO=ending position	Not used
EM_SETSRECT	Sent to set formatting rectangle of control	Not used	Long pointer to RECT data structure specifying new rectangle
EM_SETWORDBREAK*	Sent to set word break for multiline edit controls	Not used	Long pointer to application-supplied word break function
EM_UNDO	Sent to undo last edit to edit control	Not used	Not used
LB_ADDSTRING	Sent to add string to list box	Not used	Long pointer to ASCIIZ string to add
LB_DELETESTRING	Sent to delete string from list box	Index to string to delete	Not used
LB_DIR	Sent to add list of files in current directory to list box	DOS attribute value	Long pointer to file specification string (may include * and ?)
LB_GETCOUNT	Sent to get count of number of items in list box	Not used	Not used
LB_GETCURSEL	Sent to return index of current selection, if any	Not used	Not used
LB_GETSEL	Sent to return selection state of an item	Index to the item	Not used
LB_GETTEXT	Sent to copy string from list into buffer	Index to string to copy into buffer	Long pointer to buffer to receive copy of string
LB_GETTEXTLEN	Sent to determine length of string in list box	Index to string to determine length of	Not used
LB_INSERTSTRING	Sent to insert string into list box	Index to position for string, or -1 for end of list	Long pointer to ASCIIZ string to insert
LB_SELECTSTRING	Sent to change selection to first string matching prefix	Index of start point for search, -1=search all strings	Long pointer to ASCIIZ prefix string
LB_SETCURSEL	Sent to select string and scroll it into view, if necessary	Index to string to select	-1 list box set to have no selection
LB_SETSEL	Sent to set selection state of a string	0=highlight removed; non-zero=set highlight	LO=index to string or -1 for all strings in list
WM_CLEAR	Sent to delete current selection	Not used	Not used
WM_COPY	Sent to copy current selection to clipboard in CF_TEXT format	Not used	Not used
WM_CUT	Sent to perform WM_COPY and WM_CLEAR, in that order	Not used	Not used
WM_PASTE	Sent to copy clipboard data to current window at current cursor pos.	Not used	Not used

Version Info: *Applies to Windows beginning with version 2.0 only

Source: Microsoft Windows SDK Programmer's Reference 2.0, pages 508 to 510 and 519 to 586

See Also: 6.61. Format of a Windows Message
6.62. Windows General Message Numbering
6.63. Window Management Messages
6.64. Initialization Messages
6.65. Input Messages
6.66. System Information Messages
6.67. Clipboard Messages
6.69. Notification Codes
6.70. Non-Client Area Messages

6.69. NOTIFICATION CODES

Code Name	Meaning
BN_CLICKED	The button has been clicked
BN_DISABLE	The button should be drawn as disabled
BN_DOUBLECLICKED*	The user has double clicked a mouse button
BN_HILITE	The button requires highlighting
BN_PAINT	The button requires repainting
BN_UNHILITE	The button requires unhighlighting
EN_CHANGE	The user has taken an action that may have changed the content of the text
EN_ERRSPACE	The edit control is out of space
EN_HSCROLL	The user has clicked on the edit control's horiz scroll bar
EN_KILLFOCUS	The edit control has lost the input focus
EN_SETFOCUS	The edit control has obtained the input focus
EN_UPDATE*	The edit control will display altered text
EN_VSCROLL	The user has clicked on the edit control's vert scroll bar
LBN_DBLCLK	The user double clicked the mouse button over a string
LBN_ERRSPACE	Out of memory
LBN_SELCHANGE	The selection has been changed

Version Info: *Applies to versions of Windows beginning with 2.0 only

Source: Microsoft Windows SDK Programmer's Reference 2.0, pages 511 to 512 and 522 to 548

See Also:
6.61. Format of a Windows Message
6.62. Windows General Message Numbering
6.63. Window Management Messages
6.64. Initialization Messages
6.65. Input Messages
6.66. System Information Messages
6.67. Clipboard Messages
6.68. Control Messages

6.70. NON-CLIENT AREA MESSAGES

Message Name	Purpose	wParam	lParam
WM_NCACTIVATE	Sent to window when its caption bar or icon needs to be changed	0=make active; non-zero=make inactive	Not used
WM_NCCALCSIZE	Sent when size of client area needs to be calculated	Not used	Long pointer to RECT data structure
WM_NCCREATE	Sent before WM_CREATE message when window created	handle to window being created	Long pointer to CREATESTRUCT data structure for window
WM_NCDESTROY	Sent after WM_DESTROY message	Not used	Not used
WM_NCHITTEST	Sent each time mouse moved	Not used	LO=x coord of mouse, HO=y coord of mouse
WM_NCLBUTTONDBLCLK	Sent when left mouse button double clicked in non-client area	Code returned by WM_NCHITTEST	LO=x coord of mouse, HO=y coord of mouse
WM_NCLBUTTONDOWN	Sent when left mouse button is pressed in non-client area	Code returned by WM_NCHITTEST	LO=x coord of mouse, HO=y coord of mouse
WM_NCLBUTTONUP	Sent when left mouse button released in non-client area	Code returned by WM_NCHITTEST	LO=x coord of mouse, HO=y coord of mouse
WM_NCMBUTTONDBLCLK	Sent when middle mouse button double clicked in non-client area	Code returned by WM_NCHITTEST	LO=x coord of mouse, HO=y coord of mouse
WM_NCMBUTTONDOWN	Sent when middle mouse button is pressed in non-client area	Code returned by WM_NCHITTEST	LO=x coord of mouse, HO=y coord of mouse
WM_NCMBUTTONUP	Sent when middle mouse button released in non-client area	Code returned by WM_NCHITTEST	LO=x coord of mouse, HO=y coord of mouse
WM_NCMOUSEMOVE	Sent when mouse is moved in non-client area of window	Not used	LO=x coord of mouse, HO=y coord of mouse
WM_NCPAINT	Sent to window when frame needs repainting	Not used	Not used
WM_NCRBUTTONDBLCLK	Sent when right mouse button double clicked in non-client area	Code returned by WM_NCHITTEST	LO=x coord of mouse, HO=y coord of mouse
WM_NCRBUTTONDOWN	Sent when right mouse button is pressed in non-client area	Code returned by WM_NCHITTEST	LO=x coord of mouse, HO=y coord of mouse
WM_NCRBUTTONUP	Sent when right mouse button released in non-client area	Code returned by WM_NCHITTEST	LO=x coord of mouse, HO=y coord of mouse

Source: Microsoft Windows SDK Programmer's Reference 2.0, pages 513 to 514 and 576 to 584

See Also:
6.61. Format of a Windows Message
6.62. Windows General Message Numbering
6.63. Window Management Messages
6.64. Initialization Messages
6.65. Input Messages
6.66. System Information Messages
6.67. Clipboard Messages
6.68. Control Messages

6.71. WINDOWS FUNCTION SUMMARY BY VERSION

Function Name	1	2	Function Name	1	2
AccessResource	X	X	GetViewportOrg	X	X
AddAtom	X	X	GetWindow		X
AddFontResource	X	X	GetWindowDC	X	X
AdjustWindowRect	X	X	GetWindowExt	X	X
AllocResource	X	X	GetWindowLong	X	X
AnsiLower	X	X	GetWindowOrg	X	X
AnsiNext	X	X	GetWindowRect	X	X
AnsiPrev	X	X	GetWindowTask		X
AnsiToOEM	X	X	GetWindowText	X	X
AnsiUpper	X	X	GetWindowTextLength	X	X
AnyPopup	X	X	GetWindowWord	X	X
Arc	X	X	GlobalAddAtom		X
BeginPaint	X	X	GlobalAlloc	X	X
BitBlt	X	X	GlobalCompact	X	X
BringWindowToTop	X	X	GlobalDeleteAtom		X
BuildCommDCB	X	X	GlobalDiscard	X	X
CallMsgFilter	X	X	GlobalFindAtom		X
CallWindowProc	X	X	GlobalFlags	X	X
Catch	X	X	GlobalFree	X	X
ChangeClipboardChain	X	X	GlobalGetAtomName		X
ChangeMenu	X	X	GlobalHandle	X	X
CheckDlgButton	X	X	GlobalLock	X	X
CheckMenuItem	X	X	GlobalReAlloc	X	X
CheckRadioButton	X	X	GlobalSize	X	X
ChildWindowFromPoint	X	X	GlobalUnlock	X	X
Chord		X	GlobalUnwire		X
ClearCommBreak	X	X	GlobalWire		X
ClientToScreen	X	X	GrayString	X	X
ClipCursor	X	X	HIBYTE	X	X
CloseClipboard	X	X	HideCaret	X	X
CloseComm	X	X	HiliteMenuItem	X	X
CloseMetaFile	X	X	HIWORD	X	X
CloseSound	X	X	InflateRect	X	X
CloseWindow	X	X	InitAtomTable	X	X
CombineRgn	X	X	InSendMessage	X	X
CopyMetaFile	X	X	IntersectClipRect	X	X
CopyRect	X	X	IntersectRect	X	X
CountClipboardFormats	X	X	InvalidateRect	X	X
CountVoiceNotes	X	X	InvalidateRgn	X	X
CreateBitmap	X	X	InvertRect	X	X
CreateBitmapIndirect	X	X	InvertRgn	X	X
CreateBrushIndirect	X	X	IsChild	X	X
CreateCaret	X	X	IsClipboardFormatAvailable	X	X
CreateCompatibleBitmap	X	X	IsDialogMessage	X	X
CreateCompatibleDC	X	X	IsDlgButtonChecked	X	X
CreateDC	X	X	IsIconic	X	X
CreateDialog	X	X	IsRectEmpty	X	X
CreateDialogIndirect		X	IsWindow	X	X
CreateDiscardableBitmap	X	X	IsWindowEnabled	X	X
CreateEllipticRgn	X	X	IsWindowVisible	X	X
CreateEllipticRgnIndirect		X	IsZoomed		X
CreateEllipticRgnIndirect	X	X	KillTimer	X	X
CreateFont (see below)	X	X	LineDDA	X	X
CreateFontIndirect	X	X	LineTo	X	X
CreateHatchBrush	X	X	LoadAccelerators	X	X
CreateIC	X	X	LoadBitmap	X	X
CreateMenu	X	X	LoadCursor	X	X
CreateMetaFile	X	X	LoadIcon	X	X
CreatePatternBrush	X	X	LoadLibrary	X	X
CreatePen	X	X	LoadMenu	X	X
CreatePenIndirect	X	X	LoadMenuIndirect		X
CreatePolygonRgn	X	X	LoadResource	X	X
CreateRectRgn	X	X	LoadString	X	X
CreateRectRgnIndirect	X	X	LOBYTE	X	X
CreateSolidBrush	X	X	LocalAlloc	X	X
CreateWindow	X	X	LocalCompact	X	X
DefHookProc		X	LocalData	X	X
DefWindowProc	X	X	LocalDiscard	X	X
DeleteAtom	X	X	LocalFlags	X	X

(Continued)

Table 6.71. Continued

Function Name	1	2	Function Name	1	2
DeleteDC	X	X	LocalFree	X	X
DeleteMetaFile	X	X	LocalFreeze	X	X
DeleteObject	X	X	LocalHandle	X	X
Destroy Caret	X	X	LocalHandleDelta	X	X
DestroyMenu	X	X	LocalInit	X	X
DestroyWindow	X	X	LocalLock	X	X
DeviceMode	X		LocalMelt	X	X
DialogBox	X	X	LocalNotify	X	X
DialogBoxIndirect		X	LocalReAlloc	X	X
DispatchMessage	X	X	LocalShrink		X
DlgDirList	X	X	LocalSize	X	X
DlgDirSelect	X	X	LocalUnlock	X	X
DPtoLP	X	X	LockResource	X	X
DrawIcon	X	X	LockSegment	X	X
DrawMenuBar	X	X	LOWORD	X	X
DrawText	X	X	LPtoDP	X	X
Ellipse	X	X	MAKEINTATOM	X	X
EmptyClipboard	X	X	MAKEINTRESOURCE	X	X
EnableHardwareInput		X	MAKELONG	X	X
EnableMenuItem	X	X	MAKEPOINT	X	X
EnableWindow	X	X	MakeProcInstance	X	X
EndDialog	X	X	MapDialogRect	X	X
EndPaint	X	X	max	X	X
EnumChildWindows	X	X	MessageBeep	X	X
EnumClipboardFormats	X	X	MessageBox	X	X
EnumFonts	X	X	min	X	X
EnumMetaFile		X	MoveConvertWindow		X
EnumObjects	X	X	MoveTo	X	X
EnumProps	X	X	MoveWindow	X	X
EnumTaskWindows		X	OemToAnsi	X	X
EnumWindows	X	X	OffsetClipRgn	X	X
EqualRect		X	OffsetRect	X	X
EqualRgn	X	X	OffsetRgn	X	X
Escape (ABORTDOC)	X	X	OffsetViewportOrg		X
Escape (BANDINFO)		X	OffsetWindowOrg		X
Escape (DEVICEDATA)	X	X	OpenClipboard	X	X
Escape (DRAFTMODE)	X	X	OpenComm	X	X
Escape (DRAWPATTERNRECT)		X	OpenFile	X	X
Escape (ENABLEDUPLEX)		X	OpenIcon	X	X
Escape (ENABLEMANUALFEED)	X	X	OpenSound	X	X
Escape (ENABLEPAIRKERNING)	X	X	PaintRgn	X	X
Escape (ENABLERELATIVEWIDTHS)	X	X	PatBlt	X	X
Escape (EXTTEXTOUT)	X	X	PeekMessage	X	X
Escape (ENDDOC)	X	X	Pie	X	X
Escape (FLUSHOUTPUT)	X	X	PlayMetaFile	X	X
Escape (GETCOLORTABLE)	X	X	PlayMetaFileRecord		X
Escape (GETEXTENDEDTEXTMETRICS)	X	X	Polygon	X	X
Escape (GETEXTENTTABLE)	X	X	Polyline	X	X
Escape (GETPAIRKERNTABLE)	X	X	PostAppMessage	X	X
Escape (GETPHYSPAGESIZE)	X	X	PostMessage	X	X
Escape (GETPRINTINGOFFSET)	X	X	PostQuitMessage	X	X
Escape (GETSCALINGFACTOR)	X	X	PtInRect	X	X
Escape (GETRACKKERNTABLE)	X	X	PtInRegion	X	X
Escape (MFCOMMENT)		X	PtVisible	X	X
Escape (NEWFRAME)	X	X	ReadComm	X	X
Escape (NEXTBAND)	X	X	Rectangle	X	X
Escape (QUERYESCSUPPORT)	X	X	RectVisible	X	X
Escape (SELECTPAPERSOURCE)	X	X	RegisterClass	X	X
Escape (SETABORTPROC)	X	X	RegisterClipboardFormat	X	X
Escape (SETALLJUSTVALUES)		X	RegisterWindowDestroy		X
Escape (SETCHARSET)	X	X	RegisterWindowMessage	X	X
Escape (SETCOLORTABLE)	X	X	ReleaseCapture	X	X
Escape (SETCOPYCOUNT)	X	X	ReleaseDC	X	X
Escape (SETKERNTRACK)	X	X	RemoveFontResource	X	X
Escape (SETLINECAP)		X	RemoveProp	X	X
Escape (SETLINEJOIN)		X	ReplyMessage	X	X
Escape (SETMITERLIMIT)		X	RestoreDC	X	X
Escape (STARTDOC)	X	X	RGB	X	X
Escape (STRETCHBLT)	X	X	RoundRect	X	X
EscapeCommFunction	X	X	SaveDC	X	X
ExcludeClipRect	X	X	ScaleViewportExt		X
ExcludeUpdateRgn		X	ScaleWindowExt		X

(Continued)

Table 6.71. Continued

Function Name	1	2
ExtTextOut		X
FatalExit	X	X
FillRect	X	X
FillRgn	X	X
FindAtom	X	X
FindResource	X	X
FindWindow	X	X
FlashWindow	X	X
FloodFill	X	X
FlushComm	X	X
FrameRect	X	X
FrameRgn	X	X
FreeLibrary	X	X
FreeProcInstance	X	X
FreeResource	X	X
GetActiveWindow	X	X
GetAspectRatioFilter		X
GetAsyncKeyState		X
GetAtomHandle	X	X
GetAtomName	X	X
GetBitmapBits	X	X
GetBitmapDimension	X	X
GetBkColor	X	X
GetBkMode	X	X
GetBrushOrg	X	X
GetBValue	X	X
GetCapture		X
GetCaretBlinkTime	X	X
GetCaretPos		X
GetCharWidth		X
GetClassLong	X	X
GetClassName	X	X
GetClassWord	X	X
GetClientRect	X	X
GetClipboardData	X	X
GetClipboardFormatName	X	X
GetClipboardOwner	X	X
GetClipboardViewer	X	X
GetClipBox	X	X
GetCodeHandle	X	X
GetCommError	X	X
GetCommEventMask	X	X
GetCommState	X	X
GetCurrentPosition	X	X
GetCurrentTask	X	X
GetCurrentTime	X	X
GetCursorPos	X	X
GetDC	X	X
GetDCOrg		X
GetDeviceCaps	X	X
GetDlgItem	X	X
GetDlgItemInt	X	X
GetDlgItemText	X	X
GetDoubleClickTime	X	X
GetEnvironment	X	X
GetFocus	X	X
GetGValue	X	X
GetInputState		X
GetInstanceData	X	X
GetKeyboardState		X
GetKeyState	X	X
GetMapMode	X	X
GetMenu	X	X
GetMenuItemCount		X
GetMenuItemID		X
GetMenuState		X
GetMenuString	X	X
GetMessage	X	X
GetMessagePos	X	X
GetMessageTime	X	X
GetMetaFile	X	X
GetMetaFileBits	X	X

Function Name	1	2
ScreenToClient	X	X
ScrollDC		X
ScrollWindow	X	X
SelectClipRgn	X	X
SelectObject	X	X
SendDlgItemMessage	X	X
SendMessage	X	X
SetActiveWindow	X	X
SetBitmapBits	X	X
SetBitmapDimension	X	X
SetBkColor	X	X
SetBkMode	X	X
SetBrushOrg	X	X
SetCapture	X	X
SetCaretBlinkTime	X	X
SetCaretPos	X	X
SetClassLong	X	X
SetClassWord	X	X
SetClipboardData	X	X
SetClipboardViewer	X	X
SetCommBreak	X	X
SetCommEventMask	X	X
SetCommState	X	X
SetConvertHook		X
SetConvertParms		X
SetConvertWindowHeight		X
SetCursor	X	X
SetCursorPos	X	X
SetDlgItemInt	X	X
SetDlgItemText	X	X
SetDoubleClickTime		X
SetEnvironment	X	X
SetFocus	X	X
SetKeyboardState		X
SetMapMode	X	X
SetMapperFlags		X
SetMenu	X	X
SetMessageQueue		X
SetMetaFileBits	X	X
SetParent		X
SetPixel	X	X
SetPolyFillMode	X	X
SetPriority	X	X
SetProp	X	X
SetRect	X	X
SetRectEmpty	X	X
SetRectRgn		X
SetRelAbs	X	X
SetResourceHandler	X	X
SetROP2	X	X
SetScrollPos	X	X
SetScrollRange	X	X
SetSoundNoise	X	X
SetStretchBltMode	X	X
SetSwapAreaSize		X
SetSysColors	X	X
SetSysModalWindow	X	X
SetTextAlign		X
SetTextCharacterExtra	X	X
SetTextColor	X	X
SetTextJustification	X	X
SetTimer	X	X
SetViewportExt	X	X
SetViewportOrg	X	X
SetVoiceAccent	X	X
SetVoiceEnvelope	X	X
SetVoiceNote	X	X
SetVoiceQueueSize	X	X
SetVoiceSound	X	X
SetVoiceThreshold	X	X
SetWindowExt	X	X
SetWindowLong	X	X

(Continued)

Table 6.71. Continued

Function Name	1	2	Function Name	1	2
GetModuleFileName	X	X	SetWindowOrg	X	X
GetModuleHandle	X	X	SetWindowPos		X
GetModuleUsage	X	X	SetWindowsHook	X	X
GetNearestColor	X	X	SetWindowText	X	X
GetNextDlgGroupItem		X	SetWindowWord	X	X
GetNextDlgTabItem		X	ShowCaret	X	X
GetNextWindow		X	ShowCursor	X	X
GetNumTasks		X	ShowOwnedPopups		X
GetObject	X	X	ShowScrollBar		X
GetParent	X	X	ShowWindow	X	X
GetPixel	X	X	SizeofResource	X	X
GetPolyFillMode	X	X	StartSound	X	X
GetProcAddress	X	X	StopSound	X	X
GetProfileInt	X	X	StretchBlt	X	X
GetProfileString	X	X	SwapMouseButton	X	X
GetProp	X	X	SyncAllVoices	X	X
GetRelAbs	X	X	TextOut	X	X
GetROP2	X	X	Throw	X	X
GetRValue	X	X	TranslateAccelerator	X	X
GetScrollPos	X	X	TranslateCommChar	X	X
GetScrollRange	X	X	TranslateMessage	X	X
GetStockObject	X	X	UngetCommChar	X	X
GetStretchBltMode	X	X	UnhookWindowsHook		X
GetSubMenu	X	X	UnionRect	X	X
GetSysColor	X	X	UnlockData	X	X
GetSysModalWindow	X	X	UnlockResource		X
GetSystemMenu	X	X	UnlockSegment	X	X
GetSystemMetrics	X	X	UnrealizeObject	X	X
GetTempDrive	X	X	UpdateWindow	X	X
GetTempFileName	X	X	ValidateFreeSpaces		X
GetTextAlign		X	ValidateRect	X	X
GetTextCharacterExtra	X	X	ValidateRgn	X	X
GetTextColor	X	X	WaitMessage	X	X
GetTextExtent	X	X	WaitSoundState	X	X
GetTextFace	X	X	WindowFromPoint	X	X
GetTextMetrics	X	X	WinMain	X	X
GetThresholdEvent	X	X	WndProc	X	X
GetThresholdStatus	X	X	WriteComm	X	X
GetTickCount		X	WriteProfileString	X	X
GetTopWindow		X	Yield	X	X
GetUpdateRect	X	X			
GetUpdateRgn		X			
GetVersion	X	X			
GetViewportExt	X	X			

Source: Microsoft Windows SDK Programmer's References 1.0 and 2.0

See Also: 6.72. Windows Functions Summary by Name of Function
6.73. Windows Functions Summary by Type of Function

6.72. WINDOWS FUNCTION SUMMARY BY NAME OF FUNCTION

Function Name	Description	Type	Syntax (arguments)	Returns	Ref Page #
AccessResource	Sets file pointer for read access to hRefInfo	Resource manager	AccessResource(hInstance,hResInfo)	nFile	148
AddAtom	Creates atom for character string lpString	Atom manager	AddAtom(lpString)	wAtom	148
AddFontResource	Adds resource in lpFilename to system font table	Resource manager	AddFontResource(lpFilename)	nFonts	149
AdjustWindowRect	Converts client rectangle to a window rectangle	Window display	AdjustWindowRect(lpRect,lStyle,bMenu)	None	150
AllocResource	Allocates dwSize bytes of memory for hResInfo	Resource manager	AllocResource(hInstance,hResInfo,dwSize)	hMem	150
AnsiLower	Converts string lpStr to lowercase	String translation	AnsiLower(lpStr)	cChar	151
AnsiNext	Points to next character in string lpCurrentChar	String translation	AnsiNext(lpCurrentChar)	lpNextChar	151
AnsiPrev	Points to prev character in string lpStart	String translation	AnsiPrev(lpStart,lpCurrentChar)	lpPrevChar	152
AnsiToOem	Converts ANSI string to OEM char string	String translation	AnsiToOem(lpAnsiStr,lpOemStr)	bTranslated	152
AnsiUpper	Converts string lpStr to uppercase	String translation	AnsiUpper(lpStr)	cChar	153
AnyPopup	Indicates whether any popup window is visible	Window display	AnyPopup()	bVisible	153
Arc	Draws arc from X3,Y3 to X4,Y4	GDI output	Arc(hDC,X1,Y1,X2,Y2,X3,Y3,X4,Y4)	bDrawn	154
BeginPaint	Prepares window for painting	Window painting	BeginPaint(hWnd,lpPaint)	hDC	156
BitBlt	Moves bitmap from src device to dest device	GDI output	BitBlt(hDestDC,X,Y,nWidth,nHeight,hSrcDC,XSrc,YSrc,dwRop)	bDrawn	156
BringWindowToTop	Makes popup or child window the top window	Window display	BringWindowToTop(hWnd)	None	159
BuildCommDCB	Fills device control block with control codes	Communications	BuildCommDCB(lpDef,lpDCB)	nResult	160
CallMsgFilter	Passes message and code to message filter function	Window hook	CallMsgFilter(lpMsg,nCode)	bResult	160
CallWindowProc	Passes message info to lpPrevWndFunc function	Window class	CallWindowProc(lpPrevWndFunc,hWnd,wMsg,wParam,lParam)	lReply	161
Catch	Copies current exec environ to buffer lpCatchBuf	Module manager	Catch(lpCatchBuf)	nThrowBack	162
ChangeClipboardChain	Removes hWnd from clipboard viewer chain	Window clipboard	ChangeClipboardChain(hWnd,hWndNext)	bRemoved	163
ChangeMenu	Changes menu item in hMenu	Window menu	ChangeMenu(hMenu,wIDChangeItem,lpNewItem,wIDNewItem,wChange)	bChanged	163
CheckDlgButton	Changes state of button	Window dialog box	CheckDlgButton(hDlg,nIDButton,wCheck)	None	166
CheckMenuItem	Changes checkmark status of menu item	Window menu	CheckMenuItem(hMenu,wIDCheckItem,wCheck)	bOldCheck	167
CheckRadioButton	Changes checkmark to wIDCheckButton in group	Window dialog box	CheckRadioButton(hDlg,nIDFirstButton,nIDLastButton,nIDCheckButton)	None	168
ChildWindowFromPoint	Determines which child window contains Point	Window coordinate	ChildWindowFromPoint(hWndParent,Point)	hWndChild	168
Chord*	Draws a chord (ellipse insersection with line segment)	GDI output	Chord(hDC,X1,Y1,X2,Y2,X3,Y3,X4,Y4)	bDrawn	169
ClearCommBreak	Clears comm break state for nCid device	Communications	ClearCommBreak(nCid)	nResult	169
ClientToScreen	Converts client coords to equiv. screen coords	Window coordinate	ClientToScreen(hWnd,lpPoint)	None	170
ClipCursor	Restricts mouse cursor to given rectangle on screen	Window cursor	ClipCursor(lpRect)	None	170
CloseClipboard	Closes the clipboard	Window clipboard	CloseClipboard()	bClosed	171
CloseComm	Closes comm device nCid (first transmits buffer)	Communications	CloseComm(nCid)	nResult	171
CloseMetaFile	Closes metafile and creates handle	GDI metafile	CloseMetaFile(hDC)	hMF	171
CloseSound	Closes play device (first flushes voice queues)	Sound	CloseSound()	None	172
CloseWindow	Closes specified window	Window display	CloseWindow(hWnd)	None	172
CombineRgn	Combines two existing regions into new region	GDI region	CombineRgn(hDestRgn,hSrcRgn1,hSrcRgn2,nCombineMode)	nRgnType	173
CopyMetaFile	Copies metafile to lpFilename and returns new hMF	GDI metafile	CopyMetaFile(hSrcMetaFile,lpFilename)	hMF	174
CopyRect	Copies an existing rectangle	Window rectangle	CopyRect(lpDestRect,lpSourceRect)	None	174
CountClipboardFormats	Counts number of formats clipboard can render	Window clipboard	CountClipboardFormats()	nCount	174
CountVoiceNotes	Returns number of notes in voice queue	Sound	CountVoiceNotes(nVoice)	nNotes	175
CreateBitmap	Creates bitmap of specified height, width, pattern	GDI drawing	CreateBitmap(nWidth,nHeight,nPlanes,nBitCount,lpBits)	hBitmap	175
CreateBitmapIndirect	Creates bitmap from existing bitmap	GDI drawing	CreateBitmapIndirect(lpBitmap)	hBitmap	176
CreateBrushIndirect	Creates logical brush from existing brush	GDI drawing	CreateBrushIndirect(lpLogBrush)	hBrush	176
CreateCaret	Creates caret for hWnd using hBitmap	Window caret	CreateCaret(hWnd,hBitmap,nWidth,nHeight)	None	177
CreateCompatibleBitmap	Creates bitmap compatible with device hDC	GDI drawing	CreateCompatibleBitmap(hDC,nWidth,nHeight)	hBitmap	178
CreateCompatibleDC	Creates memory display context compat. with hDC	GDI display context	CreateCompatibleDC(hDC)	hMemDC	178
CreateDC	Creates display context for specified device	GDI display context	CreateDC(lpDriverName,lpDeviceName,lpOutput,lpInitData)	hDC	179
CreateDialog	Creates modeless dialog box	Window dialog box	CreateDialog(hInstance,lpTemplateName,hWndParent,lpDialogFunc)	hDlg	180
CreateDialogIndirect*	Creates modeless dialog box like one in lpDialogTemplate	Window dialog	CreateDialogIndirect(hInstance,lpDialogTemplate,hWndParent,lpDialogFunc)	hDlg	182
CreateDiscardableBitmap	Creates discardable bitmap	GDI drawing	CreateDiscardableBitmap(hDC,nWidth,nHeight)	hBitmap	184
CreateEllipticRgn	Creates elliptical region bounded by rect X1,Y1 X2,Y2	GDI region	CreateEllipticRgn(X1,Y1,X2,Y2)	hRgn	184
CreateEllipticRgnIndirect*	Creates elliptical region bounded by lpRect	GDI region	CreateEllipticRgnIndirect(lpRect)	hRgn	185
CreateFont	Creates logical font	GDI drawing	CreateFont(nHeight,nWidth,nEscapement,nOrientation,nWeight,cItalic, cUnderline, cStrikeOut, nCharSet, cOutputPrecision, cClipPrecision, cQuality, cPitchAndFamily,lpFacename)	hFont	185
CreateFontIndirect	Creates logical font like lpLogFont	GDI drawing	CreateFontIndirect(lpLogFont)	hFont	188
CreateHatchBrush	Creates logical brush with hatched pattern	GDI drawing	CreateHatchBrush(nIndex,rgbColor)	hBrush	189
CreateIC	Creates information context for device	GDI display context	CreateIC(lpDriverName,lpDeviceName,lpOutput,lpInitData)	hIC	189
CreateMenu	Creates empty menu	Window menu	CreateMenu()	hMenu	190
CreateMetaFile	Creates metafile display context	GDI metafile	CreateMetaFile(lpFilename)	hDC	191

(Continued)

Table 6.72. Continued

Function Name	Type	Description	Syntax (arguments)	Returns	Ref Page #
CreatePatternBrush	GDI drawing	Creates logical brush with hBitmap pattern	CreatePatternBrush(hBitmap)	hBrush	191
CreatePen	GDI drawing	Creates logical pen	CreatePen(nPenStyle,nWidth,rgbColor)	hPen	192
CreatePenIndirect	GDI drawing	Creates logical pen like lpLogPen	CreatePenIndirect(lpLogPen)	hPen	193
CreatePolygonRgn	GDI region	Creates polygonal region	CreatePolygonRgn(lpPoints,nCount,nPolyFillMode)	hRgn	193
CreateRectRgn	GDI region	Creates rectangular region	CreateRectRgn(X1,Y1,X2,Y2)	hRgn	194
CreateRectRgnIndirect	GDI region	Creates rectangular region sized like lpRect	CreateRectRgnIndirect(lpRect)	hRgn	194
CreateSolidBrush	GDI drawing	Creates logical brush of a solid color	CreateSolidBrush(rgbColor)	hBrush	195
CreateWindow	Window creation	Creates tiled, popup, or child window	CreateWindow(lpClassName,lpWindowName,dwStyle,X,Y,nWidth, nHeight,hWndParent,hMenu,hInstance,lpParam)	hWnd	195
DefHookProc*	Window message	Provides default hook processing of WM messages	DefHookProc(code,wParam,lParam,lplpfnNextHook)	code	206
DefWindowProc	Window default	Do default processing of messages that are ignored	DefWindowProc(hWnd,wMsg,wParam,lParam)	lReply	206
DeleteAtom	Atom manager	Deletes nAtom if its reference count is zero	DeleteAtom(nAtom)	nOldAtom	207
DeleteDC	GDI display context	Deletes specified display context	DeleteDC(hDC)	bDeleted	208
DeleteMetaFile	GDI metafile	Deletes access to metafile; frees system resources	DeleteMetaFile(hMF)	bFreed	208
DeleteObject	GDI selection	Deletes object by freeing system storage	DeleteObject(hObject)	bDeleted	208
DestroyCaret	Window caret	Destroys current caret and memory it occupied	DestroyCaret()	None	209
DestroyMenu	Window menu	Destroys hMenu and frees memory it occupied	DestroyMenu(hMenu)	bDestroyed	210
DestroyWindow	Window creation	Sends WM_DESTROY message; frees memory	DestroyWindow(hWnd)	bDestroyed	210
DeviceMode	Utility	Displays dialog box for setting printer modes	DeviceMode(hWnd,hItem,lpString,lpString)	lpString	211
DialogBox	Window dialog box	Creates modal dialog box	DialogBox(hInstance,lpTemplateName,hWndParent,lpDialogFunc)	wResult	211
DialogBoxIndirect*	Window dialog	Creates modal dialog box like hDTemplate	DialogBoxIndirect(hInstance,hDTemplate,hWndParent,lpDialogFunc)	wResult	212
DispatchMessage	Window message	Passes message to window function in MSG structure	DispatchMessage(lpMsg)	lResult	214
DlgDirList	Window dialog box	Fills nIDListBox with files matching lpPathSpec	DlgDirList(hDlg,lpPathSpec,nIDListBox,nIDStaticPath,wFiletype)	nListed	215
DlgDirSelect	Window dialog box	Copies selection from nIDListBox to lpString	DlgDirSelect(hDlg,lpString,nIDListBox)	bDirectory	217
DPtoLP	GDI conversion	Converts device points into logical points	DPtoLP(hDC,lpPoints,nCount)	bConverted	217
DrawIcon	GDI output	Draws icon with upper-left corner at X,Y	DrawIcon(hDC,X,Y,hIcon)	bDrawn	218
DrawMenuBar	Window menu	Redraws menu bar	DrawMenuBar(hWnd)	None	219
DrawText	GDI output	Draws nCount chars of lpString clipped in lpRect	DrawText(hDC,lpString,nCount,lpRect,wFormat)	Height of text	219
Ellipse	GDI drawing	Draws ellipse with center in X1,Y1 X2,Y2 rect	Ellipse(hDC,X1,Y1,X2,Y2)	bDrawn	222
EmptyClipboard	Window clipboard	Empties clipboard, frees data handles	EmptyClipboard()	bEmptied	222
EnableHardwareInput*	Window input	Enables/disables mouse and keyboard	EnableHardwareInput(fEnableInput)	bEnabled	223
EnableMenuItem	Window menu	Enables, disables, or grays menu item	EnableMenuItem(hMenu,wIDEnableItem,wEnable)	bEnabled	223
EnableWindow	Window input	Enables or disables mouse, keybd input to hWnd	EnableWindow(hWnd,bEnable)	bDone	224
EndDialog	Window dialog box	Frees resources and destroys windows of dialog box	EndDialog(hDlg,nResult)	None	225
EndPaint	Window painting	Marks end of window repainting	EndPaint(hWnd,lpPaint)	None	226
EnumChildWindows	Window display	Enumerates child windows of hWndParent	EnumChildWindows(hWndParent,lpEnumFunc,lParam)	bDone	226
EnumClipboardFormats	Window clipboard	Enumerates available clipboard formats	EnumClipboardFormats(wFormat)	wNextFormat	228
EnumFonts	GDI information	Enumerates fonts available on device	EnumFonts(hDC,lpFacename,lpFontFunc,lpData)	nResult	228
EnumMetaFile*	GDI information	Enumerates GDI calls in a metafile	EnumMetaFile(hDC,hMF,lpCallbackFunc,lpClientData)	bEnumerated	230
EnumObjects	GDI information	Enumerates objects available on device	EnumObjects(hDC,nObjectType,lpObjectFunc,lpData)	nResult	231
EnumProps	Window property	Passes each property of hWnd to lpEnumFunc	EnumProps(hWnd,lpEnumFunc)	nResult	233
EnumTaskWindows*	Window information	Enumerates all windows associated with a task	EnumTaskWindows(hTask,lpEnumFunc,lParam)	bEnumerate	235
EnumWindows	Window display	Enumerates windows on screen	EnumWindows(lpEnumFunc,lParam)	bDone	236
EqualRect*	GDI information	Determines whether two rectangles are equal	EqualRect(lpRect1,lpRect2)	bEqual	237
EqualRgn	GDI region	Determines if two regions are identical	EqualRgn(hSrcRgn1,hSrcRgn2)	bEqual	237
Escape	GDI control	Accesses device facilities not available through GDI	Escape(hDC,nEscape,nCount,lpInData,lpOutData)	nResult	238
Escape (ABORTDOC)	GDI control	Aborts current job	Escape(hDC,ABORTDOC,Null,lpstrNull,lpstrNull)	nResult	681
Escape (BANDINFO)*	GDI control	Copies banding capability info to lpIndata structure	Escape(hDC,BANDINFO,nCount,lpInData,lpOutData)	nResult	681
Escape (DEVICEDATA)	GDI control	Send data directly to printer	Escape(hDC,DEVICEDATA,nCount,lpInData,lpOutData)	nCount	683
Escape (DRAFTMODE)	GDI control	Turns draft mode ON or OFF	Escape(hDC,DRAFTMODE,2,lpDraftMode,lpstrNull)	nResult	684
Escape (DRAWPATTERNRECT)*	GDI control	Creates pattern using rules for PCL printers	Escape(hDC,DRAWPATTERNRECT,nCount,lpInData,lpstrNull)	nResult	684
Escape (ENABLEDUPLEX)*	GDI control	Enables duplex printing capabilities	Escape(hDC,ENABLEDUPLEX,nCount,lpInData,lpOutData)	nResult	686
Escape (ENABLEPAIRKERNING)	GDI control	Enables or disables kerning ability of device	Escape(hDC,ENABLEPAIRKERNING,nCount,lpInData,lpOutData)	nResult	686
Escape (ENABLERELATIVEWIDTHS)	GDI control	Enables or disables relative character widths on device	Escape(hDC,ENABLERELATIVEWIDTHS,nCount,lpInData,lpOutData)	nResult	687
Escape (ENDDOC)	GDI control	Ends print job started by EscapeSTARTDOC	Escape(hDC,ENDDOC,Null,lpstrNull,lpstrNull)	bResult	688
Escape (EXTTEXTOUT)	GDI control	More efficient TextOut for justification and kerning	Escape(hDC,EXTTEXTOUT,nCount,lpInData,lpOutData)	nResult	689
Escape (FLUSHOUTPUT)	GDI control	Flushes output in device buffer	Escape(hDC,FLUSHOUTPUT,Null,lpstrNull,lpstrNull)	bResult	690
Escape (GETCOLORTABLE)	GDI control	Copies RGB color table to lpOutData	Escape(hDC,GETCOLORTABLE,Null,lpIndex,lpColor)	nResult	691
Escape (GETEXTENDEDTEXTMETRICS)	GDI control	Fills buffer with extended text metrics for font	Escape(hDC,GETEXTENDEDTEXTMETRICS,nCount*,lpInData,lpOutData)	nCount	691

(Continued)

Function Name	Description	Type	Syntax (arguments)	Returns	Ref Page #
Escape (GETEXTENTTABLE)	Returns width of individual group of consec. chars	GDI control	Escape(hDC,GETEXTENTTABLE,nCount*,lpInData,lpOutData)	bResult	692
Escape (GETPAIRKERNTABLE)	Fills buffer at lpOutData with kerning pair table for font	GDI control	Escape(hDC,GETPAIRKERNTABLE,nCount*,lpstrNull,lpOutData)	nCount	693
Escape (GETPHYSPAGESIZE)	Copies physical page size to lpOutData POINT structure	GDI control	Escape(hDC,GETPHYSPAGESIZE,Null,lpstrNull,lpDimensions)	nResult	694
Escape (GETPRINTINGOFFSET)	Copies printing offset to lpOutData POINT structure	GDI control	Escape(hDC,GETPRINTINGOFFSET,Null,lpstrNull,lpOffset)	nResult	694
Escape (GETSCALINGFACTOR)	Returns scaling factors for x and y axes of printer	GDI control	Escape(hDC,GETSCALINGFACTOR,null,lpstrNull,lpFactors)	nResult	695
Escape (GETTRACKKERNTABLE)	Fills buffer at lpOutData with track kerning table for font	GDI control	Escape(hDC,GETTRACKKERNTABLE,nCount*,lpInData,lpOutData)	nCount	695
Escape (MFCOMMENT)*	Adds comment to metafile	GDI control	Escape(hDC,MFCOMMENT,nCount,lpComment,lpstrNull)	bResult	696
Escape (NEWFRAME)	Ends writing to a page	GDI control	Escape(hDC,NEWFRAME,Null,lpstrNull,lpstrNull)	nResult	696
Escape (NEXTBAND)	Ends writing to a band	GDI control	Escape(hDC,NEXTBAND,Null,lpstrNull,lpBandRect)	nResult	697
Escape (QUERYESCSUPPORT)	Tests whether device supports Escape	GDI control	Escape(hDC,QUERYESCSUPPORT,2,lpEscNum,lpstrNull)	nResult	698
Escape (SELECTPAPERSOURCE)	Determines and selects available paper sources	GDI control	Escape(hDC,SELECTPAPERSOURCE,2,lpInData,lpOutData)	nResult	698
Escape (SETABORTPROC)	Sets abort function for print task	GDI control	Escape(hDC,SETABORTPROC,Null,lpIAbortFunc,lpstrNull)	nResult	698
Escape (SETALLJUSTVALUES)	Sets text justification values	GDI control	Escape(hDC,SETALLJUSTVALUES,nCount,lpInData,lpOutData)	nResult	699
Escape (SETCOLORTABLE)	Sets RGB color table entry	GDI control	Escape(hDC,SETCOLORTABLE,Null,lpColorEntry,lpColor)	nResult	701
Escape (SETCOPYCOUNT)	Specifies number of copies per page to print (uncollated)	GDI control	Escape(hDC,SETCOPYCOUNT,2,lpInData,lpOutData)	bResult	702
Escape (SETKERNTRACK)	Specifies which kerning track to use	GDI control	Escape(hDC,SETKERNTRACK,2,lpInData,lpOutData)	bResult	702
Escape (SETLINECAP)	Sets line end cap	GDI control	Escape(hDC,SETLINECAP,nCount,lpInData,lpOutData)	nResult	703
Escape (SETLINEJOIN)	Sets how line segments joined	GDI control	Escape(hDC,SETLINEJOIN,nCount,lpInData,lpOutData)	nResult	704
Escape (SETMITERLIMIT)	Sets miter limit for a device	GDI control	Escape(hDC,SETMITERLIMIT,nCount,lpInData,lpOutData)	nResult	705
Escape (STARTDOC)	Starts print task	GDI control	Escape(hDC,STARTDOC,nDocLength,lpDocName,lpstrNull)	nResult	706
Escape (STRETCHBLT)	Implements StretchBit on driver level	GDI control	Escape(hDC,STRETCHBLT,nCount,lpInData,lpOutData)	bResult	707
EscapeCommFunction	Executes escape function nFunct for device nCid	Communications	EscapeCommFunction(nCid,nFunc)	nResult	238
ExcludeClipRect	Creates new clipping region for rectangle	GDI clipping rgn	ExcludeClipRect(hDC,X1,Y1,X2,Y2)	nRgnType	239
ExcludeUpdateRgn*	Excludes a region in window from clipping region for window	GDI clipping	ExcludeUpdateRgn(hDC,hWnd)	nRgnType	240
ExtTextOut*	Writes character string within rect region on display	GDI output	ExtTextOut(hDC,X,Y,wOptions,lpRect,lpString,nCount,lpDx)	bDrawn	241
FatalExit	Halts Windows and prompts through AUX	Debugging	FatalExit(Code)	Result	243
FillRect	Fills rectangle using specified brush	GDI output	FillRect(hDC,lpRect,hBrush)	None	243
FillRgn	Fills region with specified brush	GDI output	FillRgn(hDC,hRgn,hBrush)	bFilled	244
FindAtom	Retrieves atom associated with lpString	Atom manager	FindAtom(lpString)	wAtom	244
FindResource	Locates resource lpName of type lpType	Resource manager	FindResource(hInstance,lpName,lpType)	hResInfo	245
FindWindow	Returns handle of window	Window property	FindWindow(lpClassName,lpWindowName)	hWnd	246
FlashWindow	Flashes window once	Window error	FlashWindow(hWnd,bInvert)	bInverted	247
FloodFill	Fills area with current brush starting at X,Y	GDI output	FloodFill(hDC,X,Y,rgbColor)	bFilled	247
FlushComm	Flushes characters from queue of device nCid	Communications	FlushComm(nCid,nQueue)	nResult	248
FrameRect	Draws border for rectangle	GDI output	FrameRect(hDC,lpRect,hBrush)	None	249
FrameRgn	Draws border for region	GDI output	FrameRgn(hDC,hRgn,hBrush,nWidth,nHeight)	bFramed	249
FreeLibrary	Removes library module if reference count is zero	Module manager	FreeLibrary(hLibModule)	None	250
FreeProcInstance	Removes function instance at address lpProc	Module manager	FreeProcInstance(lpProc)	None	250
FreeResource	Removes resource from memory if ref count is zero	Resource manager	FreeResource(hResData)	bFreed	251
GetActiveWindow	Returns handle to active window	Window display	GetActiveWindow()	hWnd	252
GetAspectRatioFilter	Gets setting of current aspect-ratio filter		GetAspectRatioFilter(hDC)	ptDimensions	252
GetAsyncKeyState*	Determines whether key is up or down	Window input	GetAsyncKeyState(vKey)	nState	252
GetAtomHandle	Returns handle of atom string	Atom manager	GetAtomHandle(wAtom)	hMem	253
GetAtomName	Copies nSize chars of string of atom to lpBuffer	Atom manager	GetAtomName(nAtom,lpBuffer,nSize)	nLength	253
GetBitmapBits	Copies lCount bits of bitmap to lpBits buffer	GDI drawing	GetBitmapBits(hBitmap,dwCount,lpBits)	lCopied	254
GetBitmapDimension	Returns width and height of bitmap	GDI drawing	GetBitmapDimension(hBitmap)	ptDimensions	254
GetBkColor	Returns current background color of device	GDI display context	GetBkColor(hDC)	rgbColor	255
GetBkMode	Returns background mode of device	GDI display context	GetBkMode(hDC)	nBkMode	255
GetBrushOrg	Returns current brush origin	GDI display context	GetBrushOrg(hDC)	dwOrigin	255
GetBValue	Returns blue component of rgbColor	Utility	GetBValue(rgbColor)	cBlue	256
GetCapture*	Determines which window is receiving mouse input	Window input	GetCapture()	hWnd	256
GetCaretBlinkTime	Returns current caret flash rate	Window caret	GetCaretBlinkTime()	wMSeconds	257
GetCaretPos*	Returns current caret position	Window caret	GetCaretPos(lpPoint)	None	257
GetCharWidth*	Retrieves width of a character	GDI output	GetCharWidth(hDC,wFirstChar,wLastChar,lpBuffer)	bGotten	257
GetClassLong	Returns info at nIndex in WNDCLASS structure	Window class	GetClassLong(hWnd,nIndex)	Long	258
GetClassName	Copies nMaxCount chars of hWnd's class name	Window class	GetClassName(hWnd,lpClassName,nMaxCount)	nCopied	259
GetClassWord	Returns info at nIndex in WNDCLASS structure	Window class	GetClassWord(hWnd,nIndex)	word	259
GetClientRect	Copies window client area coords to lpRect	Window attribute	GetClientRect(hWnd,lpRect)	None	260
GetClipboardData	Returns data from clipboard in specified format	Window clipboard	GetClipboardData(wFormat)	hClipData	261
GetClipboardFormatName	Copies nMaxCount chars of format to lpFormatName	Window clipboard	GetClipboardFormatName(wFormat,lpFormatName,nMaxCount)	nCopied	262
GetClipboardOwner	Returns window handle of clipboard owner	Window clipboard	GetClipboardOwner()	hWnd	262

(Continued)

Table 6.72. Continued

Function Name	Description	Type	Syntax (arguments)	Returns	Ref Page #
GetClipboardViewer	Returns window handle of 1st window in viewer chn	Window clipboard	GetClipboardViewer()	hWnd	263
GetClipBox	Copies clipping rect boundary to pRect	GDI clipping rgn	GetClipBox(hDC,lpRect)	nRgnType	263
GetCodeHandle	Returns handle of code segment containing function	Module manager	GetCodeHandle(lpFunc)	hInstance	264
GetCommError	Fills lpStat buffer with status of nCid device	Communications	GetCommError(nCid,lpStat)	nError	264
GetCommEventMask	Retrieves, then clears, the event mask for nCid	Communications	GetCommEventMask(nCid,nEvtMask)	wEvent	266
GetCommState	Fills lpDCB buffer with DCB of nCid device	Communications	GetCommState(nCid,lpDCB)	nResult	266
GetCurrentPosition	Returns logical coords of current position	GDI output	GetCurrentPosition(hDC)	ptPos	267
GetCurrentTask	Returns handle of current task	Task	GetCurrentTask()	hTask	267
GetCurrentTime	Returns elapsed time since boot	Window message	GetCurrentTime()	lTime	267
GetCursorPos	Stores cursor position in POINT structure	Window cursor	GetCursorPos(lpPoint)	None	267
GetDC	Returns display context of client area for window	Window painting	GetDC(hWnd)	hDC	268
GetDCOrg*	Returns origin for display context	Window painting	GetDCOrg(hDC)	lPoint	268
GetDeviceCaps	Returns device-specific info	GDI information	GetDeviceCaps(hDC,nIndex)	nValue	269
GetDlgItem	Returns dialog control handle	Window dialog box	GetDlgItem(hDlg,nIDDlgItem)	hCtl	269
GetDlgItemInt	Translates text of nIDDlgItem to integer value	Window dialog box	GetDlgItemInt(hDlg,nIDDlgItem,lpTranslated,bSigned)	wValue	274
GetDlgItemText	Copies nMaxCount chars of control text to lpString	Window dialog box	GetDlgItemText(hDlg,nIDDlgItem,lpString,nMaxCount)	nCopied	274
GetDoubleClickTime	Returns doubleclick time for mouse	Window input	GetDoubleClickTime()	wClickTime	275
GetEnvironment	Copies device environment to lpEnviron	GDI information	GetEnvironment(lpPortName,lpEnviron,nMaxCount)	nCopied	276
GetFocus	Returns handle of window with input focus	Window input	GetFocus()	hWnd	276
GetGValue	Returns green component of rgbColor	Utility	GetGValue(rgbColor)	cGreen	277
GetInputState*	Determines whether there are input events in queue	Window input	GetInputState()	bEvent	277
GetInstanceData	Copies nCount bytes from hInstance to current Instance	Module manager	GetInstanceData(hInstance,pData,nCount)	nBytes	277
GetKeyboardState*	Copies status of virtual keys to a buffer	Window input	GetKeyboardState(lpKeyState)	none	278
GetKeyState	Returns state of virtual key	Window input	GetKeyState(nVirtKey)	nState	278
GetMapMode	Returns current mapping mode	GDI clipping rgn	GetMapMode(hDC)	nMapMode	279
GetMenu	Returns handle to window's menu	Window menu	GetMenu(hWnd)	hMenu	282
GetMenuItemCount*	Determines how many items are in hMenu	Window menu	GetMenuItemCount(hMenu)	nItems	282
GetMenuItemID*	Obtains identifier for a menu item	Window menu	GetMenuItemID(hMenu,nPos)	nID	282
GetMenuState*	Identifies top-level menu	Window menu	GetMenuState(hMenu,wID,wFlags)	wItem	283
GetMenuString	Copies nMaxCount chars of menu label to lpString	Window menu	GetMenuString(hMenu,wIDItem,lpString,nMaxCount,wFlag)	nCopied	283
GetMessage	Retrieves message	Window message	GetMessage(lpMsg,hWnd,wMsgFilterMin,wMsgFilterMax)	bContinue	284
GetMessagePos	Returns mouse position scrn coords at last message	Window message	GetMessagePos()	dwPos	285
GetMessageTime	Returns time of last message	Window message	GetMessageTime()	lTime	286
GetMetaFile	Creates handle for metafile named by lpFilename	GDI metafile	GetMetaFile(lpFilename)	hMF	287
GetMetaFileBits	Stores metafile bits in global memory block	GDI metafile	GetMetaFileBits(hMF)	hMem	287
GetModuleFileName	Copies module filename to lpFilename	Module manager	GetModuleFileName(hModule,lpFilename,nSize)	nLength	288
GetModuleHandle	Returns module handle	Module manager	GetModuleHandle(lpModuleName)	hModule	288
GetModuleUsage	Returns reference count of module hModule	Module manager	GetModuleUsage(hModule)	nCount	289
GetNearestColor	Returns device color closest to rgbColor	GDI conversion	GetNearestColor(hDC,rgbColor)	rgbSolidColor	289
GetNextDlgGroupItem*	Searches for next control in group of dialog controls	Window dialog box	GetNextDlgGroupItem(hDlg,hCtl,fPrevious)	hControl	289
GetNextDlgTabItem*	Obtains handle for first control preceding another	Window dialog box	GetNextDlgTabItem(hDlg,hCtl,fPrevious)	hControl	290
GetNextWindow*	Searches for next window handle	Window display	GetNextWindow(hWnd,wFlag)	hWnd	290
GetNumTasks	Returns number of tasks in system	Task	GetNumTasks()	nTasks	291
GetObject	Copies nCount bytes of hObject data to lpObject	GDI selection	GetObject(hObject,nCount,lpObject)	nCopied	292
GetParent	Retrieves window handle of window's parent (if any)	Window attribute	GetParent(hWnd)	hWndParent	292
GetPixel	Retrieves RGB color of pixel at X,Y	GDI output	GetPixel(hDC,X,Y)	rgbColor	293
GetPolyFillMode	Retrieves current polygon filling mode	GDI display context	GetPolyFillMode(hDC)	nPolyFillMode	293
GetProcAddress	Returns address of lpProcName function	Module manager	GetProcAddress(hModule,lpProcName)	lpAddress	294
GetProfileInt	Returns integer info from WIN.INI file	Windows init file	GetProfileInt(lpAppName,lpKeyName,nDefault)	nKeyValue	295
GetProfileString	Returns string info from WIN.INI file	Windows init file	GetProfileString(lpAppName,lpKeyName,lpDefault,lpReturnedString,nSize)	nLength	296
GetProp	Returns handle associated with lpString	Window property	GetProp(hWnd,lpString)	hData	297
GetRelAbs	Returns the relabs flag	GDI display context	GetRelAbs(hDC)	nRelAbsMode	298
GetROP2	Returns current drawing mode	GDI display context	GetROP2(hDC)	nDrawMode	299
GetRValue	Returns the red component of rgbColor	Utility	GetRValue(rgbColor)	cRed	299
GetScrollPos	Returns current position of scrollbar	Window scrolling	GetScrollPos(hWnd,nBar)	nPos	300
GetScrollRange	Copies min/max scrollbar positions	Window scrolling	GetScrollRange(hWnd,nBar,lpMinPos,lpMaxPos)	None	300
GetStockObject	Returns handle to predefined object	GDI drawing obj	GetStockObject(nIndex)	hObject	301
GetStretchBitMode	Returns current stretching mode	GDI display context	GetStretchBitMode(hDC)	nStretchMode	303

(Continued)

Function Name	Description	Type	Syntax (arguments)	Returns	Ref Page #
GetSubMenu	Returns menu handle of popup menu	Window menu	GetSubMenu(hMenu,nPos)	hPopupMenu	303
GetSysColor	Returns system color identified by nIndex	Window sys info	GetSysColor(nIndex)	rgbColor	303
GetSysModalWindow	Returns handle of system modal window, if present	Window attribute	GetSysModalWindow()	hWnd	304
GetSystemMenu	Allows access to system menu	Window menu	GetSystemMenu(hWnd,bRevert)	hSysMenu	304
GetSystemMetrics	Returns information about system metrics	Window sys info	GetSystemMetrics(nIndex)	nValue	305
GetTempDrive	Returns optimal drive letter for temp file	File I/O	GetTempDrive(cDriveLetter)	cOptDriveLetter	307
GetTempFileName	Creates temporary file name	File I/O	GetTempFileName(cDriveLetter,lpPrefixString,wUnique,lpTempFileName)	wUniqueNumber	308
GetTextAlign*	Returns status of text alignment flag	GDI text justify	GetTextAlign(hDC)	wAlignment	309
GetTextCharacterExtra	Returns current intercharacter spacing	GDI text justify	GetTextCharacterExtra(hDC)	nCharExtra	310
GetTextColor	Returns current text color	GDI display context	GetTextColor(hDC)	rgbColor	310
GetTextExtent	Computes width and height of text line in lpString	GDI text justify	GetTextExtent(hDC,lpString,nCount)	dwTextExtents	310
GetTextFace	Copies current font facename to lpFacename	GDI information	GetTextFace(hDC,nCount,lpFacename)	nCopied	311
GetTextMetrics	Fills buffer with metrics for current font	GDI information	GetTextMetrics(hDC,lpMetrics)	bRetrieved	311
GetThresholdEvent	Returns pointer to threshold flag	Sound	GetThresholdEvent()	lpInt	312
GetThresholdStatus	Returns bit mask containing threshold event status	Sound	GetThresholdStatus()	fStatus	312
GetTickCount()	Returns time since system started	Utility	GetTickCount()	dwTicks	313
GetTopWindow*	Returns handle to top-level child window	Window display	GetTopWindow(hWnd)	hWnd	313
GetUpdateRect	Copies dim of rect that needs updating to lpRect	Window painting	GetUpdateRect(hWnd,lpRect,bErase)	bUpdate	313
GetUpdateRgn*	Copies window's update region to specified region	Window painting	GetUpdateRgn(hWnd,hRgn,fErase)	sRgnType	314
GetVersion	Returns Windows version number	Module manager	GetVersion()	wVersion	315
GetViewportExt	Returns x/y extent of display context's viewport	GDI display context	GetViewportExt(hDC)	ptExtents	315
GetViewportOrg	Returns x/y coords of display context viewport org.	GDI display context	GetViewportOrg(hDC)	ptOrigin	316
GetWindow*	Searches for window in window manager's list	Window manager	GetWindow(hWnd,wCmd)	hWnd	316
GetWindowDC	Returns display context for entire window	Window painting	GetWindowDC(hWnd)	hDC	317
GetWindowExt	Returns x/y extents of display context's window	GDI display context	GetWindowExt(hDC)	ptExtents	318
GetWindowLong	Returns information about window	Window creation	GetWindowLong(hWnd,nIndex)	long	318
GetWindowOrg	Returns x/y coords of display context window origin	GDI display context	GetWindowOrg(hDC)	ptOrigin	319
GetWindowRect	Copies dimensions of entire window to lpRect	Window attribute	GetWindowRect(hWnd,lpRect)	None	319
GetWindowTask*	Returns task handle	Task	GetWindowTask(hWnd)	hTask	319
GetWindowText	Copies window's caption into lpString	Window attribute	GetWindowText(hWnd,lpString,nMaxCount)	nCopied	320
GetWindowTextLength	Returns length of window's caption or text	Window attribute	GetWindowTextLength(hWnd)	nLength	321
GetWindowWord	Returns information about window	Window creation	GetWindowWord(hWnd,nIndex)	word	321
GlobalAddAtom*	Adds global atom to the atom table	Atom manager	GlobalAddAtom(lpString)	nAtom	322
GlobalAlloc	Allocates dwBytes of memory from global heap	Memory manager	GlobalAlloc(wFlags,dwBytes)	hMem	322
GlobalCompact	Compacts global memory to free dwMinFree bytes	Memory manager	GlobalCompact(dwMinFree)	dwLargest	324
GlobalDeleteAtom*	Deletes global atom from the atom table	Atom manager	GlobalDeleteAtom(nAtom)	nDeleted	325
GlobalDiscard	Discards global memory block if ref count is zero	Memory manager	GlobalDiscard(hMem)	hOldMem	325
GlobalFindAtom*	Finds character string within atom table	Atom manager	GlobalFindAtom(lpString)	nAtom	326
GlobalFlags	Returns memory type of global memory block	Memory manager	GlobalFlags(hMem)	wFlags	326
GlobalFree	Removes global memory block if ref count is zero	Memory manager	GlobalFree(hMem)	hOldMem	327
GlobalGetAtomName	Returns copy of string associated with an atom	Atom manager	GlobalGetAtomName(nAtom,lpBuffer,nSize)	nBytes	327
GlobalHandle	Returns handle of global memory object	Memory manager	GlobalHandle(wMem)	dwMem	328
GlobalLock	Returns address of block, locks it in mem, ups ref count	Memory manager	GlobalLock(hMem)	lpAddress	328
GlobalReAlloc	Reallocates global memory block to dwBytes	Memory manager	GlobalReAlloc(hMem,dwBytes,wFlags)	hNewMem	329
GlobalSize	Returns the size of global memory block, in bytes	Memory manager	GlobalSize(hMem)	dwBytes	331
GlobalUnlock	Unlocks block, decreases reference count	Memory manager	GlobalUnlock(hMem)	bResult	331
GlobalUnwire*	Unlocks memory segment	Memory manager	GlobalUnwire(hMem)	None	332
GlobalWire*	Moves segment to low memory and locks it	Memory manager	GlobalWire(hMem)	lpSegment	332
GrayString	Writes nCount chars of lpString using hBrush to gray	GDI output	GrayString(hDC,hBrush,lpOutputFunc,lpData,nCount,X,Y,nWidth,nHeight)	bDrawn	332
HIBYTE	Returns hi-order byte of nInteger	Utility	HIBYTE(nInteger)	cHighByte	335
HideCaret	Removes system caret from window	Window caret	HideCaret(hWnd)	None	335
HiliteMenuItem	Hilites or unHilites top-level menu item	Window menu	HiliteMenuItem(hWnd,hMenu,wIDHiliteItem,wHilite)	bHilited	335
HIWORD	Returns hi-order word of lInteger	Utility	HIWORD(lInteger)	wHighWord	337
InflateRect	Resizes lpRect by X units horiz and Y units vertically	Window rectangle	InflateRect(lpRect,X,Y)	nResult	338
InitAtomTable	Initializes atom hash table	Atom manager	InitAtomTable(nSize)	bResult	338
InSendMessage	Returns True if function is processing SendMessage	Window message	InSendMessage()	bInSend	339
IntersectClipRect	Forms new clipping region from intersection	GDI clipping rgn	IntersectClipRect(hDC,X1,Y1,X2,Y2)	nRgnType	339
IntersectRect	Finds intersection of two rects, copies to lpDestRect	Window rectangle	IntersectRect(lpDestRect,lpSrc1Rect,lpSrc2Rect)	nIntersection	340
InvalidateRect	Marks lpRect for repainting	Window painting	InvalidateRect(hWnd,lpRect,bErase)	None	341

(Continued)

Table 6.72. Continued

Function Name	Description	Type	Syntax (arguments)	Returns	Ref Page #
InvalidateRgn	Marks hRgn for repainting	Window painting	InvalidateRgn(hWnd,hRgn,bErase)	None	342
InvertRect	Inverts display bits of lpRect	GDI output	InvertRect(hDC,lpRect)	nResult	343
InvertRgn	Inverts colors in hRgn	GDI output	InvertRgn(hDC,hRgn)	bInverted	343
IsChild	Returns True if window is child of hParentWnd	Window display	IsChild(hWndParent,hWnd)	bChild	343
IsClipboardFormatAvailable	Returns True if data is available in wFormat	Window clipboard	IsClipboardFormatAvailable(wFormat)	bAvailable	344
IsDialogMessage	Determines whether lpMsg is intended for modeless dialog	Window dialog box	IsDialogMessage(hDlg,lpMsg)	bUsed	344
IsDlgButtonChecked	Returns state of nIDButton	Window dialog box	IsDlgButtonChecked(hDlg,nIDButton)	wCheck	345
IsIconic	Returns status of window (iconic or open)	Window display	IsIconic(hWnd)	bIconic	345
IsRectEmpty	Determines whether lpRect is empty	Window rectangle	IsRectEmpty(lpRect)	bEmpty	346
IsWindow	Determines whether hWnd is a valid, existing window	Window creation	IsWindow(hWnd)	bExists	346
IsWindowEnabled	Returns state of hWnd input from mouse and keyboard	Window input	IsWindowEnabled(hWnd)	bEnabled	347
IsWindowVisible	Determines whether hWnd is visible	Window display	IsWindowVisible(hWnd)	bVisible	347
IsZoomed*	Determines whether window is at maximum size	Window display	IsZoomed(hWnd)	bZoomed	347
KillTimer	Kills timer event identified by hWnd and nIDEvent	Window input	KillTimer(hWnd,nIDEvent)	bKilled	348
LineDDA	Computes successive points in line X1,Y1 X2,Y2	GDI output	LineDDA(X1,Y1,X2,Y2,lpLineFunc,lpData)	None	349
LineTo	Draws line from current pos up to X,Y (but not X,Y)	GDI output	LineTo(hDC,X,Y)	bDrawn	350
LoadAccelerators	Loads accelerator table named by lpTableName	Resource manager	LoadAccelerators(hInstance,lpTableName)	hRes	351
LoadBitmap	Loads bitmap named by lpBitmapName	Resource manager	LoadBitmap(hInstance,lpBitmapName)	hBitmap	351
LoadCursor	Loads cursor named by lpCursorName	Resource manager	LoadCursor(hInstance,lpCursorName)	hCursor	352
LoadIcon	Loads icon named by lpIconName	Resource manager	LoadIcon(hInstance,lpIconName)	hIcon	353
LoadLibrary	Loads library module named by lpLibFileName	Resource manager	LoadLibrary(lpLibFileName)	hLibModule	354
LoadMenu	Loads menu named by lpMenuName	Resource manager	LoadMenu(hInstance,lpMenuName)	hMenu	355
LoadMenuIndirect*	Loads menu from lpMenuTemplate	Resource manager	LoadMenuIndirect(lpMenuTemplate)	hMenu	355
LoadResource	Loads the resource named by hResInfo	Resource manager	LoadResource(hInstance,hResInfo)	hResData	356
LoadString	Loads string wID into buffer lpBuffer	Resource manager	LoadString(hInstance,wID,lpBuffer,nBufferMax)	nSize	356
LOBYTE	Returns lo-order byte of nInteger	Utility	LOBYTE(nInteger)	cLowByte	357
LocalAlloc	Allocates wBytes of memory from local heap	Memory manager	LocalAlloc(wFlags,wBytes)	hMem	357
LocalCompact	Compacts local memory to generate wMinFree free bytes	Memory manager	LocalCompact(wMinFree)	wLargest	358
LocalDiscard	Discards local memory block hMem if ref count is zero	Memory manager	LocalDiscard(hMem)	hOldMem	359
LocalFlags	Returns memory type of block hMem	Memory manager	LocalFlags(hMem)	wFlags	359
LocalFree	Frees local memory block hMem 1 ref count is zero	Memory manager	LocalFree(hMem)	hOldMem	360
LocalFreeze	Prevents compaction of local heap	Memory manager	LocalFreeze(Dummy)	None	360
LocalHandle	Returns handle of local memory object at wMem	Memory manager	LocalHandle(wMem)	hMem	360
LocalHandleDelta	Sets entry count for each new handle table in local heap	Memory manager	LocalHandleDelta(nNewDelta)	nCurrentDelta	361
LocalInit	Initializes the local heap	Memory manager	LocalInit(wSegment,wStart,wEnd)	bResult	361
LocalLock	Returns address of block, locks block, ups ref count by 1	Memory manager	LocalLock(hMem)	pAddress	361
LocalMelt	Permits compaction of local heap	Memory manager	LocalMelt(Dummy)	None	362
LocalNotify	Sets callback function for handling notification messages	Memory manager	LocalNotify(lpNotifyFunc)	lpPrevFunc	362
LocalReAlloc	Reallocates local memory block hMem to wBytes	Memory manager	LocalReAlloc(hMem,wBytes,wFlags)	hNewMem	363
LocalShrink*	Shrinks specified memory heap	Memory manager	LocalShrink(hSeg,wSize)	wSize	363
LocalSize	Returns the size of local block hMem, in bytes	Memory manager	LocalSize(hMem)	wBytes	364
LocalUnlock	Unlocks local memory block, decreases ref count by 1	Memory manager	LocalUnlock(hMem)	bResult	366
LockData	Locks data segment in memory	Memory manager	LockData(Dummy)	hMem	366
LockResource	Returns address of hResInfo, locks it, ups ref count by 1	Resource manager	LockResource(hResData)	lpResData	367
LockSegment	Locks segment at address wSegment	Resource manager	LockSegment(wSegment)	hSegment	367
LOWORD	Returns lo-order word of lInteger	Utility	LOWORD(lInteger)	wLowWord	368
LPtoDP	Converts logical points to device points	GDI conversion	LPtoDP(hDC,lpPoints,nCount)	bConverted	368
MAKEINTATOM	Casts integer as argument for AcdAtom	Atom manager	MAKEINTATOM(wInteger)	nAtom	369
MAKEINTRESOURCE	Casts integer as argument for AcdAtom	Atom manager	MAKEINTRESOURCE(nInteger)	lpIntegerID	369
MAKELONG	Creates unsigned long integer	Utility	MAKELONG(nLowWord,nHighWord)	dwInteger	370
MAKEPOINT	Converts long value into a POINT structure	Utility	MAKEPOINT(lInteger)	ptPoint	370
MakeProcInstance	Returns address for lpProc	Module manager	MakeProcInstance(lpProc,hInstance)	lpAddress	370
MapDialogRect	Converts dialog box coords to client coords	Window dialog box	MapDialogRect(hDlg,lpRect)	None	371
max	Returns maximum value of A and B	Utility	max value 1, value 2	nMaximum	372
MessageBeep	Generates a beep when message box displayed	Window error	MessageBeep(wType)	bBeep	373
MessageBox	Creates message box window	Window error	MessageBox(hWndParent,lpText,lpCaption,wType)	nMenuItem	373
min	Returns minimum value of A and B	Utility	min value 1, value 2	nMinimum	376
MoveConvertWindow*					376
MoveTo	Moves current position to point X,Y	GDI output	MoveTo(hDC,X,Y)	ptPrevPos	376

(Continued)

Function Name	Type	Description	Syntax (arguments)	Returns	Ref Page #
MoveWindow	Window display	Causes WM_SIZE message to be sent to hWnd	MoveWindow(hWnd,X,Y,nWidth,nHeight,bRepaint)	None	377
OEMToANSI	String translation	Converts OEM char string to ANSI string	OemToAnsi(lpOemStr,lpAnsiStr)	bTranslated	378
OffsetClipRgn	GDI clipping rgn	Moves clipping region X units horiz and Y units vertically	OffsetClipRgn(hDC,X,Y)	nRgnType	378
OffsetRect	Window rectangle	Moves rectangle X units horiz and Y units vertically	OffsetRect(lpRect,X,Y)	nResult	379
OffsetRgn	GDI region	Moves region X unit horiz and Y units vertically	OffsetRgn(hRgn,X,Y)	nRgnType	380
OffsetViewportOrg*	GDI region	Modifies viewport origin relative to current values	OffsetViewportOrg(hDC,X,Y)	ptPrevPos	380
OffsetWindowOrg*	Window display	Modifies window origin relative to current values	OffsetWindowOrg(hDC,X,Y)	ptPrevPos	381
OpenClipboard	Window clipboard	Open clipboard (prevents other apps from modifying)	OpenClipboard(hWnd)	bOpened	381
OpenComm	Communications	Opens device named by lpCommName for comm use	OpenComm(lpCommName,nInQueue,nOutQueue)	nCid	382
OpenFile	File I/O	Creates,opens,reopens,or deletes file named by lpFileName	OpenFile(lpFileName,lpReOpenBuff,wStyle)	nFile	383
OpenIcon	Window display	Opens specified window	OpenIcon(hWnd)	bOpened	384
OpenSound	Sound	Opens play device for exclusive use	OpenSound()	nVoices	385
PaintRgn	GDI output	Fills hRgn with current brush	PaintRgn(hDC,hRgn)	bFilled	386
PatBlt	GDI output	Combines bit pattern with one already on device	PatBlt(hDC,X,Y,nWidth,nHeight,dwRop)	bDrawn	386
PeekMessage	Window message	Places message (if any) at lpMsg	PeekMessage(lpMsg,hWnd,wMsgFilterMin,wMsgFilterMax,bRemoveMsg)	bPresent	387
Pie	GDI output	Draws arc and connects two endpoints to center	Pie(hDC,X1,Y1,X2,Y2,X3,Y3,X4,Y4)	bDrawn	389
PlayMetaFile	GDI metafile	Plays contents of metafile on device context hDC	PlayMetaFile(hDC,hMF)	bPlayed	390
PlayMetaFileRecord*	GDI metafile	Plays metafile record by executing GDI calls	PlayMetaFileRecord(hDC,lpHandletable,lpMetaRecord,nHnd)	None	391
Polygon	GDI output	Draws polygon	Polygon(hDC,lpPoints,nCount)	bDrawn	391
Polyline	GDI output	Draws set of line segments	Polyline(hDC,lpPoints,nCount)	bDrawn	392
PostAppMessage	Window message	Posts message to application	PostAppMessage(hTask,wMsg,wParam,lParam)	bPosted	393
PostMessage	Window message	Posts message in application queue	PostMessage(hWnd,wMsg,wParam,lParam)	bPosted	393
PostQuitMessage	Window message	Posts WM_QUIT message to application	PostQuitMessage(nExitCode)	None	394
PtInRect	Window message	Determines whether point lies within lpRect	PtInRect(lpRect,Point)	bInRect	395
PtInRegion	GDI region	Determines whether X,Y is within hRgn	PtInRegion(hRgn,X,Y)	bSuccess	395
PtVisible	GDI region	Determines whether X,Y is in clipping region of hDC	PtVisible(hDC,X,Y)	bVisible	396
ReadComm	Communications	Reads up to nSize bytes from nCid into lpBuf	ReadComm(nCid,lpBuf,nSize)	nBytes	397
Rectangle	GDI output	Draws rectangle	Rectangle(hDC,X1,Y1,X2,Y2)	bDrawn	397
RectVisible	GDI clipping rgn	Determines if any part of lpRect lies within clipping rgn	RectVisible(hDC,lpRect)	bVisible	398
RegisterClass	Window class	Registers a window class	RegisterClass(lpWndClass)	bRegistered	398
RegisterClipboardFormat	Window clipboard	Registers new clipboard format	RegisterClipboardFormat(lpFormatName)	wFormat	400
RegisterWindowDestroy*	Window manager	Locks windows from destruction by other tasks	RegisterWindowDestroy(hWnd,fRegister)	bProtected	400
RegisterWindowMessage	Window message	Defines new, unique window message	RegisterWindowMessage(lpString)	wMsg	400
ReleaseCapture	Window input	Releases mouse input, restores normal processing	ReleaseCapture()	None	401
ReleaseDC	Window painting	Releases display context	ReleaseDC(hWnd,hDC)	nReleased	401
RemoveFontResource	Resource manager	Removes font from font table	RemoveFontResource(lpFilename)	bSuccess	402
RemoveProp	Window property	Removes lpString from property list	RemoveProp(hWnd,lpString)	hData	403
ReplyMessage	Window message	Replies to message without returning control	ReplyMessage(lReply)	None	403
RestoreDC	GDI display context	Restores display context to previous state	RestoreDC(hDC,nSavedDC)	bRestored	404
RGB	GDI output	Creates RGB color from individual color values	RGB(cRed,cGreen,cBlue)	DWORD	405
RoundRect	GDI output	Draws rounded rectangle	RoundRect(hDC,X1,Y1,X2,Y2,X3,Y3)	bDrawn	405
SaveDC	GDI display context	Saves current state of display context	SaveDC(hDC)	nSavedDC	407
ScaleViewportExt*	GDI region	Modifies viewport extents relative to current values	ScaleViewportExt(hDC,Xnum,Xdenom,Ynum,Ydenom)	nPrevExts	407
ScaleWindowExt*	Window display	Modifies window extents from current values	ScaleWindowExt(hDC,Xnum,Xdenom,Ynum,Ydenom)	nPrevExts	408
ScreenToClient	Window coordinate	Converts screen coords at lpPoint to client coords	ScreenToClient(hWnd,lpPoint)	None	408
ScrollDC*	GDI display context	Scrolls rectangle of bits in display context	ScrollDC(hDC,dx,dy,lprcScroll,lprcClip,hrgnUpdate,lprcUpdate)	bDidScroll	409
ScrollWindow	Window scrolling	Moves contents of client area by Xamount,Yamount	ScrollWindow(hWnd,XAmount,YAmount,lpRect,lpClipRect)	None	410
SelectClipRgn	GDI selection	Selects hRgn as current clipping region for disp context	SelectClipRgn(hDC,hRgn)	nRgnType	411
SelectObject	GDI selection	Selects hObject as current object	SelectObject(hDC,hObject)	hOldObject	412
SendDlgItemMessage	Window dialog box	Sends message to nIDDlgItem within dialog box hDlg	SendDlgItemMessage(hDlg,nIDDlgItem,wMsg,wParam,lParam)	lResult	414
SendMessage	Window message	Sends message to window or windows	SendMessage(hWnd,wMsg,wParam,lParam)	lReply	414
SetActiveWindow	Window display	Makes tiled or popup window the active window	SetActiveWindow(hWnd)	hWndPrev	415
SetBitmapBits	GDI drawing obj	Sets bitmap bits to values given at lpBits	SetBitmapBits(hBitmap,dwCount,lpBits)	bCopied	416
SetBitmapDimension	GDI drawing obj	Associates width and height with a bitmap (in .1 mm)	SetBitmapDimension(hBitmap,X,Y)	ptOldDimensions	416
SetBkColor	GDI display context	Sets background color to closest to rgbColor	SetBkColor(hDC,rgbColor)	rgbOldColor	416
SetBkMode	GDI display context	Sets background mode	SetBkMode(hDC,nBkMode)	nOldBkMode	417
SetBrushOrg	GDI display context	Sets origin of all brushes into hDC display context	SetBrushOrg(hDC,X,Y)	dwOldOrigin	418
SetCapture	Window input	Causes mouse input to be sent to hWnd	SetCapture(hWnd)	hWndPrev	418
SetCaretBlinkTime	Window caret	Establishes caret flash rate	SetCaretBlinkTime(wMSeconds)	None	419
SetCaretPos	Window caret	Moves caret to X,Y position	SetCaretPos(X,Y)	None	419
SetClassLong	Window class	Replaces long value at nIndex in WNDCLASS struct	SetClassLong(hWnd,nIndex,lNewLong)	lOldLong	420

(Continued)

Table 6.72. Continued

Function Name	Description	Type	Syntax (arguments)	Returns	Ref Page #
SetClassWord	Replaces word at nIndex in WNDCLASS struct	Window class	SetClassWord(hWnd,nIndex,wNewWord)	lOldWord	421
SetClipboardData	Copies hMem into clipboard	Window clipboard	SetClipboardData(wFormat,hMem)	hClipData	422
SetClipboardViewer	Adds hWnd to clipboard viewer chain	Window clipboard	SetClipboardViewer(hWnd)	hWndNext	424
SetCommBreak	Sets break state of device nCid and suspends transmission	Communications	SetCommBreak(nCid)	nResult	424
SetCommEventMask	Sets event mask of device nCid	Communications	SetCommEventMask(nCid,nEvtMask)	lpEvent	425
SetCommState	Sets device to state specified in lpDCB	Communications	SetCommState(lpDCB)	nResult	426
SetConvertHook*					
SetConvertWindowHeight*					
SetConvertWindowParms*					
SetCursor	Sets cursor shape to hCursor; removes if hCursor=Null	Window cursor	SetCursor(hCursor)	hOldCursor	426
SetCursorPos	Sets mouse cursor to screen coords X,Y	Window cursor	SetCursorPos(X,Y)	None	427
SetDlgItemInt	Sets text of nIDDlgItem to string representing wValue	Window dialog box	SetDlgItemInt(hDig,nIDDlgItem,wValue,bSigned)	None	427
SetDlgItemText*	Sets caption or text of nIDDlgItem to String	Window dialog box	SetDlgItemText(hDig,nIDDlgItem,lpString)	None	428
SetDoubleClickTime*	Sets mouse doubleclick time	Window input	SetDoubleClickTime(wCount)	None	429
SetEnvironment	Copies data at lpEnviron to device at lpPortName	GDI information	SetEnvironment(lpPortName,lpEnviron,nCount)	nCopied	429
SetFocus	Assigns input focus to hWnd	Window input	SetFocus(hWnd)	hWndPrev	430
SetKeyboardState*	Copies buffer to keyboard state table	Window input	SetKeyboardState(lpKeyState)	None	431
SetMapMode	Sets mapping mode of hDC	GDI display context	SetMapMode(hDC,nMapMode)	nOldMapMode	431
SetMapperFlags*	Alters algorithm used by font mapper	GDI font	SetMapperFlags(hDC,wFlag)	dwPrevFlag	433
SetMenu	Sets window menu to hMenu; removes if hMenu=Null	Window menu	SetMenu(hWnd,hMenu)	bSet	433
SetMessageQueue	Creates new message queue	Window message	SetMessageQueue(cMsg)	bNewQ	434
SetMetaFileBits	Creates memory metafile from data in memory block	GDI metafile	SetMetaFileBits(hMem)	hMF	434
SetParent*	Changes parent window of child window	Window manager	SetParent(hWndChild,hWndNewParent)	h-PrevParent	435
SetPixel	Sets pixel at X,Y to device color closest to rgbColor	GDI output	SetPixel(hDC,X,Y,rgbColor)	rgbActualColor	435
SetPolyFillMode	Sets polygon filling mode for hDC	GDI display context	SetPolyFillMode(hDC,nPolyFillMode)	nOldPolyFillMode	436
SetPriority	Sets task priority	Task	SetPriority(hTask,nChangeAmount)	nNew	437
SetProp	Copies string and data handle to property list of hWnd	Window property	SetProp(hWnd,lpString,hData)	bSet	437
SetRect	Fills RECT struct at lpRect with given coords	Window rectangle	SetRect(lpRect,X1,Y1,X2,Y2)	nResult	438
SetRectEmpty	Sets lpRect to empty rectangle (all coords zero)	Window rectangle	SetRectEmpty(lpRect)	nResult	439
SetRectRgn*	Creates rectangular region	Window rectangle	SetRectRgn(hRgn,X1,Y1,X2,Y2)	None	439
SetRelAbs	Sets the relabs flag	GDI display context	SetRelAbs(hDC,nRelAbsMode)	nOldRelAbsMode	440
SetResourceHandler	Sets function address of resource handler	Resource manager	SetResourceHandler(hInstance,lpType,lpLoadFunc)	lpLoadFunc	440
SetROP2	Sets drawing mode	GDI display context	SetROP2(hDC,nDrawMode)	nOldDrawMode	442
SetScrollPos	Sets scrollbar elevator to nPos; redraws if nonzero	Window scrolling	SetScrollPos(hWnd,nBar,nPos,bRedraw)	nOldPos	444
SetScrollRange	Sets min/max scrollbar positions for scrollbar	Window scrolling	SetScrollRange(hWnd,nBar,nMinPos,nMaxPos,bRedraw)	None	445
SetSoundNoise	Sets source and duration of noise from play device	Sound	SetSoundNoise(nSource,nDuration)	nResult	446
SetStretchBitMode	Sets stretching mode for StretchBlt function	GDI display context	SetStretchBitMode(hDC,nStretchMode)	nOldStretchMode	447
SetSwapAreaSize*	Changes amount of memory used by code segment	Memory manager	SetSwapAreaSize(rsSize)	nParagraphs	448
SetSysColors	Changes one or more system colors	Window sys info	SetSysColors(nChanges,lpSysColor,lpColorValues)	None	448
SetSysModalWindow	Makes window a system modal window	Window attribute	SetSysModalWindow(hWnd)	hPrevWnd	450
SetTextAlign*	Sets text alignment flag	GDI display context	SetTextAlign(hDC,wFlag)	wXYAlign	450
SetTextCharacterExtra	Sets amount of intercharacter spacing	GDI text justify	SetTextCharacterExtra(hDC,nCharExtra)	nOldCharExtra	452
SetTextColor	Sets text color to device color closest to rgbColor	GDI display context	SetTextColor(hDC,rgbColor)	rgbOldColor	452
SetTextJustification	Prepares GDI to justify text line	GDI text justify	SetTextJustification(hDC,nBreakExtra,nBreakCount)	nSet	453
SetTimer	Creates system timer event	Window input	SetTimer(hWnd,nIDEvent,wElapse,lpTimerFunc)	nIDNewEvent	454
SetViewportExt	Sets x/y extents of viewport for hDC	GDI display context	SetViewportExt(hDC,X,Y)	ptOldExtents	455
SetViewportOrg	Sets viewport origin for hDC	GDI display context	SetViewportOrg(hDC,X,Y)	ptOldOrigin	457
SetVoiceAccent	Places an accent in voice queue	Sound	SetVoiceAccent(nVoice,nTempo,nVolume,nMode,nPitch)	nResult	457
SetVoiceEnvelope	Places envelope in voice queue	Sound	SetVoiceEnvelope(nVoice,nShape,nRepeat)	nResult	459
SetVoiceNote	Places note in voice queue	Sound	SetVoiceNote(nVoice,nValue,nLength,nCdots)	nResult	459
SetVoiceQueueSize	Allocates nBytes of memory for voice queue	Sound	SetVoiceQueueSize(nVoice,nBytes)	nResult	460
SetVoiceSound	Places frequency and duration in voice queue	Sound	SetVoiceSound(nVoice,nFrequency,nDuration)	nResult	461
SetVoiceThreshold	Sets threshold level for voice queue	Sound	SetVoiceThreshold(nVoice,nNotes)	nResult	461
SetWindowExt	Sets x/y extents of window of hDC	GDI display context	SetWindowExt(hDC,X,Y)	ptOldExtents	461
SetWindowLong	Changes window attribute identified by nIndex	Window attribute	SetWindowLong(hWnd,nIndex,lNewLong)	lOldLong	462
SetWindowOrg	Sets window origin of hDC	GDI display context	SetWindowOrg(hDC,X,Y)	ptOldOrigin	463
SetWindowPos*	Changes size, position, ordering of window	Window manager	SetWindowPos(hWnd,hWndInsertAfter,x,y,cx,cy,wFlag)	None	464
SetWindowsHook	Installs system or application hook	Window hook	SetWindowsHook(nFilterType,lpFilterFunc)	lpPrevFilterFunc	466

(Continued)

Function Name	Description	Type	Syntax (arguments)	Returns	Ref Page #
SetWindowText	Sets window caption or text to lpString	Window attribute	SetWindowText(hWnd,lpString)	None	474
SetWindowWord	Changes window attribute specified by nIndex	Window attribute	SetWindowWord(hWnd,nIndex,wNewWord)	wOldWord	475
ShowCaret	Displays new caret or redisplays hidden caret	Window caret	ShowCaret(hWnd)	None	475
ShowCursor	Adds 1 to cursor display count if nonzero; otherwise -1	Window cursor	ShowCursor(bShow)	nCount	476
ShowOwnedPopups*	Displays or hides all popup windows	Window display	ShowOwnedPopups(hWnd,fShow)	None	477
ShowScrollBar*	Displays or hides scroll bar	Window display	ShowScrollBar(hWnd,wBar,fShow)	None	477
ShowWindow	Displays or removes window as specified by nCmdShow	Window display	ShowWindow(hWnd,nCmdShow)	bShown	478
SizeofResource	Returns size of resource hResInfo, in bytes	Resource manager	SizeofResource(hInstance,hResInfo)	wBytes	480
StartSound	Starts play in each voice queue	Sound	StartSound()	None	480
StopSound	Stops playing all voices	Sound	StopSound()	None	480
StretchBlt	Moves bitmap from source rect to destination rect	GDI output	StretchBlt(hDestDC,X,Y,nWidth,nHeight,hSrcDC,XSrc,YSrc,nSrcWidth,nSrcHeight,dwRop)	bDrawn	481
SwapMouseButton	Swaps meaning of left/right mouse buttons if bSwap=True	Window input	SwapMouseButton(bSwap)	bSwapped	483
SyncAllVoices	Places sync mark in each voice queue	Sound	SyncAllVoices()	nResult	484
TextOut	Writes character string at X,Y	GDI output	TextOut(hDC,X,Y,lpString,nCount)	bDrawn	485
Throw	Restores execution environment to values in lpCatchBuf	Module manager	Throw(lpCatchBuf,nThrowback)	None	485
TranslateAccelerator	Processes keyboard accelerators for menu commands	Window message	TranslateAccelerator(hWnd,hAccTable,lpMsg)	nTranslated	486
TranslateMessage	Translates virtual keystrokes into char messages	Window message	TranslateMessage(lpMsg)	bTranslated	487
TransmitCommChar	Places character cChar at head of transmit queue	Communications	TransmitCommChar(nCid,cChar)	nResult	488
UngetCommChar	Makes character cChar next character to be read f/ queue	Communications	UngetCommChar(nCid,cChar)	nResult	489
UnhookWindowsHook*	Removes filter function from hook chain	Window hook	UnhookWindowsHook(nHook,lpfnHook)	bUnhooked	489
UnionRect	Stores union of two rectangles	Window rectangle	UnionRect(lpDestRect,lpSrc1Rect,lpSrc2Rect)	nUnion	490
UnlockData	Unlocks data segment	Memory manager	UnlockData(Dummy)	None	490
UnlockResource*	Unlocks resource, decrements reference count	Resource manager	UnlockResource(hResData)	hSeg	491
UnlockSegment	Unlocks wSegment	Memory manager	UnlockSegment(wSegment)	hMem	491
UnrealizeObject	Directs GDI to reset origin of brush when it is selected	GDI display context	UnrealizeObject(hBrush)	bUnrealized	492
UpdateWindow	Notifies application when window needs redrawing	Window painting	UpdateWindow(hWnd)	None	492
ValidateFreeSpaces*	Determines whether free segments contain valid contents	Memory manager	ValidateFreeSpaces()	lpstrInvalid	493
ValidateRect	Releases rectangle lpRect from repainting	Window painting	ValidateRect(hWnd,lpRect)	None	493
ValidateRgn	Releases hRgn from repainting	Window painting	ValidateRgn(hWnd,hRgn)	None	494
WaitMessage	Yields control to other application	Window message	WaitMessage()	None	495
WaitSoundState	Waits until play driver enters nState	Sound	WaitSoundState(nState)	nResult	495
WindowFromPoint	Identifies window containing Point (in screen coords)	Window coordinate	WindowFromPoint(Point)	hWnd	496
WinMain	Entry point for Windows application execution	Window main	WinMain(hInstance,hPrevInstance,lpCmdLine,nCmdShow)	nExitCode	
WndProc	Processes messages sent to it	Window	WndProc(hWnd,wMsg,wParam,lParam)	lReply	496
WriteComm	Writes un to nSize bytes from buffer to device nCid	Communications	WriteComm(nCid,lpBuf,nSize)	nBytes	496
WriteProfileString	Copies lpString to WIN.INI file	Windows init file	WriteProfileString(lpApplicationName,lpKeyName,lpString)	bResult	497
Yield	Halts current task and starts any waiting task	Task	Yield()	bResult	498

Version Info: *Applicable to versions of Windows beginning with 2.0

Notes: C is case sensitive. Lowercase prefix to argument and result names are data type indicators.

Source: Microsoft Windows SDK Programmer's Reference 2.0

See Also: 6.71. Windows Function Summary by Version
6.73. Windows Function Summary by Type of Function

6.73. WINDOWS FUNCTION SUMMARY BY TYPE OF FUNCTION

Function Name	Description	Type	Syntax (arguments)	Returns	Ref Page #
MoveConvertWindow*					376
SetConvertHook*					
SetConvertParms*					
SetConvertWindowHeight*					
AddAtom	Creates atom for character string lpString	Atom manager	AddAtom(lpString)	wAtom	148
DeleteAtom	Deletes nAtom if its reference count is zero	Atom manager	DeleteAtom(nAtom)	nOldAtom	207
FindAtom	Retrieves atom associated with lpString	Atom manager	FindAtom(lpString)	wAtom	244
GetAtomHandle	Returns handle of atom string	Atom manager	GetAtomHandle(wAtom)	hMem	
GetAtomName	Copies nSize chars of string of atom to lpBuffer	Atom manager	GetAtomName(nAtom,lpBuffer,nSize)	nLength	253
GlobalAddAtom*	Adds global atom to the atom table	Atom manager	GlobalAddAtom(lpString)	nAtom	322
GlobalDeleteAtom*	Deletes global atom from the atom table	Atom manager	GlobalDeleteAtom(nAtom)	nDeleted	325
GlobalFindAtom*	Finds character string within atom table	Atom manager	GlobalFindAtom(lpString)	nAtom	326
GlobalGetAtomName	Returns copy of string associated with an atom	Atom manager	GlobalGetAtomName(nAtom,lpBuffer,nSize)	nBytes	327
InitAtomTable	Initializes atom hash table	Atom manager	InitAtomTable(nSize)	bResult	338
MAKEINTATOM	Casts integer as argument for AddAtom	Atom manager	MAKEINTATOM(wInteger)	nAtom	370
MAKEINTRESOURCE	Casts integer as argument for AddAtom	Atom manager	MAKEINTRESOURCE(nInteger)	lpIntegerID	370
BuildCommDCB	Fills device control block with control codes	Communications	BuildCommDCB(lpDef,lpDCB)	nResult	160
ClearCommBreak	Clears comm break state for nCid device	Communications	ClearCommBreak(nCid)	nResult	169
CloseComm	Closes comm device nCid (first transmits buffer)	Communications	CloseComm(nCid)	nResult	171
EscapeCommFunction	Executes escape function nFunc: for device nCid	Communications	EscapeCommFunction(nCid,nFunc)	nResult	238
FlushComm	Flushes characters from queue of device nCid	Communications	FlushComm(nCid,nQueue)	nResult	248
GetCommError	Fills lpStat buffer with status of nCid device	Communications	GetCommError(nCid,lpStat)	nError	264
GetCommEventMask	Retrieves, then clears, the event mask for nCid	Communications	GetCommEventMask(nCid,nEvtMask)	wEvent	266
GetCommState	Fills lpDCB buffer with DCB of nCid device	Communications	GetCommState(nCid,lpDCB)	nResult	266
OpenComm	Opens device named by lpCommName for comm use	Communications	OpenComm(lpCommName,nInQueue,nOutQueue)	nCid	382
ReadComm	Reads up to nSize bytes from nCid into lpBuf	Communications	ReadComm(nCid,lpBuf,nSize)	nBytes	397
SetCommBreak	Sets break state of device nCid and suspends transmission	Communications	SetCommBreak(nCid)	nResult	424
SetCommEventMask	Sets event mask of device nCid	Communications	SetCommEventMask(nCid,nEvtMask)	lpEvent	425
SetCommState	Sets device to state specified in lpDCB	Communications	SetCommState(lpDCB)	nResult	426
TransmitCommChar	Places character cChar at head of transmit queue	Communications	TransmitCommChar(nCid,cChar)	nResult	488
UngetCommChar	Makes character cChar next character to be read f/ queue	Communications	UngetCommChar(nCid,cChar)	nResult	489
WriteComm	Writes un to nSize bytes from buffer to device nCid	Communications	WriteComm(nCid,lpBuf,nSize)	nBytes	496
FatalExit	Halts Windows and prompts through AUX	Debugging	FatalExit(Code)	Result	243
GetTempDrive	Returns optimal drive letter for temp file	File I/O	GetTempDrive(cDriveLetter)	cOptDriveLetter	307
GetTempFileName	Creates temporary file name	File I/O	GetTempFileName(cDriveLetter,lpPrefixString,wUnique,lpTempFileName)	wUniqueNumber	308
OpenFile	Creates,opens,reopens,or deletes file named by lpFileName	File I/O	OpenFile(lpFileName,lpReOpenBuff,wStyle)	nFile	383
ExcludeUpdateRgn*	Excludes a region in window from clipping region for window	GDI clipping	ExcludeUpdateRgn(hDC,hWnd)	nRgnType	240
ExcludeClipRect	Creates new clipping region for rectangle	GDI clipping rgn	ExcludeClipRect(hDC,X1,Y1,X2,Y2)	nRgnType	239
GetClipBox	Copies clipping rect boundary to lpRect	GDI clipping rgn	GetClipBox(hDC,lpRect)	nRgnType	263
GetMapMode	Returns current mapping mode	GDI clipping rgn	GetMapMode(hDC)	nMapMode	282
IntersectClipRect	Forms new clipping region from intersection	GDI clipping rgn	IntersectClipRect(hDC,X1,Y1,X2,Y2)	nRgnType	339
OffsetClipRgn	Moves clipping region X units horiz and Y units vertically	GDI clipping rgn	OffsetClipRgn(hDC,X,Y)	nRgnType	378
RectVisible	Determines if any part of lpRect lies within clipping rgn	GDI clipping rgn	RectVisible(hDC,lpRect)	bVisible	398
Escape	Accesses device facilities not available through GDI	GDI control	Escape(hDC,nEscape,nCount,lpInData,lpOutData)	nResult	238
Escape (ABORTDOC)	Aborts current job	GDI control	Escape(hDC,ABORTDOC,Null,lpstrNull,lpstrNull)	nResult	681
Escape (BANDINFO)*	Copies banding capability info to lpindata structure	GDI control	Escape(hDC,BANDINFO,nCount,lpInData,lpOutData)	nResult	681
Escape (DEVICEDATA)	Send data directly to printer	GDI control	Escape(hDC,DEVICEDATA,nCount,lpInData,lpOutData)	nResult	683
Escape (DRAFTMODE)	Turns draft mode ON or OFF	GDI control	Escape(hDC,DRAFTMODE,2,lpDraftMode,lpstrNull)	nCount	684
Escape (DRAWPATTERNRECT)*	Creates pattern using rules for FCL printers	GDI control	Escape(hDC,DRAWPATTERNRECT,nCount,lpInData,lpOutData)	nResult	684
Escape (ENABLEDUPLEX)*	Enables duplex printing capabilities	GDI control	Escape(hDC,ENABLEDUPLEX,nCount,lpInData,lpOutData)	nResult	686
Escape (ENABLEPAIRKERNING)	Enables or disables kerning ability of device	GDI control	Escape(hDC,ENABLEPAIRKERNING,nCount,lpInData,lpOutData)	bResult	686
Escape (ENABLERELATIVEWIDTHS)	Enables or disables relative character widths on device	GDI control	Escape(hDC,ENABLERELATIVEWIDTHS,nCount,lpInData,lpOutData)	bResult	687
Escape (ENDDOC)	Ends print job started by EscapeSTARTDOC	GDI control	Escape(hDC,ENDDOC,Null,lpstrNull)	nResult	688
Escape (EXTTEXTOUT)	More efficient TextOut for justification and kerning	GDI control	Escape(hDC,EXTTEXTOUT,nCount,lpInData,lpOutData*)	nResult	689
Escape (FLUSHOUTPUT)	Flushes output in device buffer	GDI control	Escape(hDC,FLUSHOUTPUT,Null,lpstrNull,lpstrNull)	bResult	690
Escape (GETCOLORTABLE)	Copies RGB color table to lpOutData	GDI control	Escape(hDC,GETCOLORTABLE,Null,lpIndex,lpColor)	bResult	691
Escape (GETEXTENDEDTEXTMETRICS)	Fills buffer with extended text metrics for font	GDI control	Escape(hDC,GETEXTENDEDTEXTMETRICS,nCount*,lpInData,lpOutData)	nCount	691
Escape (GETEXTENTTABLE)	Returns width of individual group of consec chars	GDI control	Escape(hDC,GETEXTENTTABLE,nCount*,lpInData,lpOutData)	bResult	692
Escape (GETPAIRKERNTABLE)	Fills buffer at lpOutData with kerning pair table for font	GDI control	Escape(hDC,GETPAIRKERNTABLE,nCount*,lpstrNull,lpOutData)	nCount	693

(Continued)

Function Name	Description	Syntax (arguments)	Type	Returns	Ref Page #
Escape (GETPHYSPAGESIZE)	Copies physical page size to lpOutData POINT structure	Escape(hDC,GETPHYSPAGESIZE,Null,lpstrNull,lpDimensions)	GDI control	nResult	694
Escape (GETPRINTINGOFFSET)	Copies printing offset to lpOutData POINT structure	Escape(hDC,GETPRINTINGOFFSET,Null,lpstrNull,lpOffset)	GDI control	nResult	694
Escape (GETSCALINGFACTOR)	Returns scaling factors for x and y axes of printer	Escape(hDC,GETSCALINGFACTOR,null,lpstrNull,lpFactors)	GDI control	nResult	695
Escape (GETTRACKKERNTABLE)	Fills buffer at lpOutData with track kerning table for font	Escape(hDC,GETTRACKKERNTABLE,nCount*,lpInData,lpOutData)	GDI control	nCount	695
Escape (MFCOMMENT)*	Adds comment to metafile	Escape(hDC,MFCOMMENT,nCount,lpComment,lpstrNull)	GDI control	bResult	696
Escape (NEWFRAME)	Ends writing to a page	Escape(hDC,NEWFRAME,Null,lpstrNull,lpstrNull)	GDI control	nResult	696
Escape (NEXTBAND)	Ends writing to a band	Escape(hDC,NEXTBAND,Null,lpstrNull,lpBandRect)	GDI control	nResult	697
Escape (QUERYESCSUPPORT)	Tests whether device supports Escape	Escape(hDC,QUERYESCSUPPORT,2,lpEscNum,lpstrNull)	GDI control	nResult	698
Escape (SELECTPAPERSOURCE)	Determines and selects available paper sources	Escape(hDC,SELECTPAPERSOURCE,2,lpInData,lpOutData)	GDI control	nResult	698
Escape (SETABORTPROC)	Sets abort function for print task	Escape(hDC,SETABORTPROC,Null,lpIAbortFunc,lpstrNull)	GDI control	nResult	698
Escape (SETALLJUSTVALUES)	Sets text justification values	Escape(hDC,SETALLJUSTVALUES,nCount,lpInData,lpOutData)	GDI control	nResult	699
Escape (SETCOLORTABLE)	Sets RGB color table entry	Escape(hDC,SETCOLORTABLE,Null,lpColorEntry,lpColor)	GDI control	nResult	701
Escape (SETCOPYCOUNT)	Specifies number of copies per page to print (uncollated)	Escape(hDC,SETCOPYCOUNT,2,lpInData,lpOutData)	GDI control	nResult	702
Escape (SETKERNTRACK)	Specifies which kerning track to use	Escape(hDC,SETKERNTRACK,2,lpInData,lpOutData)	GDI control	bResult	702
Escape (SETLINECAP)	Sets line end cap	Escape(hDC,SETLINECAP,nCount,lpInData,lpOutData)	GDI control	nResult	703
Escape (SETLINEJOIN)	Sets how line segments joined	Escape(hDC,SETLINEJOIN,nCount,lpInData,lpOutData)	GDI control	nResult	704
Escape (SETMITERLIMIT)	Sets miter limit for a device	Escape(hDC,SETMITERLIMIT,nCount,lpInData,lpOutData)	GDI control	nResult	705
Escape (STARTDOC)	Starts print task	Escape(hDC,STARTDOC,nDocLength,lpDocName,lpstrNull)	GDI control	nResult	706
Escape (STRETCHBLT)	Implements StretchBit on driver level	Escape(hDC,STRETCHBLT,nCount,lpInData,lpInData)	GDI control	bResult	707
DPtoLP	Converts device points into logical points	DPtoLP(hDC,lpPoints,nCount)	GDI conversion	bConverted	217
GetNearestColor	Returns device color closest to rgbColor	GetNearestColor(hDC,rgbColor)	GDI conversion	rgbSolidColor	289
LPtoDP	Converts logical points to device points	LPtoDP(hDC,lpPoints,nCount)	GDI conversion	bConverted	369
CreateCompatibleDC	Creates memory display context compat. with hDC	CreateCompatibleDC(hDC)	GDI display context	hMemDC	178
CreateDC	Creates display context for specified device	CreateDC(lpDriverName,lpDeviceName,lpOutput,lpInitData)	GDI display context	hDC	179
CreateIC	Creates information context for device	CreateIC(lpDriverName,lpDeviceName,lpOutput,lpInitData)	GDI display context	hIC	189
DeleteDC	Deletes specified display context	DeleteDC(hDC)	GDI display context	bDeleted	208
GetBkColor	Returns current background color of device	GetBkColor(hDC)	GDI display context	rgbColor	255
GetBkMode	Returns background mode of device	GetBkMode(hDC)	GDI display context	nBkMode	255
GetBrushOrg	Returns current brush origin	GetBrushOrg(hDC)	GDI display context	dwOrigin	255
GetPolyFillMode	Retrieves current polygon filling mode	GetPolyFillMode(hDC)	GDI display context	nPolyFillMode	294
GetRelAbs	Returns the relabs flag	GetRelAbs(hDC)	GDI display context	nRelAbsMode	298
GetROP2	Returns current drawing mode	GetROP2(hDC)	GDI display context	nDrawMode	299
GetStretchBltMode	Returns current stretching mode	GetStretchBltMode(hDC)	GDI display context	nStretchMode	303
GetTextColor	Returns current text color	GetTextColor(hDC)	GDI display context	rgbColor	310
GetViewportExt	Returns x/y extent of display context's viewport	GetViewportExt(hDC)	GDI display context	ptExtents	315
GetViewportOrg	Returns x/y coords of display context's viewport org.	GetViewportOrg(hDC)	GDI display context	ptOrigin	316
GetWindowExt	Returns x/y extents of display context's window	GetWindowExt(hDC)	GDI display context	ptExtents	318
GetWindowOrg	Returns x/y coords of display context window origin	GetWindowOrg(hDC)	GDI display context	ptOrigin	319
RestoreDC	Restores display context to previous state	RestoreDC(hDC,nSavedDC)	GDI display context	bRestored	404
SaveDC	Saves current state of display context	SaveDC(hDC)	GDI display context	nSavedDC	407
ScrollDC*	Scrolls rectangle of bits in display context	ScrollDC(hDC,dx,dy,lprcScroll,lprcClip,hrgnUpdate,lprcUpdate)	GDI display context	bDidScroll	409
SetBkColor	Sets background color to closest to rgbColor	SetBkColor(hDC,rgbColor)	GDI display context	rgbOldColor	416
SetBkMode	Sets background mode	SetBkMode(hDC,nBkMode)	GDI display context	nOldBkMode	417
SetBrushOrg	Sets origin of all brushes into hDC display context	SetBrushOrg(hDC,X,Y)	GDI display context	dwOldOrigin	418
SetMapMode	Sets mapping mode of hDC	SetMapMode(hDC,nMapMode)	GDI display context	nOldMapMode	431
SetPolyFillMode	Sets polygon filling mode for hDC	SetPolyFillMode(hDC,nPolyFillMode)	GDI display context	nOldPolyFillMode	436
SetRelAbs	Sets the relabs flag	SetRelAbs(hDC,nRelAbsMode)	GDI display context	nOldRelAbsMode	440
SetROP2	Sets drawing mode	SetROP2(hDC,nDrawMode)	GDI display context	nOldDrawMode	442
SetStretchBltMode	Sets stretching mode for StretchBit function	SetStretchBltMode(hDC,nStretchMode)	GDI display context	nOldStretchMode	447
SetTextAlign*	Sets text alignment flag	SetTextAlign(hDC,wFlag)	GDI display context	wXYAlign	450
SetTextColor	Sets text color to device color closest to rgbColor	SetTextColor(hDC,rgbColor)	GDI display context	rgbOldColor	452
SetViewportExt	Sets x/y extents of viewport for hDC	SetViewportExt(hDC,X,Y)	GDI display context	ptOldExtents	455
SetViewportOrg	Sets viewport origin for hDC	SetViewportOrg(hDC,X,Y)	GDI display context	ptOldOrigin	457
SetWindowExt	Sets x/y extents of window of hDC	SetWindowExt(hDC,X,Y)	GDI display context	ptOldExtents	462
SetWindowOrg	Sets window origin of hDC	SetWindowOrg(hDC,X,Y)	GDI display context	ptOldOrigin	464
UnrealizeObject	Directs GDI to reset origin of brush when it is selected	UnrealizeObject(hBrush)	GDI display context	bUnrealized	492
CreateFont	Creates logical font	CreateFont(nHeight,nWidth,nEscapement,nOrientation,nWeight,cItalic, cUnderline,cStrikeOut,nCharSet,cOutputPrecision,cClipPrecision, cQuality,cPitchAndFamily,lpFacename)	GDI drawing	hFont	185

(Continued)

Table 6.73. Continued

Function Name	Description	Type	Syntax (arguments)	Returns	Ref Page #
CreateBitmap	Creates bitmap of specified height, width, pattern	GDI drawing	CreateBitmap(nWidth,nHeight,nPlanes,nBitCount,lpBits)	hBitmap	175
CreateBitmapIndirect	Creates bitmap from existing bitmap	GDI drawing	CreateBitmapIndirect(lpBitmap)	hBitmap	176
CreateBrushIndirect	Creates logical brush from existing brush	GDI drawing	CreateBrushIndirect(lpLogBrush)	hBrush	176
CreateCompatibleBitmap	Creates bitmap compatible with device hDC	GDI drawing	CreateCompatibleBitmap(hDC,nWidth,nHeight)	hBitmap	178
CreateDiscardableBitmap	Creates discardable bitmap	GDI drawing	CreateDiscardableBitmap(hDC,nWidth,nHeight)	hBitmap	184
CreateFontIndirect	Creates logical font like lpLogFont	GDI drawing	CreateFontIndirect(lpLogFont)	hFont	188
CreateHatchBrush	Creates logical brush with hatched pattern	GDI drawing	CreateHatchBrush(nIndex,rgbColor)	hBrush	189
CreatePatternBrush	Creates logical brush with hBitmap pattern	GDI drawing	CreatePatternBrush(hBitmap)	hBrush	191
CreatePen	Creates logical pen	GDI drawing	CreatePen(nPenStyle,nWidth,rgbColor)	hPen	192
CreatePenIndirect	Creates logical pen like lpLogPen	GDI drawing	CreatePenIndirect(lpLogPen)	hPen	193
CreateSolidBrush	Creates logical brush of a solid color	GDI drawing	CreateSolidBrush(rgbColor)	hBrush	195
GetBitmapBits	Copies lCount bits of bitmap to lpBits buffer	GDI drawing	GetBitmapBits(hBitmap,dwCount,lpBits)	lCopied	254
GetBitmapDimension	Returns width and height of bitmap	GDI drawing	GetBitmapDimension(hBitmap)	ptDimensions	254
GetStockObject	Returns handle to predefined object	GDI drawing obj	GetStockObject(nIndex)	hObject	301
SetBitmapBits	Sets bitmap bits to values given at lpBits	GDI drawing obj	SetBitmapBits(hBitmap,dwCount,lpBits)	bCopied	416
SetBitmapDimension	Associates width and height with a bitmap (in .1 mm)	GDI drawing obj	SetBitmapDimension(hBitmap,X,Y)	ptOldDimensions	416
SetMapperFlags*	Alters algorithm used by font mapper	GDI font	SetMapperFlags(hDC,wFlag)	dwPrevFlag	433
EnumFonts	Enumerates fonts available on device	GDI information	EnumFonts(hDC,lpFacename,lpFontFunc,lpData)	nResult	228
EnumMetaFile*	Enumerates GDI calls in a metafile	GDI information	EnumMetaFile(hDC,hMF,lpCallbackFunc,lpClientData)	bEnumerated	230
EnumObjects	Enumerates objects available on device	GDI information	EnumObjects(hDC,nObjectType,lpObjectFunc,lpData)	nResult	231
EqualRect*	Determines whether two rectangles are equal	GDI information	EqualRect(lpRect1,lpRect2)	bEqual	237
GetDeviceCaps	Returns device-specific info	GDI information	GetDeviceCaps(hDC,nIndex)	nValue	269
GetEnvironment	Copies device environment to lpEnviron	GDI information	GetEnvironment(lpPortName,lpEnviron,nMaxCount)	nCopied	276
GetTextFace	Copies current font facename to lpFacename	GDI information	GetTextFace(hDC,nCount,lpFacename)	nCopied	311
GetTextMetrics	Fills buffer with metrics for current font	GDI information	GetTextMetrics(hDC,lpMetrics)	bRetrieved	311
SetEnvironment	Copies data at lpEnviron to device at lpPortName	GDI information	SetEnvironment(lpPortName,lpEnviron,nCount)	nCopied	429
CloseMetaFile	Closes metafile and creates handle	GDI metafile	CloseMetaFile(hDC)	hMF	171
CopyMetaFile	Copies metafile to lpFilename and returns new hMF	GDI metafile	CopyMetaFile(hSrcMetaFile,lpFilename)	hMF	174
CreateMetaFile	Creates metafile display context	GDI metafile	CreateMetaFile(lpFilename)	hDC	191
DeleteMetaFile	Deletes access to metafile; frees system resources	GDI metafile	DeleteMetaFile(hMF)	bFreed	208
GetMetaFile	Creates handle for metafile named by lpFilename	GDI metafile	GetMetaFile(lpFilename)	hMF	287
GetMetaFileBits	Stores metafile bits in global memory block	GDI metafile	GetMetaFileBits(hMF)	hMem	288
PlayMetaFile	Plays contents of metafile on device context hDC	GDI metafile	PlayMetaFile(hDC,hMF)	bPlayed	390
PlayMetaFileRecord*	Plays metafile record by executing GDI calls	GDI metafile	PlayMetaFileRecord(hDC,lpHandletable,lpMetaRecord,nHnd)	None	391
SetMetaFileBits	Creates memory metafile from data in memory block	GDI metafile	SetMetaFileBits(hMem)	hMF	434
StretchBlt	Moves bitmap from source rect to destination rect	GDI output	StretchBlt(hDestDC,X,Y,nWidth,nHeight,hSrcDC,XSrc,YSrc,nSrcWidth, nSrcHeight,dwRop)	bDrawn	481
Arc	Draws arc from X3,Y3 to X4,Y4	GDI output	Arc(hDC,X1,Y1,X2,Y2,X3,Y3,X4,Y4)	bDrawn	154
BitBlt	Moves bitmap from src device to dest device	GDI output	BitBlt(hDestDC,X,Y,nWidth,nHeight,hSrcDC,XSrc,YSrc,dwRop)	bDrawn	156
Chord*	Draws a chord (ellipse insersection with line segment)	GDI output	Chord(hDC,X1,Y1,X2,Y2,X3,Y3,X4,Y4)	bDrawn	169
DrawIcon	Draws icon with upper-left corner at X,Y	GDI output	DrawIcon(hDC,X,Y,hIcon)	bDrawn	218
DrawText	Draws nCount chars of lpString clipped in lpRect	GDI output	DrawText(hDC,lpString,nCount,lpRect,wFormat)	Height of text	219
Ellipse	Draws ellipse with center in X1,Y1 X2,Y2 rect	GDI output	Ellipse(hDC,X1,Y1,X2,Y2)	bDrawn	222
ExtTextOut*	Writes character string within rect region on display	GDI output	ExtTextOut(hDC,X,Y,wOptions,lpRect,lpString,nCount,lpDx)	bDrawn	241
FillRect	Fills rectangle using specified brush	GDI output	FillRect(hDC,lpRect,hBrush)	None	243
FillRgn	Fills region with specified brush	GDI output	FillRgn(hDC,hRgn,hBrush)	bFilled	244
FloodFill	Fills area with current brush starting at X,Y	GDI output	FloodFill(hDC,X,Y,rgbColor)	bFilled	247
FrameRect	Draws border for rectangle	GDI output	FrameRect(hDC,lpRect,hBrush)	None	249
FrameRgn	Draws border for region	GDI output	FrameRgn(hDC,hRgn,hBrush,nWidth,nHeight)	bFramed	249
GetCharWidth*	Retrieves width of a character	GDI output	GetCharWidth(hDC,wFirstChar,wLastChar,lpBuffer)	bGotten	257
GetCurrentPosition	Returns logical coords of current position	GDI output	GetCurrentPosition(hDC)	ptPos	267
GetPixel	Retrieves RGB color of pixel at X,Y	GDI output	GetPixel(hDC,X,Y)	rgbColor	293
GrayString	Writes nCount chars of String using hBrush to gray	GDI output	GrayString(hDC,hBrush,lpOutputFunc,lpData,nCount,X,Y,nWidth,nHeight)	bDrawn	332
InvertRect	Inverts display bits of lpRect	GDI output	InvertRect(hDC,lpRect)	nResult	343
InvertRgn	Inverts colors in hRgn	GDI output	InvertRgn(hDC,hRgn)	bInverted	343
LineDDA	Computes successive points in line X1,Y1 X2,Y2	GDI output	LineDDA(X1,Y1,X2,Y2,lpLineFunc,lpData)	None	350
LineTo	Draws line from current pos up to X,Y (but not X,Y)	GDI output	LineTo(hDC,X,Y)	bDrawn	351
MoveTo	Moves current position to point X,Y	GDI output	MoveTo(hDC,X,Y)	ptPrevPos	376
PaintRgn	Fills hRgn with current brush	GDI output	PaintRgn(hDC,hRgn)	bFilled	386

(Continued)

Function Name	Description	Type	Syntax (arguments)	Returns	Ref Page #
PatBlt	Combines bit pattern with one already on device	GDI output	PatBlt(hDC,X,Y,nWidth,nHeight,dwRop)	bDrawn	386
Pie	Draws arc and connects two endpoints to center	GDI output	Pie(hDC,X1,Y1,X2,Y2,X3,Y3,X4,Y4)	bDrawn	389
Polygon	Draws polygon	GDI output	Polygon(hDC,lpPoints,nCount)	bDrawn	391
Polyline	Draws set of line segments	GDI output	Polyline(hDC,lpPoints,nCount)	bDrawn	392
Rectangle	Draws rectangle	GDI output	Rectangle(hDC,X1,Y1,X2,Y2)	bDrawn	397
RGB	Creates RGB color from individual color values	GDI output	RGB(cRed,cGreen,cBlue)	DWORD	405
RoundRect	Draws rounded rectangle	GDI output	RoundRect(hDC,X1,Y1,X2,Y2,X3,Y3)	bDrawn	405
SetPixel	Sets pixel at X,Y to device color closest to rgbColor	GDI output	SetPixel(hDC,X,Y,rgbColor)	rgbActualColor	435
TextOut	Writes character string at X,Y	GDI output	TextOut(hDC,X,Y,lpString,nCount)	bDrawn	485
CombineRgn	Combines two existing regions into new region	GDI region	CombineRgn(hDestRgn,hSrcRgn1,hSrcRgn2,nCombineMode)	nRgnType	173
CreateEllipticRgn	Creates elliptical region bounded by rect X1,Y1,X2,Y2	GDI region	CreateEllipticRgn(X1,Y1,X2,Y2)	hRgn	184
CreateEllipticRgnIndirect*	Creates elliptical region bounded by lpRect	GDI region	CreateEllipticRgnIndirect(lpRect)	hRgn	185
CreatePolygonRgn	Creates polygonal region	GDI region	CreatePolygonRgn(lpPoints,nCount,nPolyFillMode)	hRgn	193
CreateRectRgn	Creates rectangular region	GDI region	CreateRectRgn(X1,Y1,X2,Y2)	hRgn	194
CreateRectRgnIndirect	Creates rectangular region sized like lpRect	GDI region	CreateRectRgnIndirect(lpRect)	hRgn	194
EqualRgn	Determines if two regions are identical	GDI region	EqualRgn(hSrcRgn1,hSrcRgn2)	bEqual	237
OffsetRgn	Moves region X unit horiz and Y units vertically	GDI region	OffsetRgn(hRgn,X,Y)	nRgnType	380
OffsetViewportOrg*	Modifies viewport origin relative to current values	GDI region	OffsetViewportOrg(hDC,X,Y)	ptPrevPos	380
PtInRegion	Determines whether X,Y is within hRgn	GDI region	PtInRegion(hRgn,X,Y)	bSuccess	395
PtVisible	Determines whether X,Y is in clipping region of hDC	GDI region	PtVisible(hDC,X,Y)	bVisible	396
ScaleViewportExt*	Modifies viewport extents relative to current values	GDI region	ScaleViewportExt(hDC,Xnum,Xdenom,Ynum,Ydenom)	nPrevExts	407
DeleteObject	Deletes object by freeing system storage	GDI selection	DeleteObject(hObject)	bDeleted	208
GetObject	Copies nCount bytes of hObject data to lpObject	GDI selection	GetObject(hObject,nCount,lpObject)	nCopied	292
SelectClipRgn	Selects hRgn as current clipping region for disp context	GDI selection	SelectClipRgn(hDC,hRgn)	nRgnType	411
SelectObject	Selects hObject as current object	GDI selection	SelectObject(hDC,hObject)	hOldObject	412
GetTextAlign*	Returns status of text alignment flag	GDI text justify	GetTextAlign(hDC)	wAlignment	309
GetTextCharacterExtra	Returns current intercharacter spacing	GDI text justify	GetTextCharacterExtra(hDC)	nCharExtra	310
GetTextExtent	Computes width and height of text line in lpString	GDI text justify	GetTextExtent(hDC,lpString,nCount)	dwTextExtents	310
SetTextCharacterExtra	Sets amount of intercharacter spacing	GDI text justify	SetTextCharacterExtra(hDC,nCharExtra)	nOldCharExtra	452
SetTextJustification	Prepares GDI to justify text line	GDI text justify	SetTextJustification(hDC,nBreakExtra,nBreakCount)	nSet	453
GlobalCompact	Compacts global memory to free dwMinFree bytes	Memory manager	GlobalCompact(dwMinFree)	dwLargest	324
GlobalAlloc	Allocates dwBytes of memory from global heap	Memory manager	GlobalAlloc(wFlags,dwBytes)	hMem	322
GlobalDiscard	Discards global memory block if ref count is zero	Memory manager	GlobalDiscard(hMem)	hOldMem	325
GlobalFlags	Returns memory type of global memory block	Memory manager	GlobalFlags(hMem)	wFlags	326
GlobalFree	Removes global memory block if ref count is zero	Memory manager	GlobalFree(hMem)	hOldMem	327
GlobalHandle	Returns handle of global memory object	Memory manager	GlobalHandle(wMem)	dwMem	328
GlobalLock	Returns address of block, locks it in mem, ups ref count	Memory manager	GlobalLock(hMem)	lpAddress	328
GlobalReAlloc	Reallocates global memory block to dwBytes	Memory manager	GlobalReAlloc(hMem,dwBytes,wFlags)	hNewMem	329
GlobalSize	Returns the size of global memory block, in bytes	Memory manager	GlobalSize(hMem)	dwBytes	331
GlobalUnlock	Unlocks block, decreases reference count	Memory manager	GlobalUnlock(hMem)	bResult	331
GlobalUnwire*	Unlocks memory segment	Memory manager	GlobalUnwire(hMem)	None	332
GlobalWire*	Moves segment to low memory and locks it	Memory manager	GlobalWire(hMem)	lpSegment	332
LocalAlloc	Allocates wBytes of memory from local heap	Memory manager	LocalAlloc(wFlags,wBytes)	hMem	358
LocalCompact	Compacts local memory to generate wMinFree free bytes	Memory manager	LocalCompact(wMinFree)	wLargest	359
LocalDiscard	Discards local memory block hMem if ref count is zero	Memory manager	LocalDiscard(hMem)	hOldMem	359
LocalFlags	Returns memory type of block hMem	Memory manager	LocalFlags(hMem)	wFlags	360
LocalFree	Frees local memory block hMem if ref count is zero	Memory manager	LocalFree(hMem)	hOldMem	360
LocalFreeze	Prevents compaction of local heap	Memory manager	LocalFreeze(Dummy)	None	361
LocalHandle	Returns handle of local memory object at wMem	Memory manager	LocalHandle(wMem)	hMem	361
LocalHandleDelta	Sets entry count for each new handle table in local heap	Memory manager	LocalHandleDelta(nNewDelta)	nCurrentDelta	361
LocalInit	Initializes the local heap	Memory manager	LocalInit(wSegment,wStart,wEnd)	bResult	362
LocalLock	Returns address of block, locks block, ups ref count by 1	Memory manager	LocalLock(hMem)	pAddress	362
LocalMelt	Permits compaction of local heap	Memory manager	LocalMelt(Dummy)	None	363
LocalNotify	Sets callback function for handling notification messages	Memory manager	LocalNotify(lpNotifyFunc)	lpPrevFunc	363
LocalReAlloc	Reallocates local memory block hMem to wBytes	Memory manager	LocalReAlloc(hMem,wBytes,wFlags)	hNewMem	364
LocalShrink*	Shrinks specified memory heap	Memory manager	LocalShrink(hSeg,wSize)	wSize	366
LocalSize	Returns the size of local block hMem, in bytes	Memory manager	LocalSize(hMem)	wBytes	366
LocalUnlock	Unlocks local memory block, descreases ref count by 1	Memory manager	LocalUnlock(hMem)	bResult	367
LockData	Locks data segment in memory	Memory manager	LockData(Dummy)	hMem	367
SetSwapAreaSize*	Changes amount of memory used by code segment	Memory manager	SetSwapAreaSize(rsSize)	nParagraphs	448
UnlockData	Unlocks data segment	Memory manager	UnlockData(Dummy)	None	490

(Continued)

Table 6.73. Continued

Function Name	Type	Description	Syntax (arguments)	Returns	Ref Page #
UnlockSegment	Memory manager	Unlocks wSegment	UnlockSegment(wSegment)	hMem	491
ValidateFreeSpaces*	Memory manager	Determines whether free segments contain valid contents	ValidateFreeSpaces()	lpstrInvalid	493
Catch	Module manager	Copies current exec environ to buffer lpCatchBuf	Catch(lpCatchBuf)	nThrowBack	162
FreeLibrary	Module manager	Removes library module if reference count is zero	FreeLibrary(hLibModule)	None	250
FreeProcInstance	Module manager	Removes function instance at address lpProc	FreeProcInstance(lpProc)	None	250
GetCodeHandle	Module manager	Returns handle of code segment containing function	GetCodeHandle(lpFunc)	hInstance	264
GetInstanceData	Module manager	Copies nCount bytes from hInstance to current Instance	GetInstanceData(hInstance,pData,nCount)	nBytes	278
GetModuleFileName	Module manager	Copies module filename to lpFilename	GetModuleFileName(hModule,lpFilename,nSize)	nLength	288
GetModuleHandle	Module manager	Returns module handle	GetModuleHandle(lpModuleName)	hModule	289
GetModuleUsage	Module manager	Returns reference count of module hModule	GetModuleUsage(hModule)	nCount	289
GetProcAddress	Module manager	Returns address of lpProcName function	GetProcAddress(hModule,lpProcName)	lpAddress	295
GetVersion	Module manager	Returns Windows version number	GetVersion()	wVersion	315
MakeProcInstance	Module manager	Returns address for lpProc.	MakeProcInstance(lpProc,hInstance)	lpAddress	371
Throw	Module manager	Restores execution environment to values in lpCatchBuf	Throw(lpCatchBuf,nThrowback)	None	485
AccessResource	Resource manager	Sets file pointer for read access to hRefInfo	AccessResource(hInstance,hResInfo)	nFile	148
AddFontResource	Resource manager	Adds resource in lpFilename to system font table	AddFontResource(lpFilename)	nFonts	149
AllocResource	Resource manager	Allocates dwSize bytes of memory for hResInfo	AllocResource(hInstance,hResInfo,dwSize)	hMem	150
FindResource	Resource manager	Locates resource lpName of type lpType	FindResource(hInstance,lpName,lpType)	hResInfo	245
FreeResource	Resource manager	Removes resource from memory if ref count is zero	FreeResource(hResData)	bFreed	251
LoadAccelerators	Resource manager	Loads accelerator table named by lpTableName	LoadAccelerators(hInstance,lpTableName)	hRes	351
LoadBitmap	Resource manager	Loads bitmap named by lpBitmapName	LoadBitmap(hInstance,lpBitmapName)	hBitmap	352
LoadCursor	Resource manager	Loads cursor named by lpCursorName	LoadCursor(hInstance,lpCursorName)	hCursor	353
LoadIcon	Resource manager	Loads icon named by lpIconName	LoadIcon(hInstance,lpIconName)	hIcon	354
LoadLibrary	Resource manager	Loads library module named by lpLibFileName	LoadLibrary(lpLibFileName)	hLibModule	355
LoadMenu	Resource manager	Loads menu named by lpMenuName	LoadMenu(hInstance,lpMenuName)	hMenu	355
LoadMenuIndirect*	Resource manager	Loads menu from lpMenuTemplate	LoadMenuIndirect(lpMenuTemplate)	hMenu	356
LoadResource	Resource manager	Loads the resource named by hResInfo	LoadResource(hInstance,hResInfo)	hResData	356
LoadString	Resource manager	Loads string wID into buffer lpBuffer	LoadString(hInstance,wID,lpBuffer,nBufferMax)	nSize	357
LockResource	Resource manager	Returns address of hResInfo, locks it, ups ref count by 1	LockResource(hResData)	lpResData	368
LockSegment	Resource manager	Locks segment at address wSegment	LockSegment(wSegment)	hSegment	368
RemoveFontResource	Resource manager	Removes font from font table	RemoveFontResource(lpFilename)	bSuccess	402
SetResourceHandler	Resource manager	Sets function address of resource handler	SetResourceHandler(hInstance,lpType,lpLoadFunc)	lpLoadFunc	440
SizeofResource	Resource manager	Returns size of resource hResInfo, in bytes	SizeofResource(hInstance,hResInfo)	wBytes	480
UnlockResource*	Resource manager	Unlocks resource, decrements reference count	UnlockResource(hResData)	hSeg	491
CloseSound	Sound	Closes play device (first flushes voice queues)	CloseSound()	None	172
CountVoiceNotes	Sound	Returns number of notes in voice queue	CountVoiceNotes(nVoice)	nNotes	175
GetThresholdEvent	Sound	Returns pointer to threshold flag.	GetThresholdEvent()	lpInt	312
GetThresholdStatus	Sound	Returns bit mask containing threshold event status	GetThresholdStatus()	fStatus	312
OpenSound	Sound	Opens play device for exclusive use	OpenSound()	nVoices	385
SetSoundNoise	Sound	Sets source and duration of noise from play device	SetSoundNoise(nSource,nDuration)	nResult	446
SetVoiceAccent	Sound	Sets an accent in voice queue	SetVoiceAccent(nVoice,nTempo,nVolume,nMode,nPitch)	nResult	457
SetVoiceEnvelope	Sound	Places envelope in voice queue	SetVoiceEnvelope(nVoice,nShape,nRepeat)	nResult	459
SetVoiceNote	Sound	Places note in voice queue	SetVoiceNote(nVoice,nValue,nLength,nCdots)	nResult	459
SetVoiceQueueSize	Sound	Allocates nBytes of memory for voice queue	SetVoiceQueueSize(nVoice,nBytes)	nResult	460
SetVoiceSound	Sound	Places frequency and duration in voice queue	SetVoiceSound(nVoice,nFrequency,nDuration)	nResult	460
SetVoiceThreshold	Sound	Sets threshold level for voice queue	SetVoiceThreshold(nVoice,nNotes)	nResult	461
StartSound	Sound	Starts play in each voice queue	StartSound()	nResult	461
StopSound	Sound	Stops playing all voices	StopSound()	None	480
SyncAllVoices	Sound	Places sync mark in each voice queue	SyncAllVoices()	None	480
WaitSoundState	Sound	Waits until play driver enters nState	WaitSoundState(nState)	nResult	484
AnsiLower	String translation	Converts string lpStr to lowercase	AnsiLower(lpStr)	cChar	151
AnsiNext	String translation	Points to next character in string lpCurrentChar	AnsiNext(lpCurrentChar)	lpNextChar	151
AnsiPrev	String translation	Points to prev character in string lpStart	AnsiPrev(lpStart,lpCurrentChar)	lpPrevChar	152
ANSIToOEM	String translation	Converts ANSI string to OEM char string	AnsiToOem(lpAnsiStr,lpOemStr)	bTranslated	152
AnsiUpper	String translation	Converts string lpStr to uppercase	AnsiUpper(lpStr)	cChar	153
OEMToANSI	String translation	Converts OEM char string to ANSI string	OemToAnsi(lpOemStr,lpAnsiStr)	bTranslated	378
GetCurrentTask	Task	Returns handle of current task	GetCurrentTask()	hTask	267
GetNumTasks*	Task	Returns number of tasks in system	GetNumTasks()	nTasks	292
GetWindowTask*	Task	Returns task handle	GetWindowTask(hWnd)	hTask	319

(Continued)

Function Name	Description	Type	Syntax (arguments)	Returns	Ref Page #
Yield	Halts current task and starts any waiting task	Task	Yield()	bResult	498
SetPriority	Sets task priority	Task	SetPriority(hTask,nChangeAmount)	nNew	437
GetRValue	Returns the red component of rgbColor	Utility	GetRValue(rgbColor)	cRed	299
DeviceMode	Displays dialog box for setting printer modes	Utility	DeviceMode(hWnd,hItem,lpString,lpString)	lpString	211
GetBValue	Returns blue component of rgbColor	Utility	GetBValue(rgbColor)	cBlue	256
GetGValue	Returns green component of rgbColor	Utility	GetGValue(rgbColor)	cGreen	277
GetTickCount*	Returns time since system started	Utility	GetTickCount()	dwTicks	313
HIBYTE	Returns hi-order byte of nInteger	Utility	HIBYTE(nInteger)	cHighByte	335
HIWORD	Returns hi-order word of lInteger	Utility	HIWORD(lInteger)	wHighWord	337
LOBYTE	Returns lo-order byte of nInteger	Utility	LOBYTE(nInteger)	cLowByte	357
LOWORD	Returns lo-order word of lInteger	Utility	LOWORD(lInteger)	wLowWord	369
MAKELONG	Creates unsigned long integer	Utility	MAKELONG(nLowWord,nHighWord)	dwInteger	370
MAKEPOINT	Converts long value into a POINT structure	Utility	MAKEPOINT(lInteger)	ptPoint	371
max	Returns maximum value of A and B	Utility	max value 1, value 2	nMaximum	373
min	Returns minimum value of A and B	Utility	min value 1, value 2	nMinimum	376
WndProc	Processes messages sent to it	Window	WndProc(hWnd,wMsg,wParam,lParam)	lReply	
GetClientRect	Copies window client area coords to lpRect	Window attribute	GetClientRect(hWnd,lpRect)	None	260
GetParent	Retrieves window handle of window's parent (if any)	Window attribute	GetParent(hWnd)	hWndParent	293
GetSysModalWindow	Returns handle of system modal window, if present	Window attribute	GetSysModalWindow()	hWnd	304
GetWindowRect	Copies dimensions of entire window to lpRect	Window attribute	GetWindowRect(hWnd,lpRect)	None	319
GetWindowText	Copies window's caption into lpString	Window attribute	GetWindowText(hWnd,lpString,nMaxCount)	nCopied	320
GetWindowTextLength	Returns length of window's caption or text	Window attribute	GetWindowTextLength(hWnd)	nLength	321
SetSysModalWindow	Makes window a system modal window	Window attribute	SetSysModalWindow(hWnd)	hPrevWnd	450
SetWindowLong	Changes window attribute identified by nIndex	Window attribute	SetWindowLong(hWnd,nIndex,lNewLong)	lOldLong	463
SetWindowText	Sets window caption or text to lpString	Window attribute	SetWindowText(hWnd,lpString)	None	474
SetWindowWord	Changes window attribute specified by nIndex	Window attribute	SetWindowWord(hWnd,nIndex,wNewWord)	wOldWord	475
CreateCaret	Creates caret for hWnd using hBitmap	Window caret	CreateCaret(hWnd,hBitmap,nWidth,nHeight)	None	177
DestroyCaret	Destroys current caret and memory it occupies	Window caret	DestroyCaret()	None	209
GetCaretBlinkTime	Returns current caret flash rate	Window caret	GetCaretBlinkTime()	wMSeconds	257
GetCaretPos*	Returns current caret position	Window caret	GetCaretPos(lpPoint)	None	257
HideCaret	Removes system caret from window	Window caret	HideCaret(hWnd)	None	335
SetCaretBlinkTime	Establishes caret flash rate	Window caret	SetCaretBlinkTime(wMSeconds)	None	419
SetCaretPos	Moves caret to X,Y position	Window caret	SetCaretPos(X,Y)	None	419
ShowCaret	Displays new caret or redisplays hidden caret	Window caret	ShowCaret(hWnd)	None	475
CallWndProc	Passes message info to lpPrevWndFunc function	Window class	CallWndProc(lpPrevWndFunc,hWnd,wMsg,wParam,lParam)	lReply	161
GetClassLong	Returns info at nIndex in WNDCLASS structure	Window class	GetClassLong(hWnd,nIndex)	Long	258
GetClassName	Copies nMaxCount chars of hWnd's class name	Window class	GetClassName(hWnd,lpClassName,nMaxCount)	nCopied	259
GetClassWord	Returns info at nIndex in WNDCLASS structure	Window class	GetClassWord(hWnd,nIndex)	word	259
RegisterClass	Registers a window class	Window class	RegisterClass(lpWndClass)	bRegistered	398
SetClassLong	Replaces long value at nIndex in WNDCLASS struct	Window class	SetClassLong(hWnd,nIndex,lNewLong)	lOldLong	420
SetClassWord	Replaces word at nIndex in WNDCLASS struct	Window class	SetClassWord(hWnd,nIndex,wNewWord)	lOldWord	421
ChangeClipboardChain	Removes hWnd from clipboard viewer chain	Window clipboard	ChangeClipboardChain(hWnd,hWndNext)	bRemoved	163
CloseClipboard	Closes the clipboard	Window clipboard	CloseClipboard()	bClosed	171
CountClipboardFormats	Counts number of formats clipboard can render	Window clipboard	CountClipboardFormats()	nCount	174
EmptyClipboard	Empties clipboard, frees data handles	Window clipboard	EmptyClipboard()	bEmptied	222
EnumClipboardFormats	Enumerates available clipboard formats	Window clipboard	EnumClipboardFormats(wFormat)	wNextFormat	228
GetClipboardData	Returns data from clipboard in specified format	Window clipboard	GetClipboardData(wFormat)	hClipData	261
GetClipboardFormatName	Copies nMaxCount chars of format to lpFormatName	Window clipboard	GetClipboardFormatName(wFormat,lpFormatName,nMaxCount)	nCopied	262
GetClipboardOwner	Returns window handle of clipboard owner	Window clipboard	GetClipboardOwner()	hWnd	262
GetClipboardViewer	Returns window handle of 1st window in viewer chn	Window clipboard	GetClipboardViewer()	hWnd	263
IsClipboardFormatAvailable	Returns True if data is available in wFormat	Window clipboard	IsClipboardFormatAvailable(wFormat)	bAvailable	344
OpenClipboard	Open clipboard (prevents other apps from modifying)	Window clipboard	OpenClipboard(hWnd)	bOpened	381
RegisterClipboardFormat	Registers new clipboard format	Window clipboard	RegisterClipboardFormat(lpFormatName)	wFormat	400
SetClipboardData	Copies hMem into clipboard	Window clipboard	SetClipboardData(wFormat,hMem)	hClipData	422
SetClipboardViewer	Adds hWnd to clipboard viewer chain	Window clipboard	SetClipboardViewer(hWnd)	hWndNext	424
ChildWindowFromPoint	Determines which child window contains Point	Window coordinate	ChildWindowFromPoint(hWndParent,Point)	hWndChild	168
ClientToScreen	Converts client coords to equiv. screen coords	Window coordinate	ClientToScreen(hWnd,lpPoint)	None	170
ScreenToClient	Converts screen coords at lpPoint to client coords	Window coordinate	ScreenToClient(hWnd,lpPoint)	None	408
WindowFromPoint	Identifies window containing Point (in screen coords)	Window coordinate	WindowFromPoint(Point)	hWnd	496
CreateWindow	Creates tiled, popup, or child window	Window creation	CreateWindow(lpClassName,lpWindowName,dwStyle,X,Y,nWidth, nHeight,hWndParent,hMenu,hInstance,lpParam)	hWnd	195

(Continued)

Table 6.73. Continued

Function Name	Description	Type	Syntax (arguments)	Returns	Ref Page #
DestroyWindow	Sends WM_DESTROY message; frees memory	Window creation	DestroyWindow(hWnd)	bDestroyed	210
GetWindowLong	Returns information about window	Window creation	GetWindowLong(hWnd,nIndex)	long	318
GetWindowWord	Returns information about window	Window creation	GetWindowWord(hWnd,nIndex)	word	321
IsWindow	Determines whether hWnd is a valid, existing window	Window creation	IsWindow(hWnd)	bExists	347
ClipCursor	Restricts mouse cursor to given rectangle on screen	Window cursor	ClipCursor(lpRect)	None	170
GetCursorPos	Stores cursor position in POINT structure	Window cursor	GetCursorPos(lpPoint)	None	268
SetCursor	Sets cursor shape to hCursor; removes if hCursor=Null	Window cursor	SetCursor(hCursor)	hOldCursor	426
SetCursorPos	Sets mouse cursor to screen coords X,Y	Window cursor	SetCursorPos(X,Y)	None	427
ShowCursor	Adds 1 to cursor display count if nonzero; otherwise -1	Window cursor	ShowCursor(bShow)	nCount	476
DefWindowProc	Do default processing of messages that are ignored	Window default	DefWindowProc(hWnd,wMsg,wParam,lParam)	lReply	206
CreateDialogIndirect*	Creates modeless dialog box like one in lpDialogTemplate	Window dialog	CreateDialogIndirect(hInstance,lpDialogTemplate,hWndParent,lpDialogFunc)	hDlg	182
DialogBoxIndirect*	Creates modal dialog box like hDTemplate	Window dialog	DialogBoxIndirect(hInstance,hDTemplate,hWndParent,lpDialogFunc)	wResult	212
CheckDlgButton	Changes state of button	Window dialog box	CheckDlgButton(hDlg,nIDButton,wCheck)	None	166
CheckRadioButton	Changes checkmark to wIDCheckButton in group	Window dialog box	CheckRadioButton(hDlg,nIDFirstButton,nIDLastButton,nIDCheckButton)	None	168
CreateDialog	Creates modeless dialog box	Window dialog box	CreateDialog(hInstance,lpTemplateName,hWndParent,lpDialogFunc)	hDlg	180
DialogBox	Creates modal dialog box	Window dialog box	DialogBox(hInstance,lpTemplateName,hWndParent,lpDialogFunc)	wResult	211
DlgDirList	Fills nlDListBox with files matching lpPathSpec	Window dialog box	DlgDirList(hDlg,lpPathSpec,nlDListBox,nlDStaticPath,wFiletype)	nListed	215
DlgDirSelect	Copies selection from nlDListBox to lpString	Window dialog box	DlgDirSelect(hDlg,lpString,nlDListBox)	bDirectory	217
EndDialog	Frees resources and destroys windows of dialog box	Window dialog box	EndDialog(hDlg,nResult)	None	225
GetDlgItem	Returns dialog control handle	Window dialog box	GetDlgItem(hDlg,nIDDlgItem)	hCtl	274
GetDlgItemInt	Translates text of nIDDlgItem to integer value	Window dialog box	GetDlgItemInt(hDlg,nIDDlgItem,lpTranslated,bSigned)	wValue	274
GetDlgItemText	Copies nMaxCount chars of control text to lpString	Window dialog box	GetDlgItemText(hDlg,nIDDlgItem,lpString,nMaxCount)	nCopied	275
GetNextDlgGroupItem*	Searches for next control in group of dialog controls	Window dialog box	GetNextDlgGroupItem(hDlg,hCtl,fPrevious)	hWnd	290
GetNextDlgTabItem*	Obtains handle for first control preceding another	Window dialog box	GetNextDlgTabItem(hDlg,hCtl,fPrevious)	hControl	290
IsDialogMessage	Determines whether lpMsg is intended for modeless dialog	Window dialog box	IsDialogMessage(hDlg,lpMsg)	bUsed	345
IsDlgButtonChecked	Returns state of nIDButton	Window dialog box	IsDlgButtonChecked(hDlg,nIDButton)	wCheck	345
MapDialogRect	Converts dialog box coords to client coords	Window dialog box	MapDialogRect(hDlg,lpRect)	None	372
SendDlgItemMessage	Sends message to nlDDlgItem within dialog box hDlg	Window dialog box	SendDlgItemMessage(hDlg,nIDDlgItem,wMsg,wParam,lParam)	lResult	414
SetDlgItemInt	Sets text of nIDDlgItem to string representing wValue	Window dialog box	SetDlgItemInt(hDlg,nIDDlgItem,wValue,bSigned)	None	427
SetDlgItemText	Sets caption or text of nlDDlgItem to String	Window dialog box	SetDlgItemText(hDlg,nIDDlgItem,lpString)	None	428
AdjustWindowRect	Converts client rectangle to a window rectangle	Window display	AdjustWindowRect(lpRect,lStyle,bMenu)	None	150
AnyPopup	Indicates whether any popup window is visible	Window display	AnyPopup()	bVisible	153
BringWindowToTop	Makes popup or child window the top window	Window display	BringWindowToTop(hWnd)	None	159
CloseWindow	Closes specified window	Window display	CloseWindow(hWnd)	None	172
EnumChildWindows	Enumerates child windows of hWndParent	Window display	EnumChildWindows(hWndParent,lpEnumFunc,lParam)	bDone	226
EnumWindows	Enumerates windows on screen	Window display	EnumWindows(lpEnumFunc,lParam)	bDone	236
GetActiveWindow	Returns handle to active window	Window display	GetActiveWindow()	hWnd	252
GetNextWindow	Searches for next window handle	Window display	GetNextWindow(hWnd,wFlag)	hWnd	291
GetTopWindow*	Returns handle to top-level child window	Window display	GetTopWindow(hWnd)	hWnd	313
IsChild	Returns True if window is child of hParentWnd	Window display	IsChild(hWndParent,hWnd)	bChild	344
IsIconic	Returns status of window (iconic or open)	Window display	IsIconic(hWnd)	bIconic	346
IsWindowVisible	Determines whether hWnd is visible	Window display	IsWindowVisible(hWnd)	bVisible	347
IsZoomed*	Determines whether window is at maximum size	Window display	IsZoomed(hWnd)	bZoomed	348
MoveWindow	Causes WM_SIZE message to be sent to hWnd	Window display	MoveWindow(hWnd,X,Y,nWidth,nHeight,bRepaint)	None	377
OffsetWindowOrg*	Modifies window origin relative to current values	Window display	OffsetWindowOrg(hDC,X,Y)	ptPrevPos	381
OpenIcon	Opens specified window	Window display	OpenIcon(hWnd)	bOpened	384
ScaleWindowExt	Modifies window extents from current values	Window display	ScaleWindowExt(hDC,Xnum,Xdenom,Ynum,Ydenom)	nPrevExts	408
SetActiveWindow	Makes tiled or popup window the active window	Window display	SetActiveWindow(hWnd)	hWndPrev	415
ShowOwnedPopups*	Displays or hides all popup windows	Window display	ShowOwnedPopups(hWnd,fShow)	None	477
ShowScrollBar*	Displays or hides scrollbar	Window display	ShowScrollBar(hWnd,wBar,fShow)	None	477
ShowWindow	Displays or removes window as specified by nCmdShow	Window display	ShowWindow(hWnd,nCmdShow)	bShown	478
FlashWindow	Flashes window once	Window error	FlashWindow(hWnd,bInvert)	bInverted	247
MessageBeep	Generates a beep when message box displayed	Window error	MessageBeep(wType)	bBeep	373
MessageBox	Creates message box window	Window error	MessageBox(hWndParent,lpText,lpCaption,wType)	nMenuItem	373
CallMsgFilter	Passes message and code to message filter funct.	Window hook	CallMsgFilter(lpMsg,nCode)	bResult	161
SetWindowHook	Installs system or application hook	Window hook	SetWindowHook(nFilterType,lpFilterFunc)	lpPrevFilterFunc	466
UnhookWindowHook*	Removes filter function from hook chain	Window hook	UnhookWindowHook(nHook,lpfnHook)	bUnhooked	489
EnumTaskWindows*	Enumerates all windows associated with a task	Window information	EnumTaskWindows(hTask,lpEnumFunc,lParam)	bEnumerate	235
EnableHardwareInput*	Enables/disables mouse and keyboard	Window input	EnableHardwareInput(fEnableInput)	bEnabled	223

(Continued)

Function Name	Description	Type	Syntax (arguments)	Returns	Ref Page #
EnableWindow	Enables or disables mouse, keybd input to hWnd	Window input	EnableWindow(hWnd,bEnable)	bDone	224
GetAsyncKeyState*	Determines whether key is up or down	Window input	GetAsyncKeyState(vKey)	nState	252
GetCapture*	Determines which window is receiving mouse input	Window input	GetCapture()	hWnd	256
GetDoubleClickTime	Returns doubleclick time for mouse	Window input	GetDoubleClickTime()	wClickTime	276
GetFocus	Returns handle of window with input focus	Window input	GetFocus()	hWnd	277
GetInputState*	Determines whether there are input events in queue	Window input	GetInputState()	bEvent	277
GetKeyboardState*	Copies status of virtual keys to a buffer	Window input	GetKeyboardState(lpKeyState)	none	278
GetKeyState	Returns state of virtual key	Window input	GetKeyState(nVirtKey)	nState	279
IsWindowEnabled	Returns state of hWnd input from mouse and keyboard	Window input	IsWindowEnabled(hWnd)	bEnabled	347
KillTimer	Kills timer event identified by hWnd and nIDEvent	Window input	KillTimer(hWnd,nIDEvent)	bKilled	349
ReleaseCapture	Release mouse input, restores normal processing	Window input	ReleaseCapture()	None	401
SetCapture	Causes mouse input to be sent to hWnd	Window input	SetCapture(hWnd)	hWndPrev	418
SetDoubleClickTime*	Sets mouse doubleclick time	Window input	SetDoubleClickTime(wCount)	None	429
SetFocus	Assigns input focus to hWnd	Window input	SetFocus(hWnd)	hWndPrev	430
SetKeyboardState*	Copies buffer to keyboard state table	Window input	SetKeyboardState(lpKeyState)	None	431
SetTimer	Creates system timer event	Window input	SetTimer(hWnd,nIDEvent,wElapse,lpTimerFunc)	nIDNewEvent	454
SwapMouseButton	Swaps meaning of left/right mouse buttons if bSwap=True	Window input	SwapMouseButton(bSwap)	bSwapped	483
WinMain	Entry point for Windows application execution	Window main	WinMain(hInstance,hPrevInstance,lpCmdLine,nCmdShow)	nExitCode	
GetWindow*	Searches for window in window manager's list	Window manager	GetWindow(hWnd,wCmd)	hWnd	316
RegisterWindowDestroy*	Locks windows from destruction by other tasks	Window manager	RegisterWindowDestroy(hWnd,fRegister)	bProtected	400
SetParent*	Changes parent window of child window	Window manager	SetParent(hWndChild,hWndNewParent)	hPrevParent	435
SetWindowPos*	Changes size, position, ordering of window	Window manager	SetWindowPos(hWnd,hWndInsertAfter,x,y,cx,cy,wFlag)	None	465
ChangeMenu	Changes menu item in hMenu	Window menu	ChangeMenu(hMenu,wIDChangeItem,lpNewItem,wIDNewItem,wChange)	bChanged	163
CheckMenuItem	Changes checkmark status of menu item	Window menu	CheckMenuItem(hMenu,wIDCheckItem,wCheck)	bOldCheck	167
CreateMenu	Creates empty menu	Window menu	CreateMenu()	hMenu	190
DestroyMenu	Destroys hMenu and frees memory it occupied	Window menu	DestroyMenu(hMenu)	bDestroyed	210
DrawMenuBar	Redraws menu bar	Window menu	DrawMenuBar(hWnd)	None	219
EnableMenuItem	Enables, disables, or grays menu item	Window menu	EnableMenuItem(hMenu,wIDEnableItem,wEnable)	bEnabled	223
GetMenu	Returns handle to window's menu	Window menu	GetMenu(hWnd)	hMenu	282
GetMenuItemCount*	Determines how many items are in hMenu	Window menu	GetMenuItemCount(hMenu)	nItems	282
GetMenuItemID*	Obtains identifier for a menu item	Window menu	GetMenuItemID(hMenu,nPos)	nID	283
GetMenuState*	Identifies top-level menu	Window menu	GetMenuState(hMenu,wID,wFlags)	wItem	283
GetMenuString	Copies nMaxCount chars of menu label to lpString	Window menu	GetMenuString(hMenu,wIDItem,lpString,nMaxCount,wFlag)	nCopied	284
GetSubMenu	Returns menu handle of popup menu	Window menu	GetSubMenu(hMenu,nPos)	hPopupMenu	303
GetSystemMenu	Allows access to system menu	Window menu	GetSystemMenu(hWnd,bRevert)	hSysMenu	304
HiliteMenuItem	Hilites or unHilites top-level menu item	Window menu	HiliteMenuItem(hWnd,hMenu,wIDHiliteItem,wHilite)	bHilited	335
SetMenu	Sets window menu to hMenu; removes if hMenu=Null	Window menu	SetMenu(hWnd,hMenu)	bSet	433
DefHookProc*	Provides default hook processing of WM messages	Window message	DefHookProc(code,wParam,lParam,lplpfnNextHook)	code	206
DispatchMessage	Passes message to window function in MSG structure	Window message	DispatchMessage(lpMsg)	lResult	214
GetCurrentTime	Returns elapsed time since boot	Window message	GetCurrentTime()	lTime	267
GetMessage	Retrieves message	Window message	GetMessage(lpMsg,hWnd,wMsgFilterMin,wMsgFilterMax)	bContinue	285
GetMessagePos	Returns mouse position scrn coords at last message	Window message	GetMessagePos()	dwPos	286
GetMessageTime	Returns time of last message	Window message	GetMessageTime()	lTime	287
InSendMessage	Returns True if function is processing SendMessage	Window message	InSendMessage()	bInSend	339
PeekMessage	Places message (if any) at lpMsg	Window message	PeekMessage(lpMsg,hWnd,wMsgFilterMin,wMsgFilterMax,bRemoveMsg)	bPresent	387
PostAppMessage	Posts message to application	Window message	PostAppMessage(hTask,wMsg,wParam,lParam)	bPosted	393
PostMessage	Posts message in application queue	Window message	PostMessage(hWnd,wMsg,wParam,lParam)	bPosted	393
PostQuitMessage	Posts WM_QUIT message to application	Window message	PostQuitMessage(nExitCode)	None	394
PtInRect	Determines whether point lies within lpRect	Window message	PtInRect(lpRect,Point)	bInRect	395
RegisterWindowMessage	Defines new, unique window message	Window message	RegisterWindowMessage(lpString)	wMsg	400
ReplyMessage	Replies to message without returning control	Window message	ReplyMessage(lReply)	None	403
SendMessage	Sends message to window or windows	Window message	SendMessage(hWnd,wMsg,wParam,lParam)	lReply	414
SetMessageQueue*	Creates new message queue	Window message	SetMessageQueue(cMsg)	bNewQ	434
TranslateAccelerator	Processes keyboard accelerators for menu commands	Window message	TranslateAccelerator(hWnd,hAccTable,lpMsg)	nTranslated	486
TranslateMessage	Translates virtual keystrokes into char messages	Window message	TranslateMessage(lpMsg)	bTranslated	487
WaitMessage	Yields control to other application	Window message	WaitMessage()	None	495
BeginPaint	Prepares window for painting	Window painting	BeginPaint(hWnd,lpPaint)	hDC	156
EndPaint	Marks end of window repainting	Window painting	EndPaint(hWnd,lpPaint)	None	226
GetDC	Returns display context of client area for window	Window painting	Get DC(hWnd)	hDC	268
GetDCOrg*	Returns origin for display context	Window painting	GetDCOrg(hDC)	lPoint	269
GetUpdateRect	Copies dim of rect that needs updating to lpRect	Window painting	GetUpdateRect(hWnd,lpRect,bErase)	bUpdate	313

(Continued)

Table 6.73. Continued

Function Name	Description	Type	Syntax (arguments)	Returns	Ref Page #
GetUpdateRgn*	Copies window's update region to specified region	Window painting	GetUpdateRgn(hWnd,hRgn,fErase)	sRgnType	314
GetWindowDC	Returns display context for entire window	Window painting	GetWindowDC(hWnd)	hDC	317
InvalidateRect	Marks lpRect for repainting	Window painting	InvalidateRect(hWnd,lpRect,bErase)	None	341
InvalidateRgn	Marks hRgn for repainting	Window painting	InvalidateRgn(hWnd,hRgn,bErase)	None	342
ReleaseDC	Release display context	Window painting	ReleaseDC(hWnd,hDC)	nReleased	401
UpdateWindow	Notifies application when window needs redrawing	Window painting	UpdateWindow(hWnd)	None	492
ValidateRect	Releases rectangle lpRect from repainting	Window painting	ValidateRect(hWnd,lpRect)	None	493
ValidateRgn	Releases hRgn from repainting	Window painting	ValidateRgn(hWnd,hRgn)	None	494
EnumProps	Passes each property of hWnd to lpEnumFunc	Window property	EnumProps(hWnd,lpEnumFunc)	nResult	233
FindWindow	Returns handle of window	Window property	FindWindow(lpClassName,lpWindowName)	hWnd	246
GetProp	Returns handle associated with lpString	Window property	GetProp(hWnd,lpString)	hData	297
RemoveProp	Removes lpString from property list	Window property	RemoveProp(hWnd,lpString)	hData	403
SetProp	Copies string and data handle to property list of hWnd	Window property	SetProp(hWnd,lpString,hData)	bSet	437
CopyRect	Copies an existing rectangle	Window rectangle	CopyRect(lpDestRect,lpSourceRect)	None	174
InflateRect	Resizes lpRect by X units horiz and Y units vertically	Window rectangle	InflateRect(lpRect,X,Y)	nResult	338
IntersectRect	Finds intersection of two rects, copies to lpDestRect	Window rectangle	IntersectRect(lpDestRect,lpSrc1Rect,lpSrc2Rect)	nIntersection	340
IsRectEmpty	Determines whether lpRect is empty	Window rectangle	IsRectEmpty(lpRect)	bEmpty	346
OffsetRect	Moves rectangle X units horiz and Y units vertically	Window rectangle	OffsetRect(lpRect,X,Y)	nResult	379
SetRect	Fills RECT struct at lpRect with given coords	Window rectangle	SetRect(lpRect,X1,Y1,X2,Y2)	nResult	438
SetRectEmpty	Sets lpRect to empty rectangle (all coords zero)	Window rectangle	SetRectEmpty(lpRect)	nResult	439
SetRectRgn*	Creates rectangular region	Window rectangle	SetRectRgn(hRgn,X1,Y1,X2,Y2)	None	439
UnionRect	Stores union of two rectangles	Window rectangle	UnionRect(lpDestRect,lpSrc1Rect,lpSrc2Rect)	nUnion	490
GetScrollPos	Returns current position of scrollbar	Window scrolling	GetScrollPos(hWnd,nBar)	nPos	300
GetScrollRange	Copies min/max scrollbar positions	Window scrolling	GetScrollRange(hWnd,nBar,lpMinPos,lpMaxPos)	None	300
ScrollWindow	Moves contents of client area by Xamount,Yamount	Window scrolling	ScrollWindow(hWnd,XAmount,YAmount,lpRect,lpClipRect)	None	410
SetScrollPos	Sets scrollbar elevator to nPos; redraws if nonzero	Window scrolling	SetScrollPos(hWnd,nBar,nPos,bRedraw)	nOldPos	444
SetScrollRange	Sets min/max scrollbar positions for scroll bar	Window scrolling	SetScrollRange(hWnd,nBar,nMinPos,nMaxPos,bRedraw)	None	445
GetSysColor	Returns system color identified by nIndex	Window sys info	GetSysColor(nIndex)	rgbColor	303
GetSystemMetrics	Returns information about system metrics	Window sys info	GetSystemMetrics(nIndex)	nValue	305
SetSysColors	Changes one or more system colors	Window sys info	SetSysColors(nChanges,lpSysColor,lpColorValues)	None	448
GetProfileString	Returns string info from WIN.INI file	Windows init file	GetProfileString(lpAppName,lpKeyName,lpDefault,lpReturnedString,nSize)	nLength	296
GetProfileInt	Returns integer info from WIN.INI file	Windows init file	GetProfileInt(lpAppName,lpKeyName,nDefault)	nKeyValue	295
WriteProfileString	Copies lpString to WIN.INI file	Windows init file	WriteProfileString(lpApplicationName,lpKeyName,lpString)	bResult	497
GetAspectRatioFilter	Get setting of current aspect-ratio filter		GetAspectRatioFilter(hDC)		252

Version Info: *Applicable to versions of Windows beginning with 2.0

Notes: C is case sensitive. Lowercase prefix to argument and result names are data type indicators.

Source: Microsoft Windows SDK Programmer's Reference 2.0

See Also: 6.71. Windows Function Summary by Version
6.72. Windows Function Summary by Name of Function

6.74. DIAGNOSTIC AND ERROR CODES

Value	Message		Value	Message
1 (1)	Insufficient memory for allocation		301 (769)	Invalid task ID
2 (2)	Error reallocating memory		302 (770)	Invalid exit system call
3 (3)	Memory cannot be freed		303 (771)	Invalid BP register chain
4 (4)	Memory cannot be locked		400 (1024)	Dynamic loader/linker errors
5 (5)	Memory cannot be unlocked		401 (1025)	Error during boot process
7 (7)	Window handle not valid		402 (1026)	Error loading a module
8 (8)	Cached display contexts are busy		403 (1027)	Invalid ordinal reference
10 (16)	Clipboard already open		404 (1028)	Invalid entry name reference
13 (19)	Mouse module not valid		405 (1029)	Invalid start procedure
14 (20)	Display module not valid		406 (1030)	Invalid module handle
15 (21)	Unlocked data segment should be locked		407 (1031)	Invalid relocation record
16 (22)	Invalid lock on system queue		408 (1032)	Error saving forward reference
100 (256)	Local memory errors		409 (1033)	Error reading segment contents
103 (259)	LocalReAlloc -- invalid local heap		410 (1034)	Error reading segment contents
140 (320)	Local heap is busy		411 (1035)	Insert disk for specified file
143 (323)	Invalid local heap		412 (1036)	Error reading non-resident table
14B (331)	Invalid local heap		4FF (1279)	INT 3F handler unable to load segment
15B (347)	Invalid local heap		500 (1280)	Resource manager/user profile errors
180 (384)	Invalid local handle		501 (1281)	Missing resource table
1C0 (448)	LocalLock count overflow		502 (1282)	Bad resource type
1F0 (496)	LocalUnlock count underflow		503 (1283)	Bad resource name
200 (512)	Global memory errors		504 (1284)	Bad resource file
240 (576)	Critical section problems		505 (1285)	Error reading resource
280 (640)	Invalid global handle		600 (1536)	Atom manager errors
2C0 (704)	GlobalLock count overflow		700 (1792)	Input/Output package errors
2F0 (752)	GlobalUnlock count underflow		FFEE (65518)	Divide by zero
300 (768)	Task schedule errors			

Source: Microsoft Windows SDK Programming Tools 2.0, pages 247 to 248
Microsoft Windows Reference Manual 1.0, page 225.
(Not documented in Microsoft Windows Reference Manual 2.0)

6.75. WINDOWS LOGICAL COORDINATE MAPPING

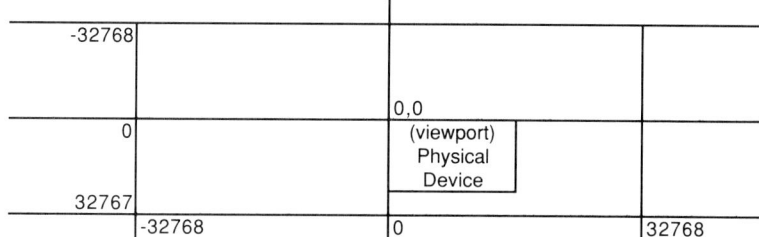

Coordinate System Transformation Equations

Variable	Meaning
xWO	The x coordinate of the window origin
yWO	The y coordinate of the window origin
xWE	The x component of the window extent
yWE	The y component of the window extent
xVO	The x coordinate of the viewport origin
yVO	The y coordinate of the viewport origin
xYE	The x component of the viewport extent
yVE	The y component of the viewport extent
Lx	The x coordinate in the logical coordinate system
Ly	The y coordinate in the logical coordinate system
Dx	The x coordinate in the physical coordinate system
Dy	The y coordinate in the physical coordinate system

Thus:
$$Dx = (Lx - xWO) * xVE/xWE + xVO$$
$$Dy = (Ly - yWO) * yVE/yWE + yVO$$
$$Lx = (Dx - xVO) (xWE/xVE) + xWO$$
$$Ly = (Dy - yVO) * yWE/yVE + yWO$$

Notes:
•The viewport generally, but not always, is the same as the physical device.
•Width and height of the viewport must be >-1 and <32768

Source: Microsoft Windows SDK Programmer's Reference 2.0, pages 88 to 90

6.76. WINDOW STYLES

Style Name	Description	Restrictions
WS_BORDER	Window that has a border	
WS_CAPTION	Window that has a caption bar	Implies WS_BORDER
WS_CHILD	Child window	Cannot be used with WS_POPUP
WS_CHILDWINDOW	Child window	
WS_CLIPCHILDREN	Exclude area occupied by child windows when drawing within parent	Used when creating parent window
WS_CLIPSIBLINGS	Clip child windows relative to one another	Used with WS_CHILD only
WS_DISABLED	Window that is initially disabled	
WS_DLGFRAME	Window with double border, no caption	
WS_GROUP**	Defines a group of controls	Group applies until next WS_GROUP
WS_HSCROLL	Window that has horizontal scrollbar	
WS_ICONIC	Window is initially iconic	For use with WS_TILED only
WS_MAXIMIZE**	Window is maximum size possible	
WS_MAXIMIZEBOX**	Window contains maximize box	
WS_MINIMIZE**	Window is minimum size possible	
WS_MINIMIZEBOX**	Window contains minimize box	
WS_OVERLAPPED**	Overlapping window	
WS_OVERLAPPEDWINDOW**	Window w/ WS_OVERLAPPED, WS_CAPTION, WS_SYSMENU, WS_THICKFRAME	
WS_POPUP	Popup window	Cannot be used with WS_CHILD
WS_POPUPWINDOW	Window having styles WS_POPUP, WS_BORDER, WS_SYSMENU	
WS_SIZEBOX*	Window that has a size box	Use with windows w/caption or scrollbars only
WS_SYSMENU	Window that has system menu box in caption bar	Use with windows w/ caption bars only
WS_TABSTOP**	Defines controls that can be moved to by tabbing	Tabbing applies until next WS_TABSTOP
WS_THICKFRAME**	Window has a thick frame, which can be used to size window	
WS_TILED*	Tiled window	
WS_TILEDWINDOW*	Window w/ WS_TILED, WS_CAPTION, WS_SYSMENU, WS_SIZEBOX	
WS_VISIBLE	Window that is initially visible	
WS_VSCROLL	Window that has vertical scrollbar	

Version Info: *Applies to Windows 1.0 only
**Applies to Windows 2.0 and later only

Source: Microsoft Windows SDK Programmer's Reference 2.0, pages 199 to 200
Microsoft Windows SDK Programmer's Reference 1.0, pages 28 to 29

See Also: 6.37. Include File Constants Definitions by Name
6.38. Include File Constants Definitions by Use
6.72. Windows Function Summary by Name of Function
6.73. Windows Function Summary by Type of Function

6.77. WINDOWS FILE TYPES

Bit is wFiletype	Meaning	Use
0 (0)	Normal File	Find all 'normal' files
1 (1)	Read-only File	Find all read-only files
2 (2)	Hidden File	Find all hidden files
4 (4)	System File	Find all System files
10 (16)	Directory File	Find all Directories
20 (32)	Archive File	Find all files with 'archive' bit set
2000 (8192)	LB_DIR flag	If set Windows puts message in apps queue
4000 (16384)	Drive bit	
8000 (32768)	Exclusive Bit	Find only files of the type listed (don't include normal files)

Notes: wFiletype is determined by ANDing together the bits for the file types
                    you want to match.

Source: Microsoft Windows SDK Programmer's Reference 2.0, page 216

See Also: 6.72. Windows Function Summary by Name of Function
                    6.73. Windows Function Summary by Type of Function

6.78. DISPLAY CONTEXT DEFAULT SETTINGS

Attribute	Default Setting
Background Color	White
Background Mode	OPAQUE
Bitmap	No default
Brush	WHITE_BRUSH
Brush Origin	(0,0)
Clipping Region	The whole display surface
Current Pen Position	(0,0)
Drawing Mode	R2_COPYPEN
Font	SYSTEM_FONT
Intercharacter spacing	0
Mapping Mode	MM_TEXT
Pen	BLACK_PEN
Polygon Filling Mode	ALTERNATE
Relabs Flag	ABSOLUTE
Stretching Mode	BLACKONWHITE
Text Color	Black
Viewport Extents	(1,1)
Viewport Orgin	(0,0)
Window Extents	(1,1)
Window Origin	(0,0)

Source: Microsoft Windows SDK Programmer's Reference 2.0, pages 92 to 93

See Also: 6.37. Include File Constants Definitions by Name
                    6.38. Include File Constants Definitions by Use

6.79. BINARY RASTER OPERATION CODES (ROP2)

Value	Function
R2_BLACK	Pixel is always black
R2_NOTMERGEPEN	Pixel is inverse of R2_MERGEPEN color
R2_MASKNOTOPEN	Pixel is combination of colors common to the display and inverse of pen
R2_NOTCOPYPEN	Pixel is inverse of pen color
R2_MASKPENNOT	Pixel is combination of colors common to the pen and inverse of display
R2_NOT	Pixel is inverse of the display color
R2_XORPEN	Pixel is combination of colors in pen and display, but not in both
R2_NOTMASKPEN	Pixel is inverse of R2_MASKPEN
R2_MASKPEN	Pixel is combination of colors common to the pen and the display
R2_NOTXORPEN	Pixel is inverse of R2_XORPEN color
R2_NOP	Pixel remains unchanged
R2_MERGENOTPEN	Pixel is a combination of display and inverse of the pen color
R2_COPYPEN	Pixel is the pen color
R2_MERGEPENNOT	Pixel is a combination of the pen and the inverse of the display color
R2_MERGEPEN	Pixel is a combination of pen and the display color
R2_WHITE	Pixel is always white

Source: Microsoft Windows SDK Programmer's Reference 2.0, page 443

See Also: 6.37. Include File Constants Definitions by Name
                       6.38. Include File Constants Definitions by Use

6.80. TERTIARY RASTER OPERATION CODES

Name	Value	Meaning
BLACKNESS	42H (66)	Dest=BLACK
DSTINVERT	550009H (5570569)	Dest=(not dest)
MERGECOPY	C000CAH (12583114)	Dest=(source AND pattern)
MERGEPAINT	BB0226H (12255782)	Dest=(source AND pattern) OR dest
NOTSRCCOPY	330008H (3342344)	Dest=(not source)
NOTSRCERASE	1100A6H (1114278)	Dest=(not source) AND (not dest)
PATCOPY	F00021 (15728673)	Dest=pattern
PATINVERT	5A0049H (5898313)	Dest=pattern XOR dest
PATPAINT	FB0A09H (16452105)	DPSnoo
SRCAND	8800C6H (8913094)	Dest=source AND dest
SRCERASE	440328H (4457256)	Dest=source AND (not dest)
SRCINVERT	660046H (6684742)	Dest=source XOR dest
SRCCOPY	CC00020 (13369376)	
SRCPAINT	EE0086H (15597702)	Dest=source OR dest
WHITENESS	FF0062H (16711778)	Dest=WHITE

Source: Microsoft Windows SDK Programmer's Reference 2.0, pages 670 to 677

See Also: 6.37. Include File Constants Definitions by Name
                       6.38. Include File Constants Definitions by Use

6.81. GDI INFORMATION INDEX DATA

Index Name	Description	Allowable Values
DRIVERVERSION	The GDI version number	100H (256)
TECHNOLOGY	The device technology used	0=vector plotter 1=raster display 2=raster printer 3=raster camera 4=character stream, PLP 5=metafile, VDM 6=display file
HORZSIZE	Width of physical display	In millimeters
VERTSIZE	Height of physical display	In millimeters
HORZRES	Width of display	In pixels
VERTRES	Height of display	In raster lines
LOGPIXELSX*	Number pixels along display width	In pixels per logical inch
LOGPIXELSY*	Number pixels along display height	In pixels per logical inch
BITSPIXEL	Number of adjacent color bits per pixel	
PLANES	Number of color planes	
NUMBRUSHES	Number of device-specific brushes	
NUMPENS	Number of device-specific pens	
NUMFONTS	Number of device-specific fonts	
NUMCOLORS	Number of entries in device's color table	
ASPECTX	Relative width of device pixel used for lines	
ASPECTY	Relative height of device pixel used f/ lines	
ASPECTXY	Diagonal width of device pixel used f/ lines	
PDEVICESIZE	Size of internal data structure PDEVICE	In bytes
CLIPCAPS	Clipping capabilities of device	0=cannot clip, 1=can clip rectangle
RASTERCAPS	Raster capabilities of device	RC_BITBLT (can transfer bitmap) RC_BANDING (requires banding support) RC_GDI20_OUTPUT (supports 2.0 features) RC_BITMAP64 (supports bitmaps >64K) RC_SCALING (capable of scaling)
CURVECAPS	Curve creation capabilities of device	Bit 0=can do circles Bit 1=can do pie wedges Bit 2=can do chord arcs Bit 3=can do ellipses Bit 4=can do wide borders Bit 5=can do styled borders Bit 6=can do wide and styled borders Bit 7=can do interiors Bits 8-15=NOT USED
LINECAPS	Line creation capabilities of device	Bit 0=RESERVED Bit 1=can do polyline Bits 2-3=RESERVED Bit 4=can do wide lines Bit 5=can do styled lines Bit 6=can do wide and styled lines Bit 7=can do interiors Bits 8-15 =NOT USED
POLYGONALCAPS	Polygonal creation capabilities of device	Bit0=can do alternate fill polygon Bit 1=can do rectangle Bit 2=can do winding number fill polygon Bit 3=can do scanline Bit 4=can do wide borders Bit 5=can do styled borders Bit 6=can do both wide and styled borders Bit 7=can do interiors Bits 8-15=NOT USED
TEXTCAPS	Text creation capabilities of device	Bit 0=can do character output precision Bit 1=can do stroke output precision Bit 2=can do stroke clip precision Bit 3=can do 90-degree character rotations Bit 4=can do any character rotation Bit 5=can do scaling independent of X and Y Bit 6=can do doubled character for scaling Bit 7=can do integer multiples for scaling Bit 8=can do any multiples for exact scaling Bit 9=can do double weight characters Bit 10=can do italics Bit 11=can do underlining Bit 12=can do strikeouts Bit 13=can do raster fonts Bit 14=can do vector fonts Bit 15=RESERVED, must be 0

Version Info: *First defined in Windows 2.0; not listed in Windows 1.0 documentation

Source: Microsoft Windows SDK Programmer's Reference 2.0, pages 270 to 273

6.82. BITMAP DATA STRUCTURES

Monochrome Bitmaps:

Pixel Order

Scan Order
Scan 0
Scan 1
...
Scan n-2
Scan n-1

Word #	Bit #	Pixel #
0	15	0
	14	1
	13	2
	12	3
	11	4
	10	5
	9	6
	8	7
	7	8
	6	9
	5	10
	4	11
	3	12
	2	13
	1	14
	0	15
1	15	16
	14	17
	13	18
	12	19
	11	20
	10	21
	9	22
	8	23
	7	24
	6	25
	5	26
	4	27
	3	28
	2	29
	1	30
	0	31

0=black
1=white

Etcetera

Table 6.82. Continued

Color Bitmaps:

Scan Order
Red Scan 0
Red Scan 1
...
Red Scan n-2
Red Scan n-1
Green Scan 0
Green Scan 1
...
Green Scan n-2
Green Scan n-1
Blue Scan 0
Blue Scan 1
...
Blue Scan n-2
Blue Scan n-1

Pixel Order

Word #	Bit #	Pixel #
0	15	0
	14	1
	13	2
	12	3
	11	4
	10	5
	9	6
	8	7
	7	8
	6	9
	5	10
	4	11
	3	12
	2	13
	1	14
	0	15
1	15	16
	14	17
	13	18
	12	19
	11	20
	10	21
	9	22
	8	23
	7	24
	6	25
	5	26
	4	27
	3	28
	2	29
	1	30
	0	31

0=color disabled
1=color enabled

Etcetera

Notes: Color bitmaps require three arrays: red, green, and blue

Source: Microsoft Windows SDK Programmer's Reference 2.0, pages 609 to 611

See Also: 6.39. BITMAP Structure Format

6.83. SYMBOLIC DEBUGGER (SYMDEB) COMMAND SUMMARY

Command Line Options:

Option	Function	Allowable Values
/m	Redirects output to secondary mono monitor	
/x	Disables the 'more' feature	
/w#	Sets memory allocation reporting level to #	0=no reporting 1=allocation messages only (default) 2=movement messages only 3=both allocation and movement messages
/@filename	Loads macro definitions from named file	
/n	Permits use of nonmaskable interrupts	
/i	Use features available on IBM compatibles	
/ffilename	Prevents named symbol file being used with executable file	
/"cmdlist"	Causes commands in list to be executed	Each command separated by semicolon

Notes:
•Options may be preceded by a hyphen instead of a forward slash
•Options may be identified with upper- or lowercase letters

Table 6.83. Continued

SYMDEB Commands:

Command	Function
a[address]	Assemble
ba[mode][size]address[value][cmdstring]	Set 80386 address breakpoint(s)
bc[idlist]	Clear breakpoint(s)
bd[idlist]	Disable breakpoint(s)
be[idlist]	Enable breakpoint(s)
bl	List breakpoint(s)
bp[id]address [value][cmdstring]	Set breakpoint
c range address	Compare
d [range]	Dump memory using previous type
da [range]	Dump memory in ASCII format
db [range]	Dump memory in bytes
dd [range]	Dump memory in double words
dg	Display global memory heap
dh	Display local memory heap for current DS
dl [range]	Dump memory as long floating point
dq	Display task queue
ds [range]	Dump memory as short floating point
dt [range]	Dump memory in 10-byte real numbers
dw [range]	Dump memory in words
e address [list]	Enter values using previous type
ea address [list]	Enter ASCII values
eb address [list]	Enter bytes
ed address [list]	Enter double words
el address [list]	Enter long floating-point values
es address [list]	Enter short floating-point values
et address [list]	Enter 10-byte real values
ew address [list]	Enter words
f range list	Fill
g [=address[address]...]	Go
h value value	Add hexadecimal values
i value	Input from port
k [value]	Backtrace stack
kt pdb [value]	Backtrace task
l [address[drive record count]]	Load
m range address	Mmove
m id[=cmdstring]	Define or execute macro
n filename[filename...]	Set name of file
o value byte	Output byte to port
p [=address][value]	Trace program instruction
q	Quit
r [register][[=]value]	Set register
s range list	Search for match
s-	Set machine debugging only
s&	Set machine and source debugging
s+	Set source debugging only
t [=address][value]	Trace program instruction
u [range]	Display unassembled instructions
v [range]	View source code lines
w [address[drive record count]]	Write to disk
x [?] symbol	Examine symbols
xo symbol	Open map or segment
z symbol value	Set symbol to value
? expression	Compute and display expression
.	Display current source code line
<filename	Redirect SYMDEB input to file
>filename	Redirect SYMDEB output to file
=filename	Redirect SYMDEB input and output
{filename	Redirect program input to file
}filename	Redirect program output to file
~filename	Redirect program input and output
![doscommand]	Execute DOS shell or command and return
* string	Comment

Source: Microsoft Windows SDK Programming Tools 2.0,
                     pages 100 to 102 and 110 to 138

—PART—
III

GENERAL PC
HARDWARE

— SECTION —
7

Keyboards,
Video Adapters,
and Peripherals

7.01. MACHINE SUMMARY AND HISTORY

		PC Class Machines					AT Class Machines		PS/2 Machines			
		PC	PC/XT	PCJr	PC Portable	Convertible	PC/AT	PC/XT 286	Model 30	Model 50	Model 60	Model 80
System	Processor	5 mhz 8088	5 mhz 8088	5 mhz 8088	5 mhz 8088	5 mhz 8088	6,8 mhz*** 80286	6 mhz 80286	8 mhz 8086	10 mhz 80286	10 mhz 80286	16 mhz 80386
	Math coprocessor	Optional	Optional	No	Optional	No	Optional	Optional	Optional	Optional	Optional	Optional
	RAM on motherboard	64K****	256K****	128K	256K	256K	512K	640K	640K	1M	1M	1M
	Maximum RAM allowed	512K****	640K	512K	640K	640K	640K,16M	640K,16M	640K	7M	15M	15M
	ROM on motherboard	40K	40K	64K	40K	40K	64K	64K	64K	128K	128K	128K
	Power supply	63.5-watt	130-watt	33-watt	130-watt	130-watt	450VA	130-watt	70-watt	not specified	not specified	not specified
Slots	8-bit PC slots	5	8	0	8	0	2	2	3	0	0	0
	16-bit AT slots	0	0	0	0	0	6		0	0	0	0
	16-bit PS/2 slots	0	0	0	0	0	0	0	0	4	8	5
	32-bit PS/2 slots	0	0	0	0	0	0	0	0	0	0	3
Drives	Drive slots †	4	4	1	2	2	3	3	2	3	4	4
	Supplied floppy drive(s)	1 180K ✷	1 360K 5.25"	None	2 360K 5.25"	2 720K 3.5"	1 1.2M 5.25"	1 360K 5.25"	1 720K 3.5"	1 1.4M 3.5"	1 1.4M 3.5"	1 1.4M 3.5"
	Supplied hard drive	None	None	None	None	None	20 Meg.	20 Meg.	20 Meg.	20 Meg.	44 Meg.	44 Meg.
	Optional hard drive	None	20 Meg.	None	None	None	40 Meg.	None	None	None	70 Meg.	70 , 115 Meg.
	Cassette	Supported	No	Supported	No	No	No	No	No	No	No	No
I/O	Parallel ports	Optional	Optional	Optional	Optional	Optional	Optional	Optional	Yes, 1	Yes, 1	Yes, 1	Yes, 1
	Serial ports	Optional	Optional	Optional	Optional	Optional	Optional	Optional	Yes, 1	Yes, 1	Yes, 1	Yes, 1
	Mouse ports	Optional	Optional	Optional	No	No	Optional	Optional	Yes	Yes	Yes	Yes
	Supplied video adapter	None	None	Built-in PCJr	Special	CGA emulation	Optional	Optional	MCGA	VGA	VGA	VGA
	Optional video adapter	MDA,CGA	MDA,CGA,EGA	None	None	None	MDA,CGA,EGA	MDA,CGA,EGA	VGA	None	None	None
	Keyboard	83-key	83-key	"chiclet"	83-key	78-key	84-key, 101/102-key	84-key, 101/102-key	101/102-key	101/102-key	101/102-key	101/102-key
Size*	Height	5.5"	5.5"	3.8"	8"	2.7"	5.6	5.5	4	5.5	23.5	23.5
	Width	19.6"	19.6"	13.9"	20"	12.8"	21.2	19.6	16	14.1	6.5	6.5
	Depth	16.1"	16.1"	11.4"	17"	14.7"	16.9	16.1	15.6	16.5	19	19
	Weight	29 lbs	32 lbs	8 lbs 4 oz	30 lbs	12.7 lbs	43 lbs	32 lbs	15.7 lbs	21 lbs	44 lbs	44 lbs
Software	Cassette BIOS support	Yes	Yes	Yes	No	No	No	No	No	No	No	No
	EGA BIOS support	No §	Yes	No	No	No	No	No	Yes	Yes	Yes	Yes
	Serial BIOS support	Yes-2 ports	Yes-2 ports	Yes	Yes-2 ports	Yes-2 ports	Yes-2 ports	Yes-2 ports	Yes-4 ports	Yes-4 ports	Yes-4 ports	Yes-4 ports
	Parallel BIOS support	Yes-2 ports	Yes-2 ports	Yes	Yes-2 ports	Yes-2 ports	Yes-2 ports	Yes-2 ports	Yes-3 ports	Yes-3 ports	Yes-3 ports	Yes-3 ports
	Hard disk BIOS support	No	Yes	No	No	No	Yes	Yes	Yes	Yes	Yes	Yes
	Recommended DOS version**	1.0	2.0	2.0	2.0	2.1	2.1	3.2	3.2	3.3	3.3	3.3
History	Introduction	Aug-81	Mar-83	Oct-83	Mar-84	Apr-86	Aug-84	Sep-86	Apr-87	Apr-87	Apr-87	Jul-87
	Updated		Jul-85			Jun-87	Apr-86				Jul-87	Jul-87
	Dropped		Jul-87				Jul-87					Sep-87

Notes:
*Case housing motherboard
**At time of introduction
***Originally 6, upgraded to 8
****Eventually upgraded to 640K
†For half-height drives
✷Other drives and sizes available
§Eventually upgraded to Yes

Source:
Byte, June 1987
Byte, August 1987
PC Magazine, May 26, 1987
PC Magazine, July 21, 1987
PCJr Technical Reference, pages 2-19, 2-135, D-1

7.02. PC, AT, AND PS/2 MEMORY USAGE SUMMARY

Address	Used By	Comments
00000 - 9FFFF	640K on system board	May be 64KB to 640KB depending upon model
A0000 - BFFFF	Display adapter reserved	EGA and VGA use all of this, CGA and MDA use portion
C0000 - DFFFF	Reserved for ROM expansion	Used for I/O channel BIOS (as in XT disk controller) C0000-C3FFF EGA BIOS C6000-C63FF PGA communications area C8000-CBFFF hard disk BIOS D0000-D7FFF cluster adapter BIOS D0000-DFFFF PCJr expansion cartridges
E0000 - EFFFF	Expansion of system ROM	As in AT, PS/2 (standard cartridges in PCJr)
F0000 - FFFFF	System ROM	May be duplicate of ROM in higher memory
100000 - 15FFFF	384K on system board	Model 50, 60, and 80 only
160000 - FDFFFF	Memory expansion	AT and PS/2 only
FE0000 - FEFFFF	RESERVED	AT and PS/2 only
FF0000 - FFFFFF	64K ROM BIOS	AT and PS/2 only

Source: IBM PS/2 Model 50 and 60 Technical Reference, page 4-181
IBM PS/2 Model 30 Technical Reference, page 1-5
IBM AT Technical Reference, page 1-8
IBM PC/XT Technical Reference, pages 1-8, 1-9

See Also: 4.002. BIOS Memory Usage Summary

7.03. I/O PORT USAGE SUMMARY

Hex Range	XT Use	AT Use	PS/2 Use	Comments
0-F	DMA controller (8237A-5)	DMA controller (8237A-5)	DMA controller	
10-1F	UNDOCUMENTED	RESERVED FOR SYSTEM BOARD	DMA controller	
20-2F	Interrupt controller (8259A)	Interrupt controller 1 (8259A)	Interrupt controller 1 (8259A)	Only ports 20, 21 actually used
30-3F	UNDOCUMENTED	Interrupt controller 1 (8259A)	UNDOCUMENTED	
40-4F	Timer (8253-5)	Timer (8254-2)	System timers	XT uses 40-43 only, PS/2 uses 40,42-44, 47 only
50-5F	Timer (8253-5)	Timer (8254-2)	UNDOCUMENTED	
60-6F	Parallel port (8255A-5)	Keyboard (8042)	Keyboard	XT uses 60-63 only, PS/2 uses 60-61, 64 only
70-7F	UNDOCUMENTED	RTC, NMI mask	RTC, NMI mask	PS/2 uses 70-71 only, reserves 74-76
80-8F	DMA page registers	DMA Page Registers (74LS612)	DMA page registers	XT uses 80-83 only, AT and PS/2 use 81-83, 87, 89-8B, 8F only
90-9F	DMA page registers	DMA page registers	I/O channel	PS/2 uses 90-94, 96-97 only
A0-AF	NMI mask register	NMI mask register	Interrupt controller 2 (8259A)	PS/2 uses A0-A1 only
B0-BF	UNDOCUMENTED	Interrupt controller 2 (8259A)	UNDOCUMENTED	
C0-CF	RESERVED	DMA controller 2 (8237A-5)	DMA controller	
D0-DF	UNDOCUMENTED	DMA controller 2 (8237A-5)	DMA controller	
E0-EF	RESERVED	RESERVED FOR SYSTEM BOARD	UNDOCUMENTED	
F0-FF	UNDOCUMENTED	Math coprocessor (80287)	Math coprocessor (80x87)	AT uses F0-F1, F8-FF only
100-10F	UNDOCUMENTED	AVAILABLE FOR I/O CHANNEL	Programmable option select	PS/2 uses 100-107 only
110-1EF	UNDOCUMENTED	AVAILABLE FOR I/O CHANNEL	UNDOCUMENTED	
1F0-1FF	UNDOCUMENTED	Fixed disk	UNDOCUMENTED	
200-20F	Game I/O adapter	Game I/O adapter	UNDOCUMENTED	Game I/O uses 200-207 only
210-21F	Expansion unit	21F RESERVED	UNDOCUMENTED	XT uses 210-217 only
220-24F	RESERVED	AVAILABLE FOR I/O CHANNEL	UNDOCUMENTED	
250-25F	UNDOCUMENTED	AVAILABLE FOR I/O CHANNEL	UNDOCUMENTED	
260-26F	UNDOCUMENTED	AVAILABLE FOR I/O CHANNEL	UNDOCUMENTED	
270-27F	Parallel printer 2	Parallel printer port 2	Parallel port 3	All use 278-27F only except PS/2 uses 278-27B
280-28F	UNDOCUMENTED	AVAILABLE FOR I/O CHANNEL	UNDOCUMENTED	
290-29F	UNDOCUMENTED	AVAILABLE FOR I/O CHANNEL	UNDOCUMENTED	
2A0-2AF	UNDOCUMENTED	AVAILABLE FOR I/O CHANNEL	UNDOCUMENTED	
2B0-2BF	Alternate EGA	Alternate EGA	UNDOCUMENTED	
2C0-2CF	Alternate EGA	Alternate EGA	UNDOCUMENTED	
2D0-2DF	Alternate EGA (3270 also uses)	Alternate EGA	UNDOCUMENTED	
2E0-2EF	UNDOCUMENTED	GPIB 0, data acquisition 0	UNDOCUMENTED	AT uses 2E1, 2E2-2E3 only
2F0-2FF	Secondary asynchronous adapter	Serial port 2	Serial port 2 (RS-232-C)	All use 2F8-2FF only
300-30F	Prototype card	Prototype card	UNDOCUMENTED	
310-31F	Prototype card	Prototype card	UNDOCUMENTED	
320-32F	Fixed disk adapter	AVAILABLE FOR I/O CHANNEL	UNDOCUMENTED	
330-33F	UNDOCUMENTED (XT/370 uses)	AVAILABLE FOR I/O CHANNEL	UNDOCUMENTED	
340-34F	UNDOCUMENTED	AVAILABLE FOR I/O CHANNEL	UNDOCUMENTED	
350-35F	UNDOCUMENTED	AVAILABLE FOR I/O CHANNEL	UNDOCUMENTED	
360-36F	UNDOCUMENTED	PC network (low address)	UNDOCUMENTED	
370-37F	Parallel printer	Parallel printer 1	Parallel port 2	All use 378-37F only except PS/2 uses 378-37B
380-38F	SDLC or second bisync controller	SDLC or second bisync controller	UNDOCUMENTED	
390-39F	UNDOCUMENTED	Cluster adapter	UNDOCUMENTED	
3A0-3AF	First bisync controller	First bisync controller	UNDOCUMENTED	
3B0-3BF	Monochrome display adapter	Monochrome display adapter	Video subsystem, parallel 1	All use 3BC-3BF for parallel port
3C0-3CF	Enhanced graphics adapter	Enhanced graphics adapter	Video subsystem	
3D0-3DF	Color graphics adapter	Color graphics adapter	Video subsystem	
3E0-3EF	3E0-3E7 RESERVED	AVAILABLE FOR I/O CHANNEL	UNDOCUMENTED	
3F0-3FF	Floppy disk adapter, 1st async	Floppy disk adapter, 1st async	Diskette drive controller, Serial 1	All use 3F0-3F7 for disk, 3F8-3FF for async communications

Legend: UNDOCUMENTED means not specifically mentioned in IBM technical reference

Notes: The AT also uses additional ports in the range 6E2-E2E1 for GPIB, Cluster, and Data Acquisition adapters

Source: IBM PC/XT Technical Reference, pages 1-24 and 1-25
   IBM PC/AT Technical Reference, pages 1-37 and 1-38
   IBM PS/2 Model 50 and 60 Technical Reference, page 1-9

7.04. PC INTERRUPT USAGE SUMMARY

Interrupt Number	Vector Address	Interrupt Name	Type	BIOS Entry Label	Comments
0H	00-03	Divide by zero exception	System	D11	
1H	04-07	Single step	System	D11	
2H	08-0B	Nonmaskable	System	NMI_INT	
3H	0C-0F	Breakpoint	System	D11	
4H	10-13	Overflow	System	D11	
5H	14-17	Print screen	BIOS	PRINT_SCREEN	See 4.001. BIOS Services Summary
6H	18-1B	RESERVED		D11	
7H	1C-1F	RESERVED		D11	
8H	20-23	Time of day service	Hardware	TIMER_INT	IRQ0 timer 0
9H	24-27	Keyboard service	Hardware	KB_INT	IRQ1 keyboard
AH	28-2B	RESERVED		D11	IRQ2 AT slave 8259
BH	2C-2F	Communications service COM2:	Hardware	D11	IRQ3 COM2:
CH	30-33	Communications service COM1:	Hardware	D11	IRQ4 COM1:
DH	34-37	Disk service/alt. printer service	Hardware	D11	IRQ5 PC: fixed disk adapter AT: LPT2
EH	38-3B	Diskette service	Hardware	DISK_INT	IRQ6 floppy disk adapter
FH	3C-3F	Printer service	Hardware	D11	IRQ7 LPT1:
10H	40-43	Video I/O	BIOS	VIDEO_IO	See 4.001. BIOS Services Summary
11H	44-47	Equipment check	BIOS	EQUIPMENT	See 4.001. BIOS Services Summary
12H	48-4B	Memory size	BIOS	MEMORY_SIZE_DETERMINE	See 4.001. BIOS Services Summary
13H	4C-4F	Disk I/O	BIOS	DISKETTE_IO	See 4.001. BIOS Services Summary
14H	50-53	Communications	BIOS	RS232_IO	See 4.001. BIOS Services Summary
15H	54-57	PC: cassette AT: extended services	BIOS	CASSETTE_IO	See 4.001. BIOS Services Summary
16H	58-5B	Keyboard I/O	BIOS	KEYBOARD_IO	See 4.001. BIOS Services Summary
17H	5C-5F	Printer	BIOS	PRINTER_IO	See 4.001. BIOS Services Summary
18H	60-63	Resident BASIC	BIOS	F600:0000	See 4.001. BIOS Services Summary
19H	64-67	Bootstrap	BIOS	BOOT_STRAP	See 4.001. BIOS Services Summary
1AH	68-6B	Time of day	BIOS	TIME_OF_DAY	See 4.001. BIOS Services Summary
1BH	6C-6F	Keyboard break	BIOS	DUMMY_RETURN	Ctrl-Break exit
1CH	70-73	Timer tick	BIOS	DUMMY_RETURN	18.2 ticks/second
1DH	74-77	Video parameters	BIOS	VIDEO_PARMS	Table address of video parameters
1EH	78-7B	Disk parameters	BIOS	DISK_BASE	Table address of disk parameters
1FH	7C-7F	Video graphics	BIOS		Table address of graphics characters
20H	80-83	Program termination	DOS		Obsolete
21H	84-87	General function services	DOS		All DOS services available through this interrupt
22H	88-8B	Terminate address	DOS		
23H	8C-8F	Ctrl-Break exit address	DOS		
24H	90-93	Critical error handler address	DOS		
25H	94-97	Absolute disk read	DOS		Read logical sector(s)
26H	98-9B	Absolute disk write	DOS		Write logical sector(s)
27H	9C-9F	Terminate/stay resident	DOS		Obsolete
28H	A0-A3	RESERVED	DOS		Idle signal
29H	A4-A7	RESERVED	DOS		TTY output
2AH	A8-AB	RESERVED	DOS		Critical section
2BH	AC-AF	RESERVED	DOS		
2CH	B0-B3	RESERVED	DOS		
2DH	B4-B7	RESERVED	DOS		
2EH	B8-BB	RESERVED	DOS		
2FH	BC-BF	RESERVED	DOS		Multiplex (print spool control)
30H	C0-C3	RESERVED	DOS		Long jump interface table address
31H	C4-C7	RESERVED	DOS		Long jump interface table address
32H	C8-CB	RESERVED	DOS		
33H	CC-CF	RESERVED	DOS		
34H	D0-D3	RESERVED	DOS		
35H	D4-D7	RESERVED	DOS		
36H	D8-DB	RESERVED	DOS		
37H	DC-DF	RESERVED	DOS		
38H	E0-E3	RESERVED	DOS		

(Continued)

Table 7.04. Continued

Interrupt Number	Vector Address	Interrupt Name	Type	BIOS Entry Label	Comments
39H	E4-E7	RESERVED	DOS		
3AH	E8-EB	RESERVED	DOS		
3BH	EC-EF	RESERVED	DOS		
3CH	F0-F3	RESERVED	DOS		
3DH	F4-F7	RESERVED	DOS		
3EH	F8-FB	RESERVED	DOS		
3FH	FC-FF	RESERVED	DOS		
40H	100-103	RESERVED	BIOS		Revectored disk I/O (Int 13)
41H	104-107	RESERVED	BIOS		Fixed disk 0 parameter table address
42H	108-10B	RESERVED	BIOS		EGA revectored video (Int 10)
43H	10C-10F	RESERVED	BIOS		EGA video parameters table address
44H	110-113	RESERVED	BIOS		EGA/PcJr 1st 128 characters table address
45H	114-117	RESERVED	BIOS		
46H	118-11B	RESERVED	BIOS		Fixed disk 1 parameter table address
47H	11C-11F	RESERVED	BIOS		
48H	120-123	RESERVED	BIOS		PcJr translate from 62-key keyboard
49H	124-127	RESERVED	BIOS		PcJr scan code translate table address
4AH	128-12B	RESERVED	BIOS		AT alarm interrupt user exit address
4BH	12C-12F	RESERVED	BIOS		
4CH	130-133	RESERVED	BIOS		
4DH	134-137	RESERVED	BIOS		
4EH	138-13B	RESERVED	BIOS		
4FH	13C-13F	RESERVED	BIOS		
50H	140-143	AT alarm interrupt	BIOS		
51H	144-147	Mouse functions	BIOS		See 5.08. INT 33H: Mouse Functions Summary
52H	148-14B	RESERVED	BIOS		
53H	14C-14F	RESERVED	BIOS		
54H	150-153	RESERVED	BIOS		
55H	154-157	RESERVED	BIOS		
56H	158-15B	RESERVED	BIOS		
57H	15C-15F	RESERVED	BIOS		
58H	160-163	RESERVED	BIOS		
59H	164-167	RESERVED	BIOS		
5AH	168-16B	Functions	PC CLUSTER		
5BH	16C-16F	Revectored in 19H	PC CLUSTER		
5CH	170-173	Network use	PC CLUSTER		NETBIOS entry point
5DH	174-177	RESERVED	BIOS		
5EH	178-17B	RESERVED	BIOS		
5FH	17C-17F	RESERVED	BIOS		
60H	180-183	RESERVED	USER PROGRAMS		
61H	184-187	RESERVED	USER PROGRAMS		
62H	188-18B	RESERVED	USER PROGRAMS		
63H	18C-18F	RESERVED	USER PROGRAMS		
64H	190-193	RESERVED	USER PROGRAMS		
65H	194-197	RESERVED	USER PROGRAMS		
66H	198-19B	RESERVED	USER PROGRAMS		
67H	19C-19F	Functions	LIM EMS		See 5.29. Expanded Memory Manager Functions Summary
68H	1A0-1A3	UNUSED	UNASSIGNED		
69H	1A4-1A7	UNUSED	UNASSIGNED		
6AH	1A8-1AB	UNUSED	UNASSIGNED		
6BH	1AC-1AF	UNUSED	UNASSIGNED		
6CH	1B0-1B3	UNUSED	UNASSIGNED		Also resume system vector
6DH	1B4-1B7	UNUSED	UNASSIGNED		
6EH	1B8-1BB	UNUSED	UNASSIGNED		
6FH	1BC-1BF	UNUSED	UNASSIGNED		
70H	1C0-1C3	PC: RESERVED AT/PS2:IRQ8 real time clock	AT BIOS	RTC_INT	IRQ8

(Continued)

Table 7.04. Continued

Interrupt Number	Vector Address	Interrupt Name	Type	BIOS Entry Label	Comments
71H	1C4-1C7	PC:RESERVED AT/PS2:IRQ9 redirected to IRQ2	AT BIOS	RE_DIRECT	IRQ9
72H	1C8-1CB	PC:RESERVED AT/PS2:IRQ10	AT BIOS	D11	IRQ10
73H	1CC-1CF	PC:RESERVED AT/PS2:IRQ11	AT BIOS	D11	IRQ11
74H	1D0-1D3	PC:RESERVED AT/PS2:IRQ12	AT BIOS	D11	IRQ12
75H	1D4-1D7	PC:RESERVED AT/PS2:IRQ13, 80287	AT BIOS	INT_287	IRQ13
76H	1D8-1DB	PC:RESERVED AT/PS2: fixed disk controller	AT BIOS	D11	IRQ14
77H	1DC-1DF	PC:RESERVED AT/PS2:IRQ15	AT BIOS	D11	IRQ15
78H-7FH	1E0-1FF	NOT USED			
80H-85H	200-217	RESERVED FOR BASIC			
86H-F0H	218-3C3	Used by BASIC			
F1H-FFH	3C4-3FF	NOT USED			

Compiled From: IBM PC/XT Technical Reference, Section 2 (see BIOS listings or page 2-4 of old XT manual for summary)
IBM PC/AT Technical Reference, Section 5 (see pages 5-5 and 5-6 for summary)
IBM DOS 3.3 Technical Reference, Section 6 (see pages 6-13 to 6-33)
IBM PS/2 and PC BIOS Technical Reference, Section 2 (see page 2-3 for summary)

See Also: 4.001. BIOS Services Summary
5.01. DOS Interrupt Usage by Version
5.08. INT 33H: Mouse Functions Summary
5.29. INT 67H: Expanded Memory Manager Functions Summary

7.05. PC KEYBOARD KEY NUMBERS AND SCAN CODES

Key Number	Hex Scan Code	Base Case	Uppercase	With Ctrl	With Alt
1	01	Esc	Esc	Esc	Suppressed
2	02	1	!	Suppressed	Extended
3	03	2	@	Nul	Extended
4	04	3	#	Suppressed	Extended
5	05	4	$	Suppressed	Extended
6	06	5	%	Suppressed	Extended
7	07	6	^	RS (30)	Extended
8	08	7	&	Suppressed	Extended
9	09	8	*	Suppressed	Extended
10	0A	9	(	Suppressed	Extended
11	0B	0	)	Suppressed	Extended
12	0C	-	_	US (31)	Extended
13	0D	=	+	Suppressed	Extended
14	0E	Backspace	Backspace	Del (127)	Suppressed
15	0F	Tab	Extended	Suppressed	Suppressed
16	10	q	Q	DC1 (17)	Extended
17	11	w	W	ETB (23)	Extended
18	12	e	E	ENQ (5)	Extended
19	13	r	R	DC2 (18)	Extended
20	14	t	T	DC4 (20)	Extended
21	15	y	Y	EM (25)	Extended
22	16	u	U	NAK (21)	Extended
23	17	i	I	HT (9)	Extended
24	18	o	O	SI (15)	Extended
25	19	p	P	DLE (16)	Extended
26	1A	[	{	Esc (27)	Suppressed
27	1B	]	}	GS (29)	Suppressed
28	1C	Enter	Enter	LF (10)	Suppressed
29	1D	Ctrl	Suppressed	Suppressed	Suppressed
30	1E	a	A	SOH (1)	Extended
31	1F	s	S	DC3 (19)	Extended
32	20	d	D	EOT (4)	Extended
33	21	f	F	ACK (6)	Extended
34	22	g	G	BEL (7)	Extended
35	23	h	H	BS (8)	Extended
36	24	j	J	LF (10)	Extended
37	25	k	K	VT (11)	Extended
38	26	l	L	FF (12)	Extended
39	27	;	:	Suppressed	Suppressed
40	28	'	"	Suppressed	Suppressed
41	29	`	~	Suppressed	Suppressed
42	2A	Left Shift	Suppressed	Suppressed	Suppressed
43	2B	\			FS (28)	Suppressed
44	2C	z	Z	SUB (26)	Extended
45	2D	x	X	CAN (24)	Extended
46	2E	c	C	ETX (3)	Extended
47	2F	v	V	SYN (22)	Extended
48	30	b	B	STX (2)	Extended
49	31	n	N	SO (14)	Extended
50	32	m	M	CR (13)	Extended
51	33	,	<	Suppressed	Suppressed
52	34	.	>	Suppressed	Suppressed
53	35	/	?	Suppressed	Suppressed
54	36	Right Shift	Suppressed	Suppressed	Suppressed
55	37	*	Print Screen	Extended	Suppressed
56	38	Alt	Suppressed	Suppressed	Suppressed
57	39	Spacebar	Spacebar	Spacebar	Spacebar
58	3A	Caps Lock	Suppressed	Suppressed	Suppressed
59	3B	F1	Extended	Extended	Extended
60	3C	F2	Extended	Extended	Extended
61	3D	F3	Extended	Extended	Extended
62	3E	F4	Extended	Extended	Extended
63	3F	F5	Extended	Extended	Extended
64	40	F6	Extended	Extended	Extended
65	41	F7	Extended	Extended	Extended
66	42	F8	Extended	Extended	Extended
67	43	F9	Extended	Extended	Extended
68	44	F10	Extended	Extended	Extended
69	45	Num Lock	Suppressed	Pause	Suppressed

(Continued)

Table 7.05. Continued

Key Number	Hex Scan Code	Base Case	Uppercase	With Ctrl	With Alt
70	46	Scroll Lock	Suppressed	Break	Suppressed
71	47	Home	NA	Clear Screen	Suppressed
72	48	Up Arrow	NA	Suppressed	Suppressed
73	49	PgUp	NA	Top of Text	Suppressed
74	4A	Numpad -	NA	Suppressed	Suppressed
75	4B	Left Arrow	NA	Extended	Suppressed
76	4C	Numpad 5	NA	Suppressed	Suppressed
77	4D	Right Arrow	NA	Extended	Suppressed
78	4E	Numpad +	NA	Suppressed	Suppressed
79	4F	End	NA	Extended	Suppressed
80	50	Down Arrow	NA	Suppressed	Suppressed
81	51	PgDn	NA	Extended	Suppressed
82	52	Ins	NA	Suppressed	Suppressed
83	53	Del	NA	Reset the system	

Notes: •Extended means first scan code returned is 00, followed by an extended ASCII code
•Suppressed indicates the key combination is not passed by the keyboard routine in BIOS

Source: IBM PC/XT Technical Reference, Section 4

See Also: 1.21. ASCII Character Set
1.23. IBM Extended Character Codes

7.06. AT 84-KEY KEY NUMBERS AND SCAN CODES

Key Number	Hex Scan Code	Base Case	Uppercase
1	29	`	~
2	02	1	!
3	03	2	@
4	04	3	#
5	05	4	$
6	06	5	%
7	07	6	^
8	08	7	&
9	09	8	*
10	0A	9	(
11	0B	0	)
12	0C	-	_
13	0D	=	+
14	2B	\		
15	0E	Backspace	Backspace
16	0F	Tab	Back Tab
17	10	q	Q
18	11	w	W
19	12	e	E
20	13	r	R
21	14	t	T
22	15	y	Y
23	16	u	U
24	17	i	I
25	18	o	O
26	19	p	P
27	1A	[	{
28	1B	]	}
30	1D	Ctrl (suppressed)	(suppressed)
31	1E	a	A
32	1F	s	S
33	20	d	D
34	21	f	F
35	22	g	G
36	23	h	H
37	24	j	J
38	25	k	K
39	26	l	L
40	27	;	:
41	28	'	"
43	1C	Enter	Enter
44	2A	(suppressed)	(suppressed)

(Continued)

Table 7.06. Continued

Key Number	Hex Scan Code	Base Case	Uppercase
46	2C	z	Z
47	2D	x	X
48	2E	c	C
49	2F	v	V
50	30	b	B
51	31	n	N
52	32	m	M
53	33	,	<
54	34	.	>
55	35	/	?
57	36	Right Shift (suppressed)	(suppressed)
58	38	Alt (suppressed)	(suppressed)
61	39	Spacebar	
64	3A	Caps Lock (suppressed)	(suppressed)
65	3C	F2	
66	3E	F4	
67	40	F6	
68	42	F8	
69	44	F10	
70	3B	F1	
71	3D	F3	
72	3F	F5	
73	41	F7	
74	43	F9	
75	E0,52	Insert	
90	01	Esc	Esc
91	47	Keypad 7	Home
92	4B	Keypad 4	←
93	4F	Keypad 1	End
95	45	Num Lock (suppressed)	(suppressed)
96	48	Keypad 8	↑
97	4C	Keypad 5	(suppressed)
98	50	Keypad 2	↓
99	52	Keypad 0	Ins
100	46	Scroll Lock (suppressed)	(suppressed)
101	49	Keypad 9	Page Up
102	4D	Keypad 6	→
103	51	Keypad 3	Page Down
104	53	Keypad .	Delete
105	54	Sys Req	
106	Not documented	Keypad *	Prt Sc
107	4A	Keypad -	
108	4E	Keypad +	

Notes: •Some key numbers and scan code numbers are missing and reserved by IBM
•Suppressed indicates key combination is not passed by the keyboard routine in BIOS

Source: IBM PC/AT Technical Reference, pages 1-44 to 1-46.4, 4-18 to 4-20, 4-33

See Also: 1.21. ASCII Character Set
1.23. IBM Extended Character Codes
7.05. PC Keyboard Key Numbers and Scan Codes
7.07. AT 101/102-key Key Numbers and Scan Codes

7.07. AT 101/102-KEY KEY NUMBERS AND SCAN CODES

Key Number	Hex Scan Code	Base Case	Uppercase
1	29	`	~
2	02	1	!
3	03	2	@
4	04	3	#
5	05	4	$
6	06	5	%
7	07	6	^
8	08	7	&
9	09	8	*
10	0A	9	(
11	0B	0	)
12	0C	-	_
13	0D	=	+
15	0E	Backspace	Backspace
16	0F	Tab	Back Tab
17	10	q	Q
18	11	w	W
19	12	e	E
20	13	r	R
21	14	t	T
22	15	y	Y
23	16	u	U
24	17	i	I
25	18	o	O
26	19	p	P
27	1A	[	{
28	1B	]	}
29	2B	\		
30	3A	Caps Lock (suppressed)	(suppressed)
31	1E	a	A
32	1F	s	S
33	20	d	D
34	21	f	F
35	22	g	G
36	23	h	H
37	24	j	J
38	25	k	K
39	26	l	L
40	27	;	:
41	28	'	"
42*	2B	#	~
43	1C	Enter	Enter
44	2A	Left Shift (suppressed)	(suppressed)
45*	D5	\		
46	2C	z	Z
47	2D	x	X
48	2E	c	C
49	2F	v	V
50	30	b	B
51	31	n	N
52	32	m	M
53	33	,	<
54	34	.	>
55	35	/	?
57	36	Right Shift (suppressed)	(suppressed)
58	1D	Left Ctrl (suppressed)	(suppressed)
60	38	Left Alt (suppressed)	(suppressed)
61	39	Spacebar	
62	E0,38	Right Alt (suppressed)	(suppressed)
64	E0,1D	Right Ctrl (suppressed)	(suppressed)
75	E0,52	Insert	
76	E0,53	Delete	

(Continued)

Table 7.07. Continued

Key Number	Hex Scan Code	Base Case	Uppercase
79	E0,4B	Left Arrow	
80	E0,47	Home	
81	EO,4F	End	
83	E0,48	Up Arrow	
84	E0,50	Down Arrow	
85	EO,49	PgUp	
86	E0,51	PgDn	
89	E0,4D	Right Arrow	
90	45,C5	NumLock (suppressed)	(suppressed)
91	47	Keypad 7	Home
92	4B	Keypad 4	Left Arrow
93	4F	Keypad 1	End
95	EO,35	Keypad /	Keypad/
96	48	Keypad 8	Up Arrow
97	4C	Keypad 5	
98	50	Keypad 2	Down Arrow
99	52	Keypad 0	Ins
100	E0,37	Keypad *	Keypad *
101	49	Keypad 9	Page Up
102	4D	Keypad 6	Right Arrow
103	51	Keypad 3	Page Down
104	53	Keypad .	Delete
105	4A	Keypad -	Keypad -
106	4E	Keypad +	Keypad +
108	E0,1C	Keypad Enter	Keypad Enter
110	01	Esc	Esc
112	3B	F1	
113	3C	F2	
114	3D	F3	
115	3E	F4	
116	3F	F5	
117	40	F6	
118	41	F7	
119	42	F8	
120	43	F9	
121	44	F10	
122	D9	F11	
123	DA	F12	
124	2A,37	Print Screen	
125	46	Scroll Lock	
126	1D,E0,45,E0,C5,9D	Pause Break	

Notes:
•Some key numbers and scan code numbers are missing and reserved by IBM
•Suppressed indicates key combination is not passed by the keyboard routine in BIOS
•*Only applicable to non-U.S. keyboards

Source:
IBM PC/AT Technical Reference, pages 1-45 to 1-46.4, 4-65 to 4-68

See Also:
1.21. ASCII Character Set
1.22. IBM ASCII Character Set
7.05. PC Keyboard Key Numbers and Scan Codes
7.06. AT 84-key Key Numbers and Scan Codes
7.08. PS/2 Key Numbers and Scan Codes

7.08. PS/2 KEY NUMBERS AND SCAN CODES

Key Number	Set 1 Make/Break	Set 2 Make/Break	Set 3 Make/Break	Base Case	Uppercase
1	29 / A9	0E / F0 0E	0E / F0 0E	`	~
2	02 / 82	16 / F0 16	16 / F0 16	1	!
3	03 / 83	1E / F0 1E	1E / F0 1E	2	@
4	04 / 84	26 / F0 26	26 / F0 26	3	#
5	05 / 85	25 / F0 25	25 / F0 25	4	$
6	06 / 86	2E / F0 2E	2E / F0 2E	5	%
7	07 / 87	36 / F0 36	36 / F0 36	6	^
8	08 / 88	3D / F0 3D	3D / F0 3D	7	&
9	09 / 89	3E / F0 3E	3E / F0 3E	8	*
10	0A / 8A	46 / F0 46	46 / F0 46	9	(
11	0B / 8B	45 / F0 45	45 / F0 45	0	)
12	0C / 8C	4E / F0 4E	4E / F0 4E	-	_
13	0D / 8D	55 / F0 55	55 / F0 55	=	+
15	0E / 8E	66 / F0 66	66 / F0 66	Backspace	
16	0F / 8F	0D / F0 0D	0D / F0 0D	Tab	
17	10 / 90	15 / F0 15	15 / F0 15	q	Q
18	11 / 91	1D / F0 1D	1D / F0 1D	w	W
19	12 / 92	24 / F0 24	24 / F0 24	e	E
20	13 / 93	2D / F0 2D	2D / F0 2D	r	R
21	14 / 94	2C / F0 2C	2C / F0 2C	t	T
22	15 / 95	35 / F0 35	35 / F0 35	y	Y
23	16 / 96	3C / F0 3C	3C / F0 3C	u	U
24	17 / 97	43 / F0 43	43 / F0 43	i	I
25	18 / 98	44 / F0 44	44 / F0 44	o	O
26	19 / 99	4D / F0 4D	4D / F0 4D	p	P
27	1A / 9A	54 / F0 54	54 / F0 54	[	{
28	1B / 9B	5B / F0 5B	5B / F0 5B	]	}
30	3A / BA	58 / F0 58	14 / F0 14	Caps Lock	
31	1E / 9E	1C / F0 1C	1C / F0 1C	a	A
32	1F / 9F	1B / F0 1B	1B / F0 1B	s	S
33	20 / A0	23 / F0 23	23 / F0 23	d	D
34	21 / A1	2B / F0 2B	2B / F0 2B	f	F
35	22 / A2	34 / F0 34	34 / F0 34	g	G
36	23 / A3	33 / F0 33	33 / F0 33	h	H
37	24 / A4	3B / F0 3B	3B / F0 3B	j	J
38	25 / A5	42 / F0 42	42 / F0 42	k	K
39	26 / A6	4B / F0 4B	4B / F0 4B	l	L
40	27 / A7	4C / F0 4C	4C / F0 4C	;	:
41	28 / A8	52 / F0 52	52 / F0 52	'	"
43	1C / 9C	5A / F0 5A	5A / F0 5A	Enter	Enter
44	2A / AA	12 / F0 12	12 / F0 12	Left Shift	
46	2C / AC	1A / F0 1A	1A / F0 1A	z	Z
47	2D / AD	22 / F0 22	22 / F0 22	x	X
48	2E / AE	21 / F0 21	21 / F0 21	c	C
49	2F / AF	2A / F0 2A	2A / F0 2A	v	V
50	30 / B0	32 / F0 32	32 / F0 32	b	B
51	31 / B1	31 / F0 31	31 / F0 31	n	N
52	32 / B2	3A / F0 3A	3A / F0 3A	m	M
53	33 / B3	41 / F0 41	41 / F0 41	,	<
54	34 / B4	49 / F0 49	49 / F0 49	.	>
55	35 / B5	4A / F0 4A	4A / F0 4A	/	?
57	36 / B6	59 / F0 59	59 / F0 59	Right Shift	
58	1D / 9D	14 / F0 14	11 / F0 11	Left Ctrl	
60	38 / B8	11 / F0 11	19 / F0 19	Left Alt	
61	39 / B9	29 / F0 29	29 / F0 29	Spacebar	
62	E0 38 / E0 B8	E0 11 / E0 F0 11	39 / F0 39	Right Alt	
64	E0 1D / E0 9D	E0 14 / E0 F0 14	58 / F0 58	Right Ctrl	
75	E0 52 / E0 D2 (base)	E0 70 / E0 F0 70 (base)	67 / F0 67	Insert	
76	E0 53 / E0 D3 (base)	E0 71 / E0 F0 71 (base)	64 / F0 64	Delete	
79	E0 4B / E0 CB (base)	E0 6B / E0 F0 6B (base)	61 / F0 61	Left Arrow	
80	E0 47 / E0 C7 (base)	E0 6C / E0 F0 6C (base)	6E / F0 6E	Home	
81	E0 4F / E0 CF (base)	E0 69 / E0 F0 69 (base)	65 / F0 65	End	
83	E0 48 / E0 C8 (base)	E0 75 / E0 F0 75 (base)	63 / F0 63	Up Arrow	
84	E0 50 / E0 D0 (base)	E0 72 / E0 F0 72 (base)	60 / F0 60	Down Arrow	
85	E0 49 / E0 C9 (base)	E0 7D / E0 F0 7D (base)	6F / F0 6F	PgUp	
86	E0 51 / E0 D1 (base)	E0 7A / E0 F0 7A (base)	6D / F0 6D	PgDn	
89	E0 4D / E0 CD (base)	E0 74 / E0 F0 74 (base)	6A / F0 6A	Right Arrow	
90	45 / C5	77 / F0 77	76 / F0 76	NumLock	
91	47 / C7	6C / F0 6C	6C / F0 6C	Keypad 7	

(Continued)

Table 7.08. Continued

Key Number	Set 1 Make/Break	Set 2 Make/Break	Set 3 Make/Break	Base Case	Uppercase
92	4B / CB	6B / F0 6B	6B / F0 6B	Keypad 4	
93	4F / CF	69 / F0 69	69 / F0 69	Keypad 1	
95	E0 35 / E0 B5 (base)	E0 4A / E0 F0 4A (base)	77 / F0 77	Keypad /	
96	48 / C8	75 / F0 75	75 / F0 75	Keypad 8	
97	4C / CC	73 / F0 73	73 / F0 73	Keypad 5	
98	50 / D0	72 / F0 72	72 / F0 72	Keypad 2	
99	52 / D2	70 / F0 70	70 / F0 70	Keypad 0	
100	37 / B7	7C / F0 7C	7E / F0 7E	Keypad *	
101	49 / C9	7D / F0 7D	7D / F0 7D	Keypad 9	
102	4D / CD	74 / F0 74	74 / F0 74	Keypad 6	
103	51 / D1	7A / F0 7A	7A / F0 7A	Keypad 3	
104	53 / D3	71 / F0 71	71 / F0 71	Keypad .	
105	4A / CA	7B / F0 7B	84 / F0 84	Keypad -	
106	4E / CE	79 / F0 79	7C / F0 7C	Keypad +	
108	E0 1C / E0 9C	E0 5A / E0 F0 5A	79 / F0 79	Keypad Enter	
110	01 / 81	76 / F0 76	08 / F0 08	Esc	
112	3B / BB	05 / F0 05	07 / F0 07	F1	
113	3C / BC	06 / F0 06	0F / F0 0F	F2	
114	3D / BD	04 / F0 04	17 / F0 17	F3	
115	3E / BE	0C / F0 0C	1F / F0 1F	F4	
116	3F / BF	03 / F0 03	27 / F0 27	F5	
117	40 / C0	0B / F0 0B	2F / F0 2F	F6	
118	41 / C1	83 / F0 83	37 / F0 37	F7	
119	42 / C2	0A / F0 0A	3F / F0 3F	F8	
120	43 / C3	01 / F0 01	47 / F0 47	F9	
121	44 / C4	09 / F0 09	4F / F0 4F	F10	
122	57 / D7	78 / F0 78	56 / F0 56	F11	
123	58 / D8	07 / F0 07	5E / F0 5E	F12	
124	E0 2A E0 37 / E0 B7 E0 AA	E0 12 E0 7C /E0 F0 7C E0 F0 12	57 / F0 57	Print Screen	
125	46 / C6	7E / F0 7E	5F / F0 5F	Scroll Lock	
126	E1 1D 45 / E1 9D C5	E1 14 77 E1 / F0 14 F0 77	62 / F0 62	Pause Break	
29 or 42*	2B / AB	5D / F0 5D	5C / F0 5C or 53 / F0 53	\	

Notes:
- *42 is only applicable to non-U.S. keyboards
- Some key numbers and scan code numbers are missing and reserved by IBM
- In set 1, shift case adds an E0 AA preceding the make code, and an E0 2A following the break code (for applicable keys only)
- In set 1, num lock case adds an E0 2A preceding the make code, and an E0 AA following the break code (for applicable keys only)
- In set 2, shift case adds an E0 F0 12 preceding the make code, and an E0 12 following the break code (for applicable keys only)
- In set 2, num lock case adds an E0 12 preceding the make code, and an E0 F0 12 following the break code (for applicable keys only)
- Set 2 is the default set

Source: IBM PS/2 Model 50 and 60 Technical Reference, pages 6-30 to 6-39

See Also:
1.21. ASCII Character Set
1.23. IBM Extended Character Codes
7.05. PC Keyboard Key Numbers and Scan Codes
7.06. AT 84-key Key Numbers and Scan Codes
7.07. AT 101/102-key Key Numbers and Scan Codes

7.09. PC & XT TYPEAHEAD BUFFER LAYOUT

Offset	Length	Name	Description
0 (0)	word	Buffer_Head	Points to next character in buffer
2 (2)	word	Buffer_Tail	Points to next blank space in buffer
4 (4)	32 bytes	Buffer_Area	Area used to store keystroke data

Notes:
•If Buffer_Head = Buffer_Tail, the buffer is empty
•Two bytes are necessary to store each keystroke, since the IBM extended keys (F1-F10, for example) consist of two byte codes. If the first byte for a keystroke is non-zero, then it represents the ASCII key and the second byte will be zero. If the first byte is zero, then it represents an extended key, and the second byte indicates the actual key pressed.
•Two low-memory words store the location of the buffer start (at 0040:0080) and one byte past its end (at 0040:0082)
•On a standard PC, the keyboard buffer is usually located at 0040:001A

Source: IBM PC/XT Technical Reference, BIOS Listing, page A-3 (original manuals only)
IBM PS/2 and PC BIOS Interface Technical Reference, Page 3-5

See Also: 4.002. BIOS Memory Usage Summary

7.10. AT KEYBOARD STATUS REGISTER

Bit Numbers

7	6	5	4	3	2	1	0	Name	Allowable Values
X								Parity error	0=odd parity (no error), 1=even parity
	X							Receive time out	0=no error, 1=keyboard did not finish
		X						Transmit time out	0=no error, 1=keyboard did not finish
			X					Inhibit switch	0=keyboard inhibited, 1=not inhibited
				X				Command/data	0=addressed as port 60H, 1=port 64H
					X			System flag	0=reset by power ON, 1=self test OK
						X		Input buffer full	0=empty, 1=full
							X	Output buffer full	0=empty, 1=full

Notes: The status register is at I/O address 64H

Source: IBM PC/AT Technical Reference, pages 1-49 to 1-50

See Also: 7.11. AT Keyboard I/O Command Summary
7.12. AT Keyboard Input Port Bit Definitions
7.13. AT Keyboard Output Port Bit Definitions

7.11. AT KEYBOARD I/O COMMAND SUMMARY

Command Value	Command Name	Comments	7	6	5	4	3	2	1	0
						Bit Numbers				
20H	Read keyboard controller									
60H	Write keyboard controller	Writes command byte -- see bitmap at right								
		RESERVED--always 0	0							
		IBM PC compatibility mode		X						
		IBM PC mode			X					
		Disable keyboard				X				
		Inhibit override					X			
		System flag						X		
		RESERVED--always 0							0	
		Enable output-buffer-full interrupt								X
AAH	Self test	55H placed in output buffer if successful								
ABH	Interface test	Returns code in output buffer as follows:								
		No error detected	0	0	0	0	0	0	0	0
		Keyboard clock line is stuck low	0	0	0	0	0	0	0	1
		Keyboard clock line is stuck high	0	0	0	0	0	0	1	0
		Keyboard data line is stuck low	0	0	0	0	0	0	1	1
		Keyboard data line is stuck high	0	0	0	0	0	1	0	0
ACH	Diagnostic dump	Sends 16 bytes of controller's RAM								
ADH	Disable keyboard feature	Sets bit 4 of controller's command byte								
AEH	Enable keyboard interface	Clears bit 4 of controller's command byte								
C0H	Read input port	Reads input port, data put in output buffer								
D0H	Read output port	Reads output port, data put in output buffer								
D1H	Write output port	Next byte placed in controller's output port								
E0H	Read test inputs	T0 and T1 inputs placed in output buffer								
F0-FFH	Pulse output port	Bits 0-3 of command determine bits to pulse								

Source:　　IBM PC/AT Technical Reference, pages 1-51 to 1-54

7.12. AT KEYBOARD INPUT PORT BIT DEFINITIONS

Bit Numbers

7	6	5	4	3	2	1	0	Function	Allowable Values
X								Keyboard inhibit switch	0=inhibited, 1=not inhibited
	X							Display switch	0=CGA, 1=MDA
		X						Manufacturing jumper status	0=jumper installed, 1=not installed
			X					System RAM	0=512K, 1=256K
				X	X	X	X	RESERVED	

Source:　　IBM PC/AT Technical Reference, page 1-55

See Also:　　7.11. AT Keyboard I/O Command Summary

7.13. AT KEYBOARD OUTPUT PORT BIT DEFINITIONS

Bit Numbers

7	6	5	4	3	2	1	0	Function	Allowable Values
X								Keyboard data output	
	X							Keyboard clock output	
		X						Input buffer empty	0=buffer full, 1=buffer empty
			X					Output buffer full	0=buffer empty, 1=buffer full
				X	X			RESERVED	
						X		Gate A20	
							X	System reset	

Source:　　IBM PC/AT Technical Reference, page 1-55

See Also:　　7.11. AT Keyboard I/O Command Summary

7.14. AT KEYBOARD TYPEMATIC RATE DEFINITIONS

Bit Numbers

7	6	5	4	3	2	1	0	Typematic Rate (±20%)
0	*	*	0	0	0	0	0	30.0
0	*	*	0	0	0	0	1	26.7
0	*	*	0	0	0	1	0	24.0
0	*	*	0	0	0	1	1	21.8
0	*	*	0	0	1	0	0	20.0
0	*	*	0	0	1	0	1	18.5
0	*	*	0	0	1	1	0	17.1
0	*	*	0	0	1	1	1	16.0
0	*	*	0	1	0	0	0	15.0
0	*	*	0	1	0	0	1	13.3
0	*	*	0	1	0	1	0	12.0
0	*	*	0	1	0	1	1	10.9
0	*	*	0	1	1	0	0	10.0
0	*	*	0	1	1	0	1	9.2
0	*	*	0	1	1	1	0	8.0
0	*	*	0	1	1	1	1	8.0
0	*	*	1	0	0	0	0	7.5
0	*	*	1	0	0	0	1	6.7
0	*	*	1	0	0	1	0	6.0
0	*	*	1	0	0	1	1	5.5
0	*	*	1	0	1	0	0	5.0
0	*	*	1	0	1	0	1	4.6
0	*	*	1	0	1	1	0	4.3
0	*	*	1	0	1	1	1	4.0
0	*	*	1	1	0	0	0	3.7
0	*	*	1	1	0	0	1	3.3
0	*	*	1	1	0	1	0	3.0
0	*	*	1	1	0	1	1	2.7
0	*	*	1	1	1	0	0	2.5
0	*	*	1	1	1	0	1	2.3
0	*	*	1	1	1	1	0	2.1
0	*	*	1	1	1	1	1	2.0

Notes: *Used to set delay (1 plus binary value * 250 milliseconds)

Source: IBM PC/AT Technical Reference, pages 4-10, 4-45

See Also: 7.11. AT Keyboard I/O Command Summary

7.15. VIDEO ADAPTER MEMORY USAGE AND OUTPUT SPECIFICATIONS

		MDA	CGA	EGA	VGA
Memory Use	Buffer Address	B0000	B8000	*	*
	Buffer Size	4 K	16 K	64 K - 256 K	256 K
	Pages in Buffer	1	4 to 8	Max of 8	Max of 8
	I/O Ports Used	3B0-3BF	3D0-3DF	3B0-3DF	3B0-3DF
Output	Bandwidth	16.257 MHz**	14.30 MHz	14.3 to 16.3 MHz	28 MHz
	Horiz. Sweep Rate	18.432 KHz**	15.75 KHz	15.7 to 21.8 KHz	31.5 KHz
	Vert. Sweep Rate	50 Hz**	60 Hz	60 Hz	50 to 70 Hz
	Max. Horiz. Pixels	720	640	*	720
	Max. Vert. Pixels	350	200	350	480
	Character Box Size	9x14	8x8	9x14 or 8x8	9x16
	Actual Character Size	7x9	7x7 or 5x7	7x9 or 7x7	7x9
System	Accesses CPU	When not refreshing	Anytime	Anytime	Anytime
	Data Transfer Rate	1.8 M/sec	1.5 M/sec	?	?
Features	Light Pen	NO	YES	YES	NO
	Composite Out	NO	YES	NO	NO
	Digital RGB Out	NO	YES	YES	NO
	Analog RGB Out	NO	NO	NO	YES
	Direct Video Out	YES	YES	YES	NO
	Color Palette	NONE	16 colors	64 colors	256 K colors
	Feature Connector	NO	NO	YES	NO
	Modulator Connector	NO	YES	NO	NO

Notes: •*B0000 for 32 K, or B8000 for 32 K, or A0000 for 64 K, or A0000 for 128 K.
Also for the EGA, a 16 K BIOS EGA extension module is mapped to processor address C0000.
•**When used with IBM Monochrome Display

Source: IBM Technical Reference Options and Adapters
IBM PS/2 Model 50 and 60 Technical Reference

See Also: 7.19. MDA Memory Map
7.22. MDA I/O Port Usage
7.23. CGA Memory Map
7.26. CGA I/O Port Usage
7.27. EGA Memory Map
7.30. EGA I/O Port Usage
7.31. VGA Memory Map
7.34. VGA I/O Port Usage

7.16. VIDEO MODES SUMMARY

BIOS Mode Details

Adapter Support

Mode #	Type	Rows	Cols	Resolution	Colors	MDA	CGA	EGA	MCGA	VGA
0	Char	25	40	320x200	16		X	X	X	X
1	Char	25	40	320x200	16		X	X	X	X
2	Char	25	80	640x200	16		X	X	X	X
3	Char	25	80	640x200	16		X	X	X	X
4	Graph	25	40	320x200	4		X	X	X	X
5	Graph	25	40	320x300	4		X	X	X	X
6	Graph	25	80	640x200	2		X	X	X	X
7	Char	25	80	720x350*	Mono	X		X		X
13	Graph	25	40	320x200	16			X		X
14	Graph	25	80	640x200	16			X		X
15	Graph	25	80	640x350	Mono			X		X
16	Graph	25	80	640x350	16			X		X
17	Graph	30	80	640x480	2				X	X
18	Graph	30	80	640x480	16					X
19	Graph	25	40	320x200	256				X	X

Notes: •EGA figures assume it has a full 256K of RAM
•Modes 8-12 are used by PCJr only
•*720x400 on VGA

Source: IBM PS/2 Model 50 and 60 Technical Reference, pages 2-11, 2-12, 4-27

7.17. VIDEO CHARACTER FONT SIZES

BIOS Mode

Mode #	Rows	Cols	Colors
0	25	40	16
1	25	40	16
2	25	80	16
3	25	80	16
7	25	80	Mono

Char Box Size

MDA	CGA	EGA	MCGA	VGA
	8x8	8x14	8x16	9x16
	8x8	8x14	8x16	9x16
	8x8	8x14	8x16	9x16
	8x8	8x14	8x16	9x16
9x14		9x14		9x16

Source: IBM PS/2 Model 50 and 60 Technical Reference,
pages 2-11, 2-12, 4-27

See Also: 7.20. MDA Character Box
7.24. CGA Character Box
7.28. EGA Character Box
7.32. VGA Character Box

7.18. VIDEO MONITOR USE SUMMARY

	MDA	CGA	EGA	MCGA	VGA
Can Use B/W TV	NO	MARGINAL	NO	NO	NO
Can Use B/W Composite Monitor	NO	YES	NO	NO	NO
Can Use IBM Monochrome Monitor	OPTIMUM	NO	YES	NO	NO
Can Use Color TV	NO	MARGINAL	NO	NO	NO
Can Use Composite Color Monitor	NO	MARGINAL	NO	NO	NO
Can Use Digital RGB Monitor	NO	OPTIMUM	OPTIMUM	NO	NO
Can Use Analog RGB Monitor	NO	NO	NO	OPTIMUM	OPTIMUM

Notes: Optimum indicates monitor for which display adapter was designed

7.19. MDA MEMORY MAP

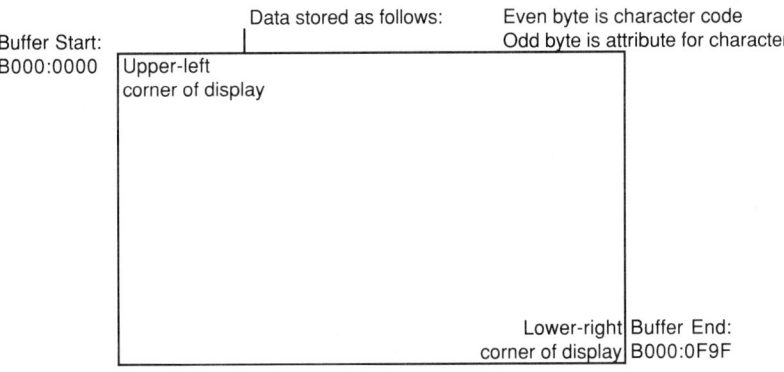

Data stored as follows: Even byte is character code
Odd byte is attribute for character

Buffer Start:
B000:0000

Upper-left corner of display

Lower-right corner of display

Buffer End:
B000:0F9F

Notes: •MDA may only be used in video mode 7 (See 7.16. Video Modes Summary)
•Additional "pages" follow sequentially in memory

Source: IBM Technical Reference Options and Adapters Volume 2, page Monochrome
Adapter 6

See Also: 7.15. Video Adapter Memory Usage and Output Specifications
7.21. MDA Character Attributes

7.20. MDA CHARACTER BOX

```
. . . . . . . . .
. . . . . . . . .
. . . X . . . . .
. . X X X . . . .
. X X . . X X . .
X X . . . . X X .
X X . . . . X X .
X X X X X X X X .
X X . . . . X X .
X X . . . . X X .
• • • • • • • • •
• • • • • • • • •
. . . . . . . . .
. . . . . . . . .
```

Character is a 7x9 pel area in a 9x14 pel box

X = pels set for a typical character "A"
• = pels set for default cursor

Notes: Pel is short for pixel element

Source: IBM Technical Reference Options and Adapters Volume 2, page
                Monochrome Display Adapter 2

See Also: 7.17. Video Character Font Sizes

7.21. MDA CHARACTER ATTRIBUTES

7	6	5	4	3	2	1	0	Function	Allowable Values
X								Blink	0=no blink, 1=blink
	X	X	X					Background	000=black background 111=white background
				X				Intensity	0=normal, 1=high intensity
					X	X	X	Foreground	000 = black character 001 = underline 111 = white character

Notes: •Invisible characters are created by placing character
                on same colored background (e.g., white on white)

Source: IBM Technical Reference Options and Adapters Volume 2, page Monochrome 6

See Also: 7.25. CGA Character Attributes
                7.29. EGA Character Attributes
                7.33. VGA Character Attributes

7.22. MDA I/O PORT USAGE

Port	Function	Comment
3B0H	NOT USED	
3B1H	NOT USED	
3B2H	NOT USED	
3B3H	NOT USED	
3B4H	6845 Index register	
3B5H	6845 Data register	
3B6H	NOT USED	
3B7H	NOT USED	
3B8H	CRT Control Port 1	Bit 0 = +high resolution mode Bit 1 = NOT USED Bit 2 = NOT USED Bit 3 = +video enable Bit 4=NOT USED Bit 5 = +enable blink Bit 6 = NOT USED Bit 7 = NOT USED
3B9H	RESERVED	
3BAH	CRT Status Port	Bit 0 = +horizontal drive Bit 1 = RESERVED Bit 2 = RESERVED Bit 3 = +black/white video
3BBH	RESERVED	
3BCH	Parallel data port	See 7.46. Printer Adapter I/O Port Usage
3BDH	Parallel status port	See 7.46. Printer Adapter I/O Port Usage
3BEH	Parallel control port	See 7.46. Printer Adapter I/O Port Usage
3BFH	NOT USED	

Source: IBM Technical Reference Options and Adapters
Volume 2, pages Monochrome 7 and 8

See Also: 7.26. CGA I/O Port Usage
7.30. EGA I/O Port Usage
7.46. Printer Adapter I/O Port Usage

7.23. CGA MEMORY MAP

For Alphanumeric Text Display (modes 0-3):

Text data stored as follows: Even byte is character code
Odd byte is attribute for character

Buffer Start:
B000:8000

Upper-left
corner of first page*

Lower-right Buffer End:
corner of first page* B000:8F9F for modes 2&3
B000:87CF for modes 0&1

(Continued)

Table 7.23. Continued

For Medium Resolution Graphics Display (320x200 all points addressable, modes 4 and 5):

Data stored as follows:
- Each pixel is two bits long
- Highest numbered pixel is LO 2 bits**
- Color of pixel is determined by 2-bit value

Buffer Start:
B000:8000

Upper-left
corner of even scans (0, 2, 4...198)

Lower-right | Buffer End:
corner of even scans | B000:9F3F

B000:9F40

MEMORY NOT USED

B000:9FFF

B000:A000

Upper-left
corner of odd scans (1,3,5...199)

Lower-right | Buffer End:
corner of odd scans | B000:BF3F

B000:BF40

MEMORY NOT USED

B000:BFFF

(Continued)

Table 7.23. Continued

For High Resolution Graphics Display (640x200 all points addressable, mode 6):

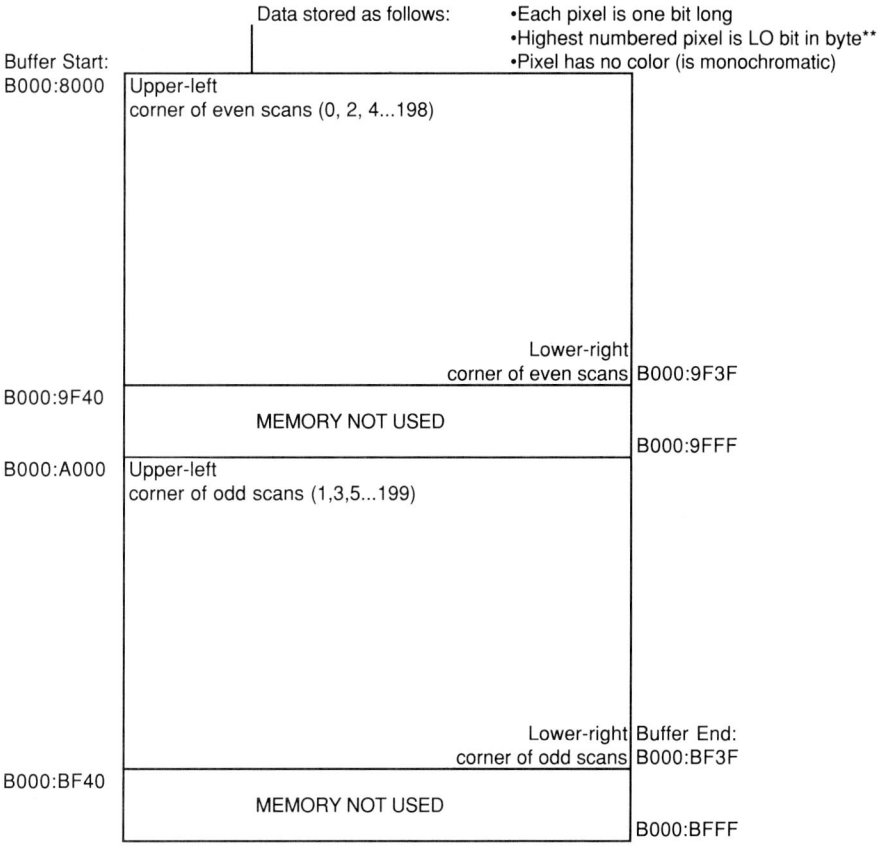

Data stored as follows:
•Each pixel is one bit long
•Highest numbered pixel is LO bit in byte**
•Pixel has no color (is monochromatic)

Buffer Start:
B000:8000

Upper-left
corner of even scans (0, 2, 4...198)

Lower-right
corner of even scans B000:9F3F

B000:9F40

MEMORY NOT USED

B000:9FFF

B000:A000   Upper-left
corner of odd scans (1,3,5...199)

Lower-right   Buffer End:
corner of odd scans B000:BF3F

B000:BF40

MEMORY NOT USED

B000:BFFF

Notes: •*Up to eight consecutive pages in modes 0 and 1, four consecutive pages in modes 2 and 3
•**In other words, the highest numbered pixel goes into the lowest bit (or bits), the lowest numbered pixel goes into the highest bit (or bits). For example:
-The first byte in medium resolution

bit number	7	6	5	4	3	2	1	0
pixel number	1		2		3		4	

-The first byte in high resolution:

bit number	7	6	5	4	3	2	1	0
pixel number	1	2	3	4	5	6	7	8

Source: IBM Technical Reference Options and Adapters Volume 2, pages Color Monitor Adapter 9 to 13

See Also: 7.15. Video Adapter Memory Usage and Output Specifications
7.25. CGA Character Attributes

7.24. CGA CHARACTER BOX

			X	X	X		
		X	X		X	X	
	X	X				X	X
	X	X				X	X
	X	X	X	X	X	X	X
	X	X				X	X
	X	X				X	X
•	•	•	•	•	•	•	•

Character is a 7x7 pel area in an 8x8 pel box

X = pels set for a typical character "A"
• = pels set for default cursor

Notes: •Pel is short for pixel element
•*Optionally, if jumper P3 inserted, character is 5x7 bit area in 8x8 box

Source: IBM Technical Reference Options and Adapters Volume 2,
pages Color Graphics Adapter 5 to 8

See Also: 7.17. Video Character Font Sizes

7.25. CGA CHARACTER ATTRIBUTES

Bit Number

7	6	5	4	3	2	1	0	Function	Allowable Values	
X								Blink	0=no blink, 1=blink	
	X	X	X					Background	000=black	
									001=blue	
									010=green	
									011=cyan	
									100=red	
									101=magenta	
									110=brown	
									111=white	
			X					Intensity	0=normal, 1=high intensity	
				X	X	X	Foreground	000=black	gray with intensity on
									001=blue	light blue with intensity on
									010=green	light green with intensity on
									011=cyan	light cyan with intensity on
									100=red	light red with intensity on
									101=magenta	light magenta with intensity on
									110=brown	yellow with intensity on
									111=white	bright white with intensity on

Notes: •Invisible characters are created by placing character
on same colored background (e.g., white on white)

Source: IBM Technical Reference Options and Adapters Volume 2, pages Color/Graphics 6 to 8

See Also: 7.21. MDA Character Attributes
7.29. EGA Character Attributes
7.33. VGA Character Attributes

7.26. CGA I/O PORT USAGE

Port	Function	7	6	5	4	3	2	1	0	Allowable Values
		Bit Numbers								
3D0	RESERVED									
3D1	RESERVED									
3D2	RESERVED									
3D3	RESERVED									
3D4	6845 index register									See 8.12. 6845 Registers
3D5	6845 data register									See 8.12. 6845 Registers
3D6	RESERVED									
3D7	RESERVED									
3D8	Mode control register (D0)	X	X							NOT USED
				X						0=blink disabled, 1=blink enabled
					X					1=640x200 graphics mode
						X				0=video signal disabled, 1=video signal enabled
							X			0=color enabled, 1=monochrome (black and white) signal
								X		0=320x200 graphics mode
									X	0=40x25 text mode, 1=80x25 text mode
3D9	Color select register (D0)	X	X							NOT USED
				X						Active color set: 0=red/green/brown, 1=cyan/magenta/white
					X					Intense colors in graphics, background colors in text mode
						X				Intense border in 40x25 text, intense background in 320x200 graphics, intensa foreground in 640x200 graphics
							X			Red border in 40x25 text, red background in 320x200 graphics, red foreground in 640x200 graphics
								X		Green border in 40x25 text, green background in 320x200 graphics, green foreground in 640x200 graphics
									X	Blue border in 40x25 text, blue background in 320x200 graphics, blue foreground in 640x200 graphics
3DA	Status register (D1)	X	X	X	X					NOT USED
						X				0=not in retrace, 1=in vertical retrace mode
							X			0=light pen switch is ON, 1=light pen switch is OFF
								X		0=no trigger, 1=positive-going edge from light pen has set trigger
									X	0=do not use memory, 1=memory may be accessed without interfering with display
3DB	Clear light pen latch									
3DC	Preset light pen latch									
3DD	RESERVED									
3DE	RESERVED									
3DF	RESERVED									

Source:

IBM Technical Reference Options and Adapters Volume 2, pages Color/Graphics 15 to 21

See Also:

7.22. MDA I/O Port Usage
7.30. EGA I/O Port Usage

7.27. EGA MEMORY MAP

For Alphanumeric Text Display (modes 0-3):

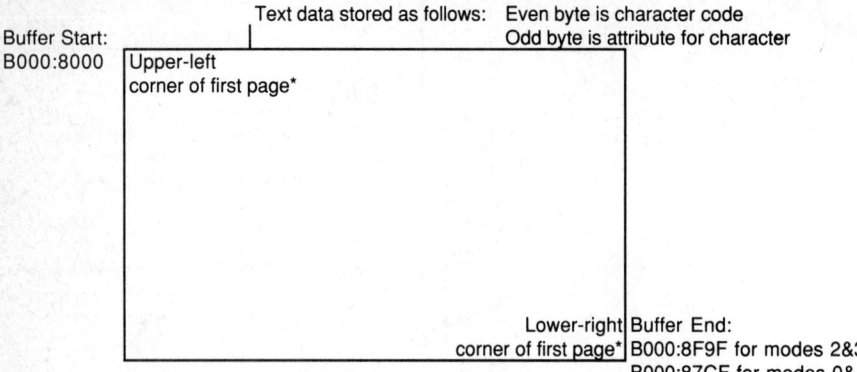

Text data stored as follows: Even byte is character code
Odd byte is attribute for character

Buffer Start:
B000:8000   Upper-left
corner of first page*

Lower-right | Buffer End:
corner of first page* | B000:8F9F for modes 2&3
B000:87CF for modes 0&1

For Medium Resolution Graphics Display (320x200 all points addressable, modes 4 and 5):

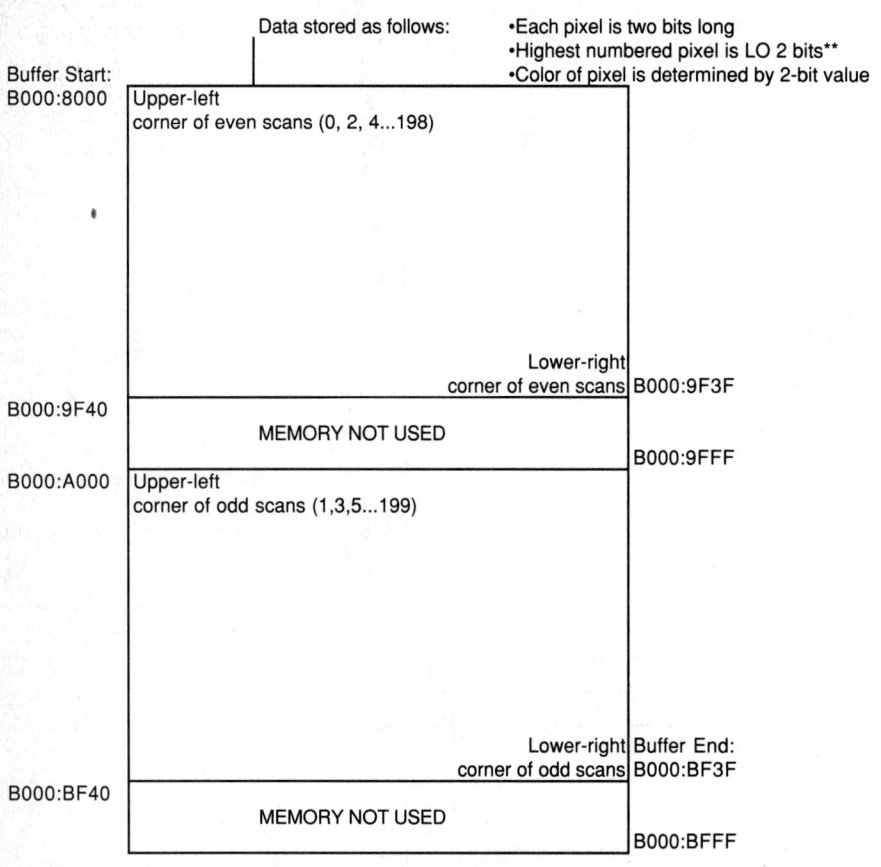

Data stored as follows:
•Each pixel is two bits long
•Highest numbered pixel is LO 2 bits**
•Color of pixel is determined by 2-bit value

Buffer Start:
B000:8000   Upper-left
corner of even scans (0, 2, 4...198)

Lower-right
corner of even scans | B000:9F3F

B000:9F40   MEMORY NOT USED

B000:9FFF

B000:A000   Upper-left
corner of odd scans (1,3,5...199)

Lower-right | Buffer End:
corner of odd scans | B000:BF3F

B000:BF40   MEMORY NOT USED

B000:BFFF

(Continued)

Table 7.27. Continued

For High Resolution Graphics Display (640x200 all points addressable, mode 6):

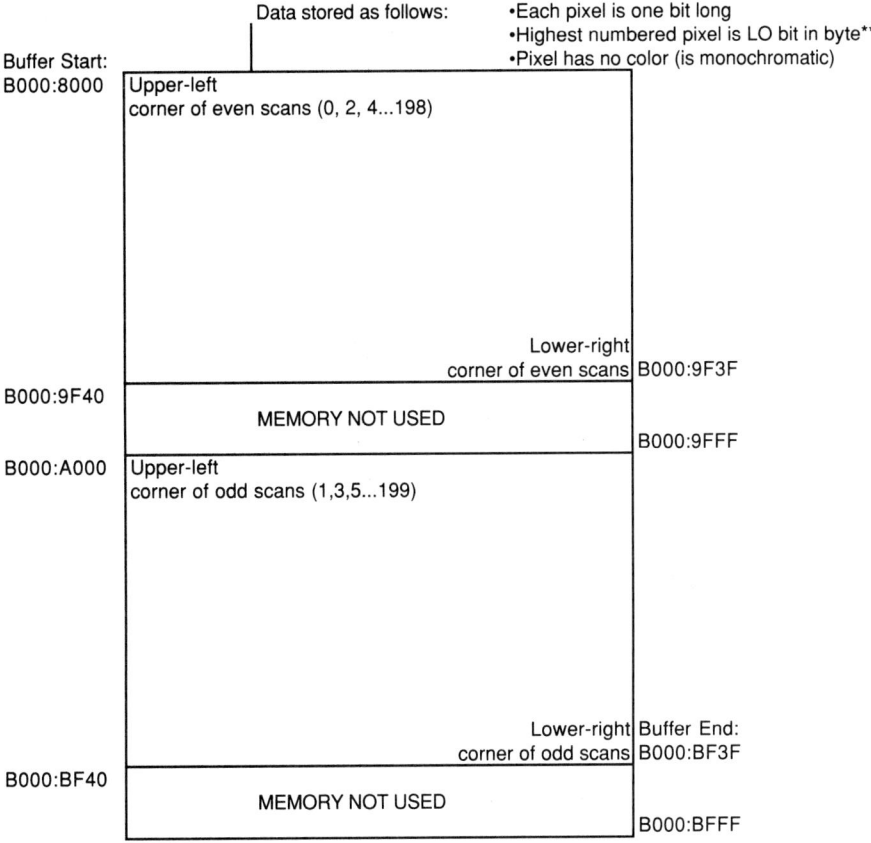

Data stored as follows:
•Each pixel is one bit long
•Highest numbered pixel is LO bit in byte**
•Pixel has no color (is monochromatic)

Buffer Start:
B000:8000 — Upper-left corner of even scans (0, 2, 4...198)

Lower-right corner of even scans B000:9F3F

B000:9F40 — MEMORY NOT USED

B000:9FFF

B000:A000 — Upper-left corner of odd scans (1,3,5...199)

Lower-right corner of odd scans — Buffer End: B000:BF3F

B000:BF40 — MEMORY NOT USED

B000:BFFF

For Medium Resolution Graphics Display (340x200 all points addressable, mode 13):

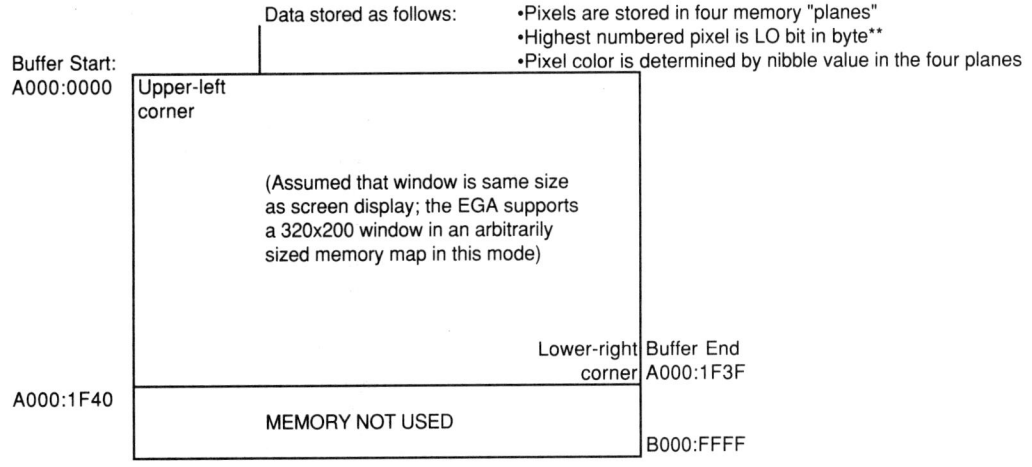

Data stored as follows:
•Pixels are stored in four memory "planes"
•Highest numbered pixel is LO bit in byte**
•Pixel color is determined by nibble value in the four planes

Buffer Start:
A000:0000 — Upper-left corner

(Assumed that window is same size as screen display; the EGA supports a 320x200 window in an arbitrarily sized memory map in this mode)

Lower-right corner — Buffer End A000:1F3F

A000:1F40 — MEMORY NOT USED

B000:FFFF

(Continued)

Table 7.27. Continued

For High Resolution Graphics Display (640x200 all points addressable, mode 14):

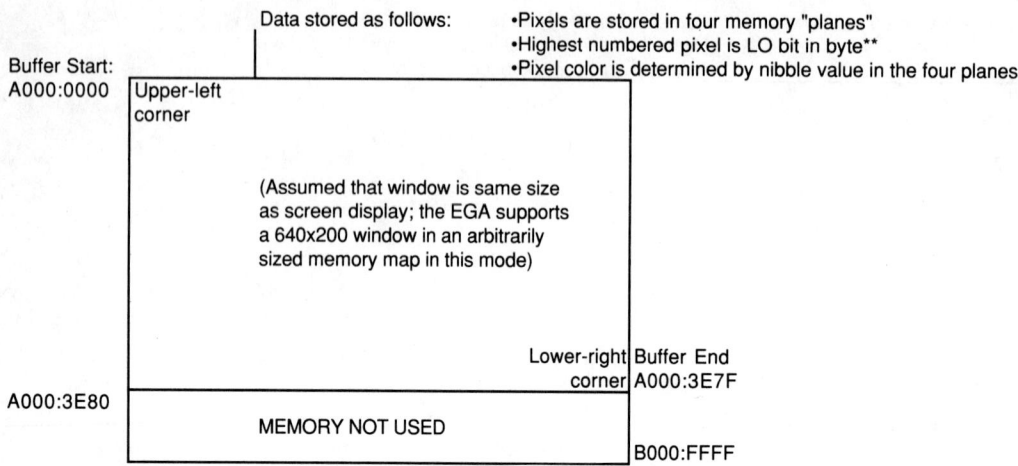

Data stored as follows:

•Pixels are stored in four memory "planes"
•Highest numbered pixel is LO bit in byte**
•Pixel color is determined by nibble value in the four planes

Buffer Start:
A000:0000

Upper-left corner

(Assumed that window is same size as screen display; the EGA supports a 640x200 window in an arbitrarily sized memory map in this mode)

Lower-right corner

Buffer End
A000:3E7F

A000:3E80

MEMORY NOT USED

B000:FFFF

For High Resolution Graphics Display (640x350 all points addressable, mode 16):

Data stored as follows:

•Pixels are stored in four memory "planes"
•Highest numbered pixel is LO bit in byte**
•Pixel color is determined by nibble value in the four planes

Buffer Start:
A000:0000

Upper-left corner

(Assumed that window is same size as screen display; the EGA supports a 640x350 window in an arbitrarily sized memory map in this mode)

Lower-right corner

Buffer End
A000:6D5F

A000:6D60

MEMORY NOT USED

B000:FFFF

(Continued)

Table 7.27. Continued

For High Resolution Graphics Display (640x350 all points addressable, mode 15):

Data stored as follows:
•Pixels are stored in four memory "planes"
•Highest numbered pixel is LO bit in byte**
•Pixel attribute is determined by nibble value in the four planes

Buffer Start:
A000:0000

Upper-left corner

(Assumed that window is same size as screen display; the EGA supports a 640x350 window in an arbitrarily sized memory map in this mode)

Lower-right corner | Buffer End A000:6D5F

A000:6D60

MEMORY NOT USED

B000:FFFF

Notes:
•When in purely EGA modes, memory organization is four planes of either 16K or 64K, and the use and definition of "pages" is up to the programmer
•*Up to eight consecutive pages in modes 0 and 1, four consecutive pages in modes 2 and 3
•**In other words, the highest numbered pixel goes into the lowest bit (or bits), the lowest numbered pixel goes into the highest bit (or bits). For example:
-The first byte in medium resolution:

bit number	7	6	5	4	3	2	1	0
pixel number	1		2		3		4	

-The first byte in high resolution:

bit number	7	6	5	4	3	2	1	0
pixel number	1	2	3	4	5	6	7	8

Source: IBM Technical Reference Options and Adapters Volume 2, pages Enhanced Adapter

See Also: 7.15. Video Adapter Memory Usage and Output Specifications
7.29. EGA Character Attributes

7.28. EGA CHARACTER BOX

For modes 7 and 15:

```
. . . . . . . . .
. . . . X . . . .
. . . X X X . . .
. . X X . X X . .
. X X . . . X X .
. X X . . . X X .
. X X X X X X X .
. X X . . . X X .
. X X . . . X X .
• • • • • • • • •
• • • • • • • • •
. . . . . . . . .
```

Character is a 7x9 pel area in a 9x14 pel box

X = pels set for a typical character "A"
• = pels set for default cursor

For modes 0-3:

```
. . X X X . . .
. X X . X X . .
X X . . . X X .
X X . . . X X .
X X X X X X X .
X X . . . X X .
X X . . . X X .
• • • • • • • •
```

Character is a 7x7 pel area in an 8x8 pel box

X = pel set for a typical character "A"
• = pels set for default cursor

Notes: Pel is short for pixel element

Source: IBM Technical Reference Options and Adapters Volume 2, page Enhanced Graphics Adapter 1

See Also: 7.17. Video Character Font Sizes

7.29. EGA CHARACTER ATTRIBUTES

For Text (modes 0-3):

7	6	5	4	3	2	1	0	Function	Allowable Values	
X								Blink	0=no blink, 1=blink	
	X	X	X					Background	000=black	
									001=blue	
									010=green	
									011=cyan	
									100=red	
									101=magenta	
									110=brown	
									111=white	
			X					Intensity	0=normal, 1=high intensity	
				X	X	X		Foreground	000=black	gray with intensity on
									001=blue	light blue with intensity on
									010=green	light green with intensity on
									011=cyan	light cyan with intensity on
									100=red	light red with intensity on
									101=magenta	light magenta with intensity on
									110=brown	yellow with intensity on
									111=white	bright white with intensity on

For Text (mode 7):

7	6	5	4	3	2	1	0	Function	Allowable Values	
X								Blink	0=no blink, 1=blink	
	X	X	X					Background	000=black	
									111=white	
			X					Intensity	0=normal, 1=high intensity	
				X	X	X		Foreground	000=black	gray with intensity on
									001=underline	
									111=white	bright white with intensity on

(Continued)

Table 7.29. Continued

For mode 15:

Pixel Plane:

3	2	1	0	Function
	0		0	Black character
	0		1	White character
	1		0	Blinking white character
	1		1	Intense white character

For modes 13,14, and 16:

Pixel Plane:

3	2	1	0	Function
X				Blue pixel component
	X			Green pixel component
		X		Red pixel component
			X	Intensity pixel component

Notes: Invisible characters in modes 0-3 and 7 are created by placing character on same colored background (e.g., white on white)

Source: IBM PS/2 Model 50 and 60 Technical Reference, pages 4-30 to 4-33

See Also: 7.21. MDA Character Attributes
7.25. CGA Character Attributes
7.33. VGA Character Attributes

7.30. EGA I/O PORT USAGE

Port	Function	Comment
3C0H	ATC index/data register	Write only
3C2H	Input status 0 register	Read only
3C4H	TS index register	Write only
3C5H	TS data register	Write only
3CAH	Graphics 2 position register	Write only
3CCH	Graphics 1 position register	Write only
3CEH	GDC index register	Write only
3CFH	GDC data register	Write only
3B4H	CRTC index register	Write only
3B5H	CRTC data register	Write only
3BAH	Input status 1 register	Read only (feature control register when written to)
3D4H	CRTC index register	Write only
3D5H	CRTC data register	Write only
3DAH	Input stats 1 register	Read only (feature control register when written to)

Source: IBM Technical Reference Options and Adapters Volume 2, pages Enhanced Graphics
IBM PS/2 Model 50 and 60 Technical Reference, pages 4-28 to 4-59

7.31. VGA MEMORY MAP

For Alphanumeric Text Display (modes 0-3):

Text data stored as follows: Even byte is character code
   Odd byte is attribute for character

Buffer Start:
B000:8000

Upper-left
corner of first page*

Lower-right
corner of first page*

Buffer End:
B000:8F9F for modes 2&3
B000:87CF for modes 0&1

For Medium Resolution Graphics Display (320x200 all points addressable, modes 4 and 5):

Data stored as follows:
•Each pixel is two bits long
•Highest numbered pixel is LO 2 bits**
•Color of pixel is determined by 2-bit value

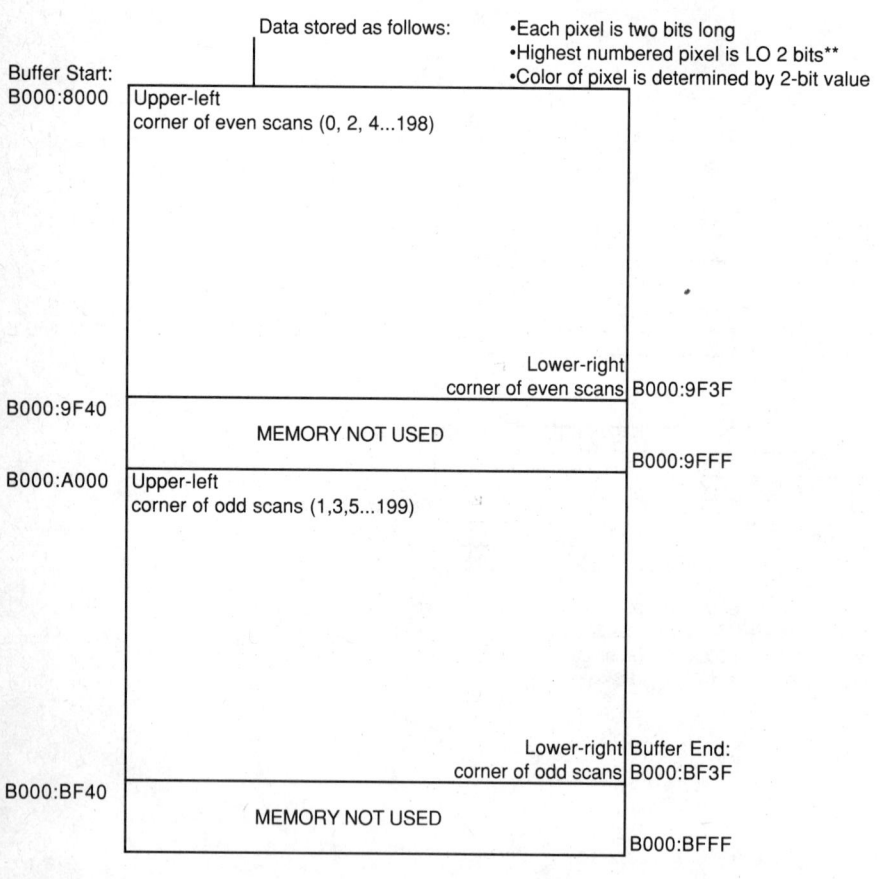

Buffer Start:
B000:8000

Upper-left
corner of even scans (0, 2, 4...198)

Lower-right
corner of even scans B000:9F3F

B000:9F40

MEMORY NOT USED

B000:9FFF

B000:A000

Upper-left
corner of odd scans (1,3,5...199)

Lower-right
corner of odd scans Buffer End:
B000:BF3F

B000:BF40

MEMORY NOT USED

B000:BFFF

(Continued)

Table 7.31. Continued

For High Resolution Graphics Display (640x200 all points addressable, mode 6):

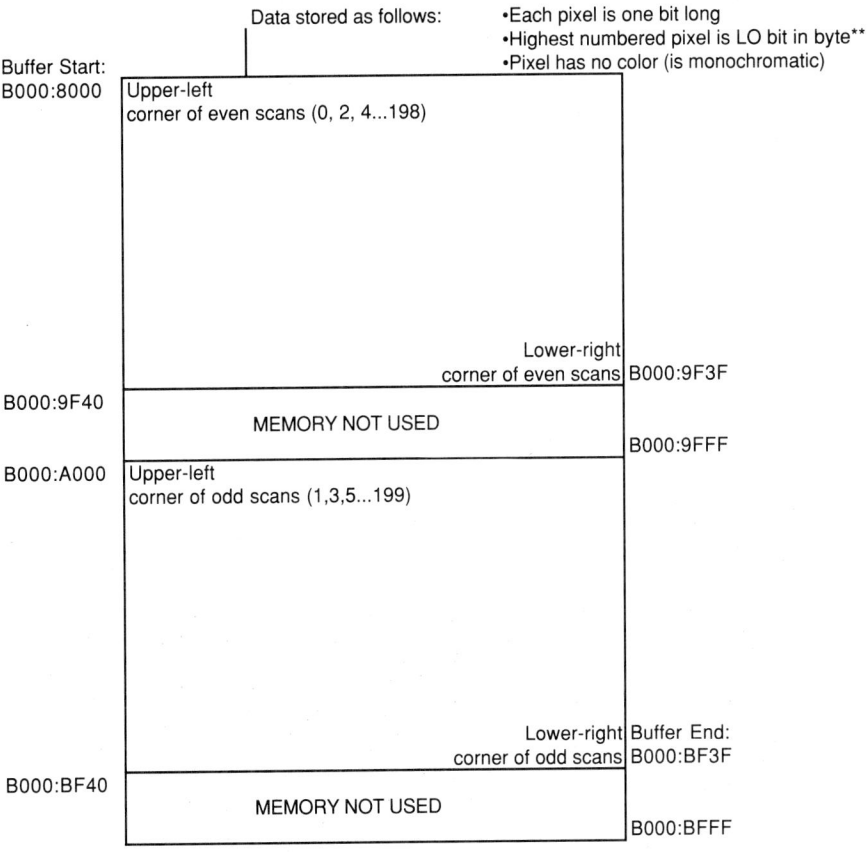

Data stored as follows:
•Each pixel is one bit long
•Highest numbered pixel is LO bit in byte**
•Pixel has no color (is monochromatic)

Buffer Start:
B000:8000

Upper-left
corner of even scans (0, 2, 4...198)

Lower-right
corner of even scans B000:9F3F

B000:9F40

MEMORY NOT USED

B000:9FFF

B000:A000

Upper-left
corner of odd scans (1,3,5...199)

Lower-right Buffer End:
corner of odd scans B000:BF3F

B000:BF40

MEMORY NOT USED

B000:BFFF

For Medium Resolution Graphics Display (340x200 all points addressable, mode 13):

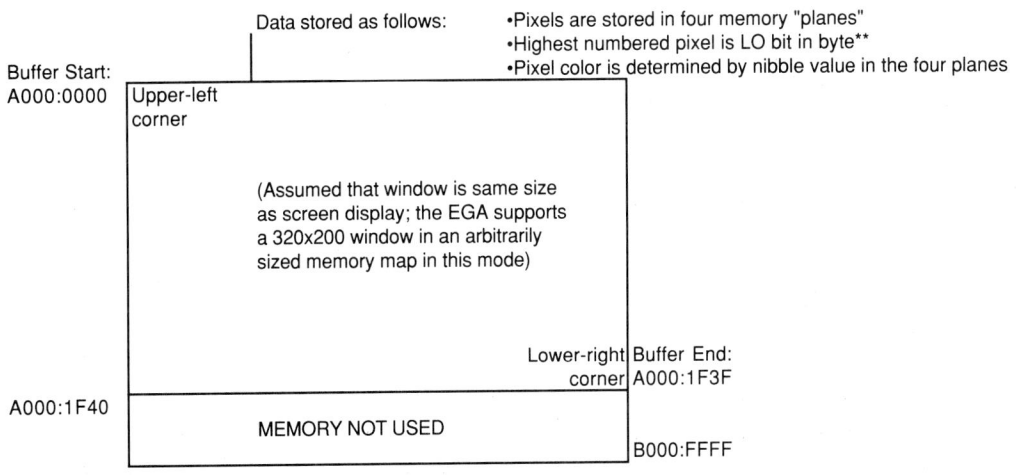

Data stored as follows:
•Pixels are stored in four memory "planes"
•Highest numbered pixel is LO bit in byte**
•Pixel color is determined by nibble value in the four planes

Buffer Start:
A000:0000

Upper-left
corner

(Assumed that window is same size
as screen display; the EGA supports
a 320x200 window in an arbitrarily
sized memory map in this mode)

Lower-right Buffer End:
corner A000:1F3F

A000:1F40

MEMORY NOT USED

B000:FFFF

(Continued)

Table 7.31. Continued

For High Resolution Graphics Display (640x200 all points addressable, mode 14):

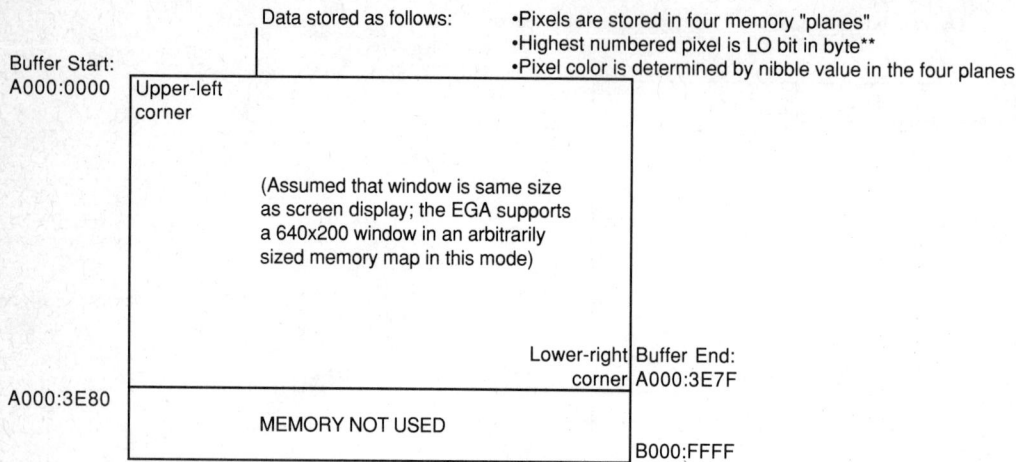

Data stored as follows: •Pixels are stored in four memory "planes"
•Highest numbered pixel is LO bit in byte**
•Pixel color is determined by nibble value in the four planes

Buffer Start:
A000:0000   Upper-left
corner

(Assumed that window is same size
as screen display; the EGA supports
a 640x200 window in an arbitrarily
sized memory map in this mode)

Lower-right | Buffer End:
corner | A000:3E7F

A000:3E80

MEMORY NOT USED

B000:FFFF

For High Resolution Graphics Display (640x350 all points addressable, mode 16):

Data stored as follows: •Pixels are stored in four memory "planes"
•Highest numbered pixel is LO bit in byte**
•Pixel color is determined by nibble value in the four planes

Buffer Start:
A000:0000   Upper-left
corner

(Assumed that window is same size
as screen display; the EGA supports
a 640x350 window in an arbitrarily
sized memory map in this mode)

Lower-right | Buffer End:
corner | A000:6D5F

A000:6D60

MEMORY NOT USED

B000:FFFF

(Continued)

Table 7.31. Continued

For High Resolution Graphics Display (640x350 all points addressable, mode 15):

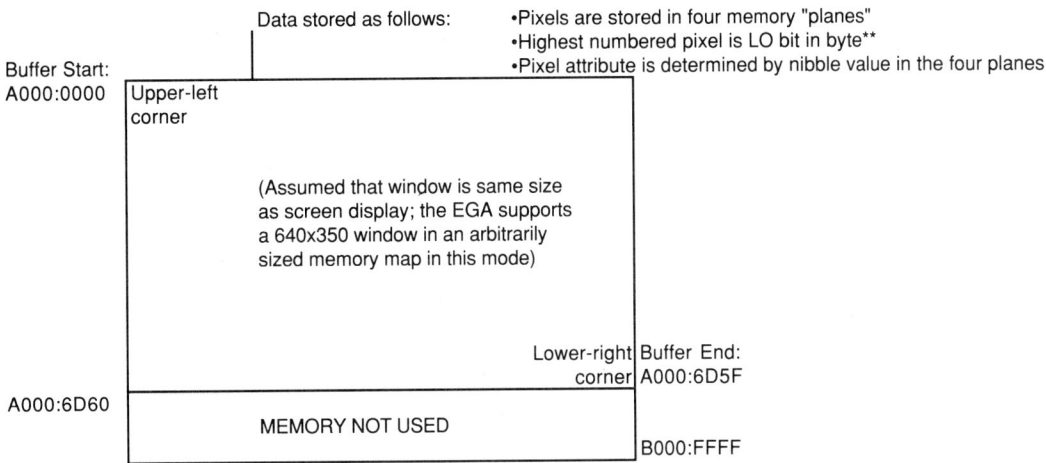

Data stored as follows:

•Pixels are stored in four memory "planes"
•Highest numbered pixel is LO bit in byte**
•Pixel attribute is determined by nibble value in the four planes

Buffer Start:
A000:0000   Upper-left corner

(Assumed that window is same size as screen display; the EGA supports a 640x350 window in an arbitrarily sized memory map in this mode)

Lower-right corner   Buffer End: A000:6D5F

A000:6D60   MEMORY NOT USED

B000:FFFF

For High Resolution Graphics Display (640x480 all points addressable, mode 17):

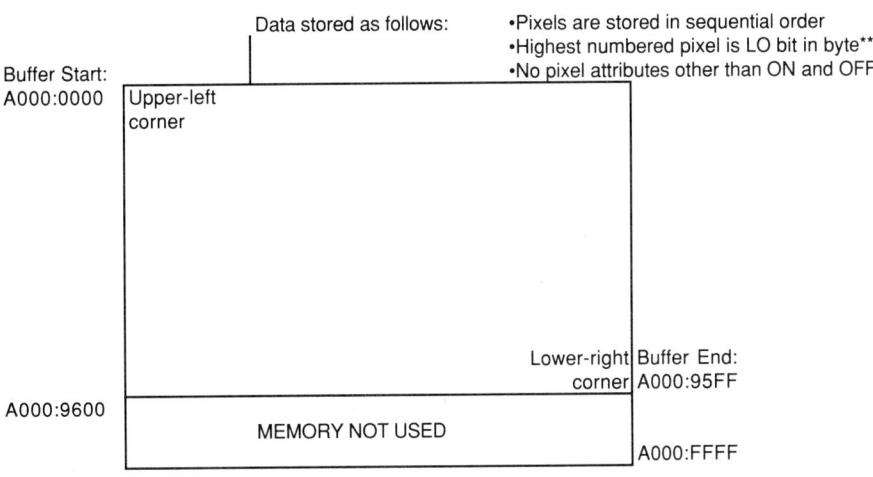

Data stored as follows:

•Pixels are stored in sequential order
•Highest numbered pixel is LO bit in byte**
•No pixel attributes other than ON and OFF

Buffer Start:
A000:0000   Upper-left corner

Lower-right corner   Buffer End: A000:95FF

A000:9600   MEMORY NOT USED

A000:FFFF

For High Resolution Graphics Display (640x480 all points addressable, mode 18):

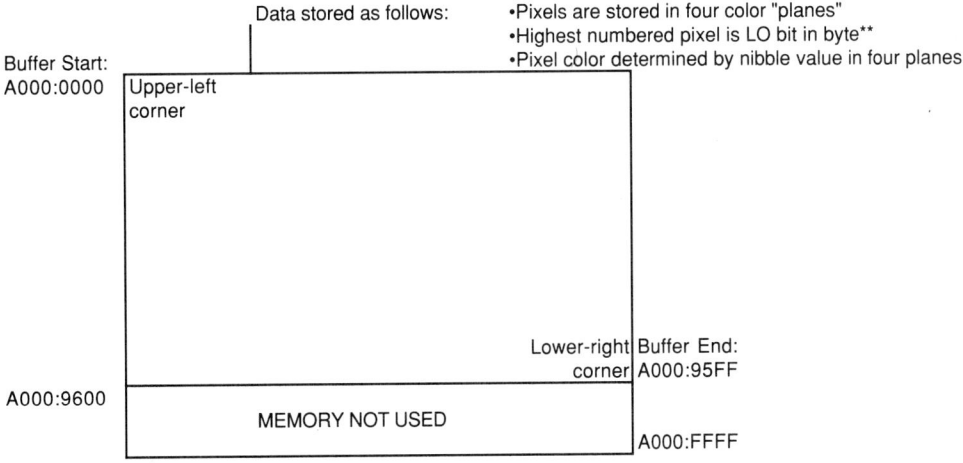

Data stored as follows:

•Pixels are stored in four color "planes"
•Highest numbered pixel is LO bit in byte**
•Pixel color determined by nibble value in four planes

Buffer Start:
A000:0000   Upper-left corner

Lower-right corner   Buffer End: A000:95FF

A000:9600   MEMORY NOT USED

A000:FFFF

(Continued)

Table 7.31. Continued

For Medium Resolution Graphics Display (320x200 all points addressable, mode 19):

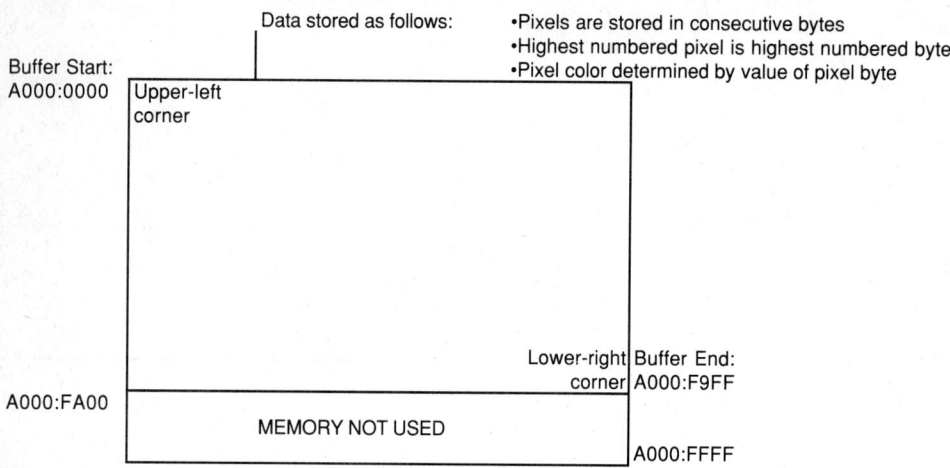

•Pixels are stored in consecutive bytes
•Highest numbered pixel is highest numbered byte
•Pixel color determined by value of pixel byte

Buffer Start:
A000:0000 — Upper-left corner

Lower-right corner — Buffer End: A000:F9FF

A000:FA00 — MEMORY NOT USED

A000:FFFF

Notes: •When in purely EGA modes, memory organization is four planes of either 16K or 64K, and the use and definition of "pages" is up to the programmer
•*Up to eight consecutive pages in modes 0 and 1, four consecutive pages in modes 2 and 3
•**In other words, the highest numbered pixel goes into the lowest bit (or bits), and the lowest numbered pixel goes into the highest bit (or bits). For example:
-The first byte in medium resolution:

bit number	7	6	5	4	3	2	1	0
pixel number	1		2		3		4	

-The first byte in high resolution:

bit number	7	6	5	4	3	2	1	0
pixel number	1	2	3	4	5	6	7	8

Source: IBM PS/2 Model 50 and 60 Technical Reference, pages 4-34 to 4-55

See Also: 7.15. Video Adapter Memory Usage and Output Specifications
7.33. VGA Character Attributes

7.32. VGA CHARACTER BOX

For modes 7 and 15:

Character is a 7x9 pel area in a 9x14 or 9x16 pel box

X = pels set for a typical character "A"
• = pels set for default cursor

For modes 0-3:

Character is a 7x7 pel area in an 8x8 or 8x14 or 9x16 pel box

X = pels set for a typical character "A"
• = pels set for default cursor

Notes: Pel is short for pixel element

Source: IBM PS/2 Model 50 and 60 Technical Reference, page 4-27

See Also: 7.17. Video Character Font Sizes

7.33. VGA CHARACTER ATTRIBUTES

For Text (modes 0-3):

7	6	5	4	3	2	1	0	Function	Allowable Values	
X								Blink	0=no blink, 1=blink	
	X	X	X					Background	000=black 001=blue 010=green 011=cyan 100=red 101=magenta 110=brown 111=white	
				X				Intensity	0=normal, 1=high intensity	
					X	X	X	Foreground	000=black 001=blue 010=green 011=cyan 100=red 101=magenta 110=brown 111=white	gray with intensity on light blue with intensity on light green with intensity on light cyan with intensity on light red with intensity on light magenta with intensity on yellow with intensity on bright white with intensity on

For Text (mode 7):

7	6	5	4	3	2	1	0	Function	Allowable Values	
X								Blink	0=no blink, 1=blink	
	X	X	X					Background	000=black 111=white	
				X				Intensity	0=normal, 1=high intensity	
					X	X	X	Foreground	000=black 001=underline 111=white	gray with intensity on bright white with intensity on

For modes 15 and 18:

Pixel Plane:

3	2	1	0	Function
		0	0	Black character
		0	1	White character
		1	0	Blinking white character
		1	1	Intense white character

For modes 13, 14, and 16:

Pixel Plane:

	Function
C0	Blue pixel component
C1	Green pixel component
C2	Red pixel component
C3	Intensity pixel component

Notes: •Invisible characters in modes 0-3 and 7 are created by placing character on same colored background (e.g., white on white)

Source: IBM PS/2 Model 50 and 60 Technical Reference, pages 4-30 to 4-39

See Also: 7.21. MDA Character Attributes
7.25. CGA Character Attributes
7.29. EGA Character Attributes

7.34. VGA I/O PORT USAGE

		I/O Port Used			
Register Name	Register Type	Color	Mono	Either	R/W
Miscellaneous output	General			3C2H	W
Miscellaneous output	General			3CCH	R
Input status register 0	General			3C2H	R
Input status register 1	General	3BAH	3DAH		R
Feature control register	General	3BAH	3DAH		W
Feature control register	General			3CAH	R
Video subsystem enable	General			3C3H	RW
Address register	Attribute			3C0H	RW
Other attribute register	Attribute			3C0H	W
Other attribute register	Attribute			3C1H	R
Index register	CRT Controller	3B4H	3D4H		RW
Other CRT controller registers	CRT Controller	3B5H	3D5H		RW
Address register	Sequencer			3C4H	RW
Other sequencer register	Sequencer			3C5H	RW
Address register	Graphics			3CEH	RW
Other graphics register	Graphics			3CFH	RW
PEL address write mode	Video DAC			3C8H	RW
PEL address read mode	Video DAC			3C7H	RW
DAC state register	Video DAC			3C7H	R
PEL data register	Video DAC			3C9H	RW
PEL mask register	Video DAC			3C6H	RW

Source: IBM PS/2 Model 50 and 60 Technical Reference,
                 pages 4-58 to 4-59

See Also: 7.22. MDA I/O Port Usage
                 7.26. CGA I/O Port Usage
                 7.30. EGA I/O Port Usage

7.35. ASYNCHRONOUS ADAPTER I/O PORT USAGE

I/O Port

Primary*	Secondary**	Used for	Comments
3F8H	2F8H	TX buffer	If bit 7 of line control register is 0
3F8H	2F8H	RX buffer	If bit 7 of line control register is 0
3F8H	2F8H	Divisor latch LO byte	If bit 7 of line control register is 1
3F9H	2F9H	Divisor latch HO byte	If bit 7 of line control register is 1
3F9H	2F9H	Interrupt enable register	
3FAH	2FAH	Interrupt identification registers	
3FBH	2FBH	Line control register	
3FCH	2FCH	Modem control register	
3FDH	2FDH	Line status register	
3FEH	2FEH	Modem status register	

Notes: •*Primary asynchronous adapter is mapped to COM1 by MS-DOS
            •**Secondary asynchronous adapter is mapped to COM2 by MS-DOS

Source: IBM Technical Reference Options and Adapters Volume 2, page Async 3

See Also: 7.36. Line Control Register
            7.37. Divisor Latch Register
            7.38. Line Status Register
            7.39. Interrupt Identification Register
            7.40. Interrupt Enable Register
            7.41. Modem Control Register
            7.42. Modem Status Register

7.36. LINE CONTROL REGISTER

Bit Number

7	6	5	4	3	2	1	0	Function	State on Reset	Allowable Values
X								Divisor latch access bit	0	1=access baud rate divisor latch
	X							Set break control	0	0=disabled, 1=enabled
		X						Stick parity	0	
			X					Even parity select	0	0=odd parity, 1=even parity
				X				Parity enable	0	0=disabled, 1=enabled
					X			Stop bits	0	0=1 stop bit, 1=1.5 (if bits 0/1=00) or 2
						X	X	Word length	00	00=5 bits 01=6 bits 10=7 bits 11=8 bits

Notes: Bits 4 and 5 affect parity only if bit 3 is enabled

Source: IBM Technical Reference Options and Adapters Volume 2, pages Async 5 to 7

See Also: 7.35. Asynchronous Adapter I/O Port Usage

7.37. DIVISOR LATCH REGISTER

Bit Number HO byte (3F9H)								Bit Number LO byte (3F8H)								Hex Value	Baud Rate Selected	Comments
7	6	5	4	3	2	1	0	7	6	5	4	3	2	1	0			
				X			X									900	50	
					X	X										600	75	
				X							X		X	X	X	417	110	.026 percent error
					X	X		X			X	X			X	359	134.5	.058 percent error
					X	X										300	150	
						X	X									180	300	
						X	X									C0	600	
							X	X								60	1200	
							X									40	1800	
								X	X	X		X				3A	2000	.69 percent error
								X	X							30	2400	
								X								20	3600	
									X	X						18	4800	
									X							10	7200	
										X	X					C	9600	

Notes: Assumes baud-rate generator with a frequency of 1.8432 MHz

Source: IBM Technical Reference Options and Adapters Volume 2, pages Async 7 to 9

See Also: 7.35. Asynchronous Adapter I/O Port Usage

7.38. LINE STATUS REGISTER

Bit Number

7	6	5	4	3	2	1	0	Function	State on Reset	Allowable Values
X								Always zero	0	No function
	X							Trans-shift-register empty	1	0=data transfer; 1=transmitter idle
		X						Trans-hold-register empty	1	0=ready; 1=transferring character
			X					Break interrupt indicator	0	0=normal receive; 1=break received
				X				Framing error indicator	0	0=normal receive; 1=framing error
					X			Parity error indicator	0	0=normal receive; 1=parity error
						X		Overrun error indicator	0	0=normal receive; 1=overrun error
							X	Receiver data ready	0	0=no data received; 1=data received

Notes: Bit 6 is read only

Source: IBM Technical Reference Options and Adapters Volume 2, pages Async 10 to 11

See Also: 7.35. Asynchronous Adapter I/O Port Usage

7.39. INTERRUPT IDENTIFICATION REGISTER

Bit Number

7	6	5	4	3	2	1	0	Function	State on Reset	Allowable Values
X	X	X	X	X				Always zero	00000	No function
					X	X		Interrupt ID	00	11=receiver line status interrupt 10=received data available interrupt 01=transmitter holding register empty interrupt 00=modem status interrupt
							X	Interrupt pending	1	0=interrupt pending; 1=no interrupt pending

Source: IBM Technical Reference Options and Adapters Volume 2, pages Async 12 to 13

See Also: 7.35. Asynchronous Adapter I/O Port Usage

7.40. INTERRUPT ENABLE REGISTER

Bit Number

7	6	5	4	3	2	1	0	Function	State on Reset	Allowable Values
X	X	X	X					Always zero	0000	No function
				X				Enable modem status Int	0	1=enable modem status interrupt; 0=disabled
					X			Receiver line status Int	0	1=enable receiver-line status interrupt; 0=disabled
						X		Transmitter holding reg empty	0	1=enable trans. holding reg. empty int; 0=disabled
							X	Received data available Int	0	1=enable received data avail. interrupt; 0=disabled

Source: IBM Technical Reference Options and Adapters Volume 2, pages Async 14 to 15

See Also: 7.35. Asynchronous Adapter I/O Port Usage

7.41. MODEM CONTROL REGISTER

Bit Number

7	6	5	4	3	2	1	0	Function	State on Reset	Allowable Values
X	X	X						Always zero	000	No function
			X					Loopback test mode	0	0=disabled; 1=enabled
				X				-OUT2 signal	0	0=-OUT2 forced high; 1=-OUT2 forced low
					X			-OUT1 signal	0	0=-OUT1 forced high; 1=-OUT1 forced low
						X		-RTS output	0	0=-RTS forced high; 1=-RTS forced low
							X	-DTR output	0	0=-DTR forced high; 1=-DTR forced low

Source: IBM Technical Reference Options and Adapters Volume 2, pages Async 15 to 16

See Also: 7.35. Asynchronous Adapter I/O Port Usage

7.42. MODEM STATUS REGISTER

Bit Number

7	6	5	4	3	2	1	0	Function	State on Reset	Allowable Values
X								-RLSD complement	Input signal	
	X							-RI complement	Input signal	
		X						-DSR complement	Input signal	
			X					-CTS complement	Input signal	
				X				Delta RLSD	0	0=no change; 1=-RLSD has changed state
					X			Trailing edge ring detector	0	0=no TE RI; 1=-RI has changed to OFF
						X		Delta DSR indicator	0	0=no change; 1=-DSR has changed state
							X	Delta CTS indicator	0	0=no change; 1=-CTS has changed state

Source: IBM Technical Reference Options and Adapters Volume 2, pages Async 16 to 18

See Also: 7.35. Asynchronous Adapter I/O Port Usage

7.43. GAME ADAPTER I/O PORT USAGE

Port	Direction	Function
201H	Write	Fire joysticks four one-shots
	Read	Read joystick position and status

Notes: Resistive inputs are read by first outputting to port 201H, then noting the amount of time they remain high by inputting continuously from port 201H

Source: IBM Technical Reference Options and Adapters Volume 2, pages Game Adapter 3 to 6

See Also: 7.44. Game Adapter AB Joystick Data Byte
7.45. Game Adapter ABCD Paddle Data Byte

7.44. GAME ADAPTER AB JOYSTICK DATA BYTE

Bit Numbers

7	6	5	4	3	2	1	0	Function
X								Status of B joystick button 2
	X							Status of B joystick button 1
		X						Status of A joystick button 2
			X					Status of A joystick button 1
				X				B joystick Y coordinate*
					X			B joystick X coordinate*
						X		A joystick Y coordinate*
							X	A joystick X coordinate*

Notes: *Coordinates are determined by the length of time the bit is held high

Source: IBM Technical Reference Options and Adapters Volume 2, page Game Adapter 6

See Also: 7.43. Game Adapter I/O Port Usage
7.45. Game Adapter ABCD Paddle Data Byte

7.45. GAME ADAPTER ABCD PADDLE DATA BYTE

Bit Numbers

7	6	5	4	3	2	1	0	Function
X								Status of D paddle button
	X							Status of C paddle button
		X						Status of B paddle button
			X					Status of A paddle button
				X				D paddle coordinate*
					X			C paddle coordinate*
						X		B paddle coordinate*
							X	A paddle coordinate*

Notes: *Coordinates are determined by the length of time the bit is held high

Source: IBM Technical Reference Options and Adapters Volume 2, page Game Adapter 6

See Also: 7.43. Game Adapter I/O Port Usage
7.44. Game Adapter AB Joystick Data Byte

7.46. PRINTER ADAPTER I/O PORT USAGE

Port	Bit Numbers 7	6	5	4	3	2	1	0	Adapter	Direction	Function
378	X								Printer	Output	Controls pin 9 (data bit 7)
		X							Printer	Output	Controls pin 8 (data bit 6)
			X						Printer	Output	Controls pin 7 (data bit 5)
				X					Printer	Output	Controls pin 6 (data bit 4)
					X				Printer	Output	Controls pin 5 (data bit 3)
						X			Printer	Output	Controls pin 4 (data bit 2)
							X		Printer	Output	Controls pin 3 (data bit 1)
								X	Printer	Output	Controls pin 2 (data bit 0)
379	X								Printer	Input	Status of pin 11 (busy)
		X							Printer	Input	Status of pin 10 (acknowledge)
			X						Printer	Input	Status of pin 12 (out of paper)
				X					Printer	Input	Status of pin 13 (select)
					X				Printer	Input	Status of pin 15 (error)
					X	X	X		Printer	Input	NOT USED
37A	X	X	X						Printer	Input	NOT USED
				X					Printer	Input	Status of IRQ Enable
					X				Printer	Input	Inverted status of pin 17 (select input)
						X			Printer	Input	Status of pin 16 (initialize printer)
							X		Printer	Input	Inverted status of pin 14 (auto feed)
								X	Printer	Input	Inverted status of pin 1 (strobe)
	X	X	X	X					Printer	Output	NOT USED
					X				Printer	Output	Inverted status of pin 17 (select input)
						X			Printer	Output	Status of pin 16 (initialize printer)
							X		Printer	Output	Inverted status of pin 14 (auto feed)
								X	Printer	Output	Inverted status of pin 1 (strobe)
3BC	X								MDA	Output	Controls pin 9 (data bit 7)
		X							MDA	Output	Controls pin 8 (data bit 6)
			X						MDA	Output	Controls pin 7 (data bit 5)
				X					MDA	Output	Controls pin 6 (data bit 4)
					X				MDA	Output	Controls pin 5 (data bit 3)
						X			MDA	Output	Controls pin 4 (data bit 2)
							X		MDA	Output	Controls pin 3 (data bit 1)
								X	MDA	Output	Controls pin 2 (data bit 0)
3BD	X								MDA	Input	Status of pin 11 (busy)
		X							MDA	Input	Status of pin 10 (acknowledge)
			X						MDA	Input	Status of pin 12 (out of paper)
				X					MDA	Input	Status of pin 13 (select)
					X				MDA	Input	Status of pin 15 (error)
					X	X	X		MDA	Input	NOT USED
3BE	X	X	X						MDA	Input	NOT USED
				X					MDA	Input	Status of IRQ Enable
					X				MDA	Input	Inverted status of pin 17 (select input)
						X			MDA	Input	Status of pin 16 (initialize printer)
							X		MDA	Input	Inverted status of pin 14 (auto feed)
								X	MDA	Input	Inverted status of pin 1 (strobe)
	X	X	X	X					MDA	Output	NOT USED
					X				MDA	Output	Inverted status of pin 17 (select input)
						X			MDA	Output	Status of pin 16 (initialize printer)
							X		MDA	Output	Inverted status of pin 14 (auto feed)
								X	MDA	Output	Inverted status of pin 1 (strobe)

Notes: •While the printer adapter and monochrome display adapter printer ports work identically, they appear at different port addresses
•The source contains incomplete material

Source: IBM Technical Reference Options and Adapters Volume 2, pages Printer Adapter 3 to 7
IBM Technical Reference Options and Adapters Volume 2, pages Monochrome Adapter 13 to 17

7.47. IBM PRINTER CONTROL CODES SUMMARY

Function Type	Function	Code Sequence in ASCII Chars	Code Sequence in Hex Bytes	Printer Type*		
				Graphics	Color	Compact
Character Style	Select char set 1	<Escape>7	1B 37	Yes	Yes	
	Select char set 2	<Escape>6	1B 36	Yes	Yes	
	10 characters per inch spacing (Compressed OFF)	<DC2>	12	Yes	Yes	Yes
	17.1 characters per inch spacing (Compressed ON)	<SI>	0F	Yes	Yes	Yes
	Doublestrike ON	<Escape> or <SI>	1B 0F	Yes	Yes	
	Doublestrike OFF	<Escape>G	1B 47	Yes	Yes	Yes
	Doublewidth ON (lines)	<Escape>H	1B 48	Yes	Yes	Yes
	Doublewidth OFF (lines)	<Escape>W<SOH>	1B 57 01	Yes	Yes	Yes
	Doublewidth by line ON	<Escape>W<Null>	1B 57 00	Yes	Yes	Yes
		<SO>	0E	Yes	Yes	Yes
	Doublewidth by line OFF	<Escape> or <SO>	1B 0E	Yes	Yes	Yes
	Emphasized printing ON	<DC4>	14	Yes	Yes	Yes
	Emphasized printing OFF	<Escape>E	1B 45	Yes	Yes	
	Subscript ON	<Escape>F	1B 46	Yes	Yes	
	Superscript ON	<Escape>S<SOH>	1B 53 01	Yes	Yes	
	Subscript/superscript OFF	<Escape>S<Null>	1B 53 00	Yes	Yes	
	Set draft quality print	<Escape>T	1B 54	Yes	Yes	
	Set text quality print	<Escape>I<SOH>	1B 49 01		Yes	
	Set letter quality print	<Escape>I<STX>	1B 49 02		Yes	
	Proportional spacing ON	<Escape>I<ETX>	1B 49 03		Yes	
	Proportional spacing OFF	<Escape>P<SOH>	1B 50 01		Yes	
	12 characters per inch spacing	<Escape>P<Null>	1B 50 00		Yes	
	Print all characters in block	<Escape>:	1B 3A		Yes	
	Print next character	<Escape>## [data]	1B 5C ## #			
	Underline ON	<Escape>^	1B 5E		Yes	
	Underline OFF	<Escape>-<SOH>	1B 2D 01	Yes	Yes	Yes
		<Escape>-<Null>	1B 2D 00	Yes	Yes	Yes
Page Settings	Ignore paper end ON	<Escape>8	1B 38	Yes	Yes	
	Ignore paper end OFF	<Escape>9	1B 39	Yes	Yes	
	Set length of page in lines	<Escape>C#	1B 43 #	Yes	Yes	Yes
	Set length of page in inches	<Escape>C<SOH>#	1B 43 00 #		Yes	
	Automatic line justification ON	<Escape>M<SOH>#	1B 4D 01		Yes	
	Automatic line justification OFF	<Escape>M<Null>	1B 4D 00		Yes	
	Perforation skip ON	<Escape>N#	1B 4E #	Yes	Yes	Yes
	Perforation skip OFF	<Escape>O	1B 4F	Yes	Yes	Yes
	Set top of page	<Escape>4	1B 34		Yes	Yes
	Set left and right margins	<Escape>X##	1B 58 # #		Yes	Yes
	Set tabs to power-on defaults	<Escape>R	1B 52		Yes	Yes
	Set horizontal tab stops	<Escape>D#...#<Null>	1B 44 #...# 00	Yes	Yes	Yes
	Set vertical tab stops	<Escape>B#...#<Null>	1B 42 #...# 00	Yes	Yes	Yes
Line Settings	Carriage return	<CR>	0D	Yes	Yes	Yes
	Line feed	<LF>	0A	Yes	Yes	Yes
	Set variable line feed to n/72 inch	<Escape>A#	1B 41 #	Yes	Yes	Yes
	Set variable line feed to n/216 inch	<Escape>J#	1B 4A #	Yes	n/144"	Yes
	Set 1/8 inch line feed	<Escape>0	1B 30	Yes	Yes	1/9"

(Continued)

Table 7.47. Continued

Function Type	Function	Code Sequence in ASCII Chars	Code Sequence in Hex Bytes	Graphics	Color	Compact
Line Settings	Set 7/72 inch line feed	<Escape>1	1B 31		6/72"	1/9"
	Start variable line feed (used after EscA)	<Escape>2	1B 32	Yes	Yes	1/6"
	Set n/216 inch line feed	<Escape>3#	1B 33 #	Yes	n/144"	
	Vertical tab	<VT>	0B	Yes	Yes	Yes
	Reverse line feed	<Escape>]	1B 5D		Yes	
	Automatic line feed ON	<Escape>5<SOH>	1B 35 01		Yes	Yes
	Automatic line feed OFF	<Escape>5<Null>	1B 35 00		Yes	
Printer Control	Ring bell	<BELL>	7	Yes	Yes	
	Clear printer buffer	<CAN>	18	Yes	Yes	Yes
	Select printer	<DC1>	11		Yes	
	Deselect printer	<DC3>	13		Yes	
	Automatic ribbon band shift	<Escape>a	1B 61		Yes	
	Select ribbon band 4 (black)	<Escape>b	1B 62		Yes	
	Select ribbon band 3	<Escape>c	1B 63		Yes	
	Space n/120 forward to next character	<Escape>d##	1B 64 # #		Yes	
	Space n/120 backward to next character	<Escape>e##	1B 65 # #		Yes	
	Select ribbon band 2	<Escape>m	1B 6D		Yes	
	Set aspect ratio to 1:1	<Escape>n<SOH>	1B 6E 01		Yes	
	Set aspect ratio to 5:6	<Escape>n<Null>	1B 6E 00		Yes	
	Deselect color printer	<Escape>Q<STX>	1B 51 02		Yes	
	Select ribbon band 1	<Escape>y	1B 79		Yes	
	Initialize function ON	<Escape>?<SOH>	1B 3F 01		Yes	
	Initialize function OFF	<Escape>?<Null>	1B 3F 00		Yes	
	Unidirectional printing ON	<Escape>U<SOH>	1B 55 01	Yes	Yes	
	Unidirectional printing OFF	<Escape>U<Null>	1B 55 00	Yes	Yes	
	Home print head	<Escape><	1B 3C	Yes	Yes	Yes
	Form feed	<FF>	0C	Yes	Yes	Yes
	Horizontal tab	<HT>	9	Yes	Yes	Yes
	Select control-value data type	<Escape>@#	1B 40#		Yes	
	Backspace	<BS>	8		Yes	
Graphics	Set to 480 bit image graphics mode	<Escape>K## [data]	1B 4B # # [data]	Yes	1108	560
	Set to 960 bit image graphics mode	<Escape>L## [data]	1B 4C # # [data]	Yes	2216	
	Set to 960 bit image graphics mode normal speed	<Escape>Y## [data]	1B 59 # # [data]	Yes	2216	
	Set to 1920 bit image graphics mode	<Escape>Z## [data]	1B 5A # # [data]	Yes	4432	

Notes:
- Characters enclosed in brackets are ASCII code names, as in <Escape>
- # should be replaced by an appropriate numeric value
- [data] indicates a bitstream of appropriately formatted data
- Numbers in "bit image graphics modes" indicate number of data bytes that follow
- *Refers to IBM Graphics Printer, IBM Color Printer, and IBM Compact Printer, respectively

Source: IBM Technical Reference Options and Adapters Volume 1, pages Graphics Printer

See Also: 1.20. ASCII Control Codes
7.48. HP LaserJet Printer Control Codes Summary

7.48. HP LASERJET PRINTER CONTROL CODES SUMMARY

Function Type	Function	Code Sequence in ASCII Chars	Code Sequence in Hex Bytes
Orientation	Portrait Mode	<Escape>&l0O	1B 26 6C 30 4F
	Landscape Mode	<Escape>&l1O	1B 26 6C 31 4F
Font Symbol Set	Roman-8	<Escape>(8U	1B 28 38 55
	USASCII	<Escape>(0U	1B 28 30 55
	Roman Ext.	<Escape>(0E	1B 28 30 45
	Danish/Norwegian	<Escape>(0D	1B 28 30 44
	British (U.K.)	<Escape>(1E	1B 28 31 45
	French	<Escape>(0F	1B 28 30 46
	German	<Escape>(0G	1B 28 30 47
	Italian	<Escape>(0I	1B 28 30 49
	Swedish/Finnish	<Escape>(0S	1B 28 30 53
	Spanish	<Escape>(1S	1B 28 31 53
	Legal	<Escape>(1U	1B 28 31 55
	Linedraw	<Escape>(0B	1B 28 30 42
	Math8	<Escape>(8M	1B 28 38 4D
	Math8a	<Escape>(0Q	1B 28 30 51
	Math8b	<Escape>(1Q	1B 28 31 51
	Math7	<Escape>(0A	1B 28 30 41
	PiFont	<Escape>(15U	1B 28 31 35 55
	PiFonta	<Escape>(2Q	1B 28 32 51
Character Spacing	Proportional	<Escape>(s1P	1B 28 73 31 50
	Fixed	<Escape>(s0P	1B 28 73 30 50
Character Pitch	10 chars per inch	<Escape>(s10H	1B 28 73 31 30 48
	12 chars per inch	<Escape>(s12H	1B 28 73 31 32 48
	16.6 chars per inch	<Escape>(s16.6H	1B 28 73 31 36 2E 36 48
	Standard Pitch (10 cpi)	<Escape>&k0S	1B 26 6B 30 53
	Compressed Pitch (16.6 cpi)	<Escape>&k2S	1B 26 6B 32 53
Character Point Size	7 point	<Escape>(s7V	1B 28 73 37 56
	8 point	<Escape>(s8V	1B 28 73 38 56
	8.5 point	<Escape>(s8.5V	1B 28 73 38 2E 35 56
	10 point	<Escape>(s10V	1B 28 73 31 30 56
	12 point	<Escape>(s12V	1B 28 73 31 32 56
	14.4 point	<Escape>(s14.4V	1B 28 73 31 34 2E 34 56
Character Style	Upright	<Escape>(s0S	1B 28 73 30 53
	Italic	<Escape>(s1S	1B 28 73 31 53
Character Weight	Light stroke	<Escape>(s-3B	1B 28 73 2D 42
	Medium stroke	<Escape>(s0B	1B 28 73 30 42
	Bold (heavy) stroke	<Escape>(s3B	1B 28 73 33 42
Character Typeface	Courier	<Escape>(s3T	1B 28 73 33 54
	Line Printer	<Escape>(s0T	1B 28 73 30 54
	Helv	<Escape>(s4T	1B 28 73 34 54
	TMS RMN	<Escape>(s5T	1B 28 73 35 54
	Prestige Elite	<Escape>(s8T	1B 28 73 38 54
	Gothic	<Escape>(s6T	1B 28 73 36 54
Page Settings	Page Length	<Escape>&l*P	1B 26 6C # 50
	Top Margin	<Escape>&l*E	1B 26 6C # 45
	Text Length	<Escape>&l*F	1B 26 6C # 46
	Clear Left/Right Margin	<Escape>9	1B 39
	Set Left Margin	<Escape>&a*L	1B 26 61 # 4C
	Set Right Margin	<Escape>&a*M	1B 26 61 # 4D
	Perforation Skip Enable	<Escape>&l0L	1B 26 6C 31 4C
	Perforation Skip Disable	<Escape>&l1L	1B 26 6C 30 4C
Line Spacing	Vertical Motion Index	<Escape>&l#C	1B 26 6C # 43
	1 line/inch	<Escape>&l1D	1B 26 6C 31 44
	2 lines/inch	<Escape>&l2D	1B 26 6C 32 44
	3 lines/inch	<Escape>&l3D	1B 26 6C 33 44
	4 lines/inch	<Escape>&l4D	1B 26 6C 34 44
	6 lines/inch	<Escape>&l6D	1B 26 6C 36 44
	8 lines/inch	<Escape>&l8D	1B 26 6C 38 44
	12 lines/inch	<Escape>&l12D	1B 26 6C 31 32 44
	16 lines/inch	<Escape>&l16D	1B 26 6C 31 36 44
	24 lines/inch	<Escape>&l24D	1B 26 6C 32 34 44
	Half line feed	<Escape>=	1B 3D
Raster Graphics	75 dpi resolution	<Escape>*t75R	1B 2A 74 37 35 52
	100 dpi resolution	<Escape>*t100R	1B 2A 74 31 30 30 52
	150 dpi resolution	<Escape>*t150R	1B 2A 74 31 35 30 52
	300 dpi resolution	<Escape>*t300R	1B 2A 74 33 30 30 52
	Start at leftmost pos.	<Escape>*r0A	1B 2A 72 30 41
	Start at current cursor	<Escape>*r1A	1B 2A 72 31 41

(Continued)

Table 7.48. Continued

Function Type	Function	Code Sequence in ASCII Chars	Code Sequence in Hex Bytes
Raster Graphics	Transfer graphic rows	<Escape>*b#W [data]	1B 2A 62 # 57 [data]
	End graphics	<Escape>*rB	1B 2A 72 42
Printer Control	Reset printer	<Escape>E	1B 45
	Selftest mode	<Escape>z	1B 7A
Cursor Positioning	Move to Row	<Escape>&a#R	1B 26 61 # 52
	Move to Column	<Escape>&a#C	1B 26 61 # 43
	Horizontal Movement	<Escape>&a#H	1B 26 61 # 48
	Vertical Movement	<Escape>&a#V	1B 26 61 # 56
Underlining	Underline ON	<Escape>&dD	1B 26 64 44
	Underline OFF	<Escape>&d@	1B 26 64 40
Miscellaneous Control	Display Functions ON	<Escape>Y	1B 59
	Display Functions OFF	<Escape>Z	1B 5A
	Transparent Print Data	<Escape>&p#X [data]	1B 26 70 # 58 [data]
	Horizontal Motion Index	<Escape>&k#H	1B 26 6B # 48
	Carriage Return=CR	<Escape>&k0G	1B 26 6B 30 47
	Carriage Return=CR+LF	<Escape>&k1G	1B 26 6B 31 47
	LF=CR+LF, FF=CR+FF	<Escape>&k2G	1B 26 6B 32 47
	Add CR to LF and FF, CR=CR+LF	<Escape>&k3G	1B 26 6B 33 47
	Enable End of Line Wrap	<Escape>&s0C	1B 26 73 30 43
	Disable End of Line Wrap	<Escape>&s1C	1B 26 73 31 43
	Number of Copies	<Escape>&1#X	1B 26 6C # 58
	Eject Page	<Escape>&l0H	1B 26 6C 30 48
	Feed From Tray	<Escape>&l1H	1B 26 6C 31 48
	Manual Feed	<Escape>&l2H	1B 26 6C 32 48
	Envelope Feed	<Escape>&l3H	1B 26 6C 33 48
Laserjet +/500+ Extensions	Graphics Horz Cursor Position	<Escape>*p#X	1B 2A 70 # 58
	Graphics Vert Cursor Position	<Escape>*p#Y	1B 2A 70 # 59
	Font ID Number	<Escape>*c#D	1B 2A 63 # 44
	ASCII Char Code Number	<Escape>*c#E	1B 2A 63 # 45
	Create Font	<Escape>)s#W [data]	1B 29 73 # 57 [data]
	Download Character	<Escape>(s#W [data]	1B 28 73 # 57 [data]
	Primary Font ID Number	<Escape>(#X	1B 28 # 58
	Secondary Font ID Number	<Escape>)#X	1B 29 # 58
	Delete all Fonts	<Escape>*c0F	1B 2A 63 30 46
	Delete all Temp Fonts	<Escape>*c1F	1B 2A 63 31 46
	Delete Last Font ID specified	<Escape>*c2F	1B 2A 63 32 46
	Delete Last Font ID & Char Code	<Escape>*c3F	1B 2A 63 33 46
	Make Temporary Font	<Escape>*c4F	1B 2A 63 34 46
	Make Permanent Font	<Escape>*c5F	1B 2A 63 35 46
	Copy/Assign	<Escape>*c6F	1B 2A 63 36 46
	Primary Font Value 0	<Escape>(0@	1B 28 30 40
	Primary Font Value 1	<Escape>(1@	1B 28 31 40
	Primary Font Value 2	<Escape>(2@	1B 28 32 40
	Primary Font Value 3	<Escape>(3@	1B 28 33 40
	Secondary Font Value 0	<Escape>)0@	1B 29 30 40
	Secondary Font Value 1	<Escape>)1@	1B 29 31 40
	Secondary Font Value 2	<Escape>)2@	1B 29 32 40
	Secondary Font Value 3	<Escape>)3@	1B 29 33 40
	Macro ID	<Escape>&f#Y	1B 26 66 # 59
	Start Macro	<Escape>&f0X	1B 26 66 30 58
	Stop Macro	<Escape>&f1X	1B 26 66 31 58
	Execute Macro	<Escape>&f2X	1B 26 66 32 58
	Call Macro	<Escape>&f3X	1B 26 66 33 58
	Enable Overlay	<Escape>&f4X	1B 26 66 34 58
	Disable Overlay	<Escape>&f5X	1B 26 66 35 58
	Delete Macros	<Escape>&f6X	1B 26 66 36 58
	Delete all Temporary Macros	<Escape>&f7X	1B 26 66 37 58
	Delete Macro ID	<Escape>&f8X	1B 26 66 38 58
	Make Macro Temporary	<Escape>&f9X	1B 26 66 39 58
	Make Macro Permanent	<Escape>&f10X	1B 26 66 31 30 58
	Push Position	<Escape>&f0S	1B 26 66 30 53
	Pop Position	<Escape>&f1S	1B 26 66 31 53
	Horz # dots in pattern	<Escape>*c#A	1B 2A 63 # 41
	Horz # decipoints in pattern	<Escape>*c#H	1B 2A 63 # 48
	Vert # dots in pattern	<Escape>*c#B	1B 2A 63 # 42
	Vert # decipoints in pattern	<Escape>*c#V	1B 2A 63 # 56
	Print Rule	<Escape>*c0P	1B 2A 63 30 50
	Print Gray Scale	<Escape>*c2P	1B 2A 63 32 50
	Print HP Pattern	<Escape>*c3P	1B 2A 63 33 50

(Continued)

Table 7.48. Continued

Function Type	Function	Code Sequence in ASCII Chars	Code Sequence in Hex Bytes
Laserjet+/500 i Extensions	Print 2% Gray Scale	<Escape>*c2G	1B 2A 63 32 47
	Print 10% Gray Scale	<Escape>*c10G	1B 2A 63 31 30 47
	Print 15% Gray Scale	<Escape>*c15G	1B 2A 63 31 35 47
	Print 30% Gray Scale	<Escape>*c30G	1B 2A 63 33 30 47
	Print 45% Gray Scale	<Escape>*c45G	1B 2A 63 34 35 47
	Print 70% Gray Scale	<Escape>*c70G	1B 2A 63 37 30 47
	Print 90% Gray Scale	<Escape>*c90G	1B 2A 63 39 30 47
	Print 100% Gray Scale	<Escape>*c100G	1B 2A 63 31 30 30 47
	HP Pattern 1 Vert Lines	<Escape>*c1G	1B 2A 63 31 47
	HP Pattern 2 Horz lines	<Escape>*c2G	1B 2A 63 32 47
	HP Pattern 3 Diagonal Lines	<Escape>*c3G	1B 2A 63 33 47
	HP Pattern 4 Diagonal Lines	<Escape>*c4G	1B 2A 63 34 47
	HP Pattern 5 Grid	<Escape>*c5G	1B 2A 63 35 47
	HP Pattern 6 Diagonal Grid	<Escape>*c6G	1B 2A 63 36 47
Laserjet 500+ Extensions	Default Stacking Position	<Escape>&l0T	1B 26 6C 30 54
	Toggle Stacking Position	<Escape>&l1T	1B 26 6C 31 54
	Eject Page	<Escape>&l0H	1B 26 6C 30 48
	Feed from Upper Cassette	<Escape>&l1H	1B 26 6C 31 48
	Manual Feed	<Escape>&l2H	1B 26 6C 32 48
	Envelope Feed	<Escape>&l3H	1B 26 6C 33 48
	Feed from Lower Cassette	<Escape>&l4H	1B 26 6C 34 48

Notes: • # should be replaced by the relevant numeric value in this chart
                    •[data] indicates a bitstream of appropriately formatted data

Source: HP Laserjet Printer Family Technical Reference Manual, pages A1-A6

See Also: 7.47. IBM Printer Control Codes Summary

7.49. AT REAL TIME CLOCK RAM CONFIGURATION USAGE

Address	Function	Comments
0H	Seconds	
1H	Second alarm	
2H	Minutes	
3H	Minute alarm	
4H	Hours	
5H	Hour alarm	
6H	Day of week	
7H	Day in month	
8H	Month	
9H	Year	
0AH	Status register A	See 7.50. AT Real Time Clock Status Register A
0BH	Status register B	See 7.51. AT Real Time Clock Status Register B
0CH	Status register C	See 7.52. AT Real Time Clock Status Register C
0DH	Status register D	See 7.53. AT Real Time Clock Status Register D
0EH	Diagnostic status byte	See 7.54. AT Real Time Clock Diagnostic Status Byte
0FH	Shutdown status byte	Defined by power-on diagnostics
10H	Disk drive type byte	See 7.55. AT Real Time Clock Diskette Drive Type Byte
11H	RESERVED	
12H	Fixed drive type byte	See 7.56. AT Real Time Clock Fixed Drive Type Byte
13H	RESERVED	
14H	Equipment byte	See 7.57. AT Real Time Clock Equipment Byte
15H	Low-base memory byte	
16H	High-base memory byte	100H=256K, 200H=512K, 280H=640K
17H	Low expansion memory byte	
18H	High expansion memory byte	200H=512K, 400H=1024K, 600-3C00H=up to 15360K
19H	Drive C extended byte	See 8.30 AT Fixed Disk Drive Types
1AH	Drive D extended byte	See 8.30 AT Fixed Disk Drive Types

(Continued)

Table 7.49. Continued

Address	Function	Comments
1BH-2DH	RESERVED	
2EH-2FH	Checksum	Checksum based on 10-2DH addresses
30H	Low expansion memory byte	
31H	High expansion memory byte	200H=512K, 400H=1024K, 600-3C00H=up to 15360K
32H	Date century byte	BCD value for century
33H	Information flags	Bit 7 set = top 128K installed, bit 6 set = first user message
34H-3FH	RESERVED	

Source: IBM PC/AT Technical Reference, pages 1-56 to 1-68

See Also: 7.50. AT Real Time Clock Status Register A
7.51. AT Real Time Clock Status Register B
7.52. AT Real Time Clock Status Register C
7.53. AT Real Time Clock Status Register D
7.54. AT Real Time Clock Diagnostic Status Byte
7.55. AT Real Time Clock Diskette Drive Type Byte
7.56. AT Real Time Clock Fixed Drive Type Byte
7.57. AT Real Time Clock Equipment Byte
8.30 AT Fixed Disk Drive Types

7.50. AT REAL TIME CLOCK STATUS REGISTER A

Bit Numbers

7	6	5	4	3	2	1	0	Name	Function	Allowable Values
X								Update in progress	Indicates update cycle in progress	0=date/time available, 1=date/time being updated
	X	X	X					22-stage divider	Identifies time-base frequency used	default=010, 32.768KHz time base
				X	X	X	X	Rate selection	Identifies divider output frequency	default=0110, 1.024KHz frequency

Source: IBM PC/AT Technical Reference, pages 1-57 to 1-58

See Also: 7.51. AT Real Time Clock Status Register B
7.52. AT Real Time Clock Status Register C
7.53. AT Real Time Clock Status Register D

7.51. AT REAL TIME CLOCK STATUS REGISTER B

Bit Numbers

7	6	5	4	3	2	1	0	Name	Function	Allowable Values
X								Set	Advances count (1-per second)	0=update normally, 1=abort update cycle
	X							Periodic Int enable	Allows interrupts at status reg A settings	0=disable int (default), 1=enable int
		X						Alarm int enable	Sets alarm interrupt	0=disabled (default), 1=enabled
			X					Update-ended Int enable	Sets end-of-update interrupt	0=disabled (default), 1=enabled
				X				Square wave enable	Sets frequency as per status reg A 0-3 bits	0=disabled (default), 1=enabled
					X			Date mode	Sets binary or BCD updates	0=BCD (default), 1=binary
						X		24/12 mode	Sets hours format in time	0=12-hour clock, 1=24-hour clock (default)
							X	Daylight savings enable	Sets clock to recognize daylight savings	0=disabled (default), 1=enabled

Source: IBM PC/AT Technical Reference, pages 1-58 to 1-59

See Also: 7.50. AT Real Time Clock Status Register A
7.52. AT Real Time Clock Status Register C
7.53. AT Real Time Clock Status Register D

7.52 AT REAL TIME CLOCK STATUS REGISTER C

Bit Numbers

7	6	5	4	3	2	1	0	Name	Function	Allowable Values
X								IRQF flag		Read only
	X							PF flag		Read only
		X						AF flag		Read only
			X					UF flag		Read only
				X	X	X	X	RESERVED		Should always be 0

Source: IBM PC/AT Technical Reference, page 1-59

See Also: 7.50. AT Real Time Clock Status Register A
7.51. AT Real Time Clock Status Register B
7.53. AT Real Time Clock Status Register D

7.53. AT REAL TIME CLOCK STATUS REGISTER D

Bit Numbers

7	6	5	4	3	2	1	0	Name	Function	Allowable Values
X								Valid RAM bit	Status of power-sense pin (bat. level)	0=battery dead, RAM invalid, 1=battery good
	X	X	X	X	X	X	X	RESERVED		Should always be 0

Source: IBM PC/AT Technical Reference, page 1-59

See Also: 7.50. AT Real Time Clock Status Register A
                   7.51. AT Real Time Clock Status Register B
                   7.52. AT Real Time Clock Status Register C

7.54. AT REAL TIME CLOCK DIAGNOSTIC STATUS BYTE

Bit Numbers

7	6	5	4	3	2	1	0	Function	Allowable Values
X								Power status of RTC chip	0=chip hasn't lost power, 1=chip has lost power
	X							Configuration record (checksum status)	0=checksum is good, 1=checksum bad
		X						Incorrect configuration information	0=valid configuration, 1=invalid configuration
			X					Memory size comparison	0=power-on check showed same memory size, 1=diff. size
				X				Fixed disk status	0=proper function, 1=adapter or drive failed initialization
					X			Time status indicator	0=time is valid, 1=time invalid
						X	X	RESERVED	

Source: IBM PC/AT Technical Reference, pages 1-59 to 1-60

See Also: 7.49. AT Real Time Clock RAM Configuration Usage

7.55. AT REAL TIME CLOCK DISKETTE DRIVE TYPE BYTE

Bit Numbers

7	6	5	4	3	2	1	0	Function	Allowable Values
X	X	X	X					Type of first diskette drive	0000=no drive, 0001=48TPI, 0010=96TPI
				X	X	X	X	Type of second diskette drive	0000=no drive, 0001=48TPI, 0010=96TPI

Source: IBM PC/AT Technical Reference, page 1-61

See Also: 7.49. AT Real Time Clock RAM Configuration Usage

7.56. AT REAL TIME CLOCK FIXED DRIVE TYPE BYTE

Bit Numbers

7	6	5	4	3	2	1	0	Function	Allowable Values
X	X	X	X					Type of first fixed drive	0000=no drive, otherwise see 8.30. AT Fixed Disk Drive Types
				X	X	X	X	Type of second fixed drive	0000=no drive, otherwise see 8.30. AT Fixed Disk Drive Types

Source: IBM PC/AT Technical Reference, page 1-62

See Also: 7.49. AT Real Time Clock RAM Configuration Usage
                   8.30. AT Fixed Disk Drive Types

7.57. AT REAL TIME CLOCK EQUIPMENT BYTE

Bit Numbers

7	6	5	4	3	2	1	0	Function	Allowable Values
X	X							Number of disk drives	00=1 drive, 01=2 drives, other values RESERVED
		X	X					Primary display type	00=display has own BIOS, 01=40 col CGA, 10=80 col CGA, 11=MDA
				X	X			NOT USED	
						X		Math coprocessor	0=not installed, 1=math coprocessor available
							X	Disk drives available	0=no disk drives available, 1=disk drives available

Source: IBM PC/AT Technical Reference, pages 1-63 to 1-64

See Also: 7.49. AT Real Time Clock RAM Configuration Usage

SECTION

8

Chips, Jumpers, Switches, and Registers

8.01. 8086 FAMILY MEMORY ADDRESSING MODES

Mode	Example	Explanation
Direct register addressing	ADD AX,CX	Uses contents of registers for operation
Indirect memory addressing	ADD AX,[CX] ADD [CX],AX	Uses CX as a relative offset to point to memory
Immediate addressing	ADD AX,123	Uses immediate value (123)
Relative memory addressing	ADD AX,[123]	Immediate value (123) is relative offset to point to memory
Indexed indirect addressing	ADD AX,[BX+SI]	Uses BX+SI as relative offset to point to memory

Source: *Programmer's Guide to the IBM PC* (Microsoft Press), Peter Norton,
                       pages 34 to 35

8.02. 8086 FAMILY INSTRUCTION SET SUMMARY

Instruction	Function	Clock Cycles**	Bytes***	Flags Affected	Undefined Flags	8088/86	80286	80386
AAA	ASCII adjust AL after add	3	1	Aux, carry	Overflow, sign, zero, parity	X	X	X
AAD	ASCII adjust before divide	14	2	Sign, zero, parity	Overflow, aux, carry	X	X	X
AAM	ASCII adjust after multiply	16	2	Sign, zero, parity	Overflow, aux, carry	X	X	X
AAS	ASCII adjust after subtract	3	1	Aux, carry	Overflow, sign, zero, parity	X	X	X
ADC accum, imm****	Add with carry	3	2 - 3	Overflow, sign, zero, aux, parity, carry	None	X	X	X
ADC mem, imm	Add with carry	7*	3 - 6	Overflow, sign, zero, aux, parity, carry	None	X	X	X
ADC mem, reg	Add with carry	7*	2 - 4	Overflow, sign, zero, aux, parity, carry	None	X	X	X
ADC reg, imm	Add with carry	3	3 - 4	Overflow, sign, zero, aux, parity, carry	None	X	X	X
ADC reg, mem	Add with carry	7*	2 - 4	Overflow, sign, zero, aux, parity, carry	None	X	X	X
ADC reg, reg	Add with carry	2	2	Overflow, sign, zero, aux, parity, carry	None	X	X	X
ADD accum, imm****	Add	3	2 - 3	Overflow, sign, zero, aux, parity, carry	None	X	X	X
ADD mem, imm	Add	7*	3 - 6	Overflow, sign, zero, aux, parity, carry	None	X	X	X
ADD mem, reg	Add	7*	2 - 4	Overflow, sign, zero, aux, parity, carry	None	X	X	X
ADD reg, imm	Add	3	3 - 4	Overflow, sign, zero, aux, parity, carry	None	X	X	X
ADD reg, mem	Add	7*	2 - 4	Overflow, sign, zero, aux, parity, carry	None	X	X	X
ADD reg, reg	Add	2	2	Overflow, sign, zero, aux, parity, carry	None	X	X	X
AND accum, imm****	Logical AND	3	2 - 3	Overflow=0, sign, zero, parity, carry=0	None	X	X	X
AND mem, imm	Logical AND	7*	3 - 6	Overflow=0, sign, zero, parity, carry=0	None	X	X	X
AND mem, reg	Logical AND	7*	2 - 4	Overflow=0, sign, zero, parity, carry=0	None	X	X	X
AND reg, imm	Logical AND	3	3 - 4	Overflow=0, sign, zero, parity, carry=0	None	X	X	X
AND reg, reg	Logical AND	2	2	Overflow=0, sign, zero, parity, carry=0	None	X	X	X
AND reg, mem	Logical AND	7*	2 - 4	Overflow=0, sign, zero, parity, carry=0	None	X	X	X
ARPL	Adjust requested privilege level	10*, 11*	2 - 3	ZF	None		X	X
BOUND reg,source	Detect array index out of range	13*	2	None	None		X	X
BSF reg, mem or reg, reg	Bit scan forward	10+bytes	3 - 4	ZF	None			X
BSR reg, mem or reg, reg	Bit scan reverse	10+bytes	3 - 4	ZF	None			X
BT	Test bit	3, 6	3 - 5	CF	None			X
BTC	Test bit and complement	6, 8	3 - 5	CF	None			X
BTR	Test bit and reset	6, 8	3 - 5	CF	None			X
BTS	Test bit and scan	6, 8	3 - 5	CF	None			X
CALL 16memptr	Call (control transfer)	11+bytes*	2 - 4	None except when task switching	None	X	X	X
CALL 16regptr	Call (control transfer)	7+bytes	2	None except when task switching	None	X	X	X
CALL 32memptr	Call (control transfer)	16+bytes	2 - 4	None except when task switching	None			X
CALL farproc	Call (control transfer)	13+bytes*	5	None except when task switching	None	X	X	X
CALL nearproc	Call (control transfer)	7+bytes	3	None except when task switching	None	X	X	X
CBW/CWDE	Convert byte to word/word to double word	2	1	None	None	X	X	X
CLC	Clear carry	2	1	Carry=0	None	X	X	X
CLD	Clear direction	2	1	Direction=0	None	X	X	X
CLI	Clear interrupt	3	1	Interrupt=0	None	X	X	X
CLTS	Clear task switched flag	5	2	TS=0 in CR0 register	None		X	X
CMC	Complement carry	2	1	Carry	None	X	X	X
CMP accum, imm****	Compare	3	2 - 3	Overflow, sign, zero, aux, parity, carry	None	X	X	X
CMP mem,imm	Compare	6*	3 - 6	Overflow, sign, zero, aux, parity, carry	None	X	X	X
CMP mem,reg	Compare	7*	2 - 4	Overflow, sign, zero, aux, parity, carry	None	X	X	X
CMP reg,imm	Compare	3	3 - 4	Overflow, sign, zero, aux, parity, carry	None	X	X	X
CMP reg,mem	Compare	6*	2 - 4	Overflow, sign, zero, aux, parity, carry	None	X	X	X
CMP reg,reg	Compare	2	2	Overflow, sign, zero, aux, parity, carry	None	X	X	X
CMPS (rep) deststr,sourcestr	Compare byte, word or double word string	5+9(rep)	1	Overflow, sign, zero, aux, parity, carry	None	X	X	X
CMPS deststr, sourcestr	Compare byte, word or double word	8	1	Overflow, sign, zero, aux, parity, carry	None	X	X	X
CLTS	Clear task switched flag	2	2	None	None		X	X
CWD/CDQ	Convert word to double word/dw to qw	2	1	None	None	X	X	X
DAA/DAS	Decimal adjust after add/subtract	3	1	Sign, zero, aux, parity, carry	None	X	X	X
DEC mem	Decrement	7*	2 - 4	Overflow, sign, zero, aux, parity	None	X	X	X
DEC reg	Decrement	2	1 - 2	Overflow, sign, zero, aux, parity	None	X	X	X
DIV 16mem	Divide	25*	2 - 4	None	Overflow, sign, zero, aux, parity, carry	X	X	X

(Continued)

Table 8.02. Continued

Instruction	Function	Clock Cycles**	Bytes***	Flags Affected	Undefined Flags	8088/86	80286	80386
DIV 16reg	Divide	22	2	None	Overflow, sign, zero, aux, parity, carry	X	X	X
DIV 8mem	Divide	17*	2 - 4	None	Overflow, sign, zero, aux, parity, carry	X	X	X
DIV 8reg	Divide	14	2	None	Overflow, sign, zero, aux, parity, carry	X	X	X
ENTER 16imm,0	Enter procedure	11	4	None	None		X	X
ENTER 16imm,1	Enter procedure	15	4	None	None		X	X
ENTER 16imm,level	Enter procedure	12+4(L)	4	None	None		X	X
ESC imm,mem	Escape to external device	9-20*	2 - 4	None	None	X	X	X
ESC imm,reg	Escape to external device	2	2	None	None	X	X	X
HLT	Halt	2	1	None	None	X	X	X
IDIV 16mem	Signed integer divide	28*	2 - 4	None	Overflow, sign, zero, aux, parity, carry	X	X	X
IDIV 16reg	Signed integer divide	25	2	None	Overflow, sign, zero, aux, parity, carry	X	X	X
IDIV 8mem	Signed integer divide	20*	2 - 4	None	Overflow, sign, zero, aux, parity, carry	X	X	X
IDIV 8reg	Signed integer divide	17	2	None	Overflow, sign, zero, aux, parity, carry	X	X	X
IMUL 16mem	Signed integer multiply	24*	2 - 4	Overflow, carry	Sign, zero, aux, parity	X	X	X
IMUL 16reg	Signed integer multiply	21	2	Overflow, carry	Sign, zero, aux, parity	X	X	X
IMUL 8mem	Signed integer multiply	16*	2 - 4	Overflow, carry	Sign, zero, aux, parity	X	X	X
IMUL 8reg	Signed integer multiply	13	2	Overflow, carry	Sign, zero, aux, parity	X	X	X
IMUL destreg,16reg,imm	Signed integer multiply	21	3 - 4	Overflow, carry	Sign, zero, aux, parity		X	X
IMUL destreg,mem,imm	Signed integer multiply	24*	3 - 4	Overflow, carry	Sign, zero, aux, parity		X	X
IN accum,DX	Input from DX port	5	1	None	None	X	X	X
IN accum,8imm	Input from port	5	2	None	None	X	X	X
INC mem	Increment	7*	2 - 4	Overflow, sign, zero, aux, parity	None	X	X	X
INC reg	Increment	2	1 - 2	Overflow, sign, zero, aux, parity	None	X	X	X
INS (rep) deststr, DX	Input string	5+4(rep)	1	None	None		X	X
INS deststr,DX	Input string	5	1	None	None		X	X
INT 8imm	Interrupt	23+bytes	1 - 2	Interrupt=0,trap=0	None	X	X	X
INTO	Interrupt on overflow	24+bytes or 3	1	Interrupt=0,trap=0	None	X	X	X
IRET	Interrupt return	17+bytes	1	All	None	X	X	X
JMP 16memptr	Unconditional jump	11+bytes*	2 - 4	None	None	X	X	X
JMP 16regptr	Unconditional jump	7+bytes	2	None	None	X	X	X
JMP 32memptr	Unconditional jump	15+bytes*	2 - 4	None	None	X	X	X
JMP far	Unconditional jump	11+bytes	5	None	None	X	X	X
JMP near	Unconditional jump	7+bytes	3	None	None	X	X	X
JMP short	Unconditional jump	7+bytes	2	None	None	X	X	X
Jxxx short	Conditional jump	7+bytes or 3	2	None	None	X	X	X
LAHF	Load AH with flags (LO byte of flags)	2	1	None	None	X	X	X
LAR	Load access rights byte	14,16*	3 - 4	ZF	None		X	X
LDS 16reg,32mem	Load pointer to DS	7*	2 - 4	None	None	X	X	X
LEA 16reg,16mem	Load effective address to register	3*	2 - 4	None	None	X	X	X
LEAVE	Leave procedure	5	1	None	None		X	X
LES 16reg,32mem	Load pointer to ES	7*	2 - 4	None	None	X	X	X
LFS	Load pointer to FS	7	3 - 4	None	None			X
LGDT	Load global descriptor table	11*	3 - 4	None	None		X	X
LGS	Load pointer to GS	7	3 - 4	None	None			X
LIDT	Load interrupt descriptor table	12*	3 - 4	None	None		X	X
LLDT	Load local descriptor table	17,19*	3 - 4	None	None		X	X
LMSW	Load machine status word	3,6*	3 - 4	None	None		X	X
LOCK	Bus lock prefix	0	1	None	None	X	X	X
LODS (rep) sourcestr	Repeat load byte/word/dword	5+4(rep)	1	None	None	X	X	X
LODS sourcestr	Load byte/word/dword	5	1	None	None	X	X	X
LOOP short	Loop	8+bytes or 4	2	None	None	X	X	X
LOOPE/LOOPZ short	Loop equal/zoom	8+bytes or 4	2	None	None	X	X	X
LOOPNE/LOOPNZ short	Loop while not equal/not zero	8+bytes or 4	2	None	None	X	X	X

(Continued)

Table 8.02. Continued

Instruction	Function	Clock Cycles**	Bytes***	Flags Affected	Undefined Flags	8088/86	80286	80386
LSL	Load segment limit	14,16*	3-4	ZF	None		X	X
LSS	Load pointer to SS	7	3-4	None	None			X
LTR	Load task register	17,19*	3-4	None	None		X	X
MOV 16reg,segreg	Move	2	2	None	None	X	X	X
MOV accum,mem****	Move	5	3	None	None	X	X	X
MOV mem,accum****	Move	3	3	None	None	X	X	X
MOV mem,imm	Move	3*	3-6	None	None	X	X	X
MOV mem,reg	Move	3*	2-4	None	None	X	X	X
MOV mem,segreg	Move	3*	2-4	None	None	X	X	X
MOV reg,imm	Move	2	2-3	None	None	X	X	X
MOV reg,mem	Move	5*	2-4	None	None	X	X	X
MOV reg,reg	Move	2	2	None	None	X	X	X
MOV segreg,16mem	Move	5*	2-4	None	None	X	X	X
MOV segreg,16reg	Move	2	2	None	None	X	X	X
MOVS (repeat) deststr,sourcestr	Move string	5+4(rep)	1	None	None	X	X	X
MOVS deststr,sourcestr	Move string	5	1	None	None	X	X	X
MOVSX	Move with sign extension	3,6	3-4	None	None			X
MOVZX	Move with zero extension	3,6	3-4	None	None			X
MUL 16mem	Multiply	24*	2-4	Overflow, carry	Sign, zero, aux, parity	X	X	X
MUL 16reg	Multiply	21	2	Overflow, carry	Sign, zero, aux, parity	X	X	X
MUL 8mem	Multiply	16*	2-4	Overflow, carry	Sign, zero, aux, parity	X	X	X
MUL 8reg	Multiply	13	2	Overflow, carry	Sign, zero, aux, parity	X	X	X
NEG mem	Change sign	7*	2-4	Overflow, sign, zero, aux, parity, carry	None	X	X	X
NEG reg	Change sign	2	2	Overflow, sign, zero, aux, parity, carry	None	X	X	X
NOP	No operation	2	1	None	None	X	X	X
NOT mem	Invert	7*	2-4	None	None	X	X	X
NOT reg	Invert	2	2	None	None	X	X	X
OR accum,imm****	Logical OR	3	2-3	Overflow=0, sign, zero, parity, carry=0	Aux	X	X	X
OR mem,imm	Logical OR	7*	3-6	Overflow=0, sign, zero, parity, carry=0	Aux	X	X	X
OR mem,reg	Logical OR	7*	2-4	Overflow=0, sign, zero, parity, carry=0	Aux	X	X	X
OR reg,imm	Logical OR	3	3-6	Overflow=0, sign, zero, parity, carry=0	Aux	X	X	X
OR reg,mem	Logical OR	7*	2-4	Overflow=0, sign, zero, parity, carry=0	Aux	X	X	X
OR reg,reg	Logical OR	2	2	Overflow=0, sign, zero, parity, carry=0	Aux	X	X	X
OUT 8immed,accum	Output to port	3	2	None	None	X	X	X
OUT DX,accum	Output to DX port	3	1	None	None	X	X	X
OUTS (rep) DX,sourcestr	Output string	5+4(rep)	1	None	None		X	X
OUTS DX,sourcestr	Output string	5	1	None	None		X	X
POP mem	Restore from stack	5*	2-4	None	None	X	X	X
POP reg	Restore from stack	5	1	None	None	X	X	X
POPA	Restore all general registers from stack	19	1	None	None		X	X
POPF	Restore flags	5	1	All	None	X	X	X
PUSH imm	Save to stack	3*	2-3	None	None		X	X
PUSH mem	Save to stack	5*	2-4	None	None	X	X	X
PUSH reg	Save to stack	3	1	None	None	X	X	X
PUSHA	Save all to stack	17	1	None	None		X	X
PUSHF	Save flags to stack	3	1	None	None	X	X	X
RCL/RCR/ROL/ROR mem,1	Rotate carry left/carry right/left/right	7*	2-4	Overflow, carry	None	X	X	X
RCL/RCR/ROL/ROR mem,CL	Rotate carry left/carry right/left/right	8*+1 per bit	2-4	Carry	Overflow	X	X	X
RCL/RCR/ROL/ROR mem,count	Rotate carry left/carry right/left/right	8*+1 per bit	3-5	Carry	Overflow		X	X
RCL/RCR/ROL/ROR reg,1	Rotate carry left/carry right/left/right	2	2	Overflow, carry	None	X	X	X
RCL/RCR/ROL/ROR reg,CL	Rotate carry left/carry right/left/right	5+1 per bit	2	Carry	Overflow	X	X	X
RCL/RCR/ROL/ROR reg,count	Rotate carry left/carry right/left/right	5+1 per bit	3	Carry	Overflow		X	X
REP	Repeat	0	1	None	None	X	X	X
REPE/REPZ	Repeat equal/zero	0	1	None	None	X	X	X
REPNE/REPNZ	Repeat not equal/not zero	0	1	None	None	X	X	X
RET (far with pop)	Return	15+bytes	3	None	None	X	X	X
RET (far, no pop)	Return	15+bytes	1	None	None	X	X	X

(Continued)

Table 8.02. Continued

Instruction	Function	Clock Cycles**	Bytes***	Flags Affected	Undefined Flags	8088/86	80286	80386
RET (near with pop)	Return	11+bytes	3	None	None	X	X	X
RET (near, no pop)	Return	11+bytes	1	None	None	X	X	X
SAHF	Store AH into flags	2	1	Sign, zero, aux, parity, carry	None	X	X	X
SAL/SHL/SAR/SHR mem,1	Shift arithmetic left/left/arithmetic right/right	7*	2 - 4	Overflow=0, sign, zero, parity, carry	Zero (SAR/SHR aux only)	X	X	X
SAL/SHL/SAR/SHR mem,CL	Shift arithmetic left/left/arithmetic right/right	8*+1 per bit	2 - 4	Sign, zero, parity, carry (SHR sign=0)	Overflow, zero (SAR/SHR overflow, aux only)	X	X	X
SAL/SHL/SAR/SHR mem,count	Shift arithmetic left/left/arithmetic right/right	8*+1 per bit	3 - 5	Sign, zero, parity, carry (SHR sign=0)	Overflow, zero (SAR/SHR overflow, aux only)		X	X
SAL/SHL/SAR/SHR reg,1	Shift arithmetic left/left/arithmetic right/right only	2	2	Overflow=0, sign, zero, parity, carry	Zero (SAR/SHR Aux only)	X	X	X
SAL/SHL/SAR/SHR reg,CL	Shift arithmetic left/left/arithmetic right/right	5+1 per bit	2	Sign, zero, parity, carry	Overflow, zero (SAR/SHR overflow, aux only)	X	X	X
SAL/SHL/SAR/SHR reg,count	Shift arithmetic left/left/arithmetic right/right	5+1 per bit	3	Sign, zero, parity, carry (SHR sign=0)	Overflow, zero (SAR/SHR overflow, aux only)		X	X
SBB accum,imm****	Subtract with borrow	3	2 - 3	Overflow, sign, zero, aux, parity, carry	None	X	X	X
SBB mem,imm	Subtract with borrow	7*	3 - 6	Overflow, sign, zero, aux, parity, carry	None	X	X	X
SBB mem,reg	Subtract with borrow	7*	2 - 4	Overflow, sign, zero, aux, parity, carry	None	X	X	X
SBB reg,imm	Subtract with borrow	3	3 - 4	Overflow, sign, zero, aux, parity, carry	None	X	X	X
SBB reg,mem	Subtract with borrow	7*	2 - 4	Overflow, sign, zero, aux, parity, carry	None	X	X	X
SBB reg,reg	Subtract with borrow	2	2	Overflow, sign, zero, aux, parity, carry	None	X	X	X
SCAS (repeat) deststr	Scan byte/word	5+8(rep)	1	Overflow, sign, zero, aux, parity, carry	None	X	X	X
SCAS deststr	Scan byte/word	7	1	Overflow, sign, zero, aux, parity, carry	None	X	X	X
SETxxx	Conditional byte set	4, 5	3 - 5	None	None			X
SGDT	Store global descriptor table	11*	3 - 4	None	None		X	X
SIDT	Store interrupt descriptor table	12*	3 - 4	None	None		X	X
SLDT	Store local descriptor table	2,3*	3 - 4	None	None		X	X
SMSW	Store machine status word	2,3*	3 - 4	None	None		X	X
STC/STD/STI	Set carry/direction/interrupt	2	1	Carry=1/DF=1/IF=1	None	X	X	X
STOS (repeat) deststr	Store byte/word	4+3(rep)	1	None	None	X	X	X
STOS deststr	Store byte/word	3	1	None	None	X	X	X
STR	Store task register	2,3*	3 - 4	None	None		X	X
SUB accum,imm****	Subtract	3	2 - 3	Overflow, sign, zero, aux, parity, carry	None	X	X	X
SUB mem,imm	Subtract	6*	3 - 6	Overflow, sign, zero, aux, parity, carry	None	X	X	X
SUB mem,reg	Subtract	7*	2 - 4	Overflow, sign, zero, aux, parity, carry	None	X	X	X
SUB reg,imm	Subtract	3	3 - 4	Overflow, sign, zero, aux, parity, carry	None	X	X	X
SUB reg,mem	Subtract	6*	2 - 4	Overflow, sign, zero, aux, parity, carry	None	X	X	X
SUB reg,reg	Subtract	2	2	Overflow, sign, zero, aux, parity, carry	None	X	X	X
TEST accum,imm****	AND function to flags	3	2 - 3	Overflow=0, sign, zero, parity, carry=0	Aux	X	X	X
TEST mem,imm	AND function to flags	6*	3 - 6	Overflow=0, sign, zero, parity, carry=0	Aux	X	X	X
TEST reg,imm	AND function to flags	3	3 - 4	Overflow=0, sign, zero, parity, carry=0	Aux	X	X	X
TEST reg,mem	AND function to flags	6*	2 - 4	Overflow=0, sign, zero, parity, carry=0	Aux	X	X	X
TEST reg,reg	AND function to flags	2	2	Overflow=0, sign, zero, parity, carry=0	Aux	X	X	X
VERR	Verify read access	14,16*	3 - 4	ZF	None		X	X
VERW	Verify write access	14,16*	3 - 4	ZF	None		X	X
WAIT	Wait for 80X87	3	1	None	None	X	X	X
XCHG accum,16reg****	Exchange	3	1	None	None	X	X	X
XCHG mem,reg	Exchange	5*	2 - 4	None	None	X	X	X
XCHG reg,reg	Exchange	3	2	None	None	X	X	X
XLAT sourcetable	Translate byte	5	1	None	None	X	X	X
XOR accum,imm****	Exclusive OR	3	2 - 3	Overflow=0, sign, zero, parity, carry=0	Aux	X	X	X
XOR mem,imm	Exclusive OR	7*	3 - 6	Overflow=0, sign, zero, parity, carry=0	Aux	X	X	X
XOR mem,reg	Exclusive OR	7*	2 - 4	Overflow=0, sign, zero, parity, carry=0	Aux	X	X	X
XOR reg,imm	Exclusive OR	3	3 - 4	Overflow=0, sign, zero, parity, carry=0	Aux	X	X	X
XOR reg,mem	Exclusive OR	7*	2 - 4	Overflow=0, sign, zero, parity, carry=0	Aux	X	X	X
XOR reg,reg	Exclusive OR	2	2	Overflow=0, sign, zero, parity, carry=0	Aux	X	X	X

(Continued)

Legend:

Reg=register
Mem=memory
Accum=accumulator (AL, AX, EAX)
Imm=immediate
Deststr=destination string
Sourcestr=source string
Segreg=segment register
Number preceding item indicates number of bits

Flags: EFLAGS is a 32 bit register in the 80386
       FLAGS (LO word of EFLAGS) is a 16 bit register

Table 8.02. Continued

Bit	Abbr.	Name
0	CF	Carry Flag
1		RESERVED
2	PF	Parity flag
3		RESERVED
4	AF	Auxiliary carry flag
5		RESERVED
6	ZF	Zero flag
7	SF	Sign flag
8	TF	Trap flag
9	IF	Interrupt enable
10	DF	Direction flag
11	OF	Overflow
12-13	IOPL	I/O privilege level
14	NT	Nested tank flag
15		RESERVED
16	RF	Resume flag (80386 only)
17	VM	Virtual 8086 mode (80386 only)
18-31		RESERVED

Notes:
- •"+Bytes" means plus additional cycle for each byte following instruction.
- •Uses additional cycle if using base indexed addressing.
- •**Clock cycles vary, depending upon actual CPU used. Timings here are typical for 8088; see your CPU Technical Reference for complete timing considerations.
- •***Number of bytes in instruction varies slightly depending on actual CPU used. Bytes shown here are for 8088/8086 except for instructions that are specific to 286 or 386.
- •****Instructions that use AL, AX, or EAX are faster than equivalent instructions using any other register.

Source: *Assembly Language Programming for the IBM PC/AT* (Robert J. Brady Co.), Leo Scanlon, pages 421 to 430
Intel Microprocessor and Peripheral Handbook Volume 1, pages 2-26 to 2-30, 2-55 to 2-59, 2-85 to 2-89, 2-117 to 2-121, 3-46 to 3-53, 4-106 to 4-119
Intel 80386 Programmer's Reference Manual, pages 17-18 to 17-174

8.03. 8086 FAMILY REGISTER SUMMARY

For 8088/8086/80286:

```
<--------------------- 16 bits --------------------->
<------- 8 bits ---------> <------- 8 bits --------->
```

			Intel name for register
AX	AH	AL	Accumulator
BX	BH	BL	Base
CX	CH	CL	Count
DX	DH	DL	Data

S P	Stack Pointer
B P	Base Pointer
S I	Source Index
D I	Destination Index
I P	Instruction Pointer
	Status Flags ---->
C S	Code Segment
D S	Data Segment
S S	Stack Segment
E S	Extra Segment

Bit Numbers

15	14	13	12	11	10	9	8	7	6	5	4	3	2	1	0
-	NT	IO	PL	OF	DF	IF	TF	SF	ZF	-	AF	-	PF	-	CF

NT=nested task	IF=interrupt flag	AF=auxiliary carry
IOPL=I/O privilege level	TF=trap flag	PF=parity flag
OF=overflow flag	SF=sign flag	CF=carry flag
DF=direction flag	ZF=zero flag	

(Continued)

Table 8.03. Continued

For 80386:

```
<----------------------- 32 bits ----------------------->     Intel name for register
<------- 16 bits --------> <------- 16 bits --------->
```

Register			Intel name for register
EAX		AX	Extended Accumulator
EBX		BX	Extended Base
ECX		CX	Extended Count
EDX		DX	Extended Data
ESP		SP	Stack Pointer
EBP		BP	Base Pointer
ESI		SI	Source Index
EDI		DI	Destination Index
EIP		IP	Instruction Pointer
EFLAGS		FLAGS	Status Flags ---->

Bit Numbers for 8086 compatible flags

15	14	13	12	11	10	9	8	7	6	5	4	3	2	1	0
-	NT	IO	PL	OF	DF	IF	TF	SF	ZF	-	AF	-	PF	-	CF

NT=nested task	IF=interrupt flag	AF=auxiliary carry
IOPL=I/O privilege level	TF=trap flag	PF=parity flag
OF=overflow flag	SF=sign flag	CF=carry flag
DF=direction flag	ZF=zero flag	

Register	Intel name for register
CS	Code Segment
SS	Stack Segment
ES	Extra Segment
DS	Data Segment (1)
FS	Data Segment (2)
GS	Data Segment (3)

Bit Numbers for extended 80386 flags

31	30	29	28	27	26	25	24	23	22	21	20	19	18	17	16
						RESERVED FOR INTEL ONLY								VM	RF

VM=virtual 8086 mode   RF=resume flag

Register	Intel name for register	
CR0	Machine Control Register	(bit 31=paging enable, bit 4=coprocessor extension type, bit 3=task switched,
CR1 RESERVED		bit 2=emulate coprocessor,bit 1=monitor coprocessor, bit 0=protection enable)
CR2	Page Fault Linear Address	(entire 32-bits used for address)
CR3	Page Directory Base Address	(bits 12-31 are page directory base register, remaining bits reserved)
GDT (48 bits)	Global Descriptor Table	
IDT (48 bits)	Interrupt Descriptor Table	
LDT	Local Descriptor Table	
TSS	Task State Segment	
DR0	Debug Register 0 (linear breakpoint address 0)	
DR1	Debug Register 1 (linear breakpoint address 1)	
DR2	Debug Register 2 (linear breakpoint address 2)	
DR3	Debug Register 3 (linear breakpoint address 3)	
DR4	Intel Reserved	
DR5	Intel Reserved	
DR6	Breakpoint status	
DR7	Breakpoint Control	
TR6	Test Control	
TR7	Test Status	

Notes: 80286 also contains GDT, IDT, LDT, and TSS registers (see 80386 registers)

Source: Intel Microprocessor and Peripheral Handbook Volume 1, pages 2-12, 2-44, 2-97, 3-5 to 3-6, and 4-2 to 4-9

8.04. 8086 FAMILY CPU CHIP VERSIONS

Chip	Clock Speed	Comments
8086	5MHz	16-bit CPU in 40-pin CERDIP or plastic DIP package
8086-1	10MHz	16-bit CPU in 40-pin CERDIP or plastic DIP package
8086-2	8MHz	16-bit CPU in 40-pin CERDIP or plastic DIP package
80C86	5MHz	16-bit CMOS CPU in 40-pin DIP or 44-pin PLCC package
80C86-2	8MHz	16-bit CMOS CPU in 40-pin DIP or 44-pin PLCC package
8088	5MHz	8-bit CPU in 40-pin CERDIP package
8088-2	8MHz	8-bit CPU in 40-pin CERDIP package
80C88	5MHz	8-bit CMOS CPU in 40-pin DIP or 44-pin PLCC package
80C88-2	8MHz	8-bit CMOS CPU in 40-pin DIP or 44-pin PLCC package
80286-6	6MHz	16-bit Protection mode CPU in 68-pin LCC or PGA package
80286-8	8MHz	16-bit Protection mode CPU in 68-pin LCC or PGA package
80286-10	10MHz	16-bit Protection mode CPU in 68-pin LCC or PGA package
80286-12	12.5MHz	16-bit Protection mode CPU in 68-pin LCC or PGA package
80386	16 or 20MHz	32-bit Protection mode CPU in 132 PGA package

Notes: Numbers are Intel numbers only. NEC makes compatible CPUs with numbers like V10, V20, etc.

Source: Intel Microprocessor and Peripheral Handbook Volume 1

See Also: 9.36. 8088 and 8086 Pinouts
9.37. 80286 Pinouts
9.38. 80386 Pinouts

8.05. 8087 FAMILY INSTRUCTION SET SUMMARY

Instruction	Function	Clock Cycles	Transfers*	Exception Flags Affected	8087	80287	80387
F2XM1	2^X-1	310-630	0	Underflow, Precision	X	X	X
FABS	Absolute value	10-17	0	Invalid	X	X	X
FADD dest, source	Add real	70-125+EA	0-6	Invalid, Denormalized, Overflow, Underflow, Precision	X	X	X
FADDP dest, source	Add real and pop	75-105	0	Invalid, Denormalized, Overflow, Underflow, Precision	X	X	X
FBLD source	Packed decimal (BCD) load	290-310+EA	5-7	Invalid	X	X	X
FBSTP	Packed decimal (BCD) store and pop	520-540+EA	6-8	Invalid	X	X	X
FCHS	Change sign	10-17	0	Invalid	X	X	X
FCLEX/FNCLEX	Clear exceptions	2-8	0	None	X	X	X
FCOM source	Compare real	40-75+EA	0-6	Invalid, Denormalized	X	X	X
FCOMP source	Compare real and pop	42-77+EA	0-6	Invalid, Denormalized	X	X	X
FCOMPP	Compare real and pop twice	45-55	0	Invalid, Denormalized	X	X	X
FCOS	Cosine	123-772	0				X
FDECSTP	Decrement stack pointer	6-12	0	None	X	X	X
FDISI/FNDISI	Disable interrupts	2-8	0	None	X	Ignored	Ignored
FDIV dest,source	Divide real	193-230+EA	0-6	Invalid, Denormalized, ZeroDivide, Overflow, Underflow, Precision	X	X	X
FDIVP dest,source	Divide real and pop	197-207	0	Invalid, Denormalized, ZeroDivide, Overflow, Underflow, Precision	X	X	X
FDIVR dest,source	Divide real reversed	194-231+EA	0-6	Invalid, Denormalized, ZeroDivide, Overflow, Underflow, Precision	X	X	X
FDIVRP dest,source	Divide real reversed and pop	198-208	0	Invalid, Denormalized, ZeroDivide, Overflow, Underflow, Precision	X	X	X
FENI/FNENI	Enable interrupts	2-8	0	None	X	Ignored	Ignored
FFREE dest	Free register	9-16	0	None	X	X	X
FIADD source	Integer add	102-143+EA	1-4	Invalid, Denormalized, Overflow, Precision	X	X	X
FICOM source	Integer compare	72-91+EA	1-4	Invalid, Denormalized	X	X	X
FICOMP source	Integer compare and pop	74-93+EA	1-4	Invalid, Denormalized	X	X	X
FIDIV source	Integer divide	224-243+EA	1-4	Invalid, Denormalized, ZeroDivide, Overflow, Underflow, Precision	X	X	X
FIDIVR source	Integer divide reversed	225-245+EA	1-4	Invalid, Denormalized, ZeroDivide, Overflow, Underflow, Precision	X	X	X
FILD source	Integer load	46-68+EA	1-6	Invalid	X	X	X
FIMUL source	Integer multiply	124-144+EA	1-4	Invalid, Denormalized, Overflow, Precision	X	X	X
FINCSTP	Increment stack pointer	6-12	0	None	X	X	X
FINIT/FNINIT	Initialize processor	2-8	0	None	X	X	X
FIST dest	Integer store	80-92+EA	2-5	Invalid, Precision	X	X	X
FISTP dest	Integer store and pop	82-105+EA	2-7	Invalid, Precision	X	X	X
FISUB source	Integer subtract	102-143+EA	1-4	Invalid, Denormalized, Overflow, Precision	X	X	X
FISUBR source	Integer subtract reversed	103-144+EA	1-4	Invalid, Denormalized, Overflow, Precision	X	X	X
FLD source	Load real	17-65+EA	0-7	Invalid, Denormalized	X	X	X
FLD1	Load +1.0	15-21	0	Invalid	X	X	X
FLDCW source	Load control word	7-14+EA	1-2	None	X	X	X
FLDENV source	Load environment	35-45+EA	7-9	None	X	X	X
FLDL2E	Load log (2^e)	15-21	0	Invalid	X	X	X
FLDL2T	Load log (2^10)	16-22	0	Invalid	X	X	X
FLDLG2	Load log (10^2)	18-24	0	Invalid	X	X	X
FLDLN2	Load log (e^2)	17-23	0	Invalid	X	X	X
FLDPI	Load pi	16-22	0	Invalid	X	X	X
FLDZ	Load +0.0	11-17	0	Invalid	X	X	X
FMUL dest,source	Multiply real	90-168+EA	0-6	Invalid, Denormalized, Overflow, Underflow, Precision	X	X	X
FMULP dest, source	Multiply real and pop	94-148	0	Invalid, Denormalized, Overflow, Underflow, Precision	X	X	X
FNOP	No operation	10-16	0	None	X	X	X
FPATAN	Partial arctangent	250-800	0	Underflow, Precision	X	X	X
FPREM	Partial remainder	15-190	0	Invalid, Denormalized, Underflow	X	X	X
FPREM1	Partial remainder (IEEE)	95-185					X
FPTAN	Partial tangent	30-540	0	Invalid, Precision	X	X	X
FRNDINT	Round to integer	16-50	0	Invalid, Precision	X	X	X
FRSTOR source	Restore saved state	205-215+EA	47-49	None	X	X	X

(Continued)

Table 8.05. Continued

Instruction	Function	Clock Cycles	Transfers*	Exception Flags Affected	8087	80287	80387
FSAVE/FNSAVE dest	Save state	205-215+EA	48-50	None	X	X	X
FSCALE	Scale	32-38	0	Invalid, Overflow, Underflow	X	X	X
FSETPM	Enter protected mode	2-8	0	None		X	X
FSIN	Sine	122-771					X
FSINCOS	Sine and cosine	194-809					X
FSQRT	Square root	180-186	0	Invalid, Denormalized, Precision	X	X	X
FST dest	Store real	15-104+EA	0-7	Invalid, Overflow, Underflow, Precision	X	X	X
FSTCW/FNSTCW dest	Store control word	12-18+EA	2-4	None	X	X	X
FSTENV/FNSTENV dest	Store environment	40-50+EA	8-10	None	X	X	X
FSTP dest	Store real and pop	17-58+EA	0-8	Invalid, Overflow, Underflow, Precision	X	X	X
FSTSW/FNSTSW dest	Store status word	12-18+EA	2-4	None	X	X	X
FSUB dest, source	Subtract real	70-125+EA	0-6	Invalid, Denormalized, Overflow, Underflow, Precision	X	X	X
FSUBP dest,source	Subtract real and pop	75-105	0	Invalid, Denormalized, Overflow, Underflow, Precision	X	X	X
FSUBR dest,source	Subtract real reversed	70-125+EA	0-6	Invalid, Denormalized, Overflow, Underflow, Precision	X	X	X
FSUBRP dest,source	Subtract real reversed and pop	75-105	0	Invalid, Denormalized, Overflow, Underflow, Precision	X	X	X
FTST	Test stack top against +0.0	38-48	0	Invalid, Denormalized	X	X	X
FUCOM	Unordered compare	24					X
FUCOMP	Unordered compare and pop	26					X
FUCOMPP	Unordered compare and pop twice	26					X
FWAIT	Wait while 8087 is busy	3+5n**	0	None	X	X	X
FXAM	Examine stack top	12-23	0	None	X	X	X
FXCH dest	Exchange registers	10-15	0	Invalid	X	X	X
FXTRACT	Extract exponent and significand	27-55	0	Invalid	X	X	X
FYL2X	Y * Log (2^X)	900-1100	0	Precision	X	X	X
FYL2XP1	Y * Log (2^X+1)	700-1000	0	Precision	X	X	X

Legend:

Dest=destination
Source=source
EA=effective address calculation

Notes:

*For 8086 only; 8088 transfers are likely to be higher; 80286 & 80386 are likely to be faster
**N=number of times CPU examines TEST line while 8087 is busy

Source:

8087 Applications and Programming for the IBM PC (Brady Books), Richard Startz, pages 244 to 258
Intel Microprocessor and Peripheral Handbook Volume 1, pages 2-140 to 2-143, 3-76 to 3-80, and 4-169 to 4-172

8.06. 8087 FAMILY REGISTER SUMMARY

```
    < -------------------------------- 80 bits --------------------------------->
    <-- 1 bit --> <------- 15 bits --------> <--------------- 64 bits --------------->   <---- 2 bits ---->
```

	Sign	Exponent	Significand		Tag field
R0	Sign	Exponent	Significand		Tag field
R1	Sign	Exponent	Significand		Tag field
R2	Sign	Exponent	Significand		Tag field
R3	Sign	Exponent	Significand		Tag field
R4	Sign	Exponent	Significand		Tag field
R5	Sign	Exponent	Significand		Tag field
R6	Sign	Exponent	Significand		Tag field
R7	Sign	Exponent	Significand		Tag field

```
         <------------------ 16 bits --------------->
```

Control register
Status register
Tag word
Instruction Pointer*
Data Pointer*

Notes: *32-bits in 8087 and 80287, 48 bits in 80387

Source: Intel Microprocessor and Peripheral Handbook Volume 1,
pages 2-125, 3-64, and 4-139

8.07. 8087 FAMILY CHIP VERSIONS

Chip	Clock Speed	Comments
8087	5MHz	In 40-pin CERDIP or plastic DIP package
8087-1	10MHz	In 40-pin CERDIP or plastic DIP package
8087-2	8MHz	In 40-pin CERDIP or plastic DIP package
80287-3	3MHz	In 40-pin DIP package
80287-6	6MHz	In 40-pin DIP package
80287-8	8MHz	In 40-pin DIP package
80287-10	10MHz	In 40-pin DIP package
80387	16MHz	In 68-pin PGA package

Notes: Numbers are Intel numbers only.

Source: Intel Microprocessor and Peripheral Handbook Volume 1

See Also: 9.39. 8087 (Coprocessor) Pinouts
9.40. 80287 (Coprocessor) Pinouts
9.41. 80387 (Coprocessor) Pinouts

8.08. 8250 I/O PORT USAGE (REGISTERS)

I/O Port	Register	Direction	Comments
3F8H	Transmit data	Output	Only if line control register bit 7 is 0
	Receive data	Input	Only if line control register bit 7 is 0
	Baud rate divisor LO byte		Only if line control register bit 7 is 1
3F9H	Baud rate divisor HO byte		Only if line control register bit 7 is 1
	Interrupt enable		Only if line control register bit 7 is 0
3FAH	Interrupt ID		
3FBH	Line control		
3FCH	Modem control		
3FDH	Line status		
3FEH	Modem status		

Source: *The IBM PC From the Inside Out* (Addison Wesley), Sargent & Shoemaker, Page 367

See Also: 4.063. INT 14H, Modem Status Byte
                          4.064. INT 14H, Com Port Parameter Byte
                          7.36. Line Control Register
                          7.37. Divisor Latch Register
                          7.38. Line Status Register
                          7.39. Interrupt Identification Register
                          7.40. Interrupt Enable Register
                          7.41. Modem Control Register
                          7.42. Modem Status Register
                          8.09. 8253 I/O Port Usage (Registers)

8.09. 8253 I/O PORT USAGE (REGISTERS)

I/O Port	Register	Direction*	Comments
40H	Timer 0	Output	
41H	Timer 1	Output	
42H	Timer 2	Output	
43H	Control word	Input	See 8.10. 8253 Control Word Byte

Source: *The IBM PC From the Inside Out* (Addison Wesley), Sargent & Shoemaker,
                        pages 2-117 to 2-121, 3-46 to 3-53, 4-106 to 4-119

See Also: 8.10. 8253 Control Word Byte

8.10. 8253 CONTROL WORD BYTE

Bit Numbers

7	6	5	4	3	2	1	0	Function	Allowable Values
X	X							Timer number	00=timer 0, 01=timer 1, 10=timer 2
		X	X					Latch, read format	00=latch current count, 01=read low byte (no latching)
									10=read high byte (no latching), 11=read low, then high byte
				X	X	X		Mode number	000=interrupt on terminal count
									001=programmable one-shot
									010=rate generator
									011=square wave generator
									100=software triggered strobe
									101=hardware triggered strobe
							X	Count type	0=binary, 1=BCD

Source: *The IBM PC From the Inside Out* (Addison Wesley), Sargent & Shoemaker, pages 241 to 242

See Also: 8.09. 8253 I/O Port Usage (Registers)

8.11. 8253 COMMAND REGISTER BYTE

Bit Numbers

7	6	5	4	3	2	1	0	Function	Comments
X	X							Select counter	00=Counter 0, 01=Counter 1 10=Counter 2, 11=Illegal
		X	X					Read/load	00=counter latch op, 11=read/load LSB, then MSB 10=read/load MSB, 01=read/load LSB
				X	X	X		Mode	000=0, 001=1, X10=2, X11=3, 100=4, 101=5
							X	BCD	0=binary counter, 1=BCD counter (4 decades)

Source: Intel Microprocessor and Peripheral Handbook, Volume 2, page 2-17

See Also: 9.47. 8253 (Programmable Interval Controller) Pinouts

8.12. 6845 REGISTERS

Register	Function	Unit	CGA 40x25	CGA 80x25	CGA graphics	MDA 80x25
R0	Horizontal total	Chars	38	71	38	61
R1	Horizontal displayed	Chars	28	50	28	50
R2	Horizontal sync position	Chars	2D	5A	2D	52
R3	Horizontal sync width	Chars	A	A	A	F
R4	Vertical total	Char rows	1F	1F	7F	19
R5	Vertical total adjust	Scan lines	6	6	6	6
R6	Vertical displayed	Char rows	19	19	64	19
R7	Vertical sync position	Char rows	1C	1C	70	19
R8	Interlace mode		2	2	2	2
R9	Max scan line address	Scan lines	7	7	1	D
R10	Cursor start	Scan lines	6	6	6	B
R11	Cursor end	Scan lines	7	7	7	C
R12	Start address high		0	0	0	0
R13	Start address low		0	0	0	0
R14	Cursor high					0
R15	Cursor low					0
R16	Light pen high					
R17	Light pen low					

Notes: Except for register numbers, all values are in hex

Source: IBM Technical Reference Options and Adapters, pages MDA 5 and CGA 17

See Also: 8.13. 6845 Port and Select Factors
9.43. 6845 (Video Controller) Pinouts

8.13. 6845 PORT AND SELECT FACTORS

Bit Numbers								Register	Function	Comments
7	6	5	4	3	2	1	0			
X								Color Select (CGA=3D9)	Not used	
		X							Active color set 320x200	00=set 1 (green/red/brown), 01=set 2 (cyan/magenta/white)
			X						Intensity/background	Intensity in graphics, background color in alphanumeric mode
				X					Intensity	Intense border in 40x25, intense background in 320x200, intense foreground in 640x200
					X				Red	Red border in 40x25, red background in 320x200, red foreground in 640x200
						X			Green	Green border in 40x25, green background in 320x200, green foreground in 640x200
							X		Blue	Blue border in 40x25, blue background in 320x200, blue foreground in 640x200
		X						Mode Cntrl (CGA=3D8)	Blink	0=no blink, 1=blink (in text modes)
			X						640x200	1=select 640x200 B/W graphics
				X					Video enable/disable	0=disable, 1=enable video
					X				Color/mono	0=color mode, 1=monochrome mode
						X			Mode	0=text, 1=320x200 graphics mode
							X		Mode	0=40x25 text, 1=80x25 text
				X				Status (CGA=3DA)	Retrace	1=raster is in vertical retrace mode
					X				Light pen	0=light pen switch on, 1=light pen switch off
						X			Light pen	1=light pen trigger set
							X		Regen-buffer	1=regen-buffer memory access can be made without interfering with display
				X				Status (MDA=3BA)	B/W video	
					X				RESERVED	
						X			RESERVED	
							X		Horizontal drive	
X	X		X		X	X		Control (MDA=3B8)	NOT USED	
		X							Enable blink	1=enabled
				X					Enable video	1=enabled
							X		High resolution mode	

Source: IBM Technical Reference Options and Adapters, pages CGA 18-21, MDA 8

See Also: 8.12. 6845 Registers
9.43. 6845 (Video Controller) Pinouts

8.14. AT J18 RAM JUMPER

Pin Number	Signal Name
1	No connection
2	-RAM SEL
3	Ground

Notes: •Connector is a 3-pin keyed Berg-strip connector (keyed on pin 3)
•To enable 2nd 256K on system board jumper pins 1 and 2
•To disable 2nd 256K on system board jumper pins 2 and 3

Source: IBM PC/AT Technical Reference, pages 1-40 to 1-41

8.15. AT DISPLAY SWITCH (SW1)

Switch Number	Function	Settings
1	Display type	ON=CGA, EGA, or PGA is primary display OFF=MDA or EGA is primary display

Notes: ON is toward front of the machine

Source: IBM PC/AT Technical Reference, page 1-41

8.16. PC SYSTEM BOARD SWITCH SETTINGS

For Switch 1:

Switch Number	Function	Settings
1	Number of drives	ON=drives installed; OFF=no drives (see switch 7/8)
2	Not used (PC1)	Must be ON (PC1)
3 & 4	Memory on system board	ON ON = 16K (PC1) or 64K (PC2) OFF ON = 32K (PC1) or 128K (PC2) ON OFF = 48K (PC1) or 192K (PC2) OFF OFF = 64K (PC1) or 256K (PC2)
5 & 6	Display adapter	ON ON = no adapter OFF ON = CGA, 40-columns ON OFF = CGA, 80 columns OFF OFF = MDA, or more than one adapter
7 & 8	Floppy drives	ON ON = 1 drive OFF ON = 2 drives ON OFF = 3 drives OFF OFF = 4 drives

For Switch 2:

Switch Number	Function	Settings
1 through 5	Memory Installed	ON ON ON ON ON = 16-64K* OFF ON ON ON ON = 96K** ON OFF ON ON ON = 128K** OFF OFF ON ON ON = 160K** ON ON OFF ON ON = 192K** OFF ON OFF ON ON = 224K** ON OFF OFF ON ON = 256K** OFF OFF OFF ON ON = 288K** ON ON ON OFF ON = 320K** OFF ON ON OFF ON = 352K** ON OFF ON OFF ON = 384K** OFF OFF ON OFF ON = 416K** ON ON OFF OFF ON = 448K** OFF ON OFF OFF ON = 480K** ON OFF OFF OFF ON = 512K** OFF OFF OFF OFF ON = 544K** ON ON ON ON OFF = 576K** OFF ON ON ON OFF = 608K** ON OFF ON ON OFF = 640K**
6 - 8	NOT USED	Must be OFF (Switch 7 reserved for 8087 on PC2)

Notes: *SW1 switches 3 & 4 control total memory
**SW1 switches 3 & 4 should be OFF

Source: IBM PC Guide to Operations, Pages Options 6 to 24

See Also: 8.17. XT System Board Switch Settings

8.17. XT SYSTEM BOARD SWITCH SETTINGS

Switch Number	Function	Settings
1	Test	ON=loops on POST routine; OFF=normal operation
2	Coprocessor	ON=8087 installed; OFF=no 8087
3 & 4	System board RAM	ON ON = 64K
		OFF ON = 128K
		ON OFF = 192K
		OFF OFF = 256K
5 & 6	Display adapter	ON ON = no adapter
		OFF ON = CGA, 40-columns
		ON OFF = CGA, 80 columns
		OFF OFF = MDA, or more than one adapter
7 & 8	Floppy drives	ON ON = 1 drive
		OFF ON = 2 drives
		ON OFF = 3 drives
		OFF OFF = 4 drives

Notes: Normal switch setting would be OFF OFF OFF OFF OFF OFF ON ON (256K, 1 floppy, MDA)

Source: IBM PC/XT Technical Reference, pages 1-13 to 1-14

8.18. PC AND XT FLOPPY DISK CONTROLLER COMMAND SUMMARY

Command Name	Command Sequence	Direction	Comments	7	6	5	4	3	2	1	0
Read Data	Command code byte 1	Write	See bit mask at right	MT	MF	SK	0	0	1	1	0
	Command code byte 2	Write	See bit mask at right	*	*	*	*	*	HD	US1	US0
	Start cylinder	Write									
	Start head	Write									
	Start sector number	Write									
	Number bytes/sector	Write	Usually 512								
	Last sector on cylinder	Write									
	Gap length	Write	Usually 3								
	Data length	Write	Used if number/bytes sector is 0								
	Status register 0	Read	See 8.19. FDC Status Register 0								
	Status register 1	Read	See 8.20. FDC Status Register 1								
	Status register 2	Read	See 8.21. FDC Status Register 2								
	Current cylinder	Read	Location after read								
	Current head	Read	Location after read								
	Current sector number	Read	Location after read								
	Number bytes/sector	Read									
Read Deleted Data	Command code byte 1	Write	See bit mask at right	MT	MF	SK	0	1	1	0	0
	Command code byte 2	Write	See bit mask at right	*	*	*	*	*	HD	US1	US0
	Start cylinder	Write									
	Start head	Write									
	Start sector number	Write									
	Number bytes/sector	Write	Usually 512								
	Last sector on cylinder	Write									
	Gap length	Write	Usually 3								
	Data length	Write	Used if number/bytes sector is 0								
	Status register 0	Read	See 8.19. FDC Status Register 0								
	Status register 1	Read	See 8.20. FDC Status Register 1								
	Status register 2	Read	See 8.21. FDC Status Register 2								
	Current cylinder	Read	Location after read								
	Current head	Read	Location after read								
	Current sector number	Read	Location after read								
	Number bytes/sector	Read									
Write Data	Command code byte 1	Write	See bit mask at right	MT	MF	0	0	0	1	0	1
	Command code byte 2	Write	See bit mask at right	*	*	*	*	*	HD	US1	US0
	Start cylinder	Write									
	Start head	Write									
	Start sector number	Write									
	Number bytes/sector	Write	Usually 512								
	Last sector on cylinder	Write									
	Gap length	Write	Usually 3								
	Data length	Write	Used if number/bytes sector is 0								
	Status register 0	Read	See 8.19. FDC Status Register 0								
	Status register 1	Read	See 8.20. FDC Status Register 1								
	Status register 2	Read	See 8.21. FDC Status Register 2								
	Current cylinder	Read	Location after write								
	Current head	Read	Location after write								
	Current sector number	Read	Location after write								
	Number bytes/sector	Read									
Write Deleted Data	Command code byte 1	Write	See bit mask at right	MT	MF	0	0	1	0	0	1
	Command code byte 2	Write	See bit mask at right	*	*	*	*	*	HD	US1	US0
	Start cylinder	Write									
	Start head	Write									
	Start sector number	Write									
	Number bytes/sector	Write	Usually 512								

(Continued)

Table 8.18. Continued

Command Name	Command Sequence	Direction	Comments	7	6	5	4	3	2	1	0
						Bit Numbers					
Write Deleted Data	Last sector on cylinder	Write									
	Gap length	Write	Usually 3								
	Data length	Write	Used if number/bytes sector is 0								
	Status register 0	Read	See 8.19. FDC Status Register 0								
	Status register 1	Read	See 8.20. FDC Status Register 1								
	Status register 2	Read	See 8.21. FDC Status Register 2								
	Current cylinder	Read	Location after write								
	Current head	Read	Location after write								
	Current sector number	Read	Location after write								
	Number bytes/sector	Read									
Read Track	Command code byte 1	Write	See bit mask at right	0 *	MF *	SK *	0 *	0 *	0 HD	1 US1	0 US0
	Command code byte 2	Write	See bit mask at right								
	Start cylinder	Write									
	Start head	Write									
	Start sector number	Write									
	Number bytes/sector	Write	Usually 512								
	Last sector on cylinder	Write									
	Gap length	Write	Usually 3								
	Data length	Write	Used if number/bytes sector is 0								
	Status register 0	Read	See 8.19. FDC Status Register 0								
	Status register 1	Read	See 8.20. FDC Status Register 1								
	Status register 2	Read	See 8.21. FDC Status Register 2								
	Current cylinder	Read	Location after read								
	Current head	Read	Location after read								
	Current sector number	Read	Location after read								
	Number bytes/sector	Read									
Read ID	Command code byte 1	Write	See bit mask at right	0 *	MF *	0 *	0 *	1 *	0 HD	1 US1	0 US0
	Command code byte 2	Write	See bit mask at right								
	Status register 0	Read	See 8.19. FDC Status Register 0								
	Status register 1	Read	See 8.20. FDC Status Register 1								
	Status register 2	Read	See 8.21. FDC Status Register 2								
	Current cylinder	Read	Location after read								
	Current head	Read	Location after read								
	Current sector number	Read	Location after read								
	Number bytes/sector	Read									
Format Track	Command code byte 1	Write	See bit mask at right	0 *	MF *	0 *	0 *	1 *	1 HD	0 US1	0 US0
	Command code byte 2	Write	See bit mask at right								
	Bytes/sector	Write	Usually 512								
	Sectors per cylinder	Write	Usually 9								
	Gap length	Write	Usually 3								
	Filler byte	Write	Data pattern to initialize sectors								
	Status register 0	Read	See 8.19. FDC Status Register 0								
	Status register 1	Read	See 8.20. FDC Status Register 1								
	Status register 2	Read	See 8.21. FDC Status Register 2								
	Current cylinder	Read	No meaning in this context								
	Current head	Read	No meaning in this context								
	Current sector number	Read	No meaning in this context								
	Number bytes/sector	Read	No meaning in this context								
Scan Equal	Command code byte 1	Write	See bit mask at right	MT *	MF *	SK *	1 *	0 *	0 HD	0 US1	1 US0
	Command code byte 2	Write	See bit mask at right								
	Start cylinder	Write									
	Start head	Write									
	Start sector number	Write									
	Number bytes/sector	Write	Usually 512								
	Last sector on cylinder	Write									
	Gap length	Write	Usually 3								
	Scan test code	Write	1=compare contiguous, 2=compare alternate								
	Status register 0	Read	See 8.19. FDC Status Register 0								
	Status register 1	Read	See 8.20. FDC Status Register 1								
	Status register 2	Read	See 8.21. FDC Status Register 2								
	Current cylinder	Read	Location after scan								
	Current head	Read	Location after scan								
	Current sector number	Read	Location after scan								
	Number bytes/sector	Read									
Scan Low or Equal	Command code byte 1	Write	See bit mask at right	MT *	MF *	SK *	1 *	1 *	0 HD	0 US1	1 US0
	Command code byte 2	Write	See bit mask at right								
	Start cylinder	Write									
	Start head	Write									
	Start sector number	Write									
	Number bytes/sector	Write	Usually 512								
	Last sector on cylinder	Write									
	Gap length	Write	Usually 3								
	Scan test code	Write	1=compare contiguous, 2=compare alternate								
	Status register 0	Read	See 8.19. FDC Status Register 0								
	Status register 1	Read	See 8.20. FDC Status Register 1								
	Status register 2	Read	See 8.21. FDC Status Register 2								
	Current cylinder	Read	Location after scan								
	Current head	Read	Location after scan								
	Current sector number	Read	Location after scan								
	Number bytes/sector	Read									

(Continued)

Table 8.18. Continued

Command Name	Command Sequence	Direction	Comments	Bit Numbers 7	6	5	4	3	2	1	0
Scan High or Equal	Command code byte 1	Write	See bit mask at right	MT	MF	SK	1	1	1	0	1
	Command code byte 2	Write	See bit mask at right	*	*	*	*	*	HD	US1	US0
	Start cylinder	Write									
	Start head	Write									
	Start sector number	Write									
	Number bytes/sector	Write	Usually 512								
	Last sector on cylinder	Write									
	Gap length	Write	Usually 3								
	Scan test code	Write	1=compare contiguous, 2=compare alternate								
	Status register 0	Read	See 8.19. FDC Status Register 0								
	Status register 1	Read	See 8.20. FDC Status Register 1								
	Status register 2	Read	See 8.21. FDC Status Register 2								
	Current cylinder	Read	Location after scan								
	Current head	Read	Location after scan								
	Current sector number	Read	Location after scan								
	Number bytes/sector	Read									
Recalibrate	Command code byte 1	Write	See bit mask at right	0	0	0	0	0	1	1	1
	Command code byte 2	Write	See bit mask at right	*	*	*	*	*	0	US1	US0
Sense Int Status	Command code byte 1	Write	See bit mask at right	0	0	0	0	1	0	0	0
	Status register 0	Read	See 8.19. FDC Status Register 0								
	Present cylinder number	Read									
Specify	Command code byte 1	Write	See bit mask at right	0	0	0	0	0	0	1	1
	Command code byte 2	Write	HO=Step Rate Time, LO=Head Unload Time	SRT	SRT	SRT	SRT	HUT	HUT	HUT	HUT
	Command code byte 3	write	Bits 1-7=Head Load Time, Bit 0=non-DMA	HLT	HLT	HLT	HLT	HLT	HLT	HLT	ND
Sense Drive Status	Command code byte 1	Write	See bit mask at right	0	0	0	0	0	1	0	0
	Command code byte 2	Write	See bit mask at right	*	*	*	*	*	HD	US1	US0
	Status register 3	Read	See 8.22. FDC Status Register 3								
Seek	Command code byte 1	Write	See bit mask at right	0	0	0	0	1	1	1	1
	Command code byte 2	Write	See bit mask at right	*	*	*	*	*	HD	US1	US0
	Cylinder to seek	Write									
Invalid	Any invalid code	Write									
	Status register 0	Read	See 8.19. FDC Status Register 0								

Legend:
* = Value ignored, may be 1 or 0
MT = multitrack operation (high=TRUE)
MF = FM mode (high=MFM, low=FM)
SK = skip deleted data address mark
HD = head number
US0 = unit select zero
US1 = unit select one

Notes: The terms "track" and "cylinder" are incorrectly used interchangeably in the IBM documentation.

Source: IBM PC/XT Technical Reference, pages 1-112 to 1-119

See Also:
8.19. PC and XT Floppy Disk Controller Status Register 0
8.20. PC and XT Floppy Disk Controller Status Register 1
8.21. PC and XT Floppy Disk Controller Status Register 2
8.22. PC and XT Floppy Disk Controller Status Register 3
8.24. XT Fixed Disk Controller Command Summary

8.19. PC AND XT FLOPPY DISK CONTROLLER STATUS REGISTER 0

Bit Numbers 7	6	5	4	3	2	1	0	Name	Function	Allowable Values
X	X							Interrupt Code	Reports status due to last command	00=normal termination
										01=abnormal termination
										10=invalid command issued
										11=abnormal termination due to change in ready state
		X						Seek end	Reports completion of seek op.	1=seek operation completed
			X					Equipment check	Set when fault received from FDD	(Also set when recalibrate fails to find track 0)
				X				Not ready	Reports FDD is not in ready state	1=not ready
					X			Head address	Reports state of head at interrupt	0=0 head, 1=1 head
						X	X	Unit select	Reports selected unit at interrupt	Bit 0=unit select 2, bit 1=unit select 1

Source: IBM PC/XT Technical Reference, page 1-120

See Also:
8.18. PC and XT Floppy Disk Controller Command Summary
8.20. PC and XT Floppy Disk Controller Status Register 1
8.21. PC and XT Floppy Disk Controller Status Register 2
8.22. PC and XT Floppy Disk Controller Status Register 3
8.24. XT Fixed Disk Controller Command Summary

8.20. PC AND XT FLOPPY DISK CONTROLLER STATUS REGISTER 1

Bit Numbers 7	6	5	4	3	2	1	0	Name	Function	Allowable Values
X								End of cylinder	Reports movement past last track	Set if FDC tries to access sector beyond final sector
	X							NOT USED		Always 0
		X						Data error	Reports CRC error in ID or data field	1=error, 0=no error
			X					Overrun	Reports FDC not serviced	1=FDC not serviced during data transfer within time limit
				X				NOT USED		Always 0
					X			No data	Reports cannot find sector or ID	1=error, 0=no error
						X		Not writable	Reports write protect signal from FDD	1=write protect during write op., 0=no error
							X	Missing address mark	Reports FDC didn't find address mark	1=missing address mark, 0=no error

Source: IBM PC/XT Technical Reference, page 1-121

See Also: 8.18.   PC and XT Floppy Disk Controller Command Summary
                  8.19.   PC and XT Floppy Disk Controller Status Register 0
                  8.21.   PC and XT Floppy Disk Controller Status Register 2
                  8.22.   PC and XT Floppy Disk Controller Status Register 3
                  8.24.   XT Fixed Disk Controller Command Summary

8.21. PC AND XT FLOPPY DISK CONTROLLER STATUS REGISTER 2

Bit Numbers 7	6	5	4	3	2	1	0	Name	Function	Allowable Values
X								NOT USED		Always 0
	X							Control mark	Reports deleted data address mark	1=deleted mark detected during read or scan, 0=no error
		X						Data error in data field	Reports CRC error in data	1=CRC error in data field, 0=no error
			X					Wrong cylinder	Track contents don't match track ID	1=error, 0=no error
				X				Scan equal hit	Reports scan found equal condition	1=scan equal, 0=scan not equal
					X			Scan not satisified	Reports scan not satisified condition	1=scan not satisified, 0=scan satisfied
						X		Bad cylinder	Track contents don't match, FFH found	1=error, 0=no error
							X	Missing address in data field	Reports FDC couldn't find mark	1=couldn't find address mark, 0=no error

Source: IBM PC/XT Technical Reference, page 1-122

See Also: 8.18.   PC and XT Floppy Disk Controller Command Summary
                  8.19.   PC and XT Floppy Disk Controller Status Register 0
                  8.20.   PC and XT Floppy Disk Controller Status Register 1
                  8.22.   PC and XT Floppy Disk Controller Status Register 3
                  8.24.   XT Fixed Disk Controller Command Summary

8.22. PC AND XT FLOPPY DISK CONTROLLER STATUS REGISTER 3

Bit Numbers

7	6	5	4	3	2	1	0	Name	Function	Allowable Values
X								Fault	FDD fault signal status	1=FDD fault, 0=no fault
	X							Write protected	FDD write protected status	1=write protected, 0=not protected
		X						Ready	FDD ready status	1=disk drive ready, 0=not ready
			X					Track 0	FDD at track zero signal	1=FDD is at track 0, 0=not at track 0
				X				Two sided	FDD two-sided media signal	1=two-sided media, 0=one-sided media
					X			Head address	FDD head selected	1=head 1, 0=head 0
						X		Unit select 1	FDD unit select 1 status	
							X	Unit select 0	FDD unit select 0 status	

Source: IBM PC/XT Technical Reference, page 1-123

See Also: 8.18. PC and XT Floppy Disk Controller Command Summary
8.19. PC and XT Floppy Disk Controller Status Register 0
8.20. PC and XT Floppy Disk Controller Status Register 1
8.21. PC and XT Floppy Disk Controller Status Register 2
8.24. XT Fixed Disk Controller Command Summary

8.23. PC AND XT FDC DISK PROGRAM CONTROL REGISTERS

Register Name	I/O Address
Data register	3F5H
Main status register	3F4H
Digital output register	3F2H

Digital Output Register:

Bit Numbers

7	6	5	4	3	2	1	0	Name	Allowable Values
						X	X	Drive select	00=A, 01=B, 10=C, 11=D
				X				Not FDC reset	
					X			Enable INT & DMA requests	
			X					Drive A motor enable	1=motor on, 0=motor off
		X						Drive B motor enable	1=motor on, 0=motor off
	X							Drive C motor enable	1=motor on, 0=motor off
X								Drive D motor enable	1=motor on, 0=motor off

Source: IBM PC/XT Technical Reference, page 1-123

See Also: 8.18. PC and XT Floppy Disk Controller Command Summary
8.24. XT Fixed Disk Controller Command Summary

8.24. XT FIXED DISK CONTROLLER COMMAND SUMMARY

Command Name	Command Sequence	Direction	Bit Numbers							
			7	6	5	4	3	2	1	0
Test Drive Ready	Command code byte 1	Write	0	0	0	0	0	0	0	0
	Command code byte 2	Write	0	0	DR	*	*	*	*	*
	Don't care	Write	*	*	*	*	*	*	*	*
	Don't care	Write	*	*	*	*	*	*	*	*
	Don't care	Write	*	*	*	*	*	*	*	*
	Don't care	Write	*	*	*	*	*	*	*	*
Recalibrate	Command code byte 1	Write	0	0	0	0	0	0	0	1
	Command code byte 2	Write	0	0	DR	*	*	*	*	*
	Don't care	Write	*	*	*	*	*	*	*	*
	Don't care	Write	*	*	*	*	*	*	*	*
	Don't care	Write	*	*	*	*	*	*	*	*
	Command Code Byte 6	Write	RT	0	0	0	0	Step option		
Request sense status	Command code byte 1	Write	0	0	0	0	0	0	1	1
	Command code byte 2	Write	0	0	DR	*	*	*	*	*
	Don't care	Write	*	*	*	*	*	*	*	*
	Don't care	Write	*	*	*	*	*	*	*	*
	Don't care	Write	*	*	*	*	*	*	*	*
	Don't care	Write	*	*	*	*	*	*	*	*
Format drive	Command code byte 1	Write	0	0	0	0	0	1	0	0
	Command code byte 2	Write	0	0	DR	Head number				
	Command code byte 3	Write	Hi cylinder	0	0	0	0	0	0	0
	Command code byte 4	Write	Lo cylinder (cylinder=10 bit value)							
	Command code byte 5	Write	0	0	0	Interleave factor (1-16)				
	Command code byte 6	Write	RT	0	0	0	0	Step option		

(Continued)

Table 8.24. Continued

Command Name	Command Sequence	Direction	Bit Numbers 7	6	5	4	3	2	1	0
Ready verify	Command code byte 1	Write	0	0	0	0	0	1	0	1
	Command code byte 2	Write	0	0	DR	Head number				
	Command code byte 3	Write	Hi cylinder		Sector number					
	Command code byte 4	Write	Lo cylinder (cylinder=10 bit value)							
	Command code byte 5	Write	Block count							
	Command code byte 6	Write	RT	RTO	0	0	0	Step option		
Format track	Command code byte 1	Write	0	0	0	0	0	1	1	0
	Command code byte 2	Write	0	0	DR	Head number				
	Command code byte 3	Write	Hi cylinder		0	0	0	0	0	0
	Command code byte 4	Write	Lo cylinder (cylinder=10 bit value)							
	Command code byte 5	Write	0	0	0	Interleave factor (1-16)				
	Command code byte 6	Write	RT	0	0	0	0	Step option		
Format bad track	Command code byte 1	Write	0	0	0	0	0	1	1	1
	Command code byte 2	Write	0	0	DR	Head number				
	Command code byte 3	Write	Hi cylinder		0	0	0	0	0	0
	Command code byte 4	Write	Lo cylinder (cylinder=10 bit value)							
	Command code byte 5	Write	0	0	0	Interleave factor (1-16)				
	Command code byte 6	Write	RT	0	0	0	0	Step option		
Read	Command code byte 1	Write	0	0	0	0	1	0	0	0
	Command code byte 2	Write	0	0	DR	Head number				
	Command code byte 3	Write	Hi cylinder		Sector number					
	Command code byte 4	Write	Lo cylinder (cylinder=10 bit value)							
	Don't care	Write	*	*	*	*	*	*	*	*
	Command code byte 6	Write	RT	RTO	0	0	0	Step option		
Write	Command code byte 1	Write	0	0	0	0	1	0	1	0
	Command code byte 2	Write	0	0	DR	Head number				
	Command code byte 3	Write	Hi cylinder		Sector number					
	Command code byte 4	Write	Lo cylinder (cylinder=10 bit value)							
	Command code byte 5	Write	Block count							
	Command code byte 6	Write	RT	0	0	0	0	Step option		
Seek	Command code byte 1	Write	0	0	0	0	1	0	1	1
	Command code byte 2	Write	0	0	DR	Head number				
	Command code byte 3	Write	Hi cylinder		0	0	0	0	0	0
	Command code byte 4	Write	Lo cylinder (cylinder=10 bit value)							
	Command code byte 5	Write	*	*	*	*	*	*	*	*
	Command code byte 6	Write	RT	0	0	0	0	Step option		
Init drive characteristics	Command code byte 1	Write	0	0	0	0	1	1	0	0
	Don't care	Write	*	*	*	*	*	*	*	*
	Don't care	Write	*	*	*	*	*	*	*	*
	Don't care	Write	*	*	*	*	*	*	*	*
	Don't care	Write	*	*	*	*	*	*	*	*
	Don't care	Write	*	*	*	*	*	*	*	*
	HO max number of cylinders	Write								
	LO max number of cylinders	Write								
	Max number of heads	Write								
	HO reduced write cylinder	Write								
	LO reduced write cylinder	Write								
	HO write precomp cylinder	Write								
	LO write precomp cylinder	Write								
	Max ECC data burst length	Write								
Read ECC Burst	Command code byte 1	Write	0	0	0	0	1	1	0	1
	Don't care	Write	*	*	*	*	*	*	*	*
	Don't care	Write	*	*	*	*	*	*	*	*
	Don't care	Write	*	*	*	*	*	*	*	*
	Don't care	Write	*	*	*	*	*	*	*	*
	Don't care	Write	*	*	*	*	*	*	*	*
Read Data from Sector Buffer	Command code byte 1	Write	0	0	0	0	1	1	1	0
	Don't care	Write	*	*	*	*	*	*	*	*
	Don't care	Write	*	*	*	*	*	*	*	*
	Don't care	Write	*	*	*	*	*	*	*	*
	Don't care	Write	*	*	*	*	*	*	*	*
	Don't care	Write	*	*	*	*	*	*	*	*
Write data to sector buffer	Command code byte 1	Write	0	0	0	0	1	1	1	1
	Don't care	Write	*	*	*	*	*	*	*	*
	Don't care	Write	*	*	*	*	*	*	*	*
	Don't care	Write	*	*	*	*	*	*	*	*
	Don't care	Write	*	*	*	*	*	*	*	*
	Don't care	Write	*	*	*	*	*	*	*	*

(Continued)

Table 8.24. Continued

Command Name	Command Sequence	Direction	Bit Numbers							
			7	6	5	4	3	2	1	0
RAM diagnostic	Command code byte 1	Write	1	1	1	0	0	0	0	0
	Don't care	Write	*	*	*	*	*	*	*	*
	Don't care	Write	*	*	*	*	*	*	*	*
	Don't care	Write	*	*	*	*	*	*	*	*
	Don't care	Write	*	*	*	*	*	*	*	*
	Don't care	Write	*	*	*	*	*	*	*	*
Drive diagnostic	Command code byte 1	Write	1	1	1	0	0	0	1	1
	Command code byte 2	Write	0	0	DR	*	*	*	*	*
	Command code byte 3	Write	*	*	*	*	*	*	*	*
	Command code byte 4	Write	*	*	*	*	*	*	*	*
	Command code byte 5	Write	*	*	*	*	*	*	*	*
	Command code byte 6	Write	RT	0	0	0	0	Step option		
Controller internal diagnostics	Command code byte 1	Write	1	1	1	0	0	1	0	0
	Don't care	Write	*	*	*	*	*	*	*	*
	Don't care	Write	*	*	*	*	*	*	*	*
	Don't care	Write	*	*	*	*	*	*	*	*
	Don't care	Write	*	*	*	*	*	*	*	*
	Don't care	Write	*	*	*	*	*	*	*	*
Read long (sector plus 4 bytes of ECC data)	Command code byte 1	Write	1	1	1	0	0	1	0	1
	Command code byte 2	Write	0	0	DR	Head number				
	Command code byte 3	Write	Hi cylinder		Sector number					
	Command code byte 4	Write	Lo cylinder (cylinder = 10 bits)							
	Command code byte 5	Write	Block count							
	Command code byte 6	Write	RT	0	0	0	0	Step option		
Write long (sector plus 4 bytes of ECC data)	Command code byte 1	Write	1	1	1	0	0	1	1	0
	Command code byte 2	Write	0	0	DR	Head number				
	Command code byte 3	Write	Hi cylinder		Sector number					
	Command code byte 4	Write	Lo cylinder (cylinder = 10 bits)							
	Command code byte 5	Write	Block count							
	Command code byte 6	Write	RT	0	0	0	0	Step option		

Legend: DR = drive (0 or 1)
RT = retries
RTO = retry option on data ECC

Notes: The terms "track" and "cylinder" are incorrectly used interchangeably in the IBM documentation.

Source: IBM PC/XT Technical Reference, pages 1-143 to 1-146

See Also: 8.18. PC and XT Floppy Disk Controller Command Summary

8.25. XT FIXED DISK CONTROLLER PORT USAGE

Port	Direction	Function
320H	Controller to system	Read data
320H	System to controller	Write data
321H	Controller to system	Read controller hardware status
321H	System to controller	Reset controller
322H	Controller to system	RESERVED
322H	System to controller	Generate controller-select pulse
323H	Controller to system	NOT USED
323H	System to controller	Write pattern to DMA and INT mask register

Source: IBM PC/XT Technical Reference, page 1-147

See Also: 7.03. I/O Port Usage Summary

8.26. XT FIXED DISK CONTROLLER DEVICE CONTROL BLOCK

Byte	7	6	5	4	3	2	1	0	Name	Allowable Values
Byte 0	X	X	X						Command class	000 and 111 are only values used
				X	X	X	X	X	Command opcode	00000=test drive ready 00001=recalibrate 00010=RESERVED 00011=request sense status 00100=format drive 00101=ready verify 00110=format track 00111=format bad track 01000=read 01001=RESERVED 01010=write 01011=seek 01100=initialize drive 01101=read ECC burst error length 01110=read data from sector buffer 01111=write data to sector buffer
Byte 1	0	0							Always zero	
			X						Drive number	
				X	X	X	X	X	Head number	
Byte 2	X	X							Hi order 2 bits of cylinder #	
			X	X	X	X	X	X	Sector number	
Byte 3	X	X	X	X	X	X	X	X	Lo order 8 bits of cylinder #	
Byte 4	X	X	X	X	X	X	X	X	Interleave or block count	Interleave must be 0-16
Byte 5	X								Retries	1=disables 4 retries by controller during ops
		X							Retry option on data ECC error	1=no rereads; 0=reread attempted
			0	0	0				Always zero	
						X	X	X	Step option	000=3 milliseconds per step 001=NOT USED 010=NOT USED 011=NOT USED 100=200 microseconds per step 101=70 microseconds per step (BIOS setting) 110=3 milliseconds per step 111=3 milliseconds per step

Source: IBM PC/XT Technical Reference, pages 1-141 to 1-146

See Also: 8.24. XT Fixed Disk Controller Command Summary

8.27. XT FIXED DISK CONTROLLER STATUS REGISTER

Bit Numbers

7	6	5	4	3	2	1	0	Name	Allowable Values
0	0							Always Zero	
		X						Logical Unit Number	0 or 1
			0	0	0			Always Zero	
						X		Error Status	0=no error, 1=error occurred
							0	Always Zero	

Source: IBM PC/XT Technical Reference, page 1-137

See Also: 8.28. XT Fixed Disk Controller Sense Bytes
8.29. XT Fixed Disk Controller Error Codes

8.28. XT FIXED DISK CONTROLLER SENSE BYTES

Byte	7	6	5	4	3	2	1	0	Name	Allowable Values
Byte 0	X								Address valid	1=address is valid
		0							Always zero	
			X	X					Error type	see 8.29. XT FDC Error Codes
					X	X	X	X	Error code	see 8.29. XT FDC Error Codes
Byte 1	0	0							Always zero	
			X						Drive number	0 or 1
				X	X	X	X	X	Head number	
Byte 2	X	X	X						HO 3 bits of cylinder #	
				X	X	X	X	X	Sector number	
Byte 3	X	X	X	X	X	X	X	X	LO 8 bits of cylinder #	

Bit Numbers spans columns 7–0.

Source: IBM PC/XT Technical Reference, page 1-137

See Also: 8.27. XT Fixed Disk Controller Status Register
8.29. XT Fixed Disk Controller Error Codes

8.29. XT FIXED DISK CONTROLLER ERROR CODES

5	4	3	2	1	0	Value	Error Description
0	0	0	0	0	0	0 (0)	No error during previous operation
0	0	0	0	0	1	1 (1)	No index signal detected from drive
0	0	0	0	1	0	2 (2)	No seek complete signal detected from drive after seek requested
0	0	0	0	1	1	3 (3)	Write fault detected from drive during previous operation
0	0	0	1	0	0	4 (4)	Drive did not respond with ready signal after being selected
0	0	0	1	0	1	5 (5)	NOT USED
0	0	0	1	1	0	6 (6)	No Track 00 signal detected from drive when it was expected
0	0	0	1	1	1	7 (7)	NOT USED
0	0	1	0	0	0	8 (8)	Drive still seeking
0	1	0	0	0	0	10 (16)	ECC error in target ID field on the disk
0	1	0	0	0	1	11 (17)	Uncorrectable ECC error in target sector during read
0	1	0	0	1	0	12 (18)	No target address mark detected on the disk
0	1	0	0	1	1	13 (19)	NOT USED
0	1	0	1	0	0	14 (20)	Sector not found (cylinder and head found correctly)
0	1	0	1	0	1	15 (21)	Seek compare error (may be cylinder and/or head address)
0	1	0	1	1	0	16 (22)	NOT USED
0	1	0	1	1	1	17 (23)	NOT USED
0	1	1	0	0	0	18 (24)	Correctable ECC error in the target field detected
0	1	1	0	0	1	19 (25)	Bad track detected during previous operation

Bit Numbers spans columns 5–0.

Source: IBM PC/XT Technical Reference, pages 1-138 to 1-139

See Also: 8.28. XT Fixed Disk Controller Sense Bytes

8.30. AT FIXED DISK DRIVE TYPES

Type	Cylinders	Heads	Write PreComp	Landing Zone
1	306	4	128	305
2	615	4	300	615
3	615	6	300	615
4	940	8	512	940
5	940	6	512	940
6	615	4	none	615
7	462	8	256	511
8	733	5	none	733
9	900	15	none	901
10	820	3	none	820
11	855	5	none	855
12	855	7	none	855
13	306	8	128	319
14	733	7	none	733
15	Extended			
16	612	4	all	663
17	977	5	300	977
18	977	7	none	977
19	1024	7	512	1023
20	733	5	300	732
21	733	7	300	732
22	733	5	300	733
23	306	4	none	336
24-255	RESERVED			

Source: IBM PC/AT Technical Reference, pages 1-63 and 1-66

See Also: 7.50. AT Real Time Clock Status Register A

8.31. PS/2 POS I/O ADDRESS SPACE

Address	Function	Comments/Bit Meanings
94 (148)	System board enable/setup register	Bit 7 set=enable functions, zero=setup functions Bit 5 set=enables VGA, zero=setup VGA
95 (149)	RESERVED	
96 (150)	Adapter enable /setup register	
97 (151)	RESERVED	
100 (256)	POS register 0 -- LO adapter ID byte	Read only
101 (257)	POS register 1 -- HO adapter ID byte	Read only
102 (258)	POS register 2 -- option select data byte 1	Read/write if implemented (bit 0=card enable)
103 (259)	POS register 3 -- option select data byte 2	Read/write if implemented
104 (260)	POS register 4 -- option select data byte 3	Read/write if implemented
105 (261)	POS register 5 -- option select data byte 4	Read/write if implemented (bit 7=channel active, bit 6=channel status)
106 (262)	POS register 6 -- LO subaddress extension	
107 (263)	POS register 7 -- HO subaddress extension	

Notes: Model 50, 60, and 80 only

Source: IBM PS/2 Model 50 and 60 Technical Reference, pages 2-21 to 2-28

See Also: 8.32. PS/2 POS Descriptor File Format
8.33. PS/2 POS ID Assignments

8.32. PS/2 POS DESCRIPTOR FILE FORMAT

Command Syntax	Function	Example	Example Explanation
ADAPTER ID number	Defines card's ID number	AdapterId 0DEAFh	Card's ID is 0DEAF hex
ADAPTER NAME string	Defines card's name	AdapterName "Thom's Hearing Aid"	Card's name is "Thom's Hearing Aid"
NUMBYTES number	Number of POS bytes used	NumBytes 2	Card uses 2 POS bytes
FIXED RESOURCES pos_setting resource_setting	Defines resources required by card	FixedResources POS[1]="XXXXXX01" int 3	Card uses first POS byte, LO 2 bits
NAMED ITEM prompt {choice...} help	Defines choices for a resource	Named_Item Prompt "Communications Port to Use:" choice "COM1" pos[0]=XXXXXX01b io 03f8h-03ffh int 4 choice "COM2" pos[0]=XXXXXX10b io 02f8h-02ffh int 3 Help "select one of the two serial ports listed"	Names an item in pos[0] used to store the user's choice of serial ports
PROMPT string	Defines a string	See Named Item, above	
CHOICE choice_name pos_setting resource_setting	Defines a named choice	See Named Item, above	
HELP string	Defines a help string	See Named Item, above	
POS[number]=bitlist	Defines one or more POS byte settings	Pos[0]=XX1XX0XX01b	X=ignored, 1=set bit, 0=clear bit
IO {range...}	Defines one or more I/O address ranges	See Named Item, above (io 03f8h-03ffh, for example)	
INT {number...}	Defines one or more interrupts used	See Named Item, above (int 4, for example)	
ARB {number...}	Defines one or more arbitration levels	ARB 1	Sets arbitration level 1
MEM {range...}	Defines one or more memory ranges	MEM 0C0000h-0CFFFFh	Card uses memory from 0C000-CFFFh

Notes:

- IO, INT, ARB, and MEM are resource_settings
- POS is a pos_setting
- Does not apply to Model 30
- File must contain at least one Card_ID, one Card_Name, and NumBytes; all else is optional

Source: IBM PS/2 Model 50 and 60 Technical Reference, pages 2-38 to 2-46

See Also: 8.33. PS/2 POS ID Assignments

8.33. PS/2 POS ID ASSIGNMENTS

ID	IBM Definition
0000	RESERVED
0001-0FFF	Bus master
5000-5FFF	Direct memory access devices
6000-6FFF	Direct program control (includes memory-mapped I/O devices)
7000-7FFF	Storage or multiple function devices
8000-80FF	Video devices
FFFF	Device not attached

Notes: These IDs are IBM guidelines only; manufacturers are free to determine their own IDs, although to do so may cause conflicts.

Source: IBM PS/2 Model 50 and 60 Technical Reference, page 2-108

See Also: 8.31. PS/2 POS I/O Address Space

8.34. PS/2 MODEL 50/60/80 DMA I/O ADDRESS MAP

Address	Function
0 (0)	Channel 0 memory address register
1 (1)	Channel 0 transfer count register
2 (2)	Channel 1 memory address register
3 (3)	Channel 1 transfer count register
4 (4)	Channel 2 memory address register
5 (5)	Channel 2 transfer count register
6 (6)	Channel 3 memory address register
7 (7)	Channel 3 transfer count register
8 (8)	Status register for channels 0-3
A (10)	Mask register (set/reset) for channels 0-3
B (11)	Mode register (write) for channels 0-3
C (12)	Clear byte pointer
D (13)	Master clear
E (14)	Clear mask register for channels 0-3
F (15)	Write mask register for channels 0-3
18 (24)	Extended function register
1A (26)	Extended function execute
81 (129)	Channel 2 page table address register (upper byte)
82 (130)	Channel 3 page table address register (upper byte)
83 (131)	Channel 1 page table address register (upper byte)
87 (135)	Channel 0 page table address register (upper byte)
89 (137)	Channel 6 page table address register (upper byte)
8A (138)	Channel 7 page table address register (upper byte)
8B (139)	Channel 5 page table address register (upper byte)
8F (143)	Channel 4 page table address register (upper byte)
C0 (192)	Channel 4 memory address register
C2 (194)	Channel 4 transfer count register
C4 (196)	Channel 5 memory address register
C6 (198)	Channel 5 transfer count register
C8 (200)	Channel 6 memory address register
CA (202)	Channel 6 transfer count register
CC (204)	Channel 7 memory address register
CE (206)	Channel 7 transfer count register
D0 (208)	Status register for channels 4-7
D4 (212)	Mask register for channels 4-7
D6 (214)	Mode register for channels 4-7
D8 (216)	Clear byte pointer
DA (218)	Master clear
DC (220)	Clear mask register for channels 4-7
DE (222)	Write mask register for channels 4-7

Notes: •Channels 0-3 follow PC/AT guidelines
•Model 30 follows XT DMA guidelines

Source: IBM PS/2 Model 50 and 60 Technical Reference, page 3-13

See Also: 8.35. PS/2 DMA Registers

8.35. PS/2 DMA REGISTERS

Register	Size	Comments	7	6	5	4	3	2	1	0	Allowable Values
						Bit Numbers					
Memory address	24 bits	1 per channel									
I/O address	16 bits	1 per channel									
Transfer count	16 bits	1 per channel									
Temporary holding	16 bits	1 for all channels									always one more than the number of DMA transfers
Mask	4 bits	1 each for channels 0-3, 4-7	X	X	X	X	X				RESERVED
										X	Mask bit (0=clear, 1=set)
								X	X		Channel select (00=0 or 4, 01=1 or 5, 10=2 or 6, 11=3 or 7)
Arbus	4 bits	1 each for channels 0 and 4	X	X	X	X					RESERVED
							X	X	X	X	Arbitration level (4-bit binary value)
Mode	8 bits	1 per channel	X	X	X	X	X				RESERVED (bit 5 must be set to 0)
								X	X		00=verify op, 01=write op, 10=read op, 11=reserved op
									X	X	00=select channel 0 or 4, 01=1 or 5, 10=2 or 6, 11=3 or 7
Status	8 bits	1 each for channels 0-3, 4-7	X								channel 3 or 7 request
				X							channel 2 or 6 request
					X						channel 1 or 5 request
						X					channel 0 or 4 request
							X				terminal count on channel 3 or 7
								X			terminal count on channel 2 or 6
									X		terminal count on channel 1 or 5
										X	terminal count on channel 0 or 4
Function	8 bits	1 for all channels (see note in source on DMA Extended Operations, page 3-18, for extended use of function register)	X	X	X	X		X	X	X	When operating as function register: program control / RESERVED / channel number
			X	X		X	X	X	X		When operating as extended mode register: RESERVED (bit 4 must be 0) / 0=8 bit transfer, 1=16-bit transfer / 0=read memory transfer, 1=write to memory transfer / 0=verify, 1=transfer data
Refresh	9 bits	Independent of DMA								X	0=I/O address equals 0000H, 1=use programmed I/O addr.

Notes: Does not apply to Model 30

Source: IBM PS/2 Model 50 and 60 Technical Reference, pages 3-14 to 3-20

See Also: 8.34. PS/2 Model 50/60/80 DMA I/O Address Map

8.36. PS/2 COUNTER REGISTERS

Register	Address	Comments	Bit Numbers								Allowable Values
			7	6	5	4	3	2	1	0	
Read/write counter 0	40 (64)										
Read/write counter 2	42 (66)										
Write control byte	43 (67)	For counter 0 and 2	X	X	X	X	X	X	X	X	SC1 and SC0: 00=counter 0, 10=counter 2 (others reserved) RW1 and RW2: 00=counter latch command 01=read/write counter bits 0-7 only 10=read/write counter bits 8-15 only 11=read/write counter bits 0=7, then 8-15 M2, M1, and M0: 000=mode 0, 001=mode 1 010=mode 2, 011=mode 3 100=mode 4, 101=mode 5 BCD: 0=16 bit binary counter, 1=BCD decimal counter
Read/write counter 3	44 (68)										
Write control byte	47 (71)	For counter 3	X	X	X	X	X	X	X	X	SC1 and SC0: 00=counter 3 (others reserved) RW1 and RW2: 00=counter latch select counter 0 01=read/write counter bits 0-7 only 10=reserved 11=reserved Must be 0

Notes: Does not apply to Model 30

Source: IBM PS/2 Model 50 and 60 Technical Reference, pages 3-29 to 3-32

8.37. PS/2 SYSTEM CONTROL PORT A (92H)

Bit Numbers

7	6	5	4	3	2	1	0	Function	Allowable Values
X	X							Disk activity light	Any bit set to 1 turns activity light on
		X			X			RESERVED	
X			X					Watchdog timer status	R/O. 0=no timeout, 1=timeout occurred
				X				RT/CMOS security lock	0=unlocked, 1=locked (done by POST)
						X		A20 active indicator	0=A20 line is inactive, 1=A20 is active
							X	Alternate CPU reset	0=system reset or write, 1=pulse alt reset pin

Notes: Does not apply to Model 30

Source: IBM PS/2 Model 50 and 60 Technical Reference, pages 4-194 to 4-195

See Also: 8.38. PS/2 System Control Port B (61H)

8.38. PS/2 SYSTEM CONTROL PORT B (61H)

Bit Numbers

7	6	5	4	3	2	1	0	Function for Write Operations	Function for Read Operations
X								1=IRQ 0 reset (timer 0 output latch)	Parity check state (1=parity check occurred)
	X							RESERVED	Channel check state (1=channel check occurred)
		X						RESERVED	Mirrors timer 2 output condition
			X					RESERVED	Toggles on each refresh request
				X				1=Enable channel check (0=disable)	Channel check status
					X			1=Enable parity check (0=disable)	Parity check status
						X		1=Enable speaker data (0=disable)	Speaker data status
							X	1=Enable timer 2 gate (0=disable)	Timer 2 gate status

Notes: Does not apply to Model 30

Source: IBM PS/2 Model 50 and 60 Technical Reference, pages 4-192 to 4-194

See Also: 8.37. PS/2 System Control Port A (92H)

8.39. PS/2 RT/CMOS AND NMI MASK (70H)

Bit Numbers

7	6	5	4	3	2	1	0	Function	Allowable Values
X								Non-maskable interrupt (NMI)	0=NMI masked, 1=NMI enabled
	X							RESERVED	
		X	X	X	X	X	X	RT/CMOS RAM address	(Used with port 71H to write to that address)

Notes: Does not apply to Model 30

Source: IBM PS/2 Model 50 and 60 Technical Reference, pages 4-194 and 4-183

— SECTION —
9

Hardware
Descriptions

9.01. 9-PIN SERIAL PORT CONNECTOR

Pin #	Description	Abbrev.	Direction*
1	Data carrier detect	DCD	In
2	Receive data	RX	In
3	Transmit data	TX	Out
4	Data terminal ready	DTR	Out
5	Signal ground	GND	
6	Data set ready	DSR	In
7	Request to send	RTS	Out
8	Clear to send	CTS	In
9	Ring indicator	RI	In

Notes: •Pin numbers refer only to DB-9P connector
•RI connection not required to operate
•*When AT configured as DTE device

Source: *Communications and Networking for the IBM PC and Compatibles*
(Brady), Larry Jordan and Bruce Churchill, page 120

See Also: 9.02. 25-Pin Serial Port Connector
9.04. RS-232C Serial Port Connector (DTE Device)

9.02. 25-PIN SERIAL PORT CONNECTOR

Pin #	Description	Abbrev.	Direction*
1	Chassis ground		
2	Transmit data	TX	Out
3	Receive data	RX	In
4	Request to send	RTS	Out
5	Clear to send	CTS	In
6	Data set ready	DSR	In
7	Signal ground	SG	
8	Carrier detect	DCD	In
9	Pos transmit current loop return**		Out
11	Neg transmit current loop data**		Out
18	Pos receive current loop data**		In
20	Data terminal ready	DTR	Out
22	Ring indicator	RI	In
25	Neg receive current loop return**		In

Notes: •RI connection not required to operate
•Pin numbers refer to DB-25P connector only
•*When PC configured as DTE device
•**Used for current loop communications only

Source: IBM Technical Reference Options and Adapters Volume 2, pages
Async 23 to 24

See Also: 9.01. 9-Pin Serial Port Connector
9.04. RS-232C Serial Port Connector (DTE Device)

9.03. PS/2 SERIAL PORT CONNECTOR

Connector	Pin Number	Direction	Model 30	Model 50/60/80
System end	1		Not connected	Not connected
(DB25)	2	Out	Transmit data	Transmit data
	3	In	Receive data	Receive data
	4	Out	Request to send	Request to send
	5	In	Clear to send	Clear to send
	6	In	Data set ready	Data set ready
	7		Signal ground	Signal ground
	8	In	RLSD	Data carrier detect
	9		Not connected	Not connected
	10		Not connected	Not connected
	11	Out	Connected to pin 20	Not connected
	12		Not connected	Not connected
	13		Not connected	Not connected
	14		Not connected	Not connected

(Continued)

Table 9.03. Continued

Connector	Pin Number	Direction	Model 30	Model 50/60/80
System end (DB25)	15		Not connected	Not connected
	16		Not connected	Not connected
	17		Not connected	Not connected
	18		Not connected	Not connected
	19		Not connected	Not connected
	20	Out	Data terminal ready	Data terminal ready
	21		Not connected	Not connected
	22	In	Ring indicate	Ring indicate
	23		Not connected	Not connected
	24		Not connected	Not connected
	25		Not connected	Not connected

Source: IBM PS/2 Model 30 Technical Reference, page 1-122
IBM PS/2 Model 50 and 60 Technical Reference, page 4-171

See Also: 9.01. 9-pin Serial Port Connector
9.02. 25-Pin Serial Port Connector
9.04. RS-232C Serial Port Connector (DTE Device)

9.04. RS-232C SERIAL PORT CONNECTOR (DTE DEVICE)

Pin #	Definition	Abbrev	Direction	Used by PC	Used by AT
1	Protective ground (chassis ground)		NA	Yes, as defined	Yes, different pin
2	Transmitted data	TX	Out	Yes, as defined	Yes, different pin
3	Received data	RX	In	Yes, as defined	Yes, different pin
4	Request to send	RTS	Out	Yes, as defined	Yes, different pin
5	Clear to send	CTS	In	Yes, as defined	Yes, different pin
6	Data set ready	DSR	In	Yes, as defined	Yes, different pin
7	Signal ground	SG	NA	Yes, as defined	Yes, different pin
8	Received line signal detector	DCD	In	Yes, as defined	Yes, different pin
9	RESERVED		NA	(+t current loop)	No
10	RESERVED		NA	No	No
11	UNASSIGNED		NA	(-t current loop)	No
12	Secondary received line signal detector		In	No	No
13	Secondary clear to send		In	No	No
14	Secondary transmitted data		Out	No	No
15	Transmission signal element timing		Out	No	No
16	Secondary received data		In	No	No
17	Receiver signal element timing		In	No	No
18	UNASSIGNED		NA	(+r current loop)	No
19	Secondary request to send		Out	No	No
20	Data terminal ready	DTR	Out	Yes, as defined	Yes, different pin
21	Signal quality detector		In	No	No
22	Ring indicator	RI	In	Yes, as defined	Yes, different pin
23	Data signal rate selector			No	No
24	Transmit signal element timing		Out	No	No
25	UNASSIGNED		NA	(-r current loop)	No

Notes: •The IBM PC and AT are normally configured as a DTE device
•While not part of the standard, a DB-25P connector is often used at the DTE device, as in the IBM PC. Its pinouts look like this:

```
1                         13
  o o o o o o o o o o o o o
    o o o o o o o o o o o o
  14                    25
```

Source: EIA Standard RS-232-C, August 1969
IBM PC/XT Technical Reference, page 1-211

See Also: 9.01. 9-Pin Serial Port Connector
9.02. 25-Pin Serial Port Connector

9.05. PS/2 15-PIN VIDEO CONNECTOR

Connector	Pin Number	Direction	Monochrome	Color
System end (DB15)	1	Out	NO PIN	Red
	2	Out	Mono	Green
	3	Out	NO PIN	Blue
	4		NO PIN	NO PIN
	5		Self test	Self test
	6		KEY	Red return*
	7		Mono return	Green return*
	8		NO PIN	Blue return*
	9		NO PIN	NO PIN
	10		Digital ground	Digital ground
	11		NO PIN	Digital ground
	12		Digital ground	NO PIN
	13	Out	HSync	HSync
	14	Out	VSync	VSync
	15		NO PIN	NO PIN

Notes: *Analog grounds

Source: IBM PS/2 Model 30 Technical Reference, page 1-78
                  IBM PS/2 Model 50 and 60 Technical Reference,
                  page 4-125

See Also: 9.10. MDA Video Connector
                  9.11. CGA RGB Connector
                  9.12. EGA RGB Connector

9.06. CGA COMPOSITE VIDEO CONNECTOR

Pin #	Description	Direction*
1	Peak to peak amplitude	Out
2	Ground	

Notes: •Video signal is approximately 1.5Vdc
                  •Pin numbers refer to RCA phono jack (1=pin, 2=shell)
                  •*From PC

Source: IBM Technical Reference Options and Adapters Volume 2,
                  page Color/Graphics 24

See Also: 9.10. MDA Video Connector
                  9.11. CGA RGB Connector
                  9.12. EGA RGB Connector

9.07. EGA FEATURE CONNECTOR

Pin Number	Signal Name	Direction
1	GND	
2	-12V	
3	+12V	
4	J1	
5	J2	
6	G'OUT	Out
7	R'OUT	Out
8	B'OUT	Out
9	ATRS/L	
10	B OUT	Out
11	G OUT	Out
12	G	In
13	R'	In
14	B	In
15	R	In
16	R OUT	Out
17	FEAT 1	Out

Pin Number	Signal Name	Direction
18	BLANK	
19	FEAT 0	Out
20	FCI	In
21	FCO	In
22	G'/I	In
23	B'/V	In
24	HIN	In
25	VIN	In
26	14 MHz	
27	Internal	Out
28	EXT OSC	Out
29	V OUT	Out
30	H OUT	Out
31	GND	
32	+5V	

Notes: •Signals preceded by a minus sign are negative true

Source: IBM Technical Reference Options and Adapters Volume 1, pages EGA 76-78

See Also: 9.12. EGA RGB Connector

9.08. CGA LIGHT PEN CONNECTOR

Pin #	Description	Direction*
1	-Light pen input	In
2	KEY (NOT USED)	
3	-Light pen switch	In
4	Chassis ground	
5	+5Vdc	Out
6	+12Vdc	Out

Notes: •Pin numbers refer to 6-pin Berg Strip on CGA board (P2)
•*From PC

Source: IBM Technical Reference Options and Adapters Volume 2, page Color/Graphics 25

See Also: 9.09. CGA RF Modulator Connector
9.10. MDA Video Connector
9.11. CGA RGB Connector
9.12. EGA RGB Connector

9.09. CGA RF MODULATOR CONNECTOR

Pin #	Description	Direction*
1	+12Vdc	Out
2	KEY (NOT USED)	
3	Composite video output	Out
4	Logic ground	

Notes: •Pin numbers refer to 4-pin Berg Strip on CGA board (P1)
•*From PC

Source: IBM Technical Reference Options and Adapters Volume 2, page Color/Graphics 25

See Also: 9.08. CGA Light Pen Connector
9.10. MDA Video Connector
9.11. CGA RGB Connector
9.12. EGA RGB Connector

9.10. MDA VIDEO CONNECTOR

Pin #	Description	Direction*
1	Ground	
2	Ground	
3	NOT USED	
4	NOT USED	
5	NOT USED	
6	+Intensity	Out
7	+Video	Out
8	+Horizontal	Out
9	-Vertical	Out

Notes: •Pin numbers refer to DB-9 connector
              •Signal voltages are 0.0 to 0.6 Vdc (0 level) and +2.4 to 3.5Vdc (1 level)
              •Parallel port pinouts are documented separately; see 9.34. Parallel Printer Connector
              •*From PC

Source: IBM Technical Reference Options and Adapters Volume 2, page Monochrome 9

See Also: 9.09. CGA RF Modulator Connector
              9.12. EGA RGB Connector
              9.13. VGA RGB Connector
              9.34. Parallel Printer Connector

9.11. CGA RGB CONNECTOR

Pin #	Description	Direction*
1	Ground	
2	Ground	
3	Red	Out
4	Green	Out
5	Blue	Out
6	+Intensity	Out
7	RESERVED	Out
8	+Horizontal drive	Out
9	-Vertical drive	Out

Notes: •Pin numbers refer to DB-9 connector
              •*From PC

Source: IBM Technical Reference Options and Adapters Volume 2,
              page Color/Graphics 24

See Also: 9.06. CGA Composite Video Connector
              9.08. CGA Light Pen Connector
              9.09. CGA RF Modulator Connector
              9.10. MDA Video Connector
              9.12. EGA RGB Connector
              9.13. VGA RGB Connector

9.12. EGA RGB CONNECTOR

Pin #	Description	Direction*
1	Ground	
2	S. red	Out
3	Red	Out
4	Green	Out
5	Blue	Out
6	Intensity/s. green	Out
7	S. blue/mono video	Out
8	Horizontal drive	Out
9	Vertical drive	Out

Notes: •Pin numbers refer to DC-9 connector
              •*From PC

Source: IBM Technical Reference Options and Adapters Volume 1,
              page Enhanced Graphics Adapter 83

See Also: 9.10. MDA Video Connector
              9.11. CGA RGB Connector

9.13. VGA RGB CONNECTOR

Pin #	Function	Mono Disp.	Color Disp.	Direction*
1	Red		Red output	Out
2	Green	Mono output	Green output	Out
3	Blue		Blue output	Out
4	RESERVED			
5	Digital ground	Self test	Self test	
6	Red return (analog ground)	KEY	Red return	
7	Green return (analog ground)	Mono return	Green return	
8	Blue return (analog ground)		Blue return	
9	Plug			
10	Digital ground	Digital ground	Digital ground	
11	RESERVED		Digital ground	
12	RESERVED	Digital ground		
13	Horizontal drive	Horizontal drive	Horizontal drive	Out
14	Vertical drive	Vertical drive	Vertical drive	Out
15	RESERVED			

Notes: •Pin numbers refer to DC-15 connector
  •*From PC

Source: IBM PS/2 Model 50 and 60 Technical Reference, page 4-125

See Also: 9.10. MDA Video Connector
  9.11. CGA RGB Connector
  9.12. EGA RGB Connector

9.14. PC & XT FLOPPY DISK CONTROLLER INTERNAL CONNECTOR

Pin Number	Signal Name	Direction
1	Ground	
2	UNUSED	
3	Ground	
4	UNUSED	
5	Ground	
6	UNUSED	
7	Ground	
8	Index	From drive
9	Ground	
10	Motor enable A	From controller
11	Ground	
12	Drive select B	From controller
13	Ground	
14	Drive select A	From controller
15	Ground	
16	Motor enable B	From controller
17	Ground	
18	Direction (stepper motor)	From controller
19	Ground	
20	Step pulse	From controller
21	Ground	
22	Write data	From controller
23	Ground	
24	Write enable	From controller
25	Ground	
26	Track 0	From drive
27	Ground	
28	Write protect	From drive
29	Ground	
30	Read data	From drive
31	Ground	
32	Select head 1	From controller
33	Ground	
34	UNUSED	

Notes: •All signals are at standard TTL levels
  •Connector is a 34-pin keyed edge connector
  (key between pins 6 and 8)
  •Even numbers are on component side of board

Source: IBM PC/XT Technical Reference, page 1-128

See Also: 9.15. PC & XT Floppy Disk Controller External Connector

9.15. PC & XT FLOPPY DISK CONTROLLER EXTERNAL CONNECTOR

Pin Number	Signal Name	Direction
1	UNUSED	
2	UNUSED	
3	UNUSED	
4	UNUSED	
5	UNUSED	
6	Index	From drive
7	Motor enable C	From controller
8	Drive select D	From controller
9	Drive select C	From controller
10	Motor enable D	From controller
11	Direction (stepper motor)	From controller
12	Step pulse	From controller
13	Write data	From controller
14	Write enable	From controller
15	Track 0	From drive
16	Write protect	From drive
17	Read data	From drive
18	Select head 1	From controller
19	NOT USED	

Pin Number	Signal Name	Direction
20	Ground	
21	Ground	
22	Ground	
23	Ground	
24	Ground	
25	Ground	
26	Ground	
27	Ground	
28	Ground	
29	Ground	
30	Ground	
31	Ground	
32	Ground	
33	Ground	
34	Ground	
35	Ground	
36	Ground	
37	Ground	

Notes: •All signals are at standard TTL levels
                 •Connector is a 37-pin D-Shell connector

Source: IBM PC/XT Technical Reference, page 1-129

See Also: 9.14. PC & XT Floppy Disk Controller Internal Connector

9.16. XT FIXED DISK CONTROLLER CONNECTOR J1

Pin Number	Signal Name	Direction
1	Ground	
2	-Reduced write current (Active Low)	From controller
3	Ground	
4	RESERVED	
5	Ground	
6	-Write gate (Active Low)	From controller
7	Ground	
8	-Seek complete (Active Low)	From drive
9	Ground	
10	-Track 00 (Active Low)	From drive
11	Ground	
12	-Write fault (Active Low)	From drive
13	Ground	
14	-Head select 0 (Active Low)	From controller
15	Ground	
16	RESERVED	
17	Ground	
18	-Head select 1 (Active Low)	From controller
19	Ground	
20	-Index (Active Low)	From drive
21	Ground	
22	-Ready (Active Low)	From drive
23	Ground	
24	-Step (Active Low)	From controller
25	Ground	
26	-Drive select 1 (Active Low)	From controller
27	Ground	
28	-Drive select 2 (Active Low)	From controller
29	Ground	
30	RESERVED	From drive
31	Ground	
32	RESERVED	From controller
33	Ground	
34	-Direction in (Active Low)	From controller

Notes: •Signals preceded by a minus sign are negative true
             •Connector is 34-pin double-row plug

See Also: 9.14. PC & XT Floppy Disk Controller Internal Connector
                9.15. PC & XT Floppy Disk Controller External Connector
                9.17. XT Fixed Disk Controller Connectors J2 and J3

Source: IBM PC/XT Technical Reference, page 1-149

9.17. XT FIXED DISK CONTROLLER CONNECTORS J2 AND J3

Pin Number	Signal Name	Direction
1	Drive select	From drive
2	Ground	
3	RESERVED	
4	Ground	
5	NO PIN (key)	
6	Ground	
7	RESERVED	
8	Ground	
9	UNUSED	
10	UNUSED	

Pin Number	Signal Name	Direction
11	Ground	
12	Ground	
13	MFM write data	From controller
14	-MFM write data (Active Low)	From controller
15	Ground	
16	Ground	
17	MFM read data	From drive
18	-MFM read data (Active Low)	From drive
19	Ground	
20	Ground	

Notes: •Signals preceded by a minus sign are negative true
•Connector is 20-pin double-row plug with key notch at pin 5

Source: IBM PC/XT Technical Reference, page 1-149

See Also: 9.14. PC & XT Floppy Disk Controller Internal Connector
9.15. PC & XT Floppy Disk Controller External Connector
9.16. XT Fixed Disk Controller Connector J1

9.18. PS/2 MODEL 30 DISKETTE DRIVE CONNECTOR

Pin Number	Direction	Signal Name
1		Signal ground
2	Out	-High density select (Active Low)
3		RESERVED
4		RESERVED
5		Signal ground
6		RESERVED
7		Signal ground
8	In	-Index (Active Low)
9		Signal ground
10	Out	-Motor enable 1 (Active Low)
11		Signal ground
12	Out	-Drive select 0 (Active Low)
13		Signal ground
14	Out	-Drive select 1 (Active Low)
15		Signal ground
16	Out	-Motor enable 0 (Active Low)
17		Signal ground
18	Out	-Direction (Active Low)
19		Signal ground
20	Out	-Step (Active Low)
21		Signal ground
22	Out	-Write data (Active Low)
23		Signal ground
24	Out	-Write enable (Active Low)
25		Signal ground
26	In	-Track 0 (Active Low)
27		Signal ground
28	In	-Write protect (Active Low)
29		Signal ground
30	In	-Read data (Active Low)
31		Signal ground
32	Out	-Head 1 select (Active Low)
33		Signal ground
34	In	-Diskette change (Active Low)
35		Ground
36		Ground
37		Ground
38	Out	+5V
39		Ground
40	Out	+12V

Notes: Drive gets power via this connector

Source: IBM PS/2 Model 30 Technical Reference, page 1-105

See Also: 9.20. PS/2 Model 50 Diskette Drive Connector

9.19. PS/2 MODEL 30 FIXED DRIVE CONNECTOR

Pin Number	Direction	Signal Name
1	Out	RESET DRV
2	In	-DISK installed
3	In/out	D0
4		Ground
5	In/out	D1
6		Ground
7	In/out	D2
8		Ground
9	In/out	D3
10		Ground
11	In/out	D4
12		Ground
13	In/out	D5
14		Ground
15	In/out	D6
16		Ground
17	In/out	D7
18		Ground
19	Out	-IOR
20		Ground
21	Out	-IOW
22		Ground
23	Out	-DISK CS
24		Ground
25	Out	A0
26		Ground
27	Out	A1
28		Ground
29	Out	A2
30	Out	+5V
31		RESERVED
32	Out	+5V
33	Out	-DACK3
34		Ground
35	In	DRQ3
36		Ground
37	In	IRQ5
38		Ground
39	In	IO CH ready
40	Out	+12V
41		Spare
42	Out	+12V
43		Spare
44	Out	+12V

Notes: Drive gets power via this connector

Source: IBM PS/2 Model 30 Technical Reference, page 1-107

See Also: 9.16. XT Fixed Disk Controller Connector J1
                 9.17. XT Fixed Disk Controller Connectors J2 and J3

9.20. PS/2 MODEL 50 DISKETTE DRIVE CONNECTOR

Connector	Pin Number	Direction	Signal
50-pin PC	1	In	2nd drive installed
Edge Connector	2	Out	-High density select (Active Low)
	3		Ground
	4		Ground
	5		Ground
	6		RESERVED
	7		Signal ground
	8	In	-Index (Active Low)
	9		Signal ground
	10	Out	-Motor enable 0 (Active Low)
	11		Signal ground
	12	Out	-Drive select 1 (Active Low)
	13		Ground
	14	Out	-Drive select 0 (Active Low)
	15		Signal ground
	16	Out	-Motor enable 1 (Active Low)
	17		Signal ground
	18	Out	-Direction (Active Low)
	19		Signal ground
	20	Out	-Step (Active Low)
	21		Signal ground
	22	Out	-Write data (Active Low)
	23		Signal ground
	24	Out	-Write enable (Active Low)
	25		Signal ground
	26	In	-Track 0 (Active Low)
	27		Signal ground
	28	In	-Write protect (Active Low)
	29		Signal ground
	30	In	-Read data (Active Low)
	31		Signal ground
	32	Out	-Head 1 select (Active Low)
	33		Signal ground
	34	In	-Diskette change (Active Low)
	35		Ground
	36		Ground
	37		Ground
	38		+5V
	39		Ground
	40		+12V
	41		RESERVED
	42		RESERVED
	43		RESERVED
	44		RESERVED
	45		RESERVED
	46		RESERVED
	47		RESERVED
	48		RESERVED
	49		RESERVED
	50		RESERVED

Source: IBM PS/2 Model 50 and 60 Technical Reference, page 4-153

See Also: 9.18. PS/2 Model 30 Diskette Drive Connector

9.21. PC & XT POWER SUPPLY CONNECTORS

Connector	Pin Number	Signal Name
5.25 floppy drive	1	+12V
	2	Ground
	3	Ground
	4	+5V
Fixed disk drive (or 2nd floppy)	1	+12V
	2	Ground
	3	Ground
	4	+5V
System board 1	1	Ground
	2	Ground
	3	-5V
	4	+5V
	5	+5V
	6	+5V
System board 2	1	Power ground
	2	KEY
	3	+12V
	4	-12V
	5	Ground
	6	Ground

Notes: Connectors are 4-pin molex connectors or 12-pin, 2-row plugs

Source: IBM PC/XT Technical Reference, pages 1-21 to 1-24

9.22. AT BATTERY CONNECTOR J21

Pin Number	Signal Name
1	Ground
2	NOT USED
3	Key
4	6 Vdc

Notes: Connector is a 4-pin keyed Berg connector (keyed on pin 3)

Source: IBM PC/AT Technical Reference, page 1-72

See Also: 9.23. AT Power Supply Connectors PS8, PS9, PS10, PS11, and PS12

9.23. AT POWER SUPPLY CONNECTORS PS8, PS9, PS10, PS11, and PS12

Connector	Pin Number	Signal Name
System board 1	1	Power good
PS8	2	+5Vdc
Back of board	3	+12Vdc
	4	-12Vdc
	5	Ground
	6	Ground
System board 2	1	Ground
PS9	2	Ground
Front of board	3	-5Vdc
	4	+5Vdc
	5	+5Vdc
	6	+5Vdc
PS10	1	+12V
1st floppy	2	Ground
	3	Ground
	4	+5V
PS11	1	+12V
2nd floppy	2	Ground
	3	Ground
	4	+5V
PS12	1	+12V
Fixed disk	2	Ground
	3	Ground
	4	+5V

Notes: Connectors are 4-pin molex connectors or 6-pin, 1-row plugs

Source: IBM PC/AT Technical Reference, pages 1-71 and 3-7

See Also: 9.22. AT Battery Connector J21

9.24. PS/2 MODEL 30 POWER SUPPLY CONNECTORS

Connector	Pin Number	Signal Name
P3	1	Power good
Rear of system	2	Ground
	3	+12V
	4	-12V
	5	Ground
	6	Ground
P4	1	Ground
Front of system	2	Ground
	3	-5V
	4	+5V
	5	+5V
	6	+5V

Notes: Connectors are 6-pin, 1-row plugs

Source: IBM PS/2 Model 30 Technical Reference, page 3-6

9.25. PS/2 MODEL 50 POWER SUPPLY CONNECTOR

Connector	Pin Number	Direction	Signal
50-pin PC	1		-12V
edge connector	2		Signal ground
	3		+12V
	4		Signal ground
	5		+12V
	6		Signal ground
	7		+12V
	8		Signal ground
	9		+12V
	10		Signal ground
	11		+12V
	12		Signal ground
	13		+12V
	14		Signal ground
	15		+5V
	16		Signal ground
	17		+5V
	18		Signal ground
	19		+5V
	20		Signal ground
	21		+5V
	22		Signal ground
	23		+5V
	24		Signal ground
	25		+5V
	26		Signal ground
	27		+5V
	28		Signal ground
	29		+5V
	30		Signal ground
	31		+5V
	32		Signal ground
	33		+5V
	34		Signal ground
	35		+5V
	36		Signal ground
	37		+5V
	38		Signal ground
	39		+5V
	40		Signal ground
	41		+5V
	42		Signal ground
	43		+5V
	44		Signal ground
	45		+5V
	46		Signal ground
	47		+5V
	48		Signal ground
	49	In	System status
	50	Out	Power good

Source: IBM PS/2 Model 50 and 60 Technical Reference, page 5-6

9.26. PS/2 MODEL 60 POWER SUPPLY CONNECTOR

Connector	Pin Number	Direction	Signal
15-pin	1		+5V
arranged as	2		Signal ground
3x5 keyed	3		+12V
matrix	4		+5V
	5		Signal ground
	6		Signal ground
	7		+5V
	8		Signal ground
	9		-12V
	10		+5V
	11		Signal ground
	12	Out	Power good
	13		+5V
	14		Signal ground
	15	In	System status

Source: IBM PS/2 Model 50 and 60 Technical Reference, page 5-7

9.27. PC & XT KEYBOARD CONNECTOR

Pin Number	Signal Name
1	+Keyboard clock (+5Vdc signal level)
2	+Keyboard data (+5Vdc signal level)
3	-Keyboard reset (not used by keyboard)
4	Ground
5	+5Vdc

Notes: Connector is a 5-pin DIN connector

Source: IBM PC/XT Technical Reference, page 1-29

See Also: 9.28. PS/2 Keyboard and Mouse Connector

9.28. PS/2 KEYBOARD AND MOUSE CONNECTOR

Connector	Pin Number	Signal Name
System end	1	+KBD DATA
(6-pin DIN)	2	RESERVED
	3	Ground
	4	+5V
	5	+KBD CLK
	6	RESERVED
	Shield	Frame ground
Keyboard end	A	RESERVED
(6-pin phone)	B	+KBD DATA
	C	Ground
	D	+KBD CLOCK
	E	+5V
	F	RESERVED
	Shield	Frame ground

Source: IBM PS/2 Model 30 Technical Reference, page 4-41

See Also: 9.27. PC & XT Keyboard Connector

9.29. AT POWER LED AND KEYLOCK CONNECTOR J20

Pin Number	Signal Name
1	LED power
2	Key
3	Ground
4	Keyboard inhibit
5	Ground

Notes: Connector is a 5-pin Berg strip

Source: IBM PC/AT Technical Reference, page 1-72

9.30. PS/2 MODEL 50/60/80 MEMORY MODULE CONNECTOR

Connector	Pin Number	Direction	Signal
30-pin	1		5V
	2	In	-Column address strobe (Active Low)
	3	In/out	D1
	4	In	A1
	5	In	A2
	6	In/out	D2
	7	In	A3
	8	In	A4
	9		Ground
	10	In/out	D3
	11	In	A5
	12	In	A6
	13	In/out	D4
	14	In	A7
	15	In	A8
	16	In/out	D5
	17	In	A9
	18		No connection
	19	In	RAS1*
	20	In/out	D6
	21	In	-Write strobe (Active Low)
	22		Ground
	23	In/out	D7
	24	Out	Presence detect 1
	25	In/out	D8
	26	Out	Presence detect 2
	27	In	Row address strobe
	28		No connection
	29	In/out	D9 (parity)
	30		+5V

Notes: *Applicable only to 512 KB modules

Source: IBM PS/2 Model 50 and 60 Technical Reference, page 4-181

9.31. PS/2 PARALLEL PORT CONNECTOR

Connector	Pin Number	Direction*	Signal
System end (DB25)	1	In/out	-STROBE (Active Low)
	2	In/out	D0
	3	In/out	D1
	4	In/out	D2
	5	In/out	D3
	6	In/out	D4
	7	In/out	D5
	8	In/out	D6
	9	In/out	D7
	10	In	-ACK (Active Low)
	11	In	BUSY
	12	In	PE
	13	In	SLCT
	14	Out	-AUTO FEED XT (Active Low)
	15	In	-ERROR (Active Low)
	16	Out	-INIT (Active Low)
	17	Out	-SLCT IN (Active Low)
	18		Ground
	19		Ground
	20		Ground
	21		Ground
	22		Ground
	23		Ground
	24		Ground
	25		Ground

Notes: *From computer

Source: IBM PS/2 Model 30 Technical Reference, page 1-126
IBM PS/2 Model 50 and 60 Technical Reference, page 4-179

See Also: 9.32. Centronics Parallel Connector
9.34. Parallel Printer Connector

9.32. CENTRONICS PARALLEL CONNECTOR

Pin #	Definition	Direction
1	-Strobe	In
2	Data 1	In
3	Data 2	In
4	Data 3	In
5	Data 4	In
6	Data 5	In
7	Data 6	In
8	Data 7	In
9	Data 8	In
10	-Acknowledge (Active Low)	Out
11	Busy	Out
12	Paper End	Out
13	Select	Out
14	-Auto Feed (Active Low)	In
15	NOT USED	
16	Logical ground	
17	Chassis ground	
18	NOT USED	
19	Ground return for -Strobe	
20	Ground return for Data 1	
21	Ground return for Data 2	
22	Ground return for Data 3	
23	Ground return for Data 4	
24	Ground return for Data 5	
25	Ground return for Data 6	
26	Ground return for Data 7	
27	Ground return for Data 8	
28	Ground return for -Acknowledge	
29	Ground return for busy	
30	Ground	
31	-Printer Init (Active Low)	In
32	-Fault (Active Low)	Out
33	Ground	
34	NOT USED	
35	Pulled up to +5V through 4.7K ohm resistor	
36	-Select In (Active Low)	In

Notes: Connector is an Amphenol 57-30360 or equivalent
(Centronics parallel)

Source: IBM Technical Reference Options and Adapters Volume 1,
pages Graphics Printer 29 to 31

See Also: 9.04. RS-232C Serial Port Connector (DTE Device)
9.31. PS/2 Parallel Port Connector
9.34. Parallel Printer Connector

9.33. GAME ADAPTER CONNECTOR

Pin #	Direction	Signal Name	Active	Function
1	Out	+5Vdc		
2	In	Button 4	High	Paddle 1 button, joystick A button
3	In	Position 0	High	Paddle 1 position, joystick A x-coordinate
4		Ground		
5		Ground		
6	In	Position 1	High	Paddle 2 position, joystick A y-coordinate
7	In	Button 5	High	Paddle 2 button
8	Out	+5Vdc		
9	Out	+5Vdc		
10	In	Button 6	High	Paddle 3 button, joystick B button
11	In	Position 2	High	Paddle 3 position, joystick B x-coordinate
12		Ground		
13	In	Position 3	High	Paddle 4 position, joystick B y-coordinate
14	In	Button 7	High	Paddle 4 button
15	Out	+5Vdc		

Notes: Connector used is a female DB-15

Source: IBM Technical Reference Options and Adapters Volume 2, pages
Game Adapter 6 and 7

9.34. PARALLEL PRINTER CONNECTOR

Pin #	Direction	Signal Name	Active	Function
1	Out	Strobe	Low	Indicates valid data available
2	Out	Data bit 0	High	Least significant bit of data byte
3	Out	Data bit 1	High	
4	Out	Data bit 2	High	
5	Out	Data bit 3	High	
6	Out	Data bit 4	High	
7	Out	Data bit 5	High	
8	Out	Data bit 6	High	
9	Out	Data bit 7	High	Most significant bit of data byte
10	In	Acknowledge	Low	Indicates data received and device is ready for more
11	In	Busy	High	Device cannot receive data
12	In	P.End	High	Device is "out of paper"
13	In	Select	High	Device is in "selected state"
14	Out	Auto Feed	Low	Device to perform line feed after each line sent
15	In	Error	Low	Device unable to perform
16	Out	Initialize printer	Low	Reset device to initial state
17	In	Select input	Low	Device can accept input
18	NA	Ground	NA	
19	NA	Ground	NA	
20	NA	Ground	NA	
21	NA	Ground	NA	
22	NA	Ground	NA	
23	NA	Ground	NA	
24	NA	Ground	NA	
25	NA	Ground	NA	

Notes:
•Connector used is a female DB-25
•The original printer adapter and monochrome display adapter parallel ports are output-only; no provision for parallel input was made until introduction of the PS/2

Source: IBM Technical Reference Options and Adapters Volume 2, page Printer Adapter 7

See Also: 9.31. PS/2 Parallel Port Connector
9.32. Centronics Parallel Connnector

9.35. PC & XT SPEAKER CONNECTOR

Pin Number	Signal Name
1	Data
2	Key
3	Ground
4	+5 Volts

Notes: Connector is a 4-pin keyed Berg connector
(keyed on pin 2)

Source: IBM PC/XT Technical Reference, page 1-20

9.36. 8088 AND 8086 PINOUTS

40-pin DIP packaging:

Pin	Signal
1	Ground
2	Address/Data 14
3	Address/Data 13
4	Address/Data 12
5	Address/Data 11
6	Address/Data 10
7	Address/Data 9
8	Address/Data 8
9	Address/Data 7
10	Address/Data 6
11	Address/Data 5
12	Address/Data 4
13	Address/Data 3
14	Address/Data 2
15	Address/Data 1
16	Address/Data 0
17	Nonmaskable Interrupt
18	Interrupt Request
19	Clock
20	Ground
21	Reset
22	Ready
23	-Test
24	Queue Status 1 (-Interrupt Acknowledge)
25	Queue Status 0 (Address Latch Enable)
26	-Status 0 (-Data Enable)
27	-Status 1 (Data Transmit/-Receive)
28	-Status 2 (Memory/-IO)
29	-Lock (-Write)
30	-Request 1 / -Grant 1 (Hold Acknowledge)
31	-Request 0 / -Grant 0 (Hold)
32	-Read
33	Min/-Max
34	-Bus High Enable / Status 7
35	Address/Data 19 / Status 6
36	Address/Data 18 / Status 5
37	Address/Data 17 / Status 4
38	Address/Data 16 / Status 3
39	Address/Data 15
40	+5V

notched end

44-pin PLCC packaging:

Top pins (1–6): +5V, No Connection, Ground, Address 13, Address 12, Address 11

Right-side / top-right pins (40–44, 1): 40 No Connection, 41 Address 15, 42 Address 16 / Status 3, 43 Address 17 / Status 4, 44 Address 18 / Status 5, Address 14

Pin	Signal
39	No Connection
38	Address 16 / Status 6
37	-Bus High Enable / Status 7
36	Min/-Max
35	-Read
34	-Request 0 / -Grant 0
33	-Request 1 / -Grant 1
32	-Lock
31	-Status 2
30	-Status 1
29	-Status 0

Pin	Signal
7	Address 10
8	Address 9
9	Address 8
10	Address 7
11	Address 6
12	Address 5
13	Address 4
14	Address 3
15	Address 2
16	Address 1
17	Address 0

notch

Bottom pins (18–28): 18 No Connection, 19 Nonmaskable Interrupt, 20 Interrupt Request, 21 Clock, 22 Ground, 23 No Connection, 24 Reset, 25 Ready, 26 -Test, 27 Queue Status 1, 28 Queue Status 0

Notes: Items in parentheses refer to function when chip is in Minimum mode (pin 33 held high)

Source: Intel Microprocessor and Peripheral Handbook Volume 1, pages 2-1 to 2-5, 2-31, 2-60, and 2-90

See Also: 9.37. 80286 Pinouts
9.38. 80386 Pinouts

9.37. 80286 PINOUTS

68-pin LCC packaging:

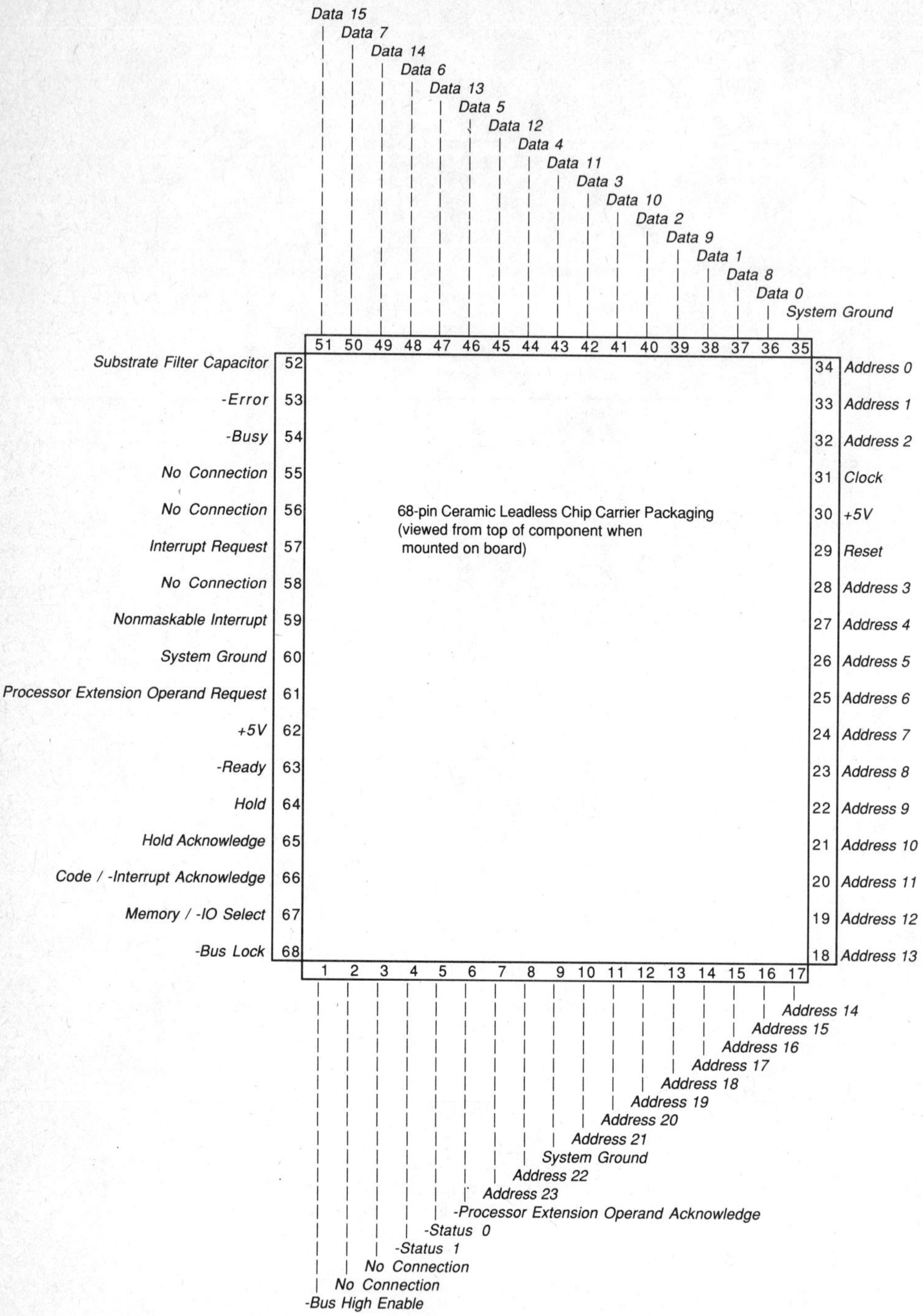

```
                                    Data 15
                                    | Data 7
                                    | | Data 14
                                    | | | Data 6
                                    | | | | Data 13
                                    | | | | | Data 5
                                    | | | | | | Data 12
                                    | | | | | | | Data 4
                                    | | | | | | | | Data 11
                                    | | | | | | | | | Data 3
                                    | | | | | | | | | | Data 10
                                    | | | | | | | | | | | Data 2
                                    | | | | | | | | | | | | Data 9
                                    | | | | | | | | | | | | | Data 1
                                    | | | | | | | | | | | | | | Data 8
                                    | | | | | | | | | | | | | | | Data 0
                                    | | | | | | | | | | | | | | | | System Ground
                                    | | | | | | | | | | | | | | | | |
                                 +---------------------------------------+
                                 | 51 50 49 48 47 46 45 44 43 42 41 40 39 38 37 36 35 |
     Substrate Filter Capacitor | 52                                  34 | Address 0
                        -Error | 53                                  33 | Address 1
                         -Busy | 54                                  32 | Address 2
                 No Connection | 55                                  31 | Clock
                 No Connection | 56   68-pin Ceramic Leadless Chip Carrier Packaging  30 | +5V
              Interrupt Request | 57   (viewed from top of component when            29 | Reset
                 No Connection | 58    mounted on board)                             28 | Address 3
           Nonmaskable Interrupt | 59                                  27 | Address 4
                 System Ground | 60                                  26 | Address 5
  Processor Extension Operand Request | 61                            25 | Address 6
                          +5V | 62                                  24 | Address 7
                        -Ready | 63                                  23 | Address 8
                          Hold | 64                                  22 | Address 9
              Hold Acknowledge | 65                                  21 | Address 10
       Code / -Interrupt Acknowledge | 66                            20 | Address 11
             Memory / -IO Select | 67                                19 | Address 12
                      -Bus Lock | 68                                  18 | Address 13
                                 | 1  2  3  4  5  6  7  8  9 10 11 12 13 14 15 16 17 |
                                 +---------------------------------------+
                                   | | | | | | | | | | | | | | | | |
                                   | | | | | | | | | | | | | | | | Address 14
                                   | | | | | | | | | | | | | | | Address 15
                                   | | | | | | | | | | | | | | Address 16
                                   | | | | | | | | | | | | | Address 17
                                   | | | | | | | | | | | | Address 18
                                   | | | | | | | | | | | Address 19
                                   | | | | | | | | | | Address 20
                                   | | | | | | | | | Address 21
                                   | | | | | | | | System Ground
                                   | | | | | | | Address 22
                                   | | | | | | Address 23
                                   | | | | | -Processor Extension Operand Acknowledge
                                   | | | | -Status 0
                                   | | | -Status 1
                                   | | No Connection
                                   | No Connection
                                   -Bus High Enable
```

(Continued)

Table 9.37. Continued

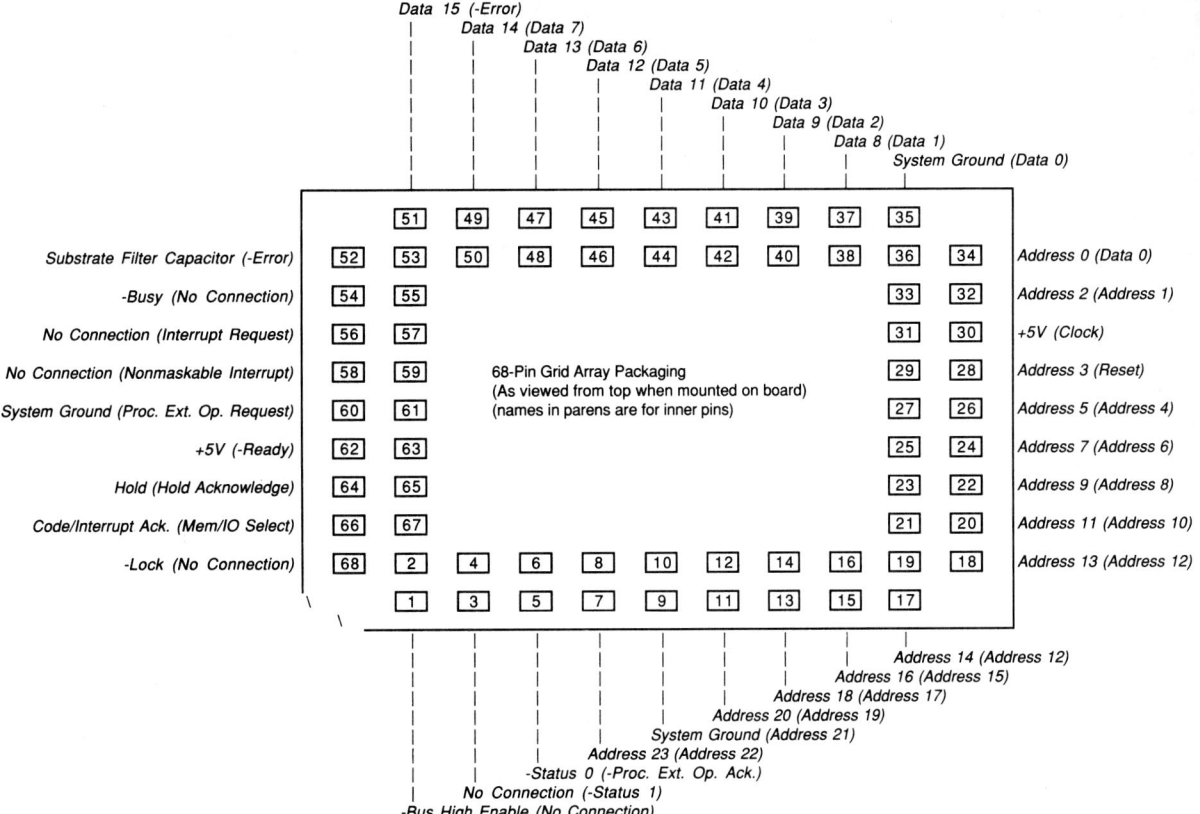

Notes: Items in parentheses refer to inner pin connections on PGA packaging

Source: Intel Microprocessor and Peripheral Handbook Volume 1, pages 3-2 to 3-4

See Also: 9.36. 8088 and 8086 Pinouts
9.38. 80386 Pinouts

9.38. 80386 PINOUTS

132-Pin Grid Array Packaging
(As viewed from top when mounted on board)

Pin	Signal
A1	Vcc (Ground)
A2	Vss (+5V)
A3	Address 3
A4	No connection
A5	Vcc (Ground)
A6	Vss (+5V)
A7	Vcc (Ground)
A8	-Error
A9	Vss (+5V)
A10	Vcc (Ground)
A11	Data/-Control
A12	Mem/-IO
A13	-Byte Enable 3
A14	Vcc (Ground)

Pin	Signal
B1	Vss (+5V)
B2	Address 5
B3	Address 4
B4	No connection
B5	Vss (+5V)
B6	No connection
B7	Int. Request
B8	Nonmask. Int.
B9	-Busy
B10	Write/-Read
B11	Vss (+5V)
B12	No connection
B13	-Byte Enable 2
B14	Vss (+5V)

Pin	Signal
C1	Address 8
C2	Address 7
C3	Address 6
C4	Address 2
C5	Vcc (Ground)
C6	No connection
C7	No connection
C8	PEREQ
C9	Reset
C10	-Lock
C11	Vss (+5V)
C12	Vcc (Ground)
C13	-Byte Enable 1
C14	-Bus Size 16

Pin	Signal
D1	Address 11
D2	Address 10
D3	Address 9
D12	Vcc (Ground)
D13	-Next Address
D14	Hold

Pin	Signal
E1	Address 14
E2	Address 13
E3	Address 12
E12	-Byte Enable 0
E13	No connection
E14	Address status

Pin	Signal
F1	Address 15
F2	Vss (+5V)
F3	Vss (+5V)
F12	Clock 2
F13	No connection
F14	Vss (+5V)

Pin	Signal
G1	Address 16
G2	Vcc (Ground)
G3	Vcc (Ground)
G12	Vcc (Ground)
G13	-Ready
G14	Vcc (Ground)

Pin	Signal
H1	Address 17
H2	Address 18
H3	Address 19
H12	Data 0
H13	Data 1
H14	Data 2

Pin	Signal
J1	Address 20
J2	Vss (+5V)
J3	Vss (+5V)
J12	Vss (+5V)
J13	Vss (+5V)
J14	Data 3

Pin	Signal
K1	Address 21
K2	Address 22
K3	Address 25
K12	Data 7
K13	Data 5
K14	Data 4

Pin	Signal
L1	Address 23
L2	Address 24
L3	Address 28
L12	Vcc (Ground)
L13	Data 8
L14	Data 6

Pin	Signal
M1	Address 26
M2	Address 29
M3	Vcc (Ground)
M4	Vss (+5V)
M5	Data 31
M6	Data 28
M7	Vcc (Ground)
M8	Vss (+5V)
M9	Data 20
M10	Vss (+5V)
M11	Data 15
M12	Data 10
M13	Vcc (Ground)
M14	Hold Ack.

Pin	Signal
N1	Address 27
N2	Address 31
N3	Vss (+5V)
N4	Vcc (Ground)
N5	Data 27
N6	Data 25
N7	Vcc (Ground)
N8	Data 23
N9	Data 21
N10	Data 17
N11	Data 16
N12	Data 12
N13	Data 11
N14	Data 9

Pin	Signal
P1	Address 30
P2	Vcc (Ground)
P3	Data 30
P4	Data 29
P5	Data 26
P6	Vss (+5V)
P7	Data 24
P8	Vcc (Ground)
P9	Data 22
P10	Data 19
P11	Data 18
P12	Data 14
P13	Data 13
P14	Vss (+5V)

Source: Intel Microprocessor and Peripheral Handbook Volume 1, pages 4-56 to 4-91

See Also: 9.36. 8088 and 8086 Pinouts
9.37. 80286 Pinouts

9.39. 8087 (COPROCESSOR) PINOUTS

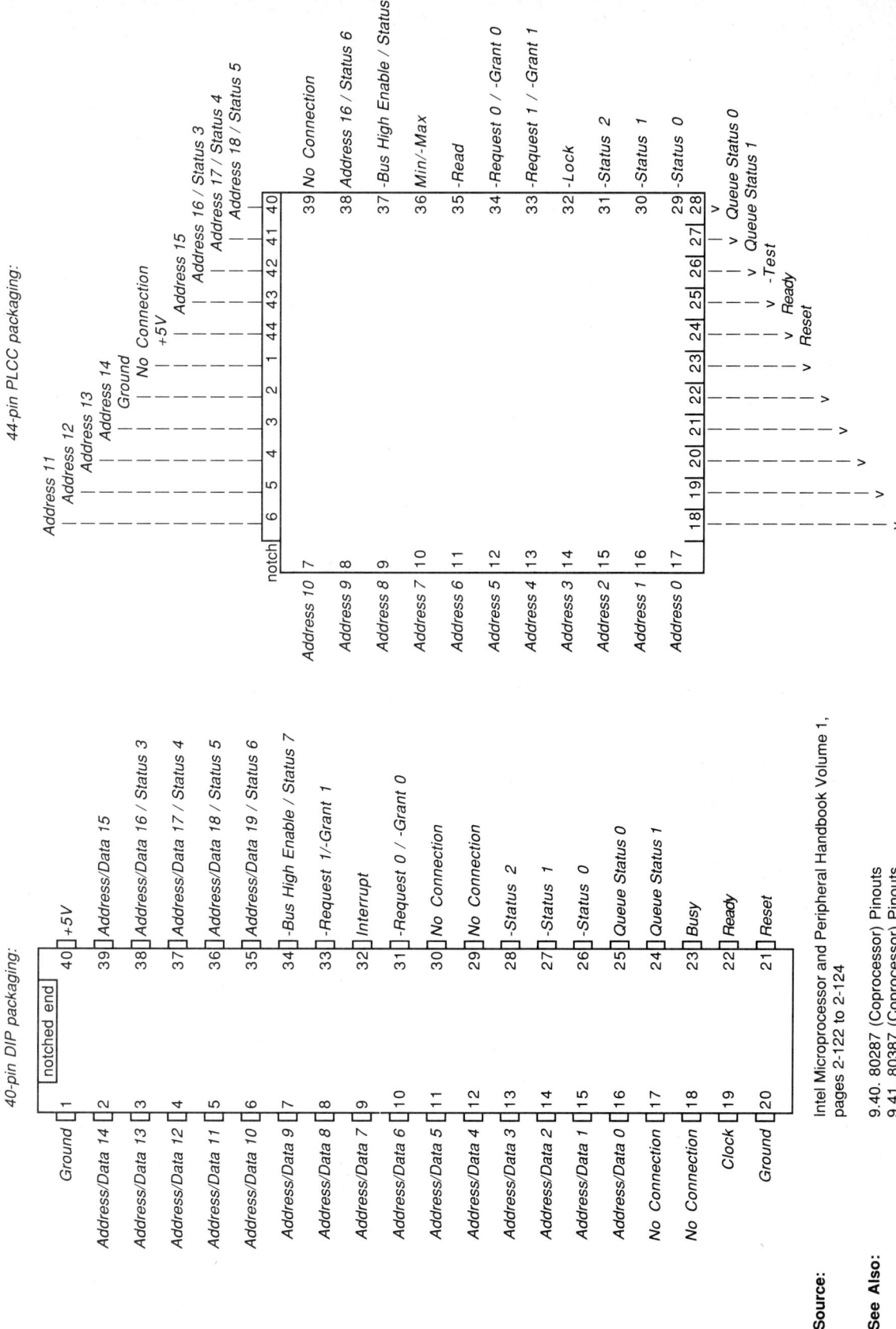

40-pin DIP packaging:

44-pin PLCC packaging:

Source: Intel Microprocessor and Peripheral Handbook Volume 1, pages 2-122 to 2-124

See Also: 9.40. 80287 (Coprocessor) Pinouts
9.41. 80387 (Coprocessor) Pinouts

9.40. 80287 (COPROCESSOR) PINOUTS

40-pin DIP packaging:

No Connection — 1	40 — No Connection
No Connection — 2	39 — Clock Mode Signal
No Connection — 3	38 — No Connection
No Connection — 4	37 — No Connection
Data 15 — 5	36 — -Processor Extension Data Channel Operand Transfer Acknowledge
Data 14 — 6	35 — Reset
Data 13 — 7	34 — -Numeric Processor Select 1
Data 12 — 8	33 — Number Processor Select 2
+5V — 9	32 — Clock
Ground — 10	31 — Command Line 1
Data 11 — 11	30 — Ground
Data 10 — 12	29 — Command Line 0
No Connection — 13	28 — -Numeric Processor Write
Data 9 — 14	27 — -Numeric Processor Read
Data 8 — 15	26 — -Error
Data 7 — 16	25 — -Busy
Data 6 — 17	24 — Processor Extension Data Channel Operating Transfer Request
Data 5 — 18	23 — Data 0
Data 4 — 19	22 — Data 1
Data 3 — 20	21 — Data 2

Source: Intel Microprocessor and Peripheral Handbook Volume 1,
                     pages 3-55 to 3-57

See Also: 9.39. 8087 (Coprocessor) Pinouts
                     9.41. 80387 (Coprocessor) Pinouts

9.41. 80387 (COPROCESSOR) PINOUTS

	K1	J1	H1	G1	F1	E1	D1	C1	B1	
L2	K2	J2	H2	G2	F2	E2	D2	C2	B2	A2
L3	K3								B3	A3
L4	K4								B4	A4
L5	K5			68-Pin Grid Array Packaging					B5	A5
L6	K6			(As viewed from top when mounted on board)					B6	A6
L7	K7								B7	A7
L8	K8								B8	A8
L9	K9								B9	A9
L10	K10	J10	H10	G10	F10	E10	D10	C10	B10	A10
	K11	J11	H11	G11	F11	E11	D11	C11	B11	

Pin	Signal
A1	No Pin
A2	Data 9
A3	Data 11
A4	Data 12
A5	Data 14
A6	Vcc +5
A7	Data 16
A8	Data 18
A9	Vcc +5
A10	Data 21
A11	No Pin

Pin	Signal
B1	Data 8
B2	Vss Ground
B3	Data 10
B4	Vcc +5
B5	Data 13
B6	Data 15
B7	Vss Ground
B8	Data 17
B9	Data 19
B10	Data 20
B11	Data 22

Pin	Signal
C1	Data 7
C2	Data 6
C10	Data 23
C11	Vss Ground
D1	Data 5
D2	Data 4
D10	Data 24
D11	Data 25
E1	Vcc +5
E2	Vss Ground
E10	Data 26

Pin	Signal
E11	Data 27
F1	Vcc +5
F2	Vss Ground
F10	Vcc +5
F11	Vss Ground
G1	Data 3
G2	Data 2
G10	Data 28
G11	Data 29
H1	Data 1
H2	Data 0

Pin	Signal
H10	Data 30
H11	Data 31
J1	Vss Ground
J2	Vcc +5
J10	Vss Ground
J11	CKM
K1	PEREQ
K2	-Busy
K3	TIE HIGH
K4	W/-R
K5	Vcc +5

Pin	Signal
K6	NPS2
K7	-ADS
K8	-Ready
K9	No connection
K10	386Clk2
K11	387Clk2
L1	No Pin
L2	-Error
L3	-ReadyO
L4	STEN
L5	Vss Ground

Pin	Signal
L6	-NPS1
L7	Vcc +5
L8	-CMD0
L9	TIE HIGH
L10	Reset In
L11	No Pin

Source: Intel Microprocessor and Peripheral Handbook Volume 1, pages 4-152 to 4-153

See Also: 9.39. 8087 (Coprocessor) Pinouts
                    9.40. 80287 (Coprocessor) Pinouts

9.42. RAM CHIP PINOUTS SUMMARY

4116 (16 KB x 1)

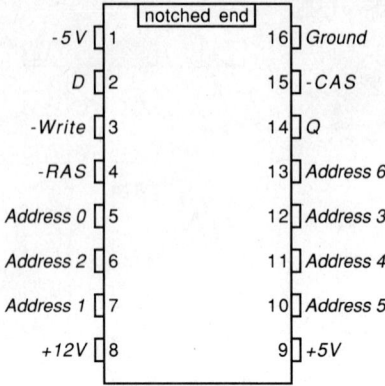

4164 (64 KB x 1)

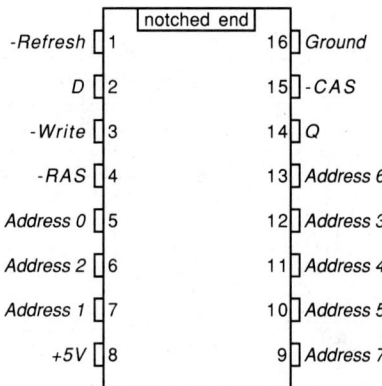

(256 KB x 1)

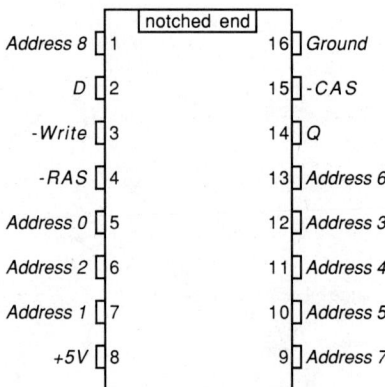

Source: *The IBM PC From the Inside Out* (Addison Wesley),
                     Sargent and Shoemaker, page 227

See Also: 9.30. PS/2 Model 50/60/80 Memory Module Connector

9.43. 6845 (VIDEO CONTROLLER) PINOUTS

40-pin DIP packaging:

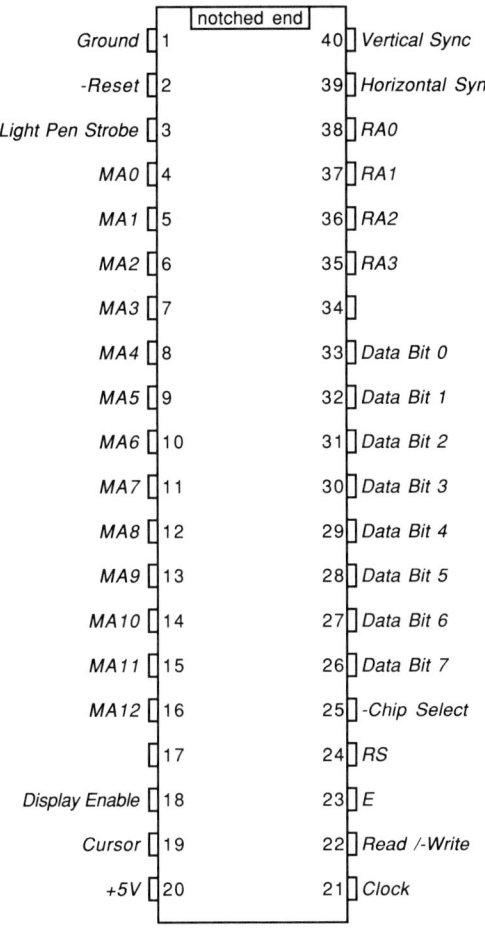

Ground	1		40	Vertical Sync
-Reset	2		39	Horizontal Sync
Light Pen Strobe	3		38	RA0
MA0	4		37	RA1
MA1	5		36	RA2
MA2	6		35	RA3
MA3	7		34	
MA4	8		33	Data Bit 0
MA5	9		32	Data Bit 1
MA6	10		31	Data Bit 2
MA7	11		30	Data Bit 3
MA8	12		29	Data Bit 4
MA9	13		28	Data Bit 5
MA10	14		27	Data Bit 6
MA11	15		26	Data Bit 7
MA12	16		25	-Chip Select
	17		24	RS
Display Enable	18		23	E
Cursor	19		22	Read /-Write
+5V	20		21	Clock

Notes: Only pins used in IBM monochrome and color adapters are shown

Source: IBM XT Technical Reference, pages D-27 and D-36

See Also: 8.12. 6845 Registers
8.13. 6845 Port and Select Factors

9.44. 8284 (CLOCK GENERATOR) PINOUTS

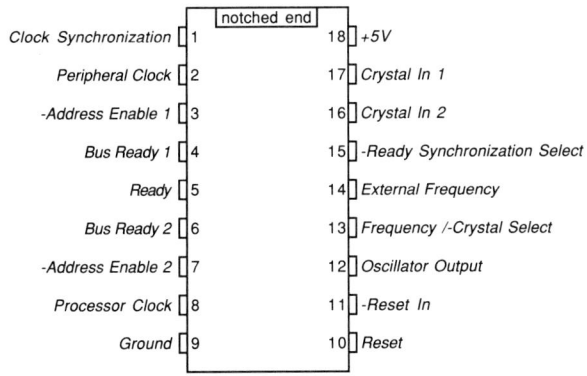

Clock Synchronization	1		18	+5V
Peripheral Clock	2		17	Crystal In 1
-Address Enable 1	3		16	Crystal In 2
Bus Ready 1	4		15	-Ready Synchronization Select
Ready	5		14	External Frequency
Bus Ready 2	6		13	Frequency /-Crystal Select
-Address Enable 2	7		12	Oscillator Output
Processor Clock	8		11	-Reset In
Ground	9		10	Reset

Notes: Available as 8284A (5 or 8MHz) and 8284A-1 (10MHz)
and available in CMOS versions 82C84A (8MHz) or 82C84A-5 (5MHz)

Source: Intel Microprocessor and Peripheral Handbook Volume 1, pages 2-144 to 2-145, 2-152 to 2-153

9.45. 8237 (DMA CONTROLLER) PINOUTS

40-pin DIP packaging:

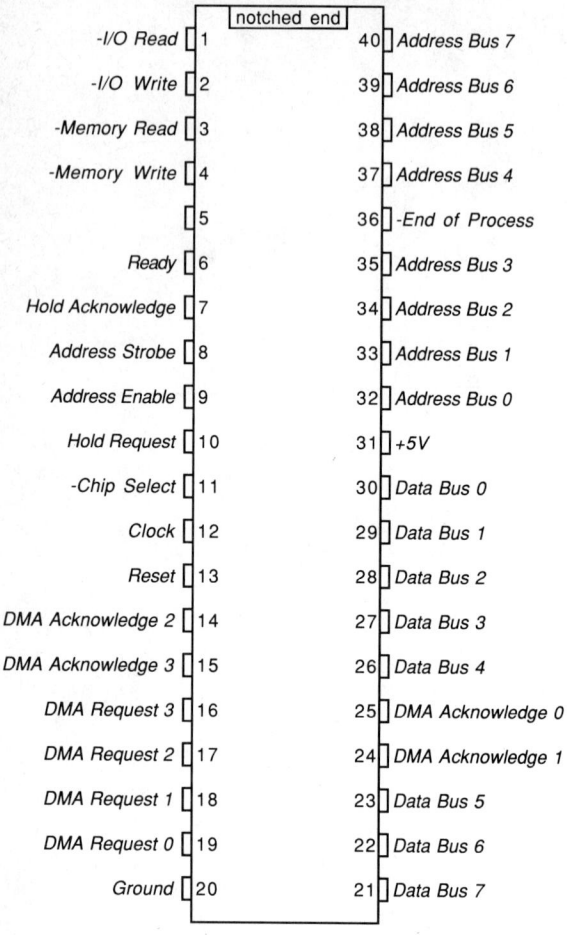

Notes:	Available as 8237A (3MHz), 8237A-4 (4MHz), 8237A-5 (5MHz) and CHMOS 82C37A-5 (5MHz)
Source:	Intel Microprocessor and Peripheral Handbook, Volume 1, pages 2-205 to 2-207 and 2-223 to 2-226
See Also:	8.34. PS/2 50/60/80 DMA I/O Address Map 8.35. PS/2 DMA Registers

9.46. 8250 (SERIAL INTERFACE CONTROLLER) PINOUTS

40-pin DIP packaging:

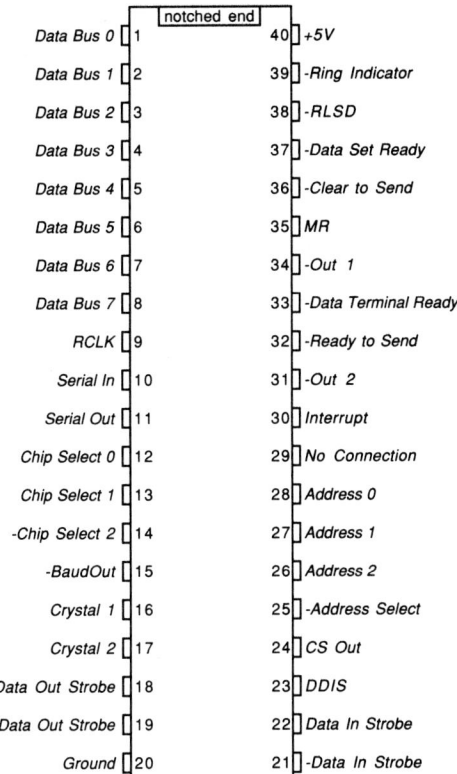

Data Bus 0 — 1	40 — +5V
Data Bus 1 — 2	39 — -Ring Indicator
Data Bus 2 — 3	38 — -RLSD
Data Bus 3 — 4	37 — -Data Set Ready
Data Bus 4 — 5	36 — -Clear to Send
Data Bus 5 — 6	35 — MR
Data Bus 6 — 7	34 — -Out 1
Data Bus 7 — 8	33 — -Data Terminal Ready
RCLK — 9	32 — -Ready to Send
Serial In — 10	31 — -Out 2
Serial Out — 11	30 — Interrupt
Chip Select 0 — 12	29 — No Connection
Chip Select 1 — 13	28 — Address 0
-Chip Select 2 — 14	27 — Address 1
-BaudOut — 15	26 — Address 2
Crystal 1 — 16	25 — -Address Select
Crystal 2 — 17	24 — CS Out
-Data Out Strobe — 18	23 — DDIS
Data Out Strobe — 19	22 — Data In Strobe
Ground — 20	21 — -Data In Strobe

Source: *The IBM PC From the Inside Out* (Addison Wesley), Sargent and Shoemaker, page 365

See Also: 8.08. 8250 I/O Port Usage (Registers)
8.09. 8253 I/O Port Usage (Registers)

9.47. 8253 (PROGRAMMABLE INTERVAL CONTROLLER) PINOUTS

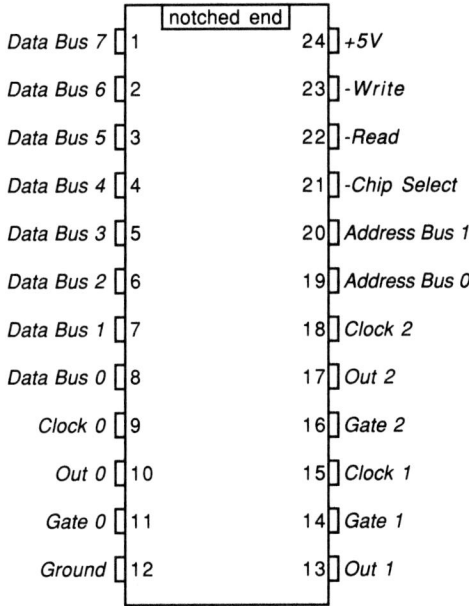

Data Bus 7 — 1	24 — +5V
Data Bus 6 — 2	23 — -Write
Data Bus 5 — 3	22 — -Read
Data Bus 4 — 4	21 — -Chip Select
Data Bus 3 — 5	20 — Address Bus 1
Data Bus 2 — 6	19 — Address Bus 0
Data Bus 1 — 7	18 — Clock 2
Data Bus 0 — 8	17 — Out 2
Clock 0 — 9	16 — Gate 2
Out 0 — 10	15 — Clock 1
Gate 0 — 11	14 — Gate 1
Ground — 12	13 — Out 1

Notes: Available as 8253, 8253-5, 8254 (8MHz), 8254-2 (10MHz), and 8254-5 (5MHz)

Source: Intel Microprocessor and Peripheral Handbook, Volume 2, pages 2-14 to 2-15 and 2-25 to 2-26

9.48. 8255 (PARALLEL INTERFACE CONTROLLER) PINOUTS

	notched end	
Port A bit 3	1	40 Port A bit 4
Port A bit 2	2	39 Port A bit 5
Port A bit 1	3	38 Port A bit 6
Port A bit 0	4	37 Port A bit 7
-Read Input	5	36 -Write Input
-Chip Select	6	35 Reset
Ground	7	34 Data Bus 0
Port Address 1	8	33 Data Bus 1
Port Address 0	9	32 Data Bus 2
Port C bit 7	10	31 Data Bus 3
Port C bit 6	11	30 Data Bus 4
Port C bit 5	12	29 Data Bus 5
Port C bit 4	13	28 Data Bus 6
Port C bit 0	14	27 Data Bus 7
Port C bit 1	15	26 +5V
Port C bit 2	16	25 Port B bit 7
Port C bit 3	17	24 Port B bit 6
Port B bit 0	18	23 Port B bit 5
Port B bit 1	19	22 Port B bit 4
Port B bit 2	20	21 Port B bit 3

Notes: Available as 8255A or CHMOS 82C55A

Source: Intel Microprocessor and Peripheral Handbook, Volume 2, pages 2-63 and 2-87 to 2-88

See Also: 8.10. 8253 Control Word Byte

9.49. 8259 (PROGRAMMABLE INTERRUPT CONTROLLER) PINOUTS

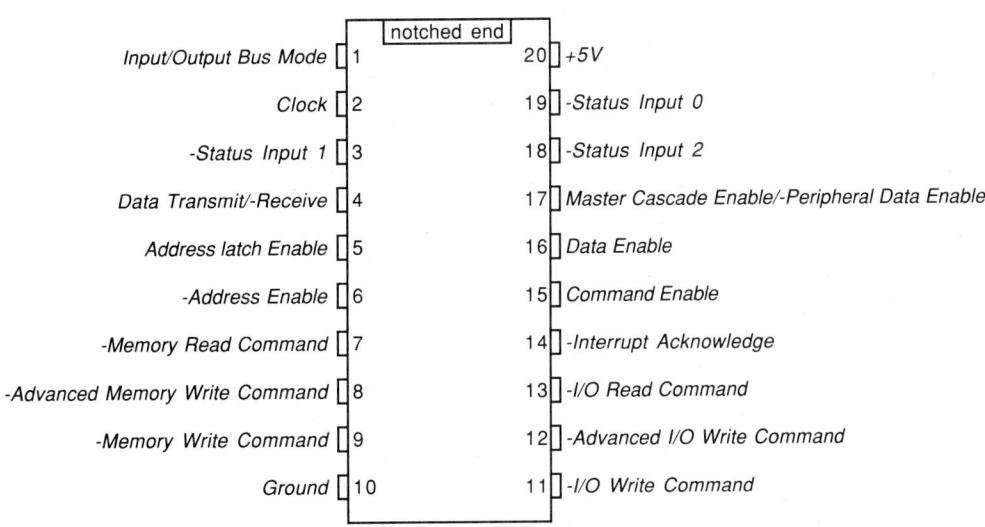

```
                        notched end
   -Chip Select  [ 1        28 ]  +5V
       -Write    [ 2        27 ]  AO Address Line
       -Read     [ 3        26 ]  -Interrupt Acknowledge
   Data Bus 7    [ 4        25 ]  Interrupt Request 7
   Data Bus 6    [ 5        24 ]  Interrupt Request 6
   Data Bus 5    [ 6        23 ]  Interrupt Request 5
   Data Bus 4    [ 7        22 ]  Interrupt Request 4
   Data Bus 3    [ 8        21 ]  Interrupt Request 3
   Data Bus 2    [ 9        20 ]  Interrupt Request 2
   Data Bus 1    [ 10       19 ]  Interrupt Request 1
   Data Bus 0    [ 11       18 ]  Interrupt Request 0
 Cascade Line 0  [ 12       17 ]  Interrupt
 Cascade Line 1  [ 13       16 ]  -Slave Program /-Enable Buffer
       Ground    [ 14       15 ]  Cascade Line 2
```

Notes: Available as 8259A, 8259A-2, 8259A-8 and CHMOS 82C59A-2

Source: Intel Microprocessor and Peripheral Handbook, Volume 1,
pages 2-234 to 2-235 and 2-258 to 2-259

See Also: 7.04. PC Interrupt Usage Summary

9.50. 8288 (BUS CONTROLLER) PINOUTS

20-pin DIP packaging:

```
                            notched end
 Input/Output Bus Mode  [ 1        20 ]  +5V
             Clock      [ 2        19 ]  -Status Input 0
      -Status Input 1   [ 3        18 ]  -Status Input 2
 Data Transmit/-Receive [ 4        17 ]  Master Cascade Enable/-Peripheral Data Enable
   Address latch Enable [ 5        16 ]  Data Enable
       -Address Enable  [ 6        15 ]  Command Enable
 -Memory Read Command   [ 7        14 ]  -Interrupt Acknowledge
 -Advanced Memory Write Command [ 8  13 ]  -I/O Read Command
 -Memory Write Command  [ 9        12 ]  -Advanced I/O Write Command
            Ground      [ 10       11 ]  -I/O Write Command
```

Notes: Available as 8288 and 82C88

Source: Intel Microprocessor and Peripheral Handbook Volume 1,
pages 2-161 to 2-163 and 2-169 to 2-170

9.51. MC146818 (AT CLOCK CONTROLLER) PINOUTS

24-pin DIP packaging

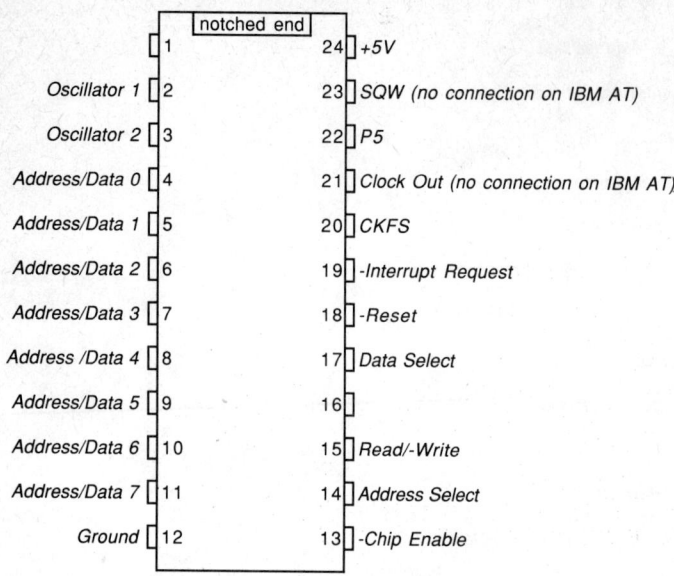

1	24 +5V
Oscillator 1 — 2	23 SQW (no connection on IBM AT)
Oscillator 2 — 3	22 P5
Address/Data 0 — 4	21 Clock Out (no connection on IBM AT)
Address/Data 1 — 5	20 CKFS
Address/Data 2 — 6	19 -Interrupt Request
Address/Data 3 — 7	18 -Reset
Address /Data 4 — 8	17 Data Select
Address/Data 5 — 9	16
Address/Data 6 — 10	15 Read/-Write
Address/Data 7 — 11	14 Address Select
Ground — 12	13 -Chip Enable

Notes: Only pins used in IBM AT are shown

Source: IBM AT Technical Reference, page 1-93

See Also:

7.49. AT Real Time Clock RAM Configuration Usage
7.50. AT Real Time Clock Status Register A
7.51. AT Real Time Clock Status Register B
7.52. AT Real Time Clock Status Register C
7.53. AT Real Time Clock Status Register D
7.54. AT Real Time Clock Diagnostic Status Byte
7.55. AT Real Time Clock Diskette Drive Type Byte
7.56. AT Real Time Clock Fixed Drive Type Byte
7.57. AT Real Time Clock Equipment Byte

9.52. PD765 (FLOPPY DISK CONTROLLER) PINOUTS

40-pin DIP packaging:

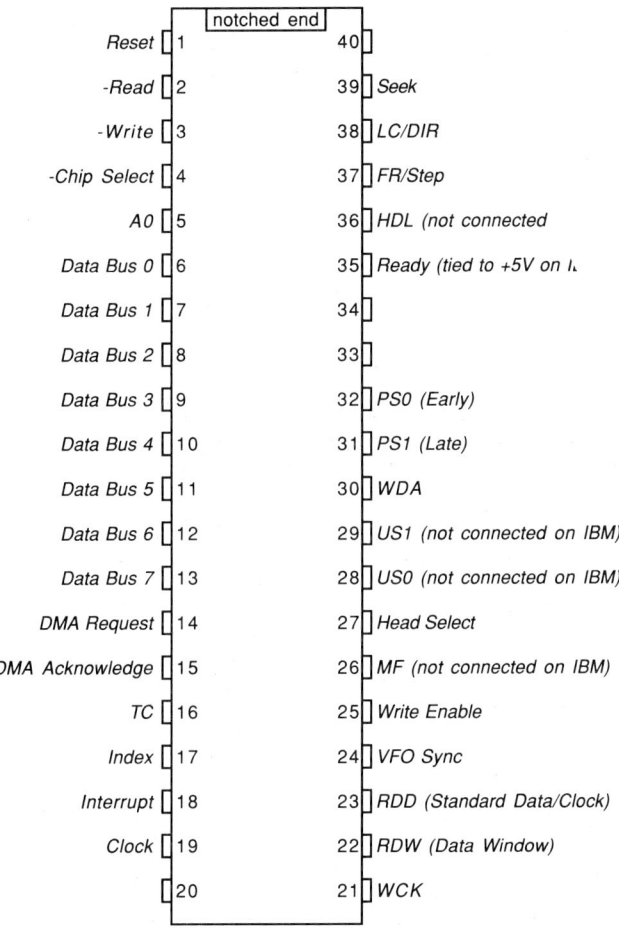

Reset — 1	40
-Read — 2	39 — Seek
-Write — 3	38 — LC/DIR
-Chip Select — 4	37 — FR/Step
A0 — 5	36 — HDL (not connected
Data Bus 0 — 6	35 — Ready (tied to +5V on I.
Data Bus 1 — 7	34
Data Bus 2 — 8	33
Data Bus 3 — 9	32 — PS0 (Early)
Data Bus 4 — 10	31 — PS1 (Late)
Data Bus 5 — 11	30 — WDA
Data Bus 6 — 12	29 — US1 (not connected on IBM)
Data Bus 7 — 13	28 — US0 (not connected on IBM)
DMA Request — 14	27 — Head Select
-DMA Acknowledge — 15	26 — MF (not connected on IBM)
TC — 16	25 — Write Enable
Index — 17	24 — VFO Sync
Interrupt — 18	23 — RDD (Standard Data/Clock)
Clock — 19	22 — RDW (Data Window)
20	21 — WCK

Notes: Only pins used in IBM floppy diskette adapters are shown

Source: IBM XT Technical Reference, pages D-46 to D-47

9.53. PC & XT ADD-ON CARD SIZE

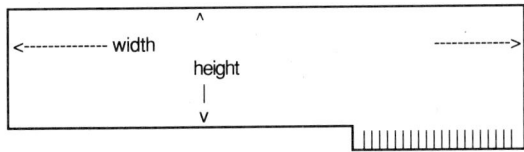

Height:	4.2 inches (106.68 mm)
Width:	13.15 inches (334.01 mm)
Pin layout:	62 pins with 100-mil card spacing

Source: Original IBM PC/XT Technical Reference, page E-4

See Also: 9.54. AT Add-on Card Size
9.55. Microchannel Card Size
9.56. PC & XT I/O Channel (System Bus) Pinouts

9.54. AT ADD-ON CARD SIZE

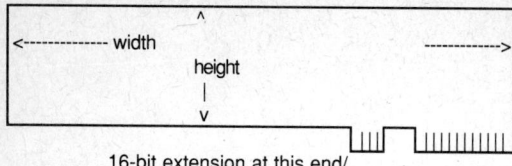

16-bit extension at this end/

Height:	4.5 inches (114 mm) -- shorter than PC/XT
Width:	13 inches (333 mm) -- same as PC/XT
Pin layout:	62 pins with 100-mil card spacing, plus 36-pin extension

Source: *IBM Personal System/2: A Business Perspective*
(John Wiley & Sons), Jim Hoskins, page 32

See Also: 9.53. PC & XT Add-on Card Size
9.55. Microchannel Card Size

9.55. MICROCHANNEL CARD SIZE

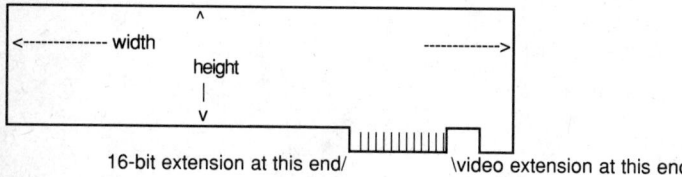

16-bit extension at this end/   \video extension at this end

Height:	3.475 inches (88.27mm)
Width:	11.50 inches (292.1mm)
Pin layout:	Dual 58-pin, 50-mil connector with 4 keyed positions
	Also allows for optional dual 10-pin video extension

Notes: Not applicable to Model 30, which uses PC/XT-style cards

Source: IBM PS/2 Model 50 and 60 Technical Reference,
pages 2-4 to 2-5 and 2-90 to 2-103

See Also: 9.53. PC & XT Add-on Card Size
9.54. AT Add-on Card Size

9.56. PC & XT I/O CHANNEL (SYSTEM BUS) PINOUTS

Pin Number	Signal Name	Description	Direction
A1	-I/O CH CK	I/O channel check; active low=parity error	Input
A2	+D7	Data bit 7	Input/output
A3	+D6	Data bit 6	Input/output
A4	+D5	Data bit 5	Input/output
A5	+D4	Data bit 4	Input/output
A6	+D3	Data bit 3	Input/output
A7	+D2	Data bit 2	Input/output
A8	+D1	Data bit 1	Input/output
A9	+D0	Data bit 0	Input/output
A10	+I/O CH RDY	I/O channel ready; pulled low to lengthen memory cycles	Input
A11	+AEN	Address enable; active high when DMA controls bus	Output
A12	+A19	Address bit 19	Output
A13	+A18	Address bit 18	Output
A14	+A17	Address bit 17	Output
A15	+A16	Address bit 16	Output
A16	+A15	Address bit 15	Output
A17	+A14	Address bit 14	Output
A18	+A13	Address bit 13	Output
A19	+A12	Address bit 12	Output
A20	+A11	Address bit 11	Output
A21	+A10	Address bit 10	Output
A22	+A9	Address bit 9	Output
A23	+A8	Address bit 8	Output
A24	+A7	Address bit 7	Output
A25	+A6	Address bit 6	Output
A26	+A5	Address bit 5	Output
A27	+A4	Address bit 4	Output
A28	+A3	Address bit 3	Output
A29	+A2	Address bit 2	Output
A30	+A1	Address bit 1	Output
A31	+A0	Address bit 0	Output
B1	GROUND		
B2	+RESET DRV	Active high to reset or initialize system logic	Output
B3	+5V		
B4	+IRQ2	Interrupt request 2	Input
B5	-5VDC		
B6	+DRQ2	DMA request 2	Input
B7	-12V		
B8	-CARD SLCTD	Card Selected; activated by cards in XT's slot J8 (Active Low)	Input
B9	+12V		
B10	GROUND		
B11	-MEMW	Memory Write (Active Low)	Output
B12	-MEMR	Memory Read (Active Low)	Output
B13	-IOW	I/O Write (Active Low)	Output
B14	-IOR	I/O Read (Active Low)	Output
B15	-DACK3	DMA Acknowledge 3 (Active Low)	Output
B16	+DRQ3	DMA Request 3	Input
B17	-DACK1	DMA Acknowledge 1 (Active Low)	Output
B18	+DRQ1	DMA Request 1	Input
B19	-DACK0	DMA Acknowledge 0 (Active Low)	Output
B20	CLOCK	System Clock (210 ns, 4.77MHz); 33% duty cycle	Output
B21	+IRQ7	Interrupt Request 7	Input
B22	+IRQ6	Interrupt Request 6	Input
B23	+IRQ5	Interrupt Request 5	Input
B24	+IRQ4	Interrupt Request 4	Input
B25	+IRQ3	Interrupt Request 3	Input
B26	-DACK2	DMA Acknowledge 2 (Active Low)	Output
B27	+T/C	Terminal Count; pulses high when DMA term. count reached	Output
B28	+ALE	Address Latch Enable	Output
B29	+5V		
B30	+OSC	High-speed clock (70 ns,14.31818MHz), 50% duty cycle	Output
B31	GROUND		

Notes: •All signals are at standard TTL levels
•Connector is a 62-pin edge connector
•A=component side of board; numbers start closest to rear panel of machine

Source: IBM PC/XT Technical Reference, pages 1-15 to 1-19

See Also: 9.57. AT I/O Channel (System Bus) Pinouts
9.58. PS/2 Model 50/60/80 Microchannel Bus Pinouts

9.57. AT I/O CHANNEL (SYSTEM BUS) PINOUTS

Pin Number	Signal Name	Description	Direction
A1	-I/O CH CK	I/O channel check; active low=parity error (Active Low)	Input
A2	+D7	Data bit 7	Input/output
A3	+D6	Data bit 6	Input/output
A4	+D5	Data bit 5	Input/output
A5	+D4	Data bit 4	Input/output
A6	+D3	Data bit 3	Input/output
A7	+D2	Data bit 2	Input/output
A8	+D1	Data bit 1	Input/output
A9	+D0	Data bit 0	Input/output
A10	+I/O CH RDY	I/O Channel ready; pulled low to lengthen memory cycles	Input
A11	+AEN	Address enable; active high when DMA controls bus	Output
A12	+A19	Address bit 19	Output
A13	+A18	Address bit 18	Output
A14	+A17	Address bit 17	Output
A15	+A16	Address bit 16	Output
A16	+A15	Address bit 15	Output
A17	+A14	Address bit 14	Output
A18	+A13	Address bit 13	Output
A19	+A12	Address bit 12	Output
A20	+A11	Address bit 11	Output
A21	+A10	Address bit 10	Output
A22	+A9	Address bit 9	Output
A23	+A8	Address bit 8	Output
A24	+A7	Address bit 7	Output
A25	+A6	Address bit 6	Output
A26	+A5	Address bit 5	Output
A27	+A4	Address bit 4	Output
A28	+A3	Address bit 3	Output
A29	+A2	Address bit 2	Output
A30	+A1	Address bit 1	Output
A31	+A0	Address bit 0	Output
B1	GROUND		
B2	+RESET DRV	Active high to reset or initialize system logic	Output
B3	+5V		
B4	+IRQ2	Interrupt request 2	Input
B5	-5VDC		
B6	+DRQ2	DMA request 2	Input
B7	-12V		
B8	-CARD SLCTD	Card selected; activated by cards in XT's slot J8	Input
B9	+12V		
B10	GROUND		
B11	-MEMW	Memory write (Active Low)	Output
B12	-MEMR	Memory read (Active Low)	Output
B13	-IOW	I/O write (Active Low)	Output
B14	-IOR	I/O read (Active Low)	Output
B15	-DACK3	DMA acknowledge 3 (Active Low)	Output
B16	+DRQ3	DMA request 3	Input
B17	-DACK1	DMA acknowledge 1 (Active Low)	Output
B18	+DRQ1	DMA request 1	Input
B19	-DACK0	DMA acknowledge 0 (Active Low)	Output
B20	CLOCK	System clock (210 ns, 4.77MHz); 33% duty cycle	Output
B21	+IRQ7	Interrupt request 7	Input
B22	+IRQ6	Interrupt request 6	Input
B23	+IRQ5	Interrupt request 5	Input
B24	+IRQ4	Interrupt request 4	Input
B25	+IRQ3	Interrupt request 3	Input
B26	-DACK2	DMA acknowledge 2 (Active Low)	Output
B27	+T/C	Terminal count; pulses high when DMA term. count reached	Output
B28	+ALE	Address latch enable	Output
B29	+5V		
B30	+OSC	High-speed clock (70 ns,14.31818MHz), 50% duty cycle	Output
B31	GROUND		
C1	SBHE	System bus high enable (data available on SD8-15)	Input/output
C2	LA23	Address bit 23	Input/output
C3	LA22	Address bit 22	Input/output
C4	LA21	Address bit 21	Input/output
C5	LA20	Address bit 20	Input/output
C6	LA19	Address bit 19	Input/output
C7	LA18	Address bit 18	Input/output

(Continued)

Table 9.57. Continued

Pin Number	Signal Name	Description	Direction
C8	LA17	Address bit 17	Input/output
C9	-MEMR	Memory read (active on all memory read cycles) (Active Low)	Input/output
C10	-MEMW	Memory write (active on all memory write cycles) (Active Low)	Input/output
C11	SD08	Data bit 8	Input/output
C12	SD09	Data bit 9	Input/output
C13	SD10	Data bit 10	Input/output
C14	SD11	Data bit 11	Input/output
C15	SD12	Data bit 12	Input/output
C16	SD13	Data bit 13	Input/output
C17	SD14	Data bit 14	Input/output
C18	SD15	Data bit 15	Input/output
D1	-MEM CS16	Memory 16-bit chip select (1 wait, 16-bit memory cycle) (Active Low)	Input
D2	-I/O CS16	I/O 16-bit chip select (1 wait, 16-bit I/O cycle) (Active Low)	Input
D3	IRQ10	Interrupt request 10	Input
D4	IRQ11	Interrupt request 11	Input
D5	IRQ12	Interrupt request 12	Input
D6	IRQ15	Interrupt request 15	Input
D7	IRQ14	Interrupt request 14	Input
D8	-DACK0	DMA acknowledge 0 (Active Low)	Output
D9	DRQ0	DMA request 0	Input
D10	-DACK5	DMA acknowledge 5 (Active Low)	Output
D11	DRQ5	DMA request 5	Input
D12	-DACK6	DMA acknowledge 6 (Active Low)	Output
D13	DRQ6	DMA request 6	Input
D14	-DACK7	DMA acknowledge 7 (Active Low)	Output
D15	DRQ7	DMA request 7	Input
D16	+5Vdc		
D17	-MASTER	Used with DRQ to gain control of system (Active Low)	Input
D18	Ground		

Notes: •All signals are at standard TTL levels
•Connector is a 62-pin edge connector with a secondary 36-pin edge connector
•A or C=component side of board; numbers start closest to rear panel of machine

Source: IBM PC/AT Technical Reference, pages 1-25 to 1-37

See Also: 9.56. PC & XT I/O Channel (System Bus) Pinouts
9.58. PS/2 Model 50/60/80 Microchannel Bus Pinouts

9.58. PS/2 MODEL 50/60/80 MICROCHANNEL BUS PINOUTS

Connector	Pin Number	Signal	Description
58-pin, 50-mil edge (component side)	A1	-CD SETUP	Card setup (Active Low)
	A2	MADE 24	Memory address enable 24
	A3	Ground	
	A4	A11	Address bit 11
	A5	A10	Address bit 10
	A6	A09	Address bit 9
	A7	+5V	
	A8	A08	Address bit 8
	A9	A07	Address bit 7
	A10	A06	Address bit 6
	A11	+5V	
	A12	A05	Address bit 5
	A13	A04	Address bit 4
	A14	A03	Address bit 3
	A15	+5V	
	A16	A02	Address bit 2
	A17	A01	Address bit 1
	A18	A00	Address bit 0
	A19	+12V	
	A20	-ADL	Address decode latch (Active Low)
	A21	-PREEMPT	Causes arbitration cycle to occur (Active Low)
	A22	-BURST	Used to signal extended use of channel (Active Low)
	A23	-12V	
	A24	ARB 00	Arbitration bus priority level bit 0
	A25	ARB 01	Arbitration bus priority level bit 1
	A26	ARB 02	Arbitration bus priority level bit 2

(Continued)

Table 9.58. Continued

Connector	Pin Number	Signal	Description
58-pin, 50-mil edge (component side)	A27	-12V	
	A28	ARB 03	Arbitration bus priority level bit 3
	A29	ARB/-GNT	High=arbitration in process, low=channel awarded
	A30	-TC	Terminal count
	A31	+5V	
	A32	-SO	Status bit 0 (Active Low)
	A33	-S1	Status bit 1 (Active Low)
	A34	M/-IO	Memory/input output
	A35	+12V	
	A36	CD CHRDY	Channel ready
	A37	D00	Data bit 0
	A38	D02	Data bit 2
	A39	+5V	
	A40	D05	Data bit 5
	A41	D06	Data bit 6
	A42	D07	Data bit 7
	A43	Ground	
	A44	-DS 16 RTN	Data size 16 return (Active Low)
	A45	-REFRESH	Memory refresh in progress when active (Active Low)
	A46	KEY	
	A47	KEY	
	A48	+5V	
	A49	D10	Data bit 10
	A50	D11	Data bit 11
	A51	D13	Data bit 13
	A52	+12V	
	A53	RESERVED	
	A54	-SBHE	System byte high enable (Active Low)
	A55	-CD DS 16	Card data size 16 (Active Low)
	A56	+5V	
	A57	-IRQ 14	Interrupt request 14 (Active Low)
	A58	-IRQ 15	Interrupt request 15 (Active Low)
58-pin, 50-mil edge (non-component side)	B1	AUDIO GND	
	B2	AUDIO	Audio sum node (2.5v peak to peak)
	B3	Ground	
	B4	14.3 MHz Osc	Clock signal
	B5	Ground	
	B6	A23	Address bit 23
	B7	A22	Address bit 22
	B8	A21	Address bit 21
	B9	Ground	
	B10	A20	Address bit 20
	B11	A19	Address bit 19
	B12	A18	Address bit 18
	B13	Ground	
	B14	A17	Address bit 17
	B15	A16	Address bit 16
	B16	A15	Address bit 15
	B17	Ground	
	B18	A14	Address bit 14
	B19	A13	Address bit 13
	B20	A12	Address bit 12
	B21	Ground	
	B22	-IRQ 9	Interrupt request 9 (Active Low)
	B23	-IRQ 3	Interrupt request 3 (Active Low)
	B24	-IRQ 4	Interrupt request 4 (Active Low)
	B25	Ground	
	B26	-IRQ 5	Interrupt request 5 (Active Low)
	B27	-IRQ 6	Interrupt request 6 (Active Low)
	B28	-IRQ 7	Interrupt request 7 (Active Low)
	B29	Ground	
	B30	RESERVED	
	B31	RESERVED	
	B32	-CHCK	Channel check (Active Low)
	B33	Ground	
	B34	-CMD	Command (data is valid on bus) (Active Low)
	B35	CHRDYRTN	Channel ready return
	B36	-CD SFDBK	Card selected feedback (Active Low)
	B37	Ground	
	B38	D1	Data bit 1
	B39	D3	Data bit 3
	B40	D4	Data bit 4
	B41	Ground	
	B42	CHRESET	Channel reset (init all adapters)
	B43	RESERVED	

(Continued)

Table 9.58. Continued

Connector	Pin Number	Signal	Description
58-pin,	B44	RESERVED	
50-mil edge	B45	Ground	
(non-	B46	Key	
component	B47	Key	
side)	B48	D8	Data bit 8
	B49	D9	Data bit 9
	B50	Ground	
	B51	D12	Data bit 12
	B52	D14	Data bit 14
	B53	D15	Data bit 15
	B54	Ground	
	B55	-IRQ 10	Interrupt request 10 (Active Low)
	B56	-IRQ 11	Interrupt request 11 (Active Low)
	B57	-IRQ 12	Interrupt request 12 (Active Low)
	B58	Ground	
Video	VA10	VSYNC	Vertical sync
Extension	VA9	HSYNC	Horizontal sync
(component	VA8	BLANK	Blank input of video DAC
side)	VA7	Ground	
	VA6	P6	PEL input 6 to video DAC
	VA5	EDCLK	Output enable for DCLK buffer
	VA4	DCLK	Video PEL clock
	VA3	Ground	
	VA2	P7	PEL input 7 to video DAC
	VA1	EVIDEO	Enable output (P0-P7)
	KEY		
Video	VB10	ESYNC	Enable VSYNC, HSYNC, BLANK
Extension	VB9	Ground	
(non-	VB8	P5	PEL input 5 to video DAC
component	VB7	P4	PEL input 4 to video DAC
side)	VB6	P3	PEL input 3 to video DAC
	VB5	Ground	
	VB4	P2	PEL input 2 to video DAC
	VB3	P1	PEL input 1 to video DAC
	VB2	P0	PEL input 0 to video DAC
	VB1	Ground	
	KEY		

Source: IBM PS/2 Model 50 and 60 Technical Reference, pages 2-5 to 2-17

See Also: 9.56. PC & XT I/O Channel (System Bus) Pinouts
9.57. AT I/O Channel (System Bus) Pinouts

Bibliography

The following works were used as primary or secondary sources of information during the compilation of this book. These works formed my desktop reference group, and I recommend them as the solid core of a reference library for anyone dealing seriously with the IBM PC family. Other valuable works also exist, and I consulted a number of them during the course of my research. But on a desert island doing PC development, these would be my first choices.

Angermeyer, John, and Jaeger, Kevin. *MS-DOS Developer's Guide.* Indianapolis, IN: Howard Sams & Company, 1986.

> A useful book. It contains information on network use, file recovery, and device drivers not found elsewhere, or at least not in as readable a form. An excellent second source for assembly-language programmers.
> (ISBN 0-672-22409-7)

Armbrust, Steven, and Forgeron, Ted. *Programmer's Reference Manual for IBM Personal Computers.* Homewood, IL: Dow Jones-Irwin, 1986.

> If you deal with DOS function calls or interrupts, this is a book you must own. Detailed, accurate, and well organized, it includes programming examples in Pascal and C for every function call. An underrated work valued by most serious programmers.
> (ISBN 0-87094-765-6)

Davies, Russ. *Mapping the IBM PC and PCjr.* Greensboro, NC: Compute! Publications, 1985.

> This is a useful compendium of highly technical information regarding the IBM PC and PCjr, but it does not include AT or PS/2 material, which lessens its current value to programmers. (ISBN 0-942386-92-2)

Duncan, Ray. *Advanced MS DOS.* Redmond, WA: Microsoft Press, 1986.

> Regarded by some as *the* DOS reference, this work is well-organized, highly readable, and relatively complete, featuring good reference sections at the end.
> (ISBN 0-914845-77-2.)

IBM Corporation. *Disk Operating System Version 3.30: Reference.* 1st ed. Boca Raton, Fl: IBM Corporation, April, 1987.

> The sections on code pages and a few of the other changes specific to version 3.3 require close attention, but the basic material is stable, accurate, and well organized.
> (IBM part number 80X0667)

IBM Corporation. *Disk Operating System Version 3.30: Technical Reference.* 1st ed. Boca Raton, FL: IBM Corporation, April, 1987.

> Like any book filled with so many facts, this volume sometimes stumbles over details. Overall, though, it's still a valuable resource.
> (IBM part number 80X0945)

IBM Corporation. *Personal System/2 and Personal Computer BIOS Interface Technical Reference.* 1st ed. Boca Raton, FL: IBM Corporation, April, 1987.

> This is now IBM's stated standard for the BIOS. The material is all here, but listings are no longer provided. Note: Subfunctions (those that use the AL register to pass a function request) are documented within the functions, but it is not always clear where one subfunction ends and another begins. Also, register use is not always identified as applying before or after the call. Make notes in the margin to help keep your bearings.
> (IBM part number 84X1514)

IBM Corporation. *Personal System/2 Model 30 Technical Reference.* 1st ed. Boca Raton, FL: IBM Corporation, January, 1987.

> BIOS listings are dropped in the PS/2 documentation, but the organization and presentation are generally better than in earlier references.
> (IBM part number 68X2201)

IBM Corporation. *Personal System/2 Model 50 and 60 Technical Reference.* 1st ed. Boca Raton, FL: IBM Corporation, April, 1987.

> This reference has no BIOS listings, but it has better organization throughout as well as more detailed presentation than earlier sources. For the programmer trying to deal with all PCs, however, the inclusion of two machines in one reference can make cross-checking a

particular item difficult. Sometimes you'll find information about both models in one place; sometimes the information is separated.
(IBM part number 68X2224)

IBM Corporation. *Technical Reference Options and Adapters.* 2 vols. Revised ed. Boca Raton, FL: IBM Corporation, April, 1984.
This is where IBM documents the PC adapter boards (especially the video and communications options). A lot of useful information is here, mixed with a lot of information appearing elsewhere in the IBM technical works.
(IBM part numbers 6137804 and 6137806)

IBM Corporation. *Technical Reference PC Network.* First Edition. Boca Raton, FL: IBM Corporation, September, 1984.
This manual is one of the many technical documents you should own if you're doing network-oriented programming, but it is heavy reading.
(IBM part number 6322916)

IBM Corporation. *Technical Reference: Personal Computer AT.* Revised ed. Boca Raton, FL: IBM Corporation, March, 1986.
Although not as well organized nor as complete as some of the other IBM references, this reference contains most of what you need to know about the PC/AT, including a full BIOS listing.
(IBM part number 6280099)

IBM Corporation. *Technical Reference: Personal Computer XT.* First Edition. Boca Raton, FL: IBM Corporation, January, 1983.
Although the data is somewhat scattered, this early reference contains everything you need to know, including full BIOS listing.
(IBM part number 6936763)

IBM Corporation. *Technical Reference: Personal Computer XT and Portable Personal Computer.* Boca Raton, FL: IBM Corporation, March, 1986.
Updated XT Technical Reference including the earlier (November 1982) BIOS listing and the most current (January 1986) BIOS listing.
(IBM part number 6280089)

Intel Corporation. *Microprocessor and Peripheral Handbook.* Volume 1—Microprocessor. Volume 2—Peripheral. Santa Clara, CA: Intel Corporation, 1987.
This is the reprint of the major data sheets, application notes, articles, and design information Intel has released to its customers. Although updated on a yearly basis, the work tends to be slightly out of date. Nevertheless, it is the best first source for information released by Intel. If what you find here isn't enough, contact Intel directly at (800) 548-4725 to find additional sources.
(Intel part number 230843)

Jourdain, Robert. *Programmer's Problem Solver for the IBM PC, XT & AT.* Bowie, MD: Robert J. Brady Co., 1986.
A useful compendium of assembly-language and BASIC routines used to drive low-level PC hardware, this book is an excellent source on how to use 8255, 8259, and other controller chips directly.
(ISBN 0-89303-787-7)

Microsoft Corporation. *Microsoft MS-DOS: Programmer's Reference* (version 3.3). Redmond, WA: Microsoft Corporation, 1987.
I prefer Microsoft's presentation and organization of its MS-DOS technical reference to IBM's, but you still need both sources.
(Document number 4106 30014-330-R04-0787)

Microsoft Corporation. *Microsoft Windows User's Guide* (version 2.0). Redmond, WA: Microsoft Corporation, 1987.
You will find minor differences between this and the earlier version, but this manual has a much better section on the more technical information, such as what goes in the WIN.INI file.
(Document number 050050051-200-R01-0887)

Microsoft Corporation. *Microsoft Windows Software Development Kit Application Style Guide* (version 2.0).Redmond, WA: Microsoft Corporation, 1987.
(Document number 050051016-200-I01-1087)

Microsoft Corporation. *Microsoft Windows Software Development Kit Programmer's Reference* (version 2.0). Redmond, WA: Microsoft Corporation, 1987.

> This reference is much, much better than the one that accompanied the original Windows 1.03 Toolkit. The organization has been improved and the index is better, which makes looking up information a lot faster. Note: Because my copy of this document, like some of the tables in this book, was based on a prerelease version of Windows 2.0, some information may have been changed or updated after the tables were compiled. (Document number 050051053-200-I02-1087)

Microsoft Corporation. *Microsoft Windows Software Development Kit Programming Tools* (version 2.0).Redmond, WA: Microsoft Corporation, 1987.
(Document number 050051051-200-I01-1087; Part number 002 00476)

Morgan, Christopher, and Waite, Mitchell. *8086/8088 16-bit Microprocessor Primer*. New York, NY: Byte/McGraw-Hill Books, 1983.

> One of the earliest books on the Intel microprocessors, this book is also one of the most approachable and understandable. Although not particularly specific to the IBM PC family, it is nevertheless a valuable reference worth owning. (ISBN 0-07-043109-4)

Norton, Peter. *The Peter Norton Programmer's Guide to the IBM PC*. Redmond, WA: Microsoft Press, 1985.

> A much better work than the one Norton is best known for writing (*Inside the IBM PC*, Robert J. Brady Co.), this book contains good material on the PCjr and the PC/AT, as well as on the base PC and PC/XT models. Like Duncan's, this book is highly recommended. (ISBN 0-14-087-144-6)

Palmer, John and Morse, Stephen. *The 8087 Primer*. New York, NY: John Wiley & Sons, 1984.

> This book contains much of the Intel technical material, made readable. A little more basic than the Startz book (see below). Uses FORTRAN programming examples.

Sargent, Murray, III and Shoemaker, Richard. *The IBM Personal Computer From the Inside Out*. Reading, MA: Addison-Wesley Publishing, 1986.

> This book, along with Peter Norton's works, is probably the best overall discussion of the PC hardware and how to drive it with software. The current (revised) edition contains information about the IBM PC/AT, but not in as much detail as one would want. (ISBN 0-201-06918-0)

Scanlon, Leo J. *Assembly Language Programming for the IBM PC-AT*. Bowie, MD: Robert J. Brady Co., 1985.

> One of the best assembly-language programming books targeted for PC and AT users, this book doesn't deal with low-level PC hardware as much as it does with BIOS and DOS functions. (ISBN 0-89303-484-3)

Startz, Richard. *8087 Applications and Programming for the IBM PC and Other PCs*. Bowie, MD: Robert J. Brady Co., 1983.

> This book is probably the best of the 8087 references that I consulted; however, the emphasis is on high-level language interface to the 8087. (ISBN 0-89303-420-7)

The Waite Group. *The PC LAN Primer*. Indianapolis, IN: Howard Sams & Company, 1986.

> This is a solid introduction to the world of LANs with a sprinkling of technical material throughout; it is not a primary source, but it is a useful introduction nonetheless. (ISBN 0-672-22448-8)

Walden, Jeff. *File Formats for Popular PC Software*. New York, NY: John Wiley & Sons, 1986.

> If data interchange is an issue, this is about the only book you'll find that even begins to cover the subject. It has detailed information about Lotus 1-2-3, dBASE, DIF, SYLK, and WordStar file formats. Although getting a little out of date, it is still a useful book. (ISBN 0-471-83671-0)

Index

Thom Hogan

Thom Hogan is a veteran of the microcomputer industry, with 11 years of experience as a developer, programmer, technical writer, marketing manager, and lecturer. He is the author of the bestselling *CP/M Users Guide*, which has sold more than 300,000 copies. He is also a frequent contributor to such computer magazines as *Bay Area Computer Currents, Macworld, InfoWorld*, and *A+*. Thom Hogan lives in Pacifica, California.

The tables in this book were prepared and submitted to Microsoft Press in electronic form. Tables were processed and formatted using Microsoft Excel for the Macintosh.

Cover design by Greg Hickman
Interior design by the staff of Microsoft Press
Principal table formatting by Colleen Tremaine,
Charles Brod, and Mark Dodge
Principal production artist: Becky Geisler-Johnson

All table composition by Microsoft Press in Helvetica, using
Microsoft Excel for the Macintosh and the Linotronic 300
laser imagesetter.